To Dad from
Kathy + Tommy + Boys

3/29/79
65 yrs. old

The World Series

A 75th Anniversary

Joseph L. Reichler, Editor

Simon and Schuster New York

Edited by—Joseph Reichler
Creative Director—Hal Evans
Designer—Joel Weltman
Art Associate—Jean Weisman
Managing Editor—John Monteleone
Assistant Managing Editor—Alfred Glossbrenner

Published by Simon and Schuster
A Division of Gulf & Western Corporation.
Simon & Schuster Building
Rockefeller Center
1230 Avenue of the Americas
New York, New York 10020

Manufactured in the United States of America.

3 4 5 6 7 8 9 10

Library of Congress Cataloging in Publication Data
The World Series: a 75th anniversary.

Includes index.
1. World Series (Baseball)—History. 2. Baseball—
United States—History. I. Reichler, Joseph L.
GV863.A1W67   796.357'782   78-8703
ISBN 0-671-24304-7

Contents

1 A Truly National Event
By Joe Durso

10 How It All Began
By Joseph L. Reichler

18 Golden Memories
By James T. Farrell

24 Iron Arms
By Joseph L. Reichler

40 Magic Mitts
By Joseph L. Reichler

46 The Babe
By Joseph L. Reichler

51 Touch 'Em All
By Joseph L. Reichler

60 Fleet Feet
By Joseph L. Reichler

66 .400 Hitters
By Joseph L. Reichler

74 In a Pinch
By Joseph L. Reichler

78 My Love Affair With Baseball
By Lillian G. Carter

81 Most Dramatic Finishes
By Joseph L. Reichler

88 Greatest Upsets
By Joseph L. Reichler

99 Stars Have Problems Too
By Joseph L. Reichler

106 Subs Who Shined
By Joseph L. Reichler

114 World Series Pressure
By Roy Campanella

118 Best World Series Teams
By Joseph L. Reichler

132 All Time All-Star
World Series Teams
By Joseph L. Reichler

142 The Black Sox Scandal
By Joseph L. Reichler

148 World Series Humor
By Joe Garagiola

152 Behind the Scenes
By Joseph L. Reichler

158 World Series Goats
By Joseph L. Reichler

167 Rhubarbs and Ejections
By Joseph L. Reichler

174 Going . . . Going . . . Gone!
By Mel Allen

179 Larry and Me
By Leo Durocher

185 The Complete Record
1903-77

270 Individual Statistics

280 The World Series Trivia Quiz

283 Credits

284 Index

Dear Fans:

No sports event in our history has consistently captured the hearts of the public as much as the World Series. Traditionally, it has been the ultimate in sports competition.

The visions of the great teams, players and extraordinary feats will always remain vivid in our minds. From the first Series between Boston and Pittsburgh in 1903 to Don Larsen's stunning perfect game in 1956 to the unforgettable drama between the Reds and Red Sox in 1975 to the spine-tingling home run performance of Reggie Jackson in 1977 the World Series has always symbolized something special.

On this diamond anniversary, we present to you THE WORLD SERIES: A 75th ANNIVERSARY, which details in words and pictures the outstanding events in the annals of what has become an international institution.

This is truly the definitive World Series publication. It covers the standout pitchers, the great pinch hitters, the interesting personalities and the most dramatic games. Almost 100 pages of records and statistics plus numerous other fascinating features and insights are included.

It is our sincere hope that THE WORLD SERIES: A 75th ANNIVERSARY will serve as a reference tool as well as a literary link to the glorious tradition of past Octobers.

Bowie K. Kuhn
Commissioner of Baseball

The World Series

A Truly National Event

BY JOSEPH DURSO

ONE AFTERNOON IN BOSTON in the autumn of 1903, the Pittsburgh Pirates tore into old Cy Young with four runs in the first inning of the first World Series game ever played. Although no one present could have known it at the time, that game marked the birth of an event and the beginning of a tradition that one day would captivate the entire nation with its pageantry, its excitement and its thrills.

The only people present at the creation were those in "the tremendous crowd of 16,242,"

sitting in the packed wooden grandstand or standing behind the ropes strung across the outfield grass. There were no radio and television networks, no satellite hookups, no microwave relays.

This was back in the time when the Common Man was still grappling with the Machine Age: less than forty summers after the Civil War; only a dozen years after the last armed conflict between the white man and the Indian at Wounded Knee. Casey Stengel was still a teen-ager in Kansas City, pumping the organ in St. Mark's Episcopal Church for twenty-five cents a day while other kids were peering at copies of **McGuffey's Reader.** Rough, tough young John McGraw was fresh from Baltimore, introducing New York to the cruel delights of "Oriole baseball."

Modern communication was a long way from creating the "media happening" and the "global village" we live in today. In fact, modern communication as we know it didn't even exist. Any "spectacular" in those simpler days was spectacular only to those hardy souls who witnessed the event from the sidelines, or to the even hardier souls who used to gather at the one place in town where bulletins might be relayed from some distant happening—the corner saloon.

Today, dramatic events like the World Series are transmitted with stunning immediacy into the living rooms of America, with 80 million spectators watching the action, live and in color, as it takes place on some ball field thousands of miles away. Yesterday, before the nation was united by coaxial cable, the same events were transmitted to places where groups of fans came together to share a drink and a less sophisticated technology.

By the time the World Series was inaugurated in 1903, technology was growing along with the popular passion for some form of recreation to spice an otherwise hard and demanding life. And at no time was the stage set so dramatically as in the quarter-century before the first World Series game.

The appearance of the typewriter at that time touched off a revolution in much the same way that radio did many years later. In 1876 came Bell's telephone, and in 1884, Mergenthaler's Linotype machine. Edison started lighting the streets in the 1880's. Daimler produced his high-speed internal-combustion engine in 1886, and Eastman his famous camera two years later. In Manhattan, brush-arc lamps were replacing the gaslights; cable cars were chasing the stagecoaches off Broadway; and the Third Avenue elevated was rocking the sidewalks of New York—and soon was offering a link to the ball parks uptown.

Fans gather at Boston's Grounds for first modern World Series in 1903.

The hot dog was there too, adding a special flavor to the public "event" of baseball. In fact, H.L. Mencken, the self-appointed guardian of society's tastes, remembered devouring "hot dogs in Baltimore way back in 1886." He also might have remembered the scene on Eutaw Street in Baltimore, where Kelly's oyster house supposedly had the fastest and slickest telegraph operator around. Perched on a little balcony halfway up the wall, the operator took the baseball scores directly off telegraph wires installed inside the restaurant and wrote them on a blackboard for the swarm of customers below.

Baseball began to grow as an "event" partially because of improved communications and partially because people had neither the time nor the money for other sports. Nor the weather, once baseball pre-empted the summertime hours. Golf, boating and horse racing were beyond the reach of the mass public. Basketball was not introduced until 1891. And when it was, it was considered a soft sport and merely a stopgap between the football and baseball seasons. Football was still pretty much of a college man's grind, more like a military exercise than a proper pastime. And boxing was often an outlaw consigned to river barges or "exhibition" halls.

So by the time the Pittsburgh Pirates ripped Cy Young for four runs in the inaugural inning of the World Series, the public was emotionally tuned in. Also technically tuned in, with excursion trains, torchlight parades and a ferociously partisan press that left no doubt as to who were the "good guys" and who were the "bad guys."

"In those days," John McGraw recalled, "it was not unusual for the papers to announce that 'the rowdy Giants, accompanied by representatives of the yellow press, got into town this morning.' We used to stay in the old Monongahela Hotel in Pittsburgh, and from there drove in open carriages to the ball park, which was in Allegheny City across the river.

"To reach the bridge, we had to pass by the public market place. If we escaped a shower of small stones and trash outside the park, we were sure to get it when we passed the market. Understand, we dressed at the hotel then, not at the ball park. If the fans started razzing, we would razz right back.

"One day we were greeted with a shower of old vegetables—potatoes, onions, tomatoes, even cantaloupes. That whole club had the skylarking spirit of college boys, and I was just as bad as any of them. On the field, though, they thought like men of affairs. Always they were on a hair's edge, ready to get into a row if anybody pulled the trigger."

To make certain that the trigger would be pulled often enough to sustain the war of nerves, McGraw would send telegrams to the next city on his New York Giants' itinerary, asking the chief of police for "protection" when they arrived. The newspapers there would duly report the request, and the Giants could always be certain of appearing before large, hostile crowds—"large" being the key word.

If the public needed any more provocation, it was promptly and regularly provided as the World Series grew into a kind of intercity war in the early decades of the century.

When McGraw's Giants played their historic "shutout" Series against Connie Mack's Philadelphia Athletics in 1905, the cocky little manager opened the war with a visual trick that would have captivated television directors half a century later. He turned his Giants loose in startling new uniforms: black flannels with white piping, boxy white caps and an immense "NY" in white across the shirts.

Connie Mack's city retaliated, though, with a trick of its own. The PHILADELPHIA NORTH AMERICAN, making more of an impact than most newspapers, erected a huge gong west of City Hall and then pealed the news of the Series across William Penn's town: one gong for a two-base hit, two for a triple, three gongs for a home run—by the Athletics, of course. It was a milestone in the annals of sports spectaculars, except for one thing: the mammoth gong tolled only five times in a week, each time for a two-bagger only, because the Giants and Athletics fired some of the strongest pitching in baseball history against each other.

Public passion? Well, after five shutouts, three by Christy Mathewson, the Giants were the world champions. And then both teams went back to Philadelphia to celebrate. Six newspapers there staged a tremendous baseball parade for the teams. Amateur and semipro clubs from three states marched the length of Broad Street with bands playing and fireworks lighting the sky. Open carriages carried the players to a great Banquet. Huge caricatures of the players were carted down the parade route. And an elephant from the Philadelphia zoo plodded along in circus fashion to symbolize Mr. Mack's White Elephants.

No white elephant was available, so a white sheet was draped over this one to perfect the symbol. Somebody suggested that they whitewash the beast to make the occasion truly memorable, but the people at the zoo drew the line at that.

"The World Series," remembered Frederick G. Lieb, who saw his first one in 1910, "developed from a post-season event—of concern largely to the interested cities—to something like the great national spectacle it is today. The country virtually shut up shop to await the result. In New York, the queue of fans started at the ticket windows of the

Rival managers Connie Mack of the A's and Giants' John McGraw (in uniform) in 1905 series.

Polo Grounds and stretched for a mile."

The newspapers did their part, too. For days before the Series, they ran pictures and stories comparing the teams, position by position. They even ran personalized comparisons by writers like Hugh Fullerton, who had amazed people in 1906 by correctly predicting the outcome of each game between the Chicago Cubs and the Chicago White Sox. Fullerton was on the staff of the CHICAGO TRIBUNE then, and even his city editor hesitated to print his forecast that the White Sox, the original "hitless wonders," would win.

They did, and Fullerton emerged as a seer with mystic vision. His vision seemed even more remarkable when he correctly called the next three Series, and by 1912 his analyses were being printed in a papers like the NEW YORK TIMES under headlines that advised: "Hugh Fullerton Favors Gardner over Herzog at Third Base." The TIMES also ran letters from angry readers denouncing Fullerton's mystic vision. And in its editorial columns the TIMES alluded to some of the momentous events of the day—Teddy Roosevelt's "Bull Moose" campaign against President Taft and Woodrow Wilson, the arrival in New York of an armada of 123 ships and the spectacular criminal trial of Lieutenant Charles Becker for complicity in the murder of a big-time gambler. Then, putting everything into perspective, it commented:

> **This is to be a week of notable incidents. As the third from the last week of the most bewildering Presidential campaign of recent memory, it should be full of political excitement. The greatest naval pageant in the history of this country will begin at the city's gates. A criminal trial of larger significance than any in late years will begin.**
>
> **Yet, who will doubt that the public interest will center on none of these, but on the games of baseball at our Polo Grounds and in Boston?**

Well, nobody in Boston doubted it. Mayor Fitzgerald, renowned as "Honey Fitz" and later as the grandfather of John F. Kennedy, personally led the Red Sox pilgrimage to New York in that October of 1912. Wearing a great stovepipe hat and a fur-collared coat, he was flanked by two brass bands and a thousand partisans. The whole cavalcade was turned into a roaring, singing mob by a celebrated bunch known as the Royal Rooters as they all boarded four special trains and invaded Mr. McGraw's town.

Mind you, there was no radio or television to "hype" the invasion. But then one was needed. The Boston crowd swept into Grand Central Station at six P.M., with the evening rush hour well under way, and promptly created one of the heaviest traffic jams in New York's memory. Later that evening, they jammed Broadway with a torchlight parade that featured Honey Fitz himself in tenor solos every couple of blocks—and the clamor was repeated the next afternoon at the Polo Grounds when the Royal Rooters crossed the diamond in formation before the opening game.

You didn't have to be inside the Polo Grounds to share in the excitement, either. Downtown, the Times Square area was clogged with people all afternoon while details of the game were flashed on a huge electric scoreboard on the facade of the Times Building. The board was sixteen feet long by seven feet high and was operated by direct wire from the ball park to the TIMES, where a man fed the play-by-play information to the board itself.

In lights, the game was reconstructed in a way that seemed magical then—a decade before the pioneering radio broadcasts of the World Series and three decades before television. Balls, strikes and outs were shown, and other lights depicted base runners as they worked their way toward home plate. Public impact? The crowd gathered one hour before Jeff Tesreau's first pitch, and traffic had to be diverted away from Times Square by hordes of policemen.

When the action switched to Fenway Park, which had just opened that season as one of the great public "stages" in baseball, it took the mounted police thirty minutes to clear the field of rooters **before** the game. Just off Newport, Rhode Island, meanwhile, President Taft was cruising aboard the yacht MAYFLOWER, and he naturally turned aside from affairs of state to inquire as to

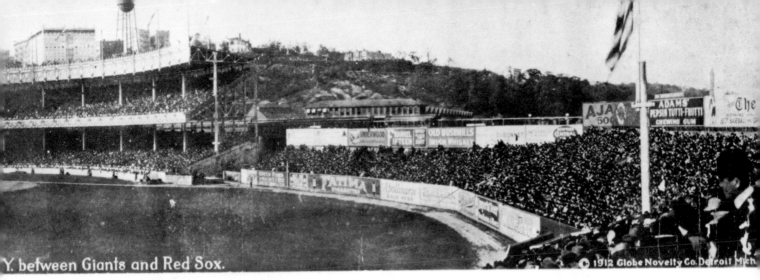

Y. between Giants and Red Sox. © 1912 Globe Novelty Co. Detroit Mich.

how the ball game was going. So the details were supplied through naval wireless at Torpedo Station—running details, as the Giants and Red Sox and their raucous disciples raged at each other for four hours.

And so another milestone was passed in the development of this national event—electric lights re-creating the Series in Times Square, wireless reports re-creating it for the President of the United States aboard his yacht. Then the century proceeded into the Roaring Twenties, and things reached a new crescendo, thanks to the pounding bat of Babe Ruth and the debut of network broadcasting.

It was a time of heroes and hoopla, a time when brokerage houses carried the betting odds and when newspapers carried endless columns of Series details, such as: "J. P. Morgan is a box-holder, as are also Harry F. Sinclair, Harry Payne Whitney, Finley J. Shepard and Charles H. Sabin."

In a box near the dugout, mystery writer Mary Roberts Rinehart entertained friends. George M. Cohan, Louis Mann and Jack Dempsey took bows. And when General John J. Pershing made an unexpected appearance, the crowd rose and cheered, as it did for Al Smith and the old brown derby. Tex Rickard, the impresario of boxing, was quoted as "leaning" toward the Yankees, as was Devereaux Milburn, the captain of the Meadowbrook polo team. But Willie Hoppe, the billiard king, stuck with the king of Broadway, Mr. McGraw, and said, "I have a hunch the Giants will win."

It was 1922, and THE NEW YORK TIMES properly covered the "event" like the revolution it was:

Radio for the first time carried the opening game of the World Series, play-by-play, direct from the Polo Grounds to great crowds throughout the eastern section of the country.

Press covering the 1922 Series between Yankees and Giants.

Throughout the broadcasting station WJZ at Newark, New Jersey, Grantland Rice, a sports writer, related his story of the game direct to an invisible audience, estimated to be five million, while WGY at Schenectady and WBZ at Springfield, Massachusetts, relayed every play of the contest.

In place of the scoreboards and megaphones of the past, amplifiers connected to radio instruments gave all the details and sidelights to thousands of enthusiasts unable to get into the Polo Grounds. Not only could the voice of the official radio observer be heard, but the voice of the umpire on the field announcing the batteries for the day mingled with the voice of a boy selling ice cream cones.

The clamor of the 40,000 baseball fans inside the Polo Grounds made radio listeners feel as if they were in the grandstand. **The cheers which greeted Babe Ruth when he stepped to the plate could be heard throughout the land.**

It was a far cry from the days of chalkboards in saloons; even a far cry from the days when bright minds at the University of Minnesota had experimented with "electronic sports" by using a spark transmitter and telegraph signals. And it was a giant step forward from the enterprising efforts of station KDKA in Pittsburgh, which in 1921 had placed a staff member in the top row of the bleachers at Forbes Field. As each inning of a ball game ended, he wrote the results on a piece of paper, leaned over the railing and dropped his message outside the fence to an accomplice, who ran to the nearest coin telephone and called in the score to the announcer in the studio.

But all that changed forever in 1923 when a young member of a jury left the Federal Court House in lower Manhattan and strolled up Broadway during the lunchtime recess.

His name was Graham McNamee, and he turned in to the building at 195 Broadway, glanced at the sign that read "Radio Station WEAF" and rode the elevator to the little two-room studio on the fourth floor. McNamee was a concert baritone who had already been praised by the critics for his "finished phrasing and excellent enunciation." Before he left the studio and returned to the jury box that afternoon, he had been hired by WEAF as a jack of all trades at thirty dollars a week. Before the summer ended, he had sat behind a microphone and described Harry Greb's assault on the world middleweight championship. Before October was over, he had sat in an open box seat and applied that "excellent enunciation" to the World Series in the gleaming new Yankee Stadium.

He was surrounded by the biggest crowds in baseball history: 62,000 in the Yankees' park and 52,000 in the Polo Grounds, across the Harlem River. By telephone lines, his perch was connected

Graham McNamee, famous broadcaster of his day, at the mike.

with crowds in crossroads and cities along the Eastern Seaboard. Stations like WJZ in New York, WMAF in South Dartmouth, Massachusetts, and WCAP in Washington, the press reported, "will also radiate the contests simultaneously with WEAF, as they will be connected by special land wires to microphones controlled by that station."

When it rained during the Series and his suit got soaked, McNamee made headlines. When he spilled a thermos of coffee and soaked his suit again, he was deluged with letters. When his first World Series was finally over, he received 1,700 letters. And when the National Broadcasting Company was organized in 1926 and the Series "went network," he received 50,000 letters.

The public's passion was aroused, no mistake about that. It was aroused when gifted writers like Franklin P. Adams invented "the saddest of words: Tinkers to Evers to Chance." It was aroused when Damon Runyon portrayed old Casey Stengel circling the bases in these words: "This is the way old Casey Stengel ran running his home run home when two were out in the ninth inning and the score was tied, and the ball still bounding inside the Yankee yard—his flanks heaving, his breath whistling, his head far back." And it was aroused, once and for all, when Graham McNamee spoke into his saucer-shaped microphone while Babe Ruth swung and "the cheers could be heard throughout the land."

On May 17, 1939, a college baseball game was played between Columbia and Princeton at Baker Field, on the north tip of Manhattan Island. The game was watched by the usual gathering of students, but what they really watched was another

Fans watching electronic scoreboard
giving pitch by pitch account of early
World Series game.

Fans viewing first televising of World Series on outdoor screens in 1947.

revolution. The game was photographed and transmitted as "live" action by one camera, and it was described by one announcer, Bill Stern. It was the first baseball game ever to be "televised," and it signaled the beginning of an exciting new era.

Three months later, the new era made the big leagues. It was August 26, 1939, at old Ebbets Field, where the Cincinnati Reds were playing a doubleheader against the Brooklyn Dodgers. This time, the action was picked up by three cameras, and the "voice" belonged to Red Barber. Not many people outside Ebbets Field saw it, but the revolution was intensifying: these were the first major-league baseball games ever covered by television.

"It was apparent," observed THE NEW YORK TIMES, in rather splendid understatement, "that considerable progress has been made in the technical requirements and apparatus for this sort of outdoor pickup where the action is fast."

The fast action was interrupted by the six grim years of World War II. But then came the postwar years and the same runaway passion of the public for some involvement with events that were not tragic and with heroes who were not armed. This time, television was ready to dramatize the excitement that baseball was ready to supply.

September 30, 1947: The place was Yankee Stadium. The occasion was the opening game of the World Series. For the first time in history, the "picture" of a Series game was carried to the public by television.

Not only that, but the National Broadcasting Company sent it all to four cities—New York, Philadelphia, Washington and Schenectady—with the commentary of three announcers—Bob Stanton, Bill Slater and Bob Edge. The director, creating a role he was to play for every World Series for the next thirty years, was Harry Coyle, who remembers, "We kept losing the picture all the time."

But Harry Coyle also remembers that they covered the scene with three cameras and used a lot of masking tape and rubber bands, trying in a crude way to contrive a "split-screen" view at times. It was primitive, of course: no zoom lens, no close-up shots, no replays, no special effects. "And when Al Gionfriddo made that catch on Joe DiMaggio in front of the bull-pen gate in left field," Coyle recalls, "he made it, and that was it."

But however primitive the technology, the public finally had the ultimate link to the event taking place in the ball park itself. Only 150,000 television sets were in use in the four cities of the little "network," but RCA estimated that the audience totaled four million. People clustered around small screens in hotel ballrooms and other places lucky enough to have television—forty years after similar crowds had thronged Times Square to follow the Series on the electric scoreboard.

After that, the milestones raced past. A World Series was first televised coast-to-coast in 1951, with Jim Britt and Russ Hodges at the microphones while the Yankees turned back the "miracle" Giants in a New York show flashed 3,000 miles to viewers in California. And in 1955, while the Dodgers were checking the Yankees and winning their first World Series, with Mel Allen and Vin Scully describing the actions of Casey Stengel and Mickey Mantle and Whitey Ford and Jackie Robinson and Duke Snider, another flourish was added: color.

Today, nearly a century after John McGraw's "Oriole baseball," the impact is nearly total. Now, two networks alternate in televising the league championship series and the World Series, while a third handles the radio broadcasts. Now, the

55,000 people inside the stadium are linked to eighty million people around the nation by a dozen cameras, a hundred technicians and staff workers, and 220 television stations.

Inside the ball park alone, two and a half miles of camera cable and three and a half miles of audio cable start the colossal trick of carrying the Series to the public. Without masking tape or rubber bands, the screen is split **four** ways. The action can be shown in "slow motion"; it can be halted by "stop action"; it can be summoned back by "instant replay," which offers **five** views of the same play.

It is a long, long time since the Pittsburgh Pirates irreverently swiped four runs from old Cy Young in the first inning of the first World Series.

It is an even longer time since the man on the balcony in the barroom posted the inning scores in chalk on his blackboard.

But in terms of public passion over the World Series, as the TIMES noted at the dawn of television, it is "apparent that considerable progress has been made...for this sort of outdoor pickup when the action is fast."

It has indeed. Thanks in part to the modern technology that has spread the spectacle far and wide, and thanks to the public's seemingly insatiable appetite for baseball, the autumn classic has earned a place in the hearts and minds of millions of Americans. Today, few people would disagree that seventy-five years after that first memorable contest in 1903, the World Series has flourished and grown into what it now is—a truly national event. ◇

How It All Began

BY JOSEPH L. REICHLER

Barney Dreyfuss

IN THE BASEBALL HALL OF FAME at Cooperstown, New York, there is no memorial to Barney Dreyfuss. There is no plaque attesting to his vision, and no statue commemorating the vital contributions to the game made by the onetime owner of the Pittsburgh Pirates. Yet Barney Dreyfuss definitely deserves a place of honor in history's pantheon of diamond greats. For Barney Dreyfuss invented the World Series, the modern version, which in October of 1978 celebrated its seventy-fifth glorious anniversary. It was in August of 1903 that Dreyfuss wrote the following letter to Henry Killilea, owner of the Boston Pilgrims:

> **The time has come for the National League and American League to organize a World Series. It is my belief that if our clubs played a series on a best-out-of-nine basis, we would create great interest in baseball, in our leagues, and in our players. I also believe it would be a financial success.**

Killilea took the letter to the Chicago office of Ban Johnson, president and organizer of the three-year-old American League.

"What do you think of the idea, Ban?" asked Killilea.

"What does Jimmy Collins [Boston's manager] think about this?" Johnson countered.

"Collins says that Cy Young and Bill Dinneen would stop Honus Wagner, Fred Clarke and those other batters."

"Then play them," snapped Johnson. "By all means, play them!"

Thus the World Series, as we know it today, was born.

There had been post-season competitions in the major leagues before 1903. The Temple Cup, instituted in 1894, was an early version of the World Series. The Cup was awarded to the winner of play-off competition between the champion and the runner-up of the old twelve-club National League. Donated by Colonel W.C. Temple of the Pittsburgh club, the Cup now resides in the National Baseball Museum at Cooperstown. The Temple Cup competition ultimately fell into disfavor when, in 1898, the fans heard rumors that the players of the two contending teams had agreed to divide the spoils equally regardless of which team won the Cup.

However, these early versions of a fall finale to the baseball campaign had lacked rules and regulations and true popular interest. Today, there is no more thrilling drama on the American scene than baseball's annual World Series in early October. People who have only a superficial interest in baseball during the playing season become all-attentive when the two major-league champions try to knock each other off in the annual Diamond Warfare. Millions and millions of people from all walks of life, in nearly all parts of the world, hold all normal activities to a minimum during World Series week. Instead, they scan newspaper sports sections or give themselves to television and radio sets in a sometimes feverish effort to keep abreast of the latest developments.

In the past seventy-five years, the World Series has made tremendous strides. Population growth, expansion, the jet age and radio and television have completely changed the autumn extravaganza. The Series is no longer a set of games viewed only by fans of the contending cities. Today it is a great international spectacle that appears on television sets in millions of homes on all seven continents. The first modern World Series, in 1903, attracted some 100,429 people. The six-game 1976 World Series was viewed, thanks largely to television, by more than 300 million.

It is almost impossible to picture baseball without this spectacular climax to the season, for what would the pennant races mean if the goal were not a place in the World Series? It is quite conceivable that without the tremendous popular interest in the World Series, major-league baseball would not have survived the destructive influence of wars and depressions. Certainly, baseball minus a World Series would lose its vibrancy.

Actually, the first modern World Series came about because of adversity and competition between the older, established National League, in business since 1876, and the newer American League, formed in 1900.

The contract-breaking, the player-jumping from league to league, the bickering and the name-calling that took place in baseball's infancy soured the fans to such an extent that the attendance in both leagues suffered drastically. Finally, in January 1903, the presidents of the two leagues met in Cincinnati and signed a peace pact. With the peace, Ban Johnson's young, battling American League finally won recognition as a legitimate major league with all the rights and privileges of the older National League circuit. The raids and counterraids between the two leagues, however, had left many unhealed wounds. Despite the cessation of hostilities, a majority of the National League diehards still wanted no truck with "those upstarts."

One National League mogul, however, did not share this intransigence. Possibly this was because he had won the most important American League concession of the peace—a pledge by Ban Johnson to keep the American League out of Pittsburgh. That N.L. mogul was Barney Dreyfuss, a man of foresight and business acumen, who just happened to own the Pittsburgh Pirates. But Dreyfuss knew that something drastic had to be done to regain the fans' interest and confidence. And so he hit upon the idea of a World Series.

Ban Johnson, originator and first President of the American League.

With an aggregation headed by such stalwarts as outfielder and manager Fred Clarke, mighty shortstop Honus Wagner, 1902 batting champion Ginger Beaumont, slugging third baseman Tommy Leach, and a pitching staff led by twenty-five-game winners Sam Leever and Deacon Charles Phillippe, Dreyfus did not for one minute believe his Pirates could be beaten by anybody, let alone a bunch from the fledgling American League.

The American League champion Boston club thought otherwise. Known as the Pilgrims or the Puritans, the team was recruited largely from top-ranking players captured in raids on National League clubs. The great Cy Young had been plucked from St. Louis, and Bill Dinneen, who ranked second only to Young on the Pilgrims' pitching staff, had been "stolen" from Boston. The club was led by the peerless third baseman Jimmy Collins, another former National Leaguer. He was abetted by Chick Stahl, a spectacular center fielder and fellow outfielders Pat Dougherty and Buck Freeman, the Babe Ruth of his day, who had led the National League with twenty-five home runs in 1899.

Dreyfuss and Killilea met in Pittsburgh early in September to draw up the plans for the first National and American League World Series. Killilea suggested a seven-game series, such as had been played for the Temple Cup. Dreyfuss maintained that seven games was too short. He held out for a best-five-out-of-nine series. The two owners agreed to split the gate. It was stipulated that neither club could use a player engaged after August 31—a restriction that has remained in World Series rules to this day.

A major problem developed, however. The American League salaries ran out on September 30, the last day of the season. But the salaries of the National League players ran to October 15. Thus it was agreed that the players take 70 percent of the receipts. That was fine with the Pittsburgh players, but the Puritans refused to play unless they were given their club's entire share of the gate. Killilea eventually appeased his athletes by promising them two weeks' extra pay in addition to a slice of the receipts.

The Pirates, with their glittering pitching staff that had hurled six consecutive shutouts during the regular season, suddenly found themselves pitching poor on the eve of the Series opener. Leever came up with a sore arm, although he tried gamely to pitch. But Ed Doheny, the Pirates' brilliant but eccentric southpaw, went berserk, nearly killing two people; he was committed to a mental hospital and never even appeared in the Series. That left Pittsburgh's pitching burden almost entirely on the shoulders of one man—Deacon Phillippe. The Deacon made a noble effort. He

Fred Clarke, Pittsburgh's manager and slugging outfielder.

hurled five complete games in thirteen days, winning his first three starts. But his mighty arm, weary from overwork, was no match for the two stalwarts Young and Dinneen. Cy won two games and Dinneen three, including the clinching game, 3-0. Boston emerged on top, five victories to three. Chick Stahl was Boston's best batsman with ten hits, and Patsy Dougherty slammed two home runs with five runs batted in. For Pittsburgh, Jimmy Sebring was tops with eleven hits. Sebring also had the distinction of hitting the first World Series home run. Boston pitchers, however, shackled the mighty Wagner. The 1903 National League batting champion with a .355 average, Honus was held to a skimpy .214 average with just one hit in his last fourteen times at bat.

With the admission price of one dollar (double the cost of a regular-season ticket), the eight games attracted 100,429 spectators. The net receipts of $55,500 were considered sensational for that day. Each winning Boston player received $1,181. Ironically, the losing Pittsburghers each pulled down $1,316. That was due to a magnanimous gesture by Dreyfuss, who tossed his entire share of the gate receipts into the players' pool.

The success of the 1903 World Series trig-

Charles "Deacon" Phillippe, who won three games for the Pirates in a losing cause.

Cy Young, baseball's biggest winner, warming up for opening game of the 1903 Series.

American League Champion Boston Pilgrims.

gered a wave of excitement among the fans, press, players and management. The club owners sensed that something tremendous had happened right under their noses and began to give serious thought to a regular interleague event to be played annually. However, if soon became clear that the time was not yet ripe. There were still smarting wounds. Though the peace between the two majors had been made late in the winter of 1902-03, there were still some National Leaguers who refused to have anything to do with the American League.

John T. Brush, owner of the New York Giants, and John McGraw, his fiery manager, were the most unconciliatory. Neither had taken too kindly to the peace agreement, and to them the entry of the American League into New York was still a festering sore. They had voiced their opposition to the 1903 post-season series, labeling it "The Bastard Series." Brush had even tried to block the enforcement of the 1903 pact by injunction proceedings in the New York State courts.

McGraw had his own reasons for his hatred of the American League, particularly its president, Ban Johnson. McGraw was the original manager and part owner of the Baltimore Americans when Johnson expanded his league eastward in 1901. The truculent manager had had frequent clashes with the league head and was serving an indefinite suspension in mid-season of 1903 when he jumped back to the National League to accept the leadership of the Giants.

The Pilgrims repeated as American League champions in 1904, beating out the New York Highlanders on the last day of the season. In the National League, the Giants, helped by the brilliant pitching of Christy Mathewson, broke Pittsburgh's three-year grip on the National League top rung. They established a new season record for victories (106), serving notice that a new power had been born. For a while, it looked as if the New York Highlanders would beat out Boston, and there was a lot of talk about a World Series involving the two Manhattan teams. Brush, backed by McGraw, said there would be no Series with the "invaders," a contemptuous word he used for manager Clark Griffith's Highlanders.

However, the Highlanders, forerunners of

John McGraw

Clark Griffith

the present-day Yankees, blew the pennant on the last day of the season on Jack Chesbro's wild pitch while the big spitballer was gunning for his forty-second victory; the Boston team therefore squeezed through by an eight-percentage-point margin. John I. Taylor, the young president of the Boston club, quickly challenged the Giants to a series, "for the baseball Championship of the World." Brush immediately declined. In an open letter to Taylor, Brush replied:

> **We won from the most important clubs in America and we are entitled to the honor of champions of the United States. There is nothing in the constitution or the playing rules of the National League that requires its victorious club to submit its championship honors to a contest with a victorious club in the minor league.**

The letter from Brush paradoxically, proved to be of tremendous value to the American League. It swung the press and public to the side of the Johnson circuit and eventually was to help establish the World Series as an annual event. Brush's own players were furious. Salaries, which had been inflated during the war between the two leagues, had subsided in 1904. Pretty good ballplayers were getting only $2,500,000 to $3,000 for the year's work. These players knew that the Pirates and Puritans had collected over $1,000 apiece out of the series the year before, and there were indignant meetings in the Giants clubhouse. Nevertheless, Brush and McGraw held their ground and there was no series.

Newspaper criticism was strong, especially in New York. Brush, a former department-store man and accustomed to dealing with people, soon realized that he was on the unpopular side of a con-troversy in which all of the nation's fans took a stand.

All winter long, he thought about the matter. Then he made his decision. In the spring of 1905 the two leagues, spurred by Brush, voted to schedule an annual series between the pennant winners of the two major leagues for the baseball championship of the world. For the new World Series, Brush proposed a lengthy code of rules and regulations which became known as the John T. Brush rules.

The series would be compulsory and would be under the jurisdiction of a three-man National Commission, composed of Garry Herrmann, chairman, and the presidents of the two majors, Ban

John T. Brush, owner of the Giants, who was responsible for the present rules governing the Series.

Johnson and Harry Pulliam. Brush's rules called for a four-out-of-seven series with 60 percent of the receipts from the first four games being set aside as a players' pool. The pool would be divided on a basis of 70 percent for the winning team and 30 percent for the losers. The Commission would take 10 percent of the receipts of the entire series. The remainder would be split evenly by the owners of the two contending clubs.

Only players engaged by their respective clubs prior to September 1 would be eligible. Umpires and scorers for the series would be appointed by the Commission. The Commission would also draw up the schedule, stipulating that the city staging the first game, and a seventh if necessary, would be obliged to post a $10,000 bond as a guarantee of its good faith and that it would live up to all the conditions. So wisely did Brush frame his rules that the code he established, with a few minor changes, still governs the World Championship Series today.

Brush's club, the Giants, and Connie Mack's Philadelphia Athletics were the first to try out the new rules in 1905. The 1905 series was won by

Christy Mathewson, Giant immortal whose three shutouts in 1905 have never been equalled.

the Giants, four games to one, under the best-four-of-seven principles.

Every game was a shutout. Three of the shutouts were hurled by Christy Mathewson, who dominated the series as no other pitcher had ever done. Within six playing days, Matty blanked the Mackmen, 3-0, 9-0 and 2-0. In each of his first two shutouts, the tall collegian from Bucknell University gave up only four hits, and in his third he allowed six hits. In the three games, he fanned eighteen batters and walked only one. Joe McGinnity pitched the other Giant shutout, while Chief Bender pitched the only shutout won by the Athletics.

The only damper on the Series was that Rube Waddell, the brilliant but erratic southpaw who won twenty-seven games for the A's that year, did not play in it. The Rube had suffered an accident a week before the start of the series—a terrific disappointment to the fans, who had been looking forward to the mound duels between Waddell and Mathewson.

The real tragedy was that Waddell was injured not on the playing field but in good-natured horseplay on a railroad platform. The Athletics were in a jubilant mood after clinching the pennant in Boston. Andy Coakley, one of the pitchers, had been given permission by Connie Mack to pitch in an exhibition game, and when he came to rejoin the team he was wearing a straw hat. Deciding that the season for straw hats had passed, the frolicsome Rube made a dive for Coakley's skimmer. In the scuffle that followed, Waddell tripped over some baggage on the platform and fell on his valuable left shoulder. Something snapped, and for several weeks Rube couldn't raise his left arm, let alone pitch. There is no doubt that the loss of the twenty-seven-game winner and baseball's strikeout king gave the Athletics a severe jolt and had much to do with their poor showing during the Series.

Outside of pitchers, the players who excelled were Mike Donlin and Roger Bresnahan of the Giants, who batted .315 and .313, respectively, the only .300 hitters of the series. Little Topsy Hartsel, Mack's leadoff man, led the A's with .294. No other player hit .250.

The series was no gold mine even with the uninflated dollar of those days. It drew 91,723 spectators, and the net gate receipts were $68,436.81. The players divided $27,434.88. The original Brush plan called for 70 percent of the purse to the winning team and 30 percent to the losers. Under this arrangement, each of the Giants received a check for $1,142 and each of the Athletics got $382. However, Ben Shibe, president of the Athletics, tossed in his owner's share, bringing the individual Athletics' shares up to $833.75.

The A's actually fared still better, thanks to the lack of confidence the Giants had in themselves. Fearing they might lose, the Giants, with the exception of McGraw, Mathewson and Bresnahan, had made secret arrangements with Athletics players to pool their shares so that each man would get the same amount. In an effort to forestall such arrangements in the future the players' purse was changed to 60 and 40 percent, and this split exists today. ◇

Chief Bender who pitched the only victory for the A's in 1905.

Golden Memories

BY JAMES T. FARRELL

Chicago National League Ball Club 1906

LOOKING BACK OVER more than sixty years as a baseball fan, many exciting plays and outstanding players readily come to mind. Like any fan, my baseball memories are something I cherish, something that is a part of me. They are one of the reasons why I love the game more now than ever before.

Yet of all my memories, the ones that often seem to stand out the most are those dealing with the World Series. Whether it's the extraordinary excitement that the post-season match-ups never fail to generate or the superb quality of play or the magnitude of the stakes that are involved, I can't really say. All I know is that the World Series is something very special and that it has consistently provided the world with some of the finest baseball ever played.

I remember, for example, the feeling I had after watching the first game of the 1977 Yankees-Dodgers Series. It was a good game, and when I got home that night, I said to myself, "That's the way baseball is supposed to be played."

And now, with the World Series celebrating its seventy-fifth anniversary in 1978, it seems like a good time to pause and reflect on the players who made it and those who didn't, on how the game has changed over the years, and on the crucial role the Series plays in baseball.

But for me, any recollection of the World Series can begin at only one place: in Chicago, just after the turn of the century.

The year was 1906, and the Series to be played that year was only the third one in the modern era. It was also the first intracity Series, and it quickly gained the status of a baseball legend.

At that time, Chicago was as hot a baseball town as you're ever likely to find on this planet. Both Chicago clubs had won the pennant in their respective leagues, and they and their followers were just burning to have the Series get under way.

The Cubs, managed by Frank Chance, "the Peerless Leader," had captured the National League pennant by setting a record still not equaled. They won 116 games and lost only 36. The White Sox, a weak-hitting club that finished the season with a team batting average of .220, gained a total of ninety victories, winning out over

taken my older brother to see some of the games that year. My older brother was collecting the pictures of ballplayers that came with certain brands of cigarettes—Sweet Caporals, Piedmonts and Capitols. Whenever he got duplicates, he would give them to me. I began to build a collection of baseball cards before I could even read.

As my interest in the game developed, one of my great hopes was to see a World Series game. But not just any game. I dreamed of seeing the Chicago White Sox play in a World Series. I yearned for them to become the Champions of the World.

Chicago White Sox 1917

the New York Highlanders by just three games. During the regular season, the White Sox hit a total of six home runs, two by the manager and center fielder, Fielder Jones. Wildfire Frank Schulte, the Cubs' right fielder, hit seven homers—a good output for a season in the era of "the dead ball." Nick Altrock, later famous as baseball's funniest clown, won twenty-one games, the most games of any pitcher on the White Sox staff. Lee Tannenhill, Sox third baseman, finished the season with a batting average of .191. Needless to say, the Cubs were the overwhelming favorites.

Yet the White Sox won the Series in six games and are now known in baseball history as "The Hitless Wonders."

I was two years old when that Series was played. My father was a baseball fan, and he had

I finally got my chance on October 6, 1917, when the White Sox met the Giants in the fourteenth World Series, at Chicago's Comiskey Park. The White Sox beat the New York Giants, 2-1, thanks to a long home run into the left-center-field bleachers by Happy Felsch. Eddie Cicotte was the winning pitcher, and Slim Sallee, a lean, gangling southpaw, took the defeat.

On that Saturday morning, my older brother Earl and I set the alarm for four A.M. We wanted to be sure to get bleacher seats for the game. We also wanted to be able to say that we had waited in line for our tickets from the early hours of the morning. We had both read that fans did this, and we figured we had to do it too, if only to uphold our credentials as real fans.

We were in that line before five A.M., but

there were already several hundred ahead of us. A few of them were kids in short pants like us, but the majority were grown men. It was evident that we could have slept longer and still have gotten tickets. But it wouldn't have been the same. We were **proud** that we had been standing in line since five A.M.

It was a chilly morning, but many fires had been built and there were vendors selling hot coffee. We enjoyed the whole scene, especially the baseball talk we overheard.

We made some money that morning, too. Several times, we sold our place in line for a dollar without having to get out of line ourselves. Finally, a man behind us told us that we had made enough money and that we'd have to sacrifice our places in-line if we sold them once more. We wouldn't have given up our places for ten times the money that we earned in this fashion, so we discontinued our business operations.

I got my second chance to see a Series game two years later. My Uncle Tom, a traveling salesman, was on the road. But he sent me a letter with a money order enclosed so that I could attend the eighth game of the 1919 World Series, which was scheduled on a weekday afternoon. This was back when the Series was a best-out-of-nine affair. Also in the envelope was another letter addressed to the priest who was the prefect of discipline at my high school. My Uncle Tom explained to the priest that a World Series ball game was an event that I would remember all my life. He asked the priest to please excuse me from classes so that I could go see the eighth game.

This was, as is well known, the clinching game for the Cincinnati Reds, who won 10-5 over the White Sox. It was a World Series that left a black mark on baseball for quite a while when it was later revealed that several White Sox players conspired to fix the outcome. Its historical significance made me even happier to have seen the game.

A lot has changed since those early years. Neither the game nor the strategy for playing it is still the same. With the ball livened up, power hitting is now the dominant factor. But years ago, the game was built on pitching. Back then, most of the pitchers who started a Series game remained on the mound until it was over. Today, however, that is rarely the case.

And then, too, there's the great improvement in gloves. It's no accident that the World Series record for errors was set in 1909, before the shape and size of baseball mitts began to change. In that Series, the Pittsburgh Pirates defeated the Detroit Tigers in seven games. The Pirates made nineteen errors, but the Tigers weren't far behind, with fifteen. Together, the thirty-four errors made by both teams set the record for the most errors ever committed in a World Series.

Although, to be fair, the modern glove obviously hasn't completely eliminated errors from Series scorecards, it has merely reduced their number. The fact is, only twice in the entire history of the World Series has a team played errorless ball. The first to accomplish this feat were the 1937 New York Yankees, who took the New York Giants in a five-game Series; and the second were the 1966 Baltimore Orioles, who rolled over the Los Angeles Dodgers in four straight games.

The many changes in the game have had at least one noticeable effect upon those of us old enough to remember the first few World Series. they make it well nigh impossible to compare players. Sometimes when I'm in a clubhouse, younger baseball writers ask me how such and such a player stacks up to Walter Johnson or Ty Cobb or Babe Ruth.

It's not an easily answered question. And frankly, I don't really like to compare a player of today with one of days gone by. Baseball can well accommodate both its heroes of yesterday and of today.

Yet comparisons are inevitable, and often they add to one's enjoyment as a fan. I'm far from immune. Outside of Jackie Robinson, I've never seen anyone run the bases the way Ty Cobb did. Nor could I say that there has ever been a smarter ballplayer than the great second baseman Eddie Collins. But for a baseball player to be great, it is sufficient that he be so according to the conditions of his times.

One such player was Napoleon Lajoie. He was so good that many people put him in a class with Honus Wagner, the legendary Pittsburgh Pirates shortstop. In 1901, Lajoie, playing with the Philadelphia Athletics, hit .401. In fact, if Ty Cobb had taken his father's advice and stayed in Georgia to study law rather than becoming a big-league ballplayer, Lajoie may well have been called "the greatest player who ever lived." As it was he was displaced as the outstanding hitter in the American League by Cobb. Lajoie was completely different than Cobb at the plate. He was infinitely graceful, and he swung the bat in a seemingly effortless way—but the ball would go like a bullet.

Unfortunately, for all his prowess, Lajoie never had a chance to play in a World Series. He did come close, though. In 1908, when he was manager and second baseman of the Cleveland Naps, the club finished second to the Detroit Tigers. They lost out for the pennant on the very last day of the season.

Another great player who never had a chance to play in the World Series was George Sisler. Tommy Holmes, the sportswriter, once said that he thought Sisler was so perfect a player that it was almost dull to watch him. He did everything right. Twice Sisler hit over .400, and he still holds

Napoleon Lajoie in the early 1900's, never had a chance to play in a World Series.

the record (257) for most hits made in a regular league season.

Among the other genuine stars who never played in a World Series are Harry Heilmann, Ted Lyons, Luke Appling, Ernie Banks and Ralph Kiner. All of these players have been elected to the Baseball Hall of Fame; but even though they have been immortalized with baseball's highest honor, the fact that they never participated in a World Series leaves something incomplete about their careers. It is somewhat like looking at an absorbing picture without a frame.

Players in every era have coveted a chance to play in the Big Show. And when you look at the stakes involved, it's no wonder. Ever since that first Series in 1903, the rewards have continued to rise.

Ralph Kiner (Inset) and Ernie Banks, both Hall of Famers, never played in a World Series.

The winning share that goes to a player on the winning team is only one of many other benefits. A Series player can now be paid for public appearances during the winter and earn extra money from commercials. But to the fans, these are just incidental advantages.

Victory in the World Series is the ultimate goal in baseball. And if a player has a decisive role in the World Series victory of his team, he has reached one of the peaks of his career. He knows that he has joined the ranks of those whose names are included not only in the history of baseball but also in baseball legend.

In Ernest Lawrence Thayer's famous poem "Casey at the Bat," five thousand eyes in Mudville were on the mighty Casey when he stepped into the batter's box. In a World Series game, a player stepping up to the plate knows that there are tens of millions of eyes on him via television. In addition to the regular fans, the audience is swelled by the thousands of viewers who, although they don't follow baseball during the season, never miss a World Series game. It has become a national spectacle. I think this is a healthy holiday. But then I'm prejudiced—I love baseball.

I begin following baseball every season when I go to Florida for two weeks to watch spring training. And by the time the playoffs begin, I am completely caught up in the excitement. By the time the World Series rolls around, I am totally immersed in the super-charged atmosphere that surrounds the baseball world. Baseball owners, executives, scouts, front-office people, former players and platoons of newspaper and magazine sportswriters all congregate for the World Series. But the games themselves are only part of the pleasure. It's also a time to renew acquaintances, to swap stories and to reminisce.

I probably like that last part best of all, for reminiscing is something unique to baseball. Oh, other sports have their great memories, too. And certainly it's enjoyable to look back on occasion at one's personal life. But for sheer power and enjoyment, no other sport and no past experience can match the memories of the summer game.

I never felt this more strongly than I did one evening after a 1973 World Series game between the Mets and the A's. After the game, I happened to be talking to Casey Stengel. Actually, Casey was doing most of the talking and I was doing most of the listening. And, as those who knew him will affirm, listening to Ol' Case could be a pleasure all its own.

We talked about the night's game, of course. But it wasn't long before the conversation turned to some of the old-time players. Players like Johnny Evers, Heinie Zimmerman, Jack Coombs, Vic Saier and Fred Mollwitz—names remembered and other names that are all but forgotten.

We talked until four A.M., but we hardly noticed the passage of time. We had entered that special world of baseball—its history, its personalities and its memories.

Sometimes, in an atmosphere like that, time itself seems to collapse. Other games and other seasons suddenly seem to be less distant. Names and faces come flooding back, and you find yourself remembering so much more about the players than the columns of statistics that flank their names in the record books. You remember the men, the personalities, whose actions shaped baseball history—the people who made it all that it is today.

And you remember the Series. Always the Series. For, after all, it is **the** central event in the baseball year—the single shining celebration about which everything else revolves. All that comes before is but preparation, and all that follows is but the laying of the groundwork for the next season and the next Series.

Today, with three-quarters of a century behind it, the World Series has become a rock-rooted tradition. It has contributed so much and become such an integral part of the game that it's simply impossible to imagine major-league baseball without it.

And a good thing, too. For if the World Series did not exist, our spirits would be the poorer for it. There would be far fewer golden moments, fewer miraculous plays and fewer immortal players to recall. The sports's continuity would somehow be broken, and baseball would never have become what it is today: the best damn game in the world. ◇

The young Casey Stengel as a New York Giant.

Iron Arms

BY JOSEPH L. REICHLER

A TOTAL OF 436 WORLD SERIES GAMES have been played since Deacon Charles Phillippe of Pittsburgh defeated Cy Young of Boston in the first game of the modern World Series on October 1, 1903. In about half of them (210), the winning pitchers have held their opponents to no more than one run. And eighty-six of the games, or about one in every five, have been shutouts. Thus, more than any other baseball skill, pitching has clearly dominated the Big Show from the beginning.

The first, and some say the best, in a long line of memorable World Series mound artists was a young fellow named Christy Mathewson. Known as "Big Six" by his admiring fans, Matty accomplished something in the 1905 Series that has never been equaled since.

Matty was in his prime that year, tall, muscular, handsome, and only twenty-five years of age. He had run up a 31-9 record as the New York Giants ran off with their second straight pennant and took on the Philadelphia Athletics, champions of the infant American League, for the World Championship.

Columbia Park in Philadelphia seated 12,000; but there were 17,955 spectators, paying a dollar apiece for the grandstand and fifty cents a head for the bleachers or standing room behind ropes in the outfield, for the first game. Mathewson, dressed in the Giants' new black uniform—a bit of John McGraw psychology—allowed the Athletics only four hits, three on ground-rule doubles, walked nobody, and struck out six. His fastball and curve were constantly on target, and so was his big pitch, the famed fadeaway. When it was over, he had pitched a shutout, giving the Giants the opener, 3-0. Philadelphia got even the next day as Chief Bender returned the favor by shutting out the Giants. The third game was delayed a day by rain, and McGraw surprised everyone by calling on Matty. Again Matty shut out the A's on just four hits, striking out eight and walking only one—the only walk he gave up in the Series. The Giants took advantage of nine hits and five Philadelphia errors to run up a 9-0 score.

Mathewson had nothing to do with the fourth-game 1-0 victory by Joe McGinnity over Ed-

Walter Johnson was a super pitcher whose feats were so fantastic that today fans wonder if he was more myth than man.

die Plank. But on Saturday, October 14, a crowd of 25,000 howling New Yorkers piled into the Polo Grounds to see if Mathewson, pitching with only one day's rest, could end it. His opponent was the tough and relentless Chief Bender. Matty gave up six hits that afternoon and Bender five, but the Giants pulled it out, 2-0 and the Series was over.

All five games had been shutouts, three of them by the incomparable Mathewson, who struck out eighteen batters in twenty-seven scoreless innings. This brilliant performance, and countless

Christy Mathewson

others that followed, inspired the late Grantland Rice to write, "There have been others who had as great an arm, others with as much nerve, and probably a few just as smart, but when it comes to a combination of all these things, there will never be another Matty. Christy Mathewson brought something to baseball that no one else had ever given to the game. He handed the game a certain touch of class, an indefinable lift in culture, brains, and personality."

It took nineteen years for the Series to pro-

duce another Super Pitcher, but when it did, it found itself with a living legend. His name was Walter Johnson, and his pitching feats were so fanciful, his achievements on the mound so implausible, that present-day fans sometimes wonder if Walter Johnson was indeed more a myth than man.

Where do you begin to relate the records that fell to the unbelievable fastball of Walter Johnson? Do you start with the most American League games—416 in 21 seasons with the

Washington Senators? Or do you begin with his unmatched 3,508 strikeouts? Perhaps you prefer his feat, in 1908, of shutting out the New York Yankees in three consecutive games? Or his lifetime total of 113 runless games? Or his 1913 performance of allowing only 1.09 earned runs per game?

You could fill a book with Johnson's feats. A league record-tying sixteen consecutive victories in 1912, fifty-six consecutive innings without allowing a single run in 1913, twenty or more victories for ten consecutive seasons, thirty victories thrice. Johnson was the undisputed king of the hill. Yet it was not until his eighteenth season, when the Senators captured their first pennant in 1924, that he finally got his chance to pitch in a World Series.

Johnson was in the evening of his career, thirty-seven years old, and getting so he'd tire in the late innings. His fastball was a shade slower than in other years, and he needed more rest between starts. So perhaps it wasn't surprising that Johnson lost the first game to John McGraw's Giants, 4-3, in twelve innings. For five innings the Senators didn't give Johnson a run. Then suddenly they tied at 2-2 in the ninth. Johnson took them past the tenth and eleventh, but then...a walk to Hank Gowdy, a single by Art Nehf, a wild throw and singles by Ross Youngs and Bill Terry...Johnson's long delayed World Series start went blooey. Yet even in defeat Johnson tied a World Series record by striking out twelve men.

At the end of four games, the teams were tied, and now it was Johnson's turn again. But he had given too much in that twelfth-inning opener. For eight innings it was close, with the Giants leading 3-2. And then they beat him, 6-2. Now, indeed, it was a sad World Series for Johnson, loser of both starts. Few expected Johnson to ever be seen in the World Series again, even after the Senators forced a seventh game by winning the sixth, 2-1.

Curly Ogden started the final game. But in the ninth, with the score tied at 3-3, manager Bucky Harris needed a pitcher. Who else but Walter Johnson could best answer to that order? "You're the best we've got, Walter," Harris said, "we've got to win or lose with you."

Johnson was in trouble from the start. Frankie Frisch tripled with no one out, and Youngs walked. But Walter bore down and struck out George Kelly and then retired Irish Meusel on a fly. The Giants put at least one man on base in the tenth, eleventh and twelfth innings, but Johnson was able to call up his reserves to keep them from crossing the plate.

It was still 3-3 when Jack Bentley retired the first Washington batter in the bottom of the twelfth. He appeared to have a second out when Muddy

Ruel raised a soft pop foul in back of the plate. But Hank Gowdy, the catcher, got his foot caught in his own mask and dropped the ball. Given a reprieve, Ruel doubled and later scored when Earl McNeely's grounder to third base hit a pebble and bounced over Freddie Lindstrom's head. The Senators won the World Series, and Walter Johnson was the winning pitcher.

Hank Gowdy

Frankie Frisch

Two years later, another magic name appeared on the World Series pitching roster—Grover Cleveland Alexander. One of the greatest right-handed pitchers ever to face a batter, Alex was a diamond hero whose superb performances have become an immortal baseball tradition. Today, though, when the name of Old Pete is mentioned, few think of the brilliant achievements of his two decades in the National League. Few remember that in two successive seasons he won more than thirty games—thirty-one in 1915 and thirty-three in 1916. Alex won 373 regular-season games, but today all are overshadowed by a single nerve-tightening, drama-packed moment that occurred in 1926, when on the downside of his career he faced Yankees slugger Tony Lazzeri.

Grover Cleveland Alexander

In 1926 Alexander was no longer the pitching ace of years gone by, but his educated right arm and cunning brain had helped give the St. Louis Cardinals their first National League pennant. Later, in the World Series with the power-packed New York Yankees, Old Pete had twice rallied a battered Redbirds team and kept their chances alive. Beaten in the first game, the Cards banked on Alexander to square matters, and he came through. Again in the sixth game, with the Yankees leading three games to two and all set to take the title, the Cards called on Alexander. Once more he conquered the awe-inspiring Murderers' Row of Ruth, Gehrig, Meusel and Lazzeri. So when the seventh and deciding game came up, Old Pete already wore the hero's mantle. He had done his job and his role was apparently over. He had brought the Cards to the doorstep of Series glory; now it was up to the others.

On the fateful afternoon of the October 10, the day of the final game, Alexander picked himself a comfortable spot in the bull pen and promptly dozed off. Jesse Haines had drawn the pitching assignment for St. Louis, opposing Waite Hoyt, and

it seemed as if Jesse would be all right.

Babe Ruth slammed Haines for a home run in the third inning, his fourth of the Series. The Cards came back in the fourth, punching over three runs. Then the Yankees produced a run in the sixth to bring the score to 3-2. The pressure became painfully acute in the seventh inning. Earle Combs opened with a single, and Mark Koenig laid down a sacrifice. Babe Ruth was purposely passed and was forced at second by Bob Meusel. As Haines pitched to Lou Gehrig, it became apparent that he was losing his stuff. Lou walked and the bases were now loaded. Tony Lazzeri was up next.

Here was the payoff point the Yankees had been waiting for. New York would have the Series in the bag. Manager Rogers Hornsby came over from second base to talk to Jesse Haines. The pitcher held up his hand. He had developed a blister; he could hardly grip the ball.

Hornsby waved to the Cardinal bull pen. Herman Bell pushed open the gate and was starting toward the mound. But Hornsby waved him back. That left only Old Pete, who hadn't warmed up at all. Now let Alexander pick up the narrative:

Babe Ruth and Tony Lazzeri loosening up before the opener of the 1926 Series against the Cardinals.

Well, I was sitting around in the bull pen, not doing anything, when someone said, "He wants you in there, Pete." I didn't find out what had happened until after the game. The bull pen in Yankee Stadium is under the bleachers, and when you're down there you can't see what's going on out on the field. All you know is what you learn from the yells of the fans overhead.

So when I came out from under the bleachers, I see the bases filled, and Lazzeri's standing in the box. Tony is up there all alone with everyone in that Sunday crowd watching him. I say to myself, "Take your time. Lazzeri isn't feeling any too good up there. Let him stew."

There have been all kinds of stories that I celebrated the night before and had a hangover when Rog called me from the bull pen to pitch to Lazzeri; that isn't the truth. After I had beaten the Yankees the day before, Rog came over to me in the clubhouse and said, "Alex, if you want to celebrate tonight, I wouldn't blame you. But go easy; I may need you tomorrow."

I said, "Okay, Rog, I'll tell you what I'll do. I'll ride back to the hotel with you and I'll meet you tomorrow and ride out to the park with you." Hell, I wanted to get that big end of the Series money as much as anyone. I had a few drinks at the hotel on Saturday night, but I was cold sober when I faced Lazzeri.

I remember Hornsby handing me the ball and saying, "We're in a tough spot and there's no place to put this guy."

"I'll take care of that," I told Rog. Bob O'Farrell, our catcher came over to talk to me. "Let's start right away where we left off yesterday," he said. Bob reminded me we'd gotten Lazzeri out four straight times Saturday with the curve ball.

I said O.K. to O'Farrell, we'll curve him. My first pitch was a curve and Tony missed. O'Farrell came out again. "Look, Aleck," he began. "This guy will be looking for that curve the next time. Let's give him a fast one." I agreed and poured one in, right under his chin. There was a crack and I knew the ball was hit hard. A pitcher can tell pretty well from the sound. I turned around to watch the ball, and all the Yankees on base were on their way. But the drive hit a tail-end fade and landed foul by several feet in the left-field bleachers. So I said to myself, "No more of that for you, my lad." I wasted a couple of pitches, then fed him a curve. Lazzeri swung and missed. Well, we were out of that jam, but there were still two innings to go.

Alexander set the Yankees down in order in the eighth and retired the first two in the ninth. And then Babe Ruth came up. Alexander, pitching carefully, walked him. Bob Meusel, a home-run hitter in his own right, was the next batter. On the first pitch to Meusel, the Babe surprised everyone by breaking for second. O'Farrell wasn't caught napping, though. His accurate throw to Hornsby had the Babe by ten feet.

Ruth picked himself up off the ground and walked away without saying a word. Old Pete also sauntered off the field. It was all in a day's work. But a day that can never be forgotten—October 10, 1926.

As Grover Cleveland Alexander so powerfully proved, it can be a mistake to underestimate a great pitcher—no matter how old he is. For example, the Philadelphia Athletics of 1929 had a crack pitching staff led by the great Lefty Grove and George Earnshaw. It was considered almost a foregone conclusion that manager Connie Mack would start one of his aces in the opener of the World Series against the Chicago Cubs. So when Al Simmons, the slugging Philadelphia outfielder, saw

Bob Meusel, strong armed outfielder and a member of the Yankees' "Murderer's Row."

George Earnshaw, Ed Rommel and Lefty Grove, three members of the Athletics' vaunted pitching staff in 1929.

Howard Ehmke warming up before the first game, he could hardly believe his eyes. After all, Ehmke was a fading veteran who had seen his best day.

"Is that fellow going to pitch for us?" Simmons asked of Mr. Mack.

"Why," replied the A's' manager, "isn't it all right with you?"

Simmons gulped. "If it's all right with you, Mr. Mack, it's all right with me," he mumbled.

The other A's players were as surprised by Mack's choice of Ehmke as was Simmons. Ehmke, with an ailing arm, had pitched only fifty-five innings all season. He had been in eleven games, completing only two. And he hadn't pitched in competition since September 11, when he needed help to beat the White Sox.

The following day—September 12—the Athletics were preparing for their final western trip. The American League pennant was pretty well in hand by then, and it looked like the Cubs would win in the National League. Connie Mack called Ehmke into his office and told the thirty-five-year old right-hander he was considering giving him his unconditional release.

For a moment or two Ehmke said nothing. Then in a low voice he said, "All right, Mr. Mack, if that's the way you want it to be. But I've always had the ambition to pitch in a World Series. My arm is not what it once was, but I honestly feel there's one more good game left in it. I'd like a chance to prove it to you."

That's all Connie Mack wanted to hear. He

had had it in mind to pitch Ehmke in the World Series opener, but he wanted to make sure Ehmke was up to it.

"Now I want you to go home," he said to Ehmke after explaining his plan. "The Cubs are coming in to play the Phillies. Sit in the stands and watch their every move. Take notes on all the hitters. Don't report until the day before the Series. You're going to pitch the first game but don't tell anybody. I don't want it known."

Ehmke didn't tell a soul, not even his wife. He remained at home, going out to Shibe Park every morning, doing running exercises, throwing a little and shagging flies. He had twenty-six days in which to get in shape.

When the Cubs came to Philadelphia to play the Phillies, he went out to Baker Bowl to look them over. He kept notes on everybody, paying particular attention to the hitters, constantly seeking to find their weaknesses.

Ehmke rejoined the Athletics in Chicago on October 7, the day before the start of the 1929 Series between the Athletics and Cubs. He reported his findings to Connie Mack. The players were surprised when Ehmke walked into the clubhouse the next morning and got into his uniform. Mack gave no hint of his first-game pitching choice during the pre-game clubhouse meeting, and Ehmke began to worry. He stayed behind when the players filed out of the room.

"Have you changed your mind, Mr. Mack?" he asked.

"Should I?" countered the aging leader of the A's.

"Why, no," replied Ehmke. "I'm ready."

"I'll have Grove warm up with you," Mack said. "I want to keep Joe McCarthy [Cubs manager] guessing."

The 50,740 spectators in Wrigley Field were no less startled than the players when they heard the public-address announcer blare out Ehmke's name. The Cubs had a formidable slugging array consisting of Rogers Hornsby, Hack Wilson, Kiki Cuyler, Riggs Stephenson and Charlie Grimm. Ehmke knew he had his work cut out for him.

Charley Root opposed Ehmke on the mound. For six innings it was a scoreless battle. In the seventh, Jimmie Foxx made good his promise to hit a home run for Ehmke. Foxx hadn't known that Ehmke would pitch the opener, but he had had a hunch. Before going to bed the night before, he had told his roommate, "If you pitch tomorrow, Howard, I'm going to hit a home run for you."

The A's now led 1-0. Ehmke, relying mostly on a wide-sweeping curve and mixing it with an occasional fastball, was compiling an impressive strikeout record. At the end of eight innings, he had

Howard Ehmke, surprise starter and winner in 1929 Series, set a strikeout record of thirteen.

tied Ed Walsh's mark of twelve, set in the 1906 World Series. The A's scored two more runs in the ninth, Bing Miller driving them in with a single.

Ehmke had only one more inning to go to record the shutout. But the Cubs rallied and scored on Stephenson's single. They had the tying runs on the bases with two out. The batter was Chick Tolson, a pinch hitter. The count on Tolson went to three balls and two strikes. Ehmke called catcher Mickey Cochrane out for a conference. "Listen, Mike," he said, "when you go back give me the sign for a fastball. I'll shake you off, but don't mind. I just want to keep that guy guessing. When it's on the way, yell for him to hit it."

Cochrane did as directed. Ehmke threw, Mickey yelled, "Hit it!" and Tolson swung and missed. The Athletics had won the opener, 3-1, and Ehmke had his record of thirteen strikeouts. Ehmke was blasted off the mound in his next start, but the A's went on to win the Series in five games. Ehmke was never to win another game in the major leagues. So this victory was not only his most important, it was also his last.

It couldn't possibly happen. A no-hitter, yes. But a perfect game in a World Series competition? Well, the idea was preposterous. Yet here was tall twenty-seven-year-old Don Larsen standing out there and almost methodically setting down the Brooklyn Dodgers' hitters in a ball game that could not be surpassed for sustained tension, a tension that became almost unbearable to the 64,519 spectators seated in vast Yankee Stadium on this Sunday, October 8, 1956.

Until the seventh inning, the fans were mild-
ly hopeful that the big guy out there might continue
pitching as he had been pitching. But whenever a
Robinson, a Snider, a Campanella or a Hodges
would come up waving a bat, the feeling in the
stands was that, "This is it. You just can't keep a
team like the world champion Brooklyn Dodgers
subdued indefinitely."

But Larsen got through the seventh without
incident, and after that you could almost hear the
crackling of the electricity in the stands. Every pitch
was **the** pitch. Now surely it would happen.

Larsen seemed the least perturbed person
in the entire stadium, with its deceiving shadows
and haze of smoke. He would just shimmy his
shoulders, shake his arm, peer at the squatting Yogi
Berra, straighten up, and with a minimum of windup throw the ball as if he and Yogi were playing
catch in the backyard.

The fans by now were sitting on a powder
keg with a lighted fuse. Every pitch brought an explosive gasp from the crowd, followed by a nervous, incomprehensible babbling that seemed to
sweep the stands in rolling waves. Then the
spectators would edge forward in their seats,
breathing softly as if something they might do
would break the spell.

Larsen got through the eighth inning
unscathed, but the toughest job lay ahead. Three
outs to go, always the toughest outs of all. The
veteran baseball writers, case-hardened over the
years, looked at each other and shrugged. They
were remembering Bill Bevens in his 1947 bid for a
no-hitter in Brooklyn, which was ruined by a double
with two down in the ninth.

But this was more than a no-hitter. A walk,
an error, a hit batsman, would tarnish Larsen's
chance to join baseball's immortals. Up to now,
twenty-four Dodgers had come to the plate and all
twenty-four had returned to the bench. Don had
some help from his teammates. In the second inning, Jackie Robinson's line shot jumped out of Andy Carey's glove but shortstop Gil McDougald fielded it. In the fifth, Mickey Mantle, whose home run
off Sal Maglie the inning before had given the
Yankees a 1-0 lead, made a spectacular backhanded catch of Gil Hodges' long drive to left center. In
the eighth, Hodges hit a tricky low liner to the left of
third base. Carey lunged and caught the ball inches
off the ground.

Now it was the ninth. Three outs to go. Carl
Furillo, first up, flied out. Roy Campanella bounced
out to McDougald. Dale Mitchell, a pinch hitter,
came out of the Dodger dugout. Larsen was no
longer nonchalant. The burden of history was on
his big-boned, slouching shoulders as he turned his
back to the batter who stood between him and
baseball's first perfect game in the World Series.

The crowd moaned as Larsen's first pitch to
Mitchell was wide. Don came back with a slider, and
Babe Pinelli, umpiring his last big-league game
behind the plate, called it a strike. Larsen got a

fastball over, and Mitchell swung and missed. Another fastball was fouled off. It was Larsen's ninety-sixth pitch of the game, and by now the crowd was screaming at every one he threw. Larsen caught Berra's signal for another fastball. He mumbled a prayer to himself: "Please get me through this." Then he pitched.

It was on the outside corner and Mitchell cocked his bat, then held up. Umpire Pinelli thrust his arm through the air in a strike motion to end a game such as none had ever pitched before. Mitchell started to complain that the pitch was outside, but nobody would hear him. Certainly not Pinelli, who was already heading for the dugout. Certainly not Berra, who was already racing toward the mound hurling himself into Larsen's arms. Certainly not Larsen, who had climbed the heights he never thought he would achieve. Certainly not the fans, who had just witnessed something that had never been seen before and quite likely never will be seen again.

Although great pitching at crucial moments or throughout a single tension-filled game has often been the dramatic focal point of the Series, there is another way a pitcher can dominate the autumn classic. He can win three games.

Today, partly because of the "lively ball," the home run, and the use of relief pitchers, this feat is rarely accomplished. In fact there hasn't been a three-game winner since Mickey Lolich of the

Don Larsen showing his pitching form which produced the only perfect game in Series history.

Charles "Babe" Adams as a rookie in 1909 who defeated the Tigers three times.

Detroit Tigers whipped the St. Louis Cardinals in 1968.

When baseball was in its infancy, though, things were different. At times, it sometimes seemed as though three-game Series winners turned up like relatives at a reading of the will. In 1903, for example, Pittsburgh's Deacon Phillippe and Boston's Bill Dineen turned in three wins apiece before Dineen finally won it for the Puritans, five games to three.

In 1905, New York's Christy Mathewson pitched the Giants to victory over the A's with three shutouts. Then, four years later, Charles "Babe" Adams also joined the ranks of three-game winners as the Pirates defeated the Detroit Tigers in 1909.

Unlike the veteran Phillippe, Babe Adams was a rookie who wasn't expected to get into the Series at all because of the Pirates' trio of big winners. The Big Three—Howard Camnitz (25-6), Vic Willis (22-12) and Lefty Al Leifield (19-8)—were Pittsburgh's pride and joy. A fourth pitcher, Nick Maddox, had a 13-8 record. Still around, but somewhat worn, was the indestructible Phillippe (8-3).

Manager Clarke stunned everybody, though, by pitching Adams in the opener. Adams, a big Missouri youngster, was used only in spots against second-division clubs, and had registered twelve victories in fifteen decisions. "Has Fred lost his senses?" moaned a Pirates fan. "What's become of our Big Three?" asked another. While on all sides there was a general lament: "Why send a boy on a man's errand?"

Actually, it was at National League president John Heydler's suggestion that Clarke sent young Adams to the mound in the opener. In Washington during the closing days of the American League campaign, Heydler watched the Senators' Dolly Gray mesmerize the heavy-hitting Tigers. Noticing Gray's motion was similar to that of Adams, Heydler sought out Clarke on the eve of the opener. "I don't know who you intend to pitch tomorrow," said Heydler, "but I saw Dolly Gray of the Senators make the Tigers throw away their bats a few days ago. And you know Gray has a remarkable pitching resemblance to Adams."

Shortly before his death in 1961, Clarke recalled that historic first game when Adams eased the Pirates' fans' fears with a 4-1 triumph over the Tigers. "Adams didn't know he was going to pitch until it was time for the warm-up," Clarke said. "Then I handed him a new ball, and his hands started to shake so much he almost dropped it. I gave him a look of contempt and said, 'What's the matter, kid, you yellow? Haven't you got any stuff in you?' "

Adams was jittery at the start, yielding a run in the first inning, but he steadied down to pitch scoreless ball the rest of the way.

"For two or three innings, I kept riding him the same way, and he really did some pitching," said Clarke. "Then I switched tactics and started to praise him. He just held 'em to six hits and beat 'em, 4-1.

"When it was over, I shook his hand and said, 'Tell me, Babe, what were you thinking about when you went out there to pitch?'

"And he said, 'I was thinking you were the meanest so-and-so I ever saw, and as soon as I won the game I was coming in and punch you in the nose.' "

With the clubs alternating in victories every other day, Adams also won the fifth game, 8-4. And when everything was on the line in the seventh, Adams was more effective than in his previous efforts. He handled the vaunted Ty Cobb and Sam Crawford with ease. Twice he retired Cobb on bouncers to the pitching mound and twice on routine outfield flies. Crawford hit only one ball hard, and it was caught by Clarke in left field. In all, Adams allowed six scattered hits and issued only one walk. His 8-0 triumph enabled him to join Dineen, Phillippe and Mathewson in the elite three-game-winners' circle.

Clarke applied psychology again before Adams' third victory—this time to the whole club. The Pirates had lost the sixth game of perhaps the roughest, rowdiest World Series ever played. Several players of both clubs were spiked, and there were a couple of fist fights.

"I knew I had to do something the night

before the final game," Fred recalled. "My boys were so wrought up and shaky, I just had to get them into a calm mood."

Clarke filled his Detroit hotel room with tubs of iced pop and beer, hired a quartet to sing, and invited a couple of fellows who had reputations as tellers of funny stories. Then he informed the players that there would be a meeting in his room that night.

"They all came in expecting a lecture," he said. "You never saw such surprised looks as when I began handing out beer and pop and the quartet started to sing. Well, we sat around two or three hours, talking and laughing and listening to the singing, never mentioning the next day.

"Finally, I told 'em, 'All right, boys, let's go to bed now. We've got a ball game tomorrow. If we win, all right. If we don't, well, that's all right, too. We've already had a good season.'

"You know, everybody showed up the next day just as loose and relaxed, and the Tigers were tight as a drum. We scalped 'em, 8-0."

It was only a year later, in 1910, that a fifth member joined the three-game-winning set. His name was Jack Coombs, a husky young pitcher from Colby College. Coombs formed one third of Connie's Mack's Athletics' Big Three, along with Chief Bender and Eddie Plank. But Plank did not pitch in the 1910 Series, because Mack, with his knowledge of the Chicago team, elected to use only right-handers, who, while they were hit rather hard, held the Cubs in all except one game. Coombs was credited with three victories. On the other hand, Chicago's star pitchers were hammered hard in every game, with Frank Baker leading the attack, both in numbers and length of drives. Only one of the five games was close, that being the one in which Mordecai Brown, after relieving Leonard "King" Cole in the ninth inning, defeated Chief Bender, 4-3, in ten innings.

The "lively ball" issue made its appearance in this Series. The first ball hit in the first game was a bounder to Joe Tinker. The Cubs shortstop threw out the runner, then demanded to see the ball, declaring something was wrong with it. The umpires examined it and found nothing wrong, but all through the game the Cubs players complained the ball was too lively. At the end of the game, several Cubs players took one of the American League balls, cut it up, and discovered for the first time the now famous "cork center." Until then, the National Leaguers were in ignorance of the fact that the American League had been using the new experimental baseball.

The Athletics won the Series in five games, with Coombs winning the second, third and fifth games. Bender easily defeated Orvie Overall in the first game, and Coombs won the second, 9-5. Jack

Jack Coombs, one of Connie Mack's big three, who won three games from the Cubs in 1910.

Coombs was wild, walking nine batters, but the Cubs, although they slapped his offerings for eight hits, could not hit when hits meant runs. The A's, with a 2-0 lead, moved into Chicago; and Mack surprised reporters when they asked him who would pitch the third game.

"Well," said Mack, "I think I'll come right back with Jack. He had rather an easy time of it yesterday."

With one day's rest, Coombs wasn't at his best. But his teammates backed him up with a fifteen-hit attack against Ed Reulbach, Harry McIntire and Jack Pfiester, and he won, 12-5. The Cubs averted a four-game sweep by winning the fourth game, which went to Brown, in relief. The victory encouraged Chicago manager Frank Chance and he threw Brown in again in the fifth game. The three-fingered right-hander was hit hard. So was Coombs, who was making his third start in six days. The Cubs matched the A's' nine hits, but Coombs won, 7-2, for his third triumph.

The Series marked the introduction of the four-umpire system. The National Commission, recognizing that umpiring in the World Series was too heavy a burden for only two men, placed four umpires on the field with excellent results.

Boston's twenty-three-year-old right-hander Smokey Joe Wood joined the three-game winners in 1912 when he led the Red Sox to victory over the Giants. Then, in 1917, Urban "Red" Faber defeated the Giants in three of the four games the White Sox won in the six-game Series. The 1920

Series between Cleveland and Brooklyn saw Elmer Smith become the first big-leaguer to hit a World Series grand-slam; and Jim Bagby was the first pitcher to hit a home run.

That Series also saw Cleveland right-hander Stan Coveleskie become the eighth pitcher to win three games in a Series. In defeating the Dodgers 3-1 in the first game, 5-1 in the fourth and 3-0 in the seventh, Coveleskie yielded fifteen hits, five in each game, and walked only two. In the first game he made only eighty-seven pitches, in the second only eighty-eight, and in the third only eighty-nine.

It wasn't until twenty-six years later that a Series hurler was able to notch three triumphs, although Louis "Bobo" Newson came within an eyelash of achieving it in 1940. That was the year the Cincinnati Reds ended a five-year American League reign by subduing the Detroit Tigers in seven games. Paul Derringer and Bucky Walters won two games apiece for the Reds, but the hero's laurels went to Newsom, who turned in two vital triumphs in a losing cause despite the anguish caused by the death of his father.

The big guy, whom the Tigers had acquired the year before from the St. Louis Browns in a ten-player trade, won the first and fifth games. It was after he had turned back the Reds, 7-2, that he learned his dad had suffered a fatal heart attack while attending the game. Nevertheless, Bobo hurled a brilliant three-hitter four days later, shutting out the Reds, 8-0. The Reds, who had captured the second and fourth games, won the sixth, 4-0,

Bobo Newsom as he looked when he starred for the Tigers in 1940.

behind Walters to even the Series at three victories each.

With only forty-eight hours' rest, Newsom returned for one more try. The Tigers jumped off to a 1-0 lead against Derringer, and Newsom protected that slim lead until the seventh, when Frank McCormick doubled and scored on a two-bagger by Jimmy Ripple. Dick Bartell, Detroit shortstop, took the relay from the outfield with his back to the plate. He was so sure that McCormick had scored that he didn't bother to turn around, even though McCormick was still six feet from the plate. The Reds weren't through. A sacrifice, a walk, and a long fly by Billy Myers sent Ripple over the plate with the run that gave the Tigers a 2-1 victory and ended Newsom's hopes of winning his third game.

Up until 1946, the pantheon of three-game winners had been reserved for right-handers. But when the Cardinals met the Red Sox that year, Harry "The Cat" Brecheen changed all that. The little left-hander from Oklahoma shut out the Red Sox in the second game, brought the contest to three games apiece with a 4-1 victory in the sixth game, and saved the seventh for his friend pitcher, Murry Dickson.

Eleven years later Lew Burdette of the Milwaukee Braves turned in a pitching masterpiece in allowing the New York Yankees only two runs in winning three games in the 1957 Series, none in the last twenty-four innings. The lean and lanky right-hander not only blanked the American League champions twice in succession, but whipped them twice in their own park, something no other pitcher has been able to do.

The Series opened at Yankee Stadium, and Warren Spahn, ace of the Braves' staff, pitched and lost the opener. "I'm kind of glad I didn't start the first game," Burdette told a reporter. "It gave me a chance to size 'em up from the bench. They're a good team, but hell they can be pitched to. I saw that."

The next day Burdette put his observations to the test and came through with a seven-hitter for a 4-2 victory. Lew allowed single runs in the second and third innings, but after the Braves opened up a 4-2 lead in the fourth, he hurled nothing but goose eggs the rest of the way. It was Burdette's turn again in the fifth game, and he responded by outdueling Whitey Ford, 1-0. Ford gave up only six hits to Burdette's seven, but Lew was always the master in the clutch. He made the Yankees hit nearly everything on the ground, striking out five and walking nobody.

The Yankees defeated Bob Buhl, 3-2. It was Spahn's turn to pitch the deciding game, but he came up with a stubborn virus and manager Fred Haney turned to Burdette. A crowd of 61,207 jammed Yankee Stadium to see whether Burdette could make it three in a row. His opponent was Don Larsen, who only a year and two days before had pitched the only perfect World Series game in history.

Burdette was in trouble immediately when leadoff batter Hank Bauer doubled, but he retired the next three batters without permitting Bauer to advance a base. The Braves jumped on Larsen for four runs in the fourth, a double by Eddie Mathews, the key hit. Burdette mowed the Yankees down in order in four of the next five innings but ran into trouble in the ninth, when three singles filled the bases, with two out. Bill Skowron, the next batter, smashed a one-bouncer to Mathews, who stepped on third and threw to first for a game-ending double play. The Braves had a 5-0 victory and the World Championship. Burdette had won three games, including two shutouts, and had chalked up an earned-run average of 0.67.

A World Series pitcher can also make his presence felt by racking up an impressive number of strikeouts. Howard Ehmke's benchmark of thirteen strikeouts in a single game in 1929 held for nearly a quarter of a century. Then, on October 2, 1953, Brooklyn Dodger Carl Erskine went Ehmke one better by striking out fourteen Yankees.

Curiously, Erskine scored eleven of his fourteen strikeouts against left-handed hitters, fanning Mickey Mantle and Joe Collins four times each. Erskine came into the ninth inning needing one more strikeout to tie and two to break the record. Don Bollweg, a left-handed pinch hitter, was batting for Phil Rizzuto. The count ran to two and two. Erskine threw a high fastball, inside. The batter swung and

missed. The 35,270 Ebbets Field patrons sent up a throaty shout.

It was only the first out in the ninth. The public-address system sounded again. Johnny Mize was pinch-hitting for pitcher Vic Raschi. Erskine remembered that "Big Jawn" had hit a three-run homer off him in the 1952 Series, a year ago almost to the day. An ideal batting stance and a level swing made Mize dangerous anywhere in the strike zone. He rarely struck out. Two uncontested curve balls crossed the plate for a zero-and-two count. Erskine wasted a pitch, Mize fouled off the next. The fifth pitch was a change-up. Mize hesitated momentarily, swung and missed, and Erskine had his fourteenth strikeout. Oh, yes, the Dodgers won, 3-2.

Erskine's record lasted exactly ten years to the day. On October 2, 1963, Sandy Koufax, also a member of the Dodgers, who now called Los Angeles their home, wiped out Erskine's record by striking out fifteen Yankees. A crowd of 69,000 at Yankee Stadium was there to see a southpaw pitching duel between Koufax and the Yankee's Whitey Ford.

Koufax, who won 25 games for the Dodgers during the regular season, setting a National League record of 306 strikeouts, had one previous World Series start—against the Chicago White Sox in 1959—losing, 1-0. The Dodgers finally got him some runs, three of them coming on a home run by Koufax' catcher, John Roseboro. Sandy did the rest. He fanned the first five he faced with his bewildering assortment of curves, fastballs and sliders. His bid to equal the Series consecutive

Carl Erskine shown when he broke Howard Ehmke World Series record in 1953.

strikeout mark of six, set by Cincinnati's Hod Eller in the 1919 Series against the White Sox, failed when Elston Howard lifted a soft pop foul to Roseboro in the second. But this didn't slow Koufax' strikeout operations. He got three in a row in the fourth and Mickey Mantle for a second time in the fifth as he retired the first fourteen batters to face him.

By the time the ninth inning came around, Koufax had thirteen strikeouts, needing only one to tie his former teammate. He got it by throwing a third strike past Phil Linz, a pinch hitter. "I knew I had tied the record when I saw the number fourteen flashed on the scoreboard," Koufax recalled. "And I debated with myself whether I should really go for fifteen. I'm such an admirer of Carl that I almost hated to take the record away from him." That he did by fanning the last Yankees batter, pinch hitter Harry Bright, with a blazing fastball. Koufax allowed six hits and would have had a shutout but for a home run by Tommy Tresh in the eighth.

In recalling how Koufax struck him out twice and had two strikes on him in his other two times at bat, Mickey Mantle said, "Koufax showed me that day that everything they said about him was true. His curve was just as tough to hit as his fastball. He threw me four or five good pitches right down the middle, but all I could do was foul them back. His fastball moved up on the hitter and his curve dropped out of sight."

October 2 appears to be a magic day for strikeout pitchers. Just five years after Koufax' fifteen against the Yankees—on October 2, 1968—Bob Gibson, perhaps the greatest pitcher ever to wear a St. Louis Cardinal uniform, struck out seventeen Detroit Tigers batters to establish a new strikeout record that is still in existence today. It was the opening game of the Series, and Bob was matched against Denny McLain in one of the most widely heralded pitching match-ups in World Series history. Both had finished brilliant seasons. Gibson had won twenty-two of thirty-one decisions but, more important, he had thirteen shutouts, with a 1.12 earned-run average, the lowest ever for a pitcher working three-hundred or more innings. McLain had won thirty-one games for the Tigers, the first to hit the thirty mark since Dizzy Dean did it with the Cardinals in 1934.

It was a scoreless game until the fourth, when two walks, a single by Mike Shannon and a double by Julian Javier, produced three Redbirds runs off McLain. Gibson struck out seven of the first nine batters to face him. Al Kaline was called out on strikes in the fourth as was Don Wert in the fifth. Gibson got two more in the sixth. Two more Tigers fanned in the seventh and when Eddie Mathews, batting for Wert in the eighth, went down swinging, he became Gibson's fourteenth strikeout victim, setting the stage for the record-breaking drama of the ninth inning.

By that time the St. Louis crowd of 54,692 knew that Gibson was only one strikeout from Koufax' record. Mickey Stanley momentarily thwarted Gibson by singling to open the ninth, but the flame-throwing Redbirds right-hander fanned Kaline for the third time, and the crowd roared as the scoreboard flashed number fifteen. Three fruitless swings by Norm Cash made Gibson the new World Series strikeout king. A moment later Willie Horton looked at the third strike for the final out of the game. The Cards had won, 4-0, and Gibson had fanned his seventeenth.

When Gibson took the mound in the 1968 Series opener against the Tigers, he already boasted a remarkable Series record. After bowing to Mel Stottlemyre and the New York Yankees in the second game of the 1964 Series, he began a string that eventually reached seven consecutive complete game victories in World Series competition. Gibson started his victory string in the fifth game of the '64 Series and then averaged his initial loss with a victory over Stottlemyre to win the seventh game and the Series for St. Louis. Three years later, the Cards were in the World Series again and Bob contributed three more victories, over the Red Sox, in seven games, becoming the first to register three triumphs since Burdette in 1957. He won the opener, 2-1, allowing but five hits in a 6-0 triumph. His third start of the Series came in the final game. This time he pitched a three-hitter and slammed a home run to bring the Championship to St. Louis with a 7-2 triumph.

If it weren't for a fielding flaw by Curt Flood, a brilliant defensive outfielder, Bob Gibson might have become the only pitcher to win three World Series games twice—and in consecutive years, at that. It was not to be, however, and Flood's misplay led to the Tigers' final 4-1 victory over the Cards in the 1968 World Series which gained Mickey Lolich, Detroit's star left-hander, the distinction of joining the Series' three-game winners. Gibson had followed up his opening-day shutout victory with an easy 10-1 triumph in the fourth game when he took on Lolich in the seventh and final game to decide the title. Lolich, pitching in the shadow of Denny McLain, had kept pace with Bob, winning the second and fifth games by scores of 8-1 and 5-3. So each was going for his third win.

Gibson began spectacularly, retiring the first ten Tigers before giving up an infield hit to Mickey Stanley. Then he retired ten more batters in a row. By this time Bob had struck out six to break the Series record of thirty-one. Not as spectacular as Gibson, Lolich nonetheless got the same results. The Cardinals nicked him for four hits and a walk through the first six innings but failed to break through for a run.

The teams went to the seventh still scoreless. When Stanley struck out and Kaline grounded out, Gibson had retired twenty of the twenty-one batters he had faced. Suddenly, a mild uprising, a disastrous mistake, and Gibson had lost control of the inning, the game and the Series. Cash lined a single to right, and Willie Horton bounced a single through the left side of the infield. Jim Northrup, who had hit a grand-slam the day before, drove the first pitch into deep center field. Flood misjudged the ball. He started in, tried to reverse himself and slipped. The ball landed behind him for a triple, scoring Cash and Horton. Another run scored on Bill Freehan's single.

Gibson was no longer invincible, but suddenly Lolich was. Buoyed by his good fortune, he mowed down the next six Cardinals. The Tigers got another run in the top of the ninth, a run Lolich didn't need, although he did give up a home run to Mike Shannon that spoiled his bid for a shutout. Mickey finished with a five-hitter to become the first left-hander to pitch three complete-game victories in the World Series. ◇

Bob Gibson as he appeared in the 1964 classic.

Magic Mitts

BY JOSEPH L. REICHLER

EVER SINCE THE WORLD SERIES became a national institution shortly after the turn of the century, the guys who slug the ball out of the park and the pitchers who turn in a shutout performance have received the lion's share of the glory. Yet superb fielding and spectacular catches have been responsible for at least as many World Series triumphs as dramatic home runs or skillful pitching.

For example, few fans will ever forget the breathtaking home run by Carlton Fisk that gave the Red Sox a twelfth-inning victory over the Reds in the sixth game of the 1975 World Series. But how many will long remember Dwight Evans' heart-stopping catch in the previous inning that saved the game for the Sox?

Cincinnati's Pete Rose was on first, via a base on balls, and there was one out when Joe Morgan poled a drive that appeared to be headed for Fenway Park's right-field bleachers. Evans raced back, made a complete circle and leaped as high as he could. He came down with the ball and crashed into the barrier. But he still had the presence of mind to throw in the direction of first base, to complete a game-saving double play.

In the 1969 upset of the highly favored Baltimore Orioles by the Miracle Mets of New York, Donn Clendenon, because of his three home runs, and little Al Weis, because of his critical four-bagger, received most of the acclaim. Yet New York center fielder Tommie Agee was at least equally responsible for the Mets' surprise win. Agee treated some 56,000 Shea Stadium viewers to a defensive display such as had never been seen before and may never be seen again.

Behind 3-0 in the fourth inning of the third game, Baltimore had put runners on first and third with one out when Frank Robinson and Boog Powell singled. Gary Gentry fanned Brooks Robinson, but Elrod Hendricks hit a towering smash to left center. Agee raced to the 396-foot sign to make a backhanded fingertip catch of Hendricks' bid for a triple. The Orioles threatened again in the seventh. Gentry disposed of the first two batters,

but suddenly developed a wild spell; he walked three batters in succession and was excused for the day. Nolan Ryan replaced him. Baltimore's Paul Blair drove a liner up the alley to right center that appeared to be headed for extra bases. Somehow Agee got there, making a headlong diving catch of the ball. Either play stands comparison with the best defensive plays in World Series competition.

Bill Mazeroski's miraculous ninth-inning home run in the final game of the 1960 Pirates-Yankees World Series brought Pittsburgh its first World Championship in thirty-five years and sent an entire state into ecstasy. But Mazeroski would never have had that starring opportunity had it not been for a pair of game-saving circus catches by his teammate, center fielder Bill Virdon.

Virdon performed the first of his feats of legerdemain in the opening game. Vernon Law was pitching and the Pirates were leading 3-1 when the Yankees came to bat in the fourth inning. Roger Maris singled and Mickey Mantle walked. Law was in trouble. But Virdon, after a long run, made a sensational one-handed grab off the wall. The play thwarted what would have been a big inning for the Yankees. Instead, New York was limited to one run, and the Pirates won, 6-4.

The Yankees won the second and third game, and the Pirates were fighting desperately to even the Series in the fourth game. It was the seventh inning, and Law again was leading 3-1. The Yankees rallied, scoring a run on a double by Bill Skowron, a single by Gil McDougald and an infield out. When Johnny Blanchard singled, Pirates manager Danny Murtaugh called on his relief ace, Roy Face. Bob Cerv greeted the little fork-ball expert with a long drive to right center. It appeared to be headed for at least two bases, which would have put the Yankees ahead. But Virdon, running at full tilt, pulled down the ball at the 407-foot marker, banging into the wall as he made the catch. The Pirates won the game, 3-2

The 1958 Series was won by the Yankees, one of the few clubs to overcome a three-games-to-one deficit, and it was a great fielding play that was largely responsible for the comeback victory. The key play occurred in the fifth game, after Milwaukee had taken a 3-1 lead in games and appeared about to make it two Series triumphs in a row over the Yankees. Lou Burdette, who had whipped the Yankees four straight times over a two-year span, was trying to wrap it up for the Braves.

The Yankees scored in the third on a home run by Gil McDougald. The Braves made their bid in the sixth. Billy Bruton led off with a single. Red Schoendienst sliced a blooper to left. But New York's Elston Howard, who had replaced Norm Siebern in left field, dashed in and made a diving, sliding one-handed grab of the ball. Bruton, already past second, was an easy double-play victim. Eddie Mathews followed with a single, which would have produced two runs had it not been for Howard's amazing catch. Encouraged by such superb fielding, Bob Turley went on to pitch a shutout, and the Yankees, in a miraculous comeback, also won the sixth and seventh games to avenge their 1957 defeat.

Among the first of the many spectacular defensive plays in the World Series was the extraordinary catch made by Harry Hooper of the Boston Red in the 1912 Series with the Giants.

Christy Mathewson, who had pitched twice without victory, was making a last effort to come up with a triumph that would give the Giants the Championship. His teammates gave him a 1-0 lead in the third inning of this deciding game, and in those days, one run was good as a million when Matty was in form. But Hugh Bedient, the Red Sox pitcher, stayed right with the Peerless One.

Josh Devore opened the Giants' fifth with a single, but was out stealing. Larry Doyle then sent a long smash to right field that had Home Run written all over it. Hooper raced across the field and threw himself over a low railing in front of the temporary bleachers. Half supported by the back of the fans, he reached high with his bare hand and made contact. Although he couldn't hold the ball, he managed to deflect it and grab it in his gloved hand before it touched the ground. It was an unbelievable catch, and for many years afterward, every great catch in a World Series was measured against it.

Whether other catches ever came up to the mark set by Harry Hooper was always a matter of debate. But there was at least one major-league manager who felt that he witnessed a catch of equal merit. The manager was the immortal John McGraw, and the catch was made by the Giants' utility outfielder Bill Cunningham on Babe Ruth in the third game of the 1922 World Series.

Yankee Whitey Witt opened the game with a single off Hugh McQuillan. Joe Dugan followed

Hall of Famer Harry Hooper
of famous Speaker-Hooper-Lewis
outfield of 1912.

41

his teammate's example in short order. Then Babe Ruth was up. The Bambino was in top form, and he smashed a drive that rocketed more than 475 feet to extreme centerfield, where the Polo Grounds was deepest.

Cunningham, who was substituting for Casey Stengel, started running as soon as he heard the crack of the bat. He had to dash around the Eddie Grant monument. and then, as he finally speared the ball between the monument and the old wooden bleachers, he stumbled and fell. But held the ball. Witt, who remained near second until after the catch was made, tagged up and raced for third. But Dugan had all he could do to get back to first.

Cunningham's play provided what proved to be the margin of victory, as both Witt and Dugan scored before McQuillan could retire the side. The Giants tagged Carl Mays for four runs in the fifth to take the game, 4-3. They ended it the next day with a 5-3 decision behind Art Nehf.

One of the most spectacular catches, and certainly the most controversial, ever made in a World Series was the one made by Sam Rice, Washington outfielder, in the eighth inning of the third game in 1925. Half the people in Griffith Stadium thought he had caught the ball; the other half thought he hadn't. It caused such a furor that the game was delayed nearly fifteen minutes. The controversy raged for days. The catch would have been even more controversial if the Senators, who won that particular game from Pittsburgh, 4-3, hadn't lost the Series anyway. If the whole works had been riding on Rice's grab of Smith's drive, it might have been the most hotly disputed play in any Series.

As long as he lived, Rice refused to confirm or deny that he had caught the ball. Virtually every one of his acquaintances, including Judge Landis, then Commissioner of Baseball, tried to pry the truth out of him. but Sam remained silent. Finally, shortly after his death on October 13, 1974, Rice's forty-nine-year-old secret ended with his own testimony from beyond his grave. The story began on Saturday, October 10—a cold, miserable day. Fred Marberry, in relief of Alex Ferguson, was trying to protect a 4-3 lead the Senators had acquired in the seventh. Rice, who had opened in center field, moved to right, and Earl McNeely took over in center. The stiff wind ripping across the field was so strong that it blew a piece off the grandstand roof.

With one out, Pittsburgh's Earl Smith sent a long drive to right center. The ball, riding with the wind, sailed toward the bleachers. Rice raced after it, and just as the ball came down, he flung up his glove. The ball and Sam disappeared together over the low barrier.

If you think Gene Tunney had a long count in his fight with Jack Dempsey, you should have clocked Rice. He was out of sight of everyone, except for his legs sticking up, longer than a TV commercial with a station break thrown in. Charlie Rigler, a National League umpire, ran for the spot, and when Rice finally reappeared with the ball in his glove, he called Smith out.

No ship that sailed the Spanish Main ever encountered more ferocious pirates than those who stormed around the ball field for the next fifteen minutes. Bill McKechnie, the Pirates' manager, appealed to the other umpires to overrule Rigler and call it a home run, but they supported their colleague. The decision stood, and Washington went on to win, 4-3. A score of Pittsburgh supporters offered affidavits that Rice had not held the ball. McKechnie carried his protest to Judge Landis, but the Commissioner stated he had no jurisdiction over a judgment call by an umpire.

For years whenever Rice was asked, "Did you or didn't you?" he would smile and say, "The umpire said I did." Finally, in December of 1974, a document surfaced in the office of Paul Kerr, president of the Hall of Fame. The letter, written by Rice in 1965 "to be opened after my death," described all the circumstances in the eighth inning when Earl Smith came to bat for Pittsburgh: "The ball was a line drive headed for the bleachers toward right center. . .I jumped as high as I could and backhanded. . .but my feet hit the barrier. . .At no

Sam Rice, was Hington's brilliant centerfielder in 1925 series.

time did I lose possession of the ball." That, hopefully, should end the nearly fifty-year-old mystery.

One of the most publicized World Series catches ever made was Al Gionfriddo's amazing grab of Joe DiMaggio's screaming drive toward the left-field bull pen in Yankee Stadium. It happened in the sixth game of the 1947 Series between the Dodgers and Yankees. Only one game from elimination, the Dodgers managed to take an 8-5 lead, and manager Burt Shotton sent Gionfriddo into left field as defensive insurance in the sixth inning. The strategy paid off immediately as the Yankees put a pair of runners on base on a pass to George Stirnweiss and a single by Yogi Berra.

Fred Lieb, the noted baseball writer and historian, described it best: "DiMaggio, the next batter, swung from the heels, and as the Yankee Clipper's powerful drive sped into the evening dusk, practically everyone in the vast crowd thought it was a homer and a tie score.

"But with the crack of the bat, little Gionfriddo raced back into deepest left. It seemed little more than what players termed 'the old college try,' but Al turned a moment before he reached the 415-foot marker and, twisting upward, caught the ball just as it was about to sail over an exit gate.

"As the crowd rocked the stadium with thunderous applause the usually placid DiMaggio, who had robbed many players of long hits, showed his displeasure by raising a dust storm as he kicked grains of sand around the infield."

Though the catch enabled the Dodgers to prolong the Series to a seventh game, the Yankees won it, 5-2. It was the fifth straight time the Yankees had conquered the Dodgers in the World Series.

The Dodgers finally broke the jinx in the 1955 Series. Johnny Podres was acclaimed, and rightfully so, as the Brooklyn hero and could easily have been elected president of that borough had he chosen to run, following his spine-tingling 2-0 triumph in the seventh game of that Series. Teammates hoisted him on their shoulders after he had retired the last batter, Elston Howard, on a grounder to Pee Wee Reese. But the climactic play actually had occurred three innings before when Sandy Amoros, a reserve outfielder, came through with his catch of a lifetime.

Tommy Byrne, who had beaten the Dodgers earlier in the Series, was Podres' mound opponent. He permitted only three hits until he gave way to Bob Grim in the sixth. But one was a fourth-inning double by Roy Campanella, which was converted to a run when Gil Hodges followed with a single. Another was a sixth-inning single, which became Brooklyn's second run on two bunts and Hodges' sacrifice fly.

Because he had used a pinch hitter for Don Zimmer, manager Walter Alston had to take the second baseman out of the game. He shifted Junior Gilliam from left field to second and sent Amoros to left field. This move proved to be the most fortuitous player shift Alston ever made. In the Yankees' half of the inning, Billy Martin walked and Gil McDougald bunted safely. The left-handed-batting Yogi Berra, normally a right-field hitter, came to bat, and Amoros moved over a bit toward center. So when Berra sliced a fly just inside the left-field foul line, it didn't seem possible that Amoros could even get near it. But the fleet-footed Cuban, racing at top speed, made a spectacular gloved-hand catch. It was an easy matter to double McDougald off first, as both Gil and Billy were by this time headed for the plate. Had the ball fallen safely, the Yankees would have tied the score and had the potential winning run in scoring position with none out.

Amoros' catch was more crucial but not more spectacular than the catch made by Willie Mays in the first game of the 1954 World Series between the New York Giants and Cleveland Indians. The catch saved the first game and paved the way for a four-game Giant sweep over the favored Indians.

The score was 2-2 in the eighth inning. Sal Maglie was locked in a pitching duel with Bob Lemon. Larry Doby led off with a walk, and Al Rosen beat out an infield hit. Vic Wertz, who already had three hits, moved menacingly toward the plate. Giants manager Leo Durocher removed Maglie and summoned Don Liddle, a left-hander, from the bull pen. Wertz's response was a terrific drive toward deepest center. The ball sailed over Mays's head and appeared on its way to the centerfield wall, some 465 feet away. But there goes Willie! Back . . . back . . . back he goes! And facing away from the plate, he takes the ball over his shoulder just short of the wall. It robbed Wertz of at least a triple.

Almost as amazing as the catch was the ensuing throw. Mays still had to turn around and get the ball away, which he somehow did before he went sprawling. Davey Williams took the throw in back of second and held Doby, who tagged up after the catch, to one base, permitting the Giants to escape the inning without a Cleveland score. The Giants won the game, 5-2, on Dusty Rhodes's pinch homer in the tenth.

Every manager has his opinion of who made the greatest catch in World Series play. Mickey Cochrane, who piloted the Detroit club to successive pennants in 1934 and 1935, always gave the nod to Jo-Jo White, the Tigers' center fielder. The play in question happened in the fifth game of the 1934 World Series between the Tigers and Cardinals. The Cards were the host club that afternoon, and they trailed 3-1 as they came to bat in the eighth inning. Tommy Bridges was the

Detroit pitcher. Virgil Davis batted for Leo Durocher and singled. Burgess Whitehead ran for him. Pepper Martin, the next batter, drove one to deep left center. Ordinarily, it would have been the left fielder's ball, but Goose Goslin, patrolling the beat, lacked the necessary speed to catch up with the drive.

From center field came Jo-Jo White, sprinting like an antelope. With Goslin urging, "Go get it, Jo-Jo! Go get it!" White raced past the Goose to the concrete wall in left field. The vast crowd, by now on its feet, gasped as Jo-Jo reached the ball with his outstretched glove, grabbed and swerved sharply to avoid hitting the wall. Had he missed the ball, the Cards would have narrowed the gap to one run, with the tying tally on third base. The threat ended, Bridges went on to win, 3-1.

The Minnesota Twins, playing in their first World Series in 1965, surprised the baseball world by taking the measure of Dodgers greats Don Drysdale and Sandy Koufax in the first two games. In the second game an unbelievable catch was made by Twins left fielder Bob Allison. The game was still scoreless in the fifth inning when Ron Fairly singled and Jim Lefebvre stroked a curving line drive to left. Allison went a long way to catch up with the ball near the fence. He reached for it and backhanded it in one final lunge, just as it was about to hit the ground. Unable to stop himself, he then slid almost

thirty feet on the wet turf with gloved hand and ball upraised in triumph.

There have been many other notable outfield catches in World Series play. Joe Di-Maggio made one on Hank Leiber to climax the 1936 Yankees-Giants Series; Terry Moore robbed Di-Maggio of an extra base with a brilliant running catch in the 1942 Yankees-Cardinals Series; Hank Bauer accounted for the final out in the 1951 Yankees-Giants series with a spectacular catch of Sal Yvars' drive with the tying run on second; Jim Rivera preserved a 1-0 victory for Chicago with an amazing catch of Charley Neal's drive in the 1959 Series between the Dodgers and White Sox; and Ron Swoboda, the Mets' right fielder, stopped the Orioles in their tracks with a charging, tumbling catch of Brooks Robinson's sinking liner in the New York-Baltimore Series of 1969.

Not all the great World Series catches belong to the outfielders. At least two of the numerous dazzling infield plays seem worthy of mention. It was a question of who was more surprised when Billy Martin made a running catch of Jackie Robinson's pop-up to the pitcher's mound. Yes, a running catch of a ball that traveled no more than sixty feet. The catch was as important as any made in the Series because it helped win the 1952 World Championship.

It was the last half of the seventh inning of

Duke Snider making tumbling catch in
1956 series.

Cleveland's Bill Wamsbsganss, author of only
unassisted triple play in World Series annals.

the seventh and final game. The Yankees were
leading 4-2. Vic Raschi had replaced Allie Reynolds
for the Yankees. Carl Furillo walked, and after
Rocky Nelson had popped up, Billy Cox singled
and Pee Wee Reese walked. The bases were loaded. It was evident that Raschi didn't have it, and
manager Casey Stengel summoned southpaw Bob
Kuzava from the bull pen to pitch to the left-handed
Duke Snider.

Kuzava got Snider to pop up for the second
out. Robinson was the next batter. He worked the
count to 3-2 before swinging at a curve and raising
a low pop-up to the right of the mound. It was Joe
Collins' ball, but the first baseman remained glued
to the spot. When Martin, playing second, saw that
neither Collins nor Kuzava was making a move
toward the ball, he dashed in, running at top speed,
and caught the ball, knee high. At least two
Dodgers would have scored if Martin had not gotten to the ball. Kuzava blanked the Dodgers the rest
of the way, to preserve the Yankees' 4-2 victory and
give them the World Championship.

Finally, the record books credit Bill Wambsganss, Cleveland second baseman, with having
made the only unassisted triple play in World Series
history. This once-in-a-lifetime feat took place in
the fifth inning of the fifth game of the 1920 Indi-
ans-Dodgers World Series. Trailing badly, the
Dodgers brought some hope to their followers by

getting the first two-batters—Pete Kilduff and Otto
Miller—on second and first via singles. Manager
Wilbert Robinson signaled for the hit-and run. Clarence Mitchell, a good-hitting pitcher, connected
solidly and sent a liner tearing over second, but
Wambsganss, noticing that the runners had taken
off with the pitch, was already on his way to the bag.
It was a simple matter for him to glove the ball and
step on second to double up Kilduff, who was on
his way to third. He turned and, to his surprise,
found Miller standing almost within reach. Wamby
coolly ambled over and put the tag on the frozen
base runner, for the third out. The Indians won the
game, 8-1, and the Series, 5-2. ◇

Babe Ruth trying out his new car (note
Babe's initials on door).

The Babe

BY JOSEPH L. REICHLER

WHAT CAN ANYONE SAY about Babe Ruth that has not already been said, except to insist that he, the Babe, not anyone else, was the greatest baseball player who ever lived. No discussion of the World Series would be complete without special mention of this most special man.

George Herman Ruth is the only man to hit three home runs in a World Series game—not once, but twice. At one time he held more than two dozen Series records, and he still owns or shares a veritable baker's dozen of hitting records. These include:

Most total bases in a Series **(22)**
Highest slugging percentage in a Series **(.744)**
Most hits in a four-game Series **(10)**
Most walks in a Series game **(4)**
Most runs scored in a four-game Series **(9)**
Most doubles in a four-game Series **(3)**
Most walks in a Series **(11)**
Scoring at least one run in the most consecutive games **(9)**
Most times reached base in one Series game **(5)** (He is also the only player to do it twice.)
Most stolen bases in one Series inning **(2)**
Highest batting average in a Series **(.625)**

But as many fans know, Ruth's talents were by no means confined to swinging a bat. He was also one of the best left-handed pitchers to ever work in the big leagues, and few played the outfield any better. Ruth was fast, he was smart, and he made catches that the best fielders in any era would have been proud to call their own. The Bambino had a sensational throwing arm, and in addition to being a superb moundsman and fielder, he also handled himself well at first base.

Yet in spite of his prowess in other areas of the game, it's as a hitter that Ruth is best remembered. Which is why it's so surprising that Babe's own most cherished accomplishment of all his World Series play was not his work at the plate but on the mound. And that was the fantastic feat of hurling 29⅔ consecutive scoreless innings in the World Series.

Before turning his talents to hitting homers, Babe Ruth was the star pitcher of the Boston Red Sox for five seasons. He posted his flinging feat in the 1916 and the 1918 Series at the expense of both the Brooklyn Dodgers and the Chicago Cubs. Not until forty-four years after the Babe's final mound appearance was his record topped. Whitey Ford, another Yankee, strung together 33⅔ scoreless innings the 1960, 1961 and 1962 World Series against Pittsburgh, Cincinnati, and San Francisco.

Babe began his string of scoreless innings on October 9, 1916, at Fenway Park, by pitching the Red Sox to a 2-1 victory over the Dodgers. The game went fourteen innings—the longest World Series game ever staged. Brooklyn's only tally came in the opening inning when Hi Myers, the Dodgers' center fielder, hit an inside-the-park home run. The ball landed in right center between Harry Hooper and Tilly Walker. Myers scored easily when Hooper fell down and Walker slipped while pursuing the ball.

Babe Ruth in a familiar batting stance.

Boston tied the score in the third when Everett "Deacon" Scott, Red Sox leadoff batter, tripled and then scored when Ruth grounded to George Cutshaw. Babe blanked the Dodgers for the remaining thirteen innings. Sherry Smith, the cagey southpaw of the Dodgers, matched the Babe's pitching through the thirteenth. The Red Sox finally broke through in the fourteenth. Dick Hoblitzell drew a walk. Mike McNally ran for him. Duffy Lewis sacrificed McNally to second. Del Gainor batted for Larry Gardner and punched a single past Mike Mowrey, Dodger third baseman, and McNally scooted all the way home from second with the run that ended the game. This enabled the twenty-one-year-old Ruth to post his first World Series victory. He allowed six hits, walked three and struck out four.

Babe's next World Series appearance came two years later, in the 1918 open when he went against Jim "Hippo" Vaughn, famed southpaw ace of the Chicago Cubs, at Wrigley Field. He stretched his string of consecutive scoreless innings to twenty-two that day as 19,274 watched him pitch a 1-0 shutout over the Cubs. Boston scored its game-winning run in the fourth inning when Dave Shean walked and reached second on George Whiteman's single. Stufy McInnis slapped a single to left, scoring Shean.

Four days later, in the fourth game of the Series, at Fenway Park, Babe again drew the pitching assignment and got his chance to eclipse the then current major-league scoreless innings record of 28⅓ innings set by the Giants' Christy Mathewson in 1905 and 1911. Ruth's mound opponent was 19-game-winner George Tyler. A crowd of 22,183 watched the Babe gain a two-run edge for himself in the fourth inning by slamming a triple to right center, scoring Dave Shean and George Whiteman, who had walked to open the inning.

Babe held the Cubs scoreless until the eighth inning, when they came to life and finally snapped the goose-egg record Ruth had begun to fashion two years earlier. Bill Killifer walked and Claude Hendrix, batting for Tyler, drove a long single into left field, sending Killifer to second. Bill McCabe ran for Hendrix. Charlie Hollocher grounded to Shean, but Killifer scored on the play. Les Mann singled home McCabe, tying the score at 2-2. Chicago made a bid for victory in the top of the ninth as Fred Merkle singled and Rollie Zeider walked with nobody out. Ruth was replaced by Joe Bush and went to right field in place of Whiteman. Bush got Bill Wortman to force Merkle at third. Sam Barber, batting for Killifer, rapped into a double play. The Red Sox won the game in their half of the ninth. Wally Schang, batting for Sam Agnew, singled and advanced to second on a passed ball. Harry Hooper bunted, but Phil Douglas threw wild to first and Schang scored. The Red Sox won, 3-2.

Under the existing rules, Ruth was credited with the victory, his third in World Series competition. All told, Ruth pitched in three Series games and worked a total of thirty-one innings. He won three games, suffered no defeats. His earned run average—a spectacular 0.87.

Of course, regardless of the Babe's personal preferences, it's as a home-run hitter that he will always be best remembered. Ruth played in five Series games for the Red Sox and in thirty-six for the Yankees, for a grand total of forty-one World Series games. During those 41 games, in 129 official times at bat, Ruth slugged a total of 15 home runs. His first was clubbed off the delivery of Shufflin' Phil Douglas of the Giants in the fourth game of the 1921 classic. Two years later, in 1923, he hit the Giants for three more. And then, on October 6,

Babe Ruth as a lefthanded pitcher with the Red Sox.

1926, he really set the world abuzz when the Yankees played the Cardinals.

Until that day, only seven players of the modern era had ever hit three home runs in one game. And no one had ever done it in a World Series game. The day before, Jesse Haines of the St. Louis Cardinals had shut out the Yankees with five hits. Ruth got one of them, an unproductive single, and he was terribly disappointed. "Haines was pitching right down my alley all afternoon," snorted the Babe in the clubhouse after the game. "I was a chump. I'll tell you one thing, though. If they pitch the same way to me tomorrow, I'll hit two out of the park."

Ruth did even better. The Cardinals; Flint Rhem started off strong, firing his fastball by Earle Combs and Mark Koenig, the first two New York batters. Then the St. Louis right-hander tried to sneak a fastball by Ruth on his first pitch. The Babe timed it perfectly. He connected for a long home run, the ball sailing over the right-field pavilion.

The Cards came back for a run in their half of the first, and the score was tied 1-1 when Babe came up again in the third. This time Rhem served Ruth a slow ball. Babe anticipated it and again swung at the first pitch. This, too, went over the grandstand roof, well toward right center and much farther than the first. Ruth had no chance to add to his home-run collection in his next time at bat, for Rhem fed him four straight balls.

Herman Bell was pitching for the Cards when Ruth came to bat in the sixth. This time the ball reached the top of the center-field bleachers for his third home run. The ball still had enough resiliency in it to bounce over a twenty-foot wall out into Grand Boulevard. It finally came down in front of the St. Louis YMCA building on Sullivan Avenue. Veteran observers called it the longest ever hit in a World Series.

This four-base firepower, devastating as it was, paled by comparison with the Babe's unparalleled slugging feat on October 9, 1928. It was unparalleled mainly because a badly crippled Ruth reached the very apex of his career to do deeds that will be remembered as long as the game lives. If there was any lingering doubt that the Babe was not the greatest slugger of all time, it was decisively put to rest in the final game of the 1928 Series when, for the second time in a World Series, he drove the ball over the right-field bleachers three times.

His first homer came in the fourth inning. Wee Willie Sherdel was pitching for the Cardinals, and he served Ruth a curve six inches inside. It was not a ball to swing at. But Babe smacked it over the right-field bleachers. The next time Sherdel faced Ruth, he planted two quick strikes that the King disdained to even swing at. He was waiting for the pitch. Next, the little southpaw tried a quick throw,

An aerial view of the Bambino's famous follow through.

sneaking the ball over the plate while the Babe's head was turned. Umpire Charley Pfirman ruled the pitch illegal. The Cards, led by manager Bill Mc-Kechnie, squawked bitterly, but the umpire's verdict stood. The count rose to two and two. Then Sherdel threw a slow outside curve, and there it was. With no perceptible effort, the Bambino met the ball and knocked it toward the right-field bleachers. The crowd gasped and groaned as the ball, flying high and never losing momentum, cleared the roof of the pavilion and disappeared. As Ruth rounded the bases, he waved his hand at the jeering crowd and saluted the fans in a mocking manner.

Grover Alexander was pitching when the Babe came to bat for the last time in the eighth. He threw a strike and then essayed a curve on the inside corner. What a mistake! The Babe met the ball squarely and drove it to right. This time the ball hit the roof of the pavilion.

It should be mentioned that Ruth performed his feats of derring-do while hobbled by a badly sprained ankle that was so swollen he could barely walk. Only his irrepressible courage and several rolls of adhesive tape made it possible for him to play at all that day. Yet not only did he duplicate his previous three-homer record, he also made a spectacular running catch that finished the last Cardinal rally and sealed the Series victory for the Yanks.

Sensing defeat as the game went on, the St.

Louis hometown crowd grew progressively nasty. They jeered and hooted whenever Ruth took his place in left field, and in the seventh inning they pelted him with bottles and refuse.

Then, at the very end of the game, Frankie Frisch hit a foul off New York's Waite Hoyt. The Babe, ignoring his throbbing ankle, dashed down the foul line and past the field boxes while St. Louis partisans filled the air with a blizzard of paper and programs, hoping to blind Ruth's vision. But in spite of the handicaps, the Bambino made a terrific one-handed running catch for the last out of the Series.

Holding the ball aloft in a picture of triumph and boyish glee, Ruth had good reason to be proud. For not only had he hit three homers in the game and made a great catch, he had also achieved the highest Series batting average ever made by a full-time player—a blistering .625. Compared to that, the Yankees' 7-3 win of the game was almost anticlimactic.

With a three-run homer against the Cubs in the first inning of the third game in 1932, Babe Ruth's Series homer record stood at fourteen. But the Babe wasn't finished yet. Although no one knew it at the time, he was about to hit his fifteenth and final home run in a World Series. And it's altogether fitting that he saved the best for last.

It came in the fifth inning of the third game of the 1932 World Series in Chicago. That autumn afternoon, the Cubs were really giving it to the Babe. They ribbed him and rode him and made him fume. And that was a bad mistake. The Babe in a good mood was bad enough, but with his dander up he was a holy terror. With one strike on him, this aging immortal, this huge potato-nosed man with the powerful shoulders, expansive chest and chorus-girl legs, barked to his tormentors in the Chicago dugout that he was going to belt one clear out of the park for a home run.

With heroic confidence, he motioned menacingly with his bat toward Wrigley Field's center-field bleachers, letting the world know what he had in mind. Chicago's Charlie Root fired another strike, and again Ruth pointed toward the bleachers. Then it happened. With Root's next pitch the Babe made good his threat. He connected and sent the ball sailing high and far. The ball finally landed in precisely the area Ruth had pointed to in what was possibly the most dramatic home run ever hit in a World Series.

THE NEW YORK TIMES made a big thing out of it the next day. "Ruth came up in the fifth," the TIMES story read, "and in no unmistakable motion the Babe notified the crowd that the nature of his retaliation would be a wallop right out of the park." Root, the victim, naturally scotched the idea that Ruth had pointed and prophesied his home run. "If Ruth had pointed to the center-field stands," he said, "I'd have knocked him on his fanny with the next pitch, believe me. He just held up two fingers to show there were only two strikes and he still had one coming."

Be that as it may, there can be no doubt that of all the great names ever to grace a World Series lineup, Babe Ruth's was the greatest of all. Forty-five years after his last Series game, the records he set in the fall classic still stand. Others have come close, but, truly, there was only one Babe Ruth! ◇

A team picture of the champion 1932 Yankees who swept the Cubs in four straight.

M. BROWN, CHICAGO NAT'L.

HOFMAN, CHICAGO NAT'L.

EVERS, CHICAGO NAT'L.

OF THE
NEW YORK NATIONALS

CHANCE, CHICAGO

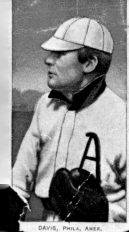

DAVIS, PHILA. AMER.

CRAWFORD, DETROIT

GIANTS

OF THE
NEW YORK NATIONALS

PIRATES

OF THE
PITTSBURG NATIONALS

WILTSE-NEW YORK

JOHNSON-WASHINGTON-AMER.

SCHMIDT DETROIT AMER.

BRANSFIELD, PHILA. NAT'L.

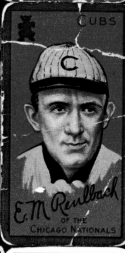

CUBS

OF THE
CHICAGO NATIONALS

DONLIN, N. Y.

JOHNSON WASH.

WRIGLEY FIELD, HOME OF "THE CUBS"

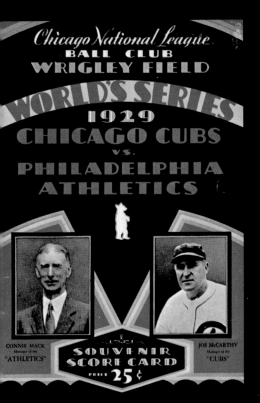

Chicago National League
BALL CLUB
WRIGLEY FIELD

WORLD'S SERIES

1929

CHICAGO CUBS
vs.
PHILADELPHIA
ATHLETICS

CONNIE MACK
Manager of the
"ATHLETICS"

JOE McCARTHY
Manager of the
"CUBS"

SOUVENIR
SCORE CARD
PRICE 25¢

YANKEES vs CUBS

WORLD'S
SERIES
OFFICIAL
PROGRAM
25¢

YANKEE STADIUM-1932

HARRY M. STEVENS, INC., Publisher

OFFICIAL
American League Ball

ATHLETICS
WORLD'S SERIES
1930

Souvenir Program   25 Cents

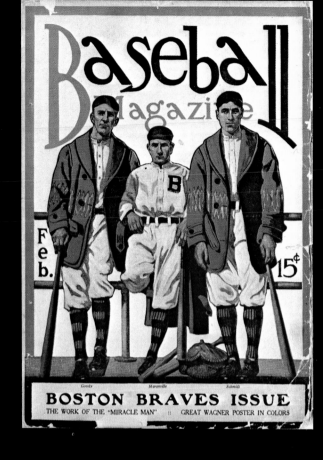

Baseball Magazine

Feb.   15¢

Gowdy   Maranville   Schmidt

BOSTON BRAVES ISSUE

THE WORK OF THE "MIRACLE MAN" :: GREAT WAGNER POSTER IN COLORS

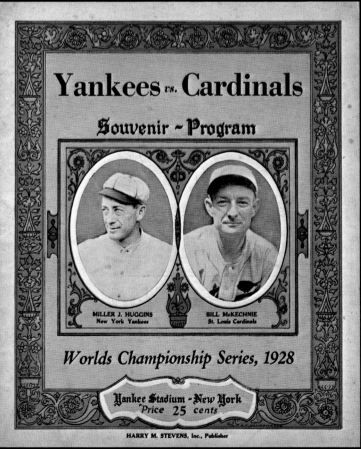

Yankees vs. Cardinals

Souvenir ~ Program

MILLER J. HUGGINS
New York Yankees

BILL McKECHNIE
St. Louis Cardinals

Worlds Championship Series, 1928

Yankee Stadium ~ New York
Price 25 cents

HARRY M. STEVENS, Inc., Publisher

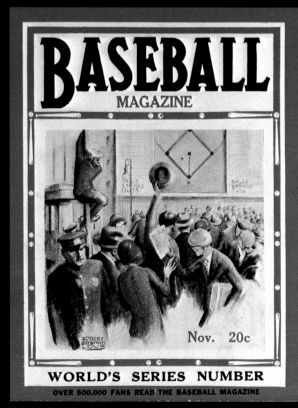

BASEBALL
MAGAZINE

BALLS
STRIKES
OUTS

BALLS
STRIKES
OUTS

ROBERT
EDWARD
LOVE

Nov.   20c

WORLD'S SERIES NUMBER
OVER 500,000 FANS READ THE BASEBALL MAGAZINE

Yankees and Reds line up for start of 1976 Series.

Top; Steve Garvey signing autographs before
1974 Series. Middle; Oakland A's line up for
1973 Series. Bottom; Cincinnati Reds line up
for the start of 1970 Series.

Top left; Don Gullett, Reds lefty pitching in 1970 Series. Top middle; Pirate, Nellie Briles delivers a hard fast ball in 1971 Series. Top right; John "Blue Moon" Odom, Oakland A's, pitching in 1972 Series. Bottom; Dodgers Sandy Koufax on the mound, follows through in the 1966 Series.

Reds Clay Carroll pitching in 1970 Series.

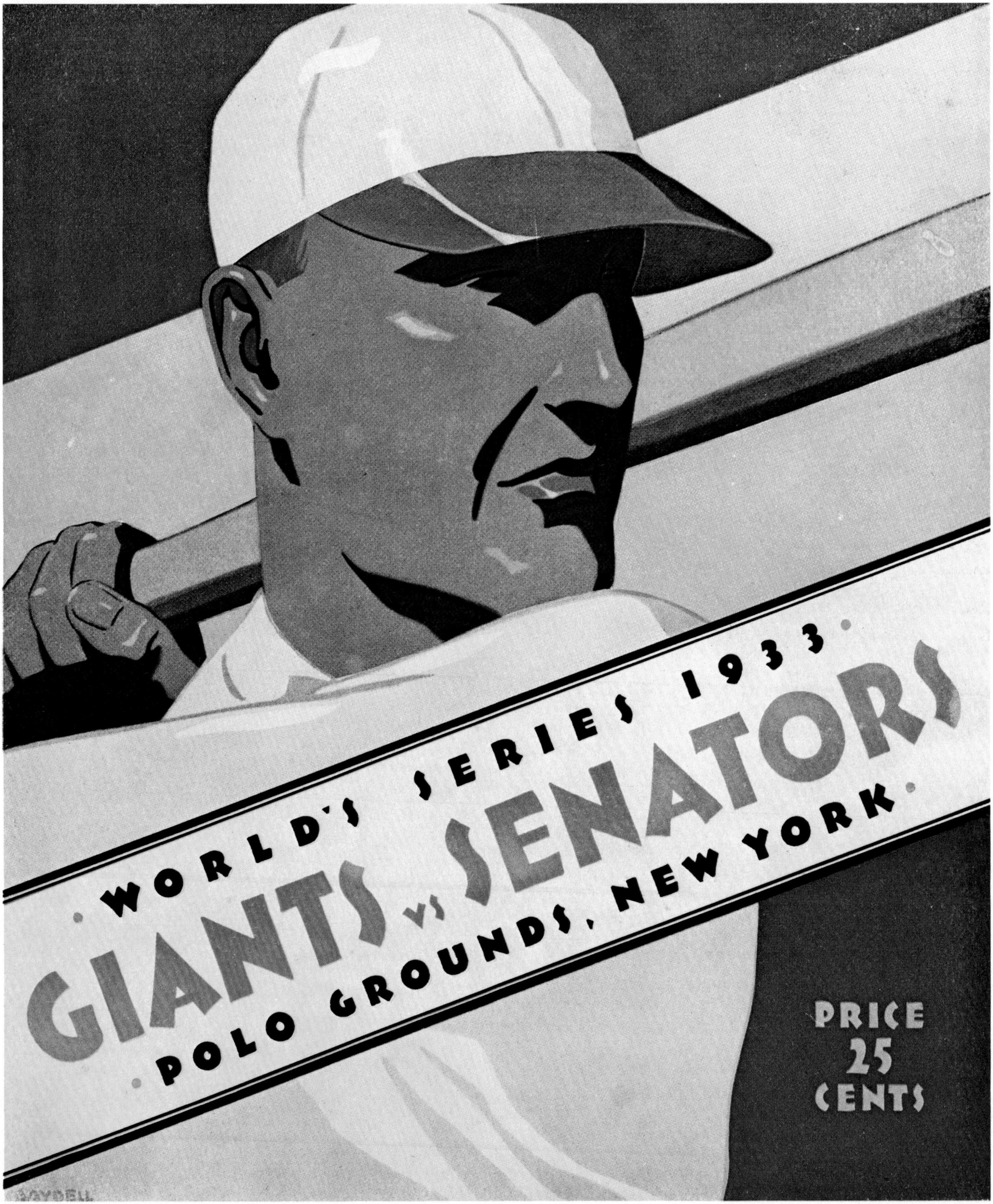
WORLD'S SERIES 1933
GIANTS vs SENATORS
POLO GROUNDS, NEW YORK
PRICE 25 CENTS
BOYDELL

Touch 'Em All!
(The Home Run)
BY JOSEPH L. REICHLER

Another angle of Babe Ruth's fabulous home run swing.

FOR EXCITEMENT AND SHEER IMPACT, nothing can ever match the lusty home run in baseball. The eternal nemesis of every pitcher, it can mean instant joy or sudden death, depending on your turn at bat. It is the only hit whose significance is always immediately obvious, the great equalizer—a brash, savage weapon designed to attain quick redemption for earlier mistakes. Long after the score has been forgotten, the memory of a home run remains vivid. The home run was the trademark of Babe Ruth, the mystique of Henry Aaron, the essence of Reggie Jackson.

It is more than proper, therefore, that home-run sluggers have been among baseball's most noticeable personalities, and that the product of their art should stand at the focal point of the game's most thrilling moments. But it wasn't always so. In the Paleolithic Era of the game, when the ball had the resiliency of an overripe potato, the home run was an incidental oddity. Managers then esteemed the bunt, the stolen base, and the sacrifice to squeeze out one run at a time. As evidence of their philosophy, the fifty-nine games that made up the first ten World Series produced a two-team total of only seventeen home runs. In the modern era, the Yankees and Dodgers alone equaled that sum in their six-game championship set of 1953 and duplicated it in 1955 and again in 1977.

Even though the emphasis on defense, pitching, and singles hitting prevailed through the first nineteen World Series, the devastating effect of the home run had a preview showing during a Series in which Frank "Home Run" Baker earned his nickname. In the 1911 Series, when Connie Mack's Athletics dumped John McGraw's Giants four games to two, Baker astonished and caused a feud between two great pitchers by smashing a home run each off Rube Marquard and the immortal Christy Mathewson on successive days. At the time, both Mathewson and Marquard were signing their names to articles written by professional ghostwriters. The articles offered expert insiders' views of the Series, and they were carried by rival newspaper syndicates. In the sixth inning of the second game, Baker exploded a two-run homer off Marquard's fastball to beat the southpaw 3-1. The following day, Mathewson, through his ghostwriter, took Rube severely to task.

"Baker's homer was due to Marquard's carelessness, wrote Matty. "Manager [John] McGraw went all over the Athletics hitters in the pre-game clubhouse talk yesterday, and paid particular attention to Baker. Marquard was told just how to pitch to him. Well, Rube pitched just what Frank likes."

The next day, Mathewson faced Baker and the A's for the second time in the Series. he carried a 1-0 lead into the ninth, giving him the distinction of having held the Athletics to only one run in forty-four World Series innings. Matty retired Eddie Collins, first batter in the ninth. And then it happened. Baker rifled Matty's fadeaway pitch into the right-field grandstand for his second home run of the Series. Baker's homer merely tied the contest, which the A's eventually won in eleven innings, but it had a noticeable effect on the crowd and a lingering influence on both teams. As one game report said, "One actually could feel in the very air that it presaged an Athletics victory." With a total of nine, Baker won the American League home-run title. But it was the two all-but-unbelievable homers against the Giants' aces, who had pitched fifty victories between them, that earned him his nickname. Frank Baker was known forever after as Home Run Baker.

Baker's homers were the first to lift fans into seventh heaven, but it was not until 1960 that a World Series was won on a home run by the last hitter. That, of course, was the dramatic sudden-death by Bill Mazeroski off the Yankees' Ralph Terry in the bottom of the ninth inning of the seventh game at Pittsburgh's Forbes Field. The 10-9 victory brought Pittsburgh its first World Championship in thirty-five years and produced mass hysteria throughout Pennsylvania. Almost completely overshadowed was the three-run homer by Hal Smith, once a Yankee farmhand, in the eight inning. His bat sent the Bucs ahead, 9-7, only to have the Yankees deadlock it in the first half of the ninth.

Another homer that time will not erase was Babe Ruth's famous "called shot" in Wrigley Field during the 1932 Yankees-Cubs Series. It was the fifth inning of the third game, with the score tied at 4-4. Ruth swung at Charlie Root's first pitch and missed. Then he pointed to the center-field bleachers. A second strike, and again Ruth showed the world where he would hit the ball. Babe connected solidly on the next pitch and sent the ball sailing—into the deepest point of the center-field bleachers, right where he'd been pointing all along. Pat Malone then replaced Charlie Root on the mound, and Lou Gehrig greeted him with another homer. New York won, 7-5, for the third win of a four-game sweep.

That was the last of the Babe's fifteen World

Babe Ruth pointing to the spot where
he intended to hit his next home run.

Series homers. Yet it was but one of many remarkable four-baggers Ruth hit in his ten fall classics.

Twice against the Cardinals, in the fourth game of both the 1926 and 1928 Series, he had blasted three home runs in St. Louis. In 1926, Babe's terrific clout off Herman Bell made history in Sportsman's Park. It hit high up in the center-field bleachers, 424 feet from home plate.

It was the longest ever hit in the old St. Louis park. Two years later, Willie Sherdel tried to sneak a quick pitch past Ruth for a third strike. Umpire Charley Pfirman wouldn't allow it, and the Babe sent Sherdel's next pitch over the right-field roof for number three of the day.

But neither the Babe nor his slugging teammate Lou Gehrig holds perhaps the most remarkable Series slugging mark. Reggie Jackson, a Yankee of later vintage, smacked five home runs in a six-game set against the Los Angeles Dodgers in 1977. More remarkable, though, was his feat of hitting each of the last four on the very first pitch—three in the sixth and final game. Besides Ruth, four others hammered four homers in a single Series: Lou Gehrig and Hank Bauer of the Yankees, Duke Snider of the Dodgers and Gene Tenace of the Oakland A's. Snider, the National League home-run leader with eleven, is the only player to do it twice—in 1952 and in 1955. Gehrig's feat in 1928 is worthy of mention. The Yankees dispatched the Cardinals in four straight, and Larrupin' Lou, in just eleven official times at bat, laced four round-trippers and a double, driving in nine runs and scoring eight. He hit .545, batting behind Ruth. The Babe hit a blistering .625 which included three home runs and three doubles among his ten hits in nineteen trips to the plate.

Still another Yankee, Mickey Mantle, holds the all-time World Series home-run record record with eighteen. The switch-hitting outfielder, batting .257 to the Babe's .326 in blue-ribbon play, went to the plate 230 times to Ruth's 129. Mantle, naturally, was involved when the Yankees and Dodgers hit a Series high of seventeen home runs in 1953. The Switcher was there again in 1955, when the same two teams equaled their previous record. Mantle broke Ruth's record dramatically in the 1964 Series. With the third game tied, Mantle drilled Cardinal relief ace Barney Schultz's first pitch into the second deck in right field for a 2-1 Yankee victory.

From 1903, when the modern interleague classic was inaugurated, through 1977, 519 homers have been rocketed into the October sky. The American League leads the National 308 to 211, a current average of slightly more than one a game. Only four times have there been World Series in which no home runs were hit, all before 1920, and there were several instances in which one side failed to find the range. The last team to go homerless in a Series was the Whiz Kids of Philadelphia in 1950.

Fact is, in the very first Series played, on October 1, 1903, right fielder Jimmy Sebring of the Pirates homered off Cy Young, the man with 511 career victories. The next day, leadoff man Pat Dougherty, the Boston left fielder, hammered not one but two home runs, to cause a frenzy in Beantown. Still, the home run was a novelty, so much so that for the next three Series not one was struck. It was not until the second game of the 1908 Series between Detroit and Chicago that a home run was recorded, and that was a windswept fly ball by Joe Tinker of the Cubs which landed in the temporary bleachers, where a rope had been stretched to protect outfielders from bottle-wielding fans. The Tigers contended that ground rules limited hits into the bleachers to doubles, but Umpire Bill Klem ruled it a home run.

Following the 1911 Series, dominated by Home Run Baker, spectators experienced a change in their thinking. Remembering how Baker had done it, they began speculating on the possibility of a home run whenever a crack hitter came up in the clutch. In 1912, Larry Doyle of the Giants and Larry Gardner of the Red Sox hit for the distance. Baker smacked his "cousin," Rube Marquard, for a third blue-ribbon round-tripper in 1913, when Fred Merkle, Giants first baseman, and Wally Schang, Athletics catcher, also connected. Hank Gowdy of the Boston Braves had a lethal wallop among his hits as his .545 batting average blew down the Athletics in 1914. And in the 1915 Series between the Red Sox and the Philadelphia Phillies, two were hit by Boston's Harry Hooper and one each by Duffy Lewis and Fred Luderus. In the 1916 Dodgers-Red Sox Series, Larry Gardner whacked two homers out of Ebbets Field on successive days, while Hy Myers, Brooklyn center fielder, stung Ruth for a round-tripper before the Babe began pitching the first of his 29⅔ consecutive scoreless World Series innings.

Benny Kauff, Giants center fielder, hit two in one game for the losing Giants in 1917, when Happy Felsch hit one for the White Sox. There was none in 1918 and only one, by Chicago's Joe Jackson, in 1919. It was in 1920, with the advent of the lively ball, that the hitters really started to reach the fences. In that Cleveland-Brooklyn Series, Elmer Smith, Indians right fielder, produced the first World Series grand slam, and his pitching mate, Sergeant Jim Bagby, became the first pitcher to insert a four-bagger into a Series box score. Babe Ruth hit his first Series homer in the first Yankees-Giants match-up of 1921. It came off Shufflin' Phil Douglas in the fourth game in a losing cause.

A jubilant Bill Mazeroski prances plateward on his Series winning home run.

Fred Merkle

In 1923, the Babe broke a Series record by hoisting three homers into the stands—but they were overshadowed by two home runs hit by Casey Stengel. This was because Casey's homers won the only two games the Giants captured in that Series. All eyes were on the Babe as the Series began, but it was irrepressible Casey who came up in the top of the ninth inning, with the score tied at 4-4, and shot a screecher to left center field. The ball rolled between the outfielders to the deepest part of Yankee Stadium. Casey puffed around the bases and collapsed over the plate, completing an astonishing inside-the-park home run.

The Yankees exploded in the second game, slamming four home runs, two by the Babe, to win 4-2. The third contest, a brilliant duel between Artie Nehf and Sam Jones, was scoreless in the seventh. Then Casey, in contrast to Mudville's strikeout hero, drove one into the right-field bleachers. The Yankees had been riding him all day. He watched the ball sail over the wall, then jogged around the bases, thumb to his nose.

Goose Goslin hit three home runs for Washington against the Giants in the 1924 Series and repeated against Pittsburgh the following year, which also saw Joe Harris of the Senators wallop three. One of the most unforgettable home runs was hit by Mule Haas in the 1929 Series during a ten-run rally by the A's against the Cubs. It was in the fourth game, with the A's leading, two games to one. Chicago had an 8-0 lead after six innings. Al Simmons opened the Athletics' seventh with a home run. A cluster of singles followed, and in no time the Cubs' lead had been cut in half. Joe McCarthy, Cubs manager, yanked Charlie Root and brought in Art Nehf, the former ace Giants southpaw, to face Haas, a left-handed hitter. With two men on base, Haas hit a line drive to center field. Hack Wilson, the Cubs' center fielder, lost the ball in the sun; it sailed over his head and caromed off the center-field fence. Haas followed Joe Boley and Max Bishop over the plate, making the score 8-7. The A's scored three additional runs that inning, to win, 10-8.

The next day, with President Herbert Hoover in the Philadelphia stands, the Cubs' Pat Malone held the A's to two hits for eight innings and led 2-0. Malone got the first man in the ninth, but issued a walk to Bishop. Haas then rifled a home run over the right-field wall, tying the score. Shortly afterwards, the A's tallied the winning run on doubles by Simmons and Bing Miller. That gave the A's the Series, four games to one.

Jimmy Foxx, Philadelphia's slugging first baseman, hit four historic Series homers, the most dramatic coming in the fifth game of the 1930 Cardinals-Athletics Series. Each team had won two games, and the first eight innings of the fifth game were a scoreless pitching duel between Burleigh

Grimes and the A's' George Earnshaw. Mickey Cochrane, first up in the ninth, walked, but Grimes retired the dangerous Al Simmons. Foxx, the next hitter, pounced on a spitter and sent it deep into the bleachers in left center. The A's won, 2-0.

In the 1931 Athletics'-Cardinals Series, the one in which Pepper Martin batted .500 and ran wild, it was George Watkins' two-run homer off Earnshaw that was the decisive blow of the Cards' 4-2 seventh-game victory in St. Louis. Two years later, in Washington, a tenth-inning homer by Mel Ott, the Giants' all-time home-run king, shot down Joe Cronin's Senators 4-3 in the fifth and final game of the 1933 Series.

A new team of Yankees came to the fore in 1936, winning four straight Series with the loss of

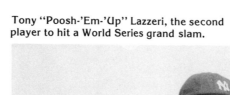
Tony "Poosh-'Em-'Up" Lazzeri, the second player to hit a World Series grand slam.

only three games. Tony Lazzeri became the second player to hit a home run with the bases full in the classic. He did it in the second game, won by the Yankees by a record 18-4 score over the Giants in the all-New York Series of 1936. Joe DiMaggio's first Series homer came in 1937. He repeated in 1938 and 1939, hit two in 1947 and tallied one each in 1949, 1950 and 1951.

A home run that tugged at the heartstrings saddened fans at Chicago's Wrigley Field in 1938. Dizzy Dean, who had been acquired from the Cardinals, was on the mound for the Cubs against the Yankees in the second game of the Series. His fastball was gone, but for seven innings he cannily held the Yankees at bay. The Yankees went into the eighth trailing 3-2. George Selkirk singled. Diz got

the next two batters. Up came Frank Crosetti, who had hit but one home run in twenty-nine previous Series games. Frank caught Dean's nothing ball and smashed it over the left-field wall. Joe Di-Maggio walloped another two-run homer in the ninth, and Dean was through.

The 1947 Yankees'-Dodgers Series is best remembered for Cookie Lavagetto's hit with two out in the ninth inning of the fourth game which not only ruined Bill Bevens' heroic bid for a no-hitter but gave the Dodgers a 3-2 victory over the Yankees. Almost forgotten is Yogi Berra's home run in the third game, the first by a pinch hitter in Series history. It was to be the first of a dozen Series homers hit by the sturdy Yankee catcher. Two years later, with the same two teams at it again,

Chuck Hiller hitting a grand slam homer for the Giants.

Tommy Henrich broke up a scintillating pitching duel between the Yankees' Allie Reynolds and Don Newcombe by rifling the Dodger right-hander's first pitch in the bottom of the ninth inning to give the Yankees a 1-0 triumph. The 1950 Series between the Phillies and Yankees produced only two home runs, but they were most important. The first, by Joe DiMaggio, broke up a 1-1 Reynolds'-Robin Roberts second-game duel in the tenth inning. The second, by Yogi Berra, ignited the Yankees' winning three-run sixth-inning rally in the final contest.

In the 1951 Giants-Yankees World Series, New York's Gil McDougald joined Elmer Smith and Tony Lazzeri in the record book, becoming the first rookie to hit a home run with the bases full. In 1953, a light-hitting second baseman with considerable World Series sock, Billy Martin, hit two home runs and batted .500, with twelve hits and eight runs batted in, to lead the Yankees to victory over the Dodgers. Martin also hit two homers in the 1956 Series against the Dodgers—but it was Berra who hogged the headlines by whacking Don Newcombe, a 27-7 winner of the Cy Young Award that year, for a grand-slam homer. That was in the second game. In the seventh and vital game, Yogi jolted Newcombe for two-run homers in both the first and third innings. That was the Series in which the Yankees smashed a dozen homers, an all-time record.

Hank Bauer hit four Series homers in 1958, three of them in winning games as the Yankees avenged the previous year's loss to Milwaukee. Chuck Essegian of the Dodgers set a pinch-hit homer record by walloping two out of the park against the White Sox in the 1959 Series. Bernie Carbo of Boston matched that feat sixteen years later, in the 1975 Series between Boston and Cincinnati. The more dramatic of Carbo's two emergency swats occurred in the eighth inning of the sixth game, regarded by many as the most exciting World Series game ever played. It came with two out and two on and forced the game into overtime. The game was won by the Red Sox on Carlton Fisk's twelfth-inning blast just inside the Fenway Park foul line. Fisk's body gyrations and his boyish jump for joy will live forever. Prior to Carbo's lifesaving home run, the most dramatic pinch-hit homer was authored by Dusty Rhodes of the Giants in the opening game of the 1954 Series with the Cleveland Indians. It came off the pitching of Bob Lemon with the score tied 2-2 in the tenth inning, for a 5-2 Giants victory. That homer got the Giants off to an upset four-game sweep over the favored Indians.

A grand slam by Chuck Hiller, the first ever to be hit by a National Leaguer in a Series game, helped the Giants to a fourth-game victory in 1962, but the Yankees were victorious in seven games. One year later, in the Dodgers' four-game rout of the Yankees, Dodger Moose Skowron became the first to hit a Series homer against his old teammates in both leagues.

Baltimore's Dave McNally became the first pitcher and twelfth player to hit a home run with the bases full when he connected in the sixth inning of the third game of the 1970 World Series with Cincinnati. Two years later, Gene Tenace, then an obscure catcher with Oakland, drilled four homers to help the A's defeat the Reds for their first of three straight World Championships. Reggie Jackson sat out the entire Series with an injury. Who would have dreamed that five years later, the irrepressible Reggie would join Babe Ruth as the only players in World Series history to slam three home runs in one game? ◇

Reggie Jackson enjoying a champagne shower after A's defeated the Dodgers.

Fleet Feet

BY JOSEPH L. REICHLER

THERE HAVE BEEN INNUMERABLE THRILLS during the nearly eight decades the World Series has been played. But one of baseball's supreme spectacles is still being reserved for future fans to marvel at and for future writers, after feverishly scanning the record books to pound their typewriters excitedly and rhapsodize: "For the first time in all World Series history, Joe Doakes today spectacularly stole home with the winning run in the ninth inning."

No, it hasn't happened yet. Not even Lou Brock has done it. Baseball's premier base stealer astounded observers by stealing seven bases in seven tries in the 1967 World Series. And as if to show it was no fluke, he stole seven more bases the following fall. But not one of them was a steal of home, let alone a steal of home in the ninth inning.

The rare theft of home, whenever it occurs, is always a crowd-tingling play. But it's even more exciting under the pulse-pounding pressure of World Series hysteria. Nothing will raise a crowd to such peaks of enthusiasm as witnessing a runner on third make a bolt toward home. The sudden dash down the line...the pitch...the slide...the tag... The suspense is sharper than a drive over the outfield fence.

As the World Series soars into its seventy-fifth year, the theft of home has been accomplished only thirteen times. Only five of these were solo steals, without any outside help. The other eight all came on one end of a double steal, which is interesting but far less exciting than an individual effort.

Tim McCarver, the St. Louis catcher, was the last player to steal home in a World Series. He crossed the plate on the back end of a double steal. It was the seventh game of the 1964 Series between the Cardinals and Yankees. Bob Gibson and Mel Stottlemyre had waged a scoreless duel until the fourth. Then the Cards got a quick run and had Mike Shannon on first and Tim McCarver on third, with two out. With Dal Maxvill at bat, Mike Shannon suddenly broke for second and beat Elston Howard's throw to Bobby Richardson. McCarver took off for home as soon as the ball left Howard's hand. He slid in under Richardson's return throw, for what was ruled a double steal.

There hasn't been a steal of home, unaided by another runner, in the last twenty-two years, and there have been only two in the last forty-three. The last to accomplish the solo feat was Jackie Robinson. This momentous event took place on September 28, 1955. It was the year of the Brooklyn Dodgers' first and only World Championship. The Yankees won the opener but not before Robinson scared them half to death with a daring steal of home that brought the Dodgers within one run of a tie.

When the Dodgers came to bat in the eighth inning, they trailed the Yankees, 6-3. Carl Furillo opened with a single, and after Gil Hodges flied out, Robinson hit a hard hopper that skidded through third baseman Gil McDougald's legs. Furillo raced to third, and Robinson took second on this miscue. Don Zimmer flied deep to center, scoring Furillo, and Robinson took second on the sacrifice. Then, as pinch hitter Frank Kellert addressed the plate, Jackie sneaked up the line and broke for home.

Whitey Ford, taken completely by surprise, tried to hurry his pitch and it came in a bit high. The ball appeared to get to the plate ahead of the runner, but Robinson slid across as catcher Yogi Berra came down on top of him with the ball. Yogi screamed wildly as late umpire Bill Summers called Robinson safe. The only other players to steal home unaided were Ty Cobb, Mike McNally, Bob Meusel and Monte Irvin.

Although he stole two intermediary bases against the Cubs in the 1908 Series, Ty Cobb had to wait until his third and last World Series before adapting his base-stealing specialty to scoring purposes. His steal of home, the first on a solo dash, came in the second game of the 1909 Series. Howard Camnitz the starting Pittsburgh pitcher, had just been removed, and Vic Willis strode to the mound to relieve him. As Willis raised his arm for the first pitch to Detroit's George Moriarty, Cobb broke for home. Catcher George Gibson didn't have a chance to nab him. Even the enemy crowd at Pittsburgh gave Ty a roaring ovation in appreciation. The Tigers won the game, 7-2, although they lost the Series, four games to three.

Bob Meusel stands alone as the only journeyman on the base paths who stole home not once but twice in World Series play. His first one was in the Yankees' first of their thirty-one Series, 1921, at the Polo Grounds. That is the only Series in which there were two steals of home. Mike McNally and Meusel turned the trick on successive days. McNally's theft came in the opening game and was a key run, inasmuch as Carl Mays was

leading the Giants' Phil Douglas 1-0 at the time. McNally doubled to left off Douglas in the fifth inning, and Wally Schang bunted him to third. Mays fanned. McNally suddenly electrified the crowd by breaking for home. And while Douglas was getting ready to pitch to center fielder Elmer Miller, catcher Frank Snyder desperately tried to jab the ball on McNally but missed. The Yankees went on to win, 3-0.

In the eighth inning the next day, with the Yankees ahead, 1-0, Meusel smashed a long single to center on which Ruth, by excellent base running, scored all the way from first. Meusel took second

Ty Cobb demonstrating his fadeaway slide as he steals a base.

on the throw-in and advanced to third on an infield out. Aaron Ward was up next, and on the first pitch Meusel lit out for home. He was aided by the fact that Nehf's pitch to Ward was outside. It was away from catcher Earl Smith, who after dropping it in the collision with Meusel, had a few choice words to say. The Yankees won, 3-0. Smith was scolded by Giants manager John McGraw and fined $200 by Commissioner Kenesaw Mountain Landis for his extemporaneous comments on the occasion. That night, McGraw growled to writer Fred Lieb, "Losing two 3-0 games is bad enough, but having them steal home on me in two consecutive days, that's what really hurts!"

Seven years later, against the Cardinals, Meusel stole home while Tony Lazzeri was swiping second base in game three at St. Louis. The theft occurred in the middle of one of the weirdest of World Series innings. The mournful frame began in a normal manner when Mark Koenig singled and was forced by Babe Ruth. Lou Gehrig, who earlier had hit an inside-the-park homer, walked. Meusel hit to Andy High, whose throw to Frankie Frisch forced Gehrig at second.

With a double play in sight, Frisch threw wildly to first, and Ruth charged for the plate. Jim Bottomley retrieved the ball and made an accurate throw to Jimmy Wilson in time to retire Ruth. The umpire called the Babe out. He reversed himself, however, when he saw that Ruth's slide had jostled the ball out of Wilson's glove. Wilson received an accidental cut on his face from Ruth's spikes. To add to his discomfiture, Wilson threw the ball into center field in an effort to head off Meusel running to second. Bob took third and Lazzeri walked. Then Lazzeri and Meusel worked their double steal. St. Louis pitcher Jesse Haines was so disgusted by this grand larceny that he stormed off the mound and disappeared under the runway.

Monte Irvin of the New York Giants performed the solo feat of stealing in the first inning of the first game of the 1951 Series with the Yankees, less than twenty-four hours after Bobby Thomson's historic playoff homer. There were two out when Irvin followed a single by Hank Thompson with a one-bagger to right center. Whitey Lockman smashed a ground-rule double into the left-field stands, scoring Thompson and sending Irving to third. With Bobby Thomson at bat, Irvin set sail for home and made it, sliding in under Allie Reynolds' high pitch. The Giants won the opener, 5-1, behind Lefty Dave Koslo, but lost the Series in six games.

Of course, not all of the spectacular World Series base running involved a steal of home. One steal that will be remembered as long as the game itself was Enos Slaughter's nonstop express run that

Monte Irvin stealing home as Yogi Berra looks quizzically at umpire's safe sign.

gave his team the 1946 Championship. The scene was the seventh game of the Series between the Cardinals and Red Sox. The score was tied 3-3 when Slaughter led off the bottom of the eighth for the Cardinals with a single. He remained on first as Boston's Bob Klinger retired the next two batters. That brought up Harry Walker, and manager Eddie Dyer gave the it-and-run sign. Walker sent a fly to shallow left center for a base hit. Roaring into second, Slaughter saw outfielder Leon Culberson juggle the ball. Full steam up, Country charged into third, where coach Mike Gonzalez was directing traffic. Gonzalez signaled to Slaughter to hold up, but the Cardinals' coach might have been a stop sign on a desert road, for all the attention Enos paid him. Slaughter swept around the hot corner as though the devil himself were after him.

Out in short left, Johnny Pesky had taken Culberson's belated relay. For a fleeting moment, the Red Sox shortstop paused. He paused too long. Johnny hadn't thought that Slaughter would dare set sail for home. Too late, he saw Enos streaking down the third-base line. Pesky's frantic throw pulled catcher Roy Partee way up the line, and Slaughter slid over the plate with the run that gave the Redbirds a 4-3 victory and their sixth World Championship.

Pesky was promptly branded as the goat, a charge that Slaughter did not agree with. "Pesky got hit with a bum rap," Slaughter still maintains today. "Because of the steal sign, I already had a pretty good jump on the pitcher when Walker hit this little floater into left center field. The play was in front of me, so I could easily see that nobody was going to catch the ball. In fact, the ball was still in the air when I came into second base. I knew third base was a cinch and I began to think I might make it all the way, especially since I knew that Culberson was not a strong thrower.

"Pesky had to go out and take the outfielder's throw and he couldn't see me, what with his back to the plate. It was up to his teammates to yell to him, but nobody did. You couldn't blame Pesky. By the time he turned around and got ready to throw, I was just a step or two away from the plate."

Eddie Collins stole fourteen bases in World Series competition, but he is best remembered for a distinguished piece of base running he turned in against the Giants in the 1917 Chicago-New York Series. Caught in the middle of a run-down play, Collins not only scored, he also made goats of three Giants players.

This piece of chicanery occurred in the fourth inning of the sixth game, right in front of the New York home crowd. Collins opened with a

Enos Slaughter sliding across the plate with winning run on his mad dash from first base.

Jackie Robinson slides across plate on successful
steal of home against the Yankees.

Eddie Collins, who beat Heinie Zimmerman in a foot race to the plate in the 1917 Series.

grounder which Heinie Zimmerman muffed for an error. Joe Jackson raised a fly to short right, but Dave Robertson dropped it for another error, allowing Collins to reach third. Happy Felsch bounced back to the mound. Collins, expecting pitcher Rube Benton to try for the double play, started for home but stopped when he saw Benton whirl toward third. Eddie immediately realized that he had no chance of returning to the bag, so he stopped midway down the line as Benton threw to Zimmerman.

Bill Rariden, the catcher, came up the line to close in on Collins, thus committing a catcher's cardinal sin of leaving home plate unprotected. Zimmerman, in possession of the ball, charged down on Collins. Just as he was about to make the tag, Collins leaped back and headed for home plate, left unguarded by Rariden, with no other Giant thoughtful enough to cover it. Although Zimmerman was forever branded as the goat, many felt the horns should have been given to Rariden. Giants manager John McGraw, though, blamed Walter Holke, maintaining that the first baseman should have covered the plate when he saw it had been left unguarded.

Although fleetness of foot was not a prerequisite in this case, Charlie Keller's spree in the final game of the 1939 Series between the Yankees and Reds merits attention. Unfortunately, the most vivid picture with the fans who saw the finale isn't one of Keller's Olympian outputs. Rather it is one of the most bizarre episodes in World Series history—the tableau in which the huge and cumbersome Ernie Lombardi lay prostrate on the ground behind the plate while Joe DiMaggio finished making an uninterrupted tour of the bases on a one-base hit.

The fantastic incident began with none out in the tenth inning and with Frank Crosetti on third and Keller on first as a result of a walk, a sacrifice and an error. DiMaggio then crashed a single to right, scoring Crosetti. Ival Goodman, the Cincinnati right fielder, allowed the hit to roll away from him. After a frantic retrieve by Goodman and a hurried relay by Frank McCormick, Lombardi dropped the throw that was meant to stop Keller and then collapsed. While the big catcher sprawled on the ground, with the ball out of his reach and with no one covering the plate, DiMaggio suddenly raced for home. Lombardi, aroused by the horrific shouts of the fans, struggled to his knees just in time to grab the ball and miss tagging DiMaggio.

Only much later was it learned that Lombardi, one of the game's outstanding catchers, was more or less the innocent victim of Keller's resounding crash as the catcher tried to tag him. Keller had inadvertently struck Lombardi in the groin and stunned him, thus causing a temporary paralyzing effect.

No base-running narrative would be complete without a recollection of Casey Stengel's home run on October 4, 1923, that gave the New York Giants a 5-4 victory over the rival Yankees. It came in the ninth inning and broke up a 4-4 tie. The victim was Joe Bush, later one of Casey's best friends. It was the first World Series game ever played at Yankee Stadium and was the only Series ever decided by an inside-the-park homer.

The hit was a drive to the fence in left center. Stengel had to beat a relay started by Bob Meusel, the outfielder with the strongest arm of his time. As Stengel rounded second, he began to wobble, and by the time he passed third he was taking both sides of the road like a Sunday driver with astigmatism. he finally sprawled safely across the plate and lay prostrate for several seconds.

A reception committee of joyous Giants met him at the plate, helped him to his feet. "What happened?" one of them asked. "Did you twist your knee?"

"No," replied Casey, "I lost a shoe passing second."

"Lost a shoe?" repeated the teammate as he looked down at Casey's two completely shod feet. "How many shoes were you wearing?"

Casey looked down in astonishment. He had been wearing a rubber sponge inside one of his shoes to protect a blister. The sponge had popped out, and under the impression he had lost a shoe, Casey had begun to favor the injured member, thus causing the weaving and wobbling. ◇

.400 Hitters

BY JOSEPH L. REICHLER

THE FABULOUS TED WILLIAMS was a bust in the World Series. Stan Musial batted .222 in 1946. Ty Cobb was an even .200 in 1907. Honus Wagner batted .222 in 1903 and Rogers Hornsby could do no better than .238 in 1926. Yet among them, these five baseball immortals captured forty major-league batting titles.

Hank Gowdy ran wild in the 1914 World Series. He teed off on Connie Mack's great Athletic pitchers as if they were rank amateurs, hitting a sizzling .545 as the Braves completed a four-game sweep. Larry McLean rapped .500 in 1913, as did Billy Martin in 1953. Tommy Thevenow batted .417 in 1926, and Emil Verban hit .412 in 1944. Substitute Al Weis surprised everyone by hitting .435 in 1969. Not a .300 hitter among them, let alone a batting champion.

How can one account for this incredible disparity? Of course, no one knows for sure, but some experts contend that the better the player is, the more he is affected by the mental strain. The stars are keenly aware that the responsibility for victory rests on their shoulders. They feel that their teammates and the fans are looking for them to carry the club to victory in the World Series, just as they did during the season. At the same time, the opposition is concentrating on stopping them. This combination of pressures is sometimes just too much.

The same is not true of a lesser light. He goes into the World Series free of mind and loose of

Hank "Old Sarge" Gowdy, batting star
of the 1914 World Series.

limb. He isn't shackled by responsibility. At least, not in the same sense as his more renowned teammates. Nobody is expecting too much of him, and the opposition isn't worrying about him.

That was the case in the 1969 Series. When the batting averages of the Baltimore Orioles and New York Mets were compared prior to the Series, Al Weis was the low man with a mark of .215. He had accumulated a total of 53 hits in 247 at-bats and had managed to hit only two homers. His chances of playing in the Series, let alone starring in it, appeared about as bright as the Mets' hopes of beating the high-flying Orioles, who boasted such clubbers as Boog Powell, Frank and Brooks Robinson, not to mention such mound artists as Jim Palmer, Dave McNally and Mike Cuellar.

But New York, aided and abetted by the inspired stickwork of Weis, produced one of the more startling upsets in the history of the classic, capturing four of the five games. Weis, getting an unexpected opportunity to play, shone the brightest. The ugly duckling batted a robust .455 in the five games, drove in three key runs and even hit a homer. For his efforts, he was presented the Babe Ruth Award as the outstanding hitter in the Series.

Another unexpected World Series hitting hero was Tommy Thevenow. In the 1926 Series between the St. Louis Cardinals and New York Yankees, Thevenow had just concluded his first full year as the Redbirds' regular shortstop, hitting a mighty .256. With such heavy hitters as Jim Bottomley, Chick Hafey, Lester Bell and the manager himself, Rogers Hornsby, gracing the lineup, Tom-

Tommy Thevenow, surprise hero of the
1926 World Series.

my was counted on only for defensive help. But the
light-hitting infielder emerged as high man for both
clubs with a .417 average.

Not too much was expected of Emil Verban
at bat in the 1944 all-St. Louis Series between the
Cardinals and Browns. Emil's .257 batting mark for
the season hardly gave any inkling of the heroics he
was to produce in the Series. But the aroused
rookie second baseman outdid himself. It appears
that after the first two games, in which the Cardinals
were the home club, the Browns unhappily sat Mrs.
Verban behind a post at Sportsman's Park in games
in which the American Leaguers were the host
club. Emil became a vengeful Cardinal. He wound
up with an average of .412, his hits being a big factor in the Cardinals' last three victories.

On the Browns' side, in 1944, the batting
leader was the equally unexpected George Mc-
Quinn, who hit a lusty .438 after a .250 season.
With the Browns hitting a lowly .183 and striking
out forty-nine times, McQuinn's bat was responsible for the Brownies making a respectable showing.
His first-game homer defeated Mort Cooper, 2-1.

One searches the list of .400 World Series
hitters in vain for such knights of the bludgeon as
Ty Cobb, Rogers Hornsby, Honus Wagner, Joe
DiMaggio, Stan Musial, Ted Williams, Henry Aaron
and Willie Mays. Instead, one encounters such
comparatively little-known players as Mark Koenig
Hank Gowdy, Jake Powell, Harry Steinfeldt and Billy Martin.

Eddie Collins, a three-time .400 hitter in World Series play.

However, the list of .400 men does include such Hall of Fame immortals as Babe Ruth, Lou Gehrig, Frank Baker, Frankie Frisch, Bill Dickey, Yogi Berra, Mickey Mantle, Roberto Clemente, Mickey Cochrane and Eddie Collins. Also such renowned swatters as Johnny Bench, Charlie Keller, Riggs Stephenson, Hack Wilson, Carl Yastrzemski, Thurman Munson, Reggie Jackson and a flock of others.

In all, seventy-six players have batted .400 or better in a World Series. Of these, that great second baseman of the Athletics and White Sox, Eddie Collins, turned the trick three times. Ruth, Gehrig, Frisch, Baker, Dickey, Berra, Phil Cavaretta, Alvin Dark, Joe Gordon and Lou Brock twice performed the feat.

After warming up by batting .429 against Frank Chance's Cubs in 1910, Collins hit .421 against John McGraw's Giants in 1913. By the time the 1917 Giants-White Sox Series arrived, Eddie had shifted to the pale hose of the Comiskey team and, despite the fact that McGraw used left-handers almost entirely in the six-game Series, Eddie, a left-handed batter, flayed them for .409.

"He's the toughest player I've ever had to contend with in a World Series," McGraw once said, "and when we played the Athletics, he was the greatest player on the field."

What recollections these .400 World Series hitters stir up as they gallop through memory's pages. Foremost of them all was Babe Ruth's .625 in the Yankees-Cardinals Series of 1928, the one in which the New York juggernaut flattened the Redbirds in four straight games. Bill McKechnie was criticized for not walking Ruth more often—the Babe had drawn only one pass in 1928, in contrast to the dozen "Annie Oakleys" he received in the 1926 World Series—but the Cardinal manager was confronted with the problem of having a .545-hitting Gehrig coming up behind Ruth.

In that four-game set in 1928, Ruth hammered out ten hits, including three homers and three doubles, in sixteen times at bat. He scored nine runs and batted in four. After warming up with doubles and singles, Babe closed with a mighty crescendo of three homers in the final game at Sportsman's Park, including the one he made after Umpire Cy Pfirman refused to permit a third strike on Bill Sherdel's quick pitch. Gehrig's bat was equally explosive. Lou strolled six times, reducing his total times at bat to eleven. But he made the most of them, clubbing four home runs, a double and a single. He knocked in nine runs and scored five.

Gehrig stormed back four years later to bat .529. He is the only player to top the .500 mark more than once. In that 1932 Series, in which the Yankee steamroller also crushed its rival in four

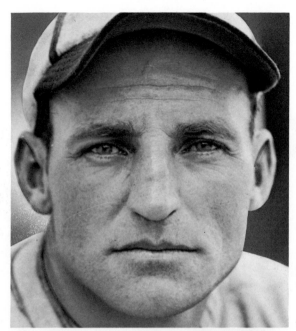

Pepper Martin, who ran wild in the 1931 World Series.

Thurman Munson batted over .500 in the 1976 Series.

straight games, Gehrig was a one-man powerhouse, accounting for fourteen runs. Lou tallied nine times and drove in eight runs. In the four games, he hit three homers, a double and five singles. "I didn't think a guy could be that good!" exclaimed Charlie Grimm, manager of the Cubs. "Every time I looked up, that big guy was on base or flying by me on a homer."

Another Series comet was Hank Gowdy's great performance against the Athletics in 1914. Gowdy's .545 ties Gehrig for second place among World Series batting averages. It was in this Series

Johnny Bench, voted Most Valuable Player of the 1976 World Series.

that Gowdy ruined the A's vaunted pitching staff, hammering out a homer, a triple, three doubles and a single in eleven times at bat to lead the Miracle Braves to a sweep. Hank also walked six times.

Thirteen players have come out of a World Series with an average of .500 or better. Johnny Bench was named the Most Valuable Player in the 1976 World Series when the Cincinnati Reds' catcher blasted Yankee pitching for two home runs, a double and a triple among his eight hits, to finish with an average of .533. In the same Series, Yankees catcher Thurman Munson hit safely in

each of the four games, accumulating nine singles for a .529 average.

At an even .500 are Pepper Martin, Vic Wertz, Billy Martin, Joe Gordon, Larry McLean, Mark Koenig and Dave Robertson. Best-remembered is the wild ride Pepper Martin took through the 1931 Series when the Cardinals faced the great Athletics, who were 107-game winners in the American League. It was the Series in which Pepper not only smacked the best pitches of Lefty Grove and George Earnshaw, but also almost got away with Mickey Cochrane's chest protector and

Billy Martin, a .500 hitter in the 1953
Series, tries unsuccessfully to avoid
tag by Roy Campanella.

shin guards. He closed the Series with five steals.

After making himself a particular nuisance to Connie Mack for four games, Martin reached his peak in the fifth contest when he drove in four of St. Louis' five runs with a homer and two singles. Had the Series ended there, Pepper would have emerged with an average of .667, but he cooled off, and by going hitless in the sixth and seventh games he reduced his average to .500.

Larry McLean's .500 for a losing cause in 1913 also was noteworthy, as the big fellow was called into the Series when McGraw's number one catcher, Chief Meyers, smashed a thumb. The Giants were no match for Connie Mack's A's that fall, and the only bright spots for McGraw were Mathewson's pitching and McLean's hitting. Larry's .500 average was especially commendable, as the

entire Giant team batted only .201.

Davey Robertson also hit .500 for a losing Giant team against the White Sox four years later, but the former New York right fielder is remembered more for his muff of a fly ball in the sixth game than for his eleven hits in twenty-two times at bat.

When the Yankees played the Pirates in 1927, the Bucs expected big trouble from Ruth and Gehrig—and got it, with a lesser amount from Bob Meusel and Tony Lazzeri. They hardly paid any attention to shortstop Mark Koenig, yet he proved the real tough baby of the Yankees' clean sweep. In four games, Koenig knocked out nine hits in eighteen times at bat.

Joe Gordon is the up-and-down man of the World Series. In the 1938 Yankees-Cubs Series,

Vic Wertz was robbed of an extra base blow by Willie Mays but still batted .500 in the 1954 Series.

Al Weis, an "Ugly Duckling," who batted over .400 in the 1969 Series.

Joe hit a brilliant .400 for New York. The next years, against the Reds' pitching, he dropped to .143. Then, in 1941, when the Yankees played the Dodgers, Gordon soared high again, and his .500 average had much to do with that five-game victory. Joe was a hitting fool, his seven safeties including a homer, a triple and a double.

A year later, when Gordon was voted the American League's Most Valuable Player, the World Series seesaw dipped low for him again. As the Cardinals won the Series, four games to one, Joe was the goat of Joe McCarthy's troupe, with the average of .095. In the Series of 1943, Gordon was halfway between his former highs and lows, hitting .235.

Two other famous Yankees, Yogi Berra and Mickey Mantle, also saw their averages go up and down like yo-yos in World Series play. Yogi's best batting figure in his first five World Series was .261 in 1951. His other marks were .158 in 1947, .063 in 1949, .200 in 1950 and .214 in 1952. Then he made a complete about face, hitting better than .300 in five of his next Series, reaching .429 in 1953 and .417 in 1955. Mantle appeared in twelve Series. But in only three did his performance reflect his true ability, although he accumulated eighteen home runs. Mickey's best showing was in the 1960 World Series when he knocked in eleven runs against the Pirates and batted an even .400. But look at some of those other figures: .200 in 1951, .208 in 1953, .200 in 1954, .167 in 1961, .120 in 1963 and .133 in 1963.

The World Series setting was a paradise to Mantle's buddy Billy Martin. The Yankees' scrappy second baseman, a .257 hitter in regular season play, batted a brilliant .500 in the 1953 Series, banging a record twelve hits. And there was a lot of TNT in those dozen hits, which included two homers, two triples and a double. He drove in eight runs, including the winning tally in the ninth inning of the final game.

Vic Wertz, a seventeen-year man in the American League, finally got his long-awaited opportunity to appear in a World Series and he made the most of it. That was in 1954 when the Giants blasted the Indians off the field in four straight. New York pitchers held the Cleveland clubbers to a .190 batting average, but they couldn't stop Wertz. Not even Willie Mays's incredible catch of his 450-foot drive failed to discourage this determined veteran. In the four games, he amassed eight hits, including a homer, a triple and a double. All of which added up to a .500 average. Had Mays not robbed Wertz of a seemingly sure three-bagger, the average would have been an astronomical .563.

The list of .400 World Series hitters is too large to single out each player individually, but special attention must be paid to one particular .400 hitter. He is Charles Dillon Stengel, better known as Casey. The year was 1923. The Yankees finally wreaked revenge on the Giants, who had whipped them in 1921 and again in 1922. Heinie Groh, the Giants' third baseman, who had murdered them with a torrid .474 batting average in 1922, was held to a paltry .182. Pancho Snyder, a .333 hitter in 1922, had only two hits in seventeen times at bat.

But the Giants did have one batting hero. He was Casey Stengel. Ol' Case simply murdered Yankee pitching, batting .417 against Waite Hoyt, Herb Pennock, Bob Shawkey and Joe Bush. He hit two home runs, and both were responsible for Giant victories—the only games won by John McGraw's team.   ◇

In a Pinch

BY JOSEPH L. REICHLER

Dusty Rhodes being greeted by Giant teammates on his game-winning pinch home run.

IT WAS WEDNESDAY, September 29, 1954. The capacity Polo Grounds crowd had settled back in their seats and prepared for a long struggle. The opener of the World Series between the New York Giants and Cleveland Indians had already gone beyond regulation time. It had been tied at 2-all since the third inning and it was now in the last half of the tenth.

Willie Mays was on second. Hank Thomp-

son was on first. There was one out as Monte Irvin strode to the plate. Leo Durocher, the Giants' manager, called him back and summoned Jim "Dusty" Rhodes from the bench. "I knew he was going to use me," Rhodes said later. "Leo knew and I knew that was my spot. The game meant something and that meant it was up to me."

Bob Lemon's first pitch was a slow curve, just above the waist. Rhodes swung and sent a lazy fly down the right-field line. Dave Pope, the Indians' right fielder, raced to the wall and watched in dismay as the ball dropped into the stands for the home run that broke up the game.

In the second game, in the fifth inning, with New York trailing 1-0, Durocher again called upon Rhodes to bat for Irvin, and again Dusty came through. This time he smacked one of Early Wynn's sliders and lifted a single to center to drive in the tying run. He remained in the game and drove in an insurance run in the 3-1 victory with a terrific home run off a Wynn knuckleball. In the third game, again answering a call to bat for Irvin, Dusty hit a pinch single with the bases loaded off Mike Garcia's fastball in the third inning to drive in the second and third runs in a 6-2 victory. His services weren't required in the fourth and final game, and Rhodes settled for a .667 batting average.

Dusty Rhodes's three hits equaled a record for pinch hits set by Bobby Brown of the New York Yankees against Brooklyn in the 1947 World Series. Rhodes's output, however, was much more telling than Brown's. The Yankee pinch hitter singled and doubled, scored one run, and drove in another. Two of his hits and both of his runs figured in games that the Yankees lost. Rhodes delivered key hits in all three games and drove in seven runs. Six were batted in as a pinch hitter.

Pinch hitting is at no time a copper-riveted cinch. But in a World Series, with the calcium glare of the spotlight shining in one's eyes, with tens of thousands of spectators watching and hundreds of thousands of dollars trembling in the balance, it is the most difficult job in baseball.

Since the beginning of the World Series, as now played, American and National League managers have called upon 871 pinch hitters. Eighty-six of these were not officially charged with a time at bat. They either walked, were hit by a pitch, or sacrificed. Of the 785 who were charged with a time at bat, 155 connected safely. That's an average of under .200.

Although teams started using pinch hitters in the first World Series seventy-five years ago, it was not until 1908 that one delivered the goods. The first to do so was Ira Thomas of Detroit. The reserve catcher was called upon by manager Hugh Jennings to bat for shortstop Charley O'Leary in the ninth against Mordecai Brown of the Cubs. Thomas singled, but the hit was wasted.

It was not until fifteen years later, in 1923, that a player came through twice in a pinch-hit role. Jack Bentley, a good hitting pitcher with the Giants, accomplished the trick against the Yankees. In 1947, twenty-four years later, Bobby Brown set the record with three pinch hits. It was also that year that the first pinch-hit homer was recorded. Since then nine other players have smashed pinch-hit home

Ira Thomas, first successful Series pinch hitter.

runs in World Series competition. Chuck Essegian did it twice for the Los Angeles Dodgers in 1959 as did Bernie Carbo for the Boston Red Sox in 1975.

Yogi Berra, holder of numerous World Series records, produced the precedent-setting clutch homer in the 1947 meeting between the New York Yankees and Brooklyn Dodgers. Yogi was to hit eleven more homers in Series play, but this was his rookie season, and he was a newcomer to the pressure-cooker atmosphere of the fall classic. To make matters worse, Yogi had been replaced as catcher in the Yankees' starting lineup for game three after going hitless in the first two games and permitting the Dodgers to run at will.

In the seventh inning of that contest, manager Bucky Harris gave the squat twenty-two-year-old Berra a chance to redeem himself. With the Yankees trailing 9-7, Yogi was called off the bench to bat for Sherman Lollar, who had replaced him behind the plate. Berra promptly slammed a home run off Ralph Branca. But even though the Yankees lost, Berra's pinch homer made record-book history.

Five years passed before another pinch hitter smashed a four-bagger in World Series play. And it was another Yankee, veteran slugger Johnny Mize, who turned the trick. Facing Dodger southpaw Preacher Roe in place of pitcher Tom Gorman in the ninth inning of game three of the 1952 Series, the left-handed-hitting Mize belted the ball into the right-field seats at Yankee Stadium. Like Berra's blow, however, Big Jawn's pinch homer availed the Yankees little, as the Dodgers prevailed 5-3.

It was a different story in the third game of the 1949 Series between the same two rivals. In that game, Mize's pinch hit, his second of the Series, was instrumental in a Yankee victory. For eight innings, fans were treated to a tense duel between New York's Tommy Byrne and Brooklyn's Ralph Branca. The Yankees took a 1-0 lead in the third inning on a pass, a single by Byrne and Phil Rizzuto's fly. But Brooklyn tied the score in the fourth on a home run by Pee Wee Reese. With Joe Page replacing Byrne, the two clubs then squared off on even terms until Yankee half of the the ninth.

With one out, Yogi Berra walked and Joe Di-Maggio fouled out. But Bobby Brown singled and Gene Woodling walked to load the bases. Johnny Mize then batted for Cliff Mapes and singled, sending Berra and Brown across the plate. After Banta replaced Branca, Jerry Coleman's single drove in the third run. This proved to be the winning marker, because, in the home half of the ninth both Luis Olmo and Roy Campanella smashed home runs before Page fanned Bruce Edwards to bring the inning to a close.

Mize was nearing the end of an illustrious career in 1952, but the thirty-nine-year-old veteran had two other homers later in that Series and batted .400 in helping the Yankees capture the seven-game set. His blast against Roe began a wave of pinch homers. Starting with his shot in 1952, five were hit in a span of four years.

Ironically, the Yankees and Allie Reynolds were the victims of the next pinch homer. It came in the opening game of the 1953 Series at Yankee Stadium. With the Bronx Bombers on top, 5-2, the Dodgers sent George Shuba to bat for pitcher Jim

Johnny Blanchard

Hughes in the sixth inning. Shuba connected for a two-run homer that pulled Brooklyn to within a run. The Yankees eventually won the game, 9-5, and went on to capture their fifth consecutive World Championship.

Another unsung performer, Hank Majeski of the Indians, whacked the fifth pinch homer in the same Series that Dusty Rhodes smashed in the fourth. It came in the fourth and final game played at Cleveland's Municipal Stadium in 1954. Batting for pitcher Ray Narleski in the fifth inning, Majeski hit a three-run homer off Don Liddle and thus earned the distinction of being the first right-handed batter to rap a pinch homer in a Series.

In 1955 Bob Cerv became the third Yankee to homer in a pinch-hitting role in the fall classic. Facing Roger Craig in the seventh inning of game five at Ebbets Field, Cerv hit a bases-empty smash, but the Dodgers won the game, 5-3. They proceeded to beat the Yankees in seven games to capture their first World Championship.

Chuck Essegian's brief rise to fame had a touch of irony to it. When the Los Angeles Dodgers arrived in Chicago to open the 1959 World Series, he discovered there was no locker for him in the visitors' clubhouse. As a result, he was forced to dress in a corner of the room. But Chuck, a journeyman outfielder who played for six major-league clubs in his six-year major-league career, had the last laugh. His pinch-hit exploits that Series earned him a special place in the record books.

After losing the opening game, the Dodgers were trailing in the second contest, 2-1, with two out in the seventh inning, when manager Walter Alston called on Essegian to bat for pitcher Johnny Podres. Chuck had struck out as a pinch hitter in game one, but this time he homered against Bob Shaw to tie the score. The Dodgers eventually won, 4-3. In the sixth and final game, Essegian hit a second pinch homer, again at Chicago's Comiskey Park. It was a ninth inning solo shot off Ray Moore, and it climaxed the Dodgers' decisive 9-3 victory.

Essegian's clouts touched off another spurt of pinch homers. In 1960, the year the Yankees outslugged Pittsburgh only to lose in seven games, Elston Howard added his name to the pinch-homer list. Casey Stengel sent him up to hit for pitcher Ryne Duren in the ninth inning of the opening game at Forbes Field. Howard responded with a two-run blast against Pirates relief ace Elroy Face, but the Yankees still wound up on the short end, 6-4. Howard came out of the Series with a .462 batting mark for thirteen at-bats.

In 1961, another Yankees catcher-outfielder and pinch-hitting hero, Johnny Blanchard, batted .400 with two homers as the New Yorkers rolled over Cincinnati in five games. The first of Blanchard's four-baggers was the tenth pinch homer in Series history. It came off Bob Purkey in the eighth inning of game three at Cincinnati's Crosley Field and tied the score at 2-all. Blanchard thus became the fifth Yankee to produce a pinch homer in Series competition, but the first to do it in a winning cause, since New York added a run in the ninth to win, 3-2.

It wasn't until fourteen years later that another man entered the select pinch-homer circle. Carl Warwick of the 1964 St. Louis Cardinals, Gonzalo Marquez of the 1972 Oakland A's and Ken Boswell of the 1973 New York Mets, each rapped three pinch hits in a single Series to tie a record, but all nine hits were singles. In the 1975 clash between Cincinnati and Boston, the Red Sox' Bernie Carbo gained the distinction of being the second player to homer twice in pinch-hitting roles in the fall classic.

Carbo hit his first in game three at Cincinnati's Riverfront Stadium. With the Reds leading 5-2, the left-swinging outfielder was sent in to bat for pitcher Reggie Cleveland, with two out in the seventh inning. He promptly tagged Clay Carroll for the eleventh pinch homer—and the first in a night game. The Red Sox later tied the score, but the Reds eventually won, 6-5, in ten innings, to take a 2 to 1 edge.

Interestingly, Carbo's smash was one of six

Bernie Carbo

home runs that night, equaling a World Series record for most round trippers in a game by both clubs. Bernie's second four-bagger rates among the most dramatic of all Series pinch homers. It came in the now legendary sixth game at Fenway Park. Trailing three games to two and only four outs from elimination, the Red Sox sent Carbo to the plate to bat for pitcher Rogelio Moret. There were two out in the eighth inning and there were two on base.

With the count at two balls and two strikes, Carbo drove the next pitch by Rawly Eastwick into the center-field seats for a record-tying second pinch homer, knotting the score at 6-all. In what ranks with World Series history's most memorable moments, Carlton Fisk hit a game-winning home run in the twelfth inning to give Boston a 7-6 triumph and send the October classic into a seventh game, which the Reds eventually won.

There has never been an inside-the-park pinch homer. Two Yankees, Gene Woodling of the 1952 champions, and Andy Carey of the 1955 pennant winners, came closest. Woodling hit his pinch three-bagger off the Dodgers' Joe Black in the first game of the 1952 Series, and Carey got his pinch triple off Brooklyn's Johnny Podres in the third game of the 1955 Series. Those three-baggers are the only ones recorded by pinch hitters in a World Series. ◇

My Love Affair with Baseball

BY LILLIAN G. CARTER

Miss Lillian Carter being hugged by Dodger
manager Tommy Lasorda.

I'VE BEEN IN LOVE with baseball for as long as I can remember. But until recently there was one ambition I had never achieved as a baseball fan. All my adult life I had wanted to see a World Series game. The World Series is baseball at its highest level, and although I felt lucky to have seen so many major- and minor-league games, I wasn't fulfilled.

Then in 1977 I was invited to attend a Series game between the New York Yankees and the Los Angeles Dodgers. The game was one of the most exciting I have ever witnessed. I remember that later, at the party after the game, someone came up and asked me why I liked baseball. I thought for a moment and then told him that I just couldn't say. I've never really stopped to analyze

why it appeals to me. All I know is that I've been a fan since I was a child. I started out watching small-town games, and over the years my enthusiasm simply continued to grow until today I am what many people would call a baseball **nut.**

Luckily, my friends understand. I can't really say that any of them love baseball quite as much as I do. But no one teases me about being so dedicated to the sport.

In fact, my enthusiasm for the game makes me somewhat unique in my family. Although Jimmy likes baseball, he unfortunately has little opportunity for it. His real love is car races. Billy also likes watching the races, but with the exception of football on TV, he doesn't follow sports all that closely.

My husband was probably the one member

of my family to come closest to matching my love for baseball. Until he died in 1953, he was as much a fan as I was, and we attended as many games as possible.

We would even go to minor-league games in Americus, Albany, and Columbus, Georgia. And since I was a Brooklyn Dodgers fan, we also used to go to New York every year to attend all the games for a week and to Cincinnati one weekend to see the Dodgers play the Reds in a doubleheader.

Our out-of-state baseball trips were a highlight of the year, and they enabled me to see many exciting baseball events in person. I was in Brooklyn, for example, when Jackie Robinson played his first game there, and he has been one of many favorites ever since. Nor will I ever forget the experience of seeing Babe Ruth hit two homers in a single game in Yankee Stadium.

If I couldn't actually go to a game, I would almost always listen to it on the radio. Mel Allen and Vince Scully were my favorite announcers. They made it both easy and fun to visualize the field and all the action in your head.

Even when I joined the Peace Corps and went to India for two years, I didn't lose contact with baseball. Although I was thousands of miles away, I was able to listen to Series games over the Voice of America. I really enjoyed that touch of home, and I was more than a little disappointed whenever emergencies at the clinic where I worked made it impossible to listen.

Of course, like any true fan, I've been elated at winning and disappointed to the point of tears when my favorite team loses. Yet my happiest and saddest moments center more around people than wins and losses. My happiest moment was seeing Hank Aaron break Babe Ruth's record by hitting his famous 715th home run. That game in Atlanta was one of the greatest I've ever witnessed. My saddest moment was the death of Lou Gehrig, a player whom I greatly admired and whom I saw many times.

My son **loves** for me to enjoy sports so much. He likes seeing me as I go around to various games. And being the President's mother doesn't really hinder me. After things have started on the field, I usually manage to avoid giving autographs by simply telling people that I came to watch the game. Most people are very polite. They understand that I don't want to be interrupted or disturbed.

Once the game begins, I look at everything: every pitch, every ball, every hit. I even like to silently argue with the umpire when he makes what I feel is a bad call. My favorite place to sit in a ball park is on the end of the ninth or tenth row near the home-team dugout. I like to be close to the field, and I enjoy hearing and seeing the players. One of the few drawbacks of being the President's mother is that I am no longer able to sit where I'd like. These days, I am placed in a box seat.

On the other hand, there are certain advantages. My favorite teams are the Los Angeles Dodgers and the Atlanta Braves (Just wait till you see what they do **next** season!), and I have had the opportunity to meet all of them.

I've also received many special mementos. I've got a baseball signed by Ralph Houk, one signed by all of the Braves, and one signed by all of the Dodgers. I've also got a special baseball hat with my name on it sent by Mr. O'Malley.

I finally got my wish to see a World Series game in October of 1977. One night out of a clear sky a young man who has been my friend for many years called me with some tremendous news. He knew of my desire to see a Series game and asked if I would like to go to Los Angeles to see the Dodgers play the Yankees. Shirley MacLaine had invited him, my personal aide, and me to be her guests.

Somehow the Dodgers' manager, Tommy Lasorda, heard I was coming. He invited me to come for the second game, the fourth of the Series, to throw out the first ball. That was on October 15, 1977, and we almost didn't make it. There were so many cars heading for the stadium that my escort had to get out of the car and direct traffic so that I could get there on time.

After the game, a very nice reception was held in my honor. I met all the players; Commissioner Kuhn; Mr. O'Malley, the owner of the Dodgers; Mr. Steinbrenner, the Yankees' owner; Cary Grant; and lots of other celebrities. Later I even went to New York for the last game, and I must confess that Reggie Jackson almost converted me with those three home runs.

But nothing could compare with my first World Series game in Los Angeles. I remember being a little anxious as to whether the catcher would be able to catch the ball I threw. But he did, and I settled back to enjoy the game.

In years past I had always watched the Series on TV. And before TV, of course, I had listened to it on the radio. Naturally I had formed a pretty good idea of what it would be like to see a Series game in person. But in spite of that, I wasn't at all prepared for the real thing. The excitement of a World Series game in person was even greater than I had imagined.

The crowds . . . everyone screaming and yelling . . . the excitement of meeting the Dodgers, Tom Lasorda, Bowie Kuhn and everyone else . . . It would have been a wonderful experience under any circumstances.

But that game was even more wonderful than I might ever have hoped, for on top of everything else—we **won!**   ◇

The Most Dramatic Finishes

BY JOSEPH L. REICHLER

THIRTY-FIVE THOUSAND, two hundred and five pairs of eyes peered into the New England darkness searching for the target area. Carlton Fisk had just swung mightily at a Pat Darcy pitch, "a sinker down and in," and had wafted it high and far toward Fenway Park's famous "Green Monster" outfield wall. You knew it had the distance, but would it be fair or foul?

A few steps from home plate, Fisk stopped and, like a boy at recess, did a slight jig, employing body English coupled with hand signals in an effort to prevent the ball from straying into foul territory. When the ball at last caromed off the foul pole for a home run, Fisk leaped ecstatically and took his romp around the bases.

Fans poured out of the stands in a veritable tidal wave of people. Security personnel made no attempt to stop them. Even the press box was in a turmoil. Veteran reporters, momentarily at least, ig-

nored their typewriters. They were marveling at the scene below.

When Fisk finally jumped on home plate, to be greeted by hysterical teammates, the curtain rang down on one of baseball's most pulsating dramas: a twelve-inning 7-6 Boston Red Sox victory over the Cincinnati Reds in the sixth game of the 1975 World Series.

It could very well be that no other game in World Series history has ever matched this one for sheer drama, excitement, suspense and importance. It was a most sensational finish to a most spectacular game. Yet, in a way, it was not wholly unexpected, for ever since its inception, the World Series has been replete with drama. It has provided heroics and heartaches, heroes and goats. It has knocked down big stars and elevated obscure figures. It has been a spectacle that Josh Devore, an old Giant outfielder, once referred to as the "World Serious." He didn't realize how right he was. What is more serious to a ballplayer, a manager, a club owner or a baseball fan than a World Series?

There hasn't been a World Series yet that

Carlton Fisk crossing plate on dramatic 12th inning home run for Boston against Cincinnati.

didn't have its share of stirring moments. Some were pulsating, some tragic, some bizarre, some even ludicrous. But each had the power to grip every fan in the ball park, every listener on the radio every viewer on television. One of the great charms of baseball is that none of its games is ever wholly devoid of excitement. A game may be one-sided; it may be sloppily played; but at some point a play is bound to happen that will bring the crowd to its feet.

You don't have to go back any further than 1977, when, in the eighth inning of the sixth game, the New York Yankees' Reggie Jackson swung at Charlie Hough's first pitch and hammered it deep into the Yankee Stadium center-field bleachers for his third home run of the game. As if sprung from a steel trap, the crowd of more than 60,000 leaped to its feet and sent up a roar that could be heard in Los Angeles.

"Reg·gie! Reg·gie! Reg·gie!" the fans shouted hysterically. And they continued to shout until Reggie Jackson emerged from the Yankees' dugout not once but twice to acknowledge their adulation. Jackson's trio of homers, all on first pitches, sealed the Dodgers' doom as they went down to their fourth defeat of the Series.

The finale of the 1912 Series between the Giants and the Red Sox rates among the top three or four most exciting games in World Series history. The Giants apparently had wrapped up the Championship by scoring a run in the top of the tenth inning. They were three outs away from victory. Center fielder Fred Snodgrass committed the Giants' first blunder when he dropped Clyde Engle's routine fly. But he immediately atoned for it with a spectacular catch of Harry Hooper's potential extra base smash. Christy Mathewson walked Steve Yerkes, bringing up the Red Sox' most dangerous hitter, Tris Speaker.

Speaker lifted a foul fly between first and home. Fred Merkle, the Giants' first baseman, went after it. But Mathewson, remembering that Merkle had missed several throws during the Series, yelled for Chief Meyers, the catcher, to take the ball. Meyers made a belated dash for it as Merkle stopped. The ball dropped untouched by hand or glove.

Given another chance, Speaker singled to drive in Engle for the trying run as Yerkes dashed to third. After Duffy Lewis was intentionally passed, Larry Gardner flied deep to right, and the winning run scored.

The 1920 World Series between Cleveland and Brooklyn is not remembered for its artistic success. But it did produce the first grand slam, the first home run by a pitcher and the first unassisted triple play—all engineered by the Indians. The next Series, though, was full of even bigger thrills. The biggest one of all came in the ninth inning of the

final game between the Giants and Yankees on October 13, 1921.

The Giants won that last battle, 1-0, with left-hander Artie Nehf pitching a four-hitter to nose out Waite Hoyt. The Giants scored their single run in the first inning, on an error by Roger Peckinpaugh. Babe Ruth, sidelined by an infected arm and a wrenched knee, went in as a pinch hitter for Wally Pipp in the ninth and grounded out. Aaron Ward drew a base on balls. Then Yankees third baseman Frank Baker drilled a sharp grounder that appeared headed for right field. Johnny Rawlings,

the Giants' second baseman, made a sprawling stop and, from a sitting position, threw out the slow-moving Baker on a close play at first. Ward, who had run with the pitch, rounded second and headed for third. First baseman George Kelly quickly rifled the ball to Frankie Frisch at third. Frisch made a lunging tag of the fleeing Ward to complete the most electrifying double play ever witnessed in a Series. It was one of those superthrills, one of the most exciting finishes in classic annals.

Most of the details of the 1941 Series between the Dodgers and Yankees fade into hazy

memory except for one play that occurred in the fourth game. To this day it is still controversial and still the subject of heated discussion among baseball fans. The Dodgers, trailing in the Series two games to one, appeared to have evened things up when they came within one strike of winning their second game. They were ahead 4-3, as the Yankees came to bat in the ninth inning at Ebbets Field.

Hugh Casey, the Dodgers' relief ace, was on the mound, and he appeared virtually untouchable. He retired the first two batters and then worked the count to three and two on Tommy Henrich. The next pitch was a vicious curve—some say it was a spitter—and Henrich swung and missed. The game apparently was over and the Series tied with two games apiece. But wait! Mickey Owen, the Dodgers' catcher, failed to hang on to the ball. It rolled through him to the backstop, and Henrich raced to first. Disaster followed in the form of three hits and a walk. Before the inning was over, the Yankees had four runs, which resulted in a 7-4 victory.

One of the most thrilling of all scenes was Enos Slaughter's scoring from first on Harry Walker's hit in the eighth inning of the seventh game of the 1946 Cardinals-Red Sox Series. There were two out when St. Louis' Walker hit the ball, and Slaughter took off as though the devil himself were after him. The hit, scored as a double, was actually no more than a long single. But Slaughter never stopped. He took everybody by surprise: Leon Culberson, who fielded the ball; Johnny Pesky, who handled the relay; and Mike Gonzalez, who was coaching at third base for the Cards. Slaughter's daring move so shocked the Red Sox players that the play at the plate wasn't even close. The run gave the Cards a 4-3 victory and the championship.

The 1949 Series between the Dodgers and the Yankees produced one of the finest pitching duels ever witnessed in a World Series. Allie Reynolds of the Yankees and Don Newcombe of the Dodgers went into the ninth inning of the opener in a scoreless deadlock. Reynolds had hurled only four complete games all season and manager Casey Stengel was taking no chances. Even though Reynolds had struck out the side in the eighth, Stengel had Joe Page heating up in the bull pen. Allie calmed his fears, though, by striking out Jackie Robinson, Gene Hermanski and Carl Furillo in the ninth.

Through nine innings, Reynolds had allowed but two hits and fanned nine. Newcombe had permitted five hits but no runs. He had eleven strikeout victims as he prepared to pitch to Tommy Henrich in the bottom of the ninth. With a two-ball and no-strike count, Newcombe served Henrich a fastball, and Tommy deposited it in the right-field stands to give Reynolds and the Yankees a 1-0 victory. The Yankees went on to win in five games. Newcombe never could shake that Yankee-itis jinx. Four more times was he to face the Yankees and not once did he go the distance.

Casey Stengel got away with murder in the 1951 Series, against the Giants. It was the ninth inning of the final game. The Giants were trailing, 4-1, but they had loaded the bases, with nobody out. The Giants' long-range right-handed hitters were coming up. Bobby Thompson, hero of the

Giants miracle only a week before, was the next hitter. After him came Monte Irvin, who already had eleven hits in the Series. Sal Yvars, a right-handed pinch hitter, was getting ready, if needed. Every bit of conventional baseball strategy called for a right-handed relief pitcher. But Ol' Case was anything but conventional. Defying all the fundamentals, he summoned Bob Kuzava, a left-hander, to face the right-handed batting trio. Kuzava retired all three on long flies and the Yankees won, 4-3.

Kuzava was the pitching hero again the following year. The Yankees led the Dodgers 4-2 in the seventh inning of the seventh game. Vic Raschi retired the first Dodger batter, but a single and two walks loaded the bases. It was evident that Raschi didn't have it, and Stengel called upon Kuzava to protect the Yankees' lead. The southpaw ran up a three-and-two count before disposing of Duke Snider on a pop-up. Kuzava next faced the right-handed Jackie Robinson and again the count went to three and two. Jackie then swung at a high curve and lifted a pop near the mound. It was first baseman Joe Collins' ball, but he appeared to lose sight of it. As Kuzava stood transfixed, Billy Martin made a desperate dash from his second-base position and, running at full speed, grabbed the ball in his gloved hand, about knee high. Two Dodgers had already crossed the plate when Martin's catch snuffed out the rally. Kuzava then blanked the Dodgers with ease in the eighth and ninth to preserve the 4-2 victory and give the title to the Bronx Bombers.

For sheer pluck, Carl Erskine's 6-5 victory over the Yankees in the fifth game of the 1952 Series had few equals. The Dodgers, thanks to a home run by Duke Snider, led 4-0 until the bottom of the fifth. Then the Yankees unloaded on Erskine with the force of a hailstorm. The lightning was supplied by Johnny Mize, who crashed a three-run homer. Carl, aided by superlative fielding plays by Carl Furillo, Andy Pafko and Billy Cox, was still in there in the seventh when Snider singled home the tying run. The score remained knotted until the eleventh when Snider drove in his fourth run with a double to put the Dodgers ahead, 6-5. Now all Erskine had to do was face Mickey Mantle, Johnny Mize and Yogi Berra. He threw Mantle out. Mize hit to the rim of the right-field stands, where Furillo made an unbelievable catch, and Berra struck out to end the game. Erskine, battered in the fifth inning, got off the floor to retire the last nineteen batters to face him.

Erskine will never forget the day he broke Howard Ehmke's World Series strikeout record. It was October 2, 1953, and the Dodgers were once again facing the Yankees. Erskine had just fanned Don Bollweg, a pinch hitter, for the first out in the ninth inning when the Ebbets Field crowd of more

Carl Erskine of the Dodgers and Johnny Mize of the Yankees, who shared heroes' laurels in 1952.

than 35,000 sent up a throaty roar. The cheering lasted longer than is customary for just an ordinary out. The pitcher looked around in surprise. The Dodgers had a 3-2 lead over the Yankees, but there were still two outs to go. So why the celebration?

Erskine was probably the only one in the park who didn't know that by fanning Bollweg he had just equaled the Series strikeout record. The news went out over the public address system, but Carl didn't hear the announcement. He had other things on his mind. Specifically, big John Mize, who was just now lumbering toward the plate to pinch-hit for pitcher Vic Raschi.

Thanks to Roy Campanella's tie-breaking home run in the eighth, the Dodgers possessed a slim one-run lead.

Erskine could only think of how easily it could be blown away by one of Mize's powerful swings. Concentrating with every nerve in his body, Carl shot over two quick strikes, both called. The next one was a wasted pitch. Then a foul. Erskine decided it was time for his specialty—a perfect change-up. Mize swung and missed, and Carl had his record fourteenth strikeout. The crowd went wild! And this time Carl Erskine knew the reason why.

The 1960 World Series was perhaps the strangest of all. The Yankees set all the records, hit

most of the homers, pitched all the shutouts and scored more than twice as many runs. But the Pirates won. They did it by coming from behind to win the seventh and deciding game of the Series, with Bill Mazeroski acting in the role of Frank Merriwell by blasting a game-winning home run in the bottom of the ninth.

Humiliated by a 12-0 score in the sixth game, the Pirates refused to quit. Even after the Yankees had overcome a 4-2 deficit and had gone ahead 7-4 in the top of the eighth, the Pirates fought back.

Gino Cimoli, a pinch hitter, singled to open Pittsburgh's eighth. Then came the break of the game. Bill Virdon slashed an apparent double-play grounder at Tony Kubek, but the ball came up hard, struck the shortstop in the throat, knocking him stunned to the ground. Dick Groat singled home one run and and Roberto Clemente singled home another. Then Hal Smith, in the game only because Smokey Burgess had gone out for a pinch hitter, smashed a home run over the left-field wall. That put the Pirates ahead, 9-7. But the Yankees overcame the deficit with two runs in the top of the ninth. Although they couldn't have known it at the time, all their efforts merely set things up for Mazeroski. Maz watched Ralph Terry deliver one ball. Then he leaned into the next pitch, a high fastball, and crashed it over the left-field wall to make Pittsburgh the world champions of baseball.

Pitching dominated the World Series of 1967 and 1968. Bob Gibson furnished the drama in both Series, although he had to share the heroics with Detroit's Mickey Lolich in '68. Gibson pitched three games against the Red Sox in 1967, winning all of them with a combined total twenty-six strikeouts and a 1.00 earned-run average. The Cardinals won the Series in seven games. The Tigers turned the tables on the Cards in 1968, winning the seventh game when Lolich outdueled Gibson, 4-1, for his third triumph. Gibson, who also hurled three complete games, obliterated Koufax's strikeout record, fanning seventeen Tigers in the opening game.

Brooks Robinson, with his sensational fielding and robust hitting, provided most of the highlights in the 1970 Series between Baltimore and Cincinnati. Robinson drove in six runs in the five-game set. And he robbed the Reds of at least that many with the most spectacular fielding by a third baseman ever witnessed in a World Series. In the sixth inning of the first game, he darted to his right for an "impossible" backhanded stop of Lee May's shot between him and the bag. Then, while still moving toward foul territory, he turned and threw in the same motion. The ball got to first base on one bounce, beating May by less than a stride. In the next inning, Robby hit a home run.

In the first inning of the third game, Robinson made a leaping grab of Tony Perez' hopper, stepped on third and fired to first for a double play. An inning later, he raced in for Tommy Helms's slow roller and nipped him with a hard throw. In the sixth, he made a diving stab of Johnny Bench's savage liner to save yet another hit. At the plate, Brooke collected nine hits, including two homers, in the five games for a .429 Series average.

Sparked by Roberto Clemente, who hit in every game for a .414 batting average, the Pirates defeated the Orioles in seven games in the 1971 Series. Steve Blass's powerful pitching performance was a real standout. Aided by Clemente's fourth-inning homer, Blass held the Orioles scoreless until the eighth, when Baltimore tied the score at 1-1 on two of the four hits given up by the young right-hander. The Pirates scored the winning

Roberto Clemente dominated the 1971 World Series with his brilliant all-around play.

run in their half of the inning on a single by Willie Stargell and Jose Pagan's hit-and-run double. Blass was untouchable in the ninth as he set the Orioles down in order, to lock up the Championship for the Pirates.

Rollie Fingers, who toiled brilliantly in relief for the Oakland A's in three straight World Series, looks upon the seventh game of the 1972 Series as the most memorable of his career. It was a tight game from the opening pitch to the last out. Blue Moon Odom started for the A's. He was opposed by the Reds' Jack Billingham. The A's got a break in the first inning when Bobby Tolan, in center field for the Reds, misjudged a fly ball by Angel Mangual, for a three-base error. Mangual scored on a bad-hop single by Gene Tenace.

The Reds tied the game in the fifth when Tony Perez doubled and later scored on a fly ball by Hal McRae. The A's went ahead 3-1 in the sixth. Bert Campaneris was on third with two out when Tenace doubled to right for the first run. Sal Bando then hit one to center, which Tolan chased. But when he fell down with a pulled hamstring muscle, the ball went over his head to score Tenace with the second run. That proved to be the winning run.

The A's hung on to that lead into the Reds' eighth. Jim Hunter was pitching by this time, having replaced Odom in the fifth. Pete Rose opened with a single and manager Dick Williams brought in Ken Holtzman, a southpaw, to face the left-handed hitting Joe Morgan. Holtzman yielded a two-bagger to Morgan and gave way to Fingers. Rollie disposed of Joe Hague, a pinch hitter, on a pop-up. Then, on orders from Williams, he intentionally walked Johnny Bench to load the bases. Tony Perez scored Rose with a long fly as the runners advanced.

The score was 3-2, but now there were two

out. Fingers got Denis Menke on a fly to left and retired the side in the ninth to give the A's their first of three straight World Series triumphs.

The Cincinnati Reds ascended the throne with a brilliant come-from-behind 4-3 victory over the Red Sox in the seventh game of the 1975 World Series. It's a Series hailed by the critics as the most exciting since the Red Sox met the Giants in 1912. After permitting the Red Sox to gain an early 3-0 lead, the Reds clawed away for a pair of runs in the sixth. They got another in the seventh and scored the winning run in the ninth on a two-out single by Joe Morgan.

However, it is the sixth game of that pulsating Series that will be best remembered. Fisk's home run, dramatic and climactic as it was, was just one of the many show-stoppers that occurred in that game. The Reds appeared to have the game, and the Series, wrapped up as they went into the eighth leading 6-3. But Bernie Carbo, pinch-hitting with two out and two on, walloped a home run to knot it up at 6-all.

Then the Red Sox seemed to have the game won in the bottom of the ninth, when they loaded the bases with one out. But George Foster threw Denny Doyle out at the plate to complete a double play. In the eleventh, Dwight Evans made a miraculous catch of Joe Morgan's bid for a homer and doubled Ken Griffey off first base, thereby setting the stage for Fisk's game-winning homer in the bottom of the twelfth. ◇

Jim "Catfish" Hunter, winner of two games in 1972.

Greatest Upsets

BY JOSEPH L. REICHLER

Dodgers finally win first World Championship in 1955.

BASEBALL'S LONG SEASON virtually guarantees that two strong teams will face each other in the World Series. There cannot be an accidental league champion in baseball. A team gets there on merit. However, there have been a number of instances where one team is a marked favorite over the other in Series play. One team may be loaded with a great number of stars and/or may have won the pennant by a huge margin. Form usually holds up in the post-season contest, but in some cases the so-called underdog has risen up and smashed down the stronger, more highly regarded club.

One of the curiosities of World Series history is that the team holding the records for most games won in both the National and American Leagues were beaten in the World Series. The 1906 Chicago Cubs, winners of 116 games, lost to the Chicago White Sox; and the 1954 Cleveland Indians, winners of 111 games, were swamped by the New York Giants.

Other big winners such as the 1931 Philadelphia Athletics and the 1969 Baltimore Orioles, who won 107 and 109 games, respectively, fell in October. The winner of the World Series is not always the acknowledged "best" team in baseball. The regular season runs through 162 games, but the World Series lasts only seven games, at the most. And anything can happen. Any team can get hot for seven games or less.

The most remarkable upset in World Series history was the totally unexpected triumph of the Boston Braves over the Philadelphia Athletics in 1914. The Braves not only beat Connie Mack's highly favored American League champions, but humiliated them in four straight. This was a Braves team that was languishing in the cellar as late as July 19. While the Athletics, losers of only four games in the Series of 1910, 1911 and 1913, had won another comparatively easy flag, defeating the second-place Boston Red Sox by 8½ games.

The Braves were not a great team by any means, but they had the momentum. As a team, they had made the most amazing climb in major-league history. From last place in mid-July, the Braves had shot up to first place on Labor Day. At the finish they led the second-place Giants by 10½ games.

Despite the Braves' big finish, the Athletics were inclined to be contemptuous of them. Connie Mack sent Chief Bender, scheduled to pitch the opener of the Series, to scout the Braves in a late-season game in New York. He learned later that the Chief had gone fishing instead. When Mack reprimanded the great pitcher, Bender replied with

a broad smile, "We don't need to scout this bush-league outfit."

The odds makers apparently agreed with Bender. They established the A's as a 3-to-1 favorite. Aside from their Big Three—Dickie Rudolph (27-10), Bill James (26-9) and Lefty Tyler (16-14)—the Braves had very little to recommend them. On the other hand, the A's boasted their "Hundred Thousand Dollar Infield" of Stuffy McInnis, Eddie Collins, Jack Barry and Frank "Home Run" Baker, plus the great pitching staff headed by Bender, Eddie Plank and Jack Coombs.

What the odds makers didn't realize was that the Braves had something else, too. They had two fiery infielders in Johnny Evers and Rabbit Maranville who fired up the entire team. And no one had counted on the batsmanship of catcher Hank Gowdy. With Rudolph pitching a five-hitter, the Braves easily won the opener, 7-1, and in the process Bender was knocked out of the box for the first time in a World Series game. Gowdy gave a preview of things to come by hitting a single, a double and a triple. The Braves were on their way. They went on to sweep the Series. Gowdy finished up with a fancy .545, his six hits including a homer, a triple and three doubles. The A's pitchers also walked him five times. Evers batted .438 and

Boston Braves miracle team of 1914.

Maranville .308. In sharp contrast, Baker led the losers with .250.

In some respects the White Sox victory over the Cubs in the all-Chicago Series of 1906 was as great an upset as that of the later Braves over the A's. The Cubs, like the A's of 1914, had been established a 3 to 1 favorite, and few of the experts gave the Sox any chance at all. With the astronomical percentage of .763, based on 166 victories against only 36 defeats, the Cubs stood heads and shoulders above anything else in their league. They finished twenty games ahead of the second-place Giants, the 1904 and 1905 pennant winners. The Sox, however, won their league championship the hard way. Stuck in the second division in mid-season, they fought their way into the race with a late-season winning streak of nineteen straight and succeeded in beating out Clark Griffith's Highlanders by three games.

However, in the club batting department the White Sox looked like a bad joke. The Cubs, with their famed Tinker-to-Evers-to-Chance combination in the infield and such outfielders as Jimmy Sheckard, Wildfire Frank Schulte and Solly Hofman, had led their league with a team batting mark of .262. The White Sox, on the other hand, were last in the American League club batting with .228. The club hit only nine home runs; Frank Isbell, the second baseman, was the top batter with .279.

The White Sox' strength was in their pitching—Ed Walsh, Nick Altrock, Frank Owen, Doc White, Frank Smith and Roy Patterson. They also had a sturdy defense, a shrewd and aggressive manager in Fielder Jones and an irrepressible will to win.

Perhaps the best break for the White Sox was an injury to George Davis, veteran captain and shortstop of the Comiskey club, on the eve of the Series. Jones moved his weak-hitting third baseman, Lee Tannehill, to shortstop, and inserted George Rohe, his infield utility man, at third base. Rohe turned out to be the batting star of the Series, winning the first and third games with key triples. So well did he do, that when Davis got back for the fourth game, Rohe remained at third base and Tannehill went to the bench. Rohe wound up tied with Jiggs Donohue, White Sox first baseman, for the batting leadership of the Series. Both men hit .333.

Starring with Rohe for the White Sox were the two Sox left-handers, Altrock and White, and young Ed Walsh, who was just coming into his own. They won all four games as the Sox took four out of six from the Cubs. Altrock won the opener 2-1 and was beaten in the third game by Mordecai Brown, 1-0. Walsh won the third game, 3-0, but needed help from White to nail down the fifth game. White won the clincher, 8-3. The Cubs' great hitters were comletely handcuffed; Solly Hofman's .306 was the top mark.

Undaunted by their defeat, the Cubs stormed back to win the pennant in both the 1907 and 1908 seasons, and each time they defeated the Detroit Tigers in the World Series. Frank Chance's three-time champions fell short in 1909, and Pittsburgh nosed them out for the pennant. Detroit, on the other hand, made it three in a row in the American League.

Pittsburgh entered the 1909 Series as the underdog, for just one reason. Everyone in baseball knew that the only type of pitcher who could beat Detroit was a fast curve-ball pitcher. The Bucs' manager, Fred Clarke, had two—Howard Camnitz, his twenty-five-game-winning ace, and a youngster named Babe Adams, who had won twelve and lost three in his rookie year. But Camnitz came down with an attack of quinsy just before the Series, and Clarke, on a hunch, decided to open with Adams.

The rest is history. Adams pitched the first, fifth and seventh games and won them all. His last victory was an 8-0 shutout that gave the Pirates the championship. Ty Cobb and Sam Crawford, Detroit's great hitters, each went hitless in four times at bat. In the three games against Adams, Cobb managed to get only one hit in eleven official times at bat.

Each of the seven World Series clashes between the Yankees and Giants was loaded with dynamite. Although the Yankees won five of the seven, all were hard fought. And none more so than the first one in 1921. Up to the time the Yankees obtained Ruth, in 1920, the Giants had been the kingpins in New York. Then along came the Babe. His exploits created a sensation, of course, much to the irritation of Giants manager, John McGraw. The Yankees then were still playing at the Polo Grounds.

Both clubs won their league pennants in 1921, and McGraw never wanted to win a World Series as badly as this one. The Yankees entered as favorites, largely because of Ruth. He had hit 59 home runs, driven in 171 runs and batted .378. Bob Meusel had hit 24 home runs with 135 RBI. And Carl Mays, Waite Hoyt and Bob Shawkey had won sixty-four games among them. The Giants had nobody to match those figures.

The Yankees got off to a great start, winning the first two games with Mays and Hoyt spinning a pair of 3-0 shutouts. In the third game, the Yankees knocked out Fred Toney and rang up four runs. No Giant had yet crossed the plate during the Series. But that was soon to change. The Giants knocked out Bob Shawkey and went ahead in the seventh with eight runs to win by a lopsided 13-5. The Giants then tied up the Series by winning the fourth game. But Hoyt beat Art Nehf, 3-1, to put the Yankees ahead again in the fifth. The Giants retaliated by winning the next three, 8-5, 2-1 and 1-0 to take the best-of-nine Series. The big show

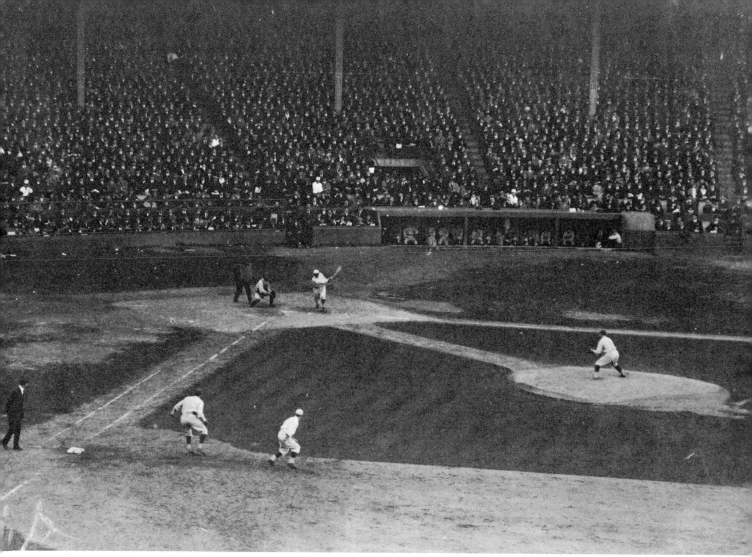

Giants upset favored Yankees in 1921.

ended with the most dramatic of all World Series double plays. Sub second baseman Johnny Rawlings, who started that double play, was the fielding and batting star of the Series. He handled thirty-seven chances without an error and collected ten hits for a .333 batting average. That 1921 victory gave McGraw the greatest satisfaction of his career.

The shoe was on the other foot in 1924 when the Giants, winners of their fourth straight pennant, were favored to beat the Senators, who had brought home their first flag since they entered the American League in 1901. The entire country, it seemed, was rooting for Washington, chiefly because of Walter Johnson. The great pitcher had pitched his heart out for mediocre Washington teams and finally landed on a champion at the age of thirty-seven in his eighteenth season in the league. But while public sentiment was with Washington, the experts gave the Senators little chance.

As if they weren't strong enough already, the Giants added four new regulars to the 1923 champions: Bill Terry, Travis Jackson, Hack Wilson and Freddy Lindstrom. Terry and Wilson

got five of the fourteen hits the Giants collected off Johnson to beat him in the first game, 4-3. The Giants drubbed Johnson again in the fifth game, 6-2. Behind by three games to two, it looked as if poor Walter had had it. Washington won the sixth game, however, 2-1. That forced a seventh game, which the Senators won in twelve innings, 4-3. Johnson hurled the last four innings, allowed no runs and received credit for the victory. The entire nation rejoiced, judging from the sacks of congratulatory mail Johnson received.

After beating the Yankees in 1926, the St. Louis Cardinals took on another powerhouse in 1931. This time it was the Philadelphia Athletics, a team with future Hall of Famers Jimmy Foxx, Al Simmons, Mickey Cochrane and Lefty Grove. The A's won the American League flag by 13½ games, with 107 victories, the most of any Philadelphia team. Simmons won the batting title with a .390 average. Grove had a phenomenal season with thirty-one victories and only four defeats. Foxx had 30 home runs and 120 runs batted in.

The Cards didn't have as many names, but they did have a kid named Pepper Martin. The rookie center fielder batted .500 with twelve hits, including a homer and four doubles. And he ran at will, stealing five bases and stretching singles into doubles. Burleigh Grimes and Bill Hallahan won two games each. The Cards won the final game 4-2. Grimes pitched shutout ball until the ninth. But with two runs and two men on, Hallahan came in and got the final out.

The 1934 Cardinals, later known as the "Gashouse Gang," were the most colorful of all St. Louis clubs, but they were considered lucky, because it took a collapse by the New York Giants for them to win the National League pennant. The Cards appeared hopelessly out of the race until the Giants dropped six of their last seven games. The Cards squeezed through on the last day. Detroit, in winning its first pennant since 1909, had built a powerful team headed by Hank Greenberg, Charley Gehringer, Goose Goslin and, of course, Mickey Cochrane, the manager and inspirational leader. The team had won 101 games, with Schoolboy Rowe, the pitching leader, winning 16 in succession. Tommy Bridges, master of the curve ball, had a 22-11 record.

The Tigers put up a valiant fight before succumbing to the steady pounding of the Cardinal bats and the pitching of the Dean Brothers, Dizzy and Paul, who won two games each. Dizzy put the final crusher on the Tigers, 11-0. This was the game when the Detroit bleacherites showered

Pepper Martin lacing a double in game against Philadelphia A's in 1931.

Ducky Medwick with fruit and Judge Landis was forced to take him out of the game so the Series could continue.

Perhaps the greatest of all the Cardinals' five World Series triumphs was the 4 to 1 success scored over the Yankees in 1942. The Yankees had set a record for. invincibility. From 1927 through 1941, the Bronx Bombers captured eight fall classics, during which they won thirty-six games and lost only four. Yet, after losing the opener of the 1942 Series to Red Ruffing, 7-4, those rollicking Redbirds dumbfounded the baseball world by smacking down Joe McCarthy's New Yorkers in the next four games.

The rout of the Yankees started in the sec-ond game, when young Johnny Beazley, a twenty-one-game-winning freshman, defeated Ernie Bonham, 4-3. Ernie White followed with a 2-0 shutout. Then came a wild Sunday game in which the Cardinals outslugged the Yankees, 9-6. Beazley repeated in the fifth game, defeating Ruffing, 4-2, to hand Red his second World Series defeat in nine decisions. With the score tied at 2-all in the ninth, Whitey Kurowski broke the deadlock with a two-run homer.

The 1954 Yankees won 103 games, highest for any of Casey Stengel's twelve seasons at Yankee Stadium. Yet they still lost the pennant by eight games. That's because the rampaging Cleveland Indians set a league record by winning

Packed stands at Navin Field, Detroit watch 12 inning thriller between Tigers and Redbirds.

111. The Indians charged into the World Series a heavy favorite over Leo Durocher's Giants, who had had to fight off a stubborn Dodger team for the top spot in the National League. The Indians had a four-star pitching staff of Bob Lemon (23-7), Early Wynn (23-11), Mike Garcia (19-8), Art Houtteman (15-7) and Bob Feller (13-3). They also had the league's batting champion in Bobby Avila and a pair of authentic sluggers in Al Rosen and Larry Doby.

Durocher's top hands were Willie Mays, Monte Irvin and Alvin Dark. And he had two great pitchers in Johnny Antonelli and Sal Maglie. Yet the experts didn't rate the Giants in the same class with their American League rivals. The experts, however, failed to consider the Giants' secret weapon: pinch hitter extraordinaire James "Dusty" Rhodes. This free soul took matters into his own hands, winning the first game with a pinch-hit homer in the tenth inning to defeat Lemon, 5-2, and coming through with key pinch hits in the second- and third-game triumphs over Wynn and Garcia. On the fourth day, the great man rested as the Giants ended the slaughter with a 7-4 victory.

Patsies in seven previous World Series, the battle-scarred Brooklyn Dodgers finally prevailed in

1955, becoming the first team to come through after losing the first two games in a seven-game set. The fact that the Yankees were the victims made it more gratifying to the Dodgers, who had lost all five previous match-ups to the Bronx Bombers. Johnny Podres was the hero of the Dodgers' triumph, winning the third and seventh games, the latter a 2-0 victory. A spectacular catch by outfielder Sandy Amoros with two Yankees on base and nobody out in the sixth inning saved Podres' shutout.

The 1960 Yankees-Pirate Series defies all logic. The Yankees hit a fantastic .338, hammered ten home runs and won by scores of 16-3, 10-0 and 12-0. But Pittsburgh won the Series, four games to three, on Bill Mazeroski's ninth-inning omer in the seventh game. New York outscored the Bucs 55 to 26, outhit them 91-60, and outhomered them 10 to 4. Bobby Richardson set two Series RBI records with six for one game and twelve for a Series. Mickey Mantle scored eight runs, drove in eleven and hit .400. Whitey Ford pitched two shutouts. No Pittsburgh pitcher ever had a complete game to his credit. But his Pirates manager Danny Murtaugh remarked afterward, "The Yankees set all the records, but they will pay off on most games won."

Brooklyn's first World Championship team managed by Walter Alston, 5th from left in lower row.

Willie Mays and Dusty Rhodes

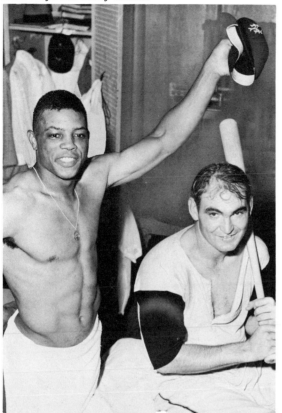

The Yankees were still regarded as something special in 1964, particularly in Series competition. The Cardinals, on the other hand, were the unexpected National League pennant winners. They were nine games behind in the middle of August, and their chances were considered nil, even by their loyal followers. But St. Louis won eight straight and Philadelphia, which looked like a cinch, lost ten in a row, putting the Cards on the World Series table on the last day.

The teams split the first four games, the Cards having to come from behind in each of their victories. Then Bob Gibson took over. After out pitching Mel Stottlemyre, 5-2, in ten innings of the fifth game, he came back to beat Stottlemyre again, 7-5, in the seventh game, to give the Redbirds another Series triumph.

One of the most astonishing feats in the World Series was the Baltimore Orioles' sweep over the Los Angeles Dodgers in 1966. The Dodgers admittedly were not a power-hitting club. But they had excellent speed, a good defense and a superb pitching staff headed by the incomparable Sandy Koufax. Baltimore manager Hank Bauer had to struggle through all season with his pitching staff,

Manager Leo Durocher of Giants responds to crowds in ticker tape parade on Broadway.

which completed only twenty-three games. Koufax alone had twenty-seven.

Dodger pitching lived up to its reputation, holding the Orioles to a club batting average of .200, lowest in history for a four-straight winner.

But the Oriole staff proved phenomenal, setting a new Series record by holding the Dodgers scoreless in the last thirty-three innings. The Dodgers scored only two runs, suffering shutouts at the hands of Jim Palmer, Wally Bunker and Dave McNally. In

Catcher Jerry Grote lifts Pitcher Jerry Koosman in a bear hug as third baseman Ed Charles does a dance of his own after Mets' fifth game win over Orioles.

addition, Moe Drabowsky, coming to the aid of McNally in the opener, set a Series record for a reliever by striking out eleven batters, six in succession, in 6⅔ innings of brilliant relief pitching.

The 1969 World Series produced one of the most startling upsets in the history of the classic as the New York Mets defeated the Baltimore Orioles, capturing four straight after losing the first game. The Series looked like a mismatch. Baltimore had the hitting and the pitching. The Orioles had won 109 games, finishing 19 games ahead of their nearest rivals in the East before taking 3 straight in the playoffs with Minnesota. They had three twenty-game winners in Jim Palmer, Dave McNally and Mike Cuellar. Boog Powell hit thirty-seven homers, Frank Robinson thirty-two, Paul Blair twenty-six and Brooks Robinson twenty-three.

Never higher than ninth since being awarded in expansion franchise in 1962, the Mets surprised everybody by winning the National League Eastern Division race handily and then swamping the Atlanta Braves in three straight games.

The Orioles, as expected, won the first game, 4-1. But there the predictability ended, for that was all they ever took. Backed by timely hitting, notably by Donn Clendenon and Al Weis; strong pitching by Jerry Koosman, Gary Gentry and Tom Seaver; and sensational fielding by Tommie Agee, Bud Harrelson and Ron Swoboda, the Mets reeled off four straight eye-popping victories to close out one of the most amazing chapters in World Series history.

A short time later, after Baltimore had captured its third consecutive American League pennant with 101 victories, manager Earl Weaver had proclaimed his team the greatest aggregation since the 1927 Yankees. The Orioles had made a shambles of the Eastern Division race, winning by twelve games and topping it off with a sweep of the three playoff games with Oakland. Pittsburgh had reached the Series by breezing to their second straight Eastern Division title and then beating the San Francisco Giants three consecutive games after losing the first.

Most experts picked the Orioles to win because the team had four twenty-game winners and Pittsburgh had none. But it was the Pirates who came through with the superior pitching in the Series. Nellie Briles pitched a two-hit 4-0 shutout in the fifth game. Steve Blass, a fifteen-game winner during the season, turned in two brilliantly pitched games, winning both. He permitted but three hits in winning the third game, 2-1, after Baltimore had won the first two. Then he defeated the Orioles in the seventh game, 2-1, with a gutsy four-hitter. Roberto Clemente stole the thunder from the Baltimore blasters, hitting safely in every game to finish with a batting average of .414.

No one can predict when next the World Series will produce a David who will rise up and slay a Goliath. But one thing is certain—it will happen. And, judging by past performances, it won't be long in coming. ◇

Mets fans rejoice over their team's surprise victory over the favored Baltimore Orioles.

Dodgers' Gil Hodges was victimized in the 1952 Series.

Stars Have Problems Too

BY JOSEPH L. REICHLER

THE POLITICIANS AND PUBLICITY HOUNDS cluttering up the field were hustled into the stands, and the contagious excitement that always accompanies the opening of a World Series began to surge through the crowd. The New York Yankees had been trading pleasantries with club house visitors. But as the ground crew began to manicure the diamond, a subtle change came over the team. Suddenly everyone was silent, as though each were wrestling with a private, personal problem. The mood was broken by a sportswriter who dropped into the dugout to give Joe DiMaggio a good-luck handshake.

"It's just another game," the fellow said.

DiMaggio, appearing in his tenth World Series, winced. "That's what they all tell you, 'It's just another game,'" Joe said. "That's bunk. I don't care how many of these things a guy has been in, he always gets butterflies in his belly when he plays in a World Series."

If DiMaggio, who appeared as unemotional as they come, admitted he was still affected by the Series jitters after playing on more Championship teams than any man in history, it's a cinch all ballplayers are seized by the same symptoms.

Rogers Hornsby once said he didn't know of a single ballplayer who didn't admit to having knots in his stomach in a World Series. "Anybody who says he isn't nervous or excited in a World Series is either crazy or a liar," he said. "I've seen pinch hitters strike out on pitches they never would have gone after during the regular season. They're pressing. They don't want to be called out on strikes in a World Series."

The stars are just as nervous—maybe even more so—than the ordinary players. In 1921, Babe Ruth's first World Series, the Bambino struck out, missing a pitch that actually hit the dirt. In 1936, Lou Gehrig of the Yankees froze at third base and didn't come home for an easy run on a base hit. Gil Hodges, the big first baseman and muscle man of the Brooklyn Dodgers, suffered the ignominy of going hitless in the full seven games of the 1952 Yankees-Dodgers Series.

Dick Groat, the Pittsburgh Pirates' shortstop and team captain, the National League's Most Valuable Player and batting champion in 1960, pulled a boner in the first game of the Series with the Yankees that left him red-faced. In the first inning of the first game, with Bill Virdon on first, Groat admitted he was so scared that he nearly froze and just scratched his foot in the batter's box. The trouble was, scratching your foot in the batter's box was the Pittsburgh club's signal for the hit-and-run play. When Groat realized what he had done, he jumped back and rubbed his forehead, which was the signal to kill the previous signal. But Virdon didn't catch Groat's new signal. He tore for second. Luckily, nobody covered the bag and he was safe. Groat's .214 batting mark was the lowest among the regulars.

The World Series carries that kind of mental strain for a week or more. The players are fighting for a pot of gold as well as the glory of the World Championship. Thousands sit in judgment of these athletes, and tens of millions follow every move on radio and television. All this adds up to pressure.

This is not to imply that great stars seldom rise to the occasion when the big chips are down. In the 1977 Series between the Yankees and Dodgers, Reggie Jackson proved that the great ones can and do meet the challenge. In the final game, under steadily mounting pressure, some of it

Yankees' Roger Maris cooled off in the '61 Series.

Rival World Series stars Ted Williams and Stan Musial exchanging views prior to '46 Series.

by his own doing, he came through with three successive home runs to single-handedly defeat the
Dodgers. Others have performed heroically, too.
Babe Ruth hit more home runs, proportionately, in
the World Series than he did during the regular
season. Lou Gehrig's cumulative batting average
for seven Series is .361. Hank Greenberg never
failed to deliver a home run in each of the four
Series in which he participated. Carl Yastrzemski
won the Triple Crown in 1967 and proceeded to
bat .400 for the Red Sox in the Series against the
Cardinals. Johnny Bench and Thurman Munson
have hit better in Series competition than in regular-
season play—and each has captured World Series
a Most Valuable Player Award.

However, a regular-season Most Valuable
Player Award, a batting title, a home-run crown or a
pitching championship is not a guarantee to stardom in a World Series. On the contrary. In many
cases, it is a bad omen, a jinx, a sure sign of dismal
performance in the post-season classic. Stan
Musial, who led the National League in batting
seven times, batted over .300 just once in four
World Series. In 1946, he hit a league-leading .365
during the regular season and a bargain-basement
.222 in the World Series.

Roger Maris topped Babe Ruth's season
home-run record in 1961, smashing sixty-one
round-trippers. He also drove in 142 runs, most in
the American League, and was duly voted the Most
Valuable Player Award. That didn't help him one bit
in the Series as he batted a frigid .105 with one
measly home run and two RBI's, even though the
Yankees annihilated the Cincinnati Reds in five
games. Mickey Mantle didn't fare much better the
following October after leading the American
League with 122 RBI's on a .321 batting average
that earned him the league's MVP. So, in the Series
with the Giants he collected only three hits in
twenty-five times at bat for an anemic .120 batting
average. Mickey didn't drive in a single run in the
seven games. Mantle enjoyed numerous pros-
perous World Series, however, as his all-time-
leading eighteen home runs and forty RBI's attest.

The most disconsolate man at the end of
the 1946 World Series between the St. Louis Cardinals and Boston Red Sox, won by St. Louis in
seven games, was Ted Williams. Long after the
final game had ended and most of his teammates
had departed, the Red Sox slugger sat in uniform in
the clubhouse, his head down, his eyes closed. Bit-
ter thoughts were in Ted's mind. It was his only
World Series chance in a glorious career stretching
through two decades, and he had muffed it. In
seven games, he made only five hits in twenty-five
times at bat, suffered five strikeouts and driven in
one run. All of his hits were singles. One was a
humble bunt, tapped down the third-base line when

Honus Wagner as he looked in 1903
when he won batting title but failed to
shine in 1903 Series.

Rogers Hornsby, National League's
MVP in 1929, didn't fare well in the
World Series vs the A's.

the Cards played manager Eddie Dyer's exaggerated "Williams Shift," leaving the entire left side of the infield unprotected. In the 1946 American League season, Williams had batted .342, smacked 38 home runs and driven in 123 runs.

In failing so dismally against Cardinals pitching, Ted certainly set no precedent. Since its inception in 1903, the Series has been an amazing leveler of luminaries, as well as a thrilling lifter of the bread-and-butter ballplayers. Williams went into the 1946 Series competition a bundle of nerves. It had been said of him that he had ice water in his veins and that he could take anything in stride. But unfortunately the 1946 Series disproved that completely.

In 1903, the great Honus Wagner, called the greatest player in National League history and regarded by all as the master shortstop of all time, represented the Pirates in the first of all modern World Series. Nobody ever accused Wagner of being nervous. He was stolid, phlegmatic. He had nerves of steel. But the importance of World Series competition got him down. Whereas in league competition he had swatted .355 to capture the first of eight batting titles, a league record, the Flying Dutchman was able to hit no better than .222 in the October games. In the last four contests, all of which the Pirates lost to Boston, Wagner managed only a feeble single in thirteen official times at bat.

Hal of famers Ty Cobb, Tris Speaker and Eddie Collins when they were teammates on the A's.

In all eight games (Boston won the Series five games to three), Honus hit nothing more dramatic than a double and was horse-collared in four games, three of them in succession.

Nobody played the game better than Ty Cobb. The Georgia Peach, regarded as the greatest all-around hitter the diamond has spawned, represented the Detroit Tigers against Mordecai Brown, Ed Reulbach, Orvie Overall and Jack Pfiester of the Chicago Cubs in the 1907 Series. "The Peach will steal the uniforms off the Chicago players," wrote one of the experts that October.

"Cobb alone will prove too much for the Chicago mound staff," shouted another master of overstatement.

Cobb stole forty-nine bases and hit .350 during the regular season to win the first of his twelve batting titles. But in the Series, Ty proved to be just about as inept as Wagner was four years earlier. He did not steal a base. He got three singles and a three-bagger in twenty trips to the plate. He did not drive in a run. He batted an even .200.

The Tigers had already lost two games when the teams shifted from Chicago to Detroit for the fourth game. The opener had ended a 3-3 tie. In the ceremony at home plate before the first game in Detroit, the fans presented manager Hughie Jennings with a giant floral tiger. Cubs manager Frank Chance scornfully looked on.

"What are you going to do with it, Hughie?" asked Chance. "Eat it?"

"No," replied Jennings. "We'll ram it down your throat."

"Who, you and Cobb?" sneered Chance. "I thought you told me he was a hitter."

"He'll hit before this is over."

"That's what you say," laughed Chance.

Chance was right, but the next year when the Tigers and Cubs met again in the Series, Cobb did hit. He batted .368 after winning his second batting title with a .324 average. It didn't help much, since the Cubs won the Series. But the next year, when the Tigers won their third straight pennant, Cobb was a flop again. He batted .377 for the season and then slumped to .231 in the Series, won by the the Pirates. Babe Adams, freshman Pittsburgh pitcher, beat the Tigers three times and retired Cobb ten of the eleven times he faced him. The Georgia Express went hitless all four times at bat in the final game won by Adams, 8-0. It was Cobbs's last appearance in Series play, although he was only twenty-two and was to continue for two more decades as baseball's best hitter.

In 1921, the great Yankees, with Babe Ruth among their stellar array for the second year, tackled the Giants. With the Bam on their side, the Yankees were expected to rend the McGraw men limb from limb. The Giants won the Championship. To be sure, Babe hit .313. But he accomplished only one homer and a mere five blows and was far from the atomic force he had been expected to be.

Ruth went into the 1921 Series suffering

from an arm infection. But he had no such handicap in the 1922 Series with the Giants, in which he was an abject failure. The Yanks never won a game, and Babe hit .118, with two blows in seventeen trips to the plate. This was to be the Babe's last nonproductive Series, however. In his next five Series appearances, he attained heights that remain unapproachable to mere mortals.

Rogers Hornsby, generally acknowledged as the greatest right-handed hitter in baseball history, suffered through cold spells in each two Series in which he participated. Rajah, the possessor of the modern major-league batting mark of .424 in a single season, was just another player in the 1929 Series between the Cubs and Athletics. He had ended the 1929 season with a flourish, hitting .380 with 40 home runs and 149 runs batted in. He was named the league's Most Valuable Player. But he contributed little to the Cubs' offense in the Series, striking out eight times and collecting only five hits in twenty-one times at bat for a .238 average. Hornsby had fared just slightly better in the 1926 Series, playing for the Cardinals when he managed seven hits in twenty-eight times at bat for .250.

What it really boils down to is that a short series of games like a World Series can find a hitter or a pitcher in a cold spell. If it happens at the wrong time, he earns the label "flop" because of all the attention concentrated on the World Series. By those standards, the National League has had a particular series of "flops" among its batting and home-run champions over the years. In all, fourteen batting champions have gotten into a World Series, and nine have hit well under .300. Jackie Robinson batted .342 in 1949 to lead the league, but his feeble .188 contributed to the Dodgers' Series loss to the Yankees. A similar fate befell Pete Reiser and the Dodgers in 1941 when Pistol Pete led the league with a .343 average only to fall to .200 in the Series.

National League home-run champions have fared even worse. The fourteen who have gotten into the World Series have hit only eight homers among them, and three of them were hit by Henry Aaron, which helped the Milwaukee Braves defeat the Yankees in the 1957 Series. Eight National League home-run champs have been held homerless in Series play, including Willie Mays, who belted forty-nine in 1962, and Willie Stargell, who slammed forty-eight in 1971.

In comparison, American League home-run champions have almost invariably come up with their share of Series homers. Babe Ruth, Lou Gehrig and Mickey Mantle were consistent in that regard. In all, the American League has had twenty-five home-run champions in the Series, and they have accounted for thirty-five home runs.

Ruth, as might be expected, hit the most as a home-run champ, four in 1928. Mantle had three in 1956, as did Carl Yastrzemski in 1967. Yastrzemski, a Triple Crown winner with Boston that year, batted .400 in the World Series against the Cardinals. In contrast, Orlando Cepeda, the National League's Most Valuable Player that year, with a .325 batting average, 111 runs batted in and 25 home runs, got just three hits in 29 times at bat for an anemic .103 average. The Baby Bull drove in just one run for the Redbirds but was spared from wearing the goat's horns because the Redbirds emerged victorious.

The greatest cold spell in Series history was sustained by Gil Hodges in the 1952 match-up between Brooklyn and New York. Hodges didn't lead the league in any category that year, but he hammered 32 home runs and drove in 102 runs on a .254 batting average. In seven October games, he went to bat twenty-one times without anything resembling a hit. Loyal Dodgers fans, suffering with Gil, said special prayers for their idol at Sunday morning mass, to no avail. He drove in just one run. Fortunately for Hodges, he had a chance in other years to make up for his miserable showing. He had some good ones, too, his best in 1953, when he hit .364 in six games. In six Series, he had five home runs.

Dolph Camilli, the Dodgers' and the National League's home-run leader in 1941, was limited to a double and two singles in seventeen trips to the plate by the Yankees in the 1941 Series. The next year, the Yankees' Joe Gordon came into the Series with the Cardinals following his greatest season when he was named the American League's Most Valuable Player. The Flash became the goat in the Yankees' first Series loss since 1926, getting two hits in twenty-one times at bat and was picked off second base for the final out in the final game. One reason why the Yankees vanquished the Dodgers in the 1949 Series was Duke Snider's failure to fathom New York pitching. The Dook of Flatbush batted a feeble .143 and equaled the record of eight strikeouts in a five-game set.

The Phillies in 1950 captured their first pennant in thirty-five years on Dick Sisler's dramatic home run in the tenth inning against the Dodgers on the final day of the season. Sisler did not enjoy his sudden fame very long. In the four-game fizzle against the Yankees that fall, Sisler was able to connect for only one safety in seventeen times at bat.

Willie Mays broke in sensationally with the Giants in 1951, but it was a different story in the World Series against the Yankees when the Say Hey Kid managed only four hits in twenty-two times at bat and banged into three double plays in one game, a Series record. Willie atoned for his poor performance three years later in the 1954 Series.

In that Series, the Giants' pitching held the Cleveland Indians' two top sluggers, Larry Doby and Al Rosen, to five hits in twenty-eight times between them. Bobby Avila, the American League's batting champion, hit only .133.

The Dodgers finally defeated the Yankees in their sixth meeting, for their first World Championship, in 1955, but New York regained the title the following year largely because Roy Campanella, the redoubtable Brooklyn catcher, was held to a .182 average. The Yankees lost to Milwaukee in 1957 but regained the title in '58 when Eddie Mathews, the Braves' slugging third baseman, batted .167 and fanned eleven times, a new Series strikeout mark. Mathews hit thirty-one home runs during the season but nary a one in the Series. The Yankees ran over Cincinnti in five games in the 1961 Series and one of the reasons was the inability of Vada Pinson, a .343 regular-season hitter, to get more than two safeties in twenty-two times a bat.

Mickey Mantle, a .400 hitter in the 1960 Series, plummeted to .120 in 1962 and .133 in 1963. The Yankees managed to win the 1962 Series in a seven-game struggle with the Giants because Orlando Cepeda, the Giants' outfielder, got only three hits for a .158 average, but they lost in four straight to the Los Angeles Dodgers in 1963. A contributing factor to the Amazing Mets' upset victory over the Orioles in 1969 was the inability of Brooks Robinson to fathom New York pit-

ching. Brooks, who atoned the next year with an amazing exhibition of hitting and fielding, was shackled with one hit in nineteen times at bat by Tom Seaver, Jerry Koosman and Company.

Another World Series hero, Joe Morgan, was anything but that in the 1972 clash between Cincinnati and Oakland when he hit a puny .125, which contributed to the Reds' loss to the Athletics. Gene Tenace was the star of that Series. He batted .348, hit four home runs and drove in nine runs. The next year, 1973, Tenace tallied only three hits, hit no homers, and his average fell to .158. Fortunately for him, the A's came from behind to overcome the Mets in seven games. Oakland's Sal Bando was the unlucky one in 1974, getting only one hit in sixteen times at bat, but again the A's came through, this time against the Dodgers, for their third consecutive world title.

The Red Sox put up a valiant fight in the 1975 Series but couldn't overcome the Reds. The failure of Cecil Cooper, who went one for nineteen, contributed substantially to the final outcome. Ron Cey did a little better for Los Angeles in 1977, but his strikeouts outnumbered his hits, five to four. The inability of the Dodgers' home-run leader to do any better, contributed to the Dodgers' Series loss to the Yankees in six games.

It's a cinch these are times the stars would rather forget but none can deny they were in illustrious company. ◇

Joe Morgan, a money player, shown crossing the plate, a rare occasion for him in the '72 Series.

Subs
Who Shined

BY JOSEPH L. REICHLER

Manager Dick Williams plants a kiss on the cheek of Gene Tenace after his fourth home run in the '72 Series.

THROUGHOUT THE YEARS, the World Series has been dominated by the exploits of the big-name heroes of the day. Mathewson, Ruth, Gehrig, Mangle, DiMaggio, Mays, Robinson, Clemente, Aaron, Gibson, Bench, Jackson and a host of others are names that will live forever in the annals of the fall classic. Yet there's another fascinating aspect to World Series tradition. And that's the sudden rise to prominence of lesser-known players whose deeds capture the headlines and, if only for a moment, become the talk of every baseball fan. The fame, though, is most often short-lived, for these instant heroes frequently fade out of sight as abruptly as they flashed into view.

This pattern of sudden rise and sudden fall began as far back as 1906. The name George Rohe, the grandfather of all dark horses, has endured in baseball literature for more than seventy years solely on the basis of four good days in the World Series of that year. A utility infielder with the Chicago White Sox, Rohe normally attracted about as much attention as a stripteaser's piano player. In 1905, his first season in the majors, he batted .212, and the following year he reached his high-water mark with .258. Neither average gave any indication of what was to come.

Rohe got his chance a few days before the 1906 Series opened. George Davis, the White Sox star shortstop, had been put out of action by a stomach ailment. So Fielder Jones, the manager, shifted Lee Tannehill from third base to shortstop and sent Rohe to the vacancy. The Sox were a decided underdog to the Chicago Cubs that year, for the Cubs had captured the National League pennant by 20 games with a total of 116 victories, a record that still stands.

No one, however, had counted on George Rohe. In dramatic contrast to his regular-season record, Rohe tied Jiggs Donahue, White Sox first baseman, for Series batting leadership with a mark of .333. In the first game, Rohe hit a three-bagger off Mordecai "Three-Fingered" Brown in the sixth inning and scored a moment later with the run that gave the American League club a 2-1 victory. The Cubs won the second game, 7-1. Then, during a scoreless duel with the stubborn Sox in the third game, Rhode struck again. This blow was even more lethal than his first.

For five innings, Ed Walsh of the Sox and Jack Pfiester of the Cubs had mowed batters down with monotonous regularity. But then the Sox' Lee Tannehill got a single. Pfiester, trying hard to prevent Walsh from getting a good ball to sacrifice, ended up issuing a walk to the spitball pitcher. Eddie Hahn was hit by a pitched ball. Cubs rooters took heart when Pfiester retired Fielder Jones on a pop foul and threw three straight strikes past Frank Isbell. It looked as though Pfiester might get out of

the inning without a score. But, as usual, no one reckoned on Rohe.

As Rohe tells it: "The first pitch was a curve that umpire Hank O'Day called a ball. Johnny Kling, who was catching, tried to distract me. 'So you're the guy who likes fastballs,' he said. 'That was a fastball you hit off Brownie in the first game. Well, you won't see any more.' So naturally, I figured Kling was trying to confuse me. I looked for the fast one and got it. The ball was a fast inside pitch, shoulder high, and I hit it right on a line. Jimmy Sheckard didn't have a chance of getting it, and it hopped right by him into the crowd."

Tannehill, Walsh and Jack O'Neill, a pinch runner, scampered home on the ground-rule triple to give the White Sox a 3-0 lead that Walsh protected to the end. The Cubs managed to stay alive by winning the next day, 1-0. But Rohe made them roll over and play dead with five hits in the two following games that wrapped up the title for the Sox, four games to two.

For a few days George Rohe's name virtually monopolized the headlines. But the fame faded fast. The following year he batted an unremarkable .213, and that winter the White Sox sold him to New Orleans. He never played major-league ball again. **Sic transit gloria.**

Nineteen hundred fourteen was the year the Boston Braves climaxed a leap from last to first by vanquishing the Philadelphia Athletics in four straight World Series games. The ease of the Braves' success over the supposedly invincible A's thrilled the nation. Hank Gowdy, the Braves' catcher, became the nation's pet. A .243 hitter with just three home runs and forty-seven runs batted in during the season, Gowdy shocked the A's by becoming the first player to hit over .500 in a Series. He wound up with a fancy .545, as his six hits included a homer, a triple and three doubles. He also drew five walks. "My regret is that I didn't walk him oftener," said Connie Mack, the A's' manager.

With many of the best players already working in the shipyards or serving in the armed forces, the 1918 classic between the Red Sox and the Cubs was strictly a war Series. But it was the shining moment for a thirty-six-year-old Boston left fielder named George Whiteman.

Bought from Toronto just before the war emergency, Whiteman saw little action during the 1918 season. But the Series was a different matter. In the first game, Whiteman's single put the winning run in scoring position and so was directly responsible for pitcher Babe Ruth's 1-0 shutout of the Cubs. Chicago came back the next day, 3-1. But in the third game, Whiteman touched off a two-run rally and sealed the decision with a sensational catch that robbed Chicago's Dode Paskert of a two-run homer two innings later. Boston won the game, 2-1.

But that wasn't all. Ruth returned to the mound in the fourth game, winning 3-2. The Bambino helped his cause with a two-run triple, the first he had hit in World Series competition. The second man to score on that swat was George Whiteman. George was also instrumental in the Red Sox' fourth triumph, a 2-1 game in which he drove in both of Boston's runs.

And what did all this get George Whiteman? A ticket back to the minors the following spring. The war was over, and as the boys came marching home there was soon no room for Whiteman. He wound up back in Houston, Texas, with his yellowing scrapbook and fading dreams.

That's usually the way it is with momentary stars. But not always. Take the case of Jack Scott, for instance. Scott was acquired by Cincinnati from Boston on the strength of his fifteen victories in 1921. Unfortunately, though, he came up with a sore arm in 1922 and was unceremoniously cut adrift by the Reds. Scott returned to his tobacco farm in Ridgeway, North Carolina, unwanted by any club and apparently finished. But Scott didn't give up. In mid-July, he decided to give his arm another try. He journeyed to New York, sought an appointment with John McGraw and asked the Giants' manager for a trial. "I'm sure I can pitch, Mr. McGraw," he pleaded. "I've been resting the arm for a couple of months now and it feels mighty good."

McGraw pondered a moment. "We're leaving on a road trip," he said, "but I'll tell you what I'll do. You can work out here with the Yankees, and I'll see how you look when we get back. How's that?"

"Fine, Mr. McGraw," Scott replied. "You won't regret this, and thanks for the chance."

Scott worked like a beaver while the Giants were away. He'd arrive at the field early in the morning and wouldn't leave until it got too dark to pitch. When McGraw returned, he looked Scott over and liked what he saw. McGraw immediately signed him to a contract.

Scott surprised everyone by winning eight and losing two during the remainder of the season. The Giants won the flag by a seven-game margin over the Cincinnati Reds and prepared to face the Yankees in the World Series. McGraw's team won the opener, 3-2, but the second contest ended in a 3-3 tie. This was the game umpire George Hildebrand called because of "darkness," although it didn't actually get too dark to play for another half hour. Judge Landis, fearful that the fan would accuse the clubs of conspiring to inflate Series revenues with the admissions that could be charged for an extra game, decreed that all of the $120,554 in game receipts be donated to local charities.

Judge Landis, Baseball's Czar, dressed in the style of his day.

McGraw named Jack Scott as his starting pitcher the next day. He was opposed by Waite Hoyt. Scott came through with a masterful four-hitter and shut out the Yankees, 3-0. Scott continued with the Giants six more years, winning another fifty-four games for them before his arm gave out at the age of thirty-seven.

There were many other unexpected heroes in the years that followed. The Yankees severely underestimated Casey Stengel when they met the Giants in the 1922 Series. Casey stung the Yanks for crucial home runs in the first and third games, helping the Giants to the only two games they won in that fall classic. A ten-year veteran and a victim of enemy bullets in World War I, thirty-four-year-old Joe Harris surprised everyone in 1925. Joe gave his Washington teammates eleven hits against the Pirates, finishing with a .440 average that included a pair of doubles and three home runs.

Tommy Thevenow completed his first full season as shortstop for the Cardinals in 1926, batting at the very bottom of the team with a miserable .256. Yet in the Series against the Yankees that year, he seemed like a different player. He put on quite a show with his glove, accepting thirty-five out of thirty-seven chances. And he got ten hits for a mark of .417, the highest on either team.

Another shortstop, Yankee Mark Koenig, had similar good fortune in 1927. Something of a goat in the 1926 loss to the Cardinals when he was held to only four hits in thirty-two times at bat, Koenig did a complete turnaround the following year. He fielded 1,000, accepting all twenty-four chances without a miscue. And he batted .500 leading all the regular hitters, including Ruth and Gehrig, with nine hits in eighteen at-bats. The Yankees swept the Series, beating the Pirates in four games.

The Cincinnati Reds outlasted the Detroit Tigers in seven grueling games in the Series of 1940. They never would have won were it not for help from two unexpected sources: reserve outfielder Jimmy Ripple and forty-year-old catcher Jimmy Wilson. Wilson, who had been serving as coach, was thrown into the breach because Ernie Lombardi, the regular catcher, had sustained an ankle injury. Ripple had appeared in only thirty-nine regular-season games, a good many as a pinch hitter.

Of the two, Ripple was the most devastating. He figured directly in each of the Reds'

four victories, hitting at a .333 clip. He hit a two-run homer in the third inning of the second game off Schoolboy Rowe to break a 2-2 tie, sending the Reds to a 5-3 victory. He doubled to drive in the eventual winning run in the 5-3 fourth-game victory. And he singled in a first-inning run that led to a 4-0 triumph in the sixth game to even the Series for the third time. It was in the finale, however, that the Cincinnati sub reached the height of his glory. With Cincinnati trailing 1-0 and a Cincinnati runner on second in the seventh inning, Ripple ripped a game-tying double and scored the winning run moments later on Billy Myers' deep fly.

Wilson, while not as spectacular as Ripple, was just as steady. Appearing in only sixteen games, with a .243 batting average during the regular season, Jimmy did not appear to be a good bet for Series stardom. Yet he caught six games, batted .353 and stole the only base of the Series. The finale was also the last game for Wilson as a player.

A curious grudge spurred a fired-up Emil Verban, rookie second baseman of the St. Louis Cardinals, to enjoy a spectacular Series in 1944

Jimmy Ripple being congratulated by Cincinnati teammate Ival Goodman after his home run in the 1940 Series.

the Dodgers was replete with heroes. Three of the least likely were Floyd (Bill) Bevens, Cookie Lavagetto and little Al Gionfriddo. Each had his day in the sun, but not one of the trio ever played in another major-league game again.

Bevens, a second-flight pitcher who had won only seven games while losing thirteen during the regular season, was making Series history by holding the Dodgers hitless through 8⅔ innings.

Floyd "Bill" Bevens was within one out of becoming first to pitch a Series no-hitter.

Harry Walker, surprise batting star of 1946 Series.

against the St. Louis Cardinals' neighboring Browns. Verban, a .257 hitter during the regular season, became furious with the Browns for giving his wife a poor seat for the family clambake. He vowed he would get even, and he did, with a vengeance. His .412 batting average led his team, and his perfect three for three helped the Cards capture the clincher, 3-1. He was flawless in the field, handling all twenty-one chances cleanly and serving as the middleman in two key double plays.

The 1946 Series is known as the "Slaughter Series" in recognition of the country boy's dazzling 270-foot dash to score the run that gave the Cardinals a World Series triumph over the Boston Red Sox. Slaughter deserves all the accolades for his daring base running, but an overlooked hero of the Cards' triumph was Harry Walker.

It was the last half of the eighth inning. The score was tied at 3-3 in this deciding game. Enos Slaughter was on first with two out. Manager Eddie Dyer gave the sign for the hit-and-run. Slaughter took off with Bob Klinger's pitch, which Walker drilled to left center. And, as everyone knows, Enos didn't stop running until he had crossed the plate with what proved to be the winning run. Walker wound up with his second hit of the game and his second double of the Series. Harry the Hat led his club with a .412 average that Series.

The 1947 Series between the Yankees and

With two out and two on in the ninth, Brooklyn manager Burt Shotton sent up pinch hitter Cookie Lavagetto. Cookie responded with a double off the right-field fence to drive in the two runs that gave the Dodgers a come-from-behind 3-2 fourth-game victory.

In the sixth game, a victory would have given the Yankees the Championship, but they were trailing 8-5 as they came to bat in the sixth.

Gionfriddo, an obscure outfielder, was sent to left field for defensive purposes. There were two runners on base and two out when Joe DiMaggio sent a screaming drive toward the left-field bull pen, apparently a home run. The five-foot-six Gionfriddo literally outran the ball. He raced to the very edge of the playing field and at the last second leaped as high as he could. With a desperate stab, he caught the ball. It was one of the most spectacular catches

Al Gionfriddo making his phenomenal catch against Joe DiMaggio in the 1947 Series.

Defensive standout, Jerry Coleman turned hitter in the 1950 Series.

in World Series history, and it certainly was a factor in the Dodgers' 8-6 triumph that forced the Series into the seventh game. The Dodgers eventually lost the Series, but that catch wrote Gionfriddo's name indelibly in the World Series Hall of Fame.

No one among the 74,065 who saw that amazing defensive play at Yankee Stadium could possibly foresee that little Gionfriddo would never again appear in a big-league box score. The same fate befell the two principals of the fourth-game drama. The World Series was also the swan song for Bevens and Lavagetto. A sore shoulder sidelined Bevens for all of the 1948 season, and he never again pitched in the majors. Lavagetto was shipped to the Oakland team in the Pacific Coast League before the start of the 1948 season. When he returned to the majors, it was as a coach and later as manager.

Jerry Coleman once confessed he was thrilled just playing on the same team with Joe DiMaggio. But in the 1950 Series, the Yankees vs. the Philadelphia Phillies', the lightly regarded Yankees second baseman led his team to a four-game sweep over the National Leaguers. The twenty-six-year-old sophomore did a superb job offensively and defensively throughout the Series. Afield, he handled twenty-three chances, including three rapid-fire double plays, without a slip. At the plate, where he wasn't expected to match strides with some of the more robust Bronx bombers in-

cluding the great DiMaggio, he played a vital role in swinging the first three encounters into the Yankees' column.

In the opener, his most determined effort with the bat was to lift a long fly to left field in the fourth inning. But it sufficed to drive home the only tally of the ball game. In the second game, he hit a double, but that wasn't his most effective move on offense. In the second inning, he drew a pass, a walk that was presently to be converted into one of the two runs the Bombers scored that afternoon. It was in the third encounter, however, that the slender Californian put out his best effort just when it was needed the most, for it was in this game that the Phils came closest to bagging one victory.

In the third inning, he pushed a single to left to drive in a run which gave the Yankees a 1-0 lead. In the eighth, with the Phils now leading 2-1, and with two out, he again drew a pass, which was soon converted into a run, tying the score. And in the ninth, it was another single to left, his third hit of the day, that drove in the winning tally that broke up the game.

Brooklyn no longer has a major-league baseball team, but nobody can take away from its citizens that memorable day—October 4, 1955—when the Dodgers won their first World Championship after seven fruitless attempts. An unheralded country kid from an obscure little upper New York State town called Witherbee was responsible. It was Johnny Podres, the winner of only nine of nineteen decisions during the season, who defeated the Yankees in Ebbets Field, after the Bronx Bombers had taken the first two games. And it was this same left-hander, five days later, who pitched the game of his life, blanking the Yankees, 2-0, in the decisive seventh game. Five times, Podres found himself in a jam as the Yankees fought bitterly to maintain their supremacy over the Dodgers. Each time he came through brilliantly.

Don Larsen, author of the only no-hitter in World Series play—a perfect game for the Yankees in 1956—and Larry Sherry, a rookie bull-pen specialist who won two games and saved two others for the Dodgers in 1959, were other surprise pitching heroes. But the biggest surprise of them all was Moe Drabowsky in the 1966 Series between Baltimore and Los Angeles, Drabowsky, pitching in his ninth season for his fourth club, was summoned from the bull pen to bail out Orioles starter Dave McNally with the bases full and one out in the third inning, Baltimore leading 4-1. Drabowsky came in to fan Wes Parker for the second out. He walked Junior Gilliam to force in a run. It was now 4-2 with the bases still clogged.

From that point, Drabowsky was simply unbeatable. He retired John Roseboro on a foul pop to end the inning. In the fourth and fifth, he

Moe Drabowsky, Baltimore relief star,
fanned 11 Dodgers, including six in
succession, in 1966 Series opener.

struck out six consecutive batters. In the seventh, the Dodgers got their only hit off him, a single by Willie Davis. Moe got the next nine batters, and the game was over. Ron Fairly, a pinch hitter, struck out in the ninth to become his eleventh strikeout victim. The Orioles went on to win the next three games by shutouts.

In 1969, the New York Mets boasted a flock of heroes as they upset the favored Baltimore Orioles in five Series games. The biggest of them all, however, was their smallest member, Al Weis. The second baseman, an adept defensive player not renowned for his hitting, stole the show from the big guys by leading all hitters with a .455 average. He drove in the decisive run in the second game and hit a home run in the fifth game to pull the Mets into a tie. His batting average for the regular season was .219.

Gene Tenace was the surprise hero of the 1972 Series between Oakland and Cincinnati. He belted a pair of home runs in his first two at-bats to give the A's a 3-2 victory in the first game. Tenace at the time was a relatively obscure catcher for Oakland. But in the Series, he collected eight hits, four of them homers, and drove in nine of the A's' total of sixteen runs in the seven games it took the A's to conquer the Reds.

Of course, in spite of the instant heroes, it will always be the big stars who attract the most attention at World Series time. For, although there have been any notable exceptions, big stars usually do come through as expected, adding further luster to their names by their Series deeds.

But every now and then, comets like Rohe, Beazley, Coleman, Drabowsky and others flash across the sky. Their fame may be short-lived, or it may linger. And they may be few and far between. But when the lightning strikes them, there can be no doubt that the entire Series is illuminated by their brilliance, however fleeting it may be. ◇

World Series Pressure

BY ROY CAMPANELLA

IS THERE SUCH A THING as World Series pressure? You bet your life there is, and don't believe anybody who tells you different. I've heard some ballplayers say the World Series is just another game to them. But I never believed them. I think they were just saying that to try to convince themselves that the Series didn't matter all that much. To me it was proof they were feeling the pressure already.

I've also heard players say the World Series was an anticlimax, especially after a tough pennant race. Winning the World Series was not too important; the important thing was winning the pennant. Even if they lost the World Series, they were still champions of their league, weren't they?

Baloney! Any player worth his salt wants to win the World Series as much as the pennant. Maybe even more. Why? First, because it's a good feeling being a member of the World Champions. Second, because they want to beat the brains out of the champions of the other league. And third, because they just don't want to lose. It's a matter of professional pride.

There are different kinds of pressure in a World Series. Some feel it at different times than others. For some, the pressure is at the beginning,

in the first game or two. They're fearful of making a mistake, of pulling a boner. I know guys who never took a pill in their life but before the start of a World Series, they had to take sleeping pills. Some players get more nervous as the Series goes on. Others don't begin to get real nervous until the sixth or seventh game. They know the games have to be won then, and the tension mounts.

I was nervous before my first Series. I was nervous before every Series. You can't help it. It's different from the regular season. I know it's just a game, but all of a sudden it becomes the most important thing in the world. Sure, the games during the regular season are important, especially in the final week of the season when you're fighting for the pennant. But in a World Series game, it seems everybody's eye are focused on you. Like the whole world was watching and waiting to see what you do.

Even before the game, everything is different. The crowd. Every seat is filled. The special cops outside and inside the ball park. No one allowed in the clubhouse. The field is crowded with cameramen and reporters. It's like a carnival. You can feel the tension all around you. It begins with the first pitching windup, and it continues until the

Roy Campanella blocking plate
against a sliding runner.

final out of the last game.

Ballplayers dream of getting into the Series, and it's not only because of the money. Everybody hopes to come away from a Series with at least one fine memory. A game-winning hit, a game-saving catch, a well-pitched ball game. Even one good play, one good hit is sometimes enough. But it's important to have one last thing to take away.

That's where the pressure comes in. Some people think that most of the pressure on the players during the Series comes from their desire to win. And when a player fails to do really well, these same folks say that the pressure got to him, that he choked up. But most of the time it's just not true.

Now, I'm not saying that it doesn't ever happen. All I'm saying is that it's a lot rarer than most people think. Tell me, how can any man who has had to overcome all kinds of pressure to make the major leagues be called a choke-up? Do you know what it means to succeed in the majors? Do you know how many crises a man has to overcome to reach the big leagues?

Sometimes a disappointing performance is just plain bad luck. Take Don Newcombe, for instance. Newk pitched the final game for us against the Yankees in '56. Yogi Berra had hit two home

runs off him, and the Yankees went on to shut us out 9-0. Afterward, people wanted to know whether I thought Newk had choked. One guy pointed out that Don had started a total of five World Series games against the Yankees and hadn't been able to win even one.

I've got to admit that I was a bit irritated at the question, because they were suggesting that maybe Don didn't have what it takes to win the big ones. But if that was true, how did he manage to win twenty-seven games in 1956 when he almost single-handedly pitched the Dodgers to a pennant? How did he earn the Cy Young Award as the best pitcher in baseball?

No, a pitcher of Don Newcombe's caliber doesn't choke under pressure. What happened to him in the World Series was bad luck, bad breaks. That's just the way it is in baseball sometimes.

Take that game he pitched against the Yankees in 1949. He lost, 1-0, to Allie Reynolds. He gave up only five hits, struck out eleven batters and didn't walk a man. It was one of the best games ever pitched in a World Series, but the other fellow pitched better. That's what I mean by luck. Or that last game in 1956. Newk was throwing good in the game. He just got hit, that's all. That could happen

to anyone. A pitcher can have all his stuff, but for some reason nobody can explain, he gets hit.

And Newcombe isn't the only pitcher who had no luck in the World Series. If I remember correctly, the Yankees twice knocked out Bob Friend in the 1960 World Series. Friend is a good pitcher, but the breaks just weren't with him in the Series. Does that mean he choked up? Don't believe it. He just got banged around, that's all. You've got to give credit to the hitters when they've got their hitting shoes on.

If it isn't bad luck, it's that other kind of pressure I was talking about earlier—the desire to make a mark, to come away from the Series with one really fine memory. Sometimes you want that big hit or to make that spectacular catch so bad that you can taste it. And that's where the trouble begins. You can feel yourself tense up. You try too hard. You feel it in every Series, no matter how many you've played.

That's what happened to Gil Hodges the Series he went twenty-one times at bat without getting a base hit. Don't let anyone tell you he could sleep nights, or that he wasn't in a cold sweat every time he came up to the plate. It wasn't that he choked up, or that he was scared. It was because he wanted to get a hit so bad, he became so anxious, that he knotted himself all up.

been hit on the hand with a pitched ball earlier in the Series and I could hardly grip a bat. Every time I swung and connected, the pain would shoot up my arm. I wanted as little of that as possible, so I figured I wouldn't take any batting practice.

Sitting in front of my locker, I could see this pitcher all by himself. He sat by his locker smoking a cigarette. Then he got up, walked over to the training table and lay down, trying to take a nap. Then he got up for a smoke. Then he walked over to the water cooler for a drink of water. Then he sat down again. Then he tried to take a nap again. Nervous? Man, was he jumpy! But you know something? That pitcher went out and beat the Yankees and pitched one of the best games of his life. Like I said, every player is nervous before every World Series. You find me one who says he ain't and I'll tell you he's a damn liar.

The Series pressure is worse if you get off to a bad start. You know everything you do is magnified. You feel the whole world is watching to see what you're going to do. It preys on your mind. Reporters gang up on you; teammates try to cheer you up. "Don't worry," they tell you, "you're gonna hit soon." But you know you don't have much time left. Every minute in the World Series is short. If you're in a batting slump, you don't have time to analyze yourself. You can't rest a day. You win the World Series or lose it in a hurry. That's when you start pressing.

World Series pressure sometimes makes you play different. I've been told by old-timers that Babe Ruth never made a wrong move on a ball field. Yet in the final game of the 1926 World Series, with two out in the ninth inning, he tried to steal second base and was thrown out. And he was the tying run. I saw Joe DiMaggio try to score from first and get thrown out by ten feet. I saw Willie Mays make a catch in deep center field for the third out, then suddenly turn and throw to the plate because he thought there were only two out. Those things happen to you in a World Series.

The World Series is just **different,** with a capital D. The excitement, the crowds, the worldwide attention—it all adds up to a lot of pressure on the players. The pressure can really be unbearable at times. And it can make players do things they wouldn't do in a regular-season game. Not out of fear or because of choking, but because of a desire to perform their very best.

One of the reasons the Dodgers had a lot of trouble winning a World Series was because we were trying too hard. The Dodgers had never won a World Series and a lot of people in Brooklyn were afraid we never would, especially if we had to play the Yankees all the time. Some of those people said we choked up every time we saw a Yankee uniform. Actually, it was just a case of being overanxious and not playing our real game.

I'll never forget one day just before a World Series game with the Yankees. The fellows had left the clubhouse for hitting and fielding practice. There were only two guys left in the clubhouse— the fellow who was to pitch that day and me. I had

I guess that's what makes the Series so special. And I know I wouldn't trade my Series experiences—pressure and all—for anything in the world. Win or lose, being in the World Series is every player's dream. And don't ever let anyone tell you otherwise. ◇

Best World Series Teams

BY JOSEPH L. REICHLER

ONNIE MACK ONCE SAID that no team could be called a true champion until it had won not one, or even two, but three league championships in a row. Connie Mack had in mind, of course, his own Philadelphia Athletics, who finally achieved the feat of winning three American League titles in succession from 1929 through 1931, after knocking on the door without success on two previous occasions.

Nine franchises have succeeded in finishing on top of their league three or more seasons in a row since the turn of the century, the period commonly known as the modern era. One of these franchises, that of the New York Yankees, won three or more titles in succession seven times, including five in a row twice. Only one other team, the 1921-24 New York Giants, was able to win the pennant more

than three straight years. The Oakland A's might have made it four in a row—or even more—had they not lost Jim "Catfish" Hunter after their third straight victory in 1974, and most of the rest of their winning crew two years later.

Selecting the most dominating of these dynasties is bound to be provocative, although hardly anyone will contest the selection of the Yankees as the most powerful aggregation of teams over a long period of time. From 1921 through 1977, the Yankees won their league's flag thirty-one times in fifty-six years, a phenomenal feat light-years away from the hopes and dreams of other clubs. After winning seven pennants in the eight years from 1936 through 1943, the Yankees rested for a while and then roared back with fourteen more league championships in sixteen years. Pennant winners in 1976 and 1977, the Yankees have constructed another powerful team that many observers predict presages yet another New York dynasty.

Next to the Yankees, the club with the most successes in the American League was Connie Mack's Philadelphia Athletics. Mr. Mack's first great team won in 1910 and 1911, missed in 1912 and won again in 1913 and 1914. After a long famine, the Athletics became a challenger again in the late 1920s. After two straight second-place finishes, they won three titles in a row and just missed a fourth with a second-place finish in 1932.

The St. Louis Cardinals did not win their first league championship until 1926, but once they

The 1927 Yankees, considered by many as the greatest of them all.

tasted the wine of victory, they continued to drink from the championship cup with regularity, winning eight more titles in the next twenty years, including three staight in 1942-44. They missed out in 1969 after finishing on top the two previous years.

John McGraw's Giants won ten National League pennants from 1903 through 1924, with four in a row in the last of those twenty-two years. Including 1925, McGraw's teams finished in the runner-up spot nine times, giving them ten first- or second-place finishes in twenty-three years. They won again in 1936 and 1937 but finished third the next year. The Giants' most persistent rivals in the early years were the Chicago Cubs, a dynasty of sorts in their own right, winning pennants in 1906, 1907, 1908 and 1910. The Cubs won a hundred or more games in each of those years except 1908, when they reached ninety-nine. Over an eleven-year period, from 1903 through 1913, they did not finish lower than third. The 1906 team won 116 games, which still stands as the most victories by any team in baseball history.

Other franchises to win three league titles in a row were the Pittsburgh Pirates of 1901-03, the Detroit Tigers of 1907-09 and the Baltimore Orioles of 1969-71.

The nomination for the greatest of these stellar World Series teams must go to the Yankees of 1927-28. Neither of these teams lost a single game to the National League. The 1927 edition was the greatest of many superb teams that wore the Yankee uniform. To be more explicit, it was the strongest machine in the history of major-league baseball. This edition of Bronx bombers had Babe Ruth at the crest of his career. Earle Combs and Bob Meusel teamed up with the Babe in the outfield; Lou Gehrig, Tony Lazzeri, Mark Koenig and Joe Dugan composed the infield, with Benny Bengough, Pat Collins and John Grabowski catching.

The Yankees had a great manager in Miller Huggins and a superb pitching staff led by Waite Hoyt, Herb Pennock, Urban Shocker, George Pipgras, Dutch Ruether and a thirty-five-year-old rookie relief ace, Wilcy Moore. They made a runaway of the pennant race, clinching the flag on Labor Day. They won 110 games and finished 19 games ahead of the second-place A's. They batted .307 as a team and they scored nearly 1,000 runs.

Never was the term "Murderers' Row" more applicable than when it was applied to Ruth, Gehrig, Meusel and Lazzeri, the players who constituted the center of the 1927 Yankees' batting order. Ruth batted .356, hit 60 home runs and drove in 164 runs. Gehrig did even better with figures of .373, 47 and 175. Meusel had only eight home runs, but he drove in 103 and batted .337. Lazzeri hit .309, with 18 homers and 102 RBI's.

And Combs, the leadoff batter, hit .356.

Legend has it that the Yankees actually won the 1927 Series from the Pirates before the first game had begun, intimidating the Steeltown players with a batting-practice display by their big hitters. The Yanks had one of their pitchers grooving the ball for his brawny teammates. With Pirates players staring open-mouthed, Ruth, Gehrig and Company hammered balls over and against the fences causing Lloyd Waner to turn to his older brother, Paul, and grasp, "Cripes, do they always hit like that?"

It's all probably true, but the Yankees won their four straight more on superior pitching than on stupendous hitting. They hit only two home runs,

both by Ruth. Waite Hoyt, the first-game winner, needed relief help in the eighth inning. Thereafter, the starters did it all. George Pipgras breezed through the second game; Pennock had a perfect game for seven and a fraction innings and settled for a three-hitter in the third; and Moore scattered ten hits in the finale.

The real four-base fireworks came the following year against the Cardinals when New York walloped a total of nine, four by Gehrig and three by Ruth, with the Babe's all coming in the final game. Never before or since have two muscle men combined to do their thing so awesomely.

Even though the Yankees had wrecked the Pirates in four straight in 1927, the Cardinals in 1928 were favored by most critics largely because the Yankees came into the Series in a crippled state. Herb Pennock was out with a sore shoulder. Earle Combs was sidelined with a broken finger. Joe Dugan had a game knee at third base, giving way often to Gene Robertson. And Tony Lazzeri could scarcely throw. As a result, he had his late-inning caddy in every game of the Series, a cocky twenty-three-year-old infield reserve named Leo Durocher.

Unfortunately for the Cardinals, Ruth and Gehrig were sound. Led by this dynamic duo, the Yankees slaughtered the Cardinals in four games, outscoring them 27 to 10. Gehrig had six hits in eleven trips—four of them homers—and drove in

Rival managers Leo Durocher and Joe McCarthy before opening of 1941 Series.

The Third Yankee dynasty began in 1949. Led by the intrepid Casey Stengel, the Yankees steamrollered to five straight world titles. Nothing like it had ever been seen in major-league history. When the Yankees made it five in a row against the Dodgers in 1953, it was their fifteenth victory in sixteen Series since 1927. They beat the Dodgers in 1949 and '52, the Phillies in 1950 and the Giants in 1951. Only the 1952 Dodgers forced the Yankees to play seven games. Allie Reynolds, Vic Raschi and Ed Lopat were the Yankee pitchers. DiMaggio continued to sparkle as late as 1951, while Phil Rizzuto, Mickey Mantle, Yogi Berra, Gil McDougald, Billy Martin and Hank Bauer emulated

nine runs in seven games, hitting .545. The Babe had ten hits in nineteen tries, including three doubles and three homers, driving in four runs as he set a Series batting average of .625. The Yankees swept by scores of 4-1, 9-3, 7-3 and 7-3; Ruth and Gehrig between them had sixteen hits, seven homers and thirteen RBI's. The Cards, as a team, had just one homer and nine runs batted in.

The Yankees cooled off somewhat after 1928, winning only once in the next six years. But they were back in 1936 when, under the direction of Joe McCarthy, New York embarked on one of baseball's greatest pennant parades. They won four straight World Championships, losing only three games. The Giants, their opponents, won two in 1936 and one in 1937. After that the Yankees rolled over both the Chicago Cubs and the Cincinnati Reds in the next two years. Gilt-edged pitching by Lefty Gomez, Red Ruffing and Monte Pearson was featured in the four triumphs. It was more than a coincidence that Joe DiMaggio joined the Yankees in 1936 and almost immediately established himself as one of the game's greatest stars. However, there were a few others responsible: Lou Gehrig, Tony Lazzeri, Bill Dickey, George Selkirk, who had replaced Babe Ruth in right field, and Red Rolfe at third base. Tommy Henrich and Charley Keller developed fast.

Casey Stengel giving instructions to his players prior to 1956 Series.

the Yankee World Series stars of the past. The veteran Johnny Mize, who failed to make a World Series in eleven National League seasons, made the last four with the Yankees. In 1952, he batted .400 and hit three homers.

The Yankees' next great machine got going in 1955 and lasted through 1964. It streaked to nine pennants in ten years, missing only in 1959, but faltered from time to time in October, coming out on the short end in five autumn clashes. The best of these teams was the 1961 edition, which rumbled over the Reds in five games. That was the season Roger Maris and Mickey Mantle hit sixty-one and fifty-four home runs, respectively, and

Whitey Ford won twenty-five games, adding two more, via shutouts, in the Series. Bobby Richardson (.391) and Moose Skowron (.353) were the hitting stars, along with Johnny Blanchard, who hit two home runs, and Lopez, who drove in seven.

After 1964, the impregnable fortress crumbled. Berra and Kubek retired at the end of the 1965 season, Richardson followed the next year, Maris, Howard and Clete Boyer were traded, and Mantle simply wore out. Ford suffered from a circulation blockage and had to quit. Like the fall of Rome, the Yankee collapse had been swift and complete. It remains to be seen whether the giant has regained its full strength.

Only one baseball club has been under the domination and management of one individual for a half century. The club, of course, was the Philadelphia Athletics and the manager was Connie Mack. The A's for extended periods overpowered the American League with marvelous teams, only to strip these teams of their talent to the point of becoming doormats for the rest of the league.

But when the A's were good, they were simply unbeatable. Take, for example, Philadelphia's two greatest representatives, the 1910-14 and the 1929-31 dynasties. Between them they won seven of Connie Mack's nine pennants and all five of his World Championships.

The list of famous players managed by Connie Mack would make a respectable Hall of Fame all by itself. In addition to Rube Waddell, one of the most brilliant of all left-handers, Mack had two of the most famous pitching triumvirates in Chief Bender, Eddie Plank and Jack Coombs, and the later trio of Lefty Grove, George Earnshaw and Swede Walberg. Two won 30 games in a season, two won 300 or more lifetime victories and four earned places in the Hall of Fame. The A's' "hundred thousand dollar" infield of Stuffy McInnis, Eddie Collins, Jack Barry and Frank "Home Run" Baker, which by today's standards would be equal to a $5-million infield, may be the best of all time. Not far behind was the 1929-32 infield of Jimmy Foxx, Max Bishop, Joe Boley and Jimmy Dykes. Outfielders? Mack was blessed with the best. Amos Strunk, Rube Oldring, Danny Murphy and Socks Seybold patrolled the outer garden for Mack's champions of 1910-14. Al Simmons, Mule Haas and Bing Miller made up the outfield of the 1929-32 A's. Mickey Cochrane, one of the game's greatest catchers, was behind the plate.

The 1910 A's were considered too inexperienced to win a pennant, but they ran away with it. Jack Coombs won thirty-one games, losing only nine. Chief Bender won twenty-three, losing only five. Eddie Collins led the league in stolen bases with eighty-one, and five A's batted .300 or better. The A's went on to overwhelm the National League champion Chicago Cubs in five games. The A's repeated in 1911. Collins hit .365; Baker led the league in home runs with 11 and in runs batted in with 115. Coombs won twenty-eight and Eddie Plank won twenty-two. In the World Series, they defeated the Giants in six games.

The A's dropped to third in 1912 but re-

The 1914 Athletics who were upset by the miracle Boston Braves.

bounded in 1913 to win the pennant and again defeat the Giants in the World Series, this time in five games. Philadelphia won its fourth pennant in five years in 1914 but was upset in the Series by the Boston Braves in four games. Connie Mack always claimed that his players that year had their minds on the Federal League instead of the World Series. Some deserted the following year to join the outlaw circuit.

Mack dismantled his world beaters before the next season got under way and it was not until a dozen years later, with a new collection of stars, that the A's were able to win again. But they ran into the mighty 1927-28 Yankees and had to wait until 1929 to win another flag. That year they won 104 games to make a cakewalk out of the race, defeating the Yankees by 18 games. They allowed the National League champion Cubs to win only one out of five games in the World Series. And these were the Cubs of Rogers Hornsby, Hack Wilson, Kiki Cuyler, Gabby Hartnett, Riggs Stephenson and Charlie Grimm.

Philadelphia won the 1930 pennant almost as easily as it did the year before. But the team met sterner opposition in the St. Louis Cardinals, just becoming known as the "Gashouse Gang." It took the A's six games to win this time. Philadelphia was led by the pitching of Grove and Earnshaw and the hitting of Foxx, Simmons and Cochrane. In 1931 the A's rolled up 107 victories, the most of any Philadelphia team, to win their third straight pennant, another runaway. Grove had the astonishing record of thirty-one victories and only four defeats. Simmons retained his batting crown with .390. The Cardinals were again the National League champions, and the Series was a chance for the A's to be the first team ever to win three World Championships in succession. But the Cardinals, led by the fiery Pepper Martin, put an end to that dream. St. Louis defeated Philadelphia in seven games.

The A's were still a magnificent club in 1932, but the Yankees were better. So Philadelphia had to be content with second place. Their era had come to an end, and like the 1914 champions, this aggregation was soon to be scattered to the winds. Within a year, the last of the wondrous A's of 1929-32 had vanished. So had the last of the Philadelphia Athletics' dynasties.

The St. Louis Cardinals have written some brilliant chapters of World Series history since Rogers Hornsby led them to their first Championship in 1926. Beginning in that year, and for twenty years thereafter, no National League club had a more powerful reign than the Cardinals. From 1926 through 1946, the Redbirds won the league championship nine times and the World Cham-

pionship six times. No National League team has won as many World Series for its home city as have the Cardinals for St. Louis. For three straight years, in 1942, 1943 and 1944, they won 105 games or more.

The 1926 Cardinals are best-remembered for the dramatic relief appearance of old Grover Cleveland "Pete" Alexander and his ensuing strikeout of Tony Lazzeri with the bases loaded in the seventh inning of the final game of the World Series. It was a great club, however, with the likes of Hornsby, Bottomley, Hafey and Wilson in the batting order supported by the pitching of Haines, Sherdel and Alexander. The 1931 champions attracted national acclaim by defeating the mighty Athletics of Foxx, Simmons, Cochrane and Grove. That was the Series in which Pepper Martin stole the show in as great a one-man onslaught as ever witnessed in a World Series. Dubbed the "Wild Horse of the Osage," Martin took the spotlight away from such illustrious teammates as Jim Bottomley, Chick Hafey, Frankie Frisch and Jimmy Wilson, getting twelve hits in the first five games, batting .500, stealing five bases, driving in five runs and scoring five. The Cards received some stout-hearted pitching from Burleigh Grimes and Bill

Burleigh Grimes, star of the Cardinal staff in 1931.

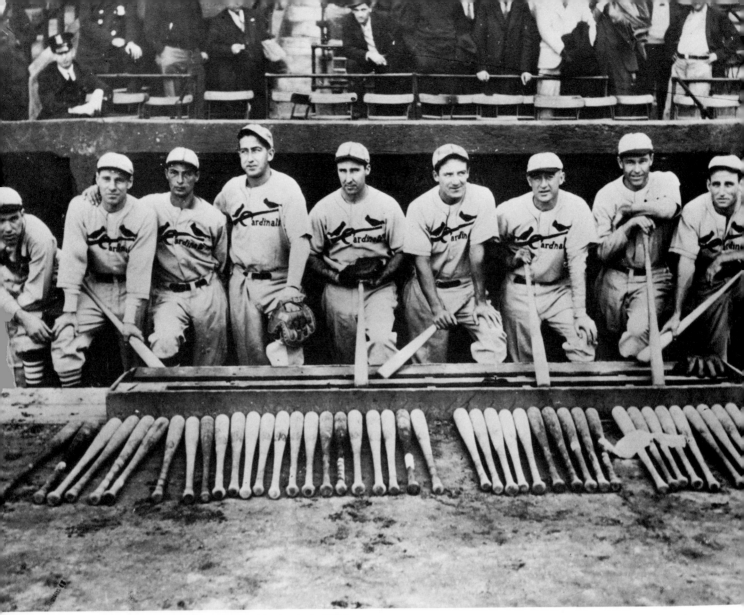

The famous Gashouse Gang of St. Louis in 1934.

Hallahan. Each won two games, and Hallahan saved one for Burleigh.

The Gashouse Gang of 1934, managed by Frisch, was the scrappiest collection of hustlers since George Stallings' Miracle Braves of 1914. They played the game to the hilt. They came from behind to beat Bill Terry's champion Giants for the pennant on the last day of the season. Then they had to win the sixth and seventh games to defeat Mickey Cochrane's Tigers in the World Series. Pepper Martin, Joe Medwick, Rip Collins and Ernie Orsatti were the Series' hitting stars. The team looked strong enough to win pennants for several more years, but tragedy and other misfortunes struck. Bill DeLancey, the young rising catching star, died suddenly. The great Dizzy Dean's arm went lame. Frisch retired, and Martin was plagued by injuries. The Cards weren't to win again until eight years later.

The champion Cards of 1942, managed by Billy Southworth, won 106 games, the most vic-tories garnered by a National League club in thirty-three years. After that, they went on to a sensa-tional victory in the World Series over the Yankees, losing the opening game and then taking four straight from the supposedly invincible Bronx Bombers. The team possessed perhaps the National League's greatest outfield in Musial, Moore and Slaughter. Marty Marion, the league's top defensive shortstop, spearheaded the infield, which had the hard-hitting rookie Whitey Kurowski at third, Johnny Hopp at first and Jimmy Brown at se-cond. Walker Cooper was the hard-hitting and accurate-throwing catcher. Johnny Beazley, who won two games in the Series, Ernie White, Max Lanier, Howie Pollet and Mort Cooper formed a solid pitching staff.

The Cardinals easily won the pennant again in 1943 but lost the World Series to the Yankees. They came back to win again in 1944 and this time they took it all with a six-game Series victory over the St. Louis Browns. In 1945, with Musial, Moore,

Slaughter and other stars in the service, they dropped to second. But they bounced back in 1946 to edge out the Dodgers in a post-season playoff and went on to defeat the Red Sox in the World Series in seven games. This was the Series in which Slaughter raced home all the way from first on a hit by Harry Walker in the eighth inning of the final game and gave the Cards a 4-3 victory. It was also the Series in which Harry "The Cat" Brecheen became the first pitcher in twenty-six years to win three World Series games.

The dynasty of the 1940s ended with Slaughter's dash, and it would be eighteen years until the Cardinals won again. Thanks largely to the pitching of Bob Gibson and the hitting and base running of Lou Brock, their newest superstars, the Cards won again in 1967. But they were beaten by the Tigers in 1968, marking the last of their twelve league championships to date.

For thirty years the Giants were the team of John J. McGraw, the little Napoleon whose fiery leadership set the example for his players. Ten times McGraw piloted the Giants to the championship of the National League. Three times they won the World Series.

The Giants also were the team of Bill Terry, Mel Ott, Leo Durocher and Alvin Dark. Terry led them to three pennants, and to one World Championship in 1933. Ott did not win anything, but Durocher brought home two pennants and one world title. Dark, who managed the Giants after they left New York for San Francisco, brought home a winner in 1962, but the team was beaten by the Yankees in the World Series.

Of all the Giant teams, the combination that ruled supreme in the National League for four successive years from 1921 through 1924 ranks at the top. Of these, the 1921 club was the best, barely edging out the 1922 club that swept the Yankees in the World Series. The 1921 club had better balance and greater power. Seven of the 1921 regulars who started the Giants on a series of four straight Championships hit better than .300. The 1922 club looked strong, with third baseman Heinie Groh a splendid addition, but it did not have the pitching of the 1921 team.

McGraw took over the reins of the Giants in mid-season of 1902, and it took him a year and a half to produce his first winner. The team that won pennants in 1904 and 1905 was led by Christy Mathewson and Joe McGinnity, two of baseball's greatest pitchers. There was no World Series in 1904, but in 1905 the Giants limited the Athletics to three runs in forty-five innings, shutting them out in four of the five games. Mathewson had three of these shutouts, McGinnity the other. Roger Bresnahan, the great catcher; Mike Donlin, the

Manager John McGraw flanked by Giant pitching stars Christy Mathewson and Joe McGinnity.

slugging outfielder; and infielders Bill Dahlen and Artie Devlin were the club's top stars.

The Giants finished second in three of the next four years, but regained first place in 1911, 1912 and 1913, only to lose in the World Series, first to the Athletics, then to the Red Sox and again to the A's. With a new machine, McGraw captured the pennant again in 1917, only to lose the World Series to the White Sox. After three more years as runners-up, McGraw put together the splendid team that won four straight pennants in 1921, 1922, 1923 and 1924.

The Giants of 1921 had a wonderful infield. The spark plug was Dave Bancroft, one of the best shortstops in the history of the organization. Frankie Frisch, playing third base before the coming of Heinie Groh from Cincinnati, wasn't quite as expert around the bag as Art Develin had been. But the Fordham Flash was sensational in the Series with the Yankees, hitting a gaudy .341. Then came George Kelly, one of the greatest first basemen the Giants ever had. Johnny Rawlings was a fill-in at second, but he proved a startling surprise. In the outfield were Ross Youngs, Irish Meusel and George Burns. The pitching was taken care of by Art Nehf, Fred Toney, Jesse Barnes and Phil Douglas. This was a club with one of the best infields of all time, a strong outfield and fine pitching. It was a game club, too, an outfit of tremendous rallying power.

The 1921 Giants literally got off the floor after dropping the first two games by 3-0 shutout scores to whip the Yankees in five of the next six games, winning the best-five-out-of-nine-game World Series. The Yankees had a 4-0 lead in the third game before the Giants had even scored their first run of the Series. But the Giants finished that day with twenty hits and a 13-5 victory and went on from there. The 1922 meeting between the two rivals was an ignoble rout. The Yankees had to settle for a ten-inning tie in five games, and their number one star, Babe Ruth, was held to a humiliating batting average of .118, with two measly hits and only one run batted in. Groh and Frisch were especially pestiferous for the Yankee pitchers. Heinie, with his bottle bat, hit a robust .474, and the Fordham Flash was right behind with .471. Nehf won two of the Giants' decisions.

The Yankees gained some measure of revenge in the 1923 head-on encounter with their interborough rival, winning the Series four games to two. Babe Ruth roared back with three home

runs and a .368 batting average. Second baseman Aaron Ward had a fantastic .417, and Bob Meusel drove in eight runs.

Frisch gave Ward quite a battle for hitting honors, coming through with a .400 average. Frankie, a tremendous money player, had another fine Series in 1924, hitting .333. But the Giants were beaten again, this time by the Washington Senators, in seven games. That was the great Giants team's last hurrah. A McGraw-led team never won again. It wasn't until nine years later that a Giants team, under a new manager, Bill Terry, was able to win another pennant.

The colorful Cubs team of Chicago, the only club that can trace its existence in the National League back to 1876 without missing a single year, has known both good years and bad. Some of their best were in the long, long ago, when they won a half dozen pennants between 1876 and 1886.

Babe Ruth caught in a rundown in second game in 1923 Series.

Their most recent pennants date back to 1932, 1935, 1938 and 1945. But easily the most glorious years were 1906-10, when the Cubs, under the leadership of Frank Chance, had perhaps their most magnetic heroes—Mordecai Brown, Johnny Kling, Johnny Evers, Joe Tinker, Ed Reulbach, Jimmy Sheckard, Wildfire Frank Schulte and others.

Starting in 1906, Chance's Cubs won three straight pennants, finished second, then won another first over a five-year span. The 1906 team won 116 games, a mark that has yet to be approached. This was the team of the famous Tinker-to-Evers-to-Chance double-play combination; the outfield of Sheckard, Schulte and Artie Hofman; the superb Kling catching; the pitching staff of Brown, Reulbach, Orvie Overall and Jack Pfiester.

It was a team that breathed fire from the first pitch to last, trampling everyone and everything on its way to the pennant. There never was before, nor has there ever been since, such a runaway. They lost only 36 of the 152 games they played, leaving the second-place Giants twenty games behind. Brown won twenty-six and lost only six. Harry Steinfeldt led the hitters with a .327 average.

Beaten by the White Sox in the World Series, the Cubs bounced back to win again in 1907. This time they won by 17½ games, finishing with 107 victories and 45 defeats. They went on to sweep the Tigers in the World Series, winning four straight after an opening-game tie. Steinfeldt led the way with a .471 batting mark.

The Cubs made it three in a row in 1908, but this time it took one of the most sensational finishes in one of the most dramatic of all pennant races to pull it off. The Cubs-Giants rivalry, always at fever pitch, reached a peak that year on September 23 in the never-to-be-forgotten game when Giants first baseman Fred Merkle failed to touch second on what appeared to be a game-winning hit against the Cubs by Al Bridwell. Because of that oversight, the game was ruled a 1-1 tie. The season ended a week later with the Giants and Cubs tied for first place. The tied game was replayed after the regular season. The Cubs won, 4-2.

It was the third straight pennant for the virtually unchanged Cubs. The Tigers were again the opponent in the World Series, and once again the Cubs emerged victorious. This time the Tigers were able to win one game. Chance led all hitters with .421, and Brown and Overall won two games each. The Cubs made a gallant bid for four straight in 1909. But although they won 104 games, they finished second to Pittsburgh. They clawed their way back, however, in 1910. Even though they lost the World Series to the Athletics, Chance's Cubs

Frank Chance, "The Peerless Leader" of the Chicago Cubs.

had established themselves as one of the great World Series teams of all time.

Only three times in World Series history has a team been able to win as many as three Series in a row. The New York Yankees of 1936-39 won four straight, and the Yankees of 1949-53 won five straight. Then, in 1972, 1973 and 1974, the Oakland A's joined the elite ranks of consecutive three-Series winners.

Oakland faced conditions that earlier legendary teams did not. To win a pennant, the A's had to win a three-out-of-five playoff, no matter how they did during the regular 162-game schedule. No other "dynasty" faced that hazard. And, in fact, the A's did finish in first place in their division five years in a row; but in 1971 they had lost a playoff to Baltimore, and in 1975 they lost to Boston, ending their reign.

Six everyday players were the backbone of their lineup through the three Championship seasons. They were Reggie Jackson, the club's top home run hitter; Joe Rudi, the leading defensive

outfielder and best-average hitter; Sal Bando, fine defensive third baseman with power; Bert Campaneris, steady shortstop and consistent hitter; Gene Tenace, catcher and long-ball hitter; and Dick Green, brilliant defensive but light-hitting second baseman. Bill North took over in center field in 1973, and Claudell Washington inherited the left-field spot in 1974 when Rudi was shifted to first.

This was a team of terrific home-run power, great speed on the bases, outstanding defense and versatility. But its true strength was pitching. There were three superb starters: Jim "Catfish" Hunter, Ken Holtzman and Vida Blue. Hunter, starting in 1971, won twenty-one games three years in a row, then upped his total to twenty-five in 1974. Holtzman won nineteen, twenty-one and nineteen in three years. Blue, a twenty-four-game-winning sensation as a rookie in 1971, won twenty in 1973, seventeen in '74 and twenty-two in '75. He was a holdout for half the 1972 season. Behind them was the best relief pitcher in the game, Rollie Fingers, working exclusively in relief, appeared in 203 games during those three Championship seasons, picking up 27 victories and 61 saves. Left-handed reliefing was done by Darold Knowles and Paul Lindblad.

In 1971, under Dick Williams, the A's won 101 games and finished far ahead in the Western Division. But the more experienced Orioles beat them in three straight in the playoffs. In 1972, they had to go five games to get past Detroit in the playoffs. They were underdogs in the World Series, but beat the Cincinnati Reds in seven games. In that Series, Tenace hit four home runs, two coming in his first two times at bat. He had hit five home runs all season.

In 1973, the A's first had to beat back the Kansas City Royals for the division title, go five games to beat the Orioles for the league championship, and finally go the limit of seven games to defeat the New York Mets in the World Series. Jackson, Rudi and Campaneris shared the hitting honors, as Holtzman was credited with two of the A's' four victories. Jackson drove in six runs. Rudi led the hitters with a .333 average. And Campaneris was voted the outstanding player of the World Series for his all-around brilliance.

In 1974 Alvin Dark succeeded Williams at the helm of the A's. The team sputtered much of the season but rose to late challenge by Texas and Kansas City to win its fourth straight division title. A four-game defeat of Baltimore put the A's into the World Series against the Los Angeles Dodgers.

Joyous Sal Bando leaps on back of pitcher Rollie Fingers, held up by catcher Dave Duncan in 1972 Series.

This proved to be the easiest World Series triumph of them all, for the A's polished off the Dodgers in five games.

The A's won their fifth division title in 1975, but the dynasty was visibly crumbling. The winter before, Hunter was declared a free agent. Hunter's absence during the regular season had no outward effect, but it hurt during the playoffs against the Red Sox, who swept all three games.

Hunter's defection was only the beginning. Owner Charlie Finley's players left the team like sailors fleeing a sinking ship. At the end of the 1976 season, Rudi, Tenace, Campaneris and Bando, having played out their option year, sold their services to other clubs. Green had retired, and

Jackson and Holtzman had been traded the previous winter because it had become quite clear to Finley that they too contemplated desertion.

Nothing lasts forever, least of all multi-Championship World Series teams. But just as surely as every dynasty is bound to fall, other teams will eventually rise to take its place. And when they do, they provide baseball with one of its most thrilling spectacles—a team of superb players whose chemistry is such that the team as a whole is even greater than the sum of its individual talents.

No one can predict just when the next great World Series team will evolve, although some say it's already in the works. But one thing is certain—another dynasty **will** appear eventually. ◇

Injured Reggie Jackson, in street clothes, joins teammates for introduction prior to 1972 Series.

The All-Time All-Star World Series Team

BY JOSEPH L. REICHLER

THE YEAR 1978 marks the seventy-fifth anniversary of the World Series, and no anniversary celebration of baseball's showcase would be complete without the selection of a real honest-to-goodness all-time All-Star World Series team. Of course, picking an All-Star team of any kind is as good a way as any to start an endless argument. The probability of finding any two persons whose selections would even partially agree is about as great as that of finding two people with identical thumbprints. But before the brickbats start flying, let it be made clear that these selections are based purely on World Series performance and not on what the athletes accomplished during their regular pennant campaigns.

This in itself should explain why so many top-flight all-time stars like Ty Cobb, Honus Wagner, Joe DiMaggio, Stan Musial, Rogers Hornsby, Bob Feller, Jackie Robinson, Willie Mays, Joe Cronin, Hack Wilson, Gabby Hartnett and Roy Campanella are not mentioned in these selections. For it just so happens that through one quirk or another these superluminaries, magnificent as they may have been at other times of their careers, somehow never managed to distinguish themselves to any great extent during their appearances in World Series competition.

Some, like the great speedball marvel Walter Johnson and his National League counterpart, Dazzy Vance, didn't make it to the fall classic until time had carried them well beyond their prime. Others, like Edd Roush, Paul Waner, Eddie

Lou Gehrig, the first baseman on the Series All-Star team.

Frankie Frisch, who twice batted .400 in Series play.

Mathews and Ted Williams, simply couldn't put it together during their brief spurts of World Series play. While still others, great stars like George Sisler, Napoleon Lajoie, Luke Appling, Ernie Banks, Ralph Kiner, Mickey Vernon, Billy Williams, Jim Bunning, Ted Lyons, Rube Waddell, Addie Joss and Harry Heilmann, never got into the autumn struggles at all.

There isn't any doubt about the Goliath of the World Series. He is Babe Ruth. He brightens its history both as a standout pitcher for the Red Sox and as its supreme hitter for the Yankees.

How about the rest? Put Ruth in his right-field position, and who would qualify to join him on the All-Star Series team? After Ruth, the choices aren't nearly as easy. It is possible to debate the claims of two or more players for virtually every position. But only one man can be named for each position. And so here's the team:

> **First Base:** Lou Gehrig, Yankees
> **Second Base:** Frank Frisch, Giants and Cardinals
> **Shortstop:** Pee Wee Reese, Dodgers
> **Third Base:** Frank "Home Run" Baker, Athletics and Yankees
> **Left Field:** Lou Brock, Cardinals
> **Center Field:** Pepper Martin, Cardinals
> **Right Field:** Babe Ruth, Red Sox and Yankees
> **Catcher:** Yogi Berra, Yankees
> **Right-handed Pitcher:** Bob Gibson, Cardinals
> **Left-handed Pitcher:** Whitey Ford, Yankees

The manager would have to be Casey Stengel, for he not only directed great teams but also managed seven of the ten victorious World Series Yankees teams. His genius in piloting five consecutive world champions from 1949 through 1954 stands today as a beacon light for all managers to stare at and ponder. His only defeats came in 1955, 1957 and 1960, but in each case it took the opposition the limit of seven games to beat him.

Some might contend that Joe McCarthy, who managed the Yankees in the 1930s and 1940s, rates number one honors. Certainly Marse Joe has excellent credentials. His Yankees teams won seven of eight October Classics, losing only to the 1942 Cardinals. His 1929 defeat as manager of the Cubs should not detract from this remarkable achievement. Connie Mack, with eight championship teams, and John McGraw, with nine, are the only other managers in contention. Mack won six world titles but McGraw only three.

At first base the pick is Lou Gehrig. But many will ask how Jimmy Foxx can be ignored. With the A's in 1929, 30 and 31, he hit .350, .333 and .348 and had four homers and eleven RBI's. Or what about Bill Terry, who hit .429 for the Giants in 1924? Or Frank Chance, who hit .421 and stole five bases for the Cubs in 1908?

Yet when everything is said and done, Gehrig surpasses them all. The immortal Iron Horse starred in practically all the Series clashes in which he appeared, recording the amazing average of .361 with ten homers over a span of seven Series. Twice he hit over .500, with .545 in 1928 and .529 in 1932. In that last Series, he dominated the Yankees' rallies that won each of the four games. He hit a two-run homer in the first game and scored three runs. In the second, his three hits accounted for all five Yankees runs. In the third game, he hit two homers, and in the last game he drove in three runs and scored two more with a single and double. Altogether, in the four games, Gehrig scored eight runs and drove in nine, with nine hits in seventeen at-bats. In all, he accounted for fourteen runs in the four-game set. In thirty-four World Series games, he drove in thirty-five runs. Other first basemen shone brightly in the World Series—Stuffy McInnis of the great Connie Mack teams of 1910-14, Charlie Grimm of the Cubs, Hank Greenberg of the Tigers, Frank McCormick of the Reds, Gil Hodges of the Dodgers. But Gehrig stands alone.

So many second basemen starred in the October classic that it is extremely difficult to name the best. Eddie Collins averaged .328 for four Series with the Athletics and two more with the White Sox. He hit over .400 three times, with a high of .429 for the A's in 1910. He stole three bases in 1913 and three more in 1917. And he fielded

Casey Stengel who managed the Yankees in ten World Series.

brilliantly in all. Charlie Gehringer averaged .321 in four World Series, including a dazzling .438 with the Miracle Braves in 1914. Joe Gordon hit .400 for the Yankees in 1938 and three years later did even better with .500. Billy Martin, although not of the caliber of some of the others, batted .500 for the Yankees in 1953 with a dozen hits and averaged .333 in five appearances. And who can forget Bill Mazeroski and his Series-winning home run for Pittsburgh in 1960?

The choice, however, is Frankie Frisch, who was always at his best when the chips were down. His average over eight Series was only .294, but he led the Giants to two Series victories over the Yankees with averages of .300 in 1921 and .471 in 1922. Although the Giants lost the next two years, Frisch did not let up, hitting .400 and .333. Ten years later, he was still the indomitable fighter as he paced the famous Gas House Gang of St. Louis to a Series victory over the Tigers, as he did three years earlier with another Cardinal team over the A's.

The World Series has produced many outstanding defensive shortstops, but few have made lasting impressions at the plate. Phil Rizzuto appeared in the most, nine, and four times batted over .300. But his overall average is .246. Alvin Dark was an almost perfect shortstop and number two hitter with the Giants in 1951 and 1954, averaging .417 and .412. But he batted only .167 with the Braves in 1948. Tommy Thevenow hit .417 with the Cards in 1926. Charlie Gelbert hit .353 with the same club in 1930 and Dick Bartell

Frank Baker earned the nickname of "Home Run Baker" for his two home runs in the 1911 Series.

PeeWee Reese finally played on a World Champion after five failures.

hit .381 with the Giants in 1936. But they were only one-year bursts. Bert Campaneris, Frank Crosetti, Leo Durocher, Jack Barry, Luis Aparicio, Dave Bancroft, Mark Belanger, Joey Sewell, Lou Boudreau and others fielded expertly in their Series appearances but didn't startle anyone with their bats.

The selection for top shortstop honors goes to Pee Wee Reese, who for three straight appearances was as dangerous a hitter as anyone in the Dodger lineup. He batted .304 in 1947, .316 in 1949 and .346 in 1952. His overall average for seven Series is .272. He was the glue of the Dodgers' infield, handling 185 of his 194 chances flawlessly and participating in 25 double plays, including the one that helped beat the Yankees in the 1955 World Series.

The third-base battle boils down to three hot corner men—Stan Hack of the Cubs, Brooks Robinson of the Orioles and Frank "Home Run" Baker of the Athletics. Other third basemen fared exceptionally well in Series play. Harry Steinfeldt hit .470 for the Cubs in 1907, driving home the winning run in the final game. Heinie Groh put on quite an exhibition in October of 1922, hitting .474 for the Giants, the all-time high for third basemen, and handled twenty chances flawlessly. Billy Werber hit .370 for the 1940 Reds. Red Rolfe is one of only a few players to hit .300 or better in four classics.

Jimmy Collins, George Rohe, Fred Lindstrom, Pie Traynor, Pete Rose, Sal Bando and Joe Dugan also have performed nobly at the hot corner.

Hack was a brilliant leadoff batter for the Cubs in three Series, batting .348 in eighteen games. In the 1938 Series against the Yankees he hit .471. Robinson, a veteran of five Series, gave one of the greatest all-around performances in the 1970 Series against the Reds. He hit .429 and smashed two home runs, but it was his fielding that had the baseball world talking all winter. Called a human vacuum, he cleaned up everything in sight, time and again robbing the Reds of seemingly certain base hits. His best play was made in the first game when he backhanded a smash by Lee May between himself and the third-base bag, and in one motion whirled and threw to Boog Powell on one bounce for the out.

The nod for the All-Star third baseman, however, goes to Baker, who set the all-time World Series batting high of .363 in six classics and five games. With the Athletics, Baker hit .429, .375 and .450 in 1910, 1911 and 1913. In 1911, he gained his celebrated sobriquet of "Home Run" Baker by hitting a two-run homer off Rube Marquard to help the A's defeat the Giants, 3-1. The next day, he homered in the ninth inning off Christy Mathewson to force the game into overtime, where it was won by the A's.

There are a number of claimants in the outfield, but only three can be chosen. Starting with left field, there is Goose Goslin, who hit .287 and seven home runs in five Series and closed his Series performance with the winning hit in Detroit in 1935. The Goose helped Washington win its first World Championship blasting three home runs in 1924, a feat he repeated in a losing cause the following year. Another stalwart was Al Simmons, who in three Series with the Athletics, hit .300, .364 and .333. Simmons sparked the A's' triumphs in 1929 and '30, and hit the homer—one of six in World Series competition—that ignited the famous ten-run inning that enabled Connie Mack's 1929 team to overcome an 8-0 Chicago lead.

It's difficult to ignore Charlie Keller—who batted .438 for the Yankees in the 1938 Series, scoring eight runs and driving in six; five of his seven hits were for extra bases, with a triple, double and three homers—or Carl Yastrzemski, who batted .400 for the Red Sox in the 1967 Series. Riggs Stephenson of the Cubs in 1929 and 1932 was outstanding. He hit .444 in 1932 and drove in seven runs attempting to stave off the Yankees' rout. Duffy Lewis hit .444 for Boston in 1915 and .353 in 1916, although his overall figure was .284. Joe Medwick was a .326 hitter in two Series, and Joe Rudi twice batted .333 for the Oakland A's.

None of the above, however, could match

Lou Brock's brilliant performances in all three of his appearances. Lou began with a modest .300 batting average in the Cards' 1964 triumph over the Yankees, although he did drive in five runs. He sizzled in 1967, banging out twelve hits against Boston pitching for a rousing .414 average. He also set a Series record with seven stolen bases. In 1968 against the Tigers, he went one better, skyrocketing to .464 on a record-tying thirteen hits that included two homers. To prove that his seven steals in '67 were no fluke, he did it again.

Despite his .257 batting average, Mickey Mantle deserves consideration for the center-field post because of his eighteen home runs, forty-two runs scored and forty runs batted in, all records. His best of twelve Series came in 1960, when he batted .400, hit three homers and drove in eleven runs. Mick's predecessor, Joe DiMaggio, batted .271 in ten Series with eight home runs and many dazzling catches in his fifty-one games. Tris Speaker did not play in as many Series, but he never failed to satisfy. He was never with a loser, batting .300 and .294 with the Red Sox in 1912 and 1915, and .320 with the Indians in 1920, Tris hit four triples in Series play, and he executed the only unassisted double play by an outfielder in the Series.

Duke Snider rates consideration for his four .300-or-better Series and his eleven home runs in thirty-six games. He was spectacular in the 1955

Lou Brock stole a record seven bases in 1967 and 1968 Series.

Pepper Martin had a brilliant Series in 1931.

Series against the Yankees, hitting four home runs and batting .320. Max Carey batted .458 for Pittsburgh in the 1925 Series, and Casey Stengel clouted two game-winning homers for the Giants and hit .417 in 1923 against the Yankees. None, however, captivated the nation as did Pepper Martin in 1931, when he almost single-handedly wrecked the powerful A's machine. He ran wild on the bases, stealing five times against Mickey Cochrane. He hit .500, scored five runs, drove in five; and among his twelve hits were four doubles and a homer. Martin also starred in the 1934 Series, getting eleven hits for a .355 average. He averaged .418 for three Series.

Ruth, of course, was in a class by himself in right field, although that position boasted some highly distinguished occupants. Roberto Clemente, Pittsburgh's brilliant flychaser, hit safely in all fourteen games he played, and in 1971 he dominated the Series as few players have ever done. In addition to batting .414 with twelve hits in twenty-nine appearances, he made several spectacular catches and uncorked a tremendous throw that had the onlookers staring in disbelief. His offensive output consisted of two doubles, a triple and two homers.

The Yankees' Hank Bauer was another outstanding World Series performer in right field. An enormous money player, Bauer holds the record for hitting safely in seventeen consecutive Series games. His four homers in 1958 helped the Yankees overcome a 3-1 Milwaukee lead in games. Henry Aaron batted .364 in two Series that included three homers and nine RBI's. Reggie Jackson was a one-man gang in 1977 with his five home runs, three in one game, his eight runs batted in, and his .450 average.

Ruth, however, was Mr. Destruction himself. In ten Series, including the three he played with the Red Sox as a pitcher, Babe hit .325, walloped fifteen homers and drove in thirty-two runs. His .625 figure in 1928 still stands as a record for a single season. He is the only player to hit three homers twice in a single game. He was, of course, a marvelous and gifted all-around player, distinguished in the outfield as well as on the mound and at bat.

Selecting the All-Star catcher poses a real problem. Do you select one on the basis of his superior work over a short period? Or one who by virtue of his good fortune appeared so often that he was able to set enduring marks? For one Series, Hank Gowdy's heroics in 1914 outstripped all the rest. Hitting against the most famous pitching staff of that time, Gowdy amassed an amazing average of .545, socked a homer, a triple and two doubles as the Boston Braves upset the favored Athletics in four straight. In two other Series, however, Gowdy went seven for thirty-one, a .226 average.

Strictly on Series performance, Wally Schang rates support. He was a world-champion catcher in three cities—Philadelphia, Boston and New York. He batted .357 with the Athletics in 1913, .444 with the Red Sox in 1918 and .318 with the Yankees in 1923. It was Schang who caught Ruth when the Babe completed his streak of 29⅔ scoreless innings in 1918. Then there is Bill Dickey, who caught in thirty-eight World Series games for dominating Yankees clubs, batting .348 in 1932 and .400 in 1938. In 1943, it was his four-bagger off Mort Cooper with Charlie Keller on base that won the final game from the Cardinals, 2-0. There's also Mickey Cochrane, who, although only .245 in five Series, was one of the Athletics' heroes of the 1929 Series when he hit .400 against Cubs pitching.

All-Star catching honors, by a thin margin, go to Yogi Berra, who has played in more World Series (14) and more games (75), has been to bat more times (259), has the most hits (71), most doubles (10), and is second to Mantle with 41 runs and 39 runs batted in. Yogi went through his first five Series as a patsy, with marks of .158, .063, .200, .261 and .214. But he roared back with averages of .429, .417, .360, .320 and .318 for an overall mark of .278. His dozen homers are topped only by Mantle and Ruth, and he is the

Babe Ruth waves to the crowd after hitting a home run in 1923 Series.

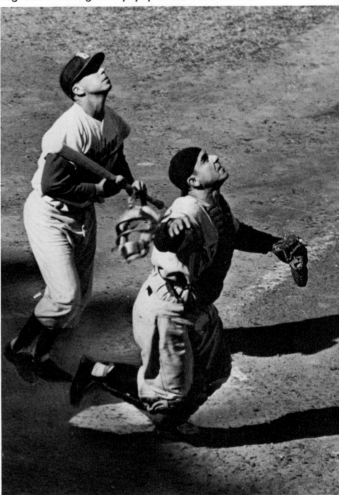

Whitey Ford, who holds the record for most consecutive scoreless innings in World Series.

Yogi Berra looking for a popup in the 1956 Series.

only player to have hit both a grand-slammer and pinch homer in a World Series.

Berra's biggest Series was in 1956 against the Dodgers. He walloped a bases-loaded home run off Don Newcombe in the second game, but the Dodgers came back to win it, 13-8. The seventh game was different. This was the one that counted, and Yogi hadn't forgotten how the Dodgers had beaten the Yankees the year before. He could still see Sandy Amoros making that catch off his slicing drive. Newcombe was on the mound again for the Dodgers. In the first inning, Berra tagged him for a two-run homer. In the third, Berra came up again with a runner on and promptly unloaded another home run off Newcombe, his third of the series and his ninth and tenth runs batted in.

The pitchers' field, left- and right-handers, is packed with standouts. Right-handers include Christy Mathewson, Bill Dinneen, Chief Bender, Smokey Joe Wood, Red Faber, Waite Hoyt, Stan Coveleski, Jack Coombs, Grover Alexander, Monte Pearson, Spud Chandler, George Earnshaw,

Bucky Walters, Buck Newsom, Allie Reynolds, Vic Raschi, Bob Gibson, Jim Palmer, Catfish Hunter, Don Sutton and Mike Torrez. Walter Johnson, in the twilight of his career, added a lustrous page to the story.

Red Ruffing was almost as certain as ever-increasing taxes in getting the all-important first-game jump for the Yankees year after year. Red opened up for the Bombers six times and lost only to Carl Hubbell of the Giants in 1936. He wound up with a 7-2 record, as did Reynolds, a Yankee of later vintage. Bender and Hoyt won six Series games each. Coombs (5-0) and Pearson (4-0) are unbeaten in Series play. Right-handers with the best Series records in recent years are Hunter and Burdette, each with a 4-2 record.

Gibson is named as the right-handed pitcher on the All-Star World Series team because, with the exception of his initial Series start, he was as close to invincible as a pitcher could be. Christy Mathewson rates a close second because of his ex-traordinary accomplishment of defeating the A's three times in 1905, all by shutouts. Although Mat-

Bob Gibson set a World Series strikeout mark for a single game in 1968.

ning, and his earned-run average was 1.88.

Lefthanded pitching heroes in World Series competition read like a Hall of Fame roster. Lefty Gomez, southpaw ace of the champion Yankees, owns an unblemished 6-0 record in October games. Herb Pennock, another Yankee Hall of Famer, captured all five of his decisions against National League clubs. Eddie Lopat, still another Yankee, won four of his five decisions.

Sandy Koufax, the Dodgers' brilliant left-hander, had a 4-3 record, but his triumphs included two shutouts, 61 strikeouts in 57 innings and an incredible .095 earned run average. Babe Ruth, as a pitcher with the Boston Red Sox, won three games without defeat during which he pitched $29\frac{2}{3}$ consecutive scoreless innings. Other outstanding lefties in World Series play included Dave McNally, 4-2; Johnny Podres, 4-1; Ken Holtzman, 4-1; Artie Nehf 4-4; Warren Spahn, 4-3; Tommy Bridges, 4-1; and Mickey Lolich, 3-0. The last two are the only southpaws to win three games in a single series.

The palm for the greatest of them all in World Series competition, however, must go to Whitey Ford. The Yankees' precocious lefthander holds a flock of World Series pitching records, most series, 11; most starts, 22; most openers, 8; most innings, 146; most strikeouts, 94; and most victories, 10.

Ford's most glittering performance, however, is his feat of stringing together $33\frac{2}{3}$ consecutive scoreless innings over a three-series stretch. He began that remarkable accomplishment by hurling successive shutouts against the Pittsburgh Pirates in the 1960 Series. He permitted only 11 hits in 18 innings, striking out eight and walking two.

Whitey was the whole show in the opening game of the 1961 Series, as he pitched his third successive shutout, beating the Cincinnati Reds, 2-0, with a brilliant two hitter that put him only $2\frac{2}{3}$ innings away from Ruth's prized pitching record of $29\frac{2}{3}$ consecutive scoreless innings. The little left-hander took care of that in his next start four days later. He went five scoreless innings before retiring with an injured ankle. Whitey added another runless inning in the opener of the 1962 Series against the San Francisco Giants before the Giants broke through for a run in the second inning of a game won by Ford and the Yankees, 6-2.

A recap of Ford's brilliant World Series performances show that he pitched the opener in eight of the 11 World Series in which he performed. He won five. He pitched the final game in three World Series. He won two. He pitched the "do-or-die" game, the vital sixth contest when his team was trailing three games to two and on the brink of defeat. The Yankees won all three of them. ◇

ty's record was a mere 5-5, he was unlucky in his losses and stunning in statistics. Over $101\frac{2}{3}$ innings in 1905 and 1911-13, Matty allowed only 76 hits and a paltry 10 bases on balls and showed an earned-run average of 1.15.

Yet, in some ways, Gibson's feats were even more remarkable. He won seven straight games for the Cards between his first and last defeat. He is the only pitcher ever to make three starts in each of three separate Series. And he completed all but his first one in three complete games. His winning scores were 2-1, 6-0 and 7-2.

Although the Cards lost the 1968 Series to the Tigers, Gibson was as impressive as ever in three starts. He struck out seventeen men in his first start, a 4-0 five-hitter, wiping out a record of fifteen strikeouts set by Sandy Koufax of the Dodgers in 1963. His second start was another five-hitter, a 10-1 victory. He struck out ten. He lost the final game, 4-1, breaking his string of seven straight victories Overall, he gave up fifty-five hits in eighty-one innings, an average of six each nine innings. He struck out ninety-two men, better than one an in-

The Black Sox Scandal

BY JOSEPH L. REICHLER

Edd Roush, starred for the Reds' in the 1919 Series.

ONE OF THE UGLIEST INCIDENTS in the history of sports took place during the infamous World Series of 1919 between the Chicago White Sox and the Cincinnati Reds. The incident will forevermore be known as the "Black Sox Scandal" because it centered on a conspiracy between professional gamblers and eight Chicago White Sox players to throw the Series to the Reds.

The gamblers, as it turned out, were at least partially successful, but not before a number of double crosses among themselves and the team they were trying to corrupt. As for the players, they were acquitted, despite their previous confessions of guilt. Yet justice was served in the end, for Judge Kenesaw Mountain Landis, the newly installed Commissioner of Baseball, barred all eight of them from professional baseball for all time.

Many versions of the Black Sox Scandal have been written, each differing with the others on some of the details. This particular story, stemming from a talk with Hall-of-Famer Ed Roush, former Cincinnati star center fielder, makes no pretense of exposing any startling new facts about the case. But it does throw light on several details that up to now have been shrouded in complete mystery.

It is now known that the gamblers and the corrupted White Sox players had agreed upon a signal to show that the "fix was in." During the first game, Chicago pitching ace Eddie Cicotte was to hit the first Cincinnati player with a ball. Cicotte, a pitcher known for his control, did just that: he hit Cincinnati's leadoff man, Morrie Rath, in the back in the bottom of the first inning.

To players not in on the conspiracy, that "misaimed" pitch seemed like a fluke. It wasn't until later that other players began to notice that something wasn't quite right with the way Chicago was playing.

One of those players was Edd Roush. In 1919, Roush was Cincinnati's brightest star. He had won the National League batting title for the second time that year, and he had just been acclaimed the greatest defensive outfielder in the game. Edd was asked when he first suspected that the 1919 Series was fixed. He answered without hesitation.

"My first suspicions came after the second game," he replied, "although it had first come to my attention after the opening game, which we won, 9-1. That evening, I was standing in front of the Sinton Hotel, where the club was stopping, breathing in the night air and wondering what tomorrow would bring. A man I knew came up to me and said, 'Roush, I want to tell you something. The Series is fixed for your club to win. There was a meeting last night in Cicotte's room and there was an argument. I was in the next room and heard the whole thing. The White Sox are going to throw it.'

"This fellow was a well-known gambler, but I always knew him to be an honest one. Yet I didn't believe his story. I just turned away without comment and walked back into the hotel and crossed the lobby. It was full of gamblers. That wasn't so strange during a World Series, but it was odd that all of them were trying to get bets down on the Reds.

"The White Sox, the whole world knew, were heavy favorites before the World Series. They had as great a club, player for player, as any club in history. They had Shoeless Joe Jackson and Happy Felsch in the outfield. Buck Weaver and Eddie Collins in the infield and Ray Schalk behind the plate. And on the mound they had Eddie Cicotte, a twenty-nine-game winner, and Claude Williams, one of the cleverest control pitchers in baseball.

"Compared with the White Sox, we were just an ordinary team. We had no World Series experience, while they had beaten the Giants in the 1917 Series with practically the same team.

"Yet the odds switched so drastically that before the first game the Reds had become 6-to-5 favorites after being a 2-to-1 underdog.

"Still I refused to believe that anything was wrong. Damned if you don't hear the silliest things at World Series time, I thought as I waited for the

Buck Weaver, a member of the Black Sox of Chicago in the 1919 Series.

elevator to take me up to my floor. The Series fixed! You hear that every year. I wonder how those rumors start. Yet there were all these strange character in the hotel lobby and outside on the street with plenty of money to offer on the Reds. It didn't make sense at the time.

"Naturally, I didn't believe anything was really wrong then, and I refused to believe everything wasn't on the up-and-up even after we won the first two games. But I must admit things were happening on the field, day after day, that seemed peculiar, to say the least. I just didn't want to—couldn't believe that anything was wrong.

"Now it was the night before the final game. We were leading in the Series, four games to three. We needed one more victory to become the champions of the world. Up to that year, the World Series had been a best-out-of-seven affair, but in 1919 the National Commission, which ruled the World Series, decided to increase it to best-out-of-nine. Their explanation was that the fans wanted to see more games.

"I was getting some fresh night air again in front of the hotel when this same fellow who had tipped me off about the fix earlier came over. He said he wanted to tell me something else. He told me an amazing story.

"He told me that a certain well-known gambler had told him eight White Sox players had been fixed to throw the Series to the Reds. He told me how a lot of gamblers, including himself, had lost a lot of money in the first games betting on the White Sox, before getting wise to what was going on. He then said that some smart crooks, angry at the double cross by the New York gamblers, began figuring out a way to get even and at the same time recoup their losses. After the first two games, they figured out a deal whereby, if they could get the Reds to throw the Series, they would clean up because by now everyone figured the Reds were all set to win.

"This was an out-and-out attempted double cross by other gamblers. My informant didn't know whether they had succeeded in reaching any of our players, but he hinted there was a strong possibility that they had. The more he talked the angrier I became. I didn't want to believe him, but it sounded convincing. Events seemed to bear out what he had told me the previous week.

"I hadn't paid any attention to the earlier rumors because they involved guys on the other team. But this time they were tampering with our players. That was a terrible thing. I was mad anyway, because losing that day meant going back to Chicago and I was anxious to get home. Hearing that gamblers were trying to fix our guys burned me worse.

"The morning of the game, we had our usual clubhouse meeting to go over the other team's hitters. I was still burning, so I stood up and said out loud so that everybody could hear, 'I hear someone in this club doesn't want to win today.' You could have heard a pin drop. 'Well, I'll be out in center field watching every move, and nobody better do anything funny. No damn crook is going to rob me of my winning share of this Series.'

"After the meeting, Pat Moran, our manager, took me aside and asked me for the details. I told him everything I knew. I was still mad, and I told him, 'I'm not going to go out and run my legs off if we have someone on the team who doesn't want to win.'

"Moran then called in Hod Eller, who was to pitch the final game for us. 'Hod,' Moran barked at Eller, 'anybody tried to bribe you?'

"Eller hesitated, then nodded his head. 'Yes,' he said, 'a feller came over to me last night and offered me five thousand-dollar bills to throw today's game. I told him to get away from me before I punched him in the nose.'

"Moran looked him in the eye and said, 'You go out there and I'll watch you and if I see anything I don't like, out you come and I'll see to it that you're through forever.'

"It worked out all right. Eller gave no sign that he was not doing anything but is best. He held Chicago to one run for seven innings and did not let up until we had a 10-1 lead. We won the final game, 10-5, but what a double double cross that attempted switch would have been. It would have been the most famous, or infamous, larceny in all sports."

According to court records, the conspiracy was begun by Billy Maharg, a former boxer from Philadelphia, and Sleepy Bill Burns, a former Cincinnati pitcher. Maharg testified that Chicago pitcher Eddie Cicotte had approached Bill Burns in mid-season. Cicotte wanted to know if Burns could raise $100,000, for he claimed to have six other players who were willing to throw the Series for that amount.

Maharg and Burns found the proposition too big to swing by themselves. So they contacted a wealthy New York underworld figure named Arnold Rothstein. Rothstein considered the proposal, but he turned them down. And that was that, as far as Maharg and Burns were concerned.

Until, that is, they ran into a man named Abe Attell sometime later. Attell was the former featherweight champion of the world (1901-1912), and after giving up boxing he had become an associate of Arnold Rothstein's. Attell told Maharg and Burns that Rothstein had changed his mind and would put up the $100,000.

The deal was then presented to the Chicago conspirators, who had now grown to eight because utility infielder Fred McMillin had overheard the plans and insisted upon being included. The others

The great White Sox team of 1919 that went bad in the Series.

were, of course, Chick Gandil, the first baseman; Swede Risberg, the shortstop; Eddie Cicotte and Claude Williams, pitchers; Shoeless Joe Jackson and happy Felsch, outfielders. Although he later claimed that he had refused to participate, third baseman Buck Weaver was aware of the conspiracy and, because he failed to blow the whistle on the others, was also linked with it.

The $100,000 was to be paid in installments of $15,000 before the first game, $20,000 before the second game, $25,000 on the fourth morning and the balance when the Series ended. Bets were offered all over the country. Agents were appointed in all major cities. Attell allegedly was quartered in a large suite at the Sinton Hotel in Cincinnati with a gang of about 12 gamblers who he said were working for Rothstein.

It is now generally accepted that Abe Attell was not working for Arnold Rothstein at all. Failing to set Rothstein's approval for the scheme, Attell had turned to other gamblers and attempted to pull the whole thing off by himself. But that wasn't the end of it: Rothstein evidently double-crossed Attell.

"Rothstein," Attell said, "told me he wanted to have nothing to do with the fix, and I took him at

his word, considering the matter dead. But when I arrived at Chicago for the Series opener I saw Nat Evans, Rothstein's partner, talking to Monty Tennes [a Chicago bookmaker]. I waited until they had finished talking. Then I approached Tennes and asked him if he was doing business with Evans.

" 'Yeah, Abe,' Tennes said. 'Evans just handed me a bonanza. He bet me twenty grand on each of the first two games. The dope took Cincinnati!'

"Right away, I knew something was up. I went right up to Evans and he confessed. He said he was acting as the go-between for Rothstein and the players. I was so angry at the double cross that I went around telling all my friends the World Series was fixed. I looked up Tennes and told him to lay off his bet, which he did."

Although Edd Roush didn't identify the mysterious stranger who tipped him off about the White Sox fix, it is thought to have been this same Monty Tennes.

I wasn't long before Maharg and Burns began to get suspicious of Abe Attell. On the morning of the first game, they went to Abe and asked for the money to give the players. Instead of giving

Judge Landis in his customary role at a game with chin resting on the railing.

it to them, Attell told them he needed all his money to make bets with. Perhaps Attell was hoping to win the $100,000 he needed to pay off the players. Or perhaps he had never intended to pay them in the first place.

At any rate, it began to look as though Attell didn't have Rothstein's backing after all. And that suspicion was later confirmed when Maharg and Burns asked him for the players' money again after Cincinnati took the opener 9-1. Again Attell stalled.

Finally Maharg and Burns were able to wrangle $10,000 out of Attell, which they gave to the players. But by this time they were convinced that Attell was lying about his Rothstein connection. They strongly suspected that Abe had put together his own gambling syndicate and was trying to swing the deal by himself.

In his confession almost a year later, Maharg was quoted as saying' "The players were restless and wanted the full amount. After Cincinnati had won the second game, Cicotte told me they would not live up to the agreement unless they got the balance of their money. Burns promised he'd get them the money after the third game.

"The White Sox got even with us by winning the third game. Burns and I lost every cent we had in our clothes. I had to hock my diamond pin to get back to Philadelphia. The upshot of the whole matter was that Attell and his gang cleaned up a fortune and the Sox players were double-crossed out of $90,000 that was coming to them.

"I heard that a new deal was made on the final game with St. Louis gamblers and that a member of the St. Louis American League team [second baseman Joe Gedeon was later expelled from baseball] was the go-between, but I know nothing about that."

Maharg's story was never proved in court. The players and a number of gamblers were subsequently indicted, but Attell fled to Canada and Burns to Mexico.

In his confession before the grand jury, Eddie Cicotte wept several times as he admitted that he had been given $10,000 for losing the first game and that the money had been placed under his pillow in his Cincinnati hotel room.

Cicotte recounted the mental anguish he had experienced since agreeing to throw the Series, and he laid much of the blame on Chick Gandil.

"Gandil told me how easy it was to make $10,000 and that no one would ever know about it. Before Gandil became a ballplayer, he was mixed up with gamblers and low characters in Arizona. That's where he got the hunch to put the fix on the Series. Abe Attell and three Pittsburgh gamblers agreed to back him. Gandil first fixed Williams and McMullin. Then he got me in on the deal and we fixed the rest."

The jurors questioned Cicotte in detail as to the manner in which games were thrown.

"It's easy to throw a game," the pitcher said. "Just the slightest hesitation on the part of the player will let a man get a hit or score a run. I did it by giving the Cincinnati batters easy balls and putting them right over the plate with nothing on them. A child could have hit them. Ray Schalk was wise the moment I started pitching. I double-crossed him on the signals.

"The fourth inning of the first game, I was driven from the mound. I pitched poor ball from the start. The score tied at one apiece. Just before I took the mound in the fourth, Gandil told me to lob them over. Duncan got on first by a walk, which brought up Kopf. I fed him a straight ball and he dribbled it to me, and I fielded it like an amateur. I held the ball too long to make a force play on Duncan, and then threw the ball to Gandil, who made a phony stab at it, stumbled over the bag and before he could recover, Kopf had it beaten. If I had been playing on the level, a double play was a cinch and the inning would have been over. I kept right on feeding straight balls, and before the inning was over five runs were across.

"The second game I pitched, I went a little better. But in the fifth inning, Duncan knocked an easy grounder to me and I let off an easy peg to Gandil, which was wide and high, just enough to pull Chick off the bag. Duncan came home with a run when I fed Kopf an easy one, which he hit to Joe Jackson. Joe helped the run on its way, when he made a poor return of the ball, throwing over Schalk's head. Neale followed with a double into Jackson's territory. Both Jackson and myself presented these two runs to them, and the game was won by the Reds. I also intercepted a throw from the outfield in one of the games that would have put a man out at the plate.

"I am through with baseball. I am going to lose myself somewhere and never touch another ball. I feel sorry to have brought this disgrace to my wife and children. I am sorry to have wrecked Mr. Comiskey's chances to win the pennant that year. I was the best pitcher in the American League last year up to the time of the World Series. But this year I can't get going. I'd give a million dollars to undo what I've done."

Joe Jackson confirmed Cicotte's story, say-ing, "Each player dealt separately with Gandil. Gandil, Risberg and McMullin were the fixers, as far as I know, and Gandil was the leader. At first all the players thought Gandil had crossed them out of the money end of the deal, but they found out later it was Attell."

Claude Williams and Happy Felsch also confessed, but Risberg, McMullin and Weaver posted bonds of $10,000 apiece and protested their innocence. Gandil, the alleged ringleader of the players, refused to appear before the grand jury. He fled to Arizona and was never heard from again.

The case, with all its complex deals and double crosses, finally went to trial on July 16, 1921. But the results were anticlimatic. In spite of the fact that American League president Ban Johnson managed to induce Bill Burns to return from Mexico and appear as the star witness for the State, and in spite of the fact that Burns corroborated Maharg's testimony and implicated Abe Attell, the State's case was weakened because it was unable to bring Attell within the jurisdiction of the court. The players, on advice of their lawyers, repudiated their confessions, and the jury brought in a verdict of "not guilty."

Judge Kenesaw Mountain Landis, the new Commissioner of Baseball, was not so easy on the players, however. He quite justly barred the eight Chicago players from every playing professional ball again. None was ever reinstated. ◇

Chick Gandil, ring leader of the Black Sox scandal.

World Series Humor

BY JOE GARAGIOLA

Joe Garagiola as he looked when he was the first
string catcher for the Cards in the 1946 Series.

RIGHT BEFORE THE SEVENTH GAME of the 1955 World Series, somebody commented to Phil Silvers that baseball was really just another part of the entertainment business. Silvers, who is a great baseball fan as well as a great comedian, just looked at the guy and then said, "You got it a little wrong, pal. In the entertainment business, you would never close a show that's drawing sixty thousand people a day."

Actually, the audience watching a World Series game these days is measured in millions, not thousands, thanks to television. The number of people watching, the prestige of the World Series,

and the money involved are all things that make the World Series the greatest pressure cooker in all of sports. But that doesn't mean that the fans and players have to leave their sense of humor back in the hotel.

Over the years, the World Series has contributed a lot to the thrills of baseball, but it has also contributed a lot to the laughs of baseball. Sometimes the two went together. In 1956, Don Larsen of the Yankees did "the impossible." He pitched a perfect game in the World Series against the Brooklyn Dodgers. After the game there was the confusion you'd expect in the Yankees'

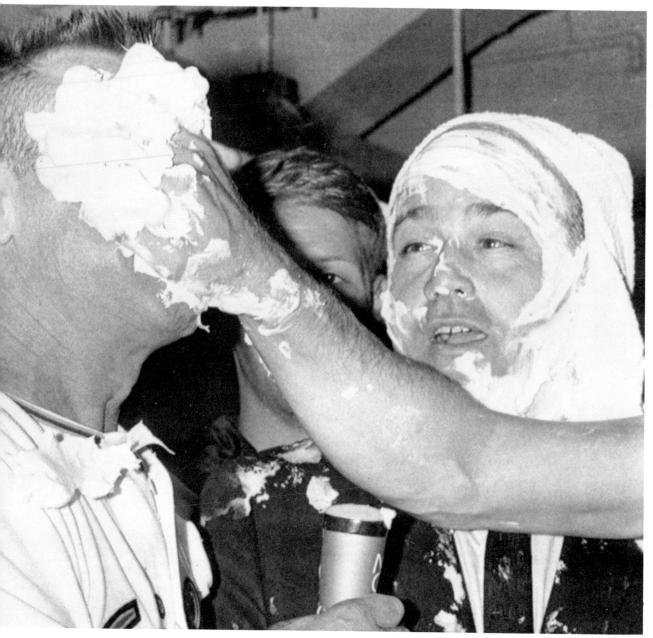

Winning manager getting a face massage after the
Orioles' four-game sweep of the Dodgers in 1964.

clubhouse, and one reporter couldn't get close enough to talk to Larsen, so he stopped manager Casey Stengel and said, "Was this the best game you ever saw Larsen pitch?" Ol' Case never missed a beat. He just said, "So far."

Lon Warneke was just a young kid of twenty-three when he was called upon to pitch for the Cubs against the Yankees in the second game of the 1932 Series. It was his first World Series, and until the day before he had never seen Yankee Stadium. Press photographers descended upon Warneke before the game and asked him to pose with his opponent, Lefty Gomez. Lon demurred. "What's the matter, Lon," asked one of the photographers, "you superstitious?" "Superstitious, hell," Warneke replied indignantly. "I just think it's unlucky."

One of the wildest World Series of them all was the one in 1934 between the St. Louis Cardinals and the Detroit Tigers. That was the year that Joe Medwick slid hard into Detroit third baseman Marvin Owen, and when he went to his position in left field the next inning the fans bombed him with fruit and garbage. It got so bad that Commissioner Kenesaw M. Landis had Medwick removed from the game. Said Medwick after the game, "I know why they threw that stuff at me. What I can't figure out is why they brought it to the ball park in the first place."

That was the same year that Dizzy Dean was pitching in the seventh game with a big lead. He decided he wanted to experiment with some new pitches, and manager Frank Frisch started to steam. When Diz kept shaking off his catcher's signs, Frisch ordered a pitcher to start warming up in the bullpen. When Dean noticed the bullpen action, he called Frisch to the mound and said, "Frank, what is that fella out there gettin' ready for? Openin' day?"

In that same World Series Dean was used as a pinch runner. Going from first to second, he didn't duck out of the way as the Tigers tried for a double play, and shortstop Billy Rogell's throw hit Diz right in the head. He went down like he'd been poleaxed, and was carried from the field and taken to the hospital. A report was issued that Diz had suffered no serious injury, and that story appeared in the papers the next day under a headline that said, "X-Rays of Dean's Head Show Nothing."

While the Giants were beating the Indians four straight in the 1954 Series, Willie Mays performed like a man from outer space. In the first game, he robbed Vic Wertz of an inside-the-park homer with an amazing over-the-head catch. In the third game, he belted three hits and knocked in two runs. In the second inning of the final game, with Wertz on second and two out, Sam Dente lined to Mays. Willie, forgetting that his catch had ended

the inning, rifled the ball home to keep Wertz from scoring. "I finally discovered Mays's weakness," observed Tony Cuccinello, Cleveland coach. "He can't count."

Some laughs have been provoked by non-combatants. During the 1956 Dodgers-Yankees World Series, the Brooklyn public-address announcer earnestly requested, "Will the fans in the front row please remove their clothing?" It was quite a while before the guffaws had died down—enough for the announcer to be heard when he repeated the request with the amendment..."from the railings."

Words can also be a problem for the players. Or, to be more exact about it, for their

Lou Brock taking off for one of seven steals in the 1967 Series.

managers. Prior to a Yankees-Dodgers World Series one year, Dodgers manager Charley Dressen angrily confronted Billy Loes, one of his starting pitchers, after Loes had made a prediction that the Series would go to seven games and that the Yankees would win it. Loes innocently claimed that he had been misquoted, which momentarily cooled Dressen down until Loes added, "I predicted they'd win it in six."

Did you know that in World Series history only thirty-six players have gotten four hits in a single game? Well, it's true. And the reason I bring it up is to illustrate a problem I myself once had in the word department. You see, I'm one of those thirty-six players. Some may find it hard to believe. But, as Casey Stengel would say, "You could look it up." Well anyway, four hits in a single Series game is kind of a nice accomplishment. So when Lou Brock got four hits in one game of the 1967 World Series, I thought I'd do the gracious thing and congratulate him after the game.

"Lou," I said, "I'm one guy who can appreciate how you feel today."

"What do you mean?" he replied.

"Well," I told him, "I once got four hits in a World Series game, too."

You know what Brock did? He laughed for a full two minutes.

Like I said, the World Series has contributed some laughs in its time. But that was one laugh I could have done without! ◇

Detroit's Schoolboy Rowe flanked by brothers Dizzy and Daffy Dean before the start of the 1934 Series.

Behind the Scenes

BY JOSEPH L. REICHLER

AFTER EVERY WORLD SERIES, fans inevitably gather at parties, around card tables or in local watering holes to recount the events, both good and bad, that took place on the field of play. Baseball insiders will get together after a Series, too. But more often than not their talk won't be limited to what took place on the field. They'll also discuss many of the things that took place behind the scenes, the stories and the incidents that usually go unreported by press or electronic media.

Some of the backstage happenings will be highly dramatic. Others will simply be amusing, such as the encounter that took place during the World Series of 1962 between the Yankees and Giants. Bobo Newsom, who pitched for practically every team in the American League, and a few in the National, was broadcasting for a Baltimore station. He agreed to meet a newspaperman for dinner at Toots Shor's, the famous saloon in New York.

While waiting for Newsom at the bar, the writer was joined by Red Smith, then working for the NEW YORK HERALD TRIBUNE. A little later, Lyall Smith of the DETROIT FREE PRESS came by. Then came Joe L. Brown of the Pittsburgh

Pirates and his dad, the famous movie star, Joe E. Brown. Finally, Harry Jones of the CLEVELAND PLAIN DEALER joined the group.

When Bob finally arrived, the writer thought he'd have some fun. "Bobo," he said, "I don't know whether you've met all these gentlemen. This is Mr. Brown, Mr. Brown, Mr. Smith, Mr. Smith, Mr. Jones."

"If there ain't nobody gonna give their right names," Newsom replied, "I ain't either."

A different circumstance and a different time. Once again Newsom was the principal character, but in this case he was surrounded by tragedy. It was in the 1940 World Series and Bobo was scheduled to pitch the opener for Detroit against Cincinnati. Before the game, he posed with his aged father as news cameras clicked. "Brought the old man all the way from Carolina to see me pitch," he explained. That day he hurled the Tigers to a 7-2 victory over the Reds. Three days later, Bobo opened the door connecting his hotel room with his father's. Mr. Newsom lay cold and still on the bed, the victim of a heart attack.

Tiger fans were stunned by the news. Their beloved Bobo would certainly be unable to pitch

Joe L. Brown, Pirates General Manager, and dad, Joe E. Brown, share a laugh together.

again in the Series. To their amazement, Newsom not only started the fifth game, but hurled an 8-0 shutout. In the clubhouse after the game, reporters were loath to question him as he sat on a stool still showing the effects of the tragedy.

"How did you do it?" one finally asked.

"My dad was lookin' down from a window in heaven tellin' me what to throw," sighed Bobo as tears coursed down his cheeks.

Schoolboy Rowe, the great Tigers pitcher, was the subject of unmerciful riding from the Cardinals' Gashouse Gang during the 1934 Series. Despite the taunts of Pepper Martin, Leo Durocher and others, he pitched a strong game and beat the Redbirds in the second game, 3-2, in twelve innings. The teams were now preparing for the sixth game. A Tigers victory, and it would be all over. Rowe was due to pitch.

A half hour before game time, manager Mickey Cochrane went into the clubhouse to see how his pitcher was doing. He found him dunking his pitching hand in a bowl of hot water. "What's the matter?" Cochrane asked.

"I slammed a door on my hand last night," Rowe said.

"You what?" Cochrane roared.

"I slammed a door on my hand. Look." And he held up the hand. It was puffed up like a balloon. Cochrane took one look and felt crushed.

"I've got nobody else to work today," he cried. "Sore hand or not, you've got to pitch."

"I'll try," said Rowe. "I don't think I can throw the curve, but I can throw the fastball all right."

With nothing but a fastball, Rowe went the full nine innings, but lost to Paul Dean, 4-3. The Cards breezed past the Tigers the next afternoon when Paul's older brother, Dizzy, wiped them out, 11-0.

An unparalleled case is that of Cliff Melton, the Giants' hope against the Yankees in the 1937 Series. Melton figured to be tough for the Yankees. Left-handers had troubled them all year. And having won twenty games in his first big-league season, Melton was definitely hot. But he was subjected to the most savage jockeying directed at a player since the Cardinals made Rowe their target three years earlier.

A shy gangling Southerner, Melton didn't say much when he reported to the Giants at training camp in 1937. It was his misfortune that he said

Bob Newsom, Tiger pitching star, in the
1940 Series.

in this art as a matter of routine. And sometimes it
could threaten to damage a lot more than a player's
ego. In the 1922 World Series between the
Yankees and the Giants, the jockeying was
especially fierce, particularly on the part of the
Giants. Johnny Rawlings, the Giants' utility infielder, was the roughest. His particular target was
Babe Ruth. After the Series, won by the Giants in a
sweep, Ruth and his fellow outfielder, Bob Meusel,
invaded the Giants' clubhouse. Both were already
in their street attire. "Where's Rawlings?" the Babe
bellowed. "I'm looking for him!"

"What's the matter, Babe?" snapped Earl
Smith, a toughie. "Can't you take it?"

Then Rawlings spoke up. "I'm right here, if
you're looking for me."

Babe took off his coat. So did Rawlings.
Jesse Barnes and Hughie McQuillan, a couple of
strong Giants pitchers, prepared to go into action.
So did Meusel. At that point, Hughie Jennings, the
Giants' coach, intervened and, fortunately for all
concerned, succeeded in ushering Ruth and
Meusel out of the room before any blows were
struck.

By the time the 1929 Series between the
Athletics and the Cubs rolled around, jockeying

Johnny Rawlings, Giants surprise hitting and fielding
star in the 1922 Series.

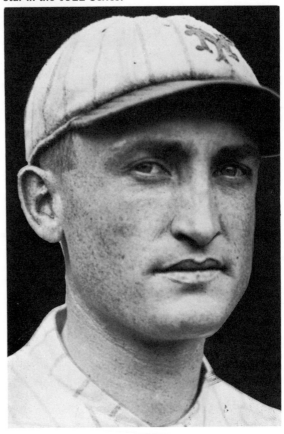

anything at all. In the one newsworthy interview he
gave the baseball writers, he sounded off at great
length against the Yankees, who had given him a
trial two years before and had unceremoniously
dropped him from their roster. The Yankees never
gave him a chance, Melton said. Nobody even
spoke to him. They were snobs, and he was glad he
was no longer with them.

The story was revived seven months later,
and now the Yankees were outraged. They were
determined to show him just how antisocial they
could be when they put their minds to it.

Nature had endowed Melton with a pair of
large ears which fanned out prominently from his
six-foot-four body. "Look, a cab with both doors
open," screamed Lefty Gomez, the Yankees'
number one jockey.

"Hey, Ump," Jack Powell shouted, "make
that monkey paint his ears green so we'll have a
background for hitting."

The insults went on and on. And Melton's
ears picked up every one. They had a telling effect,
for the Yankees battered him in both games.
Melton was never the same again.

There is very little bench jockeying today,
but in the old days players and managers engaged

had gotten so personal that Judge Landis called in managers Connie Mack and Joe McCarthy and warned them: "If this riding doesn't stop, I'll fine any player who continues it a full share. And if I can't determine who is yelling, I'll fine the manager."

The managers advised their players to tone down their remarks. Before the fifth game, Mickey Cochrane, the great Philadelphia catcher, yelled over to the Cubs' bench, "After the game, we'll serve tea in the clubhouse, girls."

"Shut your mouth, Mickey. Do you want it to cost us money?" cautioned Mr. Mack.

When Landis later walked into the A's clubhouse to congratulate the victors, he threw his arms around Cochrane and said impishly, "Now, let's have the tea, Mickey."

Physical confrontations and near battles were frequent in the early World Series. The Chicago Cubs, for example, were all tensed up in 1908 after a fierce pennant playoff with the Giants. After that famous game, the Cubs had to leave New York and go directly to Detroit to meet the Tigers in the World Series. The Cubs entered the Detroit ball park in a group. They were already in uniform because they had dressed at the hotel. As they came through a side gate down the left-field line,

Schoolboy Rowe, mainstay of Tigers' pitching staff, in 1934 Series.

Cliff Melton, victim of Yankee hitting barrage in the 1937 Series.

the Tigers were still sitting on the bench. Germany Schaefer, Detroit's scrappy third baseman, climbed out of the dugout with a ball in his hand. He fired it with all his strength at the invading enemy. Joe Tinker ran out in front of the bunch, grabbed the ball and fired it back at the Detroit bench. Fortunately the ball crashed against a wall and no one was hurt. The Cubs saved their energy for the field, winning the Series four games to one.

A crowd of some 25,000 was on hand at Fenway Park for the fifth game of the 1918 World Series between the Red Sox and Cubs. The fans sat in amazement at the sight of an empty field. The players were in uniform but were sitting in their respective clubhouses, refusing to play. Earlier, they had gone into a huddle in a strike against the National Commission, baseball's ruling body at the time. The strike was held to protest what they considered insufficient monetary rewards for playing in the Series. With the small crowds that attended this wartime Series, it was apparent that the winning and losing shares would be meager. Particularly so since a new ruling reduced the players' share to 75 percent of the players' pool, with the remainder to be divided among the players of the other first-division clubs.

Impresario Bill Veeck, dynamic head of the World Champion 1948 Cleveland Indians.

Harry Hooper of the Red Sox and Leslie Mann of the Cubs had been appointed as a two-man committee to represent the players. They demanded that the National Commission rescind the new rule, at least for this Series. They demanded a guarantee that the winning players would be paid at least $1,500 per man and the losers $1,000. The players would not leave the clubhouse, they said, until these demands were met.

An emergency meeting was held with the National Commission, consisting of Garry Herrmann and league presidents Ban Johnson of the American and John Heydler of the National. Also present were the owners of the respective clubs, the rival managers, and the mayor of Boston, Honey Fitzgerald. After an hour's debate, the players finally consented to take the field, and the fans were treated to the strange sight of the mayor coming out to home plate with an announcement.

"The players have agreed to play," he announced, "for the sake of the public and the wounded soldiers in the stands."

According to Hooper, each winning Red Sox player received $1,108.45 and each losing Cub got $574. The players gave 10 percent of their shares to war charities.

The 1918 Series wasn't the first time

players' shares had been the center of a controversy. Thirteen years earlier, in the 1905 Giants-Athletics contest, the players on both teams managed to circumvent the newly instituted John T. Brush rules. The rules declared that the winning team was to receive 75 percent of the players' pool, while the losers got the other 25 percent. The 75-25 gap, however, seemed too great to the players, so they secretly agreed to split the winners' and losers' shares down the middle for a 50-50 division of the players' pool. Only Christy Mathewson, Rogers Bresnahan of the Giants and a couple of unidentified Athletics players refused to go along. Bristol Lord, a rookie center fielder with the A's, later divulged the secret agreement.

"I had heard talk about side agreements," he related, "but I didn't know anything about it until the first day of the Series. I was a rookie and in those days rookies didn't ask questions. I was in the dugout that first day when Harry Davis, our first baseman, brought Sammy Strang, a utility outfielder with the Giants, over to meet me.

" 'This is your partner,' Davis said. 'If we win, you'll split your share with him. If the Giants win, he'll split with you.'

"That's how it was. I don't think the arrangement had any effect on the play of anybody in the Series. Both teams wanted to win, and we all gave it our best."

As it turned out, the A's, although they lost the Series, fared better at the pay window than the victorious Giants. The Giants received $1,142 apiece, while each member of the A's got $370. Under the agreement, each Giant paid his partner $386 to arrange an even split, which amounted to $756. After the Series, Connie Mack talked Ben Shibe, owner of the A's, into throwing the club's share of the Series receipts into the players' pot. Each Philadelphia player received $500 from this source, to increase his total take to $1,256.

Fred Clarke, manager of the Pirates, emerged from the 1909 Series as something of a hero for his decision to pitch Babe Adams, a rookie, in the opening game against the Tigers. Adams went on to pitch three games, and he won them all to give the Pirates the title. What was unknown at the time was that the suggestion to pitch Adams in the opener was made by John Heydler, secretary of the National League, acting as temporary league president because of the illness of Harry Pulliam.

While in Washington on business, Heydler attended a baseball game. He saw Dolly Gray of the Senators hypnotize the slugging Tigers, and he noticed a striking similarity between Gray and young Adams. Looking up Clarke on the eve of the first game, Heydler said, "I understand Camnitz [Howard Camnitz, Pittsburgh pitching ace] is out. I don't know who you have in mind to pitch tomorrow, but I saw Dolly Gray make the Tigers throw their bats away. Now Gray pitches like Adams does. You could do worse than start Adams tomorrow."

Babe Ruth is undoubtedly the greatest of all World Series standouts. He played in ten World Series and only fared poorly in one. That was the 1922 clash with the Giants. Babe couldn't seem to do anything right in that Series, and when it was over he had only a .118 average to show for it. The Giants swept that Series, and one of the victories, the first, went to Rosy Ryan in relief of Artie Nehf.

Came the ninth inning, the Yankees were trailing 3-2. But they had two runners on base with nobody out and the Babe was at bat. A hit would probably have meant a Yankees victory. So with the count two balls and one strike, John McGraw, the Giants' manager, bustled out of the dugout for a conference with catcher Hank Gowdy. Ryan, on the mound, waited anxiously while McGraw issued his instructions.

"You tell Ryan to throw the slowest ball he's got," McGraw commanded. "And don't let him get it anywhere near the plate. The big baboon will swing at anything. If Rosy gets it even close, I'll fine him a thousand dollars."

Gowdy transmitted the order to the pitcher. Ryan wound up, reared back like he was going to throw a fastball, but the ball fluttered toward home

Rosy Bill Ryan, who fanned Babe Ruth at a crucial point in the 1922 Series.

like a lazy butterfly. It actually hit the plate. Ruth, straining and eager, swung with every ounce of energy and almost threw himself off his feet as he struck out.

The Athletics defeated the Giants four games to two in the 1911 Series. The Giants stayed alive by winning the fifth game in extra innings. Larry Doyle opened the bottom of the tenth with a double, his fourth hit. With one out, Fred Merkle hit a long fly to Danny Murphy, and Doyle crossed the plate with the winning run, sliding in under Murphy's throw to the plate. Doyle missed the plate with his falling-away slide but Jack Lapp, the A's' catcher, did not notice it and walked off the field, along with the other players. Bill Klem, home-plate umpire, had noticed the omission, however, and stood at the plate without rendering a decision. After a while, with no appeal forthcoming, he strode off the field. That night, Klem confided to friends that had Lapp or any other player on the A's even nudged Doyle with the ball either at the plate or in the dugout, he would have declared Doyle out.

In the seventh inning of the third game in the 1923 Series between the Giants and Yankees, Casey Stengel hit a home run into the right-field stands at Yankee Stadium to give the Giants a 1-0 victory. Earlier, the Yankees bench had been riding Stengel, alluding to his "lucky" game-winning home run in the first game. In circling the bases, Casey saluted the Yankees and couldn't refrain from thumbing his nose at the players. After the game, Colonel Jake Ruppert, owner of the Yankees, approached Judge Landis and demanded that the Commissioner discipline Casey for such an ungentlemanly act.

Landis refused. "When a man hits a home run in a World Series game," the judge said, "he should be permitted some exuberance—particularly when his name is Casey Stengel."

Few owners could match Bill Veeck when it came to serving as a host to the press during World Series time. In 1949, he not only maintained a free restaurant and bar for 400 scribes, but added a new touch. Wives and sweethearts were invited to a continuous private party in Cleveland's Hollenden Hotel. Cabaret entertainers performed nightly, and a swing band provided dance music. In 1959, his White Sox lost to the Dodgers in six games. Riding back to the hotel after the sixth-game loss, he confided to a newspaperman who was accompanying him that if the Series had gone to the seventh game, he was going to have every reporter served breakfast in bed. Then he was going to give each man a dozen roses. He had a bouquet of flowers with him as he alighted from the cab in front of the hotel. A woman passed and Veeck handed her the flowers. She reached into her purse and handed him a dime. ◇

World Series Goats

BY JOSEPH L. REICHLER

Mickey Cochrane, victimized by
Pepper Martin's daring base-running
in the 1931 Series.

THERE ARE DARK SHADOWS spaced here and there among the bright lights of the World Series—blunders committed by star and sub alike that cost a game or even the Championship itself. With the eyes of the world upon him, an otherwise superb player who makes such a mistake may forevermore be remembered as the goat of a Series, regardless of his past triumphs and accomplishments.

Of all the players on a team, there is probably one whose position renders him more prone to the goat's horns than any other: the catcher. Whether it is because he handles the ball so much and thus has far more opportunities to make mistakes than any other player or whether it is because some mysterious force comes into play, no one knows. But whatever the reason, there seem to have been more World Series goats drawn from the ranks of catchers than from any other position on the field.

Chief Meyers, the New York Giants' big Indian catcher, earned a share of the goat's horns in the 1912 Series against the Boston Red Sox, though, to be fair, that Series is best remembered because of a muffed ball—a heartbreaking mistake that turned a solid, workmanlike Giants outfielder into the number one Goat in World Series history.

Everything, seemingly, that can happen in baseball happened in that Series, which is still generally regarded as one of the greatest ever played. For sustained suspense, for a glorious combination of great and horrible baseball, for sheer helter-skelter thrills, it was in a class by itself. It had everything, including an eleven-inning 6-6 tie which drove a scheduled seven-game Series into eight before it was over. And that eighth game wasn't settled until it went into the most bizarre inning of all time.

The stage was perfectly set for a goat or a hero on that October day in 1912 when the Giants and Red Sox clashed in the newly built Fenway Park. Each team had won three games.

Christy Mathewson, near the end of an illustrious career, was on the mound for the Giants. Hugh Bedient was the Red Sox pitcher. Mathewson had pitched twice without a victory. His first effort was the long second-game deadlock. His second tour on the mound was the loss of a five-hitter to Bedient, who gave three hits to win the fifth game, 2-1. Now the peerless Matty was making a last effort to come up with a victory.

The Giants gave him a 1-0 lead in the third inning on a single by Fred Merkle and a double by Red Murray. But the Red Sox tied it up in the seventh when a rookie named Olaf Henriksen, batting for Bedient, doubled home the tying run. Pitcher Joe Wood, who had already won two games for the Red Sox, was sent in by manager Jack Stahl to finish the contest.

At the end of the ninth, the score stood at 1-1, and for the second time in the Series a game was driven into extra innings. The Giants appeared to have won the game in the tenth when Murray doubled again and raced home on Merkle's single. Now all Matty had to do was hold the Red Sox for one more inning.

Fred Merkle, whose unfortunate blunder lost the 1908 pennant for the Giants.

The first batter was Clyde Engle, pinch-hitting for Wood. He lifted a lazy fly to left center, and Fred Snodgrass, jogging along easily, got under the ball. To the astonishment of the crowd, he allowed it to dribble through his fingers. Engle reached second base, and the excitement, which had built steadily all afternoon, became madness. Harry Hooper drove a terrific liner to center, and Snodgrass, striving to redeem his muff, made one of the most sensational catches of the Series. Matty then lost his fine control long enough to walk Steve Yerkes.

Tris Speaker, one of baseball's best hitters, strode to bat. Mathewson served him a slow, twisting fadeaway, and Speaker popped a little foul, halfway between the plate and first base. Either Chief Meyers or Fred Merkle could have caught it easily. But both stopped running for the pop-up, each thinking the other would make the catch, and the ball dropped between them. Mathewson, who could have caught the ball himself, kept shouting, "Meyers! Meyers! Take it!" Either Meyers didn't hear, or he expected Merkle to take it. In any event, Meyers didn't, and Speaker, given another chance, laced a single to right to drive Engle in with the tying run. Yerkes raced to third on the hit, and after Duffy Lewis was purposely walked, loading the bases, Larry Gardner drove Yerkes home with a long sacrifice fly to end the struggle and the Series.

"It was one of the shocks of my life when Snodgrass dropped the ball," Giants manager John John J. McGraw was to say later. "I thought surely Fred had it. When I saw the ball fall to the ground, I knew that this was going to cost us the game.

"The real sufferer was poor Matty. He was on top of his stride that day, but the boys weren't giving him any support. That was a tough game for Matty to drop. But I don't blame Snodgrass. It's something that's likely to happen to any outfielder now and then. There is no excuse, however, for not catching Speaker's ball."

Mask of Defeat

Hank Gowdy, who was acclaimed as something of a folk hero when he became the first major-leaguer to volunteer in World War I, was still bathing in the glory of his new status as a big-league regular when the Miracle Braves of Boston upset Connie Mack's seemingly invincible Philadelphia Athletics in the 1914 World Series. Gowdy, a .243 hitter during the regular season, really had himself a ball in the October extravaganza. The Athletics' pitchers simply couldn't get him out. He batted a rousing .543 for the Series, a mark that stood for fourteen years until Babe Ruth raised it to .625 in the Series of 1928.

Ten years later, though, the pendulum took a full swing in the opposite direction. The Giants were in the seventh and final game of the 1924 World Series with the Washington Senators. The

Roger Peckinpaugh committed a record eight errors in the 1925 Series.

game was tied 3-3 in the twelfth inning. The great Walter Johnson, denied a victory in two previous starts, was trying again, this time in relief. Catching for the Giants was the veteran Hank Gowdy, now called "Old Goldenrod."

After the Giants had failed to score in their half, Jack Bentley retired Ralph Miller for the first out, bringing up Muddy Ruel, the Washington catcher. Ruel, overworked from catching pratically every day, had had a poor Series at the plate, with only one hit for the seven games. He again looked to be an easy out when he raised an ordinary foul behind the plate.

Gowdy shook off his mask and started after it. But on the way, he stepped into his own discarded mask. He was still frantically trying to shake it off his foot when the ball dropped several feet from him.

"I've been in baseball thirty years and that's the first time I ever saw a catcher step into his own mask," said Christy Mathewson, then president of the Boston Braves. "Everything bad seems to happen to Giant teams in the World Series."

Gowdy's lapse proved to be a wonderful break for Washington. Ruel, his batting life spared, made the most of it by stoking a double to left. Earl McNeely hit a grounder that struck a pebble and bounded over third baseman Freddie Lindstrom's head, and Ruel came in with the run that won the

Hank Gowdy, a hero in 1914, was a goat in 1924 when he tripped over own mask reaching for a foul popup.

Fred Snodgrass, redeemed himself in the 1912 Series.

Series. Poor Old Goldenrod was elected the Goat of the 1924 Series. A hero in one Series, a goat in another.

Two Men Named Mickey

Seven years later, Philadelphia Athletics catcher Mickey Cochrane, destined to be voted into baseball's Hall of Fame, was recognized as the goat when the Cardinals' Pepper Martin, the "Wild Horse of the Osage," ran wild in the 1931 World Series. Martin batted an even .500 in the seven games, stole five bases and, in one instance, taunted Cochrane with "Here I go, Mickey!" Still Cochrane was not able to throw him out. Pepper's effrontery on the baselines caused Mickey so much concern that he batted only .180. Yes, the Cardinals copped the Series from the A's. At the annual dinner that winter, the New York writers teased Cochrane in song which went something like this:

> Watch out, Mickey, here comes Pepper Martin.
> If you don't watch out, he'll steal your jock for sartin....

Cochrane always contended he was not to blame. "How can you throw someone out who has such a long lead?" he asked. "He was almost on the base before I let go the throw."

The most famous of all World Series catching flubs was Mickey Owen's fatal passed ball in the first Yankees-Dodgers World Series in 1941. The Dodgers, in their first Series since 1920, were looking for their first World Championship in three tries. The Yankees, seasoned veterans of the October classics, took two of the first three games. But the Dodgers apparently had the Series tied up when they went into the ninth inning of the fourth game leading 4-3.

Hugh Casey was pitching in relief, the fourth Dodger hurler to appear that afternoon. It appeared he had the situation well in hand when he retired Johnny Sturm and Red Rolfe on easy grounders. Nobody on, only Tommy Henrich left. Henrich was a tough hitter, but he had gone hitless all afternoon. Casey worked carefully to three and two. Then he threw what has been described variously as a low, sharp-breaking curve and as a well-loaded spitball. Behind the plate was Mickey Owen, who had stood up well in his first year with the Dodgers as their number one catcher after coming from St. Louis. Owen had played in 128 games, had permitted two passed balls and had committed three errors.

Casey's pitch fooled Henrich completely. The batter swung and missed. Strike three! The Dodgers were leaping out of the dugout in jubilation. The game was over.

But wait. Henrich wasn't the only one fooled. The pitch, low and away, tore through Owen's mitt and careened sharply to the right. Henrich turned toward the dugout, then, hearing the shouts from his teammates, whirled around and started for first. He made it without drawing a throw.

Phil Rizzuto, a key figure in the Yankee triumph, recalls the event vividly. "I was in the dugout holding a lot of fellas' gloves—DiMag, Henrich, Keller, my own. We didn't want to lose any of them when the game was over. When Henrich swung and missed, we all got up and started toward the runway that led out of the dugout. Some of us were already into it. I know I was.

"Then we heard all that yelling and we jumped back. There was Tommy running down to first base. Owen was chasing the ball over near his own dugout. By the time he got it, Tommy was on first and there was no play."

What happened then will always remain a nightmare to the Dodgers and their followers. DiMaggio lined a single to left, with Henrich going to second. Then Keller belted a double high against the screening on top of the right-field fence. It was good for two runs. Casey, still in there, walked Bill Dickey. Then Joe Gordon followed with a two-bagger over Jimmy Wasdell's head for two more runs. In the Dodger ninth, Yankee pitcher Johnny Murphy got the stunned Brooklyn out right in order.

Owen still remembers the play as if it had occurred yesterday. "It was all my fault," he acknowledged.

"It was a great breaking curve and I should have had it. It got away from me, and by the time I got hold of it near the corner of the dugout, I couldn't have thrown anyone out at first."

Owen still marvels that Leo Durocher, the Dodger manager, did not go out to talk to Casey after that fateful pitch. "It was like a punch on the chin," said Owen. "You're stunned. You don't react. I should have gone out to the mound and stalled around a little. It was more my fault than Leo's."

In his autobiography, Durocher stated it was the only time in his life that he was too stunned to think. The next day the Yankees put the Dodgers out of their misery, 3-1.

Saved by a Win

Yogi Berra, the hero of numerous World Series, would have been the goat of the 1947 Series had the Dodgers not lost to the Yankees, four games to three. Yogi, in his first full season with the Yankees, was the number one catcher, ranking over Sherman Lollar and Aaron Robinson. But after the fourth game, Yogi had to be yanked from behind the plate. He simply couldn't cope with the Dodger speed boys.

Led by Jackie Robinson and Pee Wee Reese, the Dodgers stole seven bases against Yogi in the first four games, which wound up with two victories each for the Dodgers and the Yankees. Robinson caught the fifth game, won by the Yankees, 2-1. One of the Dodgers' three triumphs was over Bill Bevens, who would have been rewarded with a no-hitter had Berra been able to throw out a stealing Al Gionfriddo in the ninth. He didn't, and minutes later Cookie Lavagetto played the hero's role with his dramatic game-winning double.

Collision at Home

The 1975 World Series, generally regarded as one of the greatest ever to be played, was marked by brilliant base running, superlative fielding, peerless pitching, explosive hitting and last-ditch rallies that had the fans on the edge of their seats from the first game to the last.

But with all the artistic attributes, there was also controversy. The loudest shrieks of anguish came in the third game after plate umpire Larry Barnett failed to rule interference against Cincinnati pinch hitter Ed Armbruster. Armbruster and Red Sox catcher Carlton Fisk collided outside the batter's box, and Fisk's throw to second sailed into center field, setting up the game-winning situation for the Reds.

After being down by four runs in the third game, Boston had tied the score with a home run in the ninth inning to force the Reds into overtime. Boston had failed to score in the tenth, but went into the last of the inning with great expectations. Up first was Cesar Geronimo, who sent a soft single to

Mickey Owen chasing the ball after his classic muff of a third strike on Tommy Henrich in 1941.

center. next at bat was Armbruster. He dropped a bunt in front of home plate. It was not a good bunt, and Armbruster was slow to leave the box.

Fisk reached for the ball, but found the batter in his direct line of fire. He pushed Armbruster off with his gloved hand and fired to second in plenty of time. But because of the collision, the ball ended up in center field and the runners advanced to second and third.

What started out as an easy play put the Red Sox in trouble from which they could not extricate themselves. Joe Morgan promptly singled to give the Reds a 2-1 edge in victories. Cincinnati eventually emerged the winners in seven games.

Catchers Aren't Alone

Of course, catchers don't hold a monopoly on World Series whoppers. Burleigh Grimes, a pitcher, has two World Series firsts to his credit. He gave up the first grand-slam homer, and he also threw the first home-run ball to a rival pitcher—both in the same game. With the bases loaded in the first inning of the fifth game between Brooklyn and Cleveland in the 1920 Series, Elmer Smith hit a Grimes pitch into the stands for a grand-slam. Then, in the third, with two men on base, Grimes served a home run to Jim Bagby, a good hitting pitcher.

In the sixth inning of that same game, Grime's successor, Clarence Mitchell, came up with two on base. He drove a hard liner that appeared headed for center field, but Bill Wambsganss, the Indians' second baseman, speared the ball and turned it into an unassisted triple play, the only one

Hack Wilson taking a mighty swing in the 1929 Series.

of its kind in World Series history. To make the situation even more deplorable from Mitchell's point of view, the luckless pitcher hit into a double play his next at-bat. He had stroked into five outs in just two at-bats.

Roger Peckinpaugh was voted the American League's Most Valuable Player in 1925. That fall the Washington shortstop gained the goat's horns against the Pittsburgh Pirates by committing a record number of eight errors in the seven-game Series won by the Pirates. He could just as well have been the hero, although he had made seven errors before his final and decisive blunder. In the seventh game, with the Series tied at

three victories apiece, Peckinpaugh smashed a home run in the top of the eighth to give the Senators a 7-6 led behind Walter Johnson. It seemed as if Peck were going to redeem himself for his seven errors. But it wasn't to be.

With two out in the bottom of the eighth, both Earl Smith and Carson Bigbee doubled, tying the game 7-7. Eddie Moore walked, but the inning appeared to be over when Max Carey raised a pop-up to Peckinpaugh. But then Peck made his eighth error—he dropped the ball. That loaded the bases, making it possible for a double by Kiki Cuyler to bring in the winning runs.

In fairness to Peckinpaugh, the entire Series

was played in wet and miserable weather. Most of his errors were the result of low throws.

"The ball was wet and the ground was muddy," Peckinpaugh recalled. "Instead of taking the normal bounce, which Joe Judge [first baseman] could have handled with his eyes closed, those low throws skidded away from him.

"The eighth error was the most embarrassing. It's still hard to believe it really happened. It was a pop fly near the foul line, and I moved over to make the routine catch I had made hundreds of times. When I felt the ball bounce off my glove, I was the most surprised person in the world. I guess I was pressing by them. I must have tried to close my fist too soon."

Bedazzled!

How can a player bat .471 in a World Series and still be the goat? That's what happened to Hack "Sunny Boy" Wilson. Hack's failure to catch two fly balls in the outfield paved the way for a record ten-run inning that enabled the Athletics to overcome an 8-0 deficit and defeat the Cubs 10-8 in the fourth game of the 1929 World Series.

The A's had won the first two games. But the Cubs had come back to win the third and appeared to be back in the Series the next day when they shelled three Philadelphia pitchers to take what seemed like an insurmountable 8-0 lead after six and a half innings. The Cubs' Charlie Root had permitted the A's only three hits when Al Simmons opened the seventh with a home run, to polite but restrained applause. Philly manager Connie Mack was preparing to take his regulars out to give his substitutes a chance to play in a World Series, but Jimmy Foxx followed with a single, and in rapid succession came three more by Bing Miller, Jimmy Dykes and Joe Boley. Now the A's had three runs. Miller's hit was a short fly to center that Wilson lost in the sun, but nobody thought much of it at the time.

George Burns, a pinch hitter, popped out, but Max Bishop smacked another single for the A's fourth run, and the fans began to get excited as Art Nehf replaced Root on the mound. What happened next turned the Philadelphia fans into wild-eyed maniacs. Mule Haas sent a fly to center, a well-hit drive but apparently a routine out. Wilson came after the ball, but he was suddenly blinded by the sun. As he ducked away, the ball skidded on into the deepest corner of the field, and Haas rounded the bases for an inside-the-park home run. The Cubs were still leading by a run, but a walk to Mickey Cochrane and singles by Simmons and Foxx tied the score at 8-8. Jimmy Dykes's double drove in two more runs for Philadelphia, and the Cubs were crushed. The A's won again the next day to wrap up the Series.

Hack Wilson led all players on both teams

with his .471 average and handled more flies than any other player in the Series. But he forever carried the stigma of the goat of the Series. "I should have had that ball, sun or no sun," Wilson said afterward. "The sun shining over the roof of the Shibe Park stands from in back of home plate was blinding. It was so bad that Art Nehf was having a hard time catching Zach Taylor's throws back to the pitcher's box. I couldn't see the ball at all after it left Haas bat until it was almost to the ground. I started after it, but it was too late. Remember, that didn't lose the game. It helped, but we were still ahead even after it happened."

The sun, in all its brightness, also was responsible for another National League center fielder's goat's horns. In the second game of the 1966 World Series between Baltimore and Los Angeles, Willie Davis, the Dodgers' superb outfielder, committed three errors on two successive plays. These miscues helped the Orioles to a four-game sweep over the Dodgers.

Davis' stab at immortality came in the fifth inning behind Sandy Koufax, who had a scoreless duel going on with Jim Palmer. With one out and a man on, Paul Blair hit an easy pop fly toward Davis, who lost it in the sun, which put runners on second and third. Andy Etchebarren then hit a fly to center, and Davis reached for it. But he dropped the ball and, in his embarrassment, threw it past third base for another error as two runs scored and Etchebarren reached third. The game wound up 6-0 in Baltimore's favor.

Willie didn't try to alibi. "The ball hit by Blair got in a certain spot in the sun coming down and I couldn't see it," he said. "It went into my glove and dropped out as I stabbed at it. The second time, I waved my arms to show I had lost the ball, but I was closest to it and I made a stab for the ball. I guess I made the throwing error after dropping the ball because I was mad at myself and embarrassed. That was the worst thing that ever happened to me."

Curt Flood didn't even have a sun to blame for his blunder that cost the Cardinals a second straight World Series Triumph. Flood's monumental misjudgment of a fly ball took place in the seventh inning of the seventh game in the 1968 World Series between St. Louis and Detroit. Until then, it was a scoreless battle between Cardinal Bob Gibson and Tiger Mickey Lolich.

With two on and two out for Detroit, Jim Northrup hit a high fly to center. Flood, the best defensive center fielder in baseball, misjudged it, and it sailed over his head for a double, bringing in two runs. That was the turning point, the Tigers winning the game 4-1 and with it the Series. It was Lolich's third victory of the Series. The loss snapped a string of seven straight World Series triumphs for Gibson. ◇

Rhubarbs and Ejections

BY JOSEPH L. REICHLER

WITH THE STAKES SO HIGH and the pressure so intense, you'd think that the World Series would average more flared tempers and more physical confrontations per inning than any regular-season game. But, as the statistics prove, that's not the case. In fact, it's just the reverse.

The truth is, ballplayers behave differently during a World Series than they do during the regular season. They're much more docile, much more acquiescent and much more timid about questioning the umpires' judgment or challenging the opposition. Over the years there have been plenty of rhubarbs, but only about a dozen players have been ejected from a Series game for verbal or physical abuse or other forms of misconduct.

This unusually low number of disciplinary actions is due, in part, to the restraint of the players. But it is also the result of a deliberately lenient policy on the part of baseball's powers that be. The last four commissioners have instructed Series umpires to do everything they can to smooth over difficult situations, reserving banishment of players or managers as a penalty of last resort.

This policy of leniency is understandable. A player's banishment from a game during the course of a regular season, even if it weakens his team and costs a game, can usually be made up over a 162-game stretch.

But banishment of a player from a World Series game could conceivably cost a team a World Championship. Such could have been the case in the 1935 Detroit-Chicago Series when Woody English, the Cubs' only understudy to Billy Jurges at shortstop, was one of four Chicagoans exiled by umpire George Moriarty in the third game. When the Cubs tied the score in the ninth inning after strategy dictated the removal of Jurges for a pinch hitter during the rally, the team was forced to play the critical overtime innings with a third baseman, Stan Hack, at shortstop for the first time in his career. The Tigers won that game, 6-5, and the Series, four games to two.

Yet sometimes player restraint and official leniency aren't enough. Rhubarbs are an intrinsic part of baseball, and even in the World Series some have resulted in the speedy ejection of their various participants. The dubious distinction of being the first person to be thumbed out of a Series game goes to Hughie Jennings, Detroit's famed manager of the early 1900s.

It happened during the second game of the 1907 Series between the Tigers and Cubs in Chicago. The first game, a hard-fought twelve-inning tie, had only served to make the players more tense. Everyone was on edge as the second game started out as bitterly as the first. With the score tied at 1-1 in the third inning, Germany Schaefer, Detroit second baseman, was cut down trying to steal. It was a close play, and Jennings, coaching at third, charged out to umpire Hank O'Day, arguing furiously. O'Day merely waved Jennings back to his position and turned his back. Jennings started back but stopped near third base and started tearing up the grass. O'Day still ignored him. Incensed at what he considered a snub, Jennings began berating the umpire. When he failed to heed repeated warnings to cease and desist, Jennings was finally ordered off the field. Hughie didn't want to go at first, but he finally saw the light when O'Day threatened to hit him with a stiff fine in addition to the banishment.

Probably the roughest of all World Series was the riotous meeting of the Tigers and Pittsburgh pirates in 1909. It seemed as if there was an argument every inning, and George Moriarty, the pugnacious Tigers third baseman, was in the middle of almost every dispute. (Twenty-six years later, Moriarty would again be a stormy figure in a World Series, as an umpire.) In the seven games, eight players were injured, mainly by well-aimed spikes. Three of the combatants were forced out of action by their injuries, not through an umpire's judgment.

The first of three games was without casualty, though the umpire-baiting was so fierce that the National Commission, baseball's ruling body at the time, fined Fred Clarke, the Pirates' manager, and five other warriors a then imposing total of $175.

In the fourth game, though, things really got hot. John Miller, Pittsburgh second baseman, touched off a mob scene. Called out on strikes, he had to be restrained by teammates from taking a poke at umpire Bill Klem. Honus Wagner, the good-natured shortstop wizard of the Pirates, didn't go that far, but he did wave his hands contemptuously in Klem's face after a similar call. It didn't smooth his feelings an inning later when Ty Cobb slashed him across the bridge of the nose with his spikes while sliding viciously into second base. Honus retaliated by smashing the ball on top of Ty's skull.

Trouble broke out again when Miller was cut at second base by Tommy Jones's high-flying spikes. The Pittsburgh infielder, however, made only a feeble gesture at retaliation. Fifth-game out-

Woody English

bursts were strictly vocal, but the boys clashed again physically in the ninth inning of the sixth game. The Pirates, trailing 5-3, put runners on first and third. Chief Wilson bunted. Catcher Charley Schmidt fielded the dribbler, but his throw to first was wide. Tommy Jones, Detroit's first baseman, reached out to get the ball, but Wilson barged into him, flattening him like a steamroller. Jones fell as if hit by lightning and was carried off the field unconscious.

A run was scored in the course of the collision. Bill Abstein reached third, and Wilson, of course, was safe at first. Hughie Jennings called Sam Crawford in from right field to take over at first base. On the very next pitch, Crawford grabbed George Gibson's bounder and threw to the plate to head off Abstein. Schmidt, the catcher, blocked the plate sufficiently to put the tag on Abstein, but not before the runner had inflicted a spike gash on one of his legs.

There were still runners on first and second, and the two attempted a double steal. Wilson was out at third, but he too demonstrated his spike-wielding skill by doing a neat carving job on Moriarty's leg. The terrible-tempered Tigers third baseman got even the next afternoon. Bobby Byrne led off the final game for the Pirates by get-

George Moriarty

ting plunked with one of Wild Bill Donovan's errant serves, and was sacrificed to second. With Wagner at bat, Byrne lit out for third. He might have made it if Moriarty had not completely blocked the bag. Byrne crashed into him like a runaway locomotive. Moriarty was badly shaken up, but they had to carry Byrne off the field with a sprained left ankle. The mayhem didn't end there. In the next inning, Abstein was on second when Wilson bunted. Schmidt pounced on the ball and threw to Moriarty. The ball hit the third baseman's glove at the same time that Abstein's spikes ripped into his legs. Moriarty insisted on staying in the game, but he had to yield to a pinch runner after smashing a double in the bottom of the second inning. In spite of this mayhem, there were no ejections. And one might easily argue that the National Commission was perhaps **too** lenient in its anti-ejection policy.

Things were different, though, the following year when the Peerless Leader of the Cubs, became the first player to be expelled from a World Series game. Again Chicago was the scene. This time it was the third game. The Athletics, led by Connie Mack, had won the first two games, played at Philadelphia. Now, on home soil, the Cubs were striving to get back into the running. The score was tied 3-3. Harry McIntire, a side-arm spitballer, was

pitching for the Cubs. He retired the first batter, but the next four reached base. Eddie Collins singled, Frank Baker tripled, Harry David was hit by a pitched ball and Danny Murphy hammered a pitch over the right-field screen.

Umpire Tommy Connolly was assigned to the right-field foul line in the three-umpire system instituted that year. Murphy smashed a home run. Frank Chance, Chicago's player-manager, raced out from his first-base position and argued long and loud that the drive had gone foul. Several of his players joined in the debate. Chance became so abusive that Connolly finally lost patience and ordered him off the field. Stunned, Chance left without offering much resistance. Tom Needham, second-string Cubs catcher, was evicted an inning later. The two ejections prompted president Charles W. Murphy of the Cubs to issue the following statement: "I think the umpires ought to realize that players, especially managers, are under a greater strain in a Series like this than at other times and should not be so hasty in giving eviction notices."

In 1913, Art Fletcher, then a two-fisted shortstop with the Giants, was slapped with a $100 fine by the National Commission for "ungentlemanly remarks" to umpire Tommy Connolly during a game between New York and Philadelphia. Aggressive, barb-tongued Fletcher, who later became a manager with the Phillies, then a coach with the Yankees, also was a storm center in the 1917 Series between the Giants and White Sox. Several fist fights were narrowly averted by the umpires in that hotly contested Series, and Fletcher even challenged manager Clarence "Pants" Rowland of the White Sox to a bare-knuckle exchange. Rowland shrugged off the dare. In the sixth game, the clincher for the White Sox, Fletcher threw a savage block into Buck Weaver, trying to catch him off base. The players flew at each other, but umpire Cy Rigler separated them before any damaging blows were struck.

In the 1918 World Series between the Boston Red Sox and Chicago Cubs, Heinie Wagner, Red Sox coach and later the club's manager, got into a heated argument with "Hippo" Vaughn, the Cubs' husky pitcher, during the third game. Wagner became so incensed at something Vaughn yelled from the bench that he rushed into the Cubs' dugout bent on manhandling the oversized pitcher. Cubs players blocked his path, and by the time a group of Red Sox players arrived to assist their beleaguered coach, Wagner was a gory mess. The embattled coach, his baseball uniform torn to shreds, accused the Cubs' players of knocking him down and kicking him while he was flat on his back. Curiously, this particularly violent rhubarb elicited no disciplinary action from the umpires.

Umpire Tommy Connally imposed penalty on Giant shortstop Art Fletcher in 1913 Series.

Cy Rigler was the umpire again in the 1919 World Series, and his decision resulted in the ejection of White Sox catcher Ray Schalk. Looking back, it is likely that the peppery little receiver was angrier at his teammates, whom he suspected of throwing the Series to the Cincinnati Reds, than at Rigler. Schalk became involved in a dispute with Rigler over a play at the plate in the fifth game. Cincinnati was ahead, three games to one, and had just broken a scoreless game with a run when Edd Roush hit a long fly to center with two on base. Happy Felsch, the White Sox center fielder, got his hands on the ball but couldn't hold it, so Roush was credited with a three-base hit.

One run had already crossed the plate when Eddie Collins relayed Felsch's throw to Schalk, who thought he had the ball on Heinie Groh in time as he slid across the plate. Rigler called the runner safe. Schalk jumped up angrily and, hopping up and down, argued vociferously with Rigler. The arbiter patiently accepted the catcher's abuse, but his calmness deserted him when Schalk took a swipe at him with his mitt hand. The only damage done to Rigler was to his disposition, but the day was over as far as Schalk was concerned. He was replaced by Byrd Lynn.

When Judge Kenesaw Mountain Landis became Commissioner of Baseball, he ordered umpires to refrain from banishing players except when absolutely necessary. He felt it wasn't fair to

the fans who paid to see the stars, or to the teams who would be punished unduly in a short Series. To prevent such extreme hardships on the teams, players who normally would be banished during the regular season were punished merely with fines in the World Series.

This was the case with Earl Smith, the New York Giants' catcher, in the 1921 World Series with the New York Yankees. Smith engaged in a running feud with plate umpire George Moriarty—yes, the same Moriarty—that finally exploded when Moriarty called Bob Meusel safe in a clean steal of home. Smith first had to be restrained from attacking Moriarty, then from taking a punch at Meusel, who couldn't resist needling the verbose Giants catcher.

Smith remained in the game, but he was fined $200 by Judge Landis for "irregularities behind the plate," a charge the Commissioner didn't see fit to elaborate on. This was the first fine imposed on a player since the National Commissioner penalized Fletcher $100 for "ungentlemanly remarks" to Umpire Tommy Connolly in 1913.

The Giants and Yankees engaged in six interborough World Series—in 1921, 1922, 1923, 1936, 1937, 1951—and most of them were played in a businesslike fashion, with no extracurricular fuss or furor. Yankee players, as a rule, were too intent on winning to become involved in extracurricular activities. There were several, however, who allowed their emotions to get the best of them. In 1921, Babe Ruth became so in-censed at the constant riding he was getting from the opposing bench that he challenged John McGraw, the Giants' manager, to meet him out-side. Once he even invaded the enemy clubhouse to "punch that SOB on the jaw." In 1923, Ross Youngs, the great Giants right fielder, took out Aaron Ward with a rolling block to break up a dou-ble play, and the aggrieved . Yankee second baseman made threatening gestures at the base runner. The game was delayed several minutes while the two players jawed at each other, but no blows were struck.

There was so much jockeying going on be-tween the Cubs and Athletics in the 1929 World Series that Judge Landis warned both Joe McCar-thy and Connie Mack, the rival managers, to curb their squads or else be subject to a fine. The A's' chief target was Hack Wilson, the Cubs' powerful center fielder. Wilson was having a field day at bat in the Series, but the A's got the last laugh. Hack lost Mule Haas's drive for an inside-the-park homer and blamed his mistake on the sun. Thereafter, whenever Wilson came to bat, the A's went into song. The title of their ditty, of course, was "Sonny Boy"!

There was as much, maybe more, bench jockeying in the 1932 Series between the Cubs and Yankees. The issue centered around Mark Koenig, whom the Cubs had picked up from the Yankees in mid-season. Chicago couldn't have won the pen-nant without him, but the players voted him only half a share.

The ringleader in the Yankees' jockey chorus was Babe Ruth. "You cheap bums," was the mildest of Ruth's taunts. The Cubs, inflamed by Ruth's verbal assault, retaliated in kind. Their ver-biage became more vitriolic after dropping the first two games at Yankee Stadium. Each insult began with "Ya big baboon!" Ruth merely laughed. "What a cheesy dump this is!" he shouted the first time he saw Wrigley Field.

When Ruth came up in the first inning of game three, the Cubs' trainer, referring to Babe's wide girth, called out, "If I had you on my team I'd hitch you to a wagon." The Babe responded by hit-ting a three-run homer. In the fifth, Babe came to bat with a score of 4-4. This time the Chicago bench yelled out, "Big Belly!" Ruth stared mocking-ly at the Cubs' bench, then proceeded to give the Chicago players the choke-up sign—the thumb and finger at the windpipe. After he hit that home run, which some historians say he called, the Babe in rounding third made an exaggerated bow to the Cubs' bench to let them know he was still the star.

Judge Landis' second assessment of a player took place in 1933, when he plastered a fifty-dollar fine on Heinie Manush for taking a swing

Heinie Manush ejected in the 1933 Series.

at umpire Charlie Moran. Washington was playing the New York Giants in the 1933 World Series. Manush, the Senators' top slugger, was not in a par-ticularly good mood as he entered the fourth game with an .091 batting average. The Giants were leading 1-0, and Buddy Myer was on second when Manush smashed a hard shot past Bill Terry at first base. Hughie Critz, the Giants' second baseman, darted to his left for a spectacular stop back in the grass. He then whirled and threw to Carl Hubbell, who had dashed off the mound to take Critz's throw at first base. It was an extremely close play, and Moran called Manush out.

Manush was so certain he had beaten the throw that he simply returned to the bag to wait for Hubbell to return to the mound. He was flab-bergasted when Moran waved him to the bench. Finally the realization came to him. Instead of heading for the dugout, Heinie made a beeline for the umpire, shouting as he ran. When Manush got within range, he lashed out with his left hand. Moran sidestepped but wasn't quick enough, and Heinie's hand brushed his shoulder.

Moran didn't hesitate. Throwing his right thumb in the air in that old familiar gesture, the um-pire indicated in no uncertain terms that Manush was through for the day. Heinie continued to argue, and it took several minutes before order was restored and play was resumed. When the inning ended, Manush went out to his left-field position. Moran waved him off the field, but Manush stood pat. Umpire-in-chief Red Ormsby lent his vocal support to Moran, but Manush refused to budge. The partisans cheered Manush and jeered the arbiters. Ormsby finally motioned Cy Pfirman, the third-base umpire, to go out to left field to reason with Manush. After a brief discussion, Pfirman prevailed upon Manush to leave the premises. When Manush received a loser's share of the World Series cut, he learned he had been fined fifty bucks.

Fifty dollars was also the assessment against Bill Delancey, Cardinals catcher, for abusive language addressed to umpire Brick Owens in the 1934 World Series between St. Louis and Detroit. This was just the entree to the delicious scuffle that took place in the seventh and last game, which resulted in the famous Ducky Medwick fruit and vegetable shower. The Series had been replete with threats, counterthreats and verbal brickbats. Led by Dizzy Dean and Pepper Martin, the Cards rode the Tigers unmercifully. Their special targets were Schoolboy Rowe, the star pitcher, and Hank Greenberg, the slugging first baseman.

In the sixth inning of the final game, Medwick, already the Series hitting star with ten safeties, slashed a three-bagger during a two-run attack on Tommy Bridges, fourth Tigers pitcher. The issue had been decided as far back as the third inning when the Redbirds broke loose against starter Eldon Auker for seven runs, with the incomparable Dizzy Dean setting the Tigers down with monotonous regularity.

Racing into third base on his triple, Medwick slid hard into Marvin Owen as the latter crouched for the throw. The Tigers' third baseman retaliated by stepping on Medwick as Joe lay stretched on the ground. The angered base runner shot up his left foot and jammed it against Owen's shoulder. The two scrambled to their feet and started to square off, but umpire Bill Klem and Cardinals coach Mike Gonzalez stepped between them.

That seemed to settle the incident until the end of the inning when Medwick started out to his position in left field. Detroit fans began bombarding him with overripe fruit, vegetables, lunch boxes, newspapers and even bottles. Medwick retreated to the infield while groundskeepers gathered the debris. Twice Joe attempted to return to his position, only to be greeted by another bombardment. When pleas via the loudspeaker failed to halt the deluge, the umpires asked manager Frankie Frisch to withdraw Medwick from the game so play could be resumed. Frank refused, even though the score by then was Cardinals 9, Tigers 0.

Here Judge Landis took command. Sitting in a box between first and home, Landis had watched the entire proceedings with great interest.

He summoned the three umpires, the rival managers and the two principals. First he talked to Medwick, then he had a few words with Owen. When he was satisfied that he knew the facts, he turned to Medwick. "Get out of the game," he ordered. Then pointing a finger at Owen, he barked, "You stay." Medwick's ejection seemed to satisfy the fans. Medwick was not fined and later Landis explained that he ordered Medwick from the game partly to protect Medwick himself and partly for the safety of other players and spectators

The 1935 classic marked the third straight World Series in which a participant was exiled by an umpire. Only in this Series between the Cubs and Tigers, four principals were ejected. From the start, the Cubs' bench jockeys had been digging their spurs deep into Hank Greenberg, Detroit first baseman. Once in the first game, umpire George Moriarty called time, strode out to the Cubs' bench and ordered them to desist from their tactics. It did little good. Adding fuel to the fire were several close calls by Moriarty which the Cubs thought went unfairly against them. In their gibes, the players didn't neglect to mention that Moriarty was a former player and manager of the Tigers.

Oddly enough, the first man dismissed from the premises in the third game was a Detroit hireling. Tigers coach Del Baker was thumbed out for protesting a decision at third base. Then, in the sixth inning, Phil Cavarretta, the young first baseman, was out stealing on a close play. The caller was Moriarty. Cavarretta protested. Charlie Grimm, the Cubs' manager, took up the player's case and was promptly invited to leave the premises. Grimm obeyed orders, but he continued to direct the club from a passageway behind the dugout, relaying his orders via one of his coaches.

The Cubs continued to snipe away at Moriarty, and in the eighth inning he ordered Tuck Stainback, an outfielder, and Woody English, an infielder, off the bench. The next morning, Landis summoned Grimm, Stainback, English and second baseman Billy Herman, who had been one of the most vociferous hecklers although he had escaped dismissal, as well as the four umpires, to his office. The Cubs accused Moriarty of using foul language in dressing them down in the first game. Moriarty, in turn, charged the Cubs with hurling taunts at Greenberg far beyond the bounds of decency and sportsmanship.

A precedent was set for umpires when Landis fined Moriarty, along with Grimm, Stainback and English. Each was assessed $200. A $200 fine was also meted out to Frankie Crosetti, Yankee shortstop, for shoving umpire Bill Summers during the 1942 Series with the Cardinals. The run-in was precipitated by a slide play at third base. Terry

Baltimore manager Earl Weaver getting the thumb from Shag Crawford in the 1969 Series.

Moore of the Cards slid into third on Enos Slaughter's single to center, and Crosetti thought he had the runner on Joe DiMaggio's throw. Crosetti's punishment didn't end there. Commissioner Landis suspended him for thirty days at the start of the 1943 season. Mickey Livingston, Cubs catcher, also had to cough up $200 after laying hands on umpire Jocko Conlan in the 1945 Series against the Tigers, but he escaped suspension by Commissioner A.B. "Happy" Chandler.

In 1959, Charlie Dressen, then a coach with the Dodgers, was given a premature dismissal from the sixth and final game of the Series with the White Sox by Ed Hurley, an American League umpire with whom Dressen had run-ins when he managed the Washington Senators. Dressen's original target was umpire Frank Dascoli. From the Dodgers' bench, Chuck vocally differed with Dascoli's ball and strike calls on Earl Torgeson, a White Sox pinch hitter, in the fourth inning. Hurley, working at first base, which was near the Dodgers' dugout told Dressen to pipe down, whereupon Dressen

turned his attention to him. Then Hurley gave him the thumb. The thumb from Hurley wasn't all Dressen got. He also got the back of the hand from Commissioner Ford Frick with a $300 fine—$200 for profanity and $100 for "showboating tactics."

Orioles manager Earl Weaver's "crime," which resulted in his expulsion in the fourth game of the 1969 World Series, was, according to umpire Crawford "objecting too strongly on ball and strike calls."

"But I wasn't talking to you," insisted the bereaved Weaver.

"Well, one thing is sure," replied Crawford. "You won't be talking to me any more today."

Yankees manager Billy Martin did a lot of talking to umpire Bill Deegan in the fourth game of the 1976 Series—and Deegan gave back in kind, but allowed Billy to remain. Later, when Martin objected to a call by Bruce Froemming and showed his disgust by tossing a baseball onto the field, Froemming retaliated by tossing Martin off the field. ◇

The Golden Age of World Series Broadcasting

Going...
Going...
Gone!

BY MEL ALLEN

As the longtime voice of the New York Yankees, Mel Allen called the play-by-play over radio and television of more World Series than any other broadcaster. He was an unlikely candidate for a career in either baseball or broadcasting. A native of Alabama, Allen earned an undergraduate degree and a law degree from the University of Alabama. He became interested in broadcasting after handling the public-address system for the Crimson Tide football team.

Allen passed his bar examination in Alabama and headed off to New York for a vacation, stopping in at the CBS offices to get tickets to the popular radio drama Gangbusters. The receptionist heard his voice and assumed he wanted to audition for an announcer's job. She directed him to the audition studio, Mel took the test, and soon his voice was heard across the network. Allen did some news reporting and sportscasting—on one occasion he ad-libbed for fifty-two minutes in a helicopter while the start of a car race below him was delayed.

Allen had never broadcast a baseball game until CBS assigned him to provide commentary at the 1938 World Series between the Yankees and Cubs. The next year Allen became a play-by-play announcer for the Yankees, and the year after that he was named the team's principal announcer. Also, in 1940, Gillette, which then sponsored the Series and which had the right to select the broadcasters, named Allen to report the Cincinnati-Detroit World Series. In the years that followed, he broadcast a total of nineteen World Series. Allen's mellow baritone still has that familiar ring when he speaks of all that transpired beneath and within the broadcast booth.

PROBABLY BECAUSE OF MY LEGAL TRAINING, I always tried to view any game with a certain amount of objectivity. During a World Series, that task became virtually impossible. You think of Willie Mays's eighth-inning catch of the drive by Vic Wertz in the first game of the 1954 Series—the last ever played at the Polo Grounds. Or Al Gionfriddo's snatch of Joe DiMaggio's drive to keep Brooklyn alive in the 1947 Series—the last game ever played in the majors by Gionfriddo. Well, I know I have seen catches just as spectacular in the heat of the regular season pennant races, but in a four-out-of-seven Series everything is magnified.

My former broadcasting partner Phil Rizzuto, for example may have forgiven but still can't forget Eddie Stanky and their run-in at second base in the third game of the '51 Series. Stanky was attempting to steal second, Rizzuto took the throw from Yogi Berra, but had the ball kicked out of his glove by Stanky. In counterpoint to that kind of intensity, I remember Joe DiMaggio advancing to second on an error by Granny Hamner in 1950. As Joe led off second, he leaned over toward the Phillies' shortstop and offered some encouragement. I was told later that DiMaggio had simply said, "Don't let it get you down. It happens to the best of them."

The World Series then was still played on weekday afternoons in the middle of the working day for most Americans. Many businesses across the country were virtually shut down. Even during church services on the High Holidays there might be a fellow with a radio who would run up to the rabbi after the service to give him the score. The broadcast of a World Series could stop almost any kind of activity, which is a great tribute to the sport of baseball.

It also might short-circuit the nervous system of the broadcaster. Logically, you would not think that could happen. But in 1942, for example, I already had been in the booth for three different Series. In another five minutes I was to begin my fourth. I still remember sitting up there above the wooden grandstand of old Sportsman's Park in St. Louis, along with Red Barber and Bill Corum, as the Cardinals prepared to take the field against the Yankees.

I was going to provide the opening remarks for the game. As was my custom in broadcasting any game, I was sitting on the edge of my chair (you just couldn't get into the game as well if you leaned back), the microphone close to my chest, hoping I would be able to announce any play at least a split second before the crowd at the ball park registered its reaction. My audience, I always imagined, was one solitary fan sitting about three or four feet away from me.

This time, however, that crowd of one suddenly turned into a multitude in my mind as I remembered an article I had just read in TIME magazine. It was titled "50 Million Ears," and it began, "In U.S. drugstores, barbershops, lunch wagons, parlors, and pool halls, over 25 million radio listeners will cock their ears next week to listen to three men—the sportscasting trio that broadcasts the World Series." I stumbled along for several minutes on the air before I finally composed myself.

By 1960, NBC was broadcasting to about 100 million viewers over two-hundred television stations, in addition to millions more listening on radio. By then "mike fright" did not bother me, but as I prepared to open the first game of the Pirates-Yankees World Series at Forbes Field I looked over at Bob Prince and realized he was white as a sheet. He had not said a word, it seemed, in two minutes. Now Bob Prince would be the last person overcome by a case of nerves. He was a loosey-goosey kind of guy who was also the dean of practical

Grantland Rice

jokers among broadcasters. He once dove into a swimming pool from a hotel window in St. Louis. Yet here he was practically tongue-tied before his first World Series game.

I tried everything to ease the tension. Finally I said, "Bob, do you know who in our broadcasting team here is the most nervous of all right now?" He said he didn't. "Well, we are now only twenty seconds to air time," I told him, "and can you imagine how long that dadgum peacock [NBC Television's former symbol] has been waiting to spread his wings?" Prince nearly fell off his chair laughing. That broke the tension.

With broadcasters taking their work so seriously, there were bound to be blunders. Mistakes have always been a part of the broadcasting business, of course. The opening for a Yankees announcer in 1939 came when Arch McDonald's assistant, who shall remain unnamed, referred to the sponsor, which was Ivory Soap, as Ovary Soap. He failed to correct himself and was fired.

I made more than my share of errors, but none were so glaring, it seemed, as those that happened in the World Series. In the fourth game of the 1960 Series, Bill Skowron of the Yankees hit a long foul ball, at which point I said, "That brought the crowd to its collective feet." The malapropism was quoted later in the press.

In the seventh game of that Series, Yogi

The First Broadcast

The first time a Series play-by-play was broadcast directly from the scene of action was in 1922.

Charles W. Horn, chief engineer of radio station WJZ, which, though based in Newark, New Jersey, served New York City, persuaded J. C. Williver, vice-president of Western Union, to agree to lease his wires. A direct line was run between the Polo Grounds and WJZ.

Grantland Rice, the nationally known sportswriter of the NEW YORK TRIBUNE, was the play-by-play announcer in that first broadcast. The TRIBUNE splashed stories of the event all over its pages for four days prior to the Series opener.

Jack Binns, another TRI-BUNE writer, predicted, "Rice will talk to the greatest audience ever assembled to listen to one man, as it is expected that at least a million and a half people will hear his voice."

Raymond F. Guy, an engineer at WJZ, shared the announcing with Rice. Arthur Nehf of the New York Giants dueled with the Yankees' Joe Bush in the October 4th opener with the huge radio audience listening in. The Giants rallied for three runs into the eighth to win 3-2. Wilfred Ryan came in for Nehf and picked up the win. Casey Stengel played center field for the Giants and had one single in four trips.

The broadcast stirred up a great deal of interest. Retail radio stores within range set up sidewalk speakers, filling the streets with Rice's play-by-play. People as far away as Bridgeport, Connecticut, and Southampton, Long Island, picked up the broadcast.

Twice as many listeners tuned in for the second game, an estimated three million. Rice was again behind the mike. The game ended tied at 3-3. Chief Umpire George Hildebrand called the game at the end of ten innings because he feared that darkness was imminent. When it didn't get dark for another half hour, the fans raised a fuss, charging that the game had been called to extend the Series so that another game's receipts could be collected. To dispel these suspicions, the Commissioner ordered that the game's receipts, amounting to $120,000, be turned over to charity.

The Giants won the next three games to capture the Series. To this day there is no record of any radio coverage of the last two games.

When the 1923 Series rolled around, station WEAF of New York carried the full six games.

Red Barber

Berra lifted a long shot down the right-field foul line at Forbes Field. Again, I was trying to anticipate the action and call the play before the television audience could hear the reaction of the Pittsburgh crowd. If I had thought that the shot was going to stay fair, I would have been all right. I had developed the phrasing of "that ball is going, going, gone" as a means of anticipating the play while still giving me an escape in case the ball did not go out of the park. This time, however, I stated flatly that the ball was foul. By the time the words were out, Berra had broken into his home-run trot and the Yankees suddenly had the lead in the game.

My error was magnified later in SPORTS IL-LUSTRATED, which called my boner the biggest "since Clem McCarthy's historic miscall of the 1947 Kentucky Derby." This time I had the last laugh: That was **SI's** boner; Clem McCarthy's was in the 1947 Preakness.

In the early days of television broadcasting (the first televised Series was in 1947), the men behind the microphone had to be especially alert. Television productions then were not nearly as sophisticated as they are now; NBC used only three cameras to televise that Series between the Dodgers and Yankees. Moreover, the game of the week was not yet being aired. The cameramen and directors had to get their training at the World Series or the All-Star game.

Broadcasters functioned then almost as directors do now, alerting the floor manager up in the booth to aspects of the game that deserved coverage on camera. We used to debate just how much we should try to show and tell the viewer at home. Some subscribed to the principle that you shouldn't mention anything that the fan couldn't see on the screen, and that that was all the fan needed to see. I always maintained that what was shown on the television picture tube was only a small portion of what you would see if you were an astute fan actually at the ball park.

In the sixth inning of the seventh game of the 1955 World Series, for example, I noticed that Sandy Amoros, the Dodgers' left fielder, was playing farther toward center field than he normally did for Yogi Berra. I told the director to put the camera on Amoros, and pointed out on the air that the left-field line was open. Sure enough, Yogi hit the next pitch down the line in left, and Amoros made the great catch that was the defensive play of that Series.

Part of my preparation for a World Series included reading the scouting reports of the other team. These reports were provided by the Yankees. Over the years I had built enough trust with the Yankees that they knew they could turn over the scouting reports without fear of the information getting back to the opponents. I also made a point of hanging around the batting cages, and checking with the umpires before games. You could learn a lot from them that you wouldn't get anywhere else.

Sometimes I just stumbled on inside information. In the New York-Milwaukee Series of 1957, I had breakfast before the fourth game with Tom Greenwade, the scout who signed Mickey Mantle. Greenwade was an old friend who used to meet us in St. Louis and join us on the train to Kansas City during the season. Tom knew I wouldn't break a confidence, and that morning he said, "Hey, I'm worried about Mantle. He couldn't raise his arm over his head this morning to comb his hair." The day before, the Braves had tried a pick-off play on Mantle at second base. Red Schoendienst took the throw and fell heavily on Mantle sliding back to the base. There was no immediate reaction, but apparently Mantle had jammed his throwing shoulder.

He took the field later that day. But in the tenth inning, with the tying run on second base, Mantle suddenly came running in from center field. Tony Kubek took his place in center and Enos Slaughter came into the game in left field. Obviously, you don't take a player like Mantle out of the game in that situation without a compelling reason. I went ahead and broke the earlier confidence, explaining to the audience at home why Mantle may have been a defensive liability. As soon as I did, telephones began ringing in the press box. The newspaper editors, it turned out, were listening to me back in their offices. They were calling their reporters to find out why they hadn't uncovered this story the day before. It was one of the few times I

had an exclusive.

In the pressure cooker atmosphere of the World Series, the smallest plays could have major significance. How close you could come to immortality, and how close you could come to losing it all on one play. No baseball fan could forget Don Larsen's perfect World Series game on October 8, 1956. Yet very few fans probably recall the name of the Yankees' Floyd Bevens, who struggled with his control and still managed to pitch a no-hitter for $8\frac{2}{3}$ innings against the Dodgers in 1947. Then Cookie Lavagetto hit a double, and Bevens lost his chance for immortality—as well as the game, 3-2.

As a broadcaster, I fidgeted through each game, though for not the same reasons as the average fan. In those days the broadcasting assignments for a World Series still were split between the two principal announcers of the participating teams. In the Bevens—or should I say Lavagetto?—game, I did the first half; Red Barber handled the second. In 1956, Vin Scully was the principal Dodger announcer and he handled the final innings of the Larsen game.

So, as both Bevens and Larsen approached the climactic moments of their performances, I had little opportunity to comment. There was very little talk then between the two announcers. The fans of a World Series, we always reasoned, wanted the play-by-play, not the by-play of the broadcasters. That was the stature of the World Series. I therefore sat by uncomfortably as both Red and Vin departed from a tradition that I always respected—namely not referring specifically to the possibility of a no-hitter.

Of course I would let anyone with even an ounce of sense know that a no-hitter was unfolding. I might say that there have been five hits in the game, and they all belong to the Yankees, or that only six outs stand between Larsen and the pitchers' hall of fame. Obviously what I said or didn't say in the booth was not going to influence anything that happened on the field. I didn't believe in jinxes. But I knew that players on the bench don't mention a no-hitter. I just wanted to respect their dugout tradition. It's part of the romance of the game.

One controversy that engulfed me at times in my career was whether or not I was a "homer," so prejudiced in my feelings toward the Yankees that I openly rooted for them during the course of a game. The complaint seemed to be heard most from fans of losing teams, and most often seemed to be aimed at the broadcaster for the winning team. With the Yankees appearing as frequently as they did in the World Series, I was bound to be viewed as a symbol of that success. At that time also, players rarely were heard or seen on radio or television. Even in the World Series, post-game interviews normally were limited to the deciding game. Then more than now, the broadcaster was the lightning rod for the fans. The negative mail I received, which I always made a special effort to answer, blamed me for everything from stale peanuts and warm beer to the Yankees' domination of the sport.

My answer always was that, while I strive never to be prejudiced against anyone, I of course had to be partisan. You could not help but be favorably impressed by a group of players whose games you broadcast day after day and who performed so well so often. When major league baseball promoted the scoring of the game's one millionth run, my facetious thought was that, gosh, I thought the Yankees had scored a million runs all by themselves.

At the same time, however, I tried to keep my emotions in check until after a game, especially in a World Series, where loyalties were so sharply divided. What I hoped for, as probably most broadcasters did, was that the game would be a good one, something you could sink your teeth in. The feeling is similar, I imagine, to an actor hoping to get a good part in a powerful play.

Many fans, though, would not accept that analysis. I remember one man approaching me at a banquet during the off-season and telling me how much he hated my broadcasts of the Yankees. Every time he listened to me, he said, he just knew he was going to hear something else about the Yankees. I thought he was pulling my leg. In fact, he was absolutely serious.

In the 1958 World Series, in the first inning of the second game between Milwaukee and New York, the Braves scored seven runs. At that point, NBC received a telegram from a fan in Boston. It was directed to me: "Quit yapping, you Yankee lover. You're talking too much. Let me just watch the game." I was stung by the criticism and thought that maybe my disappointment at the lopsided nature of the game was reflected in my voice. The I looked more closely at the telegram and noticed it had been sent two hours before the game even started.

Not even ardent Yankee supporters could always be pleased, especially not when their emotions ran high at the World Series. When Carl Furillo hit a two-run homer off Allie Reynolds to tie the sixth game of the '53 Series in the top of the ninth, I was as excited as anyone by the drama of the moment. Almost immediately the Yankee Stadium switchboard lit up with calls from irate Yankee fans. (They had no complaints in the bottom of the ninth when I announced Billy Martin's single—his twelfth hit of the Series—to drive in the winning run.)

Controversy lingered even after I broadcast the 1963 World Series, my last from the broadcast booth. It was another Dodgers-Yankees confrontation, except this time it was across the continent rather than across town. Sandy Koufax pitched superbly in the first game, struck out fifteen, and beat Whitey Ford, 5-2. Koufax and Ford dueled again in the fourth game, with the Dodgers on the brink of sweeping the Series in consecutive games. This time, I thought, Ford outpitched Koufax. Frank Howard homered in the fifth to give the Dodgers a 1-0 lead. Then Mickey Mantle cracked a home run in the seventh to tie the game. The crowd roared, and I started to roar, too. Then I suddenly lost my voice.

What happened was that I suffered a recurrence of a nasal condition I had experienced earlier that season. At that time I was treated by the same throat doctor who cared for Frank Sinatra, and we thought we had it cleared up. But at the instant Mantle hit his home run, I felt something drip down on my vocal cords, almost as if a hand had been placed over my throat. I motioned to Vin Scully, who saw immediately that I was having trouble speaking. He took over the play-by-play and I rushed into the press box to get some hot coffee and lemon juice, hoping it would clear my throat. By the time I regained my ability to speak clearly, the game was over. The Dodgers, of course, had won, 2-1, to sweep the Series.

The speculation surrounding my sudden departure was far more dramatic than the actual event. The thrust of some accounts was the Mel Allen had become so distraught at the prospect of his beloved Yankees losing in four straight games that he choked up with emotion and was left speechless. If that were true, then how could I have broadcast the final game of the '55 Series, when Amoros made his spectacular catch and turned it into the double play that broke the back of the Yankees?

Logic defies the speculation in many ways, but to this day people still raise the memory of that afternoon in Los Angeles. Again, the World Series is an event viewed through a magnifying glass, which is what made it as exciting for broadcasters as it was for the players and fans.

No one but me (and maybe Phil Rizzuto and Jerry Coleman, my broadcast partners) will remember the regular-season game in Cleveland when I broadcast almost half a game announcing that John Kralick was pitching for the Indians, when in fact Sam McDowell was on the mound. Or the time a pinch hitter appeared in the ninth inning for the St. Louis Browns and turned out to be the same man I had said was doing the catching that game.

But no one, it seems, will ever let me forget the time I lost my voice in a World Series game. How about that? ◇

Brooks Robinson waiting for the ball at third in 1971 Series.

Overleaf; Mets Willie Mays plays in his last Series, 1973.

Johnny Bench attempts to break up double-play as A's Dick Green gets throw away in 1972 Series.

Johnny Bench puts the tag on A's Blue Moon Odom in 1972 Series.

Ken Holtzman delivers a pitch in 1974 Series.

A's Sal Bando trying to break up double play in '72 Series.

Frank Robinson waits on deck in 1970 Series.
Jubilant 1972 A's, after winning the Series.

1976 Series action at the "new" Yankee Stadium.

1947
WORLD SERIES

Dodgers

Yankees

LON KELLER

Larry and Me

BY LEO DUROCHER

MAN, THOSE YEARS WERE EXCITING. Fifty years in baseball and I loved every minute of it. Well, nearly every minute. I'm not including the year I was suspended by Happy Chandler for reasons nobody has told me yet.

There were good years and others not so good. But all were exciting. Especially the winning ones, and I was lucky enough to have my share of winning ones. I was on pennant-winning teams as a player, as a manager and as a coach. I was a teammate of Babe Ruth on a World Championship Yankees team, I was the captain of the famous Gashouse Gang of the World Champion St. Louis Cardinals and I managed World Series teams for both the Brooklyn Dodgers and the New York Giants. What more can a kid out of East Springfield, Mass., ask?

I worked for all kinds of baseball men—Ed Barrow of the Yankees, Branch Rickey of the Car-

dinals and Dodgers, Horace Stoneham of the Giants, Walter O'Malley with the Dodgers in Los Angeles—but the man who left the most profound impression was Larry MacPhail.

Leland Stanford MacPhail. That was his full name. He was a fabulous character. Brash—even brasher than me. He was loud, argumentative, autocratic, but he was also forgiving and he could charm a snake. No one had more guts and gall than Larry. One time, just after World War I, he even tried to kidnap the Kaiser—and almost succeeded. With it all, he was a hell of a baseball man. Let's face it, he was a genius. Baseball never had anyone who knew how to promote its game better. He took over a bunch of ragamuffins in Cincinnati and laid the groundwork for a championship team. He did the same in Brooklyn and he won with the New York Yankees. He introduced night baseball to the major leagues. He was the first to fly his team on a regular

Brooklyn Dodgers lineup for start of 1941 Series.

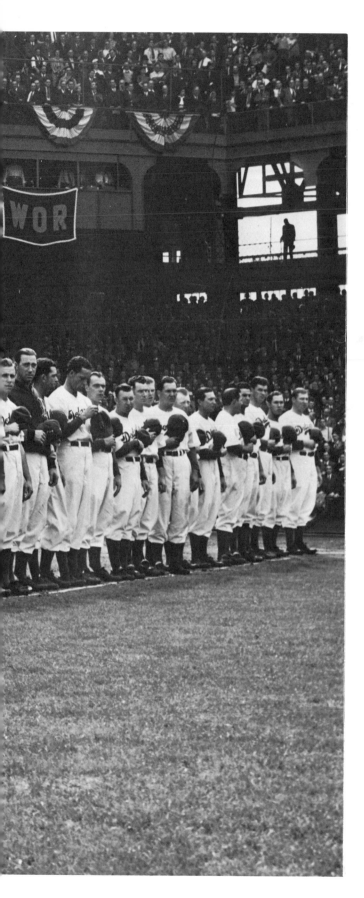

basis, and he introduced all sorts of sideshows to bring people into the ball parks.

Larry and I had a lot in common. We understood each other even though he fired me a hundred times. John McDonald was traveling secretary of the Dodgers, and he always maintained he was more of a referee than a secretary because he spent half his time trying to keep Larry and me apart. I worked on a year-to-year basis with MacPhail and at the end of each season he threatened to fire me.

The Dodgers finished third in 1939, my first year as manager, after a seventh-place finish the previous year. At the end of that '39 season, Larry and I sat down to discuss the situation for next year. Everything was going well when suddenly he began screaming. "I'm paying you to see some of your flashy fielding I've been reading so much about. But I never see it. You don't think I'm paying you just to manage the club, do you? With the players I've gotten for you, I could manage the club myself and do a damned sight better job than you have!"

"You manage the ball club?" I screamed back at him. "Don't make me laugh!"

"You're fired," he roared.

"All right, I'm fired," I yelled back. "Get somebody else to manage your lousy ball club."

Larry MacPhail.

Veterans of the 1941 Dodgers, left to right, front, Pete Reiser, Cookie Lavagetto, Dixie Walker; rear, Hugh Casey and PeeWee Reese.

The next day Larry called me and wanted to know what we could do to improve the team, as if nothing had happened.

We finished second to Cincinnati in 1940 and the cry in Brooklyn was "Wait till next year!" 1941 was going to be the year. Everybody knew it. MacPhail knew it. I knew it. The players knew it. We expected to win and we did win. The pennant was won on September 25 in Boston when Whitlow Wyatt shut out the Braves, 6-0.

It was a wild ride home. Training rules were suspended. We were really whooping it up all the way back to New York. Larry MacPhail didn't make the trip with us. He was in New York and listened to the game on the radio. He was supposed to meet the train at the 125th Street Station, but the train didn't stop there. There was a lot written at the time that I deliberately left MacPhail standing on the platform as the train roared through the station without stopping.

That wasn't exactly true. I really was unaware that MacPhail was waiting for us at the 125th Street Station, although truthfully I wouldn't have allowed the train to stop even if I knew. Here is what happened. Immediately after the game, MacPhail tried to reach me to congratulate me, but I was too busy with the press. He finally got to McDonald and told him he would be waiting at the 125th Street Station. Larry, you see, wanted to get in on the celebration. Red Barber, the voice of the Dodgers, had announced on the air what time the Dodgers would arrive at Grand Central Station. MacPhail knew that Grand Central would be packed with people waiting to greet their heroes, and he wanted to make the triumphal entry with the players into the station.

MacPhail at the time was still on good terms with Branch Rickey, then with the Cardinals, and

Dodger home run sluggers in 1941, left to right, Dixie Walker, Joe Medwick, Dolph Camilli and Pete Reiser.

Rickey happened to be in New York. The two got into a cab and rode up to 125th Street to the New York Central Station there. MacPhail was going to board the train at that point.

I didn't know this, of course—McDonald forgot to tell me—but I knew that many of the players were planning to get off at 125th Street so as not to have to fight their way through the crowd at Grand Central on 42nd Street. I felt that the fans deserved to see and greet their heroes. So I went to the conductor and told him not to stop at 125th Street but to go right on through to Grand Central. The conductor said he had orders to stop. I told him, "I don't care if you've got orders from the President. Don't stop. Go right through."

The train didn't stop at 125th Street. I roared right on through, right past MacPhail and Rickey. I didn't see them, but I was told later that Larry went berserk. He was screaming like a mad-

man. Well, after the cheering was over, I finally got back to my hotel. I was staying at the New Yorker. MacPhail was staying at the same hotel. He came to my room after I had finished an interview for the newsreel camera. There was no television at the time. McDonald was in my room.

Larry was still fuming. "McDonald," he shouted, "didn't I tell you that I would be waiting at the 125th Street Station?"

Poor John was shaking. He began to sputter. He couldn't get a single word out of his mouth.

"Wait a minute, Larry," I butted in. "I told the conductor not to stop the train."

"You're through," MacPhail roared. "You're fired!"

I couldn't believe what I heard. We had just won the pennant—the first one in twenty-one years—it was my greatest day and I was fired.

"You know what you can do with your ball

Hard-hitting outfielders Joe DiMaggio and Tommy Henrich get set for 1941 Series.

club," I shouted and took a swipe with my foot at a handy chair nearby. Unfortunately, MacPhail was resting one foot on it and he lost his balance. I didn't wait to see if he had fallen. I was out of the room in a flash.

I don't know when I went to bed that night, but along about four A.M. I was awakened by the telephone. It was McDonald. "The boss wants to see you right away," he said. "Tell him I'm asleep," I said and hung up.

I came down to the lobby later that morning and there was Larry dressed immaculately with a boutonniere in his lapel. He looked fresh as a daisy. He was smiling.

"Hey, Leo," he said, as pleasant as you please. "Let's sit down and talk. We've got to concentrate on licking the Yankees."

It was as if nothing had happened between us the night before.

Well, we didn't beat the Yankees. They beat us in five games. That was the Series in which Mickey Owen became the goat when he let a third strike get away from him that would have ended the game. Hugh Casey was the pitcher. Writers claimed that Casey threw a spitter on that third strike, but Owen and Casey both told me it was a curve ball and I believed them.

Casey was a mean, rough man. He hated everybody, particularly if you were on the other side. They used to say of me that I would order a pitcher to throw a knockdown pitch at my own mother if she were crowding the plate. Well, Casey would make sure he'd hit her—right in the head. He didn't give a damn about anybody. He didn't even care for himself. Years after he was out of baseball, he stuck a shotgun in his mouth and blew himself off the earth.

I remember a game in Pittsburgh when um-

pire George Magerkurth, my old sparring partner, called a balk on Casey. They got into a beauty of an argument and I came out to help my pitcher. It didn't do any good, though. It was still a balk, according to Mage, and it cost us a run. Casey was still livid when play was resumed. He instructed Mickey Owen, the catcher, to stay low and threw a high pitch right at Magerkurth. Mage was a big, heavy, lumbering ox, but he looked like a gazelle getting out of the way of the pitch. The big lug thought I ordered the pitch and threw me out of the game.

Now back to the 1941 World Series with the Yankees. We were ahead 4-3, with two out in the ninth, bases empty, two strikes on Tommy Henrich. Casey threw a curve, the best he ever threw, and Henrich struck out. But the ball got by Owen and skipped all the way to the screen and Henrich got to first base. The Yankees went on to score four runs to beat us. That was the whole ball of wax. Instead of the Series being all tied at two game apiece, the Yankees had a 3 to 1 edge. They wrapped it up the next day.

I remember after the Owen game seeing MacPhail standing in the clubhouse crying. It wasn't just a game to him. It was everything. He wanted nothing more in life than to beat the Yankees. Owen cried too. He took it real hard. The writers gave him a real going over. They compared his muff with boners in previous World Series.

It wasn't fair and I told the writers so. Owen didn't commit a boner. It was a mechanical error; errors happen all the time. Mickey called for a curve and Casey got a little more on the pitch than Owen expected. It was a tough pitch to handle, a curve breaking low, down around Henrich's shoes. It would have been a fourth ball, but Henrich swung at it. So you could see it was a tough pitch to handle.

I told the writers if they really wanted to get the reason why we lost the game, they should blame me, not Owen. After Henrich got on, DiMaggio singled and Keller doubled off the screen to score two runs. That's where I pulled a rock. Casey got two quick strikes on Keller and again we were only one strike away from winning.

My mistake was, for the first time in my life, I was shell-shocked. I should have gotten off the bench and gone out to the mound to talk to my pitcher. In a spot like that, especially after what happened, I've got to go out there and talk to the pitcher, slow him down. I've got to say to him, "Look, you got him where you want him. Take your time. Waste a couple of pitches; maybe he'll go after a bad one." Instead, I just sat on my ass and didn't do anything. I let Casey come right back with the pitch that Keller hit for the game winner. So, I told the writers, if you want to criticize anybody, criticize the manager.

The
World Series
The Complete Record

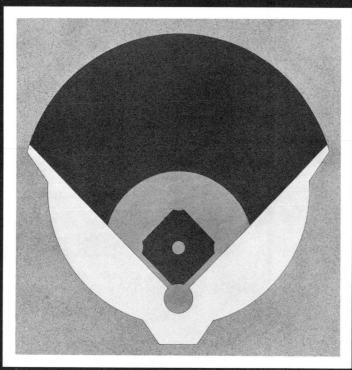

1903-77

1903

Boston Red Sox 5
Pittsburgh Pirates 3

Highlights

AFTER TWO YEARS OF FIGHTING, the 3-year-old American League and 28-year-old National League reached a settlement. Barney Dreyfuss, Pirates owner, challenged Henry Killilea, Boston Pilgrims owner, to a post-season playoff. The best-of-nine Series, played in October, was the first modern World Series.

The Pirates were weakened by injuries: Honus Wagner limping from right leg injury; Otto Krueger put out of action by late-season beaning; pitcher Ed Doheny hospitalized with a mental condition; pitcher Sam Leever suffering a sore shoulder from trap-shooting contest. Player-manager Fred Clarke had no injuries. Boston had player-manager Jimmy Collins plus an excellent mound staff led by 28-game-winner 36-year-old Cy Young.

The Pirates took four runs from Young in top of the first inning of game one. Pirate pitcher Deacon Phillippe (24 games) pitched five Series games with very little rest, winning three games. But Boston's Bill Dinneen shut out Pittsburgh in the final game for his third win to give the Series to the Pilgrims five games to three.

Game 1 Oct. 1
Pittsburgh	401 100 100 ·	7
Boston	000 000 201 ·	3

Winner-Young   Loser-Phillippe

Game 2 Oct. 2
Pittsburgh	000 000 000 ·	0
Boston	200 001 00* ·	3

Winner-Dinneen   Loser-Veil

Game 3 Oct. 3
Pittsburgh	012 000 010 ·	4
Boston	000 100 010 ·	2

Winner-Phillippe   Loser-Young

Game 4 Oct. 6
Boston	000 010 003 ·	4
Pittsburgh	100 010 30* ·	5

Winner-Phillippe   Loser-Dinneen

Game 5 Oct. 7
Boston	000 006 410 ·	11
Pittsburgh	000 000 020 ·	2

Winner-Young   Loser-Kennedy

Game 6 Oct. 8
Boston	003 020 100 ·	6
Pittsburgh	000 000 300 ·	3

Winner-Dinneen   Loser-Leever

Game 7 Oct. 10
Boston	200 202 010 ·	7
Pittsburgh	000 101 001 ·	3

Winner-Young   Loser-Phillippe

Game 8 Oct. 13
Pittsburgh	000 000 000 ·	0
Boston	000 201 00* ·	3

Winner-Dinneen   Loser-Phillippe

Total Attendance—100,420
Average Attendance—12,553
Winning Player's Share—$1,182
Losing Player's Share—$1,316

BATTING	Pos	G	AB	R	H	2B	3B	HR	RBI	BB	SO	SB	BA
Boston													
Candy LaChance	1b	8	27	5	6	2	1	0	4	3	2	0	.222
Hobe Ferris	2b	8	31	3	9	0	1	0	5	0	6	0	.290
Freddy Parent	ss	8	32	8	9	0	3	0	4	1	1	0	.281
Jimmy Collins	3b	8	36	5	9	1	2	0	1	1	1	3	.250
Buck Freeman	rf	8	32	6	9	0	3	0	4	2	2	0	.281
Chuck Stahl	cf	8	33	6	10	1	3	0	3	1	2	2	.303
Patsy Dougherty	lf	8	34	3	8	0	2	2	5	2	6	0	.235
Lou Criger	c	8	26	1	6	0	0	0	4	2	3	0	.231
Jack O'Brien	ph	2	2	0	0	0	0	0	0	0	1	0	.000
Duke Farrell	ph	2	2	0	0	0	0	0	0	1	0	0	.000
Jake Stahl	Did not play												
Cy Young	p	4	15	1	2	0	1	0	3	0	3	0	.133
Bill Dinneen	p	4	12	1	3	0	0	0	0	2	2	0	.250
Long Tom Hughes	p	1	0	0	0	0	0	0	0	0	0	0	.000
George Winter	Did not play												
Norwood Gibson	Did not play												
Team Total		8	282	39	71	4	16	2	34	14	29	5	.252

Double Plays—5   Left on Bases—55

BATTING	Pos	G	AB	R	H	2B	3B	HR	RBI	BB	SO	SB	BA
Pittsburgh													
Kitty Bransfield	1b	8	29	3	6	0	2	0	1	1	6	1	.207
Claude Ritchey	2b	8	27	2	3	1	0	0	2	4	7	1	.111
Honus Wagner	ss	8	27	2	6	1	0	0	3	3	4	3	.222
Tommy Leach	3b	8	33	3	9	0	4	0	7	1	4	1	.273
Jimmy Sebring	rf	8	30	3	11	0	1	1	3	1	4	0	**.367**
Ginger Beaumont	cf	8	34	6	9	0	1	0	1	2	4	2	.265
Fred Clarke	lf	8	34	3	9	2	1	0	2	1	5	1	.265
Eddie Phelps	c-ph	8	26	1	6	2	0	0	1	1	6	0	.231
Harry Smith	c	1	3	0	0	0	0	0	0	0	0	0	.000
Otto Krueger	Did not play												
Art Weaver	Did not play												
Joe Marshall	Did not play												
Fred Carisch	Did not play												
Deacon Phillippe	p	5	18	1	4	0	0	0	1	0	3	0	.222
Sam Leever	p	2	4	0	0	0	0	0	0	0	0	0	.000
Brickyard Kennedy	p	1	2	0	1	1	0	0	0	0	0	0	.500
Bucky Veil	p	1	2	0	0	0	0	0	0	0	2	0	.000
Gus Thompson	p	1	1	0	0	0	0	0	0	0	0	0	.000
Ed Doheny	Did not play—illness												
Kaiser Wilhelm	Did not play												
Jack Pfiester	Did not play												
Team Total		8	270	24	64	7	9	1	21	14	45	9	.237

Double Plays—5   Left on Bases—51

PITCHING	G	GS	CG	IP	H	R	ER	BB	SO	W	L	SV	ERA
Boston													
Bill Dinneen	4	4	4	35	29	8	8	8	28	3	1	0	2.06
Cy Young	4	3	3	34	31	13	7	4	17	2	1	0	**1.85**
Long Tom Hughes	1	1	0	2	4	3	2	2	0	0	1	0	9.00
Norwood Gibson	Did not play												
George Winter	Did not play												
Team Total	8	8	7	71	64	24	17	14	45	5	3	0	2.15
Pittsburgh													
Deacon Phillippe	5	5	5	44	38	19	14	3	22	3	2	0	2.86
Sam Leever	2	2	1	10	13	8	6	3	2	0	2	0	5.40
Brickyard Kennedy	1	1	0	7	11	10	4	3	3	0	1	0	5.14
Bucky Veil	1	0	0	7	6	1	1	5	1	0	0	0	1.29
Gus Thompson	1	0	0	2	3	1	1	0	1	0	0	0	4.50
Ed Doheny	Did not play—illness												
Kaiser Wilhelm	Did not play												
Jack Pfiester	Did not play												
Team Total	8	8	6	70	71	39	29	14	29	3	5	0	3.73

1905

New York Giants 4
Philadelphia Athletics 1

Highlights

THIS SERIES WAS BROUGHT ON BY pressure from the fans, who were upset at the National League's New York Giants' refusal to play the American League champion Boston Pilgrims in 1904 because of Giants manager John McGraw's dislike for American League president Ban Johnson, and Giants owner John T. Brush's hatred of the American League for putting a new club in New York in 1903.

Phenomenal pitching Series in which all five games were decided by shutouts: Christy Mathewson, the Giants' outstanding right-handed pitcher who amassed a regular-season record of 32-8 with a 1.27 ERA, won the first, third and fifth games by 3-0, 9-0 and 2-0 scores, giving up only 14 hits in his 27 innings on the mound. Chief Bender, pitching for the A's in the second game, registered the only victory over the Giants, 3-0, beating Iron Man Joe McGinnity, who gained revenge in the fourth game by turning back the A's, 1-0, on five hits, all singles.

Rube Waddell, the A's' ace pitcher, who led the majors with 287 strikeouts while garnering a 26-11 regular-season record, was scratched from the Series when he fell and injured his shoulder during some horseplay on a railroad platform.

Game 1 Oct. 9
| New York | 000 020 001 | - | 3 |
| Philadelphia | 000 000 000 | - | 0 |

Winner-Mathewson   Loser-Plank

Game 2 Oct. 10
| Philadelphia | 001 000 020 | - | 3 |
| New York | 000 000 000 | - | 0 |

Winner-Bender   Loser-McGinnity

Game 3 Oct. 12
| New York | 200 050 002 | - | 9 |
| Philadelphia | 000 000 000 | - | 0 |

Winner-Mathewson   Loser-Coakley

Game 4 Oct. 13
| Philadelphia | 000 000 000 | - | 0 |
| New York | 000 100 00* | - | 1 |

Winner-McGinnity   Loser-Plank

Game 5 Oct. 14
| Philadelphia | 000 000 000 | - | 0 |
| New York | 000 010 01* | - | 2 |

Winner-Mathewson   Loser-Bender

Total Attendance—91,723
Average Attendance—18,345
Winning Player's Share—$1,142
Losing Player's Share—$832

BATTING

	Pos	G	AB	R	H	2B	3B	HR	RBI	BB	SO	SB	BA
New York													
Dan McGann	1b	5	17	1	4	**2**	0	0	**4**	2	**7**	0	.235
Billy Gilbert	2b	5	17	1	4	0	0	0	2	0	2	1	.235
Bill Dahlen	ss	5	15	1	0	0	0	0	1	3	2	**3**	.000
Art Devlin	3b	5	16	0	4	1	0	0	1	1	3	**3**	.250
George Browne	rf	5	**22**	2	4	0	0	0	1	0	2	2	.182
Mike Donlin	cf	5	19	**4**	**5**	1	0	0	1	2	1	2	.263
Sam Mertes	lf	5	17	2	3	1	0	0	2	2	**5**	0	.176
Roger Bresnahan	c	5	16	3	**5**	**2**	0	0	1	**4**	0	1	**.313**
Sammy Strang	ph	1	3	0	0	0	0	0	0	0	1	0	.000
Frank Bowerman	Did not play												
Boileryard Clarke	Did not play												
Christy Mathewson	p	3	8	1	2	0	0	0	0	1	1	0	.250
Joe McGinnity	p	2	5	0	0	0	0	0	0	0	2	0	.000
Red Ames	p	1	0	0	0	0	0	0	0	0	0	0	.000
Hooks Wiltse	Did not play												
Dummy Taylor	Did not play												
Claude Elliott	Did not play												
Team Total		5	153	15	31	7	0	0	13	15	26	12	.203

Double Plays—3   Left on Bases—32

	Pos	G	AB	R	H	2B	3B	HR	RBI	BB	SO	SB	BA
Philadelphia													
Harry Davis	1b	5	20	0	4	1	0	0	0	0	1	0	.200
Danny Murphy	2b	5	16	0	3	1	0	0	0	0	2	0	.188
Monte Cross	ss	5	17	0	3	0	0	0	0	0	**7**	0	.176
Lave Cross	3b	5	19	0	2	0	0	0	0	1	1	0	.105
Socks Seybold	rf	5	16	0	2	0	0	0	2	0	3	0	.125
Bris Lord	cf	5	20	0	2	0	0	0	2	0	**5**	0	.100
Topsy Hartsel	lf	5	17	1	**5**	1	0	0	0	2	1	2	.294
Ossee Schreckengost	c	3	9	2	2	1	0	0	0	0	0	0	.222
Mike Powers	c	3	7	0	1	1	0	0	0	0	0	0	.143
Danny Hoffman	ph	1	1	0	0	0	0	0	0	0	1	0	.000
Jack Knight	Did not play												
Harry Barton	Did not play												
Eddie Plank	p	2	6	0	1	0	0	0	0	0	2	0	.167
Chief Bender	p	2	5	0	0	0	0	0	0	0	1	0	.000
Andy Coakley	p	1	2	0	0	0	0	0	0	0	1	0	.000
Rube Waddell	Did not play—shoulder injury												
Weldon Henley	Did not play												
Jimmy Dygert	Did not play												
Team Total		5	155	3	25	5	0	0	2	5	25	2	.161

Double Plays—2   Left on Bases—26

PITCHING

	G	GS	CG	IP	H	R	ER	BB	SO	W	L	SV	ERA
New York													
Christy Mathewson	**3**	**3**	**3**	27	14	0	0	1	**18**	3	0	0	**0.00**
Joe McGinnity	2	2	1	17	10	3	0	3	6	1	1	0	**0.00**
Red Ames	1	0	0	1	1	0	0	1	1	0	0	0	0.00
Dummy Taylor	Did not play												
Hooks Wiltse	Did not play												
Claude Elliott	Did not play												
Team Total	5	5	4	45	25	3	0	5	25	4	1	0	0.00
Philadelphia													
Eddie Plank	2	2	2	17	**14**	4	**3**	4	11	0	**2**	0	1.59
Chief Bender	2	2	2	17	9	2	2	**6**	13	1	1	0	1.06
Andy Coakley	1	1	1	9	8	**9**	2	5	2	0	1	0	2.00
Rube Waddell	Did not play—shoulder injury												
Weldon Henley	Did not play												
Jimmy Dygert	Did not play												
Team Total	5	5	5	43	31	15	7	15	26	1	4	0	1.47

1906

Chicago White Sox (A.L.) 4
Chicago Cubs (N.L.) 2

Highlights

THIS WAS THE FIRST ONE-CITY Series: Chicago Cubs vs. Chicago White Sox. The Cubs were favored 3-to-1 going in, but were defeated four games to two.

Led by Joe Tinker, Johnny Evers, Frank Chance and third baseman Harry Steinfeldt, the Cubs ripped through the N.L. with a record 116 wins. Steinfeldt alone had 83 RBI's and a .327 average. Pitcher Three Finger Brown had 26 wins and a 1.04 ERA.

The White Sox, known as "The Hitless Wonders," had a team batting average of .230—the worst in the entire A.L.

Surprisingly, the White Sox took game one, 2-1. The Cubs came back with a 7-1 win in game two. The Sox then took game three, 3-0, but the Cubs won game four, 1-0.

Game five: the Cubs hit Ed Walsh for six runs, but then "The Hitless Wonders" took eight runs from three Cubs mounds-men. Game six told the tale. The Sox knocked Three Finger Brown out of the box in his third Series appearance, scoring seven runs by the end of the second inning. White Sox couldn't be stopped then, and went on to win the game, 8-3, and the Series, four games to two.

Game 1 Oct. 9
White Sox	000 011 000 -	2
Cubs	000 001 000 -	1

Winner-Altrock Loser-Brown

Game 2 Oct. 10
Cubs	031 001 020 -	7
White Sox	000 010 000 -	1

Winner-Ruelbach Loser-Owen

Game 3 Oct. 11
White Sox	000 003 000 -	3
Cubs	000 000 000 -	0

Winner-Walsh Loser-Pfiester

Game 4 Oct. 12
Cubs	000 000 100 -	1
White Sox	000 000 000 -	0

Winner-Brown Loser-Altrock

Game 5 Oct. 13
White Sox	102 401 000 -	8
Cubs	300 102 000 -	6

Winner-Walsh Loser-Pfiester

Game 6 Oct. 14
Cubs	100 010 001 -	3
White Sox	340 000 01* -	8

Winner-White Loser-Brown

Total Attendance—99,845
Average Attendance—16,641
Winning Player's Share—$1,874
Losing Player's Share—$440

BATTING	Pos	G	AB	R	H	2B	3B	HR	RBI	BB	SO	SB	BA
Chicago White Sox													
Jiggs Donahue	1b	6	18	0	6	2	1	0	4	3	3	0	.333
Frank Isbell	2b	6	26	4	8	4	0	0	4	0	6	1	.308
George Davis	ss	3	13	4	4	3	0	0	6	0	1	1	.308
George Rohe	3b	6	21	2	7	1	2	0	4	3	1	2	**.333**
Eddie Hahn	rf	6	22	4	6	0	0	0	0	1	1	0	.273
Fielder Jones	cf	6	21	4	2	0	0	0	0	3	3	0	.095
Patsy Dougherty	lf	6	20	1	2	0	0	0	1	3	4	2	.100
Billy Sullivan	c	6	21	0	0	0	0	0	0	0	9	0	.000
Lee Tannehill	ss	3	9	1	1	0	0	0	0	0	2	0	.111
Bill O'Neill	rf	1	1	1	0	0	0	0	0	0	0	0	.000
Babe Towne	ph	1	1	0	0	0	0	0	0	0	0	0	.000
Ed McFarland	ph	1	1	0	0	0	0	0	0	0	0	0	.000
Gus Dundon	Did not play												
Hub Hart	Did not play												
Nick Altrock	p	2	4	0	1	0	0	0	0	1	1	0	.250
Ed Walsh	p	2	4	1	0	0	0	0	0	3	3	0	.000
Doc White	p	3	3	0	0	0	0	0	0	1	0	0	.000
Frank Owen	p	1	2	0	0	0	0	0	0	0	1	0	.000
Roy Patterson	Did not play												
Frank Smith	Did not play												
Lou Fiene	Did not play												
Team Total		6	187	22	37	10	3	0	19	18	35	6	.198

Double Plays—2   Left on Bases—33

BATTING	Pos	G	AB	R	H	2B	3B	HR	RBI	BB	SO	SB	BA
Chicago Cubs													
Frank Chance	1b	6	21	3	5	1	0	0	0	2	1	2	.238
Johnny Evers	2b	6	20	2	3	1	0	0	1	1	3	2	.150
Joe Tinker	ss	6	18	4	3	0	0	0	1	2	2	3	.167
Harry Steinfeldt	3b	6	20	2	5	1	0	0	2	1	0	0	.250
Wildfire Schulte	rf	6	26	1	7	3	0	0	3	1	3	0	.269
Solly Hofman	cf	6	23	3	7	1	0	0	2	3	5	1	.304
Jimmy Sheckard	lf	6	21	0	0	0	0	0	0	2	4	1	.000
Johnny Kling	c	6	17	2	3	1	0	0	0	4	3	0	.176
Pat Moran	ph	2	2	0	0	0	0	0	0	0	0	0	.000
Doc Gessler	ph	2	1	0	0	0	0	0	0	1	0	0	.000
Jimmy Slagle	Did not play												
Tom Walsh	Did not play												
Three Finger Brown	p	3	6	0	2	0	0	0	0	0	4	0	.333
Orvie Overall	p	2	4	1	1	1	0	0	0	1	1	0	.250
Ed Reulbach	p	2	3	0	0	0	0	0	1	0	1	0	.000
Jack Pfiester	p	2	2	0	0	0	0	0	0	0	1	0	.000
Carl Lundgren	Did not play												
Jack Taylor	Did not play												
Jack Harper	Did not play												
Team Total		6	184	18	36	9	0	0	11	18	28	9	.196

Double Plays—4   Left on Bases—36

PITCHING	G	GS	CG	IP	H	R	ER	BB	SO	W	L	SVB	ERA
Chicago White Sox													
Nick Altrock	2	2	**2**	18	11	2	2	2	5	1	1	0	**1.00**
Ed Walsh	2	2	1	15	7	6	2	6	17	2	0	0	1.20
Doc White	**3**	2	1	15	12	7	3	7	4	1	1	1	1.80
Frank Owen	1	0	0	6	6	3	2	3	2	0	0	0	3.00
Roy Patterson	Did not play												
Frank Smith	Did not play												
Lou Fiene	Did not play												
Team Total	6	6	4	54	36	18	9	18	28	4	2	1	1.50
Chicago Cubs													
Three Finger Brown	**3**	3	2	19½	14	8	7	4	12	1	**2**	0	3.20
Orvie Overall	2	0	0	12	10	3	3	8	8	0	0	0	2.25
Ed Reulbach	2	2	1	11	6	4	3	**8**	4	1	0	0	2.45
Jack Pfiester	2	1	1	10½	7	7	7	3	11	0	2	0	6.10
Carl Lundgren	Did not play												
Jack Taylor	Did not play												
Jack Harper	Did not play												
Team Total	6	6	4	53	37	22	20	18	35	2	4	0	3.40

1907

Chicago Cubs 4
Detroit Tigers 0

Highlights

THE CHICAGO CUBS ROARED back to take the N.L. title by a healthy margin. This time they faced the Detroit Tigers, a team with four excellent start-pitchers, a strong infield and an outfield boasting Ty Cobb, Davy Jones and Sam Crawford. Cobb, aged 20, led the A.L. with .350, 119 RBI's and 49 stolen bases.

Game one was a real landmark. In the bottom of ninth, Detroit was ahead, 3-1. But a single by Frank Chance, a hit batter (Steinfeldt) and a muff of a Johnny Evers grounder by Tigers third baseman Bill Coughlin loaded the bases and resulted in two runs by Chance and Steinfeldt to tie the score, 3-3. Then, after 12 innings of play, the stalemate was called because of darkness.

Chicago lefty Jack Pfiester allowed nine hits, but only one run in game two to win it for the Cubs, 3-1. Ed Reulbach allowed only one Tigers run as Cubs won game three, 5-1. Game four at Detroit saw the Cubs steal two bases and score three runs in the seventh without ever hitting the ball out of the infield. Disheartened, the Tigers dropped the fourth straight game, 2-0, to give Chicago the Series. Cobb had been held to a .200 average and Crawford to a .238.

Game 1 Oct. 8
Detroit	000 000 030 000 -	3
Chicago	000 100 002 000 -	3

Stopped by darkness

Game 2 Oct. 9
Detroit	010 000 000 -	1
Chicago	010 200 00* -	3

Winner-Pfiester Loser-Mullin

Game 3 Oct. 10
Detroit	000 001 000 -	1
Chicago	010 310 00* -	5

Winner-Reulbach Loser-Siever

Game 4 Oct. 11
Chicago	000 020 301 -	6
Detroit	000 100 000 -	1

Winner-Overall Loser-Donovan

Game 5 Oct. 12
Chicago	110 000 000 -	2
Detroit	000 000 000 -	0

Winner-Brown Loser-Mullin

Total Attendance—78,068
Average Attendance—15,614
Winning Player's Share—$2,143
Losing Player's Share—$1,946

BATTING

	Pos	G	AB	R	H	2B	3B	HR	RBI	BB	SO	SB	BA
Chicago													
Frank Chance	1b	4	14	3	3	1	0	0	0	3	2	3	.214
Johnny Evers	2b-ss	5	20	2	7	2	0	0	1	0	1	3	.350
Joe Tinker	ss	5	13	4	2	0	0	0	1	3	3	1	.154
Harry Steinfeldt	3b	5	17	2	8	1	1	0	2	1	2	1	**.471**
Wildfire Schulte	rf	5	20	3	5	0	0	0	2	1	2	0	.250
Jimmy Slagle	cf	5	22	3	6	0	0	0	4	2	3	6	.273
Jimmy Sheckard	lf	5	21	0	5	2	0	0	2	0	4	1	.238
Johnny Kling	c	5	19	2	4	0	0	0	1	1	4	0	.211
Del Howard	ph-1b	2	5	0	1	0	0	0	0	0	2	1	.200
Heinie Zimerman	2b	1	1	0	0	0	0	0	0	0	0	0	.000
Pat Moran	ph	1	0	0	0	0	0	0	0	0	0	0	.000
Solly Hofman		Did not play											
Orvie Overall	p	2	5	0	1	0	0	0	2	0	1	0	.200
Ed Reulbach	p	2	5	0	1	0	0	0	0	1	0	0	.200
Three Finger Brown	p	1	3	0	0	0	0	0	0	1	0	0	.000
Jack Pfiester	p	1	2	0	0	0	0	0	0	0	1	0	.000
Carl Lundgren		Did not play											
Chick Fraser		Did not play											
Kid Durbin		Did not play											
Team Total		5	167	19	43	6	1	0	16	12	26	16	.257

Double Plays—6   Left on Bases—33

	Pos	G	AB	R	H	2B	3B	HR	RBI	BB	SO	SB	BA
Detroit													
Claude Rossman	1b	5	20	1	8	0	1	0	2	1	0	1	.400
Germany Schaefer	2b	5	21	1	3	0	0	0	0	0	3	0	.143
Charley O'Leary	ss	5	17	0	1	0	0	0	0	1	3	0	.059
Bill Coughlin	3b	5	20	0	5	0	0	0	0	1	4	1	.250
Ty Cobb	rf	5	20	1	4	0	1	0	0	0	3	0	.200
Sam Crawford	cf	5	21	1	5	1	0	0	3	0	3	0	.238
Davy Jones	lf	5	17	1	6	0	0	0	0	4	0	3	.353
Boss Schmidt	c-ph	4	12	0	2	0	0	0	0	2	1	0	.167
Freddie Payne	c-pr	2	4	0	1	0	0	0	0	1	0	1	.250
Jimmy Archer	c	1	3	0	0	0	0	0	0	0	1	0	.000
Red Downs		Did not play											
Matty McIntyre		Did not play											
Bobby Lowe		Did not play											
Wild Bill Donovan	p	2	8	0	0	0	0	0	0	0	3	0	.000
George Mullin	p	2	6	0	0	0	0	0	0	0	1	0	.000
Ed Killian	p	1	2	1	1	0	0	0	0	0	0	0	.500
Ed Siever	p	1	1	0	0	0	0	0	0	0	0	0	.000
Ed Willett		Did not play											
Team Total		5	172	6	36	1	2	0	6	9	22	6	.209

Double Plays—2   Left on Bases—35

PITCHING

	G	GS	CG	IP	H	R	ER	BB	SO	W	L	SV	ERA
Chicago													
Orvie Overall	2	2	1	18	14	4	2	4	11	1	0	0	1.00
Ed Reulbach	2	1	1	12	6	1	1	3	4	1	0	0	0.75
Three Finger Brown	1	1	1	9	7	0	0	1	4	1	0	0	**0.00**
Jack Pfiester	1	1	1	9	9	1	1	1	3	1	0	0	1.00
Carl Lundgren	Did not play												
Chick Fraser	Did not play												
Kid Durbin	Did not play												
Team Total	5	5	4	48	36	6	4	9	22	4	0	0	0.75
Detroit													
Wild Bill Donovan	2	2	2	21	17	9	4	5	16	0	1	0	1.71
George Mullin	2	2	2	17	16	5	4	6	8	0	2	0	2.12
Ed Killian	1	0	0	4	3	1	1	1	1	0	0	0	2.25
Ed Siever	1	1	0	4	7	4	2	0	1	0	1	0	4.50
Ed Willett	Did not play												
Team Total	5	5	4	46	43	19	11	12	26	0	4	0	2.15

1908

Highlights

THERE WERE VERY TIGHT pennant races this year. The Chicago Cubs won their third straight mainly because of famous blunder by substitute Giants first baseman Fred Merkle, who headed for the clubhouse without bothering to touch second when he saw the Giants' "winning run" cross the plate.

The Cubs got the ball to second to make a force-out, and the umpire ruled the game a tie. When the two teams finished the season in a dead heat, the tied game was rescheduled for October 8. The Cubs took it by beating Christy Mathewson, 4-2, and earned a berth in the Series. The Detroit Tigers also had to beat the Cleveland Indians on the last day of the season to snare the A.L. title.

In a reprise of previous year, the Tigers had a first-game victory within reach and failed to grab it. The Cubs won the opener, 10-6. In game two, Chicago's Orvie Overall battled Detroit's Wild Bill Donovan through seven scoreless innings, but a wind-blown homer to right by Joe Tinker opened things up in the eighth, and the Cubs won, 6-1.

The Tigers bounced back to take game three, 8-3, powered by Ty Cobb. But even Cobb couldn't hit in game four as Chicago's Three Finger Brown pitched a 3-0 shutout. Orvie Overall repeated that feat the next game with a 2-0 shutout to win the Series for Chicago.

Game 1 Oct. 10
Chicago   004 000 105 · 10
Detroit   100 000 320 · 6
Winner-Brown Loser-Summers

Game 2 Oct. 11
Detroit   000 000 001 · 1
Chicago   000 000 06* · 6
Winner-Overall Loser-Donovan

Game 3 Oct. 12
Detroit   100 005 020 · 8
Chicago   000 300 000 · 3
Winner-Mullin Loser-Pfiester

Game 4 Oct. 13
Chicago   002 000 001 · 3
Detroit   000 000 000 · 0
Winner-Brown Loser-Summers

Game 5 Oct. 14
Chicago   100 010 000 · 2
Detroit   000 000 000 · 0
Winner-Overall Loser-Donovan

Total Attendance—62,232
Average Attendance—12,446
Winning Player's Share—$1,318
Losing Player's Share—$870

Chicago Cubs 4
Detroit Tigers 1

BATTING	Pos	G	AB	R	H	2B	3B	HR	RBI	BB	SO	SB	BA
Chicago													
Frank Chance	1b	5	19	4	8	0	0	0	2	3	1	5	.421
Johnny Evers	2b	5	20	5	7	1	0	0	2	1	2	2	.350
Joe Tinker	ss	5	19	2	5	0	0	1	4	0	2	2	.263
Harry Steinfeldt	3b	5	16	3	4	0	0	0	3	2	5	1	.250
Wildfire Schulte	rf	5	18	4	7	0	1	0	2	2	1	2	.389
Solly Hofman	cf	5	19	2	6	0	1	0	4	1	4	2	.316
Jimmy Sheckard	lf	5	21	2	5	2	0	0	1	2	3	1	.238
Johnny Kling	c	5	16	2	4	1	0	0	2	2	2	0	.250
Del Howard	ph	1	1	0	0	0	0	0	0	0	0	0	.000
Jimmy Slagle		Did not play											
Pat Moran		Did not play											
Heinie Zimmerman		Did not play											
Kid Durbin		Did not play											
Doc Marshall		Did not play											
Orvie Overall	p	3	6	0	2	0	0	0	0	0	1	0	.333
Three Finger Brown	p	2	4	0	0	0	0	0	0	0	2	0	.000
Ed Reulbach	p	2	3	0	0	0	0	0	0	0	1	0	.000
Jack Pfiester	p	1	2	0	0	0	0	0	0	0	2	0	.000
Chick Fraser		Did not play											
Carl Lundgren		Did not play											
Rube Kroh		Did not play											
Team Total		5	164	24	48	4	2	1	20	13	26	15	.293
		Double Plays—4 Left on Bases—30											
Detroit													
Claude Rossman	1b	5	19	3	4	0	0	0	3	1	4	1	.211
Germany Schaefer	2b-3b	5	16	0	2	0	0	0	0	1	4	1	.125
Charley O'Leary	ss	5	19	2	3	0	0	0	0	0	3	0	.158
Bill Coughlin	3b	5	8	0	1	0	0	0	1	0	1	0	.125
Ty Cobb	rf	5	19	3	7	1	0	0	4	1	2	2	.368
Sam Crawford	cf	5	21	2	5	1	0	0	1	1	2	0	.238
Matty McIntyre	lf	5	18	2	4	1	0	0	0	3	2	1	.222
Boss Schmidt	c	4	14	0	1	0	0	0	1	0	2	0	.071
Red Downs	2b	2	6	1	1	1	0	0	1	1	2	0	.167
Ira Thomas	ph-c	2	4	0	2	1	0	0	1	1	0	0	.500
Davy Jones	ph	3	2	1	0	0	0	0	0	1	1	0	.000
Red Killefer		Did not play											
Ed Summers	p	2	5	0	1	0	0	0	1	0	2	0	.200
Wild Bill Donovan	p	2	4	0	0	0	0	0	0	1	1	1	.000
George Mullin	p	1	3	1	1	0	0	0	1	1	0	0	.333
Ed Killian	p	1	0	0	0	0	0	0	0	0	0	0	.000
George Winter	pr-p	2	0	0	0	0	0	0	0	0	0	0	.000
Ed Willett		Did not play—ankle injury											
George Suggs		Did not play											
Team Total		5	158	15	32	5	0	0	14	12	26	6	.203
		Double Plays—5 Left on Bases—27											
George Mullin	p	1	3	1	1	0	0	0	1	1	0	0	.333
Ed Killian	p	1	0	0	0	0	0	0	0	0	0	0	.000
George Winter	pr-p	2	0	0	0	0	0	0	0	0	0	0	.000
Ed Willett		Did not play—ankle injury											
George Suggs		Did not play											
Team Total		5	158	15	32	5	0	0	14	12	26	6	.203
		Double Plays—5 Left on Bases—27											

PITCHING	G	GS	CG	IP	H	R	ER	BB	SO	W	L	SVB	ERA
Chicago													
Orvie Overall	3	2	2	18⅓	7	2	2	7	15	2	0	0	0.98
Three Finger Brown	2	1	1	11	6	1	0	1	5	2	0	0	0.00
Jack Pfiester	1	1	0	8	10	8	7	3	1	0	1	0	7.88
Ed Reulbach	2	1	0	7⅔	9	4	4	1	5	0	0	0	4.70
Chick Fraser		Did not play											
Carl Lundgren		Did not play											
Rube Kroh		Did not play											
Team Total	5	5	3	45	32	15	13	12	26	4	1	0	2.60
Detroit													
Wild Bill Donovan	2	2	2	17	17	8	8	4	10	0	2	0	4.24
Ed Summers	2	1	0	14⅔	18	8	7	4	7	0	2	0	4.30
George Mullin	1	1	1	9	1	3	0	1	8	1	0	0	0.00
Ed Killian	1	1	0	2⅓	5	4	3	3	1	0	0	0	11.57
George Winter	1	0	0	1	1	1	0	1	0	0	0	0	0.00
Ed Willett		Did not play—ankle injury											
George Suggs		Did not play											
Team Total	5	5	3	44	48	24	18	13	26	1	4	0	3.68

Ty Cobb

1909

Pittsburgh N.L. 4
Detroit A.L. 3

Highlights

THE DETROIT TIGERS WERE BACK for a third time, facing the Pittsburgh Pirates. It was a battle of the Titans between the world's two best players, Ty Cobb and Honus Wagner. Cobb, 22, led the A.L. with .377, 9 homers, 107 RBI's and 76 stolen bases. Wagner, 35, had just won his fourth straight N.L. batting title with a .399 average, set off by a league-leading 100 RBI's.

But neither giant was a Series hero. That honor went to the Pirates' 27-year-old reserve pitcher Babe Adams. Passing over Camnitz, Willis and Leifield, Pittsburgh manager Fred Clarke tapped Adams to pitch the opener. Adams allowed one hit in the top of the first, but went on to win, 4-1. Clarke sent Howie Camnitz (25 games) to the mound in game two, but the Tigers beat him, 7-2, with Cobb causing a stir with a daring steal of home in the third inning.

Honus Wagner got three hits, two RBI's and three stolen bases in game three, which the Pirates won, 8-6. The Tigers drew even with a fourth-game 5-0 shutout by George Mullin. Adams beat the Tigers a second time, 8-4, in game five. Down three games to two, the Tigers came back to take game six, 5-4, forcing the Series into a seventh game for the first time. Adams won game seven, 8-0, to give the Pirates the Championship.

Game 1 Oct. 8
Detroit   100 000 000 · 1
Pittsburgh   000 121 00* · 4
Winner-Adams   Loser-Mullin

Game 2 Oct. 9
Detroit   023 020 000 · 7
Pittsburgh   200 000 000 · 2
Winner-Donovan   Loser-Camnitz

Game 3 Oct. 11
Pittsburgh   510 000 002 · 8
Detroit   000 000 402 · 6
Winner-Maddox   Loser-Summers

Game 4 Oct. 12
Pittsburgh   000 000 000 · 0
Detroit   020 300 00* · 5
Winner-Mullin   Loser-Leifield

Game 5 Oct. 13
Detroit   100 002 010 · 4
Pittsburgh   111 000 41* · 8
Winner-Adams   Loser-Summers

Game 6 Oct. 14
Pittsburgh   300 000 001 · 4
Detroit   100 211 00* · 5
Winner-Mullin   Loser-Willis

Game 7 Oct. 16
Pittsburgh   020 203 010 · 8
Detroit   000 000 000 · 0
Winner-Adams   Loser-Donovan

Total Attendance—145,807
Average Attendance—20,830
Winning Player's Share—$1,825
Losing Player's Share—$1,275

BATTING	Pos	G	AB	R	H	2B	3B	HR	RBI	BB	SO	SB	BA
Pittsburgh													
Bill Abstein	1b	7	26	3	6	2	0	0	2	3	9	1	.231
Dots Miller	2b	7	28	2	7	1	0	0	4	2	5	3	.250
Honus Wagner	ss	7	24	4	8	2	1	0	6	4	2	6	.333
Bobby Byrne	3b	7	24	5	6	1	0	0	0	1	4	1	.250
Owen Wilson	rf	7	26	2	4	1	0	0	1	0	2	1	.154
Tommy Leach	cf-3b	7	25	8	9	4	0	0	2	2	1	1	.360
Fred Clarke	lf	7	19	7	4	0	0	2	7	5	3	3	.211
George Gibson	c	7	25	2	6	2	0	0	2	1	1	2	.240
Ham Hyatt	ph-cf	2	4	1	0	0	0	0	1	1	0	0	.000
Ed Abbaticchio	ph	1	1	0	0	0	0	0	0	0	1	0	.000
Paddy O'Connor	ph	1	1	0	0	0	0	0	0	0	1	0	.000
Mike Simon	Did not play												
Babe Adams	p	3	9	0	0	0	0	0	0	1	1	0	.000
Vic Willis	p	2	4	0	0	0	0	0	0	0	1	0	.000
Nick Maddox	p	1	4	0	0	0	0	0	0	0	1	0	.000
Deacon Phillippe	p	2	1	0	0	0	0	0	0	0	1	0	.000
Lefty Leifield	p	1	1	0	0	0	0	0	0	0	1	0	.000
Howie Camnitz	p	2	1	0	0	0	0	0	0	0	0	0	.000
Sam Leever	Did not play												
Sammy Frock	Did not play												
Chick Brandom	Did not play												
Bill Powell	Did not play												
Gene Moore	Did not play												
Team Total		7	223	34	50	13	1	2	25	20	34	18	.224

Double Plays—3   Left on Bases—44

BATTING	Pos	G	AB	R	H	2B	3B	HR	RBI	BB	SO	SB	BA
Detroit													
Tom Jones	1b	7	24	3	6	1	0	0	2	2	0	1	.250
Jim Delahanty	2b	7	26	2	9	4	0	0	4	2	5	0	.346
Donie Bush	ss	7	23	5	6	1	0	0	3	5	3	1	.261
George Moriarty	3b	7	22	4	6	1	0	0	1	3	1	0	.273
Ty Cobb	rf	7	26	3	6	3	0	0	5	2	2	2	.231
Sam Crawford	cf-1b	7	28	4	7	3	0	1	4	1	1	1	.250
Davy Jones	lf-cf	7	30	6	7	0	0	0	1	1	3	1	.233
Boss Schmidt	c	6	18	0	4	2	0	0	4	2	0	0	.222
Oscar Stanage	c	2	5	0	1	0	0	0	2	0	2	0	.200
Matty McIntyre	ph-lf	4	3	0	0	0	0	0	0	0	1	0	.000
Charley O'Leary	3b	1	3	0	0	0	0	0	0	0	0	0	.000
Heinie Beckendorf	Did not play												
George Mullin	p-ph	6	16	1	3	1	0	0	0	1	3	0	.188
Wild Bill Donovan	p	2	4	0	0	0	0	0	0	0	1	0	.000
Ed Summers	p	2	3	0	0	0	0	0	0	0	2	0	.000
Ed Willett	p	2	2	0	0	0	0	0	0	0	0	0	.000
Ralph Works	p	1	0	0	0	0	0	0	0	0	0	0	.000
Ed Killian	Did not play												
Kid Speer	Did not play												
Team Total		7	233	28	55	16	0	2	26	20	22	6	.236

Double Plays—4   Left on Bases—50

PITCHING	G	GS	CG	IP	H	R	ER	BB	SO	W	L	SVB	ERA
Pittsburgh													
Babe Adams	3	3	3	27	18	5	4	6	11	3	0	0	1.33
Vic Willis	2	1	0	11⅓	10	7	5	8	3	0	1	0	3.97
Nick Maddox	1	1	1	9	10	6	1	2	4	1	0	0	1.00
Deacon Phillippe	2	0	0	6	2	0	0	1	2	0	0	0	0.00
Lefty Leifield	1	1	0	4	7	5	5	1	0	0	1	0	11.25
Howie Camnitz	2	1	0	3⅔	8	5	4	2	2	0	1	0	9.82
Sam Leever	Did not play												
Sammy Frock	Did not play												
Chick Brandom	Did not play												
Dick Powell	Did not play												
Gene Moore	Did not play												
Team Total	7	7	4	61	55	28	19	20	22	4	3	0	2.80
Detroit													
George Mullin	4	3	3	32	23	14	8	8	20	2	1	0	2.25
Wild Bill Donovan	2	2	1	12	7	4	4	8	7	1	1	0	3.00
Ed Summers	2	2	0	7⅓	13	12	7	4	4	0	2	0	8.59
Ed Willett	2	0	0	7⅔	3	2	0	0	1	0	0	0	0.00
Ralph Works	1	0	0	2	4	2	2	0	2	0	0	0	9.00
Ed Killian	Did not play												
Kid Speer	Did not play												
Team Total	7	7	4	61	50	34	21	20	34	3	4	0	3.10

1910

Philadelphia A.L. 4
Chicago N.L. 1

Highlights

THE CHICAGO CUBS, WINNING 114 games, were back for the fourth time in five years. Tinker, Evers and Chance were still on board, but outfielders Solly Hofman and Wildfire Schulte were now offensive leaders. Three Finger Brown led pitchers with 25 wins; rookie King Cole was not far behind with 20 wins. Evers was out with a broken leg. On the A.L. side, Connie Mack had led his Philadelphia A's to their third pennant and second Series with a league record of 102 victories. The A's had Eddie Collins, 23, on second with .322, 81 RBI's and 81 stolen bases. Chief Bender, Eddie Plank, Cy Morgan, and Jack Coombs (31 games, 1.30 ERA) were the Mack moundsmen. Rube Oldring and Eddie Plank were out with injuries.

Bender beat Orvie Overall, 4-1, in game one, and Coombs beat Brown, 9-3, in game two. Mack then started Coombs in game three with only a day's rest. Chicago's Frank Chance was ejected for protesting an umpire's call. Coombs led the A's to a 12-5 victory.

The Cubs rallied to win game four, 4-3, but it was too late. The A's trounced them, 7-2, in the final game. Philadelphia had averaged .316 as a team, with Collins at .429, Baker at .409 and Coombs at .385, with three winning games on the mound.

Game 1 Oct. 17

Chicago	000 000 001	1
Philadelphia	021 000 01*	4

Winner-Bender   Loser-Overall

Game 2 Oct. 18

Chicago	100 000 101	3
Philadelphia	002 010 60*	9

Winner-Coombs   Loser-Brown

Game 3 Oct. 20

Philadelphia	125 000 400	12
Chicago	120 000 020	5

Winner-Coombs   Loser-McIntire

Game 4 Oct. 22

Philadelphia	001 200 000	3
Chicago	100 100 001	4

Winner-Brown   Loser-Bender

Game 5 Oct. 23

Philadelphia	100 010 050	7
Chicago	010 000 010	2

Winner-Coombs   Loser-Brown

Total Attendance—124,222
Average Attendance—24,844
Winning Player's Share—$2,068
Losing Player's Share—$1,375

BATTING	Pos	G	AB	R	H	2B	3B	HR	RBI	BB	SO	SB	BA
Philadelphia													
Harry Davis	1b	5	17	5	6	3	0	0	2	3	4	0	.353
Eddie Collins	2b	5	21	5	9	4	0	0	3	2	2	4	.429
Jack Barry	ss	5	17	3	4	2	0	0	3	1	3	0	.235
Frank Baker	3b	5	22	6	9	3	0	0	4	2	1	0	.409
Danny Murphy	rf	5	20	6	7	3	0	1	9	1	0	1	.350
Amos Strunk	cf	4	18	2	5	1	1	0	2	2	5	0	.278
Bris Lord	lf-cf	5	22	3	4	2	0	0	1	1	3	0	.182
Ira Thomas	c	5	12	2	3	0	0	0	1	4	1	0	.250
Topsy Hartsel	lf	1	5	2	1	0	0	0	0	0	1	2	.200
Jack Lapp	c	1	4	0	1	0	0	0	1	0	2	0	.250
Rube Oldring	Did not play—injured												
Paddy Livingston	Did not play												
Stuffy McInnis	Did not play												
Ben Houser	Did not play												
Pat Donahue	Did not play												
Claude Derrick	Did not play												
Jack Coombs	p	3	13	0	5	1	0	0	3	0	1	0	.385
Chief Bender	p	2	6	1	2	0	0	0	1	1	1	0	.333
Cy Morgan	Did not play												
Eddie Plank	Did not play												
Harry Krause	Did not play												
Jimmy Dygert	Did not play												
Tommy Atkins	Did not play												
Team Total		5	177	35	56	19	1	1	30	17	24	7	.316

Double Plays—6   Left on Bases—36

	Pos	G	AB	R	H	2B	3B	HR	RBI	BB	SO	SB	BA
Chicago													
Frank Chance	1b	5	17	1	6	1	1	0	4	0	3	0	.353
Heinie Zimmerman	2b	5	17	0	4	1	0	0	2	1	3	1	.235
Joe Tinker	ss	5	18	2	6	2	0	0	2	2	2	1	.333
Harry Steinfeldt	3b	5	20	0	2	1	0	0	1	0	4	0	.100
Wildfire Schulte	rf	5	17	3	6	3	0	0	2	2	3	0	.353
Solly Hofman	cf	5	15	2	4	0	0	0	2	4	3	0	.267
Jimmy Sheckard	lf	5	14	5	4	2	0	0	1	7	2	1	.286
Johnny Kling	c-ph	5	13	0	1	0	0	0	1	1	2	0	.077
Jimmy Archer	1b-c	3	11	1	2	1	0	0	0	0	3	0	.182
Ginger Beaumont	ph	3	2	1	0	0	0	0	0	1	1	0	.000
Tom Needham	ph	1	1	0	0	0	0	0	0	0	0	0	.000
John Kane	pr	1	0	0	0	0	0	0	0	0	0	0	.000
Johnny Evers	Did not play—injured												
Three Finger Brown	p	3	7	0	0	0	0	0	0	0	1	0	.000
King Cole	p	1	2	0	0	0	0	0	0	0	2	0	.000
Jack Pfiester	p	1	2	0	0	0	0	0	0	0	1	0	.000
Harry McIntire	p	2	1	0	0	0	0	0	0	0	1	0	.000
Orvie Overall	p	1	1	0	0	0	0	0	0	0	0	0	.000
Ed Reulbach	p	1	0	0	0	0	0	0	0	0	0	0	.000
Lew Richie	p	1	0	0	0	0	0	0	0	0	0	0	.000
Big Jeff Pfeffer	Did not play												
Orlie Weaver	Did not play												
Bill Foxen	Did not play												
Team Total		5	158	15	35	11	1	0	13	18	31	3	.222

Double Plays—3   Left on Bases—31

PITCHING	G	GS	CG	IP	H	R	ER	BB	SO	W	L	SVB	ERA
Philadelphia													
Jack Coombs	3	3	3	27	23	10	10	14	17	3	0	0	3.33
Chief Bender	2	2	2	18⅔	12	5	4	4	14	1	1	0	1.93
Cy Morgan	Did not play												
Eddie Plank	Did not play												
Harry Krause	Did not play												
Jimmy Dygert	Did not play												
Tommy Atkins	Did not play												
Team Total	5	5	5	45⅔	35	15	14	18	31	4	1	0	2.76
Chicago													
Three Finger Brown	3	2	1	18	23	16	11	7	14	1	2	0	5.50
King Cole	1	1	0	8	10	3	3	3	5	0	0	0	3.38
Jack Pfiester	1	0	0	6⅔	9	5	0	1	1	0	0	0	0.00
Harry McIntire	2	0	0	5⅓	4	5	4	3	1	0	1	0	6.75
Orvie Overall	1	1	0	3	6	3	3	1	1	0	1	0	9.00
Ed Reulbach	1	1	0	2	3	3	2	2	0	0	0	0	9.00
Lew Richie	1	0	0	1	1	0	0	0	0	0	0	0	0.00
Big Jeff Pfeffer	Did not play												
Orlie Weaver	Did not play												
Bill Foxen	Did not play												
Team Total	5	5	1	44	56	35	23	17	24	1	4	0	4.70

1911

Philadelphia A.L. 4
New York N.L. 2

Highlights

THE PHILADELPHIA A'S WERE back again, with 101 wins and their famous "$100,000 Infield" of McInnis, Collins, Barry and Baker. Facing them were John McGraw's New York Giants with Merkle, Doyle, Meyers, Fletcher, Herzog and 26-game-winner Christy Mathewson and 24-game-winner Rube Marquard.

Mathewson and Bender dueled to a 2-1 Giants win in the opener. Plank hurled a 3-1 victory over Marquard in game two. The A's' Frank Baker, A.L. home-run leader with 11 homers, added another to his tally by batting an inside fastball over the right-field fence. Baker did it again in game three as Mathewson and Coombs dueled to a 3-2 Philadelphia win, earning the nickname "Home Run Baker" for his efforts.

Six days of rain. Then Bender beat Mathewson, 4-2, in game four. McGraw put Marquard on the mound to beat Coombs, 4-3, in game five. But in game six the Giants went through three pitchers for 13 runs while Bender held New York to two runs, for the Series victory, four games to two.

Game 1 Oct. 14
Philadelphia   010 000 000 · 1
New York   000 100 10* · 2
Winner-Mathewson   Loser-Bender

Game 2 Oct. 16
New York   010 000 000 · 1
Philadelphia   100 002 00* · 3
Winner-Plank   Loser-Marquard

Game 3 Oct. 17
Philadelphia   000 000 001   02 · 3
New York   001 000 000   01 · 2
Winner-Coombs   Loser-Mathewson

Game 4 Oct. 24
New York   200 000 000 · 2
Philadelphia   000 310 00* · 4
Winner-Bender   Loser-Mathewson

Game 5 Oct. 25
Philadelphia   003 000 000   0 · 3
New York   000 000 102   1 · 4
Winner-Crandall   Loser-Plank

Game 6 Oct. 26
New York   100 000 001 · 2
Philadephia   001 401 70* · 13
Winner-Bender   Loser-Ames

Total Attendance—179,851
Average Attendance—29,975
Winning Player's Share—$3,655
Losing Player's Share—$2,436

BATTING

	Pos	G	AB	R	H	2B	3B	HR	RBI	BB	SO	SB	BA
Philadelphia													
Harry Davis	1b	6	24	3	5	1	0	0	5	0	3	0	.208
Eddie Collins	2b	6	21	4	6	1	0	0	1	2	2	2	.286
Jack Barry	ss	6	19	2	7	4	0	0	2	0	2	2	.368
Frank Baker	3b	6	24	7	9	2	0	2	5	1	5	0	**.375**
Danny Murphy	rf	6	23	4	7	3	0	0	3	0	3	0	.304
Rube Oldring	cf	6	25	2	5	2	0	1	3	0	5	0	.200
Bris Lord	lf	6	**27**	2	5	2	0	0	1	0	5	0	.185
Ira Thomas	c	4	12	1	1	0	0	0	1	1	2	0	.083
Jack Lapp	c	2	8	1	2	0	0	0	0	0	1	0	.250
Stuffy McInnis	1b	1	0	0	0	0	0	0	0	0	0	0	.000
Amos Strunk	ph	1	0	0	0	0	0	0	0	0	0	0	.000
Claude Derrick		Did not play											
Paddy Livingston		Did not play											
Topsy Hartsel		Did not play											
Chief Bender	p	3	11	0	1	0	0	0	0	0	1	0	.091
Jack Coombs	p	2	8	1	2	0	0	0	0	0	0	0	.250
Eddie Plank	p	2	3	0	0	0	0	0	0	0	2	0	.000
Cy Morgan		Did not play											
Harry Krause		Did not play											
Doc Martin		Did not play											
Dave Danforth		Did not play											
Team Total		6	205	27	50	15	0	3	21	4	31	4	.244

Double Plays—2   Left on Bases—29

	Pos	G	AB	R	H	2B	3B	HR	RBI	BB	SO	SB	BA
New York													
Fred Merkle	1b	6	20	1	3	1	0	0	1	**2**	6	0	.150
Larry Doyle	2b	6	23	3	7	3	1	0	1	2	1	2	.304
Art Fletcher	ss	6	23	1	3	1	0	0	1	0	4	0	.130
Buck Herzog	3b	6	21	3	4	2	0	0	0	2	3	2	.190
Red Murray	rf	6	21	0	0	0	0	0	0	2	5	0	.000
Fred Snodgrass	cf	6	19	1	2	0	0	0	1	**2**	7	0	.105
Josh Devore	lf	6	24	1	4	1	0	0	3	1	**8**	0	.167
Chief Meyers	c	6	20	2	6	2	0	0	2	0	3	0	.300
Beals Becker	ph	3	3	0	0	0	0	0	0	0	0	0	.000
Art Wilson	c	1	1	0	0	0	0	0	0	0	0	0	.000
Art Devlin		Did not play											
Grover Hartley		Did not play											
Gene Paulette		Did not play											
Christy Mathewson	p	3	7	0	2	0	0	0	0	1	3	0	.286
Rube Marquard	p	3	2	0	0	0	0	0	0	0	2	0	.000
Red Ames	p	2	2	0	1	0	0	0	0	0	1	0	.500
Doc Crandall	p-ph	3	2	1	1	1	0	0	1	0	**2**	0	.500
Hooks Wiltse	p	2	1	0	0	0	0	0	0	0	1	0	.000
Louis Drucke		Did not play											
Team Total		6	189	13	33	11	1	0	10	14	44	4	.175

Double Plays—2   Left on Bases—33

PITCHING

	G	GS	CG	IP	H	R	ER	BB	SO	W	L	SVB	ERA
Philadelphia													
Chief Bender	**3**	**3**	**3**	26	16	6	3	**8**	**20**	2	1	0	**1.04**
Jack Coombs	2	2	1	20	11	5	3	6	16	1	0	0	1.35
Eddie Plank	2	1	1	9⅔	6	2	2	0	8	1	1	0	1.86
Cy Morgan	Did not play												
Harry Krause	Did not play												
Doc Martin	Did not play												
Dave Danforth	Did not play												
Team Total	6	6	5	55⅔	33	13	8	14	44	4	2	0	1.29
New York													
Christy Mathewson	**3**	**3**	2	27	25	8	6	2	13	1	**2**	0	2.00
Rube Marquard	**3**	2	0	11⅔	9	6	2	1	8	0	1	0	1.54
Red Ames	2	1	0	8	6	5	2	1	6	0	1	0	2.25
Doc Crandall	2	0	0	4	2	0	0	0	2	1	0	0	0.00
Hooks Wiltse	2	0	0	3⅓	8	**8**	7	0	2	0	0	0	18.90
Louis Drucke	Did not play												
Team Total	6	6	2	54	50	27	17	4	31	2	4	0	2.83

1912

Boston A.L. 4
New York N.L. 3

Highlights

WITH SMOKEY JOE WOOD (36 games) on the mound and Duffy Lewis, Tris Speaker and Harry Hooper in the outfield, Boston won the A.L. pennant just in time to celebrate the opening of new Fenway Park. Speaker had .383 average, 90 RBI's, 10 homers and 52 stolen bases. The Red Sox faced Mc-Graw's New York Giants with Mathewson (23 games) and Marquard (26 games) on the mound.

New York rookie Jeff Tesreau lost game one to Wood, 4-3. Called because of darkness, game two ended in a 6-6 tie after 11 innings. Marquard won game three, 2-1, to even the Series. Boston came back to win the next two games, with Wood and Hugh Bedient on the mound. Game six saw Marquard win, 5-2, for New York, and the next day the Giants' batters aided Tesreau, to create an 11-4 victory, evening the Series.

The deciding game pitted Mathewson against Bedient. It was marked by a spectacular catch by Boston's Hooper on Larry Doyle and the famous "$30,000" muffed catch by Giants Fred Snodgrass on a high fly by Clyde Engle. Things went downhill for New York from then on, and Boston won the game, 3-2, and the Series.

Game 1 Oct. 8
Boston   000 001 300 · 4
New York   002 000 001 · 3
Winner-Wood   Loser-Tesreau

Game 2 Oct. 9
New York   010 100 030 10 · 6
Boston   300 010 010 10 · 6
Stopped by Darkness

Game 3 Oct. 10
New York   010 010 000 · 2
Boston   000 000 001 · 1
Winner-Marquard   Loser-O'Brien

Game 4 Oct. 11
Boston   010 100 001 · 3
New York   000 000 100 · 1
Winner-Wood   Loser-Tesreau

Game 5 Oct. 12
New York   000 000 100 · 1
Boston   002 000 00* · 2
Winner-Bedient   Loser-Mathewson

Game 6 Oct. 14
Boston   020 000 000 · 2
New York   500 000 00* · 5
Winner-Marquard   Loser-O'Brien

Game 7 Oct. 15
New York   610 002 101 · 11
Boston   010 000 210 · 4
Winner-Tesreau   Loser-Wood

Game 8 Oct. 16
New York   001 000 000 1· 2
Boston   000 000 100 2· 3
Winner-Wood   Loser-Mathewson

Total Attendance—252,037
Average Attendance—31,505
Winning Player's Share—$4,025
Losing Player's Share—$2,566

BATTING	Pos	G	AB	R	H	2B	3B	HR	RBI	BB	SO	SB	BA
Boston													
Jake Stahl	1b	8	32	3	8	2	0	0	2	0	6	2	.250
Steve Yerkes	2b	8	32	3	8	0	2	0	4	2	3	0	.250
Heinie Wagner	ss	8	30	1	5	1	0	0	0	3	6	1	.167
Larry Gardner	3b	8	28	4	5	2	1	1	4	2	5	0	.179
Harry Hooper	rf	8	31	3	9	2	1	0	2	4	4	2	.290
Tris Speaker	cf	8	30	4	9	1	2	0	2	4	2	1	.300
Duffy Lewis	lf	8	32	4	6	3	0	0	2	2	2	0	.188
Hick Cady	c	7	22	1	3	0	0	0	1	0	3	0	.136
Bill Carrigan	c	2	7	0	0	0	0	0	0	0	0	0	.000
Clyde Engle	ph	3	3	1	1	1	0	0	2	0	0	0	.333
Olaf Henriksen	pr-ph	2	1	0	1	1	0	0	1	0	0	0	1.000
Neal Ball	ph	1	1	0	0	0	0	0	0	0	1	0	.000
Hugh Bradley		Did not play											
Les Nunamaker		Did not play											
Marty Krug		Did not play											
Pinch Thomas		Did not play											
Smokey Joe Wood	p	4	7	1	2	0	0	0	1	1	0	0	.286
Hugh Bedient	p	4	6	0	0	0	0	0	0	0	0	0	.000
Ray Collins	p	2	5	0	0	0	0	0	0	0	2	0	.000
Charley Hall	p	2	4	0	3	1	0	0	0	0	1	0	.750
Buck O'Brien	p	2	2	0	0	0	0	0	0	0	2	0	.000
Larry Pape		Did not play											
Team Total		8	273	25	60	14	6	1	21	19	36	6	.220

Double Plays—5   Left on Bases—55

	Pos	G	AB	R	H	2B	3B	HR	RBI	BB	SO	SB	BA
New York													
Fred Merkle	1b	8	33	5	9	2	1	0	3	0	7	1	.273
Larry Doyle	2b	8	33	5	8	1	0	1	2	3	2	2	.242
Art Fletcher	ss	8	28	1	5	1	0	0	3	1	4	1	.179
Buck Herzog	3b	8	30	6	12	4	1	0	4	1	3	2	.400
Red Murray	rf-lf	8	31	5	10	4	1	0	5	2	2	0	.323
Fred Snodgrass	cf-lf-rf	8	33	7	7	2	0	0	2	2	5	1	.212
Josh Devore	lf	7	24	4	6	0	0	0	0	7	5	4	.250
Chief Meyers	c	8	28	2	10	0	1	0	3	2	3	1	.357
Beals Becker	pr-cf	4	4	1	0	0	0	0	0	2	0	0	.000
Moose McCormick	ph	5	4	0	1	0	0	0	1	0	0	0	.250
Art Wilson	c	2	1	0	1	0	0	0	0	0	0	0	1.000
Tillie Shafer	ss	3	0	0	0	0	0	0	0	0	0	0	.000
George Burns		Did not play											
Heinie Groh		Did not play											
Grover Hartley		Did not play											
Christy Mathewson	p	3	12	0	2	0	0	0	0	0	4	0	.167
Jeff Tesreau	p	3	8	0	3	0	0	0	2	1	3	0	.375
Rube Marquard	p	2	4	0	0	0	0	0	0	• 1	0	0	.000
Doc Crandall	p	1	1	0	0	0	0	0	0	0	1	0	.000
Red Ames	p	1	0	0	0	0	0	0	0	0	0	0	.000
Hooks Wiltse		Did not play											
Team Total		8	274	31	74	14	4	1	25	22	39	12	.270

Double Plays—4   Left on Bases—53

PITCHING	G	GS	CG	IP	H	R	ER	BB	SO	W	L	SVB	ERA
Boston													
Smokey Joe Wood	4	3	2	22	27	11	9	3	21	3	1	0	3.68
Hugh Bedient	4	2	1	18	10	2	2	7	7	1	0	0	1.00
Ray Collins	2	1	0	14⅓	14	5	3	0	6	0	0	0	1.88
Charley Hall	2	0	0	10⅔	11	6	4	9	1	0	0	0	3.38
Buck O'Brien	2	2	0	9	12	7	5	3	4	0	2	0	5.00
Larry Pape		Did not play											
Team Total	8	8	3	74	74	31	23	22	39	4	3	0	2.80
New York													
Christy Mathewson	3	3	3	28⅔	23	11	4	5	10	0	2	0	1.26
Jeff Tesreau	3	3	1	23	19	10	8	11	15	0	2	0	3.13
Rube Marquard	2	2	2	18	14	3	1	2	9	2	0	0	0.50
Doc Crandall	1	0	0	2	1	0	0	0	2	0	0	0	0.00
Red Ames	1	0	0	2	3	1	1	1	0	0	0	0	4.50
Hooks Wiltse		Did not play											
Team Total	8	8	6	73⅔	60	25	14	19	36	3	4	0	1.71

1913

Highlights

MC GRAW'S GIANTS WERE BACK for the third straight time, but the team was crippled by injuries. Despite the loss of Jack Coombs to illness, Connie Mack's Philadelphia A's were back as the A.L. champs.

Game one face-off between Rube Marquard (23 games) and Chief Bender (21 games) resulted in a 6-4 win for A's. In pre-game practice for game two, Giants catcher Chief Meyers broke a finger and Fred Merkle's bad leg gave out, forcing McGraw to adjust his lineup. Fred Snodgrass' leg problems in third inning led McGraw to unorthodox substitution of veteran pitcher Hooks Wiltse at first. The Giants dug in and won the game, 3-0, to even the Series.

Mack put Bullet Joe Bush, 23, on the mound in game three, and the A's won, 8-2. Chief Bender pitched A's to 6-5 win in game four. Now down three games to one in Series, McGraw started Mathewson in game five against Eddie Plank. It didn't help. The A's won the game, 3-1, and the Series.

Game 1 Oct. 7
Philadelphia	000 320 010 ·	6
New York	001 030 000 ·	4

Winner-Bender Loser-Marquard

Game 2 Oct. 8
New York	000 000 000 3 ·	3
Philadelphia	000 000 000 0 ·	0

Winner-Mathewson Loser-Plank

Game 3 Oct. 9
Philadelphia	320 000 210 ·	8
New York	000 010 100 ·	2

Winner-Bush Loser-Tesreau

Game 4 Oct. 10
New York	000 000 320 ·	5
Philadelphia	010 320 00* ·	6

Winner-Bender Loser-Demaree

Game 5 Oct. 11
Philadelphia	102 000 000 ·	3
New York	000 010 000 ·	1

Winner-Plank Loser-Mathewson

Total Attendance—150,992
Average Attendance—30,198
Winning Player's Share—$3,246
Losing Player's Share—$2,164

Philadelphia A.L. 4
New York N.L. 1

BATTING	Pos	G	AB	R	H	2B	3B	HR	RBI	BB	SO	SB	BA
Philadelphia													
Stuffy McInnis	1b	5	17	1	2	1	0	0	2	0	2	0	.118
Eddie Collins	2b	5	19	5	8	0	2	0	3	1	2	3	.421
Jack Barry	ss	5	20	3	6	3	0	0	2	0	0	0	.300
Frank Baker	3b	5	20	2	9	0	0	1	7	0	2	1	.450
Eddie Murphy	rf	5	22	2	5	0	0	0	0	2	0	0	.227
Amos Strunk	cf	5	17	3	2	0	0	0	0	2	2	0	.118
Rube Oldring	lf	5	22	5	6	0	1	0	0	0	1	1	.273
Wally Schang	c	4	14	2	5	0	1	1	6	0	4	0	.357
Jack Lapp	c	1	4	0	1	0	0	0	0	0	1	0	.250
Jimmy Walsh	Did not play												
Tom Daley	Did not play												
Bill Orr	Did not play												
Danny Murphy	Did not play												
Ira Thomas	Did not play												
Harry Davis	Did not play												
Doc Lavan	Did not play												
Chief Bender	p	2	8	0	0	0	0	0	0	0	1	0	.000
Eddie Plank	p	2	7	0	1	0	0	0	1	0	0	0	.143
Bullet Joe Bush	p	1	4	0	1	0	0	0	0	0	1	0	.250
Boardwalk Brown	Did not play												
Duke Houck	Did not play												
Bob Shawkey	Did not play												
Weldon Wyckoff	Did not play												
Herb Pennock	Did not play												
Jack Coombs	Did not play—illness												
Team Total		5	174	23	46	4	4	2	21	7	16	5	.204
		Double Plays—6		Left on Bases—30									
New York													
Fred Merkle	1b	4	13	3	3	0	0	1	3	1	2	0	.231
Larry Doyle	2b	5	20	1	3	0	0	0	2	0	1	0	.150
Art Fletcher	ss	5	18	1	5	0	0	0	4	1	1	1	.278
Buck Herzog	3b	5	19	1	1	0	0	0	0	0	1	0	.053
Red Murray	rf	5	16	2	4	0	0	0	1	2	2	2	.250
Tillie Shafer	cf-3b	5	19	2	3	1	1	0	1	2	3	0	.158
George Burns	lf	5	19	2	3	2	0	0	1	1	5	1	.158
Larry McLean	ph-c	5	12	0	6	0	0	0	2	0	0	0	.500
Chief Meyers	c	1	4	0	0	0	0	0	0	0	0	0	.000
Art Wilson	c	3	3	0	0	0	0	0	0	0	2	0	.000
Fred Snodgrass	1b-cf	2	3	0	1	0	0	0	0	0	0	0	.333
Moose McCormick	ph	2	2	1	1	0	0	0	0	0	0	0	.500
Eddie Grant	pr-ph	2	1	1	0	0	0	0	0	0	0	0	.000
Claude Cooper	pr	2	0	0	0	0	0	0	0	0	0	1	.000
Jim Thorpe	Did not play												
Grover Hartley	Did not play												
Christy Mathewson	p	2	5	1	3	0	0	0	1	1	0	0	.600
Doc Crandall	p-ph	4	4	0	0	0	0	0	0	0	0	0	.000
Jeff Tesreau	p	2	2	0	0	0	0	0	0	0	1	0	.000
Rube Marquard	p	2	1	0	0	0	0	0	0	0	0	0	.000
Al Demaree	p	1	1	0	0	0	0	0	0	0	0	0	.000
Hooks Wiltse	pr-1b	2	2	0	0	0	0	0	0	0	1	0	.000
Art Fromme	Did not play												
Team Total		5	164	15	33	3	1	1	15	8	19	5	.201
		Double Plays—1		Left on Bases—24									

PITCHING	G	GS	CG	IP	H	R	ER	BB	SO	W	L	SV	ERA
Philadelphia													
Eddie Plank	2	2	2	19	9	4	2	3	7	1	1	0	0.95
Chief Bender	2	2	2	18	19	9	8	1	9	2	0	0	4.00
Bullet Joe Bush	1	1	1	9	5	2	1	4	3	1	0	0	1.00
Boardwalk Brown	Did not play												
Duke Houck	Did not play												
Bob Shawkey	Did not play												
Weldon Wyckoff	Did not play												
Herb Pennock	Did not play												
Jack Coombs	Did not play—illness												
Team Total	5	5	5	46	33	15	11	8	19	4	1	0	2.15
New York													
Christy Mathewson	2	2	2	19	14	3	2	2	7	1	1	0	0.95
Rube Marquard	2	1	0	9	10	7	7	3	3	0	1	0	7.00
Jeff Tesreau	2	1	0	8 1/3	11	7	6	1	4	0	1	0	6.48
Doc Crandall	2	0	0	4 2/3	4	2	2	0	2	0	0	0	3.86
Al Demaree	1	1	0	4	7	4	2	1	0	0	1	0	4.50
Hooks Wiltse	Did not pitch												
Art Fromme	Did not play												
Team Total	5	5	2	45	46	23	19	7	16	1	4	0	3.80

1914

Boston N.L. 4
Philadelphia A.L. 0

Highlights

THE PHILADELPHIA A'S WERE first in the A.L. for the fourth time in five years. But the Boston Braves, in an astounding drive of 34 wins in 44 games, rose from the cellar in mid-July to take the N.L. flag from the New York Giants. Managed by George Stallings, the Braves had only three regular full-time players: first baseman Butch Schmidt, second baseman Johnny Evers and shortstop Rabbit Maranville. Pitchers were Dick Rudolph (27 games), Bill James (26 games) and Lefty Tyler (16 games). This phenomenal winning streak earned them the name "Miracle Braves," but Mack's club was still the heavy favorite.

Sparked by a single, a double and a triple, from catcher Hank Gowdy, the Braves rolled over the A's, 7-1, in game one. Game two was another Boston win, 1-0, with Bill James winning over Eddie Plank. A double by Gowdy in the 12th and a throwing error by Bush which sent pinch runner Mann home, gave Boston game three, 5-4. Irresistible now, the Braves went on to win game four, 3-1, with Dick Rudolph on the mound for a four-game sweep of the Series.

Game 1 Oct. 9
Boston   020 013 010 · 7
Philadelphia   010 000 000 · 1
Winner-Rudolph   Loser-Bender

Game 2 Oct. 10
Boston   000 000 001 · 1
Philadelphia   000 000 000 · 0
Winner-James   Loser-Plank

Game 3 Oct. 12
Philadelphia   100 100 000 200 · 4
Boston   010 100 000 201 · 5
Winner-James   Loser-Bush

Game 4 Oct. 13
Philadelphia   000 010 000 · 1
Boston   000 120 00* · 3
Winner-Rudolph   Loser-Shawkey

Total Attendance—111,009
Average Attendance—27,752
Winning Player's Share—$2,812
Losing Player's Share—$2,032

BATTING	Pos	G	AB	R	H	2B	3B	HR	RBI	BB	SO	SB	BA
Boston													
Butch Schmidt	1b	4	**17**	2	5	0	0	0	2	0	2	1	.294
Johnny Evers	2b	4	16	2	**7**	0	0	0	2	2	2	1	.438
Rabbit Maranville	ss	4	13	1	4	0	0	0	3	1	1	2	.308
Charlie Deal	3b	4	16	1	2	2	0	0	0	0	0	2	.125
Herbie Moran	rf	3	13	2	1	1	0	0	0	1	1	1	.077
Possum Whitted	cf	4	14	2	3	0	1	0	2	3	1	1	.214
Joe Connolly	lf	3	9	1	1	0	0	0	1	1	1	0	.111
Hank Gowdy	c	4	11	3	6	3	1	1	3	5	1	1	**.545**
Les Mann	rf-pr-ph-lf	3	7	1	2	0	0	0	1	0	1	0	.286
Ted Cather	lf	1	5	0	0	0	0	0	0	0	0	0	.000
Josh Devore	ph	1	1	0	0	0	0	0	0	0	1	0	.000
Larry Gilbert	ph	1	0	0	0	0	0	0	0	1	0	0	.000
Red Smith	Did not play—broken ankle												
Bert Whaling	Did not play												
Oscar Dugey	Did not play												
Billy Martin	Did not play												
Dick Rudolph	p	2	6	1	2	0	0	0	0	1	1	0	.333
Bill James	p	2	4	0	0	0	0	0	0	0	4	0	.000
Lefty Tyler	p	1	3	0	0	0	0	0	0	0	1	0	.000
Dick Crutcher	Did not play												
Otto Hess	Did not play												
Paul Strand	Did not play												
George Davis	Did not play												
Gene Cooreham	Did not play												
Dick Cottrell	Did not play												
Team Total		4	135	16	33	6	2	1	14	15	18	9	.244

Double Plays—4   Left on Bases—27

	Pos	G	AB	R	H	2B	3B	HR	RBI	BB	SO	SB	BA
Philadelphia													
Stuffy McInnis	1b	4	14	2	2	1	0	0	0	3	3	0	.143
Eddie Collins	2b	4	14	0	3	0	0	0	1	2	1	1	.214
Jack Barry	ss	4	14	1	1	0	0	0	0	1	1	1	.071
Frank Baker	3b	4	16	0	4	2	0	0	2	1	3	0	.250
Eddie Murphy	rf	4	16	2	3	2	0	0	0	2	2	0	.188
Amos Strunk	cf	2	7	0	2	0	0	0	0	0	2	0	.286
Rube Oldring	lf	4	15	0	1	0	0	0	0	0	5	0	.067
Wally Schang	c	4	12	1	2	1	0	0	0	1	4	0	.167
Jimmy Walsh	ph-cf	3	6	0	2	1	0	0	1	3	1	0	.333
Jack Lapp	c	1	1	0	0	0	0	0	0	0	0	0	.000
Larry Kopf	Did not play												
Chick Davies	Did not play												
Shag Thompson	Did not play												
Wickey McAvoy	Did not play												
Harry Davis	Did not play												
Ira Thomas	Did not play												
Bullet Joe Bush	p	1	5	0	0	0	0	0	0	0	2	0	.000
Eddie Plank	p	1	2	0	0	0	0	0	0	0	1	0	.000
Chief Bender	p	1	2	0	0	0	0	0	0	0	0	0	.000
Bob Shawkey	p	1	2	0	1	1	0	0	1	0	1	0	.500
Weldon Wyckoff	p	1	1	0	1	1	0	0	0	0	0	0	1.000
Herb Pennock	p	1	1	0	0	0	0	0	0	0	0	0	.000
Rube Bressler	Did not play												
Jack Coombs	Did not play												
Team Total		4	128	6	22	9	0	0	5	13	28	2	.172

Double Plays—4   Left on Bases—21

PITCHING	G	GS	CG	IP	H	R	ER	BB	SO	W	L	SV	ERA
Boston													
Dick Rudolph	**2**	**2**	**2**	18	12	2	1	4	15	2	0	0	0.50
Bill James	**2**	1	1	11	2	0	0	6	9	2	0	0	**0.00**
Lefty Tyler	1	1	0	10	8	4	4	3	4	0	0	0	3.60
Dick Crutcher	Did not play												
Otto Hess	Did not play												
George Davis	Did not play												
Paul Strand	Did not play												
Gene Cocreham	Did not play												
Dick Cottrell	Did not play												
Team Total	4	4	3	39	22	6	5	13	28	4	0	0	1.15
Philadelphia													
Bullet Joe Bush	1	1	1	11	9	5	4	4	4	0	1	0	3.27
Eddie Plank	1	1	1	9	7	1	1	4	6	0	1	0	1.00
Chief Bender	1	1	0	5⅓	8	6	6	2	3	0	1	0	10.13
Bob Shawkey	1	1	0	5	4	3	2	2	0	0	1	0	3.60
Weldon Wyckoff	1	0	0	3⅔	3	1	1	1	2	0	0	0	2.45
Herb Pennock	1	0	0	3	2	0	0	2	3	0	0	0	0.00
Rube Bressler	Did not play												
Chick Davies	Did not play												
Jack Coombs	Did not play												
Team Total	4	4	2	37	33	16	14	15	18	0	4	0	3.41

1915

Highlights

IT WAS PHILADELPHIA AND Boston again, only this time it was the Phillies against the Red Sox, not the Athletics against the Braves. The Red Sox still had Hooper, Speaker and Lewis, but their pitching staff was largely new. Righties Rube Foster (20 games) and Ernie Shore (19 games) and lefties Dutch Leonard (14 games) and a 21-year-old rookie called Babe Ruth (18 games). The Phillies had outfielder Gavvy Cravath (24 homers, 115 RBI's) leading the hitters and Grover Cleveland Alexander, 28, heading up pitchers with 31 wins.

Alexander won game one for Philadelphia, 3-1. Boston's Rube Foster pitched a three-hitter and drove in the winning run to give the Red Sox the second game, 2-1. President Woodrow Wilson watched this game, becoming the first President to see a World Series game.

With only two days' rest, Alexander pitched against Dutch Leonard but lost game three, 2-1. The Sox then took game four, 2-1. The Phils tried to come back but failed as Boston's Harry Hooper drove a ball that hopped a short fence in the ninth to ice the 5-4 win and give the Red Sox the Series, four games to one.

Game 1 Oct. 8
Boston	000 000 010 -	1
Philadelphia	000 100 02* -	3

Winner-Shore   Loser-Alexander

Game 2 Oct. 9
Boston	100 000 001 -	2
Philadelphia	000 010 000 -	1

Winner-Foster   Loser-Mayer

Game 3 Oct. 11
Philadelphia	001 000 000 -	1
Boston	000 100 001 -	2

Winner-Leonard   Loser-Alexander

Game 4 Oct. 12
Philadelphia	000 000 010 -	1
Boston	001 001 00* -	2

Winner-Shore   Loser-Chalmers

Game 5 Oct. 13
Boston	011 000 021 -	5
Philadelphia	200 200 000 -	4

Winner-Shore   Loser-Rixey

Total Attendance—143,351
Average Attendance—28,670
Winning Player's Share—$3,780
Losing Player's Share—$2,520

Boston A.L.   4
Philadelphia N.L.   1

BATTING	Pos	G	AB	R	H	2B	3B	HR	RBI	BB	SO	SB	BA
Boston													
Dick Hoblitzell	1b	5	16	1	5	0	0	0	1	0	1	1	.313
Jack Barry	2b	5	17	1	3	0	0	0	1	1	2	0	.176
Everett Scott	ss	5	18	0	1	0	0	0	0	0	3	0	.056
Larry Gardner	3b	5	17	2	4	0	1	0	4	1	0	0	.235
Harry Hooper	rf	5	20	4	7	0	0	2	3	2	4	0	.350
Tris Speaker	cf	5	17	2	5	0	1	0	0	4	1	0	.294
Duffy Lewis	lf	5	18	1	8	1	0	1	5	1	4	0	.444
Hick Cady	c-ph	4	6	0	2	0	0	0	0	1	2	0	.333
Pinch Thomas	c	2	5	0	1	0	0	0	0	0	0	0	.200
Del Gainor	ph-1b	1	3	1	1	0	0	0	0	0	0	0	.333
Olaf Henriksen	ph	2	2	0	0	0	0	0	0	0	0	0	.000
Bill Carrigan	c	1	2	0	0	0	0	0	0	1	1	0	.000
Hal Janvrin	ss	1	1	0	0	0	0	0	0	0	0	0	.000
Heinie Wagner	Did not play												
Mike McNally	Did not play												
Rube Foster	p	2	8	0	4	1	0	0	1	0	2	0	.500
Ernie Shore	p	2	5	0	1	0	0	0	0	0	3	0	.200
Dutch Leonard	p	1	3	0	0	0	0	0	0	0	2	0	.000
Babe Ruth	ph	1	1	0	0	0	0	0	0	0	0	0	.000
Smokey Joe Wood	Did not play												
Carl Mays	Did not play												
Ray Collins	Did not play												
Vean Gregg	Did not play												
Team Total		5	159	12	42	2	2	3	11	11	25	1	.264

Double Plays—2   Left on Bases—35

	Pos	G	AB	R	H	2B	3B	HR	RBI	BB	SO	SB	BA
Philadelphia													
Fred Luderus	1b	5	16	1	7	2	0	1	6	1	4	0	.438
Bert Viehoff	2b	5	16	1	1	0	0	0	0	1	5	0	.063
Dave Bancroft	ss	5	17	2	5	0	0	0	1	2	2	0	.294
Milt Stock	3b	5	17	1	2	1	0	0	0	1	0	0	.118
Gavvy Cravath	rf	5	16	2	2	1	1	0	1	2	6	0	.125
Dode Paskert	cf	5	19	2	3	0	0	0	0	1	2	0	.158
Possum Whitted	lf-1b	5	15	0	1	0	0	0	1	1	0	1	.067
Ed Burns	c	5	16	1	3	0	0	0	0	1	2	0	.188
Bobby Byrne	ph	1	1	0	0	0	0	0	0	0	0	0	.000
Bill Killefer	ph	1	1	0	0	0	0	0	0	0	0	0	.000
Beals Becker	lf	2	0	0	0	0	0	0	0	0	0	0	.000
Oscar Dugey	pr	2	0	0	0	0	0	0	0	0	0	1	.000
Bud Weiser	Did not play												
Jack Adams	Did not play												
Pete Alexander	p	2	5	0	1	0	0	0	0	0	1	0	.200
Erskine Mayer	p	2	4	0	0	0	0	0	0	0	2	0	.000
George Chalmers	p	1	3	0	1	0	0	0	0	0	1	0	.333
Eppa Rixey	p	1	2	0	1	0	0	0	0	0	0	0	.500
Al Demaree	Did not play												
George McQuillan	Did not play												
Stan Baumgartner	Did not play												
Ben Tincup	Did not play												
Team Total		5	148	10	27	4	1	1	9	10	25	2	.182

Double Plays—3   Left on Bases—23

PITCHING	G	GS	CG	IP	H	R	ER	BB	SO	W	L	SVB	ERA
Boston													
Rube Foster	2	2	2	18	12	5	4	2	13	2	0	0	2.00
Ernie Shore	2	2	2	17	12	4	4	8	6	1	1	0	2.12
Dutch Leonard	1	1	1	9	3	1	1	0	6	1	0	0	1.00
Babe Ruth	Did not play												
Smokey Joe Wood	Did not play												
Carl Mays	Did not play												
Ray Collins	Did not play												
Vean Gregg	Did not play												
Team Total	5	5	5	44	27	10	9	10	25	4	1	0	1.84
Philadelphia													
Pete Alexander	2	2	2	17⅔	3	3	4	10	1	1	0	0	1.53
Erskine Mayer	2	2	1	11⅓	16	4	3	2	7	0	1	0	2.38
George Chalmers	1	1	1	8	8	2	2	3	6	0	1	0	2.25
Eppa Rixey	1	0	0	6⅔	4	3	3	2	2	0	1	0	4.05
Al Demaree	Did not play												
George McQuillan	Did not play												
Stan Baumgartner	Did not play												
Ben Tincup	Did not play												
Team Total	5	5	4	43⅔	42	12	11	11	25	1	4	0	2.30

1916

Boston A.L. 4
Brooklyn N.L. 1

Highlights

THE BOSTON RED SOX MADE IT again, despite the loss of Tris Speaker and Smokey Joe Wood in salary disputes. Hooper and Lewis were joined by Tilly Walker in center field as Babe Ruth became the A.L.'s top southpaw with 23 wins, 9 shutouts and a 1.75 ERA. The Sox faced the Brooklyn Robins, managed by Wilbert Robinson, with Zack Wheat and Jake Daubert as star hitters and Jeff Pfeffer (25 games) and Rube Marquard on the mound. The rest of team were considered castoffs and retreads.

The Robins came close in game one, but lost, 6-5. There was a ferocious duel between Ruth and Sherry Smith in game two that lasted 14 innings and ended only when Smith walked Dick Hoblitzell and gave up a double to Del Gainor, which ended the game, 2-1, Boston.

Manager Robinson started Jack Coombs in game three, but pulled him in favor of Pfeffer in seventh, who saved game for Coombs, 4-3. Robins lost game four, 6-2, and fifth and final game, 4-1. Although the Robins lost the Series, they did have its leading batter: a right fielder named Casey Stengel (.364).

Game 1 Oct. 7
Brooklyn	000 100 004	5
Boston	001 010 31*	6

Winner-Shore   Loser-Marquard

Game 2 Oct. 9
Brooklyn	100 000 000 000 00	1
Boston	001 000 000 000 01	2

Winner-Ruth   Loser-Smith

Game 3 Oct. 10
Boston	000 002 100	3
Brooklyn	001 120 00*	4

Winner-Coombs   Loser-Mays

Game 4 Oct. 11
Boston	030 110 100	6
Brooklyn	200 000 000	2

Winner-Leonard   Loser-Marquard

Game 5 Oct. 12
Brooklyn	010 000 000	1
Boston	012 010 00*	4

Winner-Shore   Loser-Pfeffer

Total Attendance—162,859
Average Attendance—32,572
Winning Player's Share—$3,910
Losing Player's Share—$2,835

BATTING	Pos	G	AB	R	H	2B	3B	HR	RBI	BB	SO	SB	BA
Boston													
Dick Hoblitzell	1b	5	17	3	4	1	1	0	2	6	0	0	.235
Hal Janvrin	2b	5	23	2	5	3	0	0	1	0	6	0	.217
Everett Scott	ss	5	16	1	2	0	1	0	1	1	1	0	.125
Larry Gardner	3b	5	17	2	3	0	0	2	6	0	2	0	.176
Harry Hooper	rf	5	21	6	7	1	1	0	3	1	1	.333
Tilly Walker	cf	3	11	1	3	0	1	0	1	1	2	0	.273
Duffy Lewis	lf	5	17	3	6	2	1	0	1	2	1	0	.353
Pinch Thomas	c	3	7	0	1	0	1	0	0	0	1	0	.143
Chick Shorten	cf	2	7	0	4	0	0	0	2	0	1	0	.571
Hick Cady	c	2	4	1	1	0	0	0	0	3	0	0	.250
Bill Carrigan	c	1	3	0	2	0	0	0	1	0	1	0	.667
Jimmy Walsh	cf	1	3	0	0	0	0	0	0	0	0	0	.000
Del Gainor	ph	1	1	0	1	0	0	0	1	0	0	0	1.000
Olaf Henriksen	ph	1	0	1	0	0	0	0	0	1	0	0	.000
Mike McNally	pr	1	0	1	0	0	0	0	0	0	0	0	.000
Jack Barry		Did not play											
Sam Agnew		Did not play											
Heinie Wagner		Did not play											
Ernie Shore	p	2	7	0	0	0	0	0	0	0	2	0	.000
Babe Ruth	p	1	5	0	0	0	0	0	1	0	2	0	.000
Dutch Leonard	p	1	3	0	0	0	0	0	0	1	3	0	.000
Carl Mays	p	2	1	0	0	0	0	0	0	0	1	0	.000
Rube Foster	p	1	1	0	0	0	0	0	0	0	0	0	.000
Vean Gregg		Did not play											
Sad Sam Jones		Did not play											
Weldon Wyckoff		Did not play											
Team Total		5	164	21	39	7	6	2	18	18	25	1	.238

Double Plays—5   Left on Bases—28

BATTING	Pos	G	AB	R	H	2B	3B	HR	RBI	BB	SO	SB	BA
Brooklyn													
Jake Daubert	1b	4	17	1	3	0	1	0	0	2	3	0	.176
George Cutshaw	2b	5	19	2	2	1	0	0	2	1	1	0	.105
Ivy Olson	ss	5	16	1	4	0	1	0	2	2	2	0	.250
Mike Mowrey	3b	5	17	2	3	0	0	0	1	3	2	0	.176
Casey Stengel	rf-ph	4	11	2	4	0	0	0	0	0	1	0	.364
Hy Myers	cf	5	22	2	4	0	0	1	3	0	3	0	.182
Zack Wheat	lf	5	19	2	4	0	1	0	1	2	2	1	.211
Chief Meyers	c	3	10	0	2	0	1	0	0	1	0	0	.200
Jimmy Johnston	ph-rf	3	10	1	3	0	1	0	0	1	0	0	.300
Otto Miller	c	2	8	0	1	0	0	0	0	0	1	0	.125
Fred Merkle	ph-1b	3	4	0	1	0	0	0	1	2	0	0	.250
Ollie O'Mara	ph	1	1	0	0	0	0	0	0	0	1	0	.000
Gus Getz	ph	1	1	0	0	0	0	0	0	0	0	0	.000
Sherry Smith	p	1	5	0	1	0	0	0	0	0	0	0	.200
Jeff Pfeffer	p-ph	4	4	0	1	0	0	0	0	0	2	0	.250
Rube Marquard	p	2	3	0	0	0	0	0	0	0	1	0	.000
Jack Coombs	p	1	3	0	1	0	0	0	1	0	0	0	.333
Larry Cheney	p	1	0	0	0	0	0	0	0	0	0	0	.000
Nat Rucker	p	1	0	0	0	0	0	0	0	0	0	0	.000
Wheezer Dell	p	1	0	0	0	0	0	0	0	0	0	0	.000
Ed Appleton		Did not play											
Duster Mails		Did not play											
Team Total		5	170	13	34	2	5	1	11	14	19	1	.200

Double Plays—2   Left on Bases—30

PITCHING	G	GS	CG	IP	H	R	ER	BB	SO	W	L	SVB	ERA
Boston													
Ernie Shore	2	2	1	17 2/3	12	6	3	4	9	2	0	0	1.53
Babe Ruth	1	1	1	14	6	1	1	3	4	1	0	0	0.64
Dutch Leonard	1	1	1	9	5	2	1	4	3	1	0	0	1.00
Carl Mays	2	1	0	5 1/3	8	4	3	3	2	0	1	1	5.06
Rube Foster	1	0	0	3	3	0	0	0	1	0	0	0	0.00
Vean Gregg		Did not play											
Sad Sam Jones		Did not play											
Weldon Wyckoff		Did not play											
Team Total	5	5	3	49	34	13	8	14	19	4	1	1	1.47
Brooklyn													
Sherry Smith	1	1	1	13 1/3	7	2	2	6	2	0	1	0	1.35
Rube Marquard	2	2	0	11	12	9	8	6	9	0	2	0	6.55
Jeff Pfeffer	3	1	0	10 2/3	7	5	2	4	5	0	1	1	1.69
Jack Coombs	1	1	0	6 1/3	7	3	3	1	1	1	0	0	4.26
Larry Cheney	1	0	0	3	4	2	1	1	5	0	0	0	3.00
Nap Rucker	1	0	0	2	1	0	0	0	3	0	0	0	0.00
Wheezer Dell	1	0	0	1	1	0	0	0	0	0	0	0	0.00
Ed Appleton		Did not play											
Duster Mails		Did not play											
Team Total	5	5	1	47 1/3	39	21	16	18	25	1	4	1	3.04

1917

Chicago A.L. 4
New York N.L. 2

Highlights

THE CHICAGO WHITE SOX were back after eleven years, featuring Eddie Collins, Joe Jackson and Happy Felsch, with Ray Schalk behind the plate and 28-game-winner Eddie Cicotte on the mound. John McGraw's rebuilt New York Giants easily took the N.L. pennant. Ferdie Schupp (21 games) led a strong staff. Dave Robertson, George Burns, Heinie Zimmerman and Benny Kauff were standouts on offense.

Boosted by a fourth-inning homer by Felsch, Cicotte snared game one, 2-1, for Chicago. McGraw sent Schupp to the mound for game two, but after three relievers, the Sox still won, 7-2. Facing his fourth consecutive Series loss, Mc-Graw played Rube Benton in game three, beating Cicotte, 2-0, at the Polo Grounds. Schupp won game four in a 5-0 shutout of Chicago. But the White Sox took game four, 8-5.

Errors and miscues plagued the Giants in the sixth game, culminating as Chicago's Eddie Collins scooted past Giants catcher Bill Rariden in a rundown play between third and home. Third baseman Zimmerman, seeing that neither Benton nor Holke had covered the play, was forced to chase Collins with the ball, a race Collins easily won. The White Sox took the deciding game, 4-2.

Game 1 Oct. 6
New York   000 010 000 · 1
Chicago   001 100 00* · 2
Winner-Cicotte   Loser-Sallee

Game 2 Oct. 7
New York   020 000 000 · 2
Chicago   020 500 00* · 7
Winner-Faber   Loser-Anderson

Game 3 Oct. 10
Chicago   000 000 000 · 0
New York   000 200 00* · 2
Winner-Benton   Loser-Cicotte

Game 4 Oct. 11
Chicago   000 000 000 · 0
New York   000 110 12* · 5
Winner-Schupp   Loser-Faber

Game 5 Oct. 13
New York   200 200 100 · 5
Chicago   001 001 33* · 8
Winner-Faber   Loser-Sallee

Game 6 Oct. 15
Chicago   000 300 001 · 4
New York   000 020 000 · 2
Winner-Faber   Loser-Benton

Total Attendance—186,654
Average Attendance—31,109
Winning Player's Share—$3,669
Losing Player's Share—$2,442

BATTING

	Pos	G	AB	R	H	2B	3B	HR	RBI	BB	SO	SB	BA
Chicago													
Chick Gandil	1b	6	23	1	6	1	0	0	5	0	2	1	.261
Eddie Collins	2b	6	22	4	9	1	0	0	2	2	3	3	.409
Buck Weaver	ss	6	21	3	7	1	0	0	1	0	2	0	.333
Fred McMullin	3b	6	24	1	3	1	0	0	2	1	6	0	.125
Shano Collins	rf	6	21	2	6	1	0	0	0	0	2	0	.286
Happy Felsch	cf	6	22	4	6	1	0	1	3	1	5	0	.273
Joe Jackson	lf	6	23	4	7	0	0	0	2	1	0	1	.304
Ray Schalk	c	6	19	1	5	0	0	0	0	2	1	1	.263
Nemo Leibold	ph-rf	2	5	1	2	0	0	0	2	1	1	0	.400
Swede Risberg	ph	2	2	0	1	0	0	0	0	1	0	0	.500
Byrd Lynn	ph	1	1	0	0	0	0	0	0	0	1	0	.000
Eddie Murphy	Did not play												
Ted Jourdan	Did not play												
Joe Jenkins	Did not play												
Ziggy Hasbrouck	Did not play												
Bobby Byrne	Did not play												
Red Faber	p	4	7	0	1	0	0	0	0	2	3	0	.143
Eddie Cicotte	p	3	7	0	1	0	0	0	0	1	2	0	.143
Lefty Williams	p	1	0	0	0	0	0	0	0	0	0	0	.000
Dave Danforth	p	1	0	0	0	0	0	0	0	0	0	0	.000
Reb Russell	p	1	0	0	0	0	0	0	0	0	0	0	.000
Jim Scott	Did not play												
Joe Benz	Did not play												
Mellie Wolfgang	Did not play												
Team Total		6	197	21	54	6	0	1	18	11	28	6	.274

Double Plays—6   Left on Bases—39

	Pos	G	AB	R	H	2B	3B	HR	RBI	BB	SO	SB	BA
New York													
Walter Holke	1b	6	21	2	6	2	0	0	1	0	6	0	.286
Buck Herzog	2b	6	24	1	6	0	1	0	2	1	4	0	.250
Art Fletcher	ss	6	25	2	5	1	0	0	0	0	2	0	.200
Heinie Zimmerman	3b	6	25	1	3	0	0	0	0	0	0	0	.120
Dave Robertson	rf	6	22	3	11	1	1	0	1	0	0	2	.500
Benny Kauff	cf	6	25	2	4	1	0	2	5	0	2	1	.160
George Burns	lf	6	22	3	5	0	0	0	2	2	6	1	.227
Bill Rariden	c	5	13	2	5	0	0	0	2	2	1	0	.385
Lew McCarty	c-ph	3	5	1	2	0	1	0	1	0	0	0	.400
Joe Wilhoit	ph	2	1	0	0	0	0	0	0	1	0	0	.000
Jim Thorpe	rf	1	0	0	0	0	0	0	0	0	0	0	.000
Jimmy Smith	Did not play												
George Gibson	Did not play												
Hans Lobert	Did not play												
Al Baird	Did not play												
Red Murray	Did not play												
Jack Onslow	Did not play												
Slim Sallee	p	2	6	1	0	0	0	1	0	2	0	0	.167
Rube Benton	p	2	4	0	0	0	0	0	0	0	3	0	.000
Ferdie Schupp	p	2	4	0	1	0	0	0	1	0	1	0	.250
Pol Perritt	p	3	2	0	2	0	0	0	0	0	0	0	1.000
Fred Anderson	p	1	0	0	0	0	0	0	0	0	0	0	.000
Jeff Tesreau	p	1	0	0	0	0	0	0	0	0	0	0	.000
Al Demaree	Did not play												
Team Total		6	199	17	51	5	4	2	16	6	27	4	.256

Double Plays—3   Left on Bases—37

PITCHING

	G	GS	CG	IP	H	R	ER	BB	SO	W	L	SVB	ERA
Chicago													
Red Faber	4	3	2	27	21	7	7	3	9	3	1	0	2.33
Eddie Cicotte	3	2	2	23	23	6	5	2	13	1	1	0	1.95
Lefty Williams	1	0	0	1	2	1	1	0	3	0	0	0	9.00
Dave Danforth	1	0	0	1	3	2	2	0	2	0	0	0	18.00
Reb Russell	1	1	0	0	2	1	1	1	0	0	0	0	0.00
Jim Scott	Did not play												
Joe Benz	Did not play												
Mellie Wolfgang	Did not play												
Team Total	6	6	4	52	51	17	16	6	27	4	2	0	2.77
New York													
Slim Sallee	2	2	1	15⅓	20	10	9	4	4	0	2	0	5.28
Rube Benton	2	2	1	14	9	3	0	1	8	1	1	0	0.00
Ferdie Schupp	2	2	1	10⅓	11	2	2	2	9	1	0	0	1.74
Pol Perritt	3	0	0	8⅓	9	2	2	3	3	0	0	0	2.16
Fred Anderson	1	0	0	2	5	4	4	0	3	0	1	0	18.00
Jeff Tesreau	1	0	0	1	0	0	0	1	1	0	0	0	0.00
Al Demaree	Did not play												
Team Total	6	6	3	51	54	21	17	11	28	2	4	0	3.00

1918

Boston A.L. 4
Chicago N.L. 2

Highlights

WORLD WAR I CAUSED MANY players to leave for draft or war industries. The Boston Red Sox won with a jerry-built team, filling gaps with purchase of McInnis, Strunk, Schang and Bush from the A's. Ruth played outfield against right-handed pitching whenever he wasn't on the mound. Ruth batted .300, led the league with 11 homers, and won 13 games on the mound. The Chicago Cubs, weak in hitting, had an outstanding mound staff in Hippo Vaughn, Claude Hendrix and Lefty Tyler.

Ruth shut out Vaughn in game one, 1-0. Tyler took game two for the Cubs, 3-1. Submariner Carl Mays won game three from Vaughn, 2-1, with Boston's George Whiteman robbing Dode Paskert of a fourth-inning homer with a spectacular catch and Chicago's Charlie Pick stealing home in the ninth with two out.

Game four saw Ruth's streak of scoreless innings pitched in Series play broken at a record 29⅔ innings, but the Sox won anyway, 3-2. Players threatened to strike before game five because of a dispute over Series shares, but the game was played on schedule. Vaughn bested Sad Sam Jones, 3-0. Red Sox took game six, 2-1, and the Series, four games to two.

Game 1 Sept. 5
Boston	000 100 000 -	1
Chicago	000 000 000 -	0

Winner-Ruth   Loser-Vaughn

Game 2 Sept. 6
Boston	000 000 001 -	1
Chicago	030 000 00* -	3

Winner-Tyler   Loser-Bush

Game 3 Sept. 7
Boston	000 200 000 -	2
Chicago	000 010 000 -	1

Winner-Mays   Loser-Vaughn

Game 4 Sept. 9
Chicago	000 000 020 -	2
Boston	000 200 01* -	3

Winner-Ruth   Loser-Douglas

Game 5 Sept. 10
Chicago	001 000 020 -	3
Boston	000 000 000 -	0

Winner-Vaughn   Loser-Jones

Game 6 Sept. 11
Chicago	000 100 000 -	1
Boston	002 000 00* -	2

Winner-Mays   Loser-Tyler

Total Attendance—128,483
Average Attendance—21,414
Winning Player's Share—$1,103
Losing Player's Share—$671

BATTING

	Pos	G	AB	R	H	2B	3B	HR	RBI	BB	SO	SB	BA
Boston													
Stuffy McInnis	1b	6	20	2	5	0	0	0	1	1	1	0	.250
Dave Shean	2b	6	19	2	4	1	0	0	0	4	3	1	.211
Everett Scott	ss	6	21	0	2	0	0	0	1	1	1	0	.095
Fred Thomas	3b	6	16	0	2	0	0	0	0	1	2	0	.125
Harry Hooper	rf	6	20	0	4	0	0	0	0	2	2	0	.200
Amos Strunk	cf	6	23	1	4	1	1	0	0	0	5	0	.174
George Whiteman	lf	6	20	2	50	0	1	0	1	2	1	1	.250
Sam Agnew	c	4	9	0	0	0	0	0	0	0	0	0	.000
Wally Schang	ph-c	5	9	1	4	0	0	0	1	2	3	1	.444
Hack Miller	ph	1	1	0	0	0	0	0	0	0	0	0	.000
George Cochran		Did not play											
Wally Mayer		Did not play											
Jack Coffey		Did not play											
Heinie Wagner		Did not play											
Babe Ruth	p-lf	3	5	0	1	0	1	0	2	0	2	0	.200
Carl Mays	p	2	5	1	1	0	0	0	0	1	0	0	.200
Bullet Joe Bush	p	2	2	0	0	0	0	0	0	1	0	0	.000
Sad Sam Jones	p	1	1	0	0	0	0	0	0	1	0	0	.000
Jean Dubuc	ph	1	1	0	0	0	0	0	0	0	1	0	.000
Walt Kinney		Did not play											
Bill Pertica		Did not play											
Team Total		6	172	9	32	2	3	0	6	16	21	3	.186
		Double Plays—4			Left on Bases—32								
Chicago													
Fred Merkle	1b	6	18	1	5	0	0	0	1	4	3	0	.278
Charlie Pick	2b	6	18	2	7	1	0	0	0	1	1	1	**.389**
Charlie Hollocher	ss	6	21	2	4	0	1	0	1	1	1	1	.190
Charlie Deal	3b	6	17	0	3	0	0	0	0	0	1	0	.176
Max Flack	rf	6	19	2	5	0	0	0	0	4	1	1	.263
Dode Paskert	cf	6	21	0	4	1	0	0	2	2	2	0	.190
Les Mann	lf	6	22	0	5	2	0	0	2	0	0	0	.227
Bill Killefer	c	6	17	2	2	1	0	0	2	2	0	0	.118
Bob O'Farrell	ph-c	3	3	0	0	0	0	0	0	0	0	0	.000
Turner Barber	ph	3	2	0	0	0	0	0	0	0	0	0	.000
Chuck Wortman	2b	1	1	0	0	0	0	0	0	0	0	0	.000
Bill McCabe	pr-ph	3	1	1	0	0	0	0	0	0	0	0	.000
Rollie Zeider	ph-3b	2	0	0	0	0	0	0	0	2	0	0	.000
Tommy Clarke		Did not play											
Hippo Vaughn	p	3	10	0	0	0	0	0	0	0	5	0	.000
Lefty Tyler	p	3	5	0	1	0	0	0	0	2	2	0	.200
Claude Hendrix	p-ph	2	1	0	1	0	0	0	0	0	0	0	1.000
Phil Douglas	p	1	0	0	0	0	0	0	0	0	0	0	.000
Paul Carter		Did not play											
Speed Martin		Did not play											
Roy Walker		Did not play											
Team Total		6	176	10	37	5	1	0	10	18	14	3	.210
		Double Plays—7			Left on Bases—31								

PITCHING

	G	GS	CG	IP	H	R	ER	BB	SO	W	L	SVB	ERA
Boston													
Carl Mays	2	2	2	18	10	2	2	3	5	2	0	0	**1.00**
Babe Ruth	2	2	1	17	13	2	2	7	4	2	0	0	1.06
Bullet Joe Bush	2	1	1	9	7	3	3	3	0	0	1	1	3.00
Sad Sam Jones	1	1	1	9	7	3	3	5	5	0	1	0	3.00
Jean Dubuc		Did not pitch											
Walt Kinney		Did not pitch											
Bill Pertica		Did not pitch											
Team Total	6	6	5	53	37	10	10	18	14	4	2	1	1.70
Chicago													
Hippo Vaughn	3	3	3	27	17	3	3	5	17	1	2	0	1.00
Lefty Tyler	3	3	1	23	14	5	3	11	4	1	1	0	1.17
Claude Hendrix	1	0	0	1	0	0	0	0	0	0	0	0	0.00
Phil Douglas	1	0	0	1	1	1	0	0	0	0	1	0	0.00
Paul Carter		Did not play											
Speed Martin		Did not play											
Roy Walker		Did not play											
Team Total	6	6	4	52	32	9	6	16	21	2	4	0	1.04

1919

Cincinnati N.L. 5
Chicago A.L. 3

Highlights

In spite of pre-series rumors of scandal, popular interest was so high that the Series was made a best-of-nine contest. The Cincinnati Reds were good, but with Jackson, Collins, Schalk, Cicotte and Williams, the Chicago White Sox were favored 3 to 1 going in. Then the odds shifted. By game one, the Reds were favored 8 to 5. Big-time gamblers had gotten to seven White Sox players and agreed to pay them to throw the Series to the Reds.

Game one: Cicotte helped the Reds to a 9-1 win by giving up five straight hits and five runs in the fourth. Game two: Williams walked three and gave up a triple to help the Reds win, 4-2.

In game three, Dickie Kerr, a Chicago player not in on the fix, shut out the Reds, 3-0. Cicotte gave away game four, 2-0. Williams pitched game five, and the Reds won, 5-0. Then Kerr won game six for Chicago, 5-4. In a mysterious turnabout, Cicotte pitched well to win game seven, 4-1, for Chicago.

Williams was on the mound for game eight, and the Reds won, 10-5, for a five-games-to-three Series victory. Called the "Black Sox Scandal," the payoffs were later officially investigated and the guilty players were disgraced and suspended.

Game 1 Oct. 1		
Chicago	010 000 000	- 1
Cincinnati	100 500 21*	- 9
Winner-Ruether	Loser-Cicotte	

Game 2 Oct. 2		
Chicago	000 000 200	- 2
Cincinnati	000 301 00*	- 4
Winner-Sallee	Loser-Williams	

Game 3 Oct. 3		
Cincinnati	000 000 000	- 0
Chicago	020 100 00*	- 3
Winner-Kerr	Loser-Fisher	

Game 4 Oct. 4		
Cincinnati	000 020 000	- 2
Chicago	000 000 000	- 0
Winner-Ring	Loser-Cicotte	

Game 5 Oct. 6		
Cincinnati	000 004 001	- 5
Chicago	000 000 000	- 0
Winner-Eller	Loser-Williams	

Game 6 Oct. 7		
Chicago	000 013 000 1	- 5
Cincinnati	002 200 000 0	- 4
Winner-Kerr	Loser-Ring	

Game 7 Oct. 8		
Chicago	101 020 000	- 4
Cincinnati	000 001 000	- 1
Winner-Cicotte	Loser-Sallee	

Game 8 Oct. 9		
Cincinnati	410 013 010	- 10
Chicago	001 000 040	- 5
Winner-Eller	Loser-Williams	

Total Attendance—236,928
Average Attendance—29,616
Winning Player's Share—$5,207
Losing Player's Share—$3,254

BATTING	Pos	G	AB	R	H	2B	3B	HR	RBI	BB	SO	SB	BA
Cincinnati													
Jake Daubert	1b	8	29	4	7	0	1	0	1	1	2	1	.241
Morrie Rath	2b	8	31	5	7	1	0	0	2	4	1	**2**	.226
Larry Kopf	ss	8	27	3	6	0	**2**	0	3	3	2	0	.222
Heinie Groh	3b	8	29	**6**	5	2	0	0	2	**6**	4	0	.172
Greasy Neale	rf	8	28	3	10	1	1	0	4	2	**5**	1	.357
Edd Roush	cf	8	28	**6**	6	2	1	0	7	3	0	**2**	.214
Pat Duncan	lf	8	26	3	7	2	0	0	**8**	2	2	0	.269
Bill Rariden	c	5	19	0	4	0	0	0	2	0	0	1	.211
Ivy Wingo	c	3	7	1	4	0	0	0	1	3	1	0	.571
Sherry Magee	ph	2	2	0	1	0	0	0	0	0	0	0	.500
Jimmy Smith	pr	1	0	0	0	0	0	0	0	0	0	0	.000
Rube Bressler	Did not play												
Hank Schreiber	Did not play												
Nick Allen	Did not play												
Charlie See	Did not play												
Hod Eller	p	2	7	2	2	1	0	0	0	0	2	0	.286
Dutch Ruether	p-ph	3	6	2	4	1	**2**	0	4	1	0	0	.667
Jimmy Ring	p	2	5	0	0	0	0	0	0	0	2	0	.000
Slim Sallee	p	2	4	0	0	0	0	0	0	0	0	0	.000
Ray Fisher	p	2	2	0	1	0	0	0	0	0	0	0	.500
Dolf Luque	p	2	1	0	0	0	0	0	0	0	1	0	.000
Roy Mitchell	Did not play												
Ed Gerner	Did not play												
Team Total		8	251	35	64	10	7	0	34	25	22	7	.255
		Double Plays—7					Left on Bases—46						
Chicago													
Chick Gardil	1b	8	30	1	7	0	1	0	5	1	3	1	.233
Eddie Collins	2b	8	31	2	7	1	0	0	1	1	2	1	.226
Swede Risberg	ss	8	25	3	2	0	1	0	0	5	3	1	.080
Buck Weaver	3b	8	**34**	4	11	**4**	1	0	0	0	2	0	.324
Nemo Leibold	rf-ph-cf	5	18	0	1	0	0	0	0	2	3	1	.056
Happy Felsch	cf-rf	8	26	2	5	1	0	0	3	1	4	0	.192
Joe Jackson	lf	8	32	5	**12**	3	0	**1**	6	1	2	0	**.375**
Ray Schalk	c	8	23	1	7	0	0	0	2	4	2	1	.304
Shano Collins	rf-cf	4	16	2	4	1	0	0	0	0	0	0	.250
Fred McMullin	ph	2	2	0	1	0	0	0	0	0	0	0	.500
Eddie Murphy	ph	3	2	0	0	0	0	0	0	0	1	0	.000
Byrd Lynn	c	1	1	0	0	0	0	0	0	0	0	0	.000
Joe Jenkins	Did not play												
Hervey McClellan	Did not play												
Eddie Cicotte	p	3	8	0	0	0	0	0	0	0	3	0	.000
Dickie Kerr	p	2	6	0	1	0	0	0	0	0	0	0	.167
Lefty Williams	p	3	5	0	1	0	0	0	0	0	3	0	.200
Roy Wilkinson	p	2	2	0	0	0	0	0	0	0	1	0	.000
Bill James	p	1	2	0	0	0	0	0	0	0	1	0	.000
Grover Lowdermilk	p	1	0	0	0	0	0	0	0	0	0	0	.000
Erskine Mayer	p	1	0	0	0	0	0	0	0	0	0	0	.000
Red Faber	Did not play												
John Sullivan	Did not play												
Team Total		8	263	20	59	10	3	1	17	15	30	5	.224
		Double Plays—9					Left on Bases—52						

PITCHING	G	GS	CG	IP	H	R	ER	BB	SO	W	L	SVB	ERA
Cincinnati													
Hod Eller	2	2	**2**	18	13	5	4	2	**15**	**2**	0	0	2.00
Dutch Ruetler	2	2	1	14	12	5	4	4	1	1	0	0	2.57
Jimmy Ring	2	1	1	14	7	1	1	6	4	1	1	0	**0.64**
Slim Sallee	2	2	1	13⅓	**19**	6	2	1	2	1	1	0	1.35
Ray Fisher	2	1	0	7⅔	7	3	2	2	2	0	1	0	2.35
Dolf Luque	2	0	0	5	1	0	0	0	6	0	0	0	0.00
Rube Bressler	Did not play												
Roy Mitchell	Did not play												
Ed Gerner	Did not play												
Team Total	8	8	5	72	59	20	13	15	30	5	3	0	1.62
Chicago													
Eddie Cicotte	**3**	**3**	**2**	21⅔	19	9	7	5	7	1	2	0	2.91
Dickie Kerr	2	2	**2**	19	14	4	3	3	6	**2**	0	0	1.42
Lefty Williams	**3**	**3**	1	16⅓	12	**12**	**12**	**8**	4	0	**3**	0	6.61
Roy Wilkinson	2	0	0	7⅓	9	4	1	4	3	0	0	0	1.23
Bill James	1	0	0	4⅔	8	4	3	3	2	0	0	0	5.79
Grover Lowdermilk	1	0	0	1	2	1	1	1	0	0	0	0	9.00
Erskine Mayer	1	0	0	1	0	1	0	1	0	0	0	0	0.00
Red Faber	Did not play												
John Sullivan	Did not play												
Team Total	8	8	5	71	64	35	27	25	22	3	5	0	3.42

1920

Cleveland N.L. 5
Brooklyn N.L. 2

Highlights

THE BLACK SOX SCANDAL BROKE in September, causing the suspension of the crooked White Sox players. As a result, the Cleveland Indians won the A.L. flag by two games. The Indians, managed by Tris Speaker (.388), had pitching aces Jim Bagby, Stan Coveleski and Ray Caldwell. Their opponents, the Brooklyn Robins, had outfielder Zack Wheat and a strong staff headed by Burleigh Grimes (23 games).

Games one was a duel between the Robins' Rube Marquard and Coveleski, a 3-1 victory for Cleveland. Grimes used his spitball to shut out Bagby (31 games), 3-0, for Brooklyn in game two. The Robins won the third game, 2-1, with Sherry Smith on mound.

The Indians then came from behind to take the next four games and the Championship. Coveleski won game four, 5-1. In game five, Cleveland's Elmer Smith hit the first grand-slam homer in Series history, while teammate Jim Bagby became the first pitcher to hit a homer in the Series. With men on first and second and no outs, Cleveland's second baseman Bill Wambsganss leapt up to catch a ball hit by Clarence Mitchell, stepped on second, and tagged an astounded Otto Miller near second for the first and only unassisted triple play in Series history. Cleveland won, 8-1. Duster Mails shut out the Robins, 1-0, in game six, and Coveleski finished things up with his third five-hitter the next day, 3-0.

Game 1 Oct. 5
Cleveland	020 100 000 ·	3
Brooklyn	000 000 100 ·	1

Winner-Coveleski Loser-Marquard

Game 2 Oct. 6
Cleveland	000 000 000 ·	0
Brooklyn	101 010 00* ·	3

Winner-Grimes Loser-Bagby

Game 3 Oct. 7
Cleveland	000 100 000 ·	1
Brooklyn	200 000 00* ·	2

Winner-S. Smith Loser-Caldwell

Game 4 Oct. 9
Brooklyn	000 100 000 ·	1
Cleveland	202 001 00* ·	5

Winner-Coveleski Loser-Cadore

Game 5 Oct. 10
Brooklyn	000 000 001 ·	1
Cleveland	400 310 00* ·	8

Winner-Bagby Loser-Grimes

Game 6 Oct. 11
Brooklyn	000 000 000 ·	0
Cleveland	000 001 00* ·	1

Winner-Mails Loser-S. Smith

Game 7 Oct. 12
Brooklyn	000 000 000 ·	0
Cleveland	000 110 10* ·	3

Winner-Coveleski Loser-Grimes

Total Attendance—178,737
Average Attendance—25,534
Winning Player's Share—$4,168
Losing Player's Share—$2,419

BATTING

Cleveland	Pos	G	AB	R	H	2B	3B	HR	RBI	BB	SO	SB	BA
Doc Johnston	ph-1b	5	11	1	3	0	0	0	0	2	1	1	.273
Bill Wambsganss	2b	7	26	3	4	0	0	0	1	2	1	0	.154
Joe Sewell	ss	7	23	0	4	0	0	0	0	2	1	0	.174
Larry Gardner	3b	7	24	1	5	1	0	0	2	1	1	0	.208
Elmer Smith	ph-rf	5	13	1	4	0	1	1	5	1	1	0	.308
Tris Speaker	cf	7	25	6	8	2	1	0	1	3	1	0	.320
Charlie Jamieson	ph-lf	6	15	2	5	1	0	0	1	1	0	1	.333
Steve O'Neill	c	7	21	1	7	3	0	0	2	4	3	0	.333
Joe Evans	lf-ph	4	13	0	4	0	0	0	0	1	0	0	.308
George Burns	lb-ph	5	10	1	3	1	0	0	2	3	3	0	.300
Smokey Joe Wood	rf-ph	4	10	2	2	1	0	0	0	1	2	0	.200
Jack Graney	ph-rf-lf	3	3	0	0	0	0	0	0	0	2	0	.000
Les Nunamaker	ph-c	2	2	0	1	0	0	0	0	0	0	0	.500
Harry Lunte	2b	1	0	0	0	0	0	0	0	0	0	0	.000
Pinch Thomas	c	1	0	0	0	0	0	0	0	0	0	0	.000
Stan Coveleski	p	3	10	2	1	0	0	0	0	0	4	0	.100
Jim Bagby	p	2	6	1	2	0	0	1	3	0	0	0	.333
Duster Mails	p	2	5	0	0	0	0	0	0	0	1	0	.000
George Uhle	p	2	0	0	0	0	0	0	0	0	0	0	.000
Ray Caldwell	p	1	0	0	0	0	0	0	0	0	0	0	.000
Guy Morton		Did not play											
Bob Clark		Did not play											
George Ellison		Did not play											
Team Total		7	217	21	53	9	2	2	17	21	21	2	.244

Double Plays—8 Triple Play—1 (Wambsganss unassisted) Left on Bases—43

Brooklyn	Pos	G	AB	R	H	2B	3B	HR	RBI	BB	SO	SB	BA
Ed Konetchy	1b	7	23	0	4	0	1	0	2	3	2	0	.174
Pete Kilduff	2b	7	21	0	2	0	0	0	0	1	4	0	.095
Ivy Olson	ss	7	25	2	8	1	0	0	0	3	1	0	.320
Jimmy Johnston	3b	4	14	2	3	0	0	0	0	0	2	1	.214
Tommy Griffith	rf	7	21	1	4	2	0	0	3	0	2	0	.190
Hy Myers	cf	7	26	0	6	0	0	0	1	0	1	0	.231
Zack Wheat	lf	7	27	2	9	2	0	0	2	1	2	0	.333
Otto Miller	c	6	14	0	2	0	0	0	1	1	2	0	.143
Jack Sheehan	3b	3	11	0	2	0	0	0	0	0	1	0	.182
Ernie Krueger	c-ph	4	6	0	1	0	0	0	0	0	0	0	.167
Bernie Neis	pr-rf	4	5	0	0	0	0	0	0	1	0	0	.000
Bill Lamar	ph	3	3	0	0	0	0	0	0	0	0	0	.000
Ray Schmandt	ph	1	1	0	0	0	0	0	0	0	0	0	.000
Bill McCabe	pr	1	0	0	0	0	0	0	0	0	0	0	.000
Rowdy Elliott		Did not play											
Chuck Ward		Did not play											
Zack Taylor		Did not play											
Burleigh Grimes	p	3	6	1	2	0	0	0	0	0	0	0	.333
Sherry Smith	p	2	6	0	0	0	0	0	0	0	2	0	.000
Clarence Mitchell	p-ph	2	3	0	1	0	0	0	0	0	0	0	.333
Rube Marquard	p	2	1	0	0	0	0	0	0	0	0	0	.000
Al Mamaux	p	3	1	0	0	0	0	0	0	0	1	0	.000
Jeff Pfeffer	p	1	1	0	0	0	0	0	0	0	0	0	.000
Leon Cadore	p	2	0	0	0	0	0	0	0	0	0	0	.000
George Mohart		Did not play											
Johnny Miljus		Did not play											
Team Total		7	215	8	44	5	1	0	8	10	20	1	.205

Double Plays—5 Left on Bases—39

PITCHING

Cleveland	G	GS	CG	IP	H	R	ER	BB	SO	W	L	SVB	ERA
Stan Coveleski	3	3	3	27	15	2	2	2	8	3	0	0	0.67
Dusty Mails	2	1	1	15⅔	6	0	0	6	6	1	0	0	0.00
Jim Bagby	2	2	1	15	20	4	3	1	3	1	1	0	1.80
George Uhle	2	0	0	3	1	0	0	3	0	0	0	0	0.00
Ray Caldwell	1	1	0	⅓	2	2	1	1	0	0	1	0	27.00
Guy Morton		Did not play											
Bob Clark		Did not play											
George Ellison		Did not play											
Team Total	7	7	5	61	44	8	6	10	20	5	2	0	0.88

Brooklyn	G	GS	CG	IP	H	R	ER	BB	SO	W	L	SVB	ERA
Burleigh Grimes	3	3	1	19⅓	23	10	9	9	4	1	2	0	4.19
Sherry Smith	2	2	2	17	10	2	1	3	3	1	1	0	0.53
Rube Marquard	2	1	0	9	7	3	1	3	6	0	1	0	1.00
Clarence Mitchell	1	0	0	4⅔	3	1	0	3	0	0	0	0	0.00
Al Mamaux	3	0	0	4	2	2	2	0	5	0	0	0	4.50
Jeff Pfeffer	1	0	0	3	4	1	1	2	1	0	0	0	3.00
Leon Cadore	2	1	0	2	4	2	2	1	1	0	1	0	9.00
George Mohart		Did not play											
Johnny Miljus		Did not play											
Team Total	7	7	3	59	53	21	16	21	21	2	5	0	2.44

1921

New York N.L. 5
New York A.L. 3

Highlights

WHEN JOHN MC GRAW AGREED to let the Yankees use the Polo Grounds in 1913, he didn't feel they'd be much of a threat. But with a winning season in 1919 and the acquisition of Babe Ruth from Boston, the Yanks began outdrawing the Giants. Then both teams won pennants, and the stage was set for an all-New York, all-Polo Grounds Series.

Yankee submariner Carl Mays shut out the Giants, 3-0, in game one, and Yankees Waite Hoyt did the same in game two. The Giants turned it around in game three with a 13-5 win, knocking out Bob Shawkey and forcing the Yankees to send in three other pitchers. A homer by Ruth in game four almost opened things up, but the Mays-Douglas duel ended with a 4-2 Giants win. Ruth beat out a bunt in game five to give Waite Hoyt the edge he needed to win it, 3-1.

Ruth was sidelined by an infected arm and a bad knee and the Yanks lost game six, 8-5. Mays lost to Douglas, 2-1, in game seven to give the Giants a four-to-three lead in games. Hoyt did his job well in game eight, but even a pinch-hit appearance by Ruth couldn't turn the game into a win. The Giants took it, 1-0, and won the best-of-nine Series, five games to three.

Game 1 Oct. 5
Yankees	100 011 000	- 3
Giants	000 000 000	- 0

Winner-Mays Loser-Douglas

Game 2 Oct. 6
Giants	000 000 000	- 0
Yankees	000 100 02*	- 3

Winner-Hoyt Loser-Nehf

Game 3 Oct. 7
Yankees	004 000 010	- 5
Giants	004 000 81*	- 13

Winner-Barnes Loser-Quinn

Game 4 Oct. 9
Giants	000 000 031	- 4
Yankees	000 010 001	- 2

Winner-Douglas Loser-Mays

Game 5 Oct. 10
Yankees	001 200 000	- 3
Giants	100 000 000	- 1

Winner-Hoyt Loser-Nehf

Game 6 Oct. 11
Giants	030 401 000	- 8
Yankees	320 000 000	- 5

Winner-Barnes Loser-Shawkey

Game 7 Oct. 12
Yankees	010 000 000	- 1
Giants	000 100 10*	- 2

Winner-Douglas Loser-Mays

Game 8 Oct. 13
Giants	100 000 000	- 1
Yankees	000 000 000	- 0

Winner-Nehf Loser-Hoyt

Total Attendance—269,976
Average Attendance—33,747
Winning Player's Share—$5,265
Losing Player's Share—$3,510

BATTING

	Pos	G	AB	R	H	2B	3B	HR	RBI	BB	SO	SB	BA
New York Giants													
George Kelly	1b	8	30	3	7	1	0	0	4	3	10	0	.233
Johnny Rawlings	2b	8	30	2	10	3	0	0	4	0	3	0	.333
Dave Bancroft	ss	8	33	3	5	1	0	0	3	1	5	0	.152
Frankie Frisch	3b	8	30	5	9	0	1	0	1	4	3	3	.300
Ross Youngs	rf	8	25	3	7	1	1	0	4	7	2	2	.280
George Burns	cf	8	33	2	11	4	1	0	2	3	5	1	.333
Irish Meusel	lf	8	29	4	10	2	1	1	7	2	3	1	.345
Frank Snyder	c-ph	7	22	4	8	1	0	1	3	0	2	0	**.364**
Earl Smith	ph-c	3	7	0	0	0	0	0	0	1	0	0	.000
Eddie Brown	Did not play												
Bill Cunningham	Did not play												
Mike Gonzalez	Did not play												
Casey Stengel	Did not play												
Alex Gaston	Did not play												
Wally Kopf	Did not play												
Art Nehf	p	3	9	0	0	0	0	0	0	1	3	0	.000
Jesse Arnes	p	3	9	3	4	0	0	0	0	0	0	0	.444
Phil Douglas	p	3	7	0	0	0	0	0	0	0	2	0	.000
Fred Toney	p	2	0	0	0	0	0	0	0	0	0	0	.000
Rosy Ryan	Did not play												
Slim Sallee	Did not play												
Red Shea	Did not play												
Red Causey	Did not play												
Team Total		8	264	29	71	13	4	2	28	22	38	7	.269

Double Plays—4 Left on Bases—54

	Pos	G	AB	R	H	2B	3B	HR	RBI	BB	SO	SB	BA
New York Yankees													
Wally Pipp	1b	8	26	1	4	1	0	0	2	2	3	1	.154
Aaron Ward	2b	8	26	1	6	0	0	0	4	2	6	0	.231
Roger Peckinpaugh	ss	8	28	2	5	1	0	0	0	4	3	0	.179
Mike McNally	3b	7	20	3	4	1	0	0	1	1	3	2	.200
Bob Meusel	rf	8	30	3	6	2	0	0	3	2	5	1	.200
Elmer Miller	cf	8	31	3	5	1	0	0	2	2	5	0	.161
Babe Ruth	lf-ph	6	16	3	5	0	0	1	4	5	8	2	.313
Wally Schang	c	8	21	1	6	1	1	0	1	5	3	0	.286
Chick Fewster	pr-lf	4	10	3	2	0	1	0	2	3	3	0	.200
Frank Baker	ph-3b	4	8	0	2	0	0	0	0	1	0	0	.250
Al DeVormer	pr-c	2	1	0	0	0	0	0	0	0	0	0	.000
Bragg Roth	Did not play												
Chicken Hawks	Did not play												
Johnny Mitchell	Did not play												
Waite Hoyt	p	3	9	0	2	0	0	0	1	0	1	0	.222
Carl Mays	p	3	9	0	1	0	0	0	0	0	1	0	.111
Bob Shawkey	p	2	4	2	2	0	0	0	0	0	1	0	.500
Jack Quinn	p	1	2	0	0	0	0	0	0	0	1	0	.000
Harry Harper	p	1	0	0	0	0	0	0	0	0	0	0	.000
Tom Rogers	p	1	0	0	0	0	0	0	0	0	0	0	.000
Bill Piercy	p	1	0	0	0	0	0	0	0	0	0	0	.000
Rip Collins	p	1	0	0	0	0	0	0	0	0	0	0	.000
	Did not play												
Team Total		8	241	22	50	7	1	2	20	27	44	6	.207

Double Plays—8 Left on Bases—43

PITCHING

	G	GS	CG	IP	H	R	ER	BB	SO	W	L	SVB	ERA
New York Giants													
Art Nehf	**3**	**3**	**3**	26	13	6	4	**13**	8	1	**2**	0	1.38
Phil Douglas	**3**	**3**	2	26	**20**	6	6	5	17	**2**	1	0	2.07
Jesse Barnes	**3**	0	0	16⅓	10	3	3	6	**18**	**2**	0	0	1.65
Fred Toney	2	2	0	2⅔	7	7	7	3	1	0	0	0	23.63
Rosy Ryan	Did not play												
Slim Sallee	Did not play												
Red Shea	Did not play												
Red Causey	Did not play												
Team Total	8	8	5	71	50	22	20	27	44	5	3	0	2.53
New York Yankees													
Waite Hoyt	**3**	**3**	**3**	27	18	2	0	11	**18**	**2**	1	0	**0.00**
Carl Mays	**3**	**3**	**3**	26	**20**	6	5	0	9	1	**2**	0	1.73
Bob Shawkey	2	1	0	9	13	9	7	6	5	0	1	0	7.00
Jack Quinn	1	0	0	3⅔	8	4	4	2	2	0	1	0	9.82
Harry Harper	1	1	0	1⅓	3	3	3	2	1	0	0	0	20.25
Tom Rogers	1	0	0	1⅓	3	1	1	0	1	0	0	0	6.75
Bill Piercy	1	0	0	2	0	0	0	2	0	0	0	0	0.00
Rip Collins	1	0	0	⅔	4	4	4	1	0	0	0	0	54.00
Alex Ferguson	Did not play												
Team Total	8	8	6	70	71	29	24	22	38	3	5	0	3.09

Frankie Frisch

1922

New York N.L. 4
New York A.L. 0

Highlights

THE SERIES REVERTED TO BEST of seven games this year, with the Giants versus the Yankees at the Polo Grounds. Babe Ruth and Bob Meusel, the foundation of the Yanks' offense, were sidelined until May 20 by Commissioner Landis for making an unauthorized barnstorming trip after the 1921 Series. The Yankees acquired Everett Scott, Joe Dugan, Joe Bush, and Sad Sam Jones from the Red Sox and Whitey Witt from the A's. The Giants had Frankie Frisch (.327, 31 stolen bases), George Kelly, Dave Bancroft, Ross Youngs and Casey Stengel—all at .321 or better. Art Nehf (19 wins) and Rosy Ryan (17 wins) were on the mound.

The Giants won the Series in four straight (3-2, 3-3, 3-0, 4-3 and 5-3), holding Ruth to .118 with no homers. Game two was called because of darkness by umpire George Hildebrand. Forty-five minutes of sunlight were still left and fans were furious. So furious that Commissioner Landis ordered entire game receipts ($120,000) donated to military hospitals for disabled veterans.

Game 1 Oct. 4
Yankees	000 001 100 ·	2
Giants	000 000 03* ·	3

Winner-Ryan Loser-Bush

Game 2 Oct. 5
Giants	300 000 000 0 ·	3
Yankees	100 100 010 0 ·	3

Stopped by darkness

Game 3 Oct. 6
Yankees	000 000 000 ·	0
Giants	002 000 10* ·	3

Winner-J. Scott Loser-Jones

Game 4 Oct. 7
Giants	000 040 000 ·	4
Yankees	200 000 100 ·	3

Winner-McQuillan Loser-Mays

Game 5 Oct. 8
Yankees	100 010 100 ·	3
Giants	020 000 03* ·	5

Winner-Nehf Loser-Bush

BATTING	Pos	G	AB	R	H	2B	3B	HR	RBI	BB	SO	SB	BA
New York Giants													
George Kelly	1b	5	18	0	5	0	0	0	2	0	3	0	.278
Frankie Frisch	2b	5	17	3	8	1	0	0	2	1	0	1	.471
Dave Bancroft	ss	5	19	4	4	0	0	0	2	2	1	0	.211
Heinie Groh	3b	5	19	4	9	1	0	0	0	2	1	0	.474
Ross Youngs	rf	5	16	2	6	0	0	0	2	3	1	0	.375
Bill Cunningham	pr-cf	4	10	0	2	0	0	0	2	2	1	0	.200
Irish Meusel	lf	5	20	3	5	0	0	1	7	0	1	0	.250
Frank Snyder	c	4	15	1	5	0	0	0	0	0	1	0	.333
Earl Smith	ph-c	4	7	0	1	0	0	0	0	0	2	0	.143
Casey Stengel	cf	2	5	0	2	0	0	0	0	0	1	0	.400
Lee King	cf	2	1	0	1	0	0	0	0	1	0	0	1.000
Johnny Rawlings		Did not play											
Dave Robertson		Did not play											
Alex Gaston		Did not play											
Jesse Barnes	p	1	4	0	0	0	0	0	0	0	1	0	.000
Jack Scott	p	1	4	0	1	0	0	0	0	0	1	0	.250
Hugh McQuillan	p	1	4	1	1	1	0	0	0	0	1	0	.250
Art Nehf	p	2	3	0	0	0	0	0	0	2	0	0	.000
Rosy Ryan	p	1	0	0	0	0	0	0	0	0	0	0	.000
Claude Jonnard		Did not play											
Virgil Barnes		Did not play											
Carmen Hill		Did not play											
Clint Blume		Did not play											
Team Total		5	162	18	50	2	1	1	18	12	15	1	.309

Double Plays—4   Left on Bases—32

	Pos	G	AB	R	H	2B	3B	HR	RBI	BB	SO	SB	BA
New York Yankees													
Wally Pipp	1b	5	21	0	6	1	0	0	3	0	2	1	.286
Aaron Ward	2b	5	13	2	2	0	0	2	3	3	3	0	.154
Everett Scott	ss	5	14	0	2	0	0	0	1	1	0	0	.143
Joe Dugan	3b	5	20	4	5	1	0	0	0	0	1	0	.250
Babe Ruth	rf	5	17	1	2	1	0	0	1	2	3	0	.118
Whitey Witt	cf	5	18	1	4	1	1	0	0	1	2	0	.222
Bob Meusel	lf	5	20	2	6	1	0	0	2	1	3	1	.300
Wally Schang	c	5	16	0	3	1	0	0	0	0	3	0	.188
Norm McMillan	ph-cf	1	2	0	0	0	0	0	0	0	0	0	.000
Elmer Smith	ph	2	2	0	0	0	0	0	0	0	2	0	.000
Frank Baker	ph	1	1	0	0	0	0	0	0	0	0	0	.000
Mike McNally	2b	1	0	0	0	0	0	0	0	0	0	0	.000
Fred Hofmann		Did not play											
Al DeVormer		Did not play											
Camp Skinner		Did not play											
Bullet Joe Bush	p	2	6	0	1	0	0	0	1	0	0	0	.167
Bob Shawkey	p	1	4	0	0	0	0	0	0	0	1	0	.000
Waite Hoyt	p	2	2	0	1	0	0	0	0	0	0	0	.500
Carl Mays	p	1	2	0	0	0	0	0	0	0	0	0	.000
Sad Sam Jones	p	2	0	0	0	0	0	0	0	0	0	0	.000
George Murray		Did not play											
Lefty O'Doul		Did not play											
Team Total		5	158	11	32	6	1	2	11	8	20	2	.203

Double Plays—7   Left on Bases—25

PITCHING	G	GS	CG	IP	H	R	ER	BB	SO	W	L	SVB	ERA
New York Giants													
Art Nehf	2	2	1	16	11	5	4	3	6	1	0	0	2.25
Jesse Barnes	1	1	1	10	8	3	2	2	6	0	0	0	1.80
Jack Scott	1	1	1	9	4	0	0	1	2	1	0	0	0.00
Hugh McQuillan	1	1	1	9	8	3	3	2	4	1	0	0	3.00
Rosy Ryan	1	0	0	2	1	0	0	0	2	1	0	0	0.00
Claude Jonnard		Did not play											
Virgil Barnes		Did not play											
Carmen Hill		Did not play											
Clint Blume		Did not play											
Team Total	5	5	4	46	32	11	9	8	20	4	0	0	1.76
New York Yankees													
Bullet Joe Bush	2	2	1	15	21	8	8	5	6	0	2	0	4.80
Bob Shawkey	1	1	1	10	8	3	2	4	4	0	0	0	2.70
Waite Hoyt	2	1	0	8	11	3	1	2	4	0	1	0	1.13
Carl Mays	1	1	0	8	9	4	4	2	1	0	1	0	4.50
Sad Sam Jones	2	0	0	2	1	0	0	1	0	0	0	0	0.00
George Murray		Did not play											
Lefty O'Doul		Did not play											
Team Total	5	5	2	43	50	18	16	12	15	0	4	0	3.35

Total Attendance—185,947
Average Attendance—37,189
Winning Player's Share—$4,470
Losing Player's Share—$3.225

1923

New York A.L. 4
New York N.L. 2

Highlights

THE YANKEES WERE EVICTED from the Polo Grounds by the Giants, so they built Yankee Stadium and christened it by winning their third A.L. pennant. With Babe Ruth (.393, 41 homers, 130 RBI's) and a solid mound staff, the Yankees faced McGraw's New York Giants in the Series.

Game one was knotted at 4-4 when Giants center fielder Casey Stengel knocked one deep into left center. As he rounded second, his shoe came undone and he hobbled home to score the winning run just ahead of Bob Meusel's throw from outfield. Ruth's two homers helped win game two, 4-2, for the Yanks. Casey Stengel's homer in game three was the only score, and as he rounded the bases Casey thumbed his nose at the Yankees' bench.

The Yankees knocked 16-game-winner Jack Scott and two relievers out of box with six runs in the second inning of game four, laying groundwork for an 8-4 victory. In game five, the Yanks sailed to a 8-1 win.

With the Yanks ahead in Series at three games to two, McGraw put Nehf on mound in game six. After seven innings, Giants led by 4-1, but Nehf, tiring, loaded the bases and then walked Joe Bush to force in one run. Pitcher Rosy Ryan could do no better. A walk to Dugan and a Meusel single, aided by a wild throw by Giants Bill Cunningham, gave Yankees the game, 6-4, and their first World Championship.

Game 1 Oct. 10
Giants   004 000 001 - 5
Yankees   120 000 100 - 4
Winner-Ryan   Loser-Bush

Game 2 Oct. 11
Yankees   010 210 000 - 4
Giants   010 001 000 - 2
Winner-Pennock   Loser-McQuillan

Game 3 Oct. 12
Giants   000 000 100 - 1
Yankees   000 000 000 - 0
Winner-Nehf   Loser-Jones

Game 4 Oct. 13
Yankees   061 100 000 - 8
Giants   000 000 031 - 4
Winner-Shawkey   Loser-J. Scott

Game 5 Oct. 14
Giants   010 000 000 - 1
Yankees   340 100 00* - 8
Winner-Bush   Loser-Bentley

Game 6 Oct. 15
Yankees   100 000 050 - 6
Giants   100 111 000 - 4
Winner-Pennock   Loser-Nehf

Total Attendance—301,430
Average Attendance—50,238
Winning Player's Share—$6,143
Losing Player's Share—$4,113

BATTING	Pos	G	AB	R	H	2B	3B	HR	RBI	BB	SO	SB	BA
New York Yankees													
Wally Pipp	1b	6	20	2	5	0	0	0	2	4	1	0	.250
Aaron Ward	2b	6	24	4	10	0	0	1	2	1	3	1	.417
Everett Scott	ss	6	22	2	7	0	0	0	3	0	1	0	.318
Joe Dugan	3b	6	25	5	7	2	1	1	5	3	0	0	.280
Babe Ruth	rf-1b	6	19	8	7	1	1	3	3	8	6	0	.368
Whitey Witt	cf	6	25	1	6	2	0	0	4	1	1	0	.240
Bob Meusel	lf	6	26	1	7	1	2	0	8	0	3	0	.269
Wally Schang	c	6	22	3	7	1	0	0	1	2	0	.318
Hinkey Haines	rf-cf-ph	2	1	1	0	0	0	0	0	0	0	0	.000
Fred Hofmann	ph	2	1	0	0	0	0	0	0	1	0	0	.000
Harvey Hendrick	ph	1	1	0	0	0	0	0	0	0	0	0	.000
Ernie Johnson	ss-pr	2	0	1	0	0	0	0	0	0	0	0	.000
Elmer Smith	Did not play												
Benny Bengough	Did not play												
Mike McNally	Did not play												
Mike Gazella	Did not play												
Bullet Joe Bush	p-ph	4	7	2	3	1	0	0	1	1	1	0	.429
Herb Pennock	p	3	6	0	0	0	0	0	0	0	2	0	.000
Bob Shawkey	p	1	3	0	1	0	0	0	1	0	0	0	.333
Sad Sam Jones	p	2	2	0	0	0	0	0	0	0	1	0	.000
Waite Hoyt	p	1	1	0	0	0	0	0	0	0	1	0	.000
Carl Mays	Did not play												
George Pipgras	Did not play												
Oscar Roettger	Did not play												
Team Total		6	205	30	60	8	4	5	29	20	22	1	.293

Double Plays—6   Left on Bases—43

	Pos	G	AB	R	H	2B	3B	HR	RBI	BB	SO	SB	BA
New York Giants													
George Kelly	1b	6	22	1	4	0	0	0	1	1	2	0	.182
Frankie Frisch	2b	6	25	2	10	0	1	0	1	0	0	0	.400
Dave Bancroft	ss	6	24	1	2	0	0	0	1	1	2	1	.083
Heinie Groh	3b	6	22	3	4	0	1	0	2	3	1	0	.182
Ross Youngs	rf	6	23	2	8	0	0	1	3	2	0	0	.348
Casey Stengel	cf-ph	6	12	3	5	0	0	2	4	4	0	0	.417
Irish Meusel	lf	6	25	3	7	1	1	1	2	0	2	0	.280
Frank Snyder	c	5	17	1	2	0	0	0	1	2	2	0	.118
Bill Cunningham	cf-ph	4	7	0	1	0	0	0	0	1	0	0	.143
Hank Gowdy	c	3	4	0	0	0	0	0	0	0	1	0	.000
Jimmy O'Connell	ph	2	1	0	0	0	0	0	0	0	1	0	.000
Travis Jackson	ph	1	1	0	0	0	0	0	0	0	0	0	.000
Freddie Maguire	pr	2	0	1	0	0	0	0	0	0	0	0	.000
Alex Gaston	Did not play												
Ralph Shinners	Did not play												
Art Nehf	p	2	6	0	1	0	0	0	0	0	4	0	.167
Jack Bentley	p-ph	5	5	0	3	1	0	0	0	0	0	0	.600
Hugh McQuillan	p	2	3	0	0	0	0	0	0	0	1	0	.000
Rosy Ryan	p	3	2	0	0	0	0	0	0	0	1	0	.000
Virgil Barnes	p	2	1	0	0	0	0	0	0	0	1	0	.000
Jack Scott	p	2	1	0	0	0	0	0	0	0	0	0	.000
Claude Jonnard	p	2	0	0	0	0	0	0	0	0	0	0	.000
Mule Watson	p	1	0	0	0	0	0	0	0	0	0	0	.000
Dinty Gearin	pr	1	0	0	0	0	0	0	0	0	0	0	.000
Team Total		6	201	17	47	2	3	5	17	12	18	1	.234

Double Plays—8   Left on Bases—35

PITCHING	G	GS	CG	IP	H	R	ER	BB	SO	W	L	SVB	ERA
New York Yankees													
Herb Pennock	3	2	1	17⅓	19	7	7	1	8	2	0	1	3.63
Bullet Joe Bush	3	1	1	16⅔	1	2	2	4	5	1	0	1.08
Sad Sam Jones	2	1	0	10	5	1	1	2	3	0	1	1	0.90
Bob Shawkey	1	1	0	7⅔	12	3	3	4	2	1	0	0	3.52
Waite Hoyt	1	1	0	2⅓	4	4	4	1	0	0	0	15.43
Carl Mays	Did not play												
George Pipgras	Did not play												
Oscar Roettger	Did not play												
Team Total	6	6	2	54	47	17	17	12	18	4	2	2	2.83
New York Giants													
Art Nehf	2	2	1	16⅓	10	5	5	6	7	1	1	0	2.76
Rosy Ryan	3	0	0	9⅓	11	4	1	3	3	1	0	0	0.96
Hugh McQuillan	2	1	0	9	11	5	5	4	3	0	1	0	5.00
Jack Bentley	2	1	0	6⅔	10	8	7	4	1	0	1	0	9.45
Virgil Barnes	2	0	0	4⅔	4	0	0	4	0	0	0	0.00
Jack Scott	2	1	0	3	9	5	4	1	2	0	1	0	12.00
Claude Jonnard	2	0	0	2	1	0	0	1	1	0	0	0.00
Mule Watson	1	1	0	2	4	3	3	1	1	0	0	13.50
Dinty Gearin	Did not play												
Team Total	6	6	1	53	60	30	25	20	22	2	4	0	4.25

1924

Highlights

THE WASHINGTON SENATORS won their first A.L. pennant largely because of the skill of "Boy Wonder" player-manager Bucky Harris, 27. Outfielders Goose Goslin and Sam Rice supplied the hits; Walter Johnson, 36, used his fastball to win 23 games, leading the league with 158 strikeouts.

It was Johnson versus Nehf in game one, a 4-3 twelfth-inning Giants win. Homers by Goslin and Harris helped the Senators come back in game two, 4-3. Eight pitchers, four per team, appeared in game three, a 6-4 New York victory. The Senators returned to win game four, 7-4, with Goslin going four for four for the day, with a three-run homer. Johnson lost what was scheduled as his last Series game, 6-2.

A 2-1 Washington win in game six evened the Series at three games apiece. Score was 0-0 in game seven until Bucky Harris hit a homer, but the Giants connected too. Harris then hit a routine grounder that hit a pebble and suddenly popped up over Fred Lindstrom's head, and the score was 3-3. Harris put Johnson in, and at the bottom of the twelfth, Giants catcher Hank Gowdy, tripping over a face mask, muffed a foul pop-up by Muddy Ruel. Ruel then doubled and, when a second easy grounder suddenly popped up over Lindstrom's head, scored the winning run to give the Senators and Walter Johnson their first World Championship.

Game 1 Oct. 4
New York   010 100 000 002 · 4
Washington   000 001 001 001 · 3
Winner-Nehf   Loser-Johnson

Game 2 Oct. 5
New York   000 000 102 · 3
Washington   200 010 001 · 4
Winner-Zachary   Loser-Bentley

Game 3 Oct. 6
Washington   000 200 011 · 4
New York   021 101 01* · 6
Winner-McQuillan   Loser-Marberry

Game 4 Oct. 7
Washington   003 020 020 · 7
New York   100 001 011 · 4
Winner-Mogridge   Loser-Barnes

Game 5 Oct. 8
Washington   000 100 010 · 2
New York   001 020 03* · 6
Winner-Bentley   Loser-Johnson

Game 6 Oct. 9
New York   100 000 000 · 1
Washington   000 020 00* · 2
Winner-Zachary   Loser-Nehf

Game 7 Oct. 10
New York   000 003 000 000 · 3
Washington   000 100 020 001 · 4
Winner-Johnson   Loser-Bentley

Total Attendance—283,665
Average Attendance—40,524
Winning Player's Share—$5,970
Losing Player's Share—$3,820

Washington A.L. 4
New York N.L. 3

BATTING	Pos	G	AB	R	H	2B	3B	HR	RBI	BB	SO	SB	BA
Washington													
Joe Judge	1b	7	26	4	10	1	0	0	0	5	2	0	.385
Bucky Harris	2b	7	33	5	11	0	0	2	7	1	4	0	.333
Roger Peckinpaugh	ss	4	12	1	5	2	0	0	2	1	0	1	.417
Ossie Bluege	3b-ss	7	26	2	5	0	0	0	2	3	4	1	.192
Sam Rice	rf	7	29	2	6	0	0	0	1	3	2	2	.207
Earl McNeely	cf-ph	7	27	4	6	3	0	0	1	4	4	1	.222
Goose Goslin	lf	7	32	4	11	1	0	3	7	0	7	0	.344
Muddy Ruel	c	7	21	2	2	1	0	0	0	6	1	0	.095
Ralph Miller	3b	4	11	0	2	0	0	0	0	2	1	0	.182
Nemo Leibold	cf-ph	3	6	1	1	1	0	0	0	1	0	0	.167
Tommy Taylor	pr-3b	3	2	0	0	0	0	0	0	0	2	0	.000
Mule Shirley	ph-pr	3	2	1	1	0	0	0	0	1	0	0	.500
Bennie Tate	ph	3	0	0	0	0	0	0	0	1	3	0	.000
Showboat Fisher	Did not play												
Pinky Hargrave	Did not play												
Walter Johnson	p	3	9	0	1	0	0	0	0	0	0	0	.111
Tom Zachary	p	2	5	0	0	0	0	0	0	1	3	0	.000
George Mogridge	p	2	5	0	0	0	0	0	0	0	5	0	.000
Firpo Marberry	p	4	2	0	0	0	0	0	0	0	0	0	.000
Allen Russell	p	1	0	0	0	0	0	0	0	0	0	0	.000
Joe Martina	p	1	0	0	0	0	0	0	0	0	0	0	.000
By Speece	p	1	0	0	0	0	0	0	0	0	0	0	.000
Curly Ogden	p	1	0	0	0	0	0	0	0	0	0	0	.000
Paul Zahniser	Did not play												
Team Total		7	248	26	61	9	0	5	24	29	34	5	.246

Double Plays—10   Left on Bases—57

	Pos	G	AB	R	H	2B	3B	HR	RBI	BB	SO	SB	BA
New York Giants													
Bill Terry	1b-ph	5	14	3	6	0	1	1	1	3	1	0	.429
Frankie Frisch	2b-3b	7	30	1	10	4	1	0	0	4	1	1	.333
Travis Jackson	ss	7	27	3	2	0	0	0	1	1	4	1	.074
Fred Lindstrom	3b	7	30	1	10	2	0	0	4	3	6	0	.333
Ross Youngs	rf-lf	7	27	3	5	1	0	0	2	5	6	1	.185
George Kelly	cf-2b-1b	7	31	7	9	1	0	1	4	1	8	0	.290
Hack Wilson	lf-cf	7	30	1	7	1	0	0	3	1	9	0	.233
Hank Gowdy	c	7	27	4	7	0	0	0	2	2	2	0	.259
Irish Meusel	lf-rf	4	13	0	2	0	0	0	1	2	0	0	.154
Billy Southworth	pr-cf-ph	5	1	1	0	0	0	0	0	0	0	0	.000
Heinie Groh	ph	1	1	0	1	0	0	0	0	0	0	0	1.000
Frank Snyder	ph	1	1	0	0	0	0	0	0	0	0	0	.000
Jimmy O'Connell	Did not play												
Art Nehf	p	3	7	1	3	0	0	0	0	0	0	0	.429
Jack Bentley	p-ph	5	7	1	2	0	0	1	2	1	1	0	.286
Virgil Barnes	p	2	4	0	0	0	0	0	0	1	2	0	.000
Rosy Ryan	p	2	2	1	1	0	0	1	1	0	0	0	.500
Hugh McQuillan	p	3	1	0	1	0	0	0	0	1	1	0	.100
Harry Baldwin	p	1	0	0	0	0	0	0	0	0	0	0	.000
Wayland Dean	p	1	0	0	0	0	0	0	0	0	0	0	.000
Mule Watson	p	1	0	0	0	0	0	0	0	0	0	0	.000
Claude Jonnard	p	1	0	0	0	0	0	0	0	0	0	0	.000
Walter Huntzinger	Did not play												
Ernie Maun	Did not play												
Team Total		7	253	27	66	9	2	4	22	25	40	3	.261

Double Plays—4   Left on Bases—59

PITCHING	G	GS	CG	IP	H	R	ER	BB	SO	W	L	SV	ERA
Washington													
Walter Johnson	3	2	2	24	30	10	6	11	20	1	2	0	2.25
Tom Zachary	2	2	1	17²/₃	13	4	4	3	3	2	0	0	2.04
George Mogridge	2	1	0	12	7	5	3	6	5	1	0	0	2.25
Firpo Marberry	4	1	0	8	9	5	1	4	10	0	1	2	1.13
Allen Russell	1	0	0	3	4	2	1	0	0	0	0	0	3.00
Joe Martina	1	0	0	1	0	0	0	0	1	0	0	0	0.00
By Speece	1	0	0	1	3	1	1	0	0	0	0	0	9.00
Curly Ogden	1	1	0	¹/₃	0	0	0	1	1	0	0	0	0.00
Paul Zahniser	Did not play												
Team Total	7	7	3	67	66	27	16	25	40	4	3	2	2.15
New York													
Art Nehf	3	2	1	19²/₃	15	5	4	9	7	1	1	0	1.83
Jack Bentley	3	2	1	17	18	7	7	8	10	1	2	0	3.71
Virgil Barnes	2	2	0	12²/₃	15	8	8	1	9	0	1	0	5.68
Hugh McQuillan	3	1	0	7	2	2	2	6	2	1	0	1	2.57
Rosy Ryan	2	0	0	5²/₃	7	2	2	4	3	0	0	0	3.18
Harry Baldwin	1	0	0	2	1	0	0	0	1	0	0	0	0.00
Wayland Dean	1	0	0	2	3	2	1	0	2	0	0	0	4.50
Mule Watson	1	0	0	²/₃	0	0	0	0	0	0	0	1	0.00
Claude Jonnard	1	0	0	0	0	0	0	1	0	0	0	0	0.00
Walter Huntzinger	Did not play												
Ernie Maun	Did not play												
Team Total	7	7	2	66²/₃	61	26	24	29	34	3	4	2	3.24

1925

Pittsburgh N.L. 4
Washington A.L. 3

Highlights

PIE TRAYNOR, KIKI CUYLER, MAX Carey, Glenn Wright, Clyde Barnhart and George Grantham powered the Pitttsburgh Pirates to their first N.L. pennant since 1909. Facing them were the Washington Senators with Sam Rice, Goose Goslin, Roger Peckinpaugh (the A.L.'s MVP at .294), spitballer Stan Coveleski and 20-gamewinner Walter Johnson, 37.

Johnson beat Lee Meadows, 4-1, in the opener. In game two, all players wore black armbands to commemorate the death of Christy Mathewson, who had died during night. An eighthinning muff of an easy grounder by Peckinpaugh and a homer by Cuyler put the Senators away, 3-2. The Senators took game three, 4-3, with Sam Rice making a disputed catch of an apparent homer when he disappeared over the fence and reappeared with the ball. Game four: homers by Goslin and Harris highlighted a 4-0 Washington win. Pirates came back, 6-3, in game five.

Pittsburgh also took game six, 3-2. The deciding game was played in drizzling rain. Two errors and a homer by Peckinpaugh helped Pittsburgh win, 9-7, for first Championship in sixteen years.

Game 1 Oct. 7
Washington	010 020 001 -	4
Pittsburgh	000 010 000 -	1

Winner-Johnson   Loser-Meadows

Game 2 Oct. 8
Washington	010 000 001 -	2
Pittsburgh	000 100 02* -	3

Winner-Aldridge   Loser-Coveleski

Game 3 Oct. 10
Pittsburgh	010 101 000	-3
Washington	001 001 20*	4

Winner-Ferguson   Loser-Kremer

Game 4 Oct. 11
Pittsburgh	000 000 000 -	0
Washington	004 000 00* -	4

Winner-Johnson   Loser-Yde

Game 5 Oct. 12
Pittsburgh	002 000 211 -	6
Washington	100 100 100 -	3

Winner-Aldridge   Loser-Coveleski

Game 6 Oct. 13
Washington	110 000 000 -	2
Pittsburgh	002 010 00* -	3

Winner-Kremer   Loser-Ferguson

Game 7 Oct. 15
Washington	400 200 010 -	7
Pittsburgh	003 010 23* -	9

Winner-Kremer   Loser-Johnson

Total Attendance—282,848
Average Attendance—40,407
Winning Player's Share—$5,333
Losing Player's Share—$3,735

BATTING

	Pos	G	AB	R	H	2B	3B	HR	RBI	BB	SO	SB	BA
Pittsburgh													
George Grantham	1b-ph	5	15	0	2	0	0	0	0	0	3	1	.133
Eddie Moore	2b	7	26	7	6	1	0	1	2	5	2	0	.231
Glenn Wright	ss	7	27	3	5	1	0	1	3	1	4	0	.185
Pie Traynor	3b	7	26	2	9	0	2	1	4	3	1	1	.346
Kiki Cuyler	rf	7	26	3	7	3	0	1	6	1	4	0	.269
Max Carey	cf	7	24	6	11	4	0	0	2	2	3	3	.458
Clyde Barnhart	lf	7	28	1	7	1	0	0	5	3	5	1	.250
Earl Smith	c	6	20	0	7	1	0	0	0	1	2	0	.350
Stuffy McInnis	ph-1b	4	14	0	4	0	0	0	1	0	2	0	.286
Johnny Gooch	c	3	3	0	0	0	0	0	0	0	0	0	.000
Carson Bigbee	pr-ph-lf	4	3	1	1	1	0	0	1	0	0	1	.333
Johnny Rawlings	Did not play												
Fresco Thompson	Did not play												
Roy Spencer	Did not play												
Jewel Ens	Did not play												
Mule Haas	Did not play												
Ray Kremer	p	3	7	0	1	0	0	0	1	0	5	0	.143
Vic Aldridge	p	3	7	0	0	0	0	0	0	0	0	0	.000
Johnny Morrison	p	3	2	1	1	0	0	0	0	0	0	0	.500
Lee Meadows	p	1	1	0	0	0	0	0	0	1	1	0	.000
Emil Yde	p-pr	2	1	1	0	0	0	0	0	0	0	0	.000
Babe Adams	p	1	0	0	0	0	0	0	0	0	0	0	.000
Red Oldham	p	1	0	0	0	0	0	0	0	0	0	0	.000
Tom Sheehan	Did not play												
Bud Culloton	Did not play												
Team Total		7	230	25	61	12	2	4	25	17	32	7	.265

Double Plays—4   Left on Bases—54

	Pos	G	AB	R	H	2B	3B	HR	RBI	BB	SO	SB	BA
Washington													
Joe Judge	1b	7	23	2	4	1	0	1	3	3	2	0	.174
Bucky Harris	2b	7	23	2	2	0	0	0	0	1	3	0	.087
Roger Peckinpaugh	ss	7	24	1	6	1	0	1	3	1	2	1	.250
Ossie Bluege	3b	5	18	2	5	1	0	0	2	0	4	0	.278
Joe Harris	rf	7	25	5	11	2	0	3	6	3	4	0	.440
Sam Rice	cf-rf	7	33	5	12	0	0	0	3	0	1	0	.364
Goose Goslin	lf	7	26	6	8	1	0	3	6	3	3	0	.308
Muddy Ruel	c	7	19	0	6	1	0	0	1	3	2	0	.316
Buddy Myer	3b	3	8	0	2	0	0	0	0	1	2	0	.250
Hank Severeid	c	1	3	0	1	0	0	0	0	0	0	0	.333
Nemo Leibold	ph	3	2	1	1	1	0	0	0	1	0	0	.500
Spence Adams	ph-2b	2	1	0	0	0	0	0	0	0	0	0	.000
Bobby Veach	ph	2	1	0	0	0	0	0	0	1	0	0	.000
Earl McNeely	cf-pr	4	0	2	0	0	0	0	0	0	0	1	.000
Everett Scott	Did not play												
Bennie Tate	Did not play												
Tex Jeanes	Did not play												
Walter Johnson	p	3	11	0	1	0	0	0	0	0	3	0	.091
Alex Ferguson	p	2	4	0	0	0	0	0	0	0	3	0	.000
Stan Coveleski	p	2	3	0	0	0	0	0	0	1	2	0	.000
Firpo Marberry	p	2	0	0	0	0	0	0	0	0	0	0	.000
Win Ballou	p	2	0	0	0	0	0	0	0	0	0	0	.000
Tom Zachary	p	1	0	0	0	0	0	0	0	0	0	0	.000
Dutch Ruether	ph	1	1	0	0	0	0	0	0	0	1	0	.000
Allen Russell	Did not play												
Team Total		7	225	26	59	8	0	8	25	17	32	2	.262

Double Plays—8   Left on Bases—46

PITCHING

	G	GS	CG	IP	H	R	ER	BB	SO	W	L	SV	ERA
Pittsburgh													
Ray Kremer	3	2	2	21	17	7	7	4	9	2	1	0	3.00
Vic Aldridge	3	3	2	18⅓	18	9	9	9	9	2	0	0	4.42
Johnny Morrison	3	1	0	9⅓	11	3	3	1	7	0	0	0	2.89
Lee Meadows	1	1	0	8	6	3	3	0	4	0	1	0	3.38
Emil Yde	1	1	0	2⅓	5	4	3	3	1	0	1	0	11.57
Babe Adams	1	0	0	1	2	0	0	0	0	0	0	0	0.00
Red Oldham	1	0	0	1	0	0	0	0	2	0	0	1	0.00
Tom Sheehan	Did not play												
Bud Culloton	Did not play												
Team Total	7	7	4	61	59	26	25	17	32	4	3	1	3.69
Washington													
Walter Johnson	3	3	3	26	26	10	6	4	15	2	1	0	2.08
Stan Coveleski	2	2	0	14⅓	16	7	6	5	3	0	2	0	3.77
Alex Ferguson	2	2	1	14	13	6	5	6	11	1	1	0	3.21
Firpo Marberry	2	0	0	2⅓	3	0	0	0	2	0	0	1	0.00
Win Ballou	2	0	0	1⅔	0	0	0	1	1	0	0	0	0.00
Tom Zachary	1	0	0	1⅔	3	2	2	1	0	0	0	0	10.80
Dutch Ruether	Did not pitch												
Allen Russell	Did not play												
Team Total	7	7	4	60	61	25	19	17	32	3	4	1	2.85

1926

St. Louis N.L. 4
New York A.L. 3

Highlights

THE ST. LOUIS CARDINALS WON their first N.L. flag since 1888, with the help of player-manager Rogers Hornsby, Sunny Jim Bottomley and Les Bell. Pitchers were Flint Rhem, Bill Sherdel, Jesse Haines and 30-year-old Grover Cleveland Alexander. Their opponents were the New York Yankees, including Ruth, Meusel, Dugan, Pennock, Hoyt, Sam Jones, Shawkey, Gehrig (23 years old), Lazzeri, Koenig, Combs and pitcher Urban Shocker.

The Yankees won game one, 2-1. Pete Alexander won game two for the Cards, 6-2. Haines hurled a five-hitter to give the Cards game three, 4-0. Then Ruth hit three homers in game four to lead the Yankees to a 10-5 win. The Yankees took game five, 3-2, behind Herb Pennock.

Alexander won game six, 10-2, tying Series at three apiece. Hornsby started Haines in game seven. But with the score at 3-2, in favor or St. Louis in the seventh, with two out and three Yankees on base, Haines, who had a blister on his index finger, was in trouble. Hornsby pulled him and sent Alexander to the mound. Old Pete struck out Lazzeri to end the rally. With the score still 3-2, Alexander got Combs and Koenig and walked Ruth. Ruth decided to steal but was easily tagged to end the game and give the Series to St. Louis.

Game 1 Oct. 2
St. Louis   100 000 000 · 1
New York   100 001 00* · 2
Winner-Pennock   Loser-Sherdel

Game 2 Oct. 3
St. Louis   002 000 301 · 6
New York   020 000 000 · 2
Winner-Alexander   Loser-Shocker

Game 3 Oct. 5
New York   000 000 000 · 0
St. Louis   000 310 00* · 4
Winner-Haines   Loser-Ruether

Game 4 Oct. 6
New York   101 142 100 · 10
St. Louis   100 300 001 · 5
Winner-Hoyt   Loser-Reinhart

Game 5 Oct. 7
New York   000 001 001   1 · 3
St. Louis   000 100 100   0 · 2
Winner-Pennock   Loser-Sherdel

Game 6 Oct. 9
St. Louis   300 010 501 · 10
New York   000 100 100 · 2
Winner-Alexander   Loser-Shawkey

Game 7 Oct. 10
St. Louis   000 300 000 · 3
New York   001 001 000 · 2
Winner-Haines   Loser-Hoyt

Total Attendance—328,051
Average Attendance—46,864
Winning Player's Share—$5,585
Losing Player's Share—$3,418

BATTING	Pos	G	AB	R	H	2B	3B	HR	RBI	BB	SO	SB	BA
St. Louis													
Jim Bottomley	1b	7	29	4	10	3	0	0	5	1	2	0	.345
Rogers Hornsby	2b	7	28	2	7	1	0	0	4	2	2	1	.250
Tommy Thevenow	ss	7	24	5	10	1	0	1	4	0	1	0	.417
Les Bell	3b	7	27	4	7	1	0	1	6	2	5	0	.259
Billy Southworth	rf	7	29	6	10	1	1	1	4	0	0	1	.345
Taylor Douthit	cf	4	15	3	4	2	0	0	1	3	2	0	.267
Chick Hafey	lf	7	27	2	5	2	0	0	0	0	7	0	.185
Bob O'Farrell	c	7	23	2	7	1	0	0	2	2	2	0	.304
Wattie Holm	ph-rf-cf	5	16	1	2	0	0	0	1	1	2	0	.125
Jake Flowers	ph	3	3	0	0	0	0	0	0	0	1	0	.000
Specs Toporcer	ph	1	0	0	0	0	0	0	0	1	0	0	.000
Ray Blades		Did not play—injured											
Ernie Vick		Did not play											
Pete Alexander	p	3	7	1	0	0	0	0	0	0	2	0	.000
Bill Sherdel	p	2	5	0	0	0	0	0	0	0	2	0	.000
Jesse Haines	p	3	5	1	3	0	0	1	2	0	1	0	.600
Flint Rhem	p	1	1	0	0	0	0	0	0	0	1	0	.000
Hi Bell	p	1	0	0	0	0	0	0	0	0	0	0	.000
Wild Bill Hallahan	p	1	0	0	0	0	0	0	0	0	0	0	.000
Vic Keen	p	1	0	0	0	0	0	0	0	0	0	0	.000
Art Reinhart	p	1	0	0	0	0	0	0	0	0	0	0	.000
Allan Sothoron		Did not play											
Syl Johnson		Did not play											
Ed Clough		Did not play											
Team Total		7	239	31	65	12	1	4	30	11	30	2	.272

Double Plays—6   Left on Bases-43

	Pos	G	AB	R	H	2B	3B	HR	RBI	BB	SO	SB	BA
New York													
Lou Gehrig	1b	7	23	1	8	2	0	0	4	5	4	0	.348
Tony Lazzeri	2b	7	26	2	5	1	0	0	3	1	6	0	.192
Mark Koenig	ss	7	32	2	4	1	0	0	2	0	6	0	.125
Joe Dugan	3b	7	24	2	8	1	0	0	2	1	1	0	.333
Babe Ruth	rf-lf	7	20	6	6	0	0	4	5	11	2	1	.300
Earle Combs	cf	7	28	3	10	2	0	0	2	5	2	0	.357
Bob Meusel	lf-rf	7	21	3	5	1	1	0	0	6	1	0	.238
Hank Severeid	c	7	22	1	6	1	0	0	1	1	2	0	.273
Ben Paschal	ph	5	4	0	1	0	0	0	1	1	2	0	.250
Pat Collins	c	3	2	0	0	0	0	0	0	0	1	0	.000
Mike Gazella	3b	1	0	0	0	0	0	0	0	0	0	0	.000
Spence Adams	pr	2	0	0	0	0	0	0	0	0	0	0	.000
Benny Bengough		Did not play—shoulder injury											
Roy Carlyle		Did not play											
Aaron Ward		Did not play											
Herb Pennock	p	3	7	1	1	1	0	0	0	0	0	0	.143
Waite Hoyt	p	2	6	0	0	0	0	0	0	0	1	0	.000
Dutch Ruether	p-ph	3	4	0	0	0	0	0	0	0	0	0	.000
Bob Shawkey	p	3	2	0	0	0	0	0	0	0	1	0	.000
Urban Shocker	p	2	2	0	0	0	0	0	0	0	2	0	.000
Myles Thomas	p	2	0	0	0	0	0	0	0	0	0	0	.000
Sad Sam Jones	p	1	0	0	0	0	0	0	0	0	0	0	.000
Walter Beall		Did not play											
Garland Braxton		Did not play											
Herb McQuaid		Did not play											
Team Total		7	223	21	54	10	1	4	20	31	31	1	.242

Double Plays—3   Left on Bases—55

PITCHING	G	GS	CG	IP	H	R	ER	BB	SO	W	L	SV	ERA
St. Louis													
Pete Alexander	3	2	2	20⅓	12	4	3	4	17	2	0	1	1.33
Bill Sherdel	2	2	1	17	15	5	4	8	3	0	2	0	2.12
Jesse Haines	3	2	1	16⅔	13	2	2	9	5	2	0	0	1.08
Flint Rhem	1	1	0	4	7	3	3	2	4	0	0	0	6.75
Hi Bell	1	0	0	2	4	2	2	1	1	0	0	0	9.00
Wild Bill Hallahan	1	0	0	2	2	1	1	3	1	0	0	0	4.50
Vic Keen	1	0	0	1	0	0	0	0	0	0	0	0	0.00
Art Reinhart	1	0	0	0	1	4	4	4	0	0	1	0	0.00
Syl Johnson		Did not play											
Allan Sothoron		Did not play											
Ed Clough		Did not play											
Team Total	7	7	4	63	54	21	19	31	31	4	3	1	2.71
New York													
Herb Pennock	3	2	2	22	13	3	3	4	8	2	0	0	1.23
Waite Hoyt	2	2	1	15	19	8	2	1	10	1	1	0	1.20
Bob Shawkey	3	1	0	10	8	7	6	2	7	0	1	0	5.40
Urban Shocker	2	1	0	7⅔	13	7	5	0	3	0	1	0	5.87
Dutch Ruether	1	1	0	4⅓	7	4	2	2	1	0	1	0	4.16
Myles Thomas	2	0	0	3	3	1	1	0	0	0	0	0	3.00
Sad Sam Jones	1	0	0	1	2	1	1	2	1	0	0	0	9.00
Walter Beall		Did not play											
Garland Braxton		Did not play											
Herb McQuaid		Did not play											
Team Total	7	7	3	63	65	31	20	11	30	3	4	0	2.86

1927

New York A.L. 4
Pittsburgh N.L. 0

Highlights

THIS WAS THE SERIES IN WHICH the Pittsburgh Pirates were reportedly unnerved by watching the New York Yankees at batting practice before game one. The Yankees' "Murderer's Row" included Ruth, Gehrig, Meusel and Lazzeri. Pirates manager Donie Bush had brothers Paul and Lloyd Waner, a.k.a. "Big Poison" (.380 and 131 RBI's) and "Little Poison" (.355), as well as Pie Traynor and Glenn Wright.

Game one went to New York, 5-4, and game two to New York, 6-2, thanks to George Pipgras. Control pitcher Herb Pennock won game three for the Yanks, 3-1, to put the Bucs down three to zero in games.

The Pirates managed to tie game four, 3-3, in the seventh with Johnny Miljus on the mound, but the Yankees were unstoppable, and the game ended in an 8-1 New York victory.

Game 1 Oct. 5

New York	103 010 000 -	5
Pittsburgh	101 010 010 -	4

Winner-Hoyt   Loser-Kremer

Game 2 Oct. 6

New York	003 000 030 -	6
Pittsburgh	100 000 010 -	2

Winner-Pipgras   Loser-Aldridge

Game 3 Oct. 7

Pittsburgh	000 000 010 -	1
New York	200 000 60* -	8

Winner-Pennock   Loser-Meadows

Game 4 Oct. 8

Pittsburgh	100 000 200 -	3
New York	100 020 001 -	4

Winner-Moore   Loser-Miljus

BATTING	Pos	G	AB	R	H	2B	3B	HR	RBI	BB	SO	SB	BA
New York													
Lou Gehrig	1b	4	13	2	4	2	2	0	4	3	3	0	.308
Tony Lazzeri	2b	4	15	1	4	1	0	0	2	1	4	0	.267
Mark Koenig	ss	4	18	5	9	2	0	0	2	0	2	0	**.500**
Joe Dugan	3b	4	15	2	3	0	0	0	0	0	0	0	.200
Babe Ruth	rf	4	15	4	6	0	0	2	7	2	2	1	.400
Earle Combs	cf	4	16	6	5	0	0	0	2	1	2	0	.313
Bob Meusel	lf	4	17	1	2	0	0	0	1	1	7	1	.118
Pat Collins	c	2	5	0	3	1	0	0	0	3	0	0	.600
Benny Bengough	c	2	4	1	0	0	0	0	0	1	0	0	.000
Johnny Grabowski	c	1	2	0	0	0	0	0	0	0	0	0	.000
Cedric Durst	ph	1	1	0	0	0	0	0	0	0	0	0	.000
Ray Morehart		Did not play											
Mike Gazella		Did not play											
Ben Paschal		Did not play											
Julie Wera		Did not play											
Wilcy Moore	p	2	5	0	1	0	0	0	0	0	3	0	.200
Herb Pennock	p	1	4	1	0	0	0	0	1	0	1	0	.000
George Pipgras	p	1	3	0	1	0	0	0	0	1	1	0	.333
Waite Hoyt	p	1	3	0	0	0	0	0	0	0	0	0	.000
Dutch Ruether		Did not play											
Urban Shocker		Did not play											
Myles Thomas		Did not play											
Bob Shawkey		Did not play											
Joe Giard		Did not play											
Team Total		4	136	23	38	6	2	2	19	13	25	2	.279

Double Plays—4   Left on Bases—29

	Pos	G	AB	R	H	2B	3B	HR	RBI	BB	SO	SB	BA
Pittsburgh													
Joe Harris	1b	4	15	0	3	0	0	0	1	0	0	0	.200
George Grantham	2b	3	11	0	4	1	0	0	0	1	1	0	.364
Glenn Wright	ss	4	13	1	2	0	0	0	2	0	0	0	.154
Pie Traynor	3b	4	15	1	3	1	0	0	0	1	1	0	.200
Paul Waner	rf	4	15	0	5	1	0	0	3	0	1	0	.333
Lloyd Waner	cf	4	15	5	6	1	1	0	0	1	0	0	.400
Clyde Barnhart	lf	4	16	0	5	1	0	0	4	0	0	0	.313
Earl Smith	c-ph	3	8	0	0	0	0	0	0	0	0	0	.000
Johnny Gouch	c	3	5	0	0	0	0	0	0	1	1	0	.000
Hal Rhyne	2b	1	4	0	0	0	0	0	0	0	0	0	.000
Fred Brickell	ph	2	1	0	0	0	0	0	0	0	0	0	.000
Roy Spencer	ph-c	1	1	0	0	0	0	0	0	0	0	0	.000
Heinie Groh	ph	1	1	0	0	0	0	0	0	0	0	0	.000
Kiki Cuyler		Did not play											
Joe Cronie		Did not play											
Vic Aldridge	p	1	2	0	0	0	0	0	0	0	0	0	.000
Johnny Miljus	p	2	2	0	0	0	0	0	0	0	2	0	.000
Lee Meadows	p	1	2	0	0	0	0	0	0	0	0	0	.000
Ray Kremer	p	1	2	1	1	1	0	0	0	0	1	0	.500
Carmen Hill	p	1	1	0	0	0	0	0	0	1	0	0	.000
Mike Cvengros	p	2	0	0	0	0	0	0	0	0	0	0	.000
Joe Dawson	p	1	0	0	0	0	0	0	0	0	0	0	.000
Emil Yde	pr	1	0	1	0	0	0	0	0	0	0	0	.000
Team Total		4	130	10	29	6	1	0	10	4	7	0	.223

Double Plays—2   Left on Bases—23

PITCHING	G	GS	CG	IP	H	R	ER	BB	SO	W	L	SV	ERA
New York													
Wilcy Moore	2	1	1	10²/₃	11	3	1	2	2	1	0	1	**0.84**
Herb Pennock	1	1	1	9	3	1	1	0	1	1	0	0	1.00
George Pipgras	1	1	1	9	7	2	2	1	2	1	0	0	2.00
Waite Hoyt	1	1	0	7¹/₃	8	4	4	1	2	1	0	0	4.91
Urban Shocker		Did not play											
Dutch Ruether		Did not play											
Myles Thomas		Did not play											
Bob Shawkey		Did not play											
Joe Giard		Did not play											
Team Total	4	4	3	36	29	10	8	4	7	4	0	1	2.00
Pittsburgh													
Vic Aldridge	1	1	0	7¹/₃	10	6	6	4	4	0	1	0	7.36
Johnny Miljus	2	0	0	6²/₃	4	1	1	4	6	0	1	0	1.35
Lee Meadows	1	1	0	6¹/₃	7	7	7	1	6	0	1	0	9.95
Carmen Hill	1	1	0	6	9	3	3	1	6	0	0	0	4.50
Ray Kremer	1	1	0	5	5	5	2	3	1	0	1	0	3.60
Mike Cvengros	2	0	0	2¹/₃	3	1	1	0	2	0	0	0	3.86
Joe Dawson	1	0	0	1	0	0	0	0	0	0	0	0	0.00
Emil Yde		Did not pitch											
Team Total	4	4	0	34²/₃	38	23	20	13	25	0	4	0	5.19

1928

New York A.L. 4
St. Louis N.L. 0

Highlights

AFTER BEATING THE YANKEES in 1926, St. Louis Cardinals owner Sam Breadon broke up and re-formed his team. Hornsby was traded to the Giants for Frankie Frisch, and Rabbit Maranville was put into the shortstop spot, with Jim Bottomley and Chick Hafey in the outfield. Bill Sherdel (age 31), Jesse Haines (age 34) and Pete Alexander (age 41) made up the pitching staff. Their opponents were an injury-ridden Yankees team: pitcher Herb Pennock and second baseman Lazzeri both had bad arms; Earle Combs, a broken finger; and Babe Ruth, a bad ankle.

Waite Hoyt won the opener, 4-1, with two doubles and a single by Ruth. Alexander was knocked out of the box by the Yankees in a 9-3 win of game two. Game three: Ruth hit two singles and Gehrig two homers to power the Yanks to a 7-3 victory. Game four was the coup de grace for St. Louis. Ruth hit three homers and Gehrig one, in a game that ended at 7-3, for New York's second consecutive sweep of the Series.

Game 1	Oct. 4		
St. Louis	000 000 100	·	1
New York	100 200 01*	·	4
Winner-Hoyt	Loser-Sherdel		

Game 2	Oct. 5		
St. Louis	030 000 000	·	3
New York	314 000 10*	·	9
Winner-Pipgras	Loser Alexander		

Game 3	Oct. 7		
New York	010 203 100	·	7
St. Louis	200 010 000	·	3
Winner-Zachary	Loser-Haines		

Game 4	Oct. 9		
New York	000 100 420	·	7
St. Louis	001 100 001	·	3
Winner-Hoyt	Loser Sherdel		

Total Attendance—199,072
Average Attendance—49,768
Winning Player's Share—$5,532
Losing Player's Share—$4,197

BATTING	Pos	G	AB	R	H	2B	3B	HR	RBI	BB	SO	SB	BA
New York													
Lou Gehrig	1b	4	11	5	6	1	0	4	9	6	0	0	.545
Tony Lazzeri	2b	4	12	2	3	1	0	0	0	1	0	2	.250
Mark Koenig	ss	4	19	1	3	0	0	0	0	0	1	0	.158
Gene Robertson	3b-ph	3	8	1	1	0	0	0	2	1	0	0	.125
Babe Ruth	rf-lf	4	16	9	10	3	0	3	4	1	2	0	.625
Ben Paschal	cf-ph	3	10	0	2	0	0	0	1	1	0	0	.200
Bob Meusel	lf-rf	4	15	5	3	1	0	1	3	2	5	2	.200
Benny Bengough	c	4	13	1	3	0	0	0	1	1	1	0	.231
Cedric Durst	cf	4	8	3	3	0	0	1	2	0	1	0	.375
Joe Dugan	3b	3	6	0	1	0	0	0	1	0	0	0	.167
Leo Durocher	2b	4	2	0	0	0	0	0	0	0	1	0	.000
Pat Collins	c	1	1	0	1	1	0	0	0	0	0	0	1.000
Earle Combs	ph	1	0	0	0	0	0	0	0	1	0	0	.000
Johnny Grabowski	Did not play												
Mike Gazella	Did not play												
Bill Dickey	Did not play												
Waite Hoyt	p	2	7	0	1	0	0	0	0	0	0	0	.143
Tom Zachary	p	1	4	0	0	0	0	0	0	0	1	0	.000
George Pipgras	p	1	2	0	0	0	0	0	0	1	0	0	.000
Herb Pennock	Did not play—illness												
Fred Heimach	Did not play												
Myles Homas	Did not play												
Rosy Ryan	Did not play												
Team Total		4	134	27	37	7	0	9	25	13	12	4	.276

Double Plays—3   Left on Bases—24

BATTING	Pos	G	AB	R	H	2B	3B	HR	RBI	BB	SO	SB	BA
St. Louis													
Jim Bottomley	1b	4	14	1	3	0	1	1	3	2	6	0	.214
Frankie Frisch	2b	4	13	1	3	0	0	0	1	2	2	2	.231
Rabbit Maranville	ss	4	13	2	4	1	0	0	0	1	1	1	.308
Andy High	3b	4	17	1	5	2	0	0	1	1	3	0	.294
George Harper	rf	3	9	1	1	0	0	0	0	2	2	0	.111
Taylor Douthit	cf	4	11	1	1	0	0	0	0	1	1	0	.091
Chick Hafey	lf	4	15	0	3	0	0	0	0	1	4	0	.200
Jimmie Wilson	c	4	11	1	1	1	0	0	1	0	3	0	.091
Ernie Orsatti	ph-cf	4	7	1	2	1	0	0	1	0	3	0	.286
Wattie Holm	ph-rf	3	6	0	1	0	0	0	1	0	1	0	.167
Earl Smith	c	1	4	0	3	0	0	0	0	0	0	0	.750
Ray Blades	ph	1	1	0	0	0	0	0	0	0	1	0	.000
Pepper Martin	pr	1	0	1	0	0	0	0	0	0	0	0	.000
Tommy Thevenow	ss	1	0	0	0	0	0	0	0	0	0	0	.000
Wally Roettger	Did not play—broken leg												
Howie Williamson	Did not play												
Bill Sherdel	p	2	5	0	0	0	0	0	0	0	2	0	.000
Jesse Haines	p	1	2	0	0	0	0	0	0	0	0	0	.000
Clarence Mitchell	p	1	2	0	0	0	0	0	0	0	0	0	.000
Pete Alexander	p	2	1	0	0	0	0	0	0	1	0	0	.000
Syl Johnson	p	2	0	0	0	0	0	0	0	0	0	0	.000
Flint Rhem	p	1	0	0	0	0	0	0	0	0	0	0	.000
Fred Frankhouse	Did not play												
Art Reinhart	Did not play												
Hal Haid	Did not play												
Team Total		4	131	10	27	5	1	1	9	11	29	3	.207

Double Plays—3   Left on Bases—27

PITCHING	G	GS	CG	IP	H	R	ER	BB	SO	W	L	SV	ERA
New York													
Waite Hoyt	2	2	2	18	14	4	3	6	14	2	0	0	1.50
George Pipgras	1	1	1	9	4	3	2	4	8	1	0	0	2.00
Tom Zachary	1	1	1	9	9	3	3	1	7	1	0	0	3.00
Herb Pennock	Did not play—illness												
Fred Heimach	Did not play												
Myles Thomas	Did not play												
Rosy Ryan	Did not play												
Team Total	4	4	4	36	27	10	8	11	29	4	0	0	2.00
St. Louis													
Bill Sherdel	2	2	0	13⅓	15	7	7	3	3	0	2	0	4.73
Jesse Haines	1	1	0	6	6	6	3	3	3	0	1	0	4.50
Clarence Mitchell	1	0	0	5⅔	2	1	1	2	2	0	0	0	1.59
Pete Alexander	2	1	0	5	10	11	11	4	2	0	1	0	19.80
Syl Johnson	2	0	0	2	4	2	1	1	1	0	0	0	4.50
Flint Rhem	1	0	0	2	0	0	0	0	1	0	0	0	0.00
Fred Frankhouse	Did not play												
Art Reinhart	Did not play												
Hal Haid	Did not play												
Team Total	4	4	0	34	37	27	23	13	12	0	4	0	6.09

1929

Highlights

AFTER FIFTEEN YEARS, CONNIE Mack finally had another winning Philadelphia team: Jimmie Foxx, Al Simmons, Mickey Cochrane, pitchers George Earnshaw, Lefty Grove and a host of other good players. They faced the Chicago Cubs.

Surprising everyone, Mack started Howard Ehmke in game one. The gamble paid off in a 3-1 Philadelphia victory. Earnshaw and Grove combined to beat the Cubs, 9-3, in game two. But the Cubs bounced back to win game three, 3-1.

With an 8-0 lead at the 6½-inning mark in game four, the Cubs looked like sure winners. But Al Simmons homered, and successive singles by Foxx, Bing Miller, Jimmy Dykes and Joe Boley made the score 8-3. Cubs manager Joe McCarthy began substituting pitchers, but nothing could prevent the 10-8 Athletics win.

In game five, Chicago's Pat Malone held on to a 2-0 lead through eight innings, but the A's refused to be stopped, and a single by Bishop, a homer by Haas and doubles by Simmons and Miller ended the game, 3-2, to give Connie Mack's team the Championship.

Game 1 Oct. 8
Philadelphia	000 000 102 ·	3
Chicago	000 000 001 ·	1

Winner-Ehmke Loser-Root

Game 2 Oct. 9
Philadelphia	003 300 120 ·	9
Chicago	000 030 000 ·	3

Winner-Earnshaw Loser-Malone

Game 3 Oct. 11
Chicago	000 003 000 ·	3
Philadelphia	000 010 000 ·	1

Winner-Bush Loser-Earnshaw

Game 4 Oct. 12
Chicago	000 205 100 ·	8
Philadelphia	000 000 100 * ·	10

Winner-Rommel Loser-Blake

Game 5 Oct. 14
Chicago	000 200 000 ·	2
Philadelphia	000 000 003 ·	3

Winner-Walberg Loser-Malone

Total Attendance—190,490
Average Attendance—38,098
Winning Player's Share—$5,621
Losing Player's Share—$3,782

Philadelphia A.L. 4
Chicago N.L. 1

BATTING	Pos	G	AB	R	H	2B	3B	HR	RBI	BB	SO	SB	BA
Philadelphia													
Jimmy Foxx	1b	5	20	5	7	1	0	2	5	1	1	0	.350
Max Bishop	2b	5	21	2	4	0	0	0	1	2	3	0	.190
Joe Boley	ss	5	17	1	4	0	0	0	1	0	3	0	.235
Jimmy Dykes	3b	5	19	2	8	1	0	0	4	1	1	0	.421
Bing Miller	rf	5	19	1	7	1	0	0	4	0	2	0	.368
Mule Haas	cf	5	21	3	5	0	0	2	6	1	3	0	.238
Al Simmons	lf	5	20	6	6	1	0	2	5	1	4	0	.300
Mickey Cochrane	c	5	15	5	6	1	0	0	0	7	0	0	.400
George Burns	ph	1	2	0	0	0	0	0	0	0	1	0	.000
Walt French	ph	1	1	0	0	0	0	0	0	0	1	0	.000
Homer Summa	ph	1	1	0	0	0	0	0	0	0	0	0	.000
Sammy Hale	Did not play												
Cy Perkins	Did not play												
Jim Cronin	Did not play												
Bevo LeBourveau	Did not play												
Eddie Collins	Did not play												
George Earnshaw	p	2	5	1	0	0	0	0	0	0	4	0	.000
Howard Ehmke	p	2	5	0	1	0	0	0	0	0	0	0	.200
Lefty Grove	p	2	2	0	0	0	0	0	0	0	1	0	.000
Jack Quinn	p	1	2	0	0	0	0	0	0	0	2	0	.000
Rube Walberg	p	2	1	0	0	0	0	0	0	0	0	0	.000
Eddie Rommel	p	1	0	0	0	0	0	0	0	0	0	0	.000
Bill Shores	Did not play												
Carroll Yerkes	Did not play												
Bill Breckinridge	Did not play												
Team Total		5	171	26	48	5	0	6	26	13	27	0	.281

Double Plays—2   Left on Bases—35

	Pos	G	AB	R	H	2B	3B	HR	RBI	BB	SO	SB	BA
Chicago													
Charlie Grimm	1b	5	18	2	7	0	0	1	4	1	2	0	.389
Rogers Hornsby	2b	5	21	4	5	1	1	0	1	1	8	0	.238
Woody English	ss	5	21	1	4	2	0	0	1	6	0	0	.190
Norm McMillan	3b	5	20	0	2	0	0	0	0	2	6	1	.100
Kiki Cuyler	rf	5	20	4	6	1	0	0	4	1	7	0	.300
Hack Wilson	cf	5	17	2	8	0	1	0	0	4	3	0	.471
Riggs Stephenson	lf	5	19	3	6	1	0	0	3	2	2	0	.316
Zack Taylor	c	5	17	0	3	0	0	0	3	0	3	0	.176
Gabby Hartnett	ph	3	3	0	0	0	0	0	0	0	3	0	.000
Mike Gonzalez	c-ph	2	1	0	0	0	0	0	0	0	1	0	.000
Cliff Heathcote	ph	2	1	0	0	0	0	0	0	0	0	0	.000
Chuck Tolson	ph	1	1	0	0	0	0	0	0	0	1	0	.000
Footsie Blair	ph	1	1	0	0	0	0	0	0	0	0	0	.000
Clyde Beck	Did not play												
Johnny Schulte	Did not play												
Johnny Moore	Did not play												
Charlie Root	p	2	5	0	0	0	0	0	0	0	3	0	.000
Pat Malone	p	3	4	0	1	1	0	0	0	0	2	0	.250
Guy Bush	p	2	3	1	0	0	0	0	0	1	3	0	.000
Sheriff Blake	p	2	1	0	1	0	0	0	0	0	0	0	1.000
Hal Carlson	p	2	0	0	0	0	0	0	0	0	0	0	.000
Art Nehf	p	2	0	0	0	0	0	0	0	0	0	0	.000
Mike Cvengros	Did not play												
Ken Penner	Did not play												
Hank Grampp	Did not play												
Team Total		5	173	17	43	6	2	1	15	13	50	1	.249

Double Plays—4   Left on Bases—36

PITCHING	G	GS	CG	IP	H	R	ER	BB	SO	W	L	SV	ERA
Philadelphia													
George Earnshaw	2	2	1	13⅔	14	6	4	6	17	1	1	0	2.63
Howard Ehmke	2	2	1	12⅔	14	3	2	3	13	1	0	0	1.42
Lefty Grove	2	0	0	6⅓	3	0	0	1	10	0	0	2	0.00
Rube Walberg	2	0	0	6⅓	3	1	0	0	8	1	0	0	0.00
Jack Quinn	1	1	0	5	7	6	5	2	2	0	0	0	9.00
Eddie Rommel	1	0	0	1	2	1	1	1	0	1	0	0	9.00
Bill Shores	Did not play												
Carroll Yerkes	Did not play												
Bill Breckinridge	Did not play												
Team Total	5	5	2	45	43	17	12	13	50	4	1	2	2.40

	G	GS	CG	IP	H	R	ER	BB	SO	W	L	SV	ERA
Chicago													
Charlie Root	2	2	0	13⅓	12	7	7	2	8	0	1	0	4.73
Pat Malone	3	2	1	13	12	9	6	7	11	0	2	0	4.15
Guy Bush	2	1	1	11	12	3	1	2	4	1	0	0	0.82
Hal Carlson	2	0	0	4	7	3	3	1	3	0	0	0	6.75
Sheriff Blake	2	0	0	1⅓	4	2	2	0	1	0	1	0	13.50
Art Nehf	2	0	0	1	1	2	2	1	0	0	0	0	18.00
Mike Cvengros	Did not play												
Ken Penner	Did not play												
Hank Grampp	Did not play												
Team Total	5	5	2	43⅔	48	26	21	13	27	1	4	0	4.33

1930

Philadelphia A.L. 4
St. Louis N.L. 2

Highlights

ST. LOUIS HAD .300 HITTERS AT all eight starting positions and a team average of .314, with Frisch, Hafey, Bottomley and George Watkins leading the way. They also had lefty Bill Hallahan, spitballer Burleigh Grimes and knuckleballer Jesse Haines on the mound, but little depth to the staff. The Philadelphia A's had hitters like Simmons, Foxx, Cochrane, as well as ace hurlers Lefty Grove and George Earnshaw.

It was Grove's fastball versus Grimes's spitball in game one, with the A's winning, 5-2. In game two, the A's continued winning, to pin a 6-1 loss on Flint Rhem. The Cards came back to take game three, 5-0, with Bill Hallahan on the mound. Haines then threw a 3-1 win in game four to even the Series.

Earnshaw and Grimes dueled to a scoreless eighth inning, when Mack pulled Earnshaw and sent in Lefty Grove. Grimes was doing well for the Cards when a walk to Cochrane and a Foxx homer led to the 2-0 Philadelphia win. Mack used Earnshaw after only a day's rest in game six, and forgetting how tired he was, he pitched the A's to a 7-1 win and the World Championship.

Game 1 Oct. 1
St. Louis	002 000 000	- 2
Philadelphia	010 101 11*	- 5

Winner-Grove   Loser-Grimes

Game 2 Oct. 2
St. Louis	010 000 000	- 1
Philadelphia	202 200 00*	- 6

Winner-Earnshaw   Loser-Rhem

Game 3 Oct. 4
Philadelphia	000 000 000	- 0
St. Louis	000 110 21*	- 5

Winner-Hallahan   Loser-Walberg

Game 4 Oct. 5
Philadelphia	100 000 000	- 1
St. Louis	001 200 00*	- 3

Winner-Haines   Loser-Grove

Game 5 Oct. 6
Philadelphia	000 000 002	- 2
St. Louis	000 000 000	- 0

Winner-Grove   Loser-Grimes

Game 6 Oct. 8
St. Louis	000 000 001	- 1
Philadelphia	201 211 00*	- 7

Winner-Earnshaw   Loser-Hallahan

Total Attendance—212,619
Average Attendance—35,437
Winning Player's Share—$5,038
Losing Player's Share—$3,537

BATTING

Philadelphia	Pos	G	AB	R	H	2B	3B	HR	RBI	BB	SO	SB	BA
Jimmy Foxx	1b	6	21	3	7	2	1	1	3	2	4	0	.333
Max Bishop	2b	6	18	5	4	0	0	0	0	7	3	0	.222
Joe Boley	ss	6	21	1	2	0	0	0	1	0	1	0	.095
Jimmy Dykes	3b	6	18	2	4	3	0	1	5	5	3	0	.222
Bing Miller	rf	6	21	0	3	2	0	0	3	0	4	0	.143
Mule Haas	cf	6	18	1	2	0	1	0	1	1	3	0	.111
Al Simmons	lf-cf	6	22	4	8	2	0	2	4	2	2	0	**.364**
Mickey Cochrane	c	6	18	5	4	1	0	2	4	5	2	0	.222
Jim Moore	ph-lf	3	3	0	1	0	0	0	0	1	1	0	.333
Eric McNair	ph	1	1	0	0	0	0	0	0	0	0	0	.000
Dib Williams	Did not play												
Wally Schang	Did not play												
Homer Summa	Did not play												
Cy Perkins	Did not play												
Pinky Higgins	Did not play												
Eddie Collins	Did not play												
George Earnshaw	p	3	9	0	0	0	0	0	0	0	5	0	.000
Lefty Grove	p	3	6	0	0	0	0	0	0	0	3	0	.000
Rube Walberg	p	1	2	0	0	0	0	0	0	0	1	0	.000
Jack Quinn	p	1	0	0	0	0	0	0	0	0	0	0	.000
Bill Shores	p	1	0	0	0	0	0	0	0	0	1	0	.000
Roy Mahaffey	Did not play												
Eddie Rommel	Did not play												
Charlie Perkins	Did not play												
Team Total		6	178	21	35	10	2	6	21	24	32	0	.197

Double Plays—2   Left on Bases—36

St. Louis	Pos	G	AB	R	H	2B	3B	HR	RBI	BB	SO	SB	BA
Jim Bottomley	1b	6	22	1	1	0	0	0	0	2	9	0	.045
Frankie Frisch	2b	6	24	0	5	2	0	0	0	0	0	1	.208
Charlie Gelbert	ss	6	17	2	6	0	1	0	2	3	3	0	.353
Sparky Adams	3b	6	21	0	3	0	0	0	1	0	4	0	.143
George Watkins	rf	4	12	2	2	0	0	1	1	1	3	0	.167
Taylor Douthit	cf	6	24	1	2	0	0	1	2	0	2	0	.083
Chick Hafey	lf	6	22	2	6	5	0	0	2	1	3	0	.273
Jimmy Wilson	c	4	15	0	4	1	0	0	2	0	1	0	.267
Ray Blades	rf-ph	5	9	2	1	0	0	0	0	2	2	0	.111
Gus Mancuso	c	2	7	1	2	0	0	0	0	1	2	0	.286
Andy High	ph-3b	2	1	1	0	0	0	0	0	1	0	0	.500
Showboat Fisher	ph	2	2	0	1	1	0	0	0	0	1	0	.500
Ernie Orsatti	ph	1	1	0	0	0	0	0	0	0	0	0	.000
George Puccinelli	ph	1	1	0	0	0	0	0	0	0	0	0	.000
Burleigh Grimes	p	2	5	0	2	0	0	0	0	0	1	0	.400
Wild Bill Hallahan	p	2	2	0	0	0	0	0	0	1	1	0	.000
Jesse Haines	p	1	2	0	1	0	0	0	1	0	0	0	.500
Jim Lindsey	p	2	1	0	1	0	0	0	0	0	0	0	1.000
Flint Rhem	p	1	1	0	0	0	0	0	0	0	0	0	.000
Syl Johnson	p	2	0	0	0	0	0	0	0	0	1	0	.000
Hi Bell	p	1	0	0	0	0	0	0	0	0	0	0	.000
Al Grabowski	Did not play												
Team Total		6	190	12	38	10	1	2	11	11	33	1	.200

Double Plays—4   Left on Bases—37

PITCHING

Philadelphia	G	GS	CG	IP	H	R	ER	BB	SO	W	L	SV	ERA
George Earnshaw	3	3	2	25	13	2	2	7	19	2	0	0	0.72
Lefty Grove	3	2	2	19	15	5	3	3	10	2	1	0	1.42
Rube Walberg	1	1	0	4⅔	4	2	2	1	3	0	1	0	3.86
Jack Quinn	1	0	0	2	3	1	1	0	1	0	0	0	4.50
Bill Shores	1	0	0	1⅓	3	2	2	0	0	0	0	0	13.50
Roy Mahaffey	Did not play												
Eddie Rommel	Did not play												
Charlie Perkins	Did not play												
Team Total	6	6	4	52	38	12	10	11	33	4	2	0	1.73

St. Louis	G	GS	CG	IP	H	R	ER	BB	SO	W	L	SV	ERA
Burleigh Grimes	2	2	2	17	10	7	7	6	13	0	2	0	3.71
Wild Bill Hallahan	2	2	1	11	9	2	2	8	8	1	1	0	1.64
Jesse Haines	1	1	1	9	4	1	1	4	2	1	0	0	1.00
Syl Johnson	2	0	0	5	4	4	4	3	4	0	0	0	7.20
Jim Lindsey	2	0	0	4⅔	4	1	1	1	2	0	0	0	1.93
Flint Rhem	1	1	0	3⅓	7	6	4	2	3	0	1	0	10.80
Hi Bell	1	0	0	1	0	0	0	0	0	0	0	0	0.00
Al Grabowski	Did not play												
Team Total	6	6	4	51	35	21	19	24	32	2	4	0	3.35

1931

St. Louis N.L. 4
Philadelphia A.L. 3

Highlights

WITH FRANKIE FRISCH, CHICK Hafey, Jim Bottomley and 21-year-old "Wild Horse of the Osage" Pepper Martin, the St. Louis Cardinals again won the N.L. pennant. Their opponents were once more the Philadelphia A's with Foxx, Simmons, Cochrane, Mule Haas and pitchers Grove and Earnshaw. However, thanks in large measure to Pepper Martin, the results this time were different.

The Cards lost the opener, 6-2. But in game two, Martin stretched a single into a double with a dramatic steal in the second and then stole third and came home on Jimmie Wilson's fly to center to make it 1-0. Martin continued stealing and again crossed the plate to lead the Cards to a 2-0 victory. Game three was a 5-2 Cardinal win. But Earnshaw shut out the Cards 3-0 in game four. In game five, Martin beat out a bunt in the fourth, hit a homer in the sixth, singled in the eighth and drove in four runs to fashion a 5-1 St. Louis victory.

The Cards lost game six, 8-1, as Martin hit a slump. He remained hitless in the final game too, but other Cards batters made up for it, so it was 4-0, St. Louis, at the end of the third. The A's got two across in the ninth, but it was too late. St. Louis won, 4-2, as Pepper Martin raced in from center field to catch a Max Bishop line drive for the final out.

Game 1 Oct. 1
| Philadelphia | 004 000 200 | - | 6 |
| St. Louis | 200 000 000 | - | 2 |
Winner-Grove   Loser-Derringer

Game 2 Oct. 2
| Philadelphia | 000 000 000 | - | 0 |
| St. Louis | 010 000 10* | - | 2 |
Winner-Hallahan   Loser-Earnshaw

Game 3 Oct. 5
| St. Louis | 020 200 001 | - | 5 |
| Philadephia | 000 000 002 | - | 2 |
Winner-Grimes   Loser-Grove

Game 4 Oct. 6
| St. Louis | 000 000 000 | - | 0 |
| Philadelphia | 100 002 00* | - | 3 |
Winner-Earnshaw   Loser-Johnson

Game 5 Oct. 7
| St. Louis | 100 002 011 | - | 5 |
| Philadelphia | 000 000 100 | - | 1 |
Winner-Hallahan   Loser-Hoyt

Game 6 Oct. 9
| Philadelphia | 000 040 400 | - | 8 |
| St. Louis | 000 001 000 | - | 1 |
Winner-Grove   Loser-Derringer

Game 7 Oct. 10
| Philadelphia | 000 000 002 | - | 2 |
| St. Louis | 202 000 00* | - | 4 |
Winner-Grimes   Loser-Earnshaw

Total Attendance—231,567
Average Attendance—33,081
Winning Player's Share—$4,468
Losing Player's Share—$3,023

BATTING

	Pos	G	AB	R	H	2B	3B	HR	RBI	BB	SO	SB	BA
St. Louis													
Jim Bottomley	1b	7	25	2	4	1	0	0	2	2	5	0	.160
Frankie Frisch	2b	7	27	2	7	2	0	0	1	1	2	1	.259
Charlie Gelbert	ss	7	23	0	6	1	0	0	3	0	4	0	.261
Andy High	3b-pr	4	15	3	4	0	0	0	0	0	2	0	.267
George Watkins	rf-pr	5	14	4	4	1	0	1	2	2	1	1	.286
Pepper Martin	cf	7	24	5	12	4	0	1	5	2	3	5	.500
Chick Hafey	lf	6	24	1	4	0	0	0	0	0	5	1	.167
Jimmie Wilson	c	7	23	0	5	0	0	0	2	1	1	0	.217
Wally Roettger	rf	3	14	1	4	1	0	0	0	0	3	0	.286
Jake Flowers	ph-3b	5	11	1	1	1	0	0	0	1	0	0	.091
Sparky Adams	3b	2	4	0	1	0	0	0	0	0	1	0	.250
Ernie Orsatti	lf	3	3	0	0	0	0	0	0	0	3	0	.000
Ray Blades	ph	2	2	0	0	0	0	0	0	0	2	0	.000
Ripper Collins	ph	2	2	0	0	0	0	0	0	0	1	0	.000
Gus Mancuso	ph-c	2	1	0	0	0	0	0	0	0	0	0	.000
Mike Gonzalez	Did not play												
Burleigh Grimes	p	2	7	0	2	0	0	0	2	0	2	0	.286
wild Bill Hallahan	p	3	6	0	0	0	0	0	0	0	3	0	.000
Paul Derringer	p	3	2	0	0	0	0	0	0	0	1	0	.000
Syl Johnson	p	3	2	0	0	0	0	0	0	0	2	0	.000
Jim Lindsey	p	2	0	0	0	0	0	0	0	0	0	0	.000
Flint Rhem	p	1	0	0	0	0	0	0	0	0	0	0	.000
Jesse Haines	Did not play												
Allyn Stout	Did not play												
Tony Kaufmann	Did not play												
Team Total		7	229	19	54	11	0	2	17	9	41	8	.236

Double Plays—7   Left on Bases—40

	Pos	G	AB	R	H	2B	3B	HR	RBI	BB	SO	SB	BA
Philadelphia													
Jimmie Foxx	1b	7	23	3	8	0	0	1	3	6	5	0	.348
Max Bishop	2b	7	27	4	4	0	0	0	0	3	5	0	.148
Dib Williams	ss	7	25	2	8	1	0	0	1	2	9	0	.320
Jimmy Dykes	3b	7	22	2	5	0	0	0	2	5	1	0	.227
Bing Miller	rf	7	26	3	7	1	0	0	1	0	4	0	.269
Mule Haas	cf	7	23	1	3	1	0	0	2	3	5	0	.130
Al Simmons	lf-cf	7	27	4	9	2	0	2	8	3	3	0	.333
Mickey Cochrane	c	7	25	2	4	0	0	0	1	5	2	0	.160
Jim Moore	ph-lf	2	3	0	1	0	0	0	0	0	1	0	.333
Eric McNair	pr-ph-2b	2	2	1	0	0	0	0	0	0	1	0	.000
Doc Cramer	ph	2	2	0	1	0	0	0	0	2	0	0	.500
Joe Boley	ph	1	1	0	0	0	0	0	0	0	1	0	.000
Johnnie Heving	ph	1	1	0	0	0	0	0	0	0	0	0	.000
Phil Todt	ph	1	0	0	0	0	0	0	0	1	0	0	.000
Joe Palmisano	Did not play												
Lefty Grove	p	3	10	0	0	0	0	0	0	0	7	0	.000
George Earnshaw	p	3	8	0	0	0	0	0	0	0	2	0	.000
Waite Hoyt	p	1	2	0	0	0	0	0	0	0	0	0	.000
Rube Walbert	p	2	0	0	0	0	0	0	0	0	0	0	.000
roy Mahaffey	p	1	0	0	0	0	0	0	0	0	0	0	.000
Eddie Rommel	p	1	0	0	0	0	0	0	0	0	0	0	.000
Hank McDonald	Did not play												
Jim Peterson	Did not play												
Lew Krausse	Did not play												
Team Total		7	227	22	50	5	0	3	20	28	46	0	.220

Double Plays—4   Left on Bases—52

PITCHING

	G	GS	CG	IP	H	R	ER	BB	SO	W	L	SV	ERA
St. Louis													
Wild Bill Hallahan	3	2	2	18⅓	12	1	1	8	12	2	0	1	0.49
Burleigh Grimes	2	2	1	17⅔	9	4	4	9	11	2	0	0	2.04
Paul Derringer	3	2	0	12⅔	14	10	6	7	14	0	2	0	4.26
Syl Johnson	3	1	0	9	10	3	3	1	6	0	1	0	3.00
Jim Lindsey	2	0	0	3⅓	4	4	2	3	2	0	0	0	5.40
Flint Rhem	1	0	0	1	1	0	0	0	1	0	0	0	0.00
Jesse Haines	Did not play												
Allyn Stout	Did not play												
Tony Kaufmann	Did not play												
Team Total	7	7	3	62	50	22	16	28	46	4	3	1	2.32
Philadelphia													
Lefty Grove	3	3	2	26	28	7	7	2	16	2	1	0	2.42
George Earnshaw	3	3	2	24	12	6	5	4	20	1	2	0	1.88
Waite Hoyt	1	1	0	6	7	3	3	0	1	0	1	0	4.50
Rube Walberg	2	0	0	3	3	1	1	2	4	0	0	0	3.00
Roy Mahaffey	1	0	0	1	1	1	1	1	0	0	0	0	9.00
Eddie Rommel	1	0	0	1	3	1	1	0	0	0	0	0	9.00
Hank McDonald	Did not play												
Jim Peterson	Did not play												
Lew Krausse	Did not play												
Team Total	7	7	4	61	54	19	18	9	41	3	4	0	2.66

Al Simmons

1932

New York A.L. 4
Chicago N.L. 0

Highlights

AFTER A HIATUS OF THREE years, the Yankees were back, with Ruth, Gehrig, Lazzeri and Combs, as well as newcomers Bill Dickey, Frankie Crosetti, Ben Chapman and pitchers Lefty Gomez, Red Ruffing and Johnny Allen. Chicago Cubs manager Rogers Hornsby was fired by team owner Bill Veeck. First baseman Charlie Grimm was give the manager job and kept the team in first place with Gabby Hartnett, Kiki Cuyler, Billy Herman and Riggs Stephenson and pitchers like Lon Warneke, Guy Bush, Charlie Root and Pat Malone.

The Cubs picked up Mark Koenig from the Yankees in late August, voting him only a half share of pennant and Series money. Koenig's Yankees teammates were outraged; the Cubs' decision was the cause of much bitterness throughout the Series.

The Yankees rolled over the Cubs in four games. But there was one remarkable incident in game three when Babe Ruth, playing in his last Series, "called his shot" by first pointing to the center-field stands and hitting a homer off Charlie Root into that area.

Game 1	Sept. 28			
Chicago	200 000 220	·	6	
New York	000 305 31*	·	12	
Winner-Ruffing	Loser-Bush			

Game 2	Sept. 29			
Chicago	101 000 000	·	2	
New York	202 010 00*	·	5	
Winner-Gomez	Loser Warneke			

Game 3	Oct. 1			
New York	301 020 001	·	7	
Chicago	102 100 001	·	5	
Winner-Pipgras	Loser-Root			

Game 4	Oct. 2			
New York	102 002 404	·	13	
Chicago	400 001 001	·	6	
Winner-W. Moore	Loser-May			

Total Attendance—191,998
Average Attendance—48,000
Winning Player's Share—$5,232
Losing Player's Share—$4,245

BATTING	Pos	G	AB	R	H	2B	3B	HR	RBI	BB	SO	SB	BA
New York													
Lou Gehrig	1b	4	17	9	9	1	0	3	8	2	1	0	.529
Tony Lazzeri	2b	4	17	4	5	0	0	2	5	2	1	0	.294
Frankie Crosetti	ss	4	15	2	2	1	0	0	0	2	3	0	.133
Joe Sewell	3b	4	15	4	5	1	0	0	3	4	0	0	.333
Babe Ruth	rf-lf	4	15	6	5	0	0	2	6	4	3	0	.333
Earle Combs	cf	4	16	8	6	1	0	1	4	4	3	0	.375
Ben Chapman	lf-rf	4	17	1	5	2	0	0	6	2	4	0	.294
Bill Dickey	c	4	16	2	7	0	0	0	4	2	1	0	.438
Sammy Byrd	lf	1	0	0	0	0	0	0	0	0	0	0	.000
Myril Hoag	pr	1	0	1	0	0	0	0	0	0	0	0	.000
Lyn Lary		Did not play											
Art Jorgens		Did not play											
Doc Farrell		Did not play											
George Pipgras	p	1	5	0	0	0	0	0	0	0	5	0	.000
Red Ruffing	p-ph	2	4	0	0	0	0	0	0	1	1	0	.000
Lefty Gomez	p	1	3	0	0	0	0	0	0	0	2	0	.000
Wilcy Moore	p	1	3	0	1	0	0	0	0	0	2	0	.333
Herb Pennock	p	2	1	0	0	0	0	0	0	0	0	0	.000
Johnny Allen	p	1	0	0	0	0	0	0	0	0	0	0	.000
Danny MacFayden		Did not play											
Jumbo Brown		Did not play											
Ed Wells		Did not play											
Charlie Devens		Did not play											
Team Total		4	144	37	45	6	0	8	36	23	26	0	.313

Double Plays—1   Left on Bases—33

	Pos	G	AB	R	H	2B	3B	HR	RBI	BB	SO	SB	BA
Chicago													
Charlie Grimm	1b	4	15	2	5	2	0	0	1	2	2	0	.333
Billy Herman	2b	4	18	5	4	1	0	0	1	1	3	0	.222
Billy Jurges	ss	3	11	1	4	1	0	0	1	0	1	2	.364
Woody English	3b	4	17	2	3	0	0	0	1	2	2	0	.176
Kiki Cuyler	rf	4	18	2	5	1	1	1	2	0	3	1	.278
Johnny Moore	cf	2	7	1	0	0	0	0	0	2	1	0	.000
Riggs Stephenson	lf	4	18	2	8	1	0	0	4	0	0	0	.444
Gabby Hartnett	c	4	16	2	5	2	0	1	1	1	3	0	.313
Frank Demaree	cf	2	7	1	2	0	0	1	4	1	0	0	.286
Mark Koenig	ss-ph	2	4	1	1	0	1	0	1	1	0	0	.250
Rollie Hemsley	ph-c	3	3	0	0	0	0	0	0	0	3	0	.000
Marv Gudat	ph	2	2	0	0	0	0	0	0	0	1	0	.000
Stan Hack	pr	1	0	0	0	0	0	0	0	0	0	0	.000
Zack Taylor		Did not play											
Lon Warneke	p	2	4	0	0	0	0	0	0	0	3	0	.000
Jakie May	p	2	2	0	0	0	0	0	0	0	0	0	.000
Charlie Root	p	1	2	0	0	0	0	0	0	0	1	0	.000
Guy Bush	p	2	1	0	0	0	0	0	0	1	0	0	.000
Burleigh Grimes	p	2	1	0	0	0	0	0	0	0	1	0	.000
Pat Malone	p	1	0	0	0	0	0	0	0	0	0	0	.000
Bud Tinning	p	2	0	0	0	0	0	0	0	0	0	0	.000
Bob Smith	p	1	0	0	0	0	0	0	0	0	0	0	.000
Leroy Herrmann		Did not play											
Team Total		4	146	19	37	8	2	3	16	11	24	3	.253

Double Plays—7   Left on Bases—31

PITCHING	G	GS	CG	IP	H	R	ER	BB	SO	W	L	SV	ERA
New York													
Red Ruffing	1	1	1	9	10	6	4	6	10	1	0	0	4.00
Lefty Gomez	1	1	1	9	9	2	1	1	8	1	0	0	1.00
George Pipgras	1	1	0	8	9	5	4	3	1	1	0	0	4.50
Wilcy Moore	1	0	0	5⅓	2	1	0	0	1	1	0	0	0.00
Herb Pennock	2	0	0	4	2	1	1	1	4	0	0	2	2.25
Johnny Allen	1	1	0	⅔	5	4	3	0	0	0	0	0	40.50
Danny MacFayden		Did not play											
Jumbo Brown		Did not play											
Ed Wells		Did not play											
Charlie Devens		Did not play											
Team Total	4	4	2	36	37	19	13	11	24	4	0	2	3.25
Chicago													
Lon Warneke	2	1	1	10⅔	15	7	7	5	8	0	1	0	5.91
Guy Bush	2	2	0	5⅔	5	9	9	6	2	0	1	0	14.29
Jakie May	2	0	0	4⅔	9	7	6	3	4	0	1	0	11.57
Charlie Root	1	1	0	4⅓	6	6	5	3	4	0	1	0	10.38
Pat Malone	1	0	0	2⅔	1	0	0	4	4	0	0	0	0.00
Burleigh Grimes	2	0	0	2⅔	7	7	7	2	0	0	0	0	23.63
Bud Tinning	2	0	0	2⅓	0	0	0	0	3	0	0	0	0.00
Bob Smith	1	0	0	1	2	1	1	0	1	0	0	0	9.00
Leroy Hermann		Did not play											
Team Total	4	4	1	34	45	37	35	23	26	0	4	0	9.26

1933

New York N.L. 4
Washington A.L. 1

Highlights

As MANAGER OF THE WASHINGton Senators, Joe Cronin, 26, carefully stocked up on hitters like Joel Kuhel and Heinie Manush and pitchers like General Crowder and Earl Whitehill. At 34, Bill Terry had taken over from John McGraw as manager of the Giants, and he and outfielder Mel Ott led the batting order, while Carl Hubbell, Hal Schumacher and Freddie Fitzsimmons handled the mound chores.

Hubbell won game one, 4-2. Aided by a two-run Mel Ott homer, New York also won game two as Schumacher allowed only five hits on the way to a 6-1 triumph. The Senators came back to win game three, 4-0. But with Hubbell on the mound again, the Giants broke through a ninth-inning tie to take game four, 2-1.

The Senators were down 3-0 in game five when Fred Schulte's three-run homer tied things up. But then at the top of the tenth Mel Ott hit a homer to nail down the 4-3 victory and the Giants' first Series crown since 1922.

Game 1 Oct. 3
Washington	000 100 001 · 2
New York	202 000 00* · 4

Winner-Hubbell   Loser-Stewart

Game 2 Oct. 4
Washington	001 000 000 · 1
New York	000 006 00* · 6

Winner-Schumacher   Loser-Crowder

Game 3 Oct. 5
New York	000 000 000 · 0
Washington	210 000 10* · 4

Winner-Whitehill   Loser-Fitzsimmons

Game 4 Oct. 6
New York	000 100 000 01 · 2
Washington	000 000 100 00 · 1

Winner-Hubbell   Loser-Weaver

Game 5 Oct. 7
New York	020 001 000 1 · 4
Washington	000 003 000 0 · 3

Winner-Luque   Loser-Russell

Total Attendance—164,076
Average Attendance—32,815
Winning Player's Share—$4,257
Losing Player's Share—$3,010

BATTING	Pos	G	AB	R	H	2B	3B	HR	RBI	BB	SO	SB	BA
New York													
Bill Terry	1b	5	22	3	6	1	0	1	1	0	0	0	.273
Hughie Critz	2b	5	22	2	3	0	0	0	0	1	0	0	.136
Blondy Ryan	ss	5	18	0	5	0	0	0	1	1	5	0	.278
Travis Jackson	3b	5	18	3	4	1	0	0	2	1	3	0	.222
Mel Ott	rf	5	18	3	7	0	0	2	4	4	4	0	.389
Kiddo Davis	cf	5	19	1	7	1	0	0	0	0	3	0	.368
Jo-Jo Moore	lf	5	22	1	5	1	0	0	1	1	3	0	.227
Gus Mancuso	c	5	17	2	2	1	0	0	2	3	0	0	.118
Homer Peel	cf-ph	2	2	0	1	0	0	0	0	0	0	0	.500
Lefty O'Doul	ph	1	1	1	1	0	0	0	2	0	0	0	1.000
Johnny Vergez	Did not play-appendicitis												
Bernie James	Did not play												
Paul Richards	Did not play												
Chuck Dressen	Did not play												
Harry Danning	Did not play												
Carl Hubbell	p	2	7	0	2	0	0	0	0	0	0	0	.286
Hal Schumacher	p	2	7	0	2	0	0	0	3	0	3	0	.286
Freddie Fitzsimmons	p	1	2	0	1	0	0	0	0	0	0	0	.500
Dolf Luque	p	1	1	0	1	0	0	0	0	0	0	0	1.000
Hi Bell	p	1	0	0	0	0	0	0	0	0	0	0	.000
Roy Parmalee	Did not play												
Glenn Spencer	Did not play												
Watty Clark	Did not play												
Jack Salveson	Did not play												
Team Total		5	176	16	47	5	0	3	16	11	21	0	.267
	Double Plays—5			Left on Bases—39									
Washington													
Joe Kuhel	1b	5	20	1	3	0	0	0	1	1	4	0	.150
Buddy Myer	2b	5	20	2	6	1	0	0	2	2	3	0	.300
Joe Cronin	ss	5	22	1	7	0	0	0	2	0	2	0	.318
Ossie Bluege	3b	5	16	1	2	1	0	0	0	1	6	0	.125
Goose Goslin	rf-lf	5	20	2	5	1	0	1	1	1	3	0	.250
Fred Schulte	cf	5	21	1	7	1	0	1	4	1	1	0	.333
Heinie Manush	lf	5	18	2	2	0	0	0	0	2	1	0	.111
Luke Sewell	c	5	17	1	3	0	0	0	1	2	0	1	.176
Dave Harris	ph-rf	3	2	0	0	0	0	0	2	0	0	0	.000
Cliff Bolton	ph	2	2	0	0	0	0	0	0	0	0	0	.000
Sam Rice	ph	1	1	0	1	0	0	0	0	0	0	0	1.000
John Kerr	pr	1	0	0	0	0	0	0	0	0	0	0	.000
Bob Boken	Did not play												
Moe Berg	Did not play												
General Crowder	p	2	4	0	1	0	0	0	0	0	0	0	.250
Monty Weaver	p	1	4	0	0	0	0	0	0	0	2	0	.000
Earl Whitehill	p	1	3	0	0	0	0	0	0	0	0	0	.000
Jack Russell	p	3	2	0	0	0	0	0	0	1	2	0	.000
Lefty Stewart	p	1	1	0	0	0	0	0	0	0	1	0	.000
Alex McColl	p	1	0	0	0	0	0	0	0	0	0	0	.000
Tommy Thomas	p	2	0	0	0	0	0	0	0	0	0	0	.000
Ed Chapman	Did not play												
Team Total		5	173	11	37	4	0	2	11	13	25	1	.214
	Double Plays—4			Left on Bases—37									

PITCHING	G	GS	CG	IP	H	R	ER	BB	SO	W	L	SV	ERA
New York													
Carl Hubbell	2	2	2	20	13	3	0	6	15	2	0	0	0.00
Hal Schumacher	2	2	1	14 2/3	13	4	4	5	3	1	0	0	2.45
Freddie Fitzsimmons	1	1	0	7	9	4	4	0	2	0	1	0	5.14
Dolf Luque	1	0	0	4 1/3	2	0	0	2	5	1	0	0	0.00
Hi Bell	1	0	0	1	0	0	0	0	0	0	0	0	0.00
Roy Parmalee	Did not play												
Glenn Spencer	Did not play												
Watty Clark	Did not play												
Jack Salveson	Did not play												
Team Total	5	5	3	47	37	11	8	13	25	4	1	0	1.53
Washington													
General Crowder	2	2	0	11	16	9	9	5	7	0	1	0	7.36
Monty Weaver	1	1	0	10 1/3	11	2	2	4	3	0	1	0	1.74
Jack Russell	3	0	0	10 1/3	8	1	1	0	7	0	1	0	0.87
Earl Whitehill	1	1	1	9	5	0	0	2	2	1	0	0	0.00
Lefty Stewart	1	1	0	2	6	4	2	0	0	0	1	0	9.00
Alex McColl	1	0	0	2	0	0	0	0	0	0	0	0	0.00
Tommy Thomas	2	0	0	1 1/3	1	0	0	0	2	0	0	0	0.00
Ed Chapman	Did not play												
Team Total	5	5	1	46	47	16	14	11	21	1	4	0	2.74

1934

St. Louis N.L. 4
Detroit A.L. 3

Highlights

THE ST. LOUIS CARDINALS, THE same team that was christened "The Gashouse Gang" the following year, took first place in the N.L. on the last two days of the season. The Detroit Tigers, led by catcher-manager Mickey Cochrane, had a team batting average of .300. This was the first pennant for Detroit since 1909.

Game four was at St. Louis. Cardinal Dizzy Dean, pinch-running in the fourth inning, failed to slide into second and and was hit in the head by shortstop Billy Rogell's throw. Diz was carried off the field on a stretcher. X rays showed no damage, and Dean pitched game five the next day.

Each team had won three games, so the Series was forced to a seventh. Score was 9-0, St. Louis, in the sixth inning. Cardinal Ducky Medwick slid into third base hard and wrestled with Detroit's Marv Owen. Home-team fans were furious. When Medwick took his position in left at the bottom of the inning, fans pelted him with garbage. Medwick tried to take his position three times, but each time had to retreat to dugout. Commissioner Landis was forced to order Medwick from the game. But it made little difference to the Cards, for St. Louis won the game, 11-0, and the Series.

BATTING	Pos	G	AB	R	H	2B	3B	HR	RBI	BB	SO	SB	BA
St. Louis													
Ripper Collins	1b	7	30	4	11	1	0	0	3	1	2	0	.367
Frankie Frisch	2b	7	31	2	6	1	0	0	4	0	1	0	.194
Leo Durocher	ss	7	27	4	7	1	1	0	0	0	0	0	.259
Pepper Martin	3b	7	31	8	11	3	1	0	4	3	3	2	.355
Jack Rothrock	rf	7	30	3	7	3	1	0	6	1	2	0	.233
Ernie Orsatti	cf-ph	7	22	3	7	0	1	0	2	3	1	0	.318
Joe Medwick	lf	7	29	4	11	0	1	1	5	1	7	0	**.379**
Bill DeLancey	c	7	29	3	5	3	0	1	4	2	8	0	.172
Chick Fullis	cf-lf	3	5	0	2	0	0	0	0	0	0	0	.400
Spud Davis	ph	2	2	0	2	0	0	0	1	0	0	0	1.000
Pat Crawford	ph	2	2	0	0	0	0	0	0	0	0	0	.000
Burgess Whitehead	pr-ss	1	0	0	0	0	0	0	0	0	0	0	.000
Francis Healy	Did not play												.250
Dizzy Dean	p-pr	4	12	3	3	2	0	0	1	0	3	0	.250
Paul Dean	p	2	6	0	1	0	0	0	2	0	1	0	.167
Wild Bill Hallahan	p	1	3	0	0	0	0	0	0	0	1	0	.000
Bill Walker	p	2	2	0	0	0	0	0	0	0	2	0	.000
Tex Carleton	p	2	1	0	0	0	0	0	0	0	0	0	.000
Dazzy Vance	p	1	0	0	0	0	0	0	0	0	0	0	.000
Jim Mooney	p	1	0	0	0	0	0	0	0	0	0	0	.000
Jesse Haines	p	1	0	0	0	0	0	0	0	0	0	0	.000
Team Total		7	262	34	73	14	5	2	32	11	31	2	.279

Double Plays—2   Left on Bases—49

Detroit													
Hank Greenberg	1b	7	28	4	9	2	1	1	7	4	9	1	.321
Charlie Gehringer	2b	7	29	5	11	1	0	1	2	3	0	1	**.379**
Billy Rogell	ss	7	29	3	8	1	0	0	4	1	4	1	.276
Marv Owen	3b	7	29	0	2	0	0	0	1	0	5	1	.069
Pete Fox	rf	7	28	1	8	6	0	0	2	1	4	0	.286
Jo-Jo White	cf	7	23	6	3	0	0	0	0	8	4	1	.130
Goose Goslin	lf	7	29	2	7	1	0	0	2	3	1	0	.241
Mickey Cochrane	c	7	28	2	6	1	0	0	1	4	3	0	.214
Gee Walker	ph	3	3	0	1	0	0	0	0	1	0	0	.333
Frank Doljack	ph-cf	2	2	0	0	0	0	0	0	0	0	0	.000
Ray Hayworth	c	2	0	0	0	0	0	0	0	0	0	0	.000
Flea Clifton	Did not play												
Heinie Schuble	Did not play												
Schoolboy Rowe	p	3	7	0	0	0	0	0	0	0	5	0	.000
Tommy Bridges	p	3	7	0	1	0	0	0	0	1	4	0	.143
Eldon Auker	p	2	4	0	0	0	0	0	0	0	2	0	.000
Chief Hogsett	p	3	3	0	0	0	0	0	0	0	1	0	.000
General Crowder	p	2	1	0	0	0	0	0	0	0	0	0	.000
Firpo Marberry	p	2	0	0	0	0	0	0	0	0	0	0	.000
Vic Sorrell	Did not play												
Carl Fischer	Did not play												
Luke Hamlin	Did not play												
Team Total		7	250	23	56	12	1	2	20	25	43	5	.224

Double Plays—6   Left on Bases—64

PITCHING	G	GS	CG	IP	H	R	ER	BB	SO	W	L	SV	ERA
St. Louis													
Dizzy Dean	3	3	2	26	20	6	5	5	17	2	1	0	1.73
Paul Dean	2	2	2	18	15	4	2	7	11	2	0	0	**1.00**
Wild Bill Hallahan	1	1	0	8⅓	6	2	2	4	6	0	0	0	2.16
Bill Walker	2	0	0	6⅓	6	7	5	6	2	0	2	0	7.11
Tex Carlton	2	1	0	3⅔	5	3	3	2	2	0	0	0	7.36
Dazzy Vance	1	0	0	1⅓	2	1	0	1	3	0	0	0	0.00
Jim Mooney	1	0	0	1	1	0	0	0	0	0	0	0	0.00
Jesse Haines	1	0	0	⅔	1	0	0	0	2	0	0	0	0.00
Team Total	7	7	4	65⅓	56	23	17	25	43	4	3	0	2.34
Detroit													
Schoolboy Rowe	3	2	2	21⅓	19	8	7	0	12	1	1	0	2.95
Tommy Bridges	3	2	1	17⅓	21	9	7	1	12	1	1	0	3.63
Eldon Auker	2	2	1	11⅓	16	8	7	5	2	1	1	0	5.56
Chief Hogsett	3	0	0	7⅓	6	1	1	3	3	0	0	0	1.23
General Crowder	2	1	0	6	6	4	1	1	2	0	1	0	1.50
Firpo Marberry	2	0	0	1⅔	5	4	4	1	0	0	0	0	21.60
Vic Sorrell	Did not play												
Carl Fischer	Did not play												
Luke Hamlin	Did not play												
Team Total	7	7	4	65	73	34	27	11	31	3	4	0	3.74

Game 1 Oct. 3
St. Louis   021 014 000 · 8
Detroit   001 001 010 · 3
Winner-J. Dean   Loser-Crowder

Game 2 Oct. 4
St. Louis   011 000 000 000 · 2
Detroit   000 100 001 001 · 3
Winner-Rowe   Loser-W. Walker

Game 3 Oct. 5
Detroit   000 000 001 · 1
St. Louis   110 020 00* · 4
Winner-P. Dean   Loser-Bridges

Game 4 Oct. 6
Detroit   003 100 150 · 10
St. Louis   011 200 000 · 4
Winner-Auker   Loser-W. Walker

Game 5 Oct. 7
Detroit   010 002 000 · 3
St. Louis   000 000 100 · 1
Winner-Bridges   Loser-J. Dean

Game 6 Oct. 8
St. Louis   100 020 100 · 4
Detroit   001 002 000 · 3
Winner-P. Dean   Loser-Rowe

Game 7 Oct. 9
St. Louis   007 002 200 · 11
Detroit   000 000 000 · 0
Winner-J. Dean   Loser-Auker

Total Attendance—281,510
Average Attendance—40,216
Winning Player's Share—$5,390
Losing Player's Share-$3,355

1935

Detroit A.L. 4
Chicago N.L. 2

Highlights

MANAGED BY CATCHER MICKEY Cochrane (.319), the Detroit Tigers were back again. Hank Greenberg, Charlie Gehringer and Goose Goslin were the main hitters, and Tommy Bridges, Schoolboy Rowe, Eldon Auker and General Crowder were the heart of the mound staff. Their opponents, the Chicago Cubs, had a stronger staff, headed by Bill Lee and Lon Warneke. Gabby Hartnett and Billy Herman led the Cubs' attack.

Warneke shut out Rowe, 3-0, in the opener, but Detroit evened things in game two, 8-3. Greenberg broke a wrist in this game, and so was unable to help the Tigers for the rest of the Series. But even so, the Tigers won game three, 6-5, and then used Crowder to beat Tex Carleton, 2-1, in game four.

Warneke pitched the Cubs to a 2-0 lead in game five, when an injured shoulder forced him from the mound in the seventh. Bill Lee took over and saved the 3-1 win for Chicago. Game six was tied 3-3 after eight innings, when Cubs third baseman Stan Hack led off with a triple. Detroit's Tommy Bridges got the next three Cubs batters, and the Tigers went on to win the game and the Series with a Goslin single that scored Cochrane.

Game 1 Oct. 2
Chicago	200 000 001	-	3
Detroit	000 000 000	-	0

Winner-Warneke Loser-Rowe

Game 2 Oct. 3
Chicago	000 010 200	-	3
Detroit	400 300 10*	-	8

Winner-Bridges Loser-Root

Game 3 Oct. 4
Detroit	000 001 040	01	- 6
Chicago	020 010 002	00	- 5

Winner-Rowe Loser-French

Game 4 Oct. 5
Detroit	001 001 000	-	2
Chicago	010 000 000	-	1

Winner-Crowder Loser-Carleton

Game 5 Oct. 6
Detroit	000 000 001	-	1
Chicago	002 000 10*	-	3

Winner-Warneke Loser-Rowe

Game 6 Oct. 7
Chicago	001 020 000	-	3
Detroit	100 101 001	-	4

Winner-Bridges Loser-French

Total Attendance—286,672
Average Attendance—47,779
Winning Player's Share—$6,545
Losing Player's Share—$4,199

BATTING	Pos	G	AB	R	H	2B	3B	HR	RBI	BB	SO	SB	BA
Detroit													
Marv Owen	3b-1b	6	20	2	1	0	0	0	1	2	3	0	.050
Charlie Gehringer	2b	6	24	4	9	3	0	0	4	2	1	1	.375
Billy Rogell	ss	6	24	1	7	2	0	0	1	2	5	0	.292
Flea Clifton	3b	4	16	1	0	0	0	0	0	2	4	0	.000
Pete Fox	rf	6	26	1	10	3	1	0	4	0	1	0	**.385**
Jo-Jo White	cf	5	19	3	5	0	0	0	1	5	7	0	.263
Goose Goslin	lf	6	22	2	6	1	0	0	3	5	0	0	.273
Mickey Cochrane	c	6	24	3	7	1	0	0	1	4	1	0	.292
Hank Greenberg	1b	2	6	1	1	0	0	1	2	1	0	0	.167
Gee Walker	ph-cf	3	4	1	1	0	0	0	0	1	0	0	.250
Ray Hayworth	Did not play												
Heinie Schuble	Did not play												
Frank Reiber	Did not play												
Hugh Shelley	Did not play												
Schoolboy Rowe	p	3	8	0	2	1	0	0	0	0	1	0	.250
Tommy Bridges	p	2	8	1	1	0	0	0	1	0	3	0	.125
General Crowder	p	1	3	1	1	0	0	0	0	1	0	0	.333
Eldon Auker	p	1	2	0	0	0	0	0	0	0	1	0	.000
Chief Hogsett	p	1	0	0	0	0	0	0	0	0	0	0	.000
Joe Sullivan	Did not play												
Vic Sorrell	Did not play												
Roxie Lawson	Did not play												
Team Total		6	206	21	51	11	1	1	18	25	27	1	.249

Double Plays—7   Left on Bases—51

	Pos	G	AB	R	H	2B	3B	HR	RBI	BB	SO	SB	BA
Chicago Cubs													
Phil Cavarretta	1b	6	24	1	3	0	0	0	0	0	5	0	.125
Billy Herman	2b	6	24	3	8	2	1	1	6	0	2	0	.333
Billy Jurges	ss	6	16	3	4	0	0	0	1	4	4	0	.250
Stan Hack	3b-ss	6	22	2	5	1	1	0	0	2	2	1	.227
Frank Demaree	rf-cf	6	24	2	6	1	0	2	2	1	4	0	.250
Fred Lindstrom	cf-3b	4	15	0	3	1	0	0	0	1	1	0	.200
Augie Galan	lf	6	25	2	4	1	0	0	2	2	2	0	.160
Gabby Hartnett	c	6	24	1	7	0	0	1	2	0	3	0	.292
Chuck Klein	ph-rf-cf	5	12	2	4	0	0	1	2	0	2	0	.333
Ken O'Dea	ph	1	1	0	1	0	0	0	1	0	0	0	1.000
Walter Stephenson	ph	1	1	0	0	0	0	0	0	0	1	0	.000
Tuck Stainback	Did not play												
Woody English	Did not play												
Charlie Grimm	Did not play												
Lon Warneke	p	3	5	0	1	0	0	0	0	0	0	0	.200
Larry French	p	2	4	1	1	0	0	0	0	0	2	0	.250
Fabian Kowalik	p	1	2	1	1	0	0	0	0	0	0	0	.500
Roy Henshaw	p	1	1	0	0	0	0	0	0	0	0	0	.000
Bill Lee	p	2	5	0	0	0	0	0	1	0	0	0	.000
Tex Carleton	p	1	1	0	0	0	0	0	0	1	1	0	.000
Charlie Root	p	2	0	0	0	0	0	0	0	0	0	0	.000
Clyde Shoun	Did not play												
Hugh Casey	Did not play												
Team Total		6	202	18	48	6	2	5	17	11	29	1	.238

Double Plays—5   Left on Bases—38

PITCHING	G	GS	CG	IP	H	R	ER	BB	SO	W	L	SV	ERA
Detroit													
Schoolboy Rowe	3	2	2	21	19	8	6	1	14	1	2	0	2.57
Tommy Bridges	2	2	2	18	18	6	5	4	9	2	0	0	2.50
General Crowder	1	1	1	9	5	1	1	3	5	1	0	0	1.00
Eldon Auker	1	1	0	6	6	3	2	2	1	0	0	0	3.00
Chief Hogsett	1	0	0	1	0	0	0	1	0	0	0	0	0.00
Joe Sullivan	Did not play												
Vic Sorrell	Did not play												
Roxie Lawson	Did not play												
Team Total	6	6	5	55	48	18	14	11	29	4	2	0	2.29
Chicago													
Lon Warneke	3	2	1	16⅔	9	1	1	4	5	2	0	0	0.54
Larry French	2	1	1	10⅔	15	5	4	2	8	0	2	0	3.38
Bill Lee	2	1	0	10⅓	11	5	4	5	5	0	0	1	3.48
Tex Carleton	1	1	0	7	6	2	1	7	4	0	1	0	1.29
Fabian Kowalik	1	0	0	4⅓	3	1	1	1	1	0	0	0	2.10
Roy Henshaw	1	0	0	3⅔	2	3	3	5	2	0	0	0	7.36
Charlie Root	2	1	0	2	5	4	4	1	2	0	1	0	18.00
Clyde Shoun	Did not play												
Hugh Casey	Did not play												
Team Total	6	6	2	54⅓	51	21	18	25	27	2	4	1	2.96

1936

Highlights

THIS WAS THE FIRST SUBWAY Series in thirteen years. The Yankees no longer had Ruth, but their offensive line up was still very powerful: Gehrig, Lazzeri and Dickey while Crosetti was still at short and Red Ruffing and Lefty Gomez still led the mound staff. Yankees newcomers: George Selkirk, Jake Powell, Red Rolfe, Monte Pearson, Bump Hadley and, appearing in the majors for the first time this season, Joe DiMaggio (.323, 29 homers and 125 RBI's). New York Giants Mel Ott and Carl Hubbell headed up the opposition.

Hubbell won the opener, 6-1, at the Polo Grounds, but the Yanks overpowered the Giants, 18-4, in game two, a game in which Tony Lazzeri hit the second grand-slam homer in Series history. Pat Malone relieved Hadley in eighth to save a 2-1 Yankees win in game three. Carl Hubbell tried to turn things around in game four, but he was bested, 5-2, by Pearson.

The Giants then won game five, 5-4, but the Yankees took game six, 13-5, to win both the game and the Series.

Game 1 Sept. 30
Yankees   001 000 000 · 1
Giants   000 011 04* · 6
Winner-Hubbell   Loser-Ruffing

Game 2 Oct. 2
Yankees   207 001 206 · 18
Giants   010 300 000 · 4
Winner-Gomez   Loser-Schumacher

Game 3 Oct. 3
Giants   000 010 000 · 1
Yankees   010 000 01* · 2
Winner-Hadley   Loser-Fitzsimmons

Game 4 Oct. 4
Giants   ·000 100 010 · 2
Yankees   013 000 01* · 5
Winner-Pearson   Loser-Hubbell

Game 5 Oct. 5
Giants   300 001 000   1 · 5
Yankees   011 002 000   0 · 4
Winner- Schumacher   Loser-Malone

Game 6 Oct. 6
Yankees   021 200 017 · 13
Giants   200 010 110 · 5
Winner-Gomez   Loser-Fitzsimmons

Total Attendance—302,924
Average Attendance—50,487
Winning Player's Share—$6,431
Losing Player's Share—$4,656

BATTING	Pos	G	AB	R	H	2B	3B	HR	RBI	BB	SO	SB	BA
New York Yankees													
Lou Gehrig	1b	6	24	5	7	1	0	2	7	3	2	0	.292
Tony Lazzeri	2b	6	20	4	5	0	0	1	7	4	4	0	.250
Frankie Crosetti	ss	6	26	5	7	2	0	0	3	3	5	0	.269
Red Rolfe	3b	6	25	5	10	0	0	0	4	3	1	0	.400
George Selkirk	rf	6	24	6	8	0	1	2	3	4	4	0	.333
Joe DiMaggio	cf	6	26	3	9	3	0	0	3	1	3	0	.346
Jake Powell	lf	6	22	8	10	1	0	1	5	4	4	1	.455
Bill Dickey	c	6	25	5	3	0	0	1	5	3	4	0	.120
Roy Johnson	pr-ph	2	1	0	0	0	0	0	0	0	1	0	.000
Bob Seeds	pr	1	0	0	0	0	0	0	0	0	0	0	.000
Joe Glenn	Did not play												
Jack Saltzgaver	Did not play												
Art Jorgens	Did not play												
Don Heffner	Did not play												
Lefty Gomez	p	2	8	1	2	0	0	0	3	0	3	0	.250
Red Ruffing	p-ph	3	5	0	0	0	0	0	0	1	2	0	.000
Monte Pearson	p	1	4	0	2	1	0	0	0	0	0	0	.500
Johnny Murphy	p	1	2	1	1	0	0	0	0	1	0	1	.500
Bump Hadley	p	1	2	0	0	0	0	0	0	0	1	0	.000
Pat Malone	p	2	1	0	1	0	0	0	0	0	0	0	1.000
Johnny Broaca	Did not play												
Jumbo Brown	Did not play												
Kemp Wicker	Did not play												
Team Total		6	215	43	65	8	1	7	41	26	35	1	.302

Double Plays—2   Left on Bases—43

BATTING	Pos	G	AB	R	H	2B	3B	HR	RBI	BB	SO	SB	BA
New York Giants													
Bill Terry	1b	6	25	1	6	0	0	0	5	1	4	0	.240
Burgess Whitehead	2b	6	21	1	1	0	0	0	2	1	3	0	.048
Dick Bartell	ss	6	21	5	8	3	0	1	3	4	4	0	.381
Travis Jackson	3b	6	21	1	4	0	0	0	1	1	3	0	.190
Mel Ott	rf	6	23	4	7	2	0	1	3	3	1	0	.304
Jimmy Ripple	cf-ph	5	12	2	4	0	0	1	3	3	3	0	.333
Jo-Jo Moore	lf	6	28	4	6	2	0	1	1	1	4	0	.214
Gus Mancuso	c	6	19	3	5	2	0	0	1	3	3	0	.263
Hank Leiber	cf	2	6	0	0	0	0	0	0	2	0	0	.000
Sam Leslie	ph	3	3	0	2	0	0	0	0	0	0	0	.667
Mark Koenig	ph-2b	3	3	0	1	0	0	0	0	0	1	0	.333
Kiddo Davis	ph-pr	4	2	2	1	0	0	0	0	0	0	0	.500
Harry Danning	ph-c	2	2	0	0	0	0	0	0	0	1	0	.000
Eddie Mayo	3b	1	1	0	0	0	0	0	0	0	0	0	.000
Roy Spencer	Did not play												
Carl Hubbell	p	2	6	0	2	0	0	0	1	0	0	0	.333
Freddie Fitzsimmons	p	2	4	0	2	0	0	0	0	0	1	0	.500
Hal Schumacher	p	2	4	0	0	0	0	0	0	1	3	0	.000
Slick Castleman	p	1	2	0	1	0	0	0	0	0	0	0	.500
Dick Coffman	p	2	0	0	0	0	0	0	0	0	0	0	.000
Frank Gabler	p	2	0	0	0	0	0	0	0	1	0	0	.000
Harry Gumbert	p	2	0	0	0	0	0	0	0	0	0	0	.000
Al Smith	p	1	0	0	0	0	0	0	0	0	0	0	.000
Team Total		6	203	23	50	9	0	4	20	21	33	0	.246

Double Plays—7   Left on Bases—46

PITCHING	G	GS	CG	IP	H	R	ER	BB	SO	W	L	SV	ERA
New York Yankees													
Lefty Gomez	2	2	1	15⅓	14	8	8	11	9	2	0	0	4.70
Red Ruffing	2	2	0	14	16	10	7	5	12	0	1	0	4.50
Monte Pearson	1	1	1	9	7	2	2	2	7	1	0	0	2.00
Bump Hadley	1	1	0	8	10	1	1	1	2	1	0	0	1.12
Pat Malone	2	0	0	5	2	1	1	1	2	0	1	1	1.80
Johnny Murphy	1	0	0	2⅔	1	1	1	1	1	0	0	1	3.38
Johnny Broaca	Did not play												
Jumbo Brown	Did not play												
Kemp Wicker	Did not play												
Team Total	6	6	2	54	50	23	20	21	33	4	2	2	3.36
New York Giants													
Carl Hubbell	2	2	1	16	15	5	4	2	10	1	1	0	2.25
Hal Schumacher	2	2	1	12	13	9	7	10	11	1	1	0	5.25
Freddie Fitzsimmons	2	2	1	11⅔	13	7	7	2	6	0	2	0	5.40
Frank Gablerman	2	0	0	5	7	4	4	4	0	0	0	0	7.20
Slick Castleman	1	0	0	4⅓	3	1	1	2	5	0	0	0	2.08
Harry Gumbert	2	0	0	2	7	8	8	4	2	0	0	0	36.00
Dick Coffman	2	0	0	1⅔	5	6	6	1	1	0	0	0	32.40
Al Smith	1	0	0	⅓	2	3	3	1	0	0	0	0	81.00
Team Total	6	6	3	53	65	43	40	26	35	2	4	0	6.79

Hal Schumacher and Lefty Gomez

1937

New York A.L. 4
New York N.L. 1

Highlights

POWER WAS THE NAME OF THE Yankees' game this year. Among the big bats were Gehrig (.351, 37 homers and 159 RBI's), DiMaggio (.346, 46 homers and 167 RBI's), Bill Dickey, George Selkirk and a host of others. Lefty Gomez and Red Ruffing were the main pitchers. The opposition was the New York Giants with Carl Hubbell and Cliff Melton on the mound.

After an auspicious start, Hubbell was knocked out of the box in the opener as the Yankees ran up an 8-1 victory. Melton met a similar fate in game two as the Yankees knocked him out too, 8-1. With Schumacher facing Pearson, the Giants lost game three, 5-1. Hubbell returned in game four for a six-hitter that ended in a 7-3 Giants victory.

The fifth game finished it as Lefty Gomez beat Melton, Al Smith and Don Brennan, 4-2, to win the Series for the Yankees. Tony Lazzeri closed out twelve seasons with the Yankees with the Series top batting average of .400.

Game 1 Oct. 6
Giants	000 010 000 ·	1
Yankees	000 007 01* ·	8

Winner-Gomez Loser-Hubbell

Game 2 Oct. 7
Giants	100 000 000 ·	1
Yankees	000 024 20* ·	8

Winner-Ruffing Loser-Melton

Game 3 Oct. 8
Yankees	012 110 000 ·	5
Giants	000 000 100 ·	1

Winner-Pearson Loser-Schumacher

Game 4 Oct. 9
Yankees	101 000 001 ·	3
Giants	060 000 10* ·	7

Winner-Hubbell Loser-Hadley

Game 5 Oct. 10
Yankees	011 020 000 ·	4
Giants	002 000 000 ·	2

Winner-Gomez Loser-Melton

Total Attendance—238,142
Average Attendance—47,628
Winning Player's Share—$6,471
Losing Player's Share—$4,490

BATTING	Pos	G	AB	R	H	2B	3B	HR	RBI	BB	SO	SB	BA
New York Yankees													
Lou Gehrig	1b	5	17	4	5	1	1	1	3	5	4	0	.294
Tony Lazzeri	2b	5	15	3	6	0	1	1	2	3	3	0	**.400**
Frankie Crosetti	ss	5	21	2	1	0	0	0	0	3	2	0	.048
Red Rolfe	3b	5	20	3	6	2	1	0	1	3	2	0	.300
George Selkirk	rf	5	19	5	5	1	0	0	6	2	0	0	.263
Joe DiMaggio	cf	5	22	2	6	0	0	1	4	0	3	0	.273
Myril Hoag	lf	5	20	4	6	1	0	1	2	0	1	0	.300
Bill Dickey	c	5	19	3	4	0	1	0	3	2	2	0	.211
Jake Powell	ph	1	1	0	0	0	0	0	0	0	1	0	.000
Tommy Henrich	Did not play—injured												
Don Heffner	Did not play												
Joe Glenn	Did not play												
Jack Saltzgaver	Did not play												
Art Jorgens	Did not play												
Lefty Gomez	p	2	6	2	1	0	0	0	1	2	1	0	.167
Red Ruffing	p	1	4	0	2	1	0	0	3	0	0	0	.500
Monte Pearson	p	1	3	0	0	0	0	0	0	1	1	0	.000
Ivy Andrews	p	1	2	0	0	0	0	0	0	0	1	0	.000
Bump Hadley	p	1	0	0	0	0	0	0	0	0	0	0	.000
Johnny Murphy	p	1	0	0	0	0	0	0	0	0	0	0	.000
Kemp Wicker	p	1	0	0	0	0	0	0	0	0	0	0	.000
Pat Malone	Did not play												
Frank Makosky	Did not play												
Spud Chandler	Did not play												
Team Total		5	169	28	42	6	4	4	25	21	21	0	.249

Double Plays—2 Left on Bases—36

BATTING	Pos	G	AB	R	H	2B	3B	HR	RBI	BB	SO	SB	BA
New York Giants													
Johnny McCarthy	1b	5	19	1	4	1	0	0	1	1	2	0	.211
Burgess Whitehead	2b	5	16	1	4	2	0	0	0	2	0	1	.250
Dick Bartell	ss	5	21	3	5	1	0	0	1	0	3	0	.238
Mel Ott	3b	5	20	1	4	0	0	1	3	1	4	0	.200
Jimmy Ripple	lf	5	17	2	5	0	0	0	0	3	1	0	.294
Hank Leiber	cf	3	11	2	4	0	0	0	2	1	1	0	.364
Jo-Jo Moore	lf	5	23	1	9	1	0	0	1	0	1	0	.391
Harry Danning	c	3	12	0	3	1	0	0	2	0	2	0	.250
Gus Mancuso	c-ph	3	8	0	0	0	0	0	1	0	1	0	.000
Lou Chiozza	cf	2	7	0	2	0	0	0	0	1	1	0	.286
Wally Berger	ph	3	3	0	0	0	0	0	0	0	1	0	.000
Sam Leslie	ph	2	1	0	0	0	0	0	0	1	0	0	.000
Blondy Ryan	ph	1	1	0	0	0	0	0	0	0	1	0	.000
Mickey Haslin	Did not play												
Ed Madjeski	Did not play												
Carl Hubbell	p	2	6	1	0	0	0	0	1	0	0	0	.000
Cliff Melton	p	3	2	0	0	0	0	0	0	1	1	0	.000
Dick Coffman	p	2	1	0	0	0	0	0	0	0	1	0	.000
Hal Schumacher	p	1	1	0	0	0	0	0	0	0	1	0	.000
Don Brennan	p	2	0	0	0	0	0	0	0	0	0	0	.000
Harry Gumbert	p	2	0	0	0	0	0	0	0	0	0	0	.000
Al Smith	p	2	0	0	0	0	0	0	0	0	0	0	.000
Slick Castleman	Did not play—arm injury												
Tom Baker	Did not play												
Team Total		5	169	12	40	6	0	1	12	11	21	1	.237

Double Plays—5 Left on Bases—36

PITCHING	G	GS	CG	IP	H	R	ER	BB	SO	W	L	SV	ERA
New York Yankees													
Lefty Gomez	2	2	2	18	16	3	3	2	8	2	0	0	1.50
Red Ruffing	1	1	1	9	7	1	1	3	8	1	0	0	**1.00**
Monte Pearson	1	1	0	8⅔	5	1	1	2	4	1	0	0	1.04
Ivy Andrews	1	0	0	5⅔	6	2	2	4	1	0	0	0	3.18
Bump Hadley	1	1	0	1⅓	6	5	5	0	0	0	1	0	33.75
Kemp Wicker	1	0	0	1	6	0	0	0	0	0	0	0	0.00
Johnny Murphy	1	0	0	⅓	0	0	0	0	0	0	0	1	0.00
Pat Malone	Did not play												
Spud Chandler	Did not play												
Frank Makosky	Did not play												
Team Total	5	5	3	44	40	12	12	11	21	4	1	1	2.45
New York Giants													
Carl Hubbell	2	2	1	14⅓	12	10	6	4	7	1	1	0	3.77
Cliff Melton	3	2	0	11	12	6	6	6	7	0	2	0	4.91
Hal Schumacher	1	1	0	6	9	5	4	4	3	0	1	0	6.00
Dick Coffman	2	0	0	4⅓	2	2	2	5	1	0	0	0	4.15
Don Brennan	2	0	0	3	1	0	0	1	1	0	0	0	0.00
Al Smith	2	0	0	3	2	1	1	0	1	0	0	0	3.00
Harry Gumbert	2	0	0	1⅓	4	4	4	1	1	0	0	0	27.00
Slick Castleman	Did not play—arm injury												
Tom Baker	Did not play												
Team Total	5	5	1	43	42	28	23	21	21	1	4	0	4.81

1938

Highlights

THE NEW YORK YANKEES VIRtually sailed to the A.L. pennant with the same basic lineup as the previous year. Newcomers were Joe Gordon at second and Tommy Henrich in right. The Chicago Cubs, though, had to slug it out with the Pirates in the last days of the season. They had few powerful bats. Only Stan Hack and Carl Reynolds hit .300. Pitching was by Bill Lee and Clay Bryant, with occasional help from Dizzy Dean.

Red Ruffing beat Bill Lee in game one, 3-1. Dizzy Dean used a variety of pitches and sppeds to outfox Yankees batters in game two, but Yanks finally caught on in the eighth inning and knocked him out with a 6-3 score. The Cubs lost game three, 5-2, as both Dickey and Gordon hit homers. As in the 1932 match-up, the Cubs were down 3-0 in the Series, and as before, they couldn't reverse the trend.

Chicago ran through six pitchers during the final game, but a Crosetti triple that brought in three runs, a four-run Yankee eighth, and a homer by Henrich sealed their fate, 8-3, for a second sweep of the Series by the New York Yankees over the Chicago Cubs.

Game 1 Oct. 5

New York	020 000 100 ·	3
Chicago	001 000 000 ·	1
Winner-Ruffing	Loser-Lee	

Game 2 Oct. 6

New York	020 000 022 ·	6
Chicago	102 000 000 ·	3
Winner-Gomez	Loser-Dean	

Game 3 Oct. 8

Chicago	000 010 010 ·	2
New York	000 022 01* ·	5
Winner-Pearson	Loser-Bryant	

Game 4 Oct. 9

Chicago	000 100 020 ·	3
New York	030 001 04* ·	8
Winner-Ruffing	Loser-Lee	

Total Attendance—200,833
Average Attendance—50,208
Winning Player's Share—$5,783
Losing Player's Share—$4,675

BATTING

	Pos	G	AB	R	H	2B	3B	HR	RBI	BB	SO	SB	BA
New York													
Lou Gehrig	1b	4	14	4	4	0	0	0	0	2	3	0	.286
Joe Gordon	2b	4	15	3	6	2	0	1	6	1	3	1	.400
Frankie Crosetti	ss	4	16	1	4	2	1	1	6	2	4	0	.250
Red Rolfe	3b	4	18	0	3	0	0	0	1	0	3	1	.167
Tommy Henrich	rf	4	16	3	4	1	0	1	1	0	1	0	.250
Joe DiMaggio	cf	4	15	4	4	0	0	1	2	1	1	0	.267
George Selkirk	lf	3	10	0	2	0	0	0	1	2	1	0	.200
Bill Dickey	c	4	15	2	6	0	0	1	2	1	0	1	.400
Myril Hoag	ph-lf	2	5	3	2	1	0	0	1	0	0	0	.400
Jack Powell	lf	1	0	0	0	0	0	0	0	0	0	0	.000
Bill Knickerbocker		Did not play											
Joe Glenn		Did not play											
Babe Pahlgren		Did not play											
Art Jorgens		Did not play											
Red Ruffing	p	2	6	1	1	0	0	0	1	1	0	0	.167
Monte Pearson	p	1	3	1	1	0	0	0	0	1	0	0	.333
Lefty Gomez	p	1	2	0	0	0	0	0	0	0	0	0	.000
Johnny Murphy	p	1	0	0	0	0	0	0	0	0	0	0	.000
Spud Chandler		Did not play											
Bump Hadley		Did not play											
Steve Sundra		Did not play											
Wes Ferrell		Did not play											
Ivy Andrews		Did not play											
Team Total		4	135	22	37	6	1	5	21	11	16	3	.274

Double Plays—4   Left on Bases—24

	Pos	G	AB	R	H	2B	3B	HR	RBI	BB	SO	SB	BA
Chicago													
Ripper Collins	1b	4	15	1	2	0	0	0	0	0	3	0	.133
Billy Herman	2b	4	16	1	3	0	0	0	0	1	4	0	.188
Billy Jurges	ss	4	13	0	3	1	0	0	0	1	3	0	.231
Stan Hack	3b	4	17	3	8	1	0	0	1	1	2	0	.471
Phil Cararretta	rf	4	13	1	6	1	0	0	0	0	2	0	.462
Joe Marty	cf	3	12	1	6	1	0	1	5	0	2	0	.500
Frank Demaree	lf-rf	3	10	1	1	0	0	0	0	1	2	0	.100
Gabby Hartnett	c	3	11	0	1	0	1	0	0	0	2	0	.091
Carl Reynolds	cf-lf-ph	4	12	0	0	0	0	0	0	1	3	0	.000
Ken O'Dea	ph-c	3	5	1	1	0	0	1	2	1	0	0	.200
Augie Galan	ph	2	2	0	0	0	0	0	0	0	1	0	.000
Tony Lazzeri	ph	2	2	0	0	0	0	0	0	0	1	0	.000
Bob Gabark		Did not play											
Jim Asbell		Did not play											
Dizzy Dean	p	2	3	0	2	0	0	0	0	0	0	0	.667
Bill Lee	p	2	3	0	0	0	0	0	0	0	1	0	.000
Clay Bryant	p	1	2	0	0	0	0	0	0	0	1	0	.000
Larry French	p	3	0	0	0	0	0	0	0	0	0	0	.000
Jack Russell	p	2	0	0	0	0	0	0	0	0	0	0	.000
Tex Carleton	p	1	0	0	0	0	0	0	0	0	0	0	.000
Vance Page	p	1	0	0	0	0	0	0	0	0	0	0	.000
Charlie Root	p	1	0	0	0	0	0	0	0	0	0	0	.000
Team Total		4	136	9	33	4	1	2	8	6	26	0	.243

Double Plays—3   Left on Bases—26

PITCHING

	G	GS	CG	IP	H	R	ER	BB	SO	W	L	SV	ERA
New York Yankees													
Red Ruffing	2	2	2	18	17	4	3	2	11	2	0	0	1.50
Monte Pearson	1	1	1	9	5	2	1	2	9	1	0	0	1.00
Lefty Gomez	1	1	0	7	9	3	3	1	5	1	0	0	3.86
Johnny Murphy	1	0	0	2	2	0	0	1	1	0	0	1	0.00
Spud Chandler		Did not play											
Bump Hadley		Did not play											
Steve Sundra		Did not play											
Wes Ferrell		Did not play											
Ivy Andrews		Did not play											
Team Total	4	4	3	36	33	9	7	6	26	4	0	1	1.75
Chicago													
Bill Lee	2	2	0	11	15	6	3	1	8	0	2	0	2.45
Dizzy Dean	2	1	0	8⅓	8	6	6	1	2	0	1	0	6.48
Clay Bryant	1	1	0	5⅓	6	4	4	5	3	0	1	0	6.75
Larry French	3	0	0	3⅓	1	1	1	1	2	0	0	0	2.70
Charlie Root	1	0	0	3	3	1	1	0	0	0	0	0	3.00
Jack Russell	2	0	0	1⅔	1	0	0	1	0	0	0	0	0.00
Vance Page	1	0	0	1⅓	2	2	2	0	0	0	0	0	13.50
Tex Carleton	1	0	0	0	1	2	2	2	0	0	0	0	0.00
Team Total	4	4	0	34	37	22	19	11	16	0	4	0	5.03

1939

Highlights

A VICTIM OF A RARE FORM OF polio, Lou Gehrig left the Yankees' lineup in May. But with DiMaggio, Gordon, Dickey, Selkirk, Rolfe and rookie Charlie Keller at bat, the Yankees still had power to win the A.L. flag 17 games ahead of Boston, their fourth straight pennant. The Cincinnati Reds won the N.L. pennant for the first time since 1919, powered by Ival Goodman, Frank McCormick, Ernie Lombardi and pitchers Bucky Walters and Paul Derringer.

The Yankees won the opener, 2-1, and game two, 4-0. In game two, Yankee righty Monte Pearson had almost pitched perfect game when Ernie Lombardi touched him for a clean single in the top of eighth. The Reds got ten hits and three runs in game three. The Yanks got only five hits. But those five included homers by DiMaggio and Dickey and two homers by Keller. The Yanks won game three, 7-3.

In game four, Keller accidently kicked catcher Ernie Lombardi in the groin as he crossed the plate. Lombardi fell to ground stunned as DiMaggio tore home to ice the 7-4 game and give the Yankees an unprecedented fourth consecutive World Championship.

Game 1 Oct. 4
Cincinnati	000 100 000	· 1
New York	000 010 001	· 2

Winner-Ruffing Loser-Derringer

Game 2 Oct. 5
Cincinnati	000 000 000	· 0
New York	003 100 00*	· 4

Winner-Pearson Loser-Walters

Game 3 Oct. 7
New York	202 030 000	· 7
Cincinnati	120 000 000	· 3

Winner-Hadley Loser-Thompson

Game 4 Oct. 8
New York	000 000 202	3	· 7
Cincinnati	000 000 310	0	· 4

Winner-Murphy Loser-Walters

Total Attendance—183,849
Average Attendance—45,962
Winning Player's Share—$5,542
Losing Player's Share—$4,193

New York A.L. 4
Cincinnati N.L. 0

BATTING	Pos	G	AB	R	H	2B	3B	HR	RBI	BB	SO	SB	BA
New York													
Babe Dahlgren	1b	4	14	2	3	**2**	0	1	2	0	4	0	.214
Joe Gordon	2b	4	14	1	2	0	0	0	1	0	2	0	.143
Frankie Crosetti	ss	4	16	2	1	0	0	0	1	2	2	0	.063
Red Rolfe	3b	4	16	2	2	0	0	0	0	0	0	0	.125
Charlie Keller	rf	4	16	**8**	7	1	**1**	3	6	1	2	0	**.438**
Joe DiMaggio	cf	4	16	3	5	0	0	1	3	1	1	0	.313
George Selkirk	lf	4	12	0	2	1	0	0	0	3	2	0	.167
Bill Dickey	c	4	15	2	4	0	0	2	5	1	2	0	.267
Tommy Henrich	Did not play												
Buddy Rosar	Did not play												
Jake Powell	Did not play												
Lou Gehrig	Did not play—illness												
Bill Knickerbocker	Did not play												
Art Jorgens	Did not play												
Red Ruffing	p	1	3	0	1	0	0	0	0	0	1	0	.333
Bump Hadley	p	1	3	0	0	0	0	0	0	0	0	0	.000
Johnny Murphy	p	1	2	0	0	0	0	0	0	0	1	0	.000
Monte Pearson	p	1	2	0	0	0	0	0	0	0	1	0	.000
Lefty Gomez	p	1	1	0	0	0	0	0	0	0	0	0	.000
Oral Hildebrand	p	1	1	0	0	0	0	0	0	0	1	0	.000
Steve Sundra	p	1	0	0	0	0	0	0	0	1	0	0	.000
Atley Donald	Did not play												
Marius Russo	Did not play												
Spud Chandler	Did not play												
Team Total		4	131	20	27	4	1	7	18	9	20	0	.206

Double Plays—5   Left on Bases—16

	Pos	G	AB	R	H	2B	3B	HR	RBI	BB	SO	SB	BA
Cincinnati													
Frank McCormick	1b	4	15	1	6	1	0	0	1	0	1	0	.400
Lonny Frey	2b	4	17	0	0	0	0	0	0	1	4	0	.000
Billy Myers	ss	4	12	2	4	0	1	0	0	2	3	0	.333
Bill Werber	3b	4	16	1	4	0	0	0	2	2	0	0	.250
Ival Goodman	rf	4	15	3	5	1	0	0	1	1	2	1	.333
Harry Craft	cf	4	11	0	1	0	0	0	0	0	6	0	.091
Wally Berger	lf-cf	4	15	0	0	0	0	0	1	0	4	0	.000
Ernie Lombardi	c	4	14	0	3	0	0	0	2	0	1	0	.214
Al Simmons	lf	1	4	1	1	1	0	0	0	0	0	0	.250
Willard Hershberger	c-ph	3	2	0	1	0	0	0	1	0	0	0	.500
Frenchy Bordagaray	pr	2	0	0	0	0	0	0	0	0	0	0	.000
Nino Bongiovanni	ph	1	1	0	0	0	0	0	0	0	0	0	.000
Lee Gamble	ph	1	1	0	0	0	0	0	0	0	1	0	.000
Eddie Joost	Did not play												
Lew Riggs	Did not play												
Les Scarsella	Did not play												
Paul Derringer	p	2	5	0	1	0	0	0	0	0	0	0	.200
Bucky Walters	p	2	3	0	0	0	0	0	0	0	0	0	.000
Junior Thompson	p	1	1	0	1	0	0	0	0	0	0	0	1.000
Whitey Moore	p	1	1	0	0	0	0	0	0	0	0	0	.000
Lee Gibson	p	1	0	0	0	0	0	0	0	0	0	0	.000
Johnny Vander Meer	Did not play												
Johnny Niggerling	Did not play												
Milt Shoffner	Did not play												
Hank Johnson	Did not play												
Team Total		4	133	8	27	3	1	0	8	6	22	1	.203

Double Plays—1   Left on Bases—23

PITCHING	G	GS	CG	IP	H	R	ER	BB	SO	W	L	SV	ERA
New York													
Monte Pearson	1	1	1	9	2	0	0	1	8	1	0	0	**0.00**
Red Ruffing	1	1	1	9	4	1	1	1	4	1	0	0	1.00
Bump Hadley	1	0	0	8	7	2	2	3	2	1	0	0	2.25
Oral Hildebrand	1	1	0	4	2	0	0	0	3	0	0	0	0.00
Johnny Murphy	1	0	0	3⅓	5	1	1	0	2	1	0	0	2.70
Steve Sundra	1	0	0	2⅔	4	3	0	1	2	0	0	0	0.00
Lefty Gomez	1	1	0	1	3	1	1	0	1	0	0	0	9.00
Atley Donald	Did not play												
Marius Russo	Did not play												
Spud Chandler	Did not play												
Team Total	4	4	2	37	27	8	5	6	22	4	0	0	1.22

	G	GS	CG	IP	H	R	ER	BB	SO	W	L	SV	ERA
Cincinnati													
Paul Derringer	**2**	**2**	1	15⅓	9	4	4	3	**9**	0	1	0	2.35
Bucky Walters	**2**	1	1	11	**13**	9	6	1	6	0	**2**	0	4.91
Junior Thompson	1	1	0	4⅔	5	7	7	4	3	0	1	0	13.50
Whitey Moore	1	0	0	3	0	0	0	0	2	0	0	0	0.00
Lee Grissom	1	0	0	1⅓	0	0	0	1	0	0	0	0	0.00
Johnny Vander Meer	Did not play												
Johnny Niggerling	Did not play												
Milt Shoffner	Did not play												
Hank Johnson	Did not play												
Team Total	4	4	2	35⅓	27	20	17	9	20	0	4	0	4.33

1940

Cincinnati N.L. 4
Detroit A.L. 3

Highlights

THE CINCINNATI REDS REPEATED as N.L. champs, but their A.L. opponents were not Yankees. The New York team finished third, after four consecutive Series titles. In their place was a beefed-up Detroit Tigers team featuring Hank Greenberg (41 homers and 150 RBI's) in left, Rudy York (33 homers and 134 RBI's) at first, plus Charlie Gehringer and Barney McCosky, both over .300. Head of mound staff was Bobo Newsom with 21 wins and Schoolboy Rowe with 16.

Newsom beat Derringer, 7-2, in game one. But that night tragedy struck as Bobo's father died of a heart attack. The Reds evened the Series by winning game two, 5-3, but the Tigers took game three, 7-4. Then Derringer pitched a five-hitter to give the Reds a 5-2 fourth-game victory. Just days after his father's death, Bobo Newsom hurled a three-hit shutout to give Detroit an 8-0 win in game five.

In game six, Reds pitcher Bucky Walters threw a five-hit 4-0 shutout, hitting a homer and scoring one of the runs himself. The Reds went on to win game seven behind Derringer, 2-1, for the Series title.

Game 1	Oct. 2		
Detroit		050 020 000 · 7	
Cincinnati		000 100 010 · 2	
Winner-Newsom		Loser-Derringer	

Game 2	Oct. 3		
Detroit		200 001 000 · 3	
Cincinnati		022 100 00* · 5	
Winner-Walters		Loser-Rowe	

Game 3	Oct. 4		
Cincinnati		100 000 012 · 4	
Detroit		000 100 42* · 7	
Winner-Bridges		Loser-Turner	

Game 4	Oct. 5		
Cincinnati		201 100 010 · 5	
Detroit		001 001 000 · 2	
Winner-Derringer		Loser-Trout	

Game 5	Oct. 6		
Cincinnati		000 000 000 · 0	
Detroit		003 400 01* · 8	
Winner-Newsom		Loser-Thompson	

Game 6	Oct. 7		
Detroit		000 000 000 · 0	
Cincinnati		200 001 01* · 4	
Winner-Walters		Loser-Rowe	

Game 7	Oct. 8		
Detroit		001 000 000 · 1	
Cincinnati		000 000 20* · 2	
Winner-Derringer		Loser-Newsom	

Total Attendance—281,927
Average Attendance—40,275
Winning Player's Share—$5,804
Losing Player's Share—$3,532

BATTING	Pos	G	AB	R	H	2B	3B	HR	RBI	BB	SO	SB	BA
Cincinnati													
Frank McCormick	1b	7	28	2	6	1	0	0	0	1	1	0	.214
Eddie Joost	2b	7	25	0	5	0	0	0	2	1	2	0	.200
Billy Myers	ss	7	23	0	3	0	0	0	2	2	5	0	.130
Bill Werber	3b	7	27	5	10	4	0	0	2	4	2	0	.370
Ival Goodman	rf	7	29	5	8	2	0	0	5	0	3	0	.276
Mike McCormick	cf	7	29	1	9	3	0	0	2	1	6	0	.310
Jimmy Ripple	lf	7	21	3	7	2	0	1	6	4	2	0	.333
Jimmie Wilson	c	6	17	2	6	0	0	0	0	1	2	1	.353
Bill Baker	c	3	4	1	1	0	0	0	0	0	1	0	.250
Ernie Lombardi	ph-c	2	3	0	1	1	0	0	0	1	0	0	.333
Lonnie Frey	ph-pr-2b	3	2	0	0	0	0	0	0	0	0	0	.000
Morrie Arnovich	ph-lf	1	1	0	0	0	0	0	0	0	0	0	.000
Lew Riggs	ph	3	3	1	0	0	0	0	0	0	2	0	.000
Harry Craft	ph	1	1	0	0	0	0	0	0	0	0	0	.000
Bucky Walters	p	2	7	2	2	1	0	1	2	0	1	0	.286
Paul Derringer	p	3	7	0	0	0	0	0	0	0	1	0	.000
Whitey Moore	p	3	2	0	0	0	0	0	0	0	1	0	.000
Jim Turner	p	1	2	0	0	0	0	0	0	0	0	0	.000
Junior Thompson	p	1	1	0	0	0	0	0	0	0	1	0	.000
Joe Beggs	p	1	0	0	0	0	0	0	0	0	0	0	.000
Johnny Hutchings	p	1	0	0	0	0	0	0	0	0	0	0	.000
Elmer Riddle	p	1	0	0	0	0	0	0	0	0	0	0	.000
Johnny Vander Meer	p	1	0	0	0	0	0	0	0	0	0	0	.000
Milt Shoffner	Did not play												
Witt Guise	Did not play												
Team Total		7	232	22	58	14	0	2	21	15	30	1	.250

Double Plays—9   Left on Bases—49

BATTING	Pos	G	AB	R	H	2B	3B	HR	RBI	BB	SO	SB	BA
Detroit													
Rudy York	1b	7	26	3	6	0	1	1	2	4	7	0	.231
Charlie Gehringer	2b	7	28	3	6	0	0	0	1	2	0	0	.214
Dick Bartell	ss	7	26	2	7	2	0	0	3	3	3	0	.269
Pinky Higgins	3b	7	24	2	8	3	1	1	6	3	3	0	.333
Bruce Campbell	rf	7	25	4	9	1	0	1	5	4	4	0	.360
Barney McCosky	cf	7	23	5	7	1	0	0	1	7	4	0	.304
Hank Greenberg	lf	7	28	5	10	2	1	1	6	2	5	0	.357
Billy Sullivan	c-ph	5	13	3	2	0	0	0	0	5	2	0	.154
Birdie Tebbetts	c-ph	4	11	0	0	0	0	0	0	0	0	0	.000
Frank Croucher	ss	1	0	0	0	0	0	0	0	0	0	0	.000
Earl Averill	ph	3	3	0	0	0	0	0	0	0	0	0	.000
Pete Fox	ph	1	1	0	0	0	0	0	0	0	0	0	.000
Dutch Meyer	Did not play												
Tuck Stainbach	Did not play												
Bobo Newsom	p	3	10	1	1	0	0	0	0	0	1	0	.100
Johnny Gorsica	p	2	4	0	0	0	0	0	0	0	2	0	.000
Tommy Bridges	p	1	3	0	0	0	0	0	0	0	1	0	.000
Schoolboy Rowe	p	2	1	0	0	0	0	0	0	0	1	0	.000
Clay Smith	p	1	1	0	0	0	0	0	0	0	1	0	.000
Dizzy Trout	p	1	1	0	0	0	0	0	0	0	0	0	.000
Fred Hutchinson	p	1	0	0	0	0	0	0	0	0	0	0	.000
Archie McKain	p	1	0	0	0	0	0	0	0	0	0	0	.000
Hal Newhouser	Did not play												
Al Benton	Did not play												
Tom Seats	Did not play												
Team Total		7	228	28	56	9	3	4	24	30	30	0	.246

Double Plays—4   Left on Bases—50

PITCHING	G	GS	CG	IP	H	R	ER	BB	SO	W	L	SV	ERA
Cincinnati													
Paul Derringer	3	3	2	19⅓	17	8	6	10	6	2	1	0	2.79
Bucky Walters	2	2	2	18	8	3	3	6	6	2	0	0	1.50
Whitey Moore	3	0	0	8⅓	8	3	3	6	7	0	0	0	3.24
Jim Turner	1	1	0	6	8	5	5	0	4	0	1	0	7.50
Junior Thompson	1	1	0	3⅓	8	6	6	4	2	0	1	0	16.20
Johnny Vander Meer	1	0	0	3	2	0	0	3	2	0	0	0	0.00
Joe Beggs	1	0	0	1	3	2	1	0	1	0	0	0	9.00
Johnny Hutchings	1	0	0	1	2	1	1	1	0	0	0	0	9.00
Elmer Riddle	1	0	0	1	0	0	0	0	2	0	0	0	0.00
Milt Shoffner	Did not play												
Witt Guise	Did not play												
Team Total	7	7	4	61	56	28	25	30	30	4	3	0	3.69
Detroit													
Bobo Newsom	3	3	3	26	18	4	4	4	17	2	1	0	1.38
Johnny Gorsica	2	0	0	11⅓	6	1	1	4	4	0	0	0	0.79
Tommy Bridges	1	1	1	9	10	4	3	1	5	1	0	0	3.00
Clay Smith	1	0	0	4	1	1	1	3	1	0	0	0	2.25
Schoolboy Rowe	2	2	0	3⅔	12	7	7	1	1	0	2	0	17.18
Archie McKain	1	0	0	3	4	1	1	0	0	0	0	0	3.00
Dizzy Trout	1	1	0	2	6	3	2	1	1	0	1	0	9.00
Fred Hutchinson	1	0	0	1	1	1	1	1	1	0	0	0	9.00
Hal Newhouser	Did not play												
Al Benton	Did not play												
Tom Seats	Did not play												
Team Total	7	7	4	60	58	22	20	15	30	3	4	0	3.00

New York A.L. 4
Brooklyn N.L. 1

Highlights

GUIDED BY 35-YEAR-OLD LEO Durocher, the Brooklyn Dodgers won their first pennant in 21 years. They had batting champs Pete Reiser, Dixie Walker, Joe Medwick, Billy Herman, Cookie Lavagetto, Pee Wee Reese, Mickey Owen and N.L. MVP Dolph Camilli. Their pitching staff was headed by Kirby Higbe and Whit Wyatt, both 22-game winners, with Hugh Casey in relief. Back in top form were their A.L. opponents, the New York Yankees, with DiMaggio, Keller, Henrich, Gordon, Dickey, Rolfe, Ruffing, Gomez, Murphy and rookies Johnny Sturm and Phil Rizzuto.

After two days, both teams had won one by the identical score of 3-2. The Dodgers lost game three, 2-1, a game in which a ball hit by Yankees pitcher Marius Russo smashed Freddie Fitzsimmons' kneecap, forcing him from the mound.

In top of the ninth in game four, Hugh Casey needed only one out to seal the Dodgers' victory when he pitched a curve to Henrich, who swung and missed. But catcher Mickey Owen let the pitch get past him and Heinrich made it to first. That opened things up for the Yankees, who went on to win, 7-4, and put the Dodgers down three games to one in the Series. Game five finished it as Yankees won, 3-1, to secure their ninth World Championship.

Game 1 Oct. 1
Brooklyn	000 010 100 -	2
New York	010 101 00* -	3

Winner-Ruffing   Loser-Davis

Game 2 Oct. 2
Brooklyn	000 021 000 -	3
New York	011 000 000 -	2

Winner-Wyatt   Loser-Chandler

Game 3 Oct. 4
New York	000 000 020 -	2
Brooklyn	000 000 010 -	1

Winner-Russo   Loser-Casey

Game 4 Oct. 5
New York	100 200 004 -	7
Brooklyn	000 220 000 -	4

Winner-Murphy   Loser-Casey

Game 5 Oct. 6
New York	020 010 000 -	3
Brooklyn	001 000 000 -	1

Winner-Bonham   Loser-Wyatt

Total Attendance—235,773
Average Attendance—47,155
Winning Player's Share—$5,943
Losing Player's Share—$4,829

BATTING

	Pos	G	AB	R	H	2B	3B	HR	RBI	BB	SO	SB	BA
New York													
Johnny Sturm	1b	5	21	0	6	0	0	0	2	0	2	1	.286
Joe Gordon	2b	5	14	2	7	1	1	1	5	7	0	0	.500
Phil Rizzuto	ss	5	18	0	2	0	0	0	0	3	1	1	.111
Red Rolfe	3b	5	20	2	6	0	0	0	0	2	1	0	.300
Tommy Henrich	rf	5	18	4	3	1	0	1	1	3	3	0	.167
Joe DiMaggio	cf	5	19	1	5	0	0	0	1	2	2	0	.263
Charlie Keller	lf	5	18	5	7	2	0	0	5	3	1	0	.389
Bill Dickey	c	5	18	3	3	1	0	0	1	3	1	0	.167
George Selkirk	ph	2	2	0	1	0	0	0	0	0	0	0	.500
Buddy Rosar	c	1	1	0	0	0	0	0	0	0	0	0	.000
Frenchy Bordagaray	pr	1	0	0	0	0	0	0	0	0	0	0	.000
Jerry Priddy	Did not play												
Frankie Crosetti	Did not play												
Ken Silvestri	Did not play												
Ernie Bonham	p	1	4	0	0	0	0	0	0	0	4	0	.000
Marius Russo	p	1	4	0	0	0	0	0	0	0	1	0	.000
Red Ruffing	p	1	3	0	0	0	0	0	0	0	0	0	.000
Spud Chandler	p	1	2	0	1	0	0	0	0	1	0	0	.500
Johnny Murphy	p	2	2	0	0	0	0	0	0	0	1	0	.000
Atley Donald	p	1	2	0	0	0	0	0	0	0	1	0	.000
Marv Breuer	p	1	1	0	0	0	0	0	0	0	0	0	.000
Lefty Gomez	Did not play												
Steve Peek	Did not play												
Charley Stanceau	Did not play												
Norm Branch	Did not play												
Team Total		5	166	17	41	5	1	2	16	23	18	2	.247

Double Plays—7   Left on Bases—42

	Pos	G	AB	R	H	2B	3B	HR	RBI	BB	SO	SB	BA
Brooklyn													
Dolph Camilli	1b	5	18	1	3	1	0	0	1	1	6	0	.167
Billy Herman	2b	4	8	0	1	0	0	0	0	2	0	0	.125
Pee Wee Reese	ss	5	20	1	4	0	0	0	2	0	0	0	.200
Cookie Lavagetto	3b	3	10	1	1	0	0	0	0	2	0	0	.100
Dixie Walker	rf	5	18	3	4	2	0	0	0	2	1	0	.222
Pete Reiser	cf	5	20	1	4	1	1	1	3	1	6	0	.200
Joe Medwick	lf	5	17	1	4	1	0	0	0	1	2	0	.235
Mickey Owen	c	5	12	1	2	0	0	1	0	2	3	0	.167
Lew Riggs	ph-3b	3	8	0	2	0	0	0	1	1	1	0	.250
Pete Coscarart	2b	3	7	1	0	0	0	0	0	1	2	0	.000
Jimmy Wasdell	ph-lf	3	5	0	1	1	0	0	2	0	0	0	.200
Augie Galan	ph	2	2	0	0	0	0	0	0	0	1	0	.000
Herman Franks	c	1	1	0	0	0	0	0	0	0	0	0	.000
Leo Durocher	Did not play												
Whit Wyatt	p	2	6	1	1	1	0	0	0	0	1	0	.167
Hugh Casey	p	3	2	0	1	0	0	0	0	0	1	0	.500
Curt Davis	p	1	2	0	0	0	0	0	0	0	0	0	.000
Freddie Fitzsimmons	p	1	2	0	0	0	0	0	0	0	0	0	.000
Kirby Higbe	p	1	1	0	1	0	0	0	0	0	0	0	1.000
Johnny Allen	p	3	0	0	0	0	0	0	0	0	0	0	.000
Larry French	p	2	0	0	0	0	0	0	0	0	0	0	.000
Luke Hamlin	Did not play												
Newt Kimball	Did not play												
Tom Drake	Did not play												
Ed Albosta	Did not play												
Team Total		5	159	11	29	7	2	1	11	14	21	0	.182

Double Plays—5   Left on Bases—27

PITCHING

	G	GS	CG	IP	H	R	ER	BB	SO	W	L	SV	ERA
New York													
Ernie Bonham	1	1	1	9	4	1	1	2	2	1	0	0	1.00
Red Ruffing	1	1	1	9	6	2	1	3	5	1	0	0	1.00
Marius Russo	1	1	1	9	4	1	1	2	5	1	0	0	1.00
Johnny Murphy	2	0	0	6	2	0	0	1	3	1	0	0	0.00
Spud Chandler	1	1	0	5	4	3	2	2	2	0	1	0	3.60
Atley Donald	1	1	0	4	6	4	4	3	2	0	0	0	9.00
Marv Breuer	1	0	0	3	3	0	0	1	2	0	0	0	0.00
Lefty Gomez	Did not play												
Steve Peek	Did not play												
Charley Stanceau	Did not play												
Norm Branch	Did not play												
Team Total	5	5	3	45	29	11	9	14	21	4	1	0	1.80
Brooklyn													
Whit Wyatt	2	2	2	18	15	5	5	10	14	1	1	0	2.50
Freddie Fitzsimmons	1	1	0	7	4	0	0	3	1	0	0	0	0.00
Hugh Casey	3	0	0	5⅓	9	6	2	2	1	0	2	0	3.38
Curt Davis	1	1	0	5⅓	6	3	3	3	1	0	1	0	5.06
Johnny Allen	3	0	0	3⅔	1	0	0	3	0	0	0	0	0.00
Kirby Higbe	1	1	0	3⅔	6	3	3	2	1	0	0	0	7.36
Larry French	2	0	0	1	0	0	0	0	0	0	0	0	0.00
Luke Hamlin	Did not play												
Newt Kimball	Did not play												
Tom Drake	Did not play												
Ed Albosta	Did not play												
Team Total	5	5	2	44	41	17	13	23	18	1	4	0	2.66

1942

St. Louis N.L. 4
New York A.L. 1

Highlights

FROM 1942 THROUGH 1946 the St. Louis Cardinals captured three World Championships in four Series appearances. Their first step was inauspicious as they lost, 7-4, to the Yankees, committing four errors and failing to hit safely until two outs in the eighth inning. But these '42 Cards were a young team that learned quickly.

Enos Slaughter made a rally-ending throw in the ninth inning of the second game, cutting down Tuck Stainback at third, to preserve a 4-3 victory and even the Series.

The Cards displayed splendid defense in game three, when in successive innings outfielders Terry Moore, Stan Musial and Slaughter made sensational catches off the bats of Joe DiMaggio, Joe Gordon and Charlie Keller to save a 2-0 victory.

The Cards continued their late-inning heroics in games four and five, with their bats. In their 9-6 victory in game four, Walker Cooper singled home Slaughter in the seventh inning with what proved to be the deciding run. In game five's 4-2 clincher, Whitey Kurowski slammed a ninth-inning two-run home run to send the Yanks home losers for the first time in nine successive World Series appearances. Their previous loss was in 1926, when the Cards edged them, 4-3.

Game 1 Sept. 30
New York	000 110 032 ·	7
St. Louis	000 000 004 ·	4

Winner-Ruffing Loser-M. Cooper

Game 2 Oct. 1
New York	000 000 030 ·	3
St. Louis	200 000 11* ·	4

Winner-Beazley Loser-Bonham

Game 3 Oct. 3
St. Louis	001 000 001 ·	2
New York	000 000 000 ·	0

Winner-White Loser-Chandler

Game 4 Oct. 4
St. Louis	000 600 201 ·	9
New York	100 005 000 ·	6

Winner-Lanier Loser-Donald

Game 5 Oct. 5
St. Louis	000 101 002 ·	4
New York	100 100 000 ·	2

Winner-Beazley Loser-Ruffing

Total Attendance—277,101
Average Attendance—55,420
Winning Player's Share—$6,193
Losing Player's Share—$3,352

BATTING

	Pos	G	AB	R	H	2B	3B	HR	RBI	BB	SO	SB	BA
St. Louis													
Johnny Hopp	1b	5	17	3	3	0	0	0	0	1	1	0	.176
Jimmy Brown	2b	5	20	2	6	0	0	0	1	3	0	0	.300
Marty Marion	ss	5	18	2	2	0	1	0	3	1	2	0	.111
Whitey Kurowski	3b	5	15	3	4	0	1	1	5	2	3	0	.267
Enos Slaughter	rf	5	19	3	5	1	0	1	2	3	2	0	.263
Terry Moore	cf	5	17	2	5	1	0	0	2	2	3	0	.294
Stan Musial	lf	5	18	2	4	1	0	0	2	4	0	0	.222
Walker Cooper	c	5	21	3	6	1	0	0	4	0	1	0	.286
Ray Sanders	ph	2	1	1	0	0	0	0	0	1	0	0	.000
Ken O'Dea	ph	1	1	0	1	0	0	0	1	0	0	0	1.000
Harry Walker	ph	1	1	0	0	0	0	0	0	0	1	0	.000
Creepy Crespi	pr	1	0	1	0	0	0	0	0	0	0	0	.000
Coaker Triplett	Did not play												
Sam Narron	Did not play												
Johnny Beazley	p	2	7	0	1	0	0	0	0	0	5	0	.143
Mort Cooper	p	2	5	1	1	0	0	0	2	0	1	0	.200
Ernie White	p	1	2	0	0	0	0	0	0	0	0	0	.000
Max Lanier	p	2	1	0	1	0	0	0	0	1	0	0	1.000
Harry Gumbert	p	2	0	0	0	0	0	0	0	0	0	0	.000
Howie Pollet	p	1	0	0	0	0	0	0	0	0	0	0	.000
Howie Krist	Did not play												
Murry Dickson	Did not play												
Whitey Moore	Did not play												
Team Total		5	163	23	39	4	2	2	23	17	19	0	.239

Double Plays—3   Left on Bases—32

	Pos	G	AB	R	H	2B	3B	HR	RBI	BB	SO	SB	BA
New York													
Jerry Priddy	3b-1b	3	10	0	1	1	0	0	1	1	0	6	.100
Joe Gordon	2b	5	21	1	2	1	0	0	0	0	7	0	.095
Phil Rizzuto	ss	5	21	2	8	0	0	1	1	2	1	2	.381
Red Rolfe	3b	4	17	5	6	2	0	0	0	1	2	0	.353
Roy Cullenbine	rf	5	19	3	5	1	0	0	2	1	2	1	.263
Joe DiMaggio	cf	5	21	3	7	0	0	0	3	0	1	0	.333
Charlie Keller	lf	5	20	2	4	0	0	2	5	1	3	0	.200
Bill Dickey	c	5	19	1	5	0	0	0	1	1	0	0	.263
Buddy Hassett	1b	3	9	1	3	1	0	0	2	0	1	0	.333
Frankie Crosetti	3b	1	3	0	0	0	0	0	0	0	1	0	.000
Buddy Rosar	ph	1	1	0	1	0	0	0	0	0	0	0	1.000
George Selkirk	ph	1	1	0	0	0	0	0	0	0	0	0	.000
Tuck Stainback	pr	2	0	0	0	0	0	0	0	0	0	0	.000
Rollie Hemsley	Did not play												
Tommy Henrich	Not in series—military												
Red Ruffing	p-ph	4	9	0	2	0	0	0	0	0	2	0	.222
Ernie Bonham	p	2	2	0	0	0	0	0	0	1	0	0	.000
Spud Chandler	p	2	2	0	0	0	0	0	0	0	1	0	.000
Atley Donald	p	1	2	0	0	0	0	0	0	0	0	0	.000
Hank Borowy	p	1	1	0	0	0	0	0	0	0	1	0	.000
Marv Breuer	p	1	0	0	0	0	0	0	0	0	0	0	.000
Jim Turner	p	1	0	0	0	0	0	0	0	0	0	0	.000
Lefty Gomez	Did not play												
Marius Russo	Did not play												
Johnny Murphy	Did not play												
Johnny Lindell	Did not play												
Team Total		5	178	18	44	6	0	3	14	8	22	3	.247

Double Plays—2   Left on Bases—34

PITCHING

	G	GS	CG	IP	H	R	ER	BB	SO	W	L	SV	ERA
St. Louis													
Johnny Beazley	2	2	2	18	17	5	5	3	6	2	0	0	2.50
Mort Cooper	2	2	0	13	17	10	8	4	9	0	1	0	5.54
Ernie White	1	1	1	9	6	0	0	6	1	1	0	0	0.00
Max Lanier	2	0	0	4	3	2	0	1	1	1	0	0	0.00
Harry Gumbert	2	0	0	⅔	1	1	0	0	0	0	0	0	0.00
Howie Pollet	1	0	0	⅓	0	0	0	0	0	0	0	0	0.00
Howie Krist	Did not play												
Murry Dickson	Did not play												
Whitey Moore	Did not play												
Team Total	5	5	3	45	44	18	13	8	22	4	1	0	2.60
New York													
Red Ruffing	2	2	1	17⅔	14	8	8	7	11	1	1	0	4.08
Ernie Bonham	2	1	1	11	9	5	5	3	3	0	1	0	4.09
Spud Chandler	2	1	0	8⅓	5	1	1	1	3	0	1	1	1.08
Hank Borowy	1	1	0	3	6	6	6	3	1	0	0	0	18.00
Atley Donald	1	0	0	3	3	2	2	2	1	0	1	0	6.00
Jim Turner	1	0	0	1	0	0	0	1	0	0	0	0	0.00
Marv Breuer	1	0	0	0	2	1	0	0	0	0	0	0	0.00
Lefty Gomez	Did not play												
Marius Russo	Did not play												
Johnny Murphy	Did not play												
Johnny Lindell	Did not play												
Team Total	5	5	2	44	39	23	22	17	19	1	4	1	4.50

1943

New York A.L. 4
St. Louis N.L. 1

Highlights

BOTH TEAMS WERE DEPLETED by the call to arms. The Yanks lost Joe DiMaggio, Phil Rizzuto, Red Ruffing and Buddy Hassett. The Cards lost Enos Slaughter, Terry Moore, Jimmy Brown, Johnny Beazley and Howie Pollet to the military, and general manager Branch Rickey, who left to take over the Brooklyn Dodgers.

The Cards and Yanks traded victories in the first two games, first a 4-2 victory by the Yanks and then a 4-3 victory by the Cards. The Cards' pitcher-catcher brothers, Mort and Walker Cooper, lost their father on the morning of the game.

The Yanks dominated the rest of the Series, running off 6-2, 2-1 and 2-0 victories. Their pitching staff posted an outstanding 1.46 ERA, and held all the Cards' regulars under .300 at the plate except Marty Marion, who hit .357.

Wartime limitations on travel changed the scheduling format; the first three games were played in New York and all necessary remaining games in St. Louis.

Game 1 Oct. 5
St. Louis	010 010 000 - 2
New York	000 202 00* - 4
Winner-Chandler	Loser-Lanier

Game 2 Oct. 6
St. Louis	001 300 000 - 4
New York	000 100 002 - 3
Winner-M. Cooper	Loser-Bonham

Game 3 Oct. 7
St. Louis	000 200 000 - 2
New York	000 001 05* - 6
Winner-Borowy	Loser-Brazle

Game 4 Oct. 10
New York	000 100 010 - 2
St. Louis	000 000 100 - 1
Winner-Russo	Loser-Brecheen

Game 5 Oct. 11
New York	000 002 000 - 2
St. Louis	000 000 000 - 0
Winner-Chandler	Loser-M. Cooper

Total Attendance—277,312
Average Attendance—55,462
Winning Player's Share—$6,139
Losing Player's Share—$4,322

BATTING	Pos	G	AB	R	H	2B	3B	HR	RBI	BB	SO	SB	BA
New York													
Nick Etten	1b	5	19	0	2	0	0	0	2	1	2	0	.105
Joe Gordon	2b	5	17	2	4	1	0	1	2	3	3	0	.235
Frankie Crosetti	ss	5	18	4	5	0	0	0	1	2	3	1	.278
Billy Johnson	3b	5	20	3	6	1	1	0	3	0	3	0	.300
Johnny Lindell	cf-rf	4	9	1	1	0	0	0	0	1	4	0	.111
Tuck Stainback	rf-cf	5	17	0	3	0	0	0	0	0	2	0	.176
Charlie Keller	lf	5	18	3	4	0	1	0	2	2	5	1	.222
Bill Dickey	c	5	18	1	5	0	0	1	4	2	2	0	.278
Bud Methany	rf	2	8	0	1	0	0	0	0	0	2	0	.125
Snuffy Stirnweiss	ph	1	1	1	0	0	0	0	0	0	0	0	.000
Roy Weatherly	ph	1	1	0	0	0	0	0	0	0	0	0	.000
Ken Sears		Did not play											
Rollie Hemsley		Did not play											
Oscar Grimes		Did not play											
Spud Chandler	p	2	6	0	1	0	0	0	0	0	2	0	.167
Marius Russo	p	1	3	1	2	2	0	0	0	1	1	0	.667
Hank Borowy	p	1	2	1	1	1	0	0	0	0	1	0	.500
Ernie Bonham	p	1	2	0	0	0	0	0	0	0	0	0	.000
Johnny Murphy	p	2	0	0	0	0	0	0	0	0	0	0	.000
Butch Wensloff		Did not play											
Bill Zuber		Did not play											
Atley Donald		Did not play											
Jim Turner		Did not play											
Tommy Byrne		Did not play											
Marv Breuer		Did not play											
Team Total		5	159	17	35	5	2	2	14	12	30	2	.220
		Double Plays—3		Left on Bases—30									
St. Louis													
Ray Sanders	1b	5	17	3	5	0	0	1	2	3	4	0	.294
Lou Klein	2b	5	22	0	3	0	0	0	0	1	2	0	.136
Marty Marion	ss	5	14	1	5	2	0	1	2	3	1	1	**.357**
Whitey Kurowski	3b	5	18	2	4	1	0	0	1	0	3	0	.222
Stan Musial	rf	5	18	2	5	0	0	0	2	2	2	0	.278
Harry Walker	cf-ph	5	18	0	3	1	0	0	0	0	2	0	.167
Danny Litwhiler	lf-ph	5	15	0	4	1	0	0	2	2	4	0	.267
Walker Cooper	c	5	17	1	5	0	0	0	0	0	1	0	.294
Debs Garms	ph-lf	2	5	0	0	0	0	0	0	0	2	0	.000
Johnny Hopp	cf	1	4	0	0	0	0	0	0	0	1	0	.000
Ken O'Dea	ph-c	2	3	0	2	0	0	0	0	0	0	0	.667
Frank Demaree	ph	1	1	0	0	0	0	0	0	0	0	0	.000
Sam Narron	ph	1	1	0	0	0	0	0	0	0	0	0	.000
George Fallon		Did not play											
Mort Cooper	p	2	5	0	0	0	0	0	0	0	3	0	.000
Max Lanier	p	3	4	0	1	0	0	0	1	0	0	0	.250
Al Brazle	p	1	3	0	0	0	0	0	0	0	1	0	.000
Harry Brecheen	p	3	0	0	0	0	0	0	0	0	0	0	.000
Murry Dickson	p	1	0	0	0	0	0	0	0	0	0	0	.000
Howie Krist	p	1	0	0	0	0	0	0	0	0	0	0	.000
Ernie White	pr	1	0	0	0	0	0	0	0	0	0	0	.000
Harry Gumbert		Did not play											
George Munger		Did not play											
Team Total		5	165	9	37	5	0	2	8	11	26	1	.224
		Double Plays—4		Left on Bases—37									

PITCHING	G	GS	CG	IP	H	R	ER	BB	SO	W	L	SV	ERA
New York													
Spud Chandler	2	2	2	18	17	2	1	3	10	2	0	0	0.50
Marius Russo	1	1	1	9	7	1	0	1	2	1	0	0	**0.00**
Hank Borowy	1	1	0	8	6	2	2	3	4	1	0	0	2.25
Ernie Bonham	1	1	0	8	6	4	4	3	9	0	1	0	4.50
Johnny Murphy	2	0	0	2	1	0	0	1	1	0	0	1	0.00
Butch Wensloff		Did not play											
Bill Zuber		Did not play											
Atley Donald		Did not play											
Jim Turner		Did not play											
Tommy Byrne		Did not play											
Marv Breuer		Did not play											
Team Total	5	5	3	45	37	9	7	11	26	4	1	1	1.46
St. Louis													
Mort Cooper	2	2	1	16	11	5	**5**	3	10	1	1	0	2.81
Max Lanier	**3**	2	0	15⅓	13	5	3	3	13	0	1	0	1.76
Al Brazle	1	1	0	7⅓	5	6	3	2	4	0	1	0	3.68
Harry Brecheen	**3**	0	0	3⅔	5	1	1	3	3	0	1	0	2.45
Murry Dickson	1	0	0	⅔	0	0	0	1	0	0	0	0	0.00
Howie Krist	1	0	0	0	1	0	0	0	0	0	0	0	0.00
Harry Gumbert		Did not play											
George Munger		Did not play											
Ernie White		Did not pitch											
Team Total	5	5	1	43	35	17	12	12	30	1	4	0	2.51

1944

St. Louis N.L. 4
St. Louis A.L. 2

Highlights

THE ONE AND ONLY ALL-ST. Louis Series turned out to be a cakewalk for the Cardinals, who trounced their American League rivals, four games to two, and a disappointment to the Browns, who barely made their only Series appearance by edging out the Yankees on the last day of the season. In game one, the Browns made two hits stand up for a 2-1 victory but then dropped the second game, 3-2, in eleven innings. Rookie Cardinal reliever Blix Donnelly was the star of this extra-inning drama as he picked up the victory by pitching four shutout innings and striking out seven. The Cards lost game three, 6-2, but came back to take three straight, holding the Browns to three runs over the last 27 innings.

Browns made ten errors and batted only .183 in the six games while surprisingly, their pitching staff held up against the hard-hitting Cardinals lineup with a respectable 1.49 ERA.

Sportman's Park, site of the Series, was owned by the Browns but used by both clubs.

Game 1	Oct. 4		
Browns	000 200 000	-	2
Cardinals	000 000 001	-	1
Winner-Galehouse	Loser-M. Cooper		

Game 2	Oct. 5		
Browns	000 000 200 00	-	2
Cardinals	001 100 000 01	-	3
Winner-Donnelly	Loser-Muncrief		

Game 3	Oct. 6		
Cardinals	100 000 100	-	2
Browns	004 000 20*	-	6
Winner-Kramer	Loser-Wilks		

Game 4	Oct. 7		
Cardinals	202 001 000	-	5
Browns	000 000 010	-	1
Winner-Brecheen	Loser-Jakucki		

Game 5	Oct. 8		
Cardinals	000 001 010	-	2
Browns	000 000 000	-	0
Winner-M. Cooper	Loser-Galehouse		

Game 6	Oct. 9		
Browns	010 000 000	-	1
Cardinals	000 300 00*	-	3
Winner-Lanier	Loser-Potter		

Total Attendance—206,708
Average Attendance—34,451
Winning Player's Share—$4,626
Losing Player's Share—$2,744

BATTING	Pos	G	AB	R	H	2B	3B	HR	RBI	BB	SO	SB	BA
St. Louis Cardinals													
Ray Sanders	1b	6	21	5	6	0	0	1	1	5	8	0	.286
Emil Verban	2b	6	17	1	7	0	0	0	2	2	0	0	.412
Marty Marion	ss	6	22	1	5	3	0	0	2	2	3	0	.227
Whitey Kurowski	3b	6	23	2	5	1	0	0	1	1	4	0	.217
Stan Musial	rf	6	23	2	7	2	0	1	2	2	0	0	.304
Johnny Hopp	cf	6	27	2	5	0	0	0	0	0	8	0	.185
Danny Litwhiler	lf	6	20	2	4	1	0	1	1	2	7	0	.200
Walker Cooper	c	6	22	1	7	2	1	0	2	3	2	0	.318
Augie Bergamo	ph-lf	3	6	0	0	0	0	0	1	2	3	0	.000
George Fallon	2b	2	2	0	0	0	0	0	0	0	1	0	.000
Ken O'Dea	ph	3	3	0	1	0	0	0	2	2	0	0	.333
Debs Garms	ph	2	2	0	0	0	0	0	0	0	0	0	.000
Pepper Martin		Did not play											
Bob Keely		Did not play											
Mort Cooper	p	2	4	0	0	0	0	0	0	0	2	0	.000
Max Lanier	p	2	4	0	2	0	0	0	1	0	0	0	.500
Harry Brecheen	p	1	4	0	0	0	0	0	0	0	1	0	.000
Ted Wilks	p	2	2	0	0	0	0	0	0	0	2	0	.000
Blix Donnelly	p	2	1	0	0	0	0	0	0	0	1	0	.000
Freddie Schmidt	p	1	1	0	0	0	0	0	0	0	1	0	.000
Bud Byerly	p	1	0	0	0	0	0	0	0	0	0	0	.000
Al Jurisich	p	1	0	0	0	0	0	0	0	0	0	0	.000
George Munger		Not in series—military service											
Team Total		6	204	16	49	9	1	3	15	19	43	0	.240
		Double Plays—3			Left on Bases—51								
St. Louis Browns													
George McQuinn	1b	6	16	2	7	2	0	1	5	7	2	0	**.438**
Don Gutteridge	2b	6	21	1	3	1	0	0	0	3	5	0	.143
Vern Stephens	ss	6	22	2	5	1	0	0	0	3	3	0	.227
Mark Christman	3b	6	22	0	2	0	0	0	1	0	6	0	.091
Gene Moore	rf	6	22	4	4	0	0	0	0	3	6	0	.182
Mike Kreevich	cf	6	26	0	6	3	0	0	0	0	5	0	.231
Chet Laabs	lf-ph	5	15	1	3	1	1	0	0	2	6	0	.200
Red Hayworth	c	6	17	1	2	1	0	0	1	3	1	0	.118
Al Zarilla	ph-lf	4	10	1	1	0	0	0	1	0	4	0	.100
Frank Mancuso	ph-c	2	3	0	2	0	0	0	0	1	0	0	.667
Floyd Baker	ph-2b	2	2	0	0	0	0	0	0	0	2	0	.000
Milt Byrnes	ph	3	2	0	0	0	0	0	0	1	2	0	.000
Mike Chartak	ph	2	2	0	0	0	0	0	0	0	2	0	.000
Ellis Clary	ph	1	1	0	0	0	0	0	0	0	0	0	.000
Tom Turner	ph	1	1	0	0	0	0	0	0	0	0	0	.000
Denny Galehouse	p	2	5	0	1	0	0	0	0	1	1	0	.200
Jack Kramer	p	2	4	0	0	0	0	0	0	0	2	0	.000
Neis Potter	p	2	4	0	0	0	0	0	0	0	1	0	.000
Bob Muncrief	p	2	1	0	0	0	0	0	0	0	1	0	.000
Al Hollingsworth	p	1	1	0	0	0	0	0	0	0	0	0	.000
Sig Jakucki	p	1	0	0	0	0	0	0	0	0	0	0	.000
Tex Shirley	pr-p	2	0	0	0	0	0	0	0	0	0	0	.000
George Caster		Did not play											
Willis Hudlin		Did not play											
Sam Zoldak		Did not play											
Team Total		6	197	12	36	9	1	1	9	23	49	0	.183
		Double Plays—4			Left on Bases—44								

PITCHING	G	GS	CG	IP	H	R	ER	BB	SO	W	L	SV	ERA
St. Louis Cardinals													
Mort Cooper	2	2	1	16	9	2	2	5	16	1	1	0	1.13
Max Lanier	2	2	0	12⅓	8	3	3	8	11	1	0	0	2.79
Harry Brecheen	1	1	1	9	9	1	1	4	4	1	0	0	1.00
Ted Wilks	2	1	0	6⅓	5	4	4	3	7	0	1	1	5.68
Blix Donnelly	2	0	0	6	2	0	0	1	9	1	0	0	0.00
Freddy Schmidt	1	0	0	3⅓	1	0	0	1	1	0	0	0	0.00
Bud Byerly	1	0	0	1⅓	0	0	0	0	1	0	0	0	0.00
Al Jurisich	1	0	0	⅔	2	2	2	1	0	0	0	0	27.00
George Munger	Not in series—military service												
Team Total	6	6	2	55	36	12	12	23	49	4	2	1	1.96
St. Louis Browns													
Denny Galehouse	2	2	2	18	13	3	3	5	15	1	1	0	1.50
Jack Kramer	2	1	1	11	9	2	0	4	12	1	0	0	0.00
Neis Potter	2	2	0	9⅔	10	5	1	3	6	0	1	0	0.93
Bob Muncrief	2	0	0	6⅔	5	1	1	4	4	0	1	0	1.35
Al Hollingsworth	1	0	0	4	5	1	1	2	1	0	0	0	2.25
Sig Jakucki	1	1	0	3	5	4	3	0	4	0	1	0	9.00
Tex Shirley	1	0	0	2	2	0	0	1	1	0	0	0	0.00
George Caster	Did not play												
Willis Hudlin	Did not play												
Sam Zoldak	Did not play												
Team Total	6	6	3	54⅓	49	16	9	19	43	2	4	0	1.49

1945

Detroit A.L. 4
Chicago N.L. 3

Highlights

VIRGIL TRUCKS AND HANK Greenberg, two World War II veterans, returned to the Tigers in time to help make them World Champions. Greenberg rejoined the team from the Army Air Force after the war in Europe ended in May; Trucks, who got his discharge from the Navy after the Japanese surrender in August, came aboard on the last day of the season to pitch the pennant clincher for the Tigers. The duo combined their talents in the second game of the Series to gain the Tigers their initial victory: Trucks went the route, scattering seven hits and striking out four, while Greenberg slammed a three-run homer in the fifth to provide the margin of victory, 4-1.

The final war Series also marked the last World Series appearance of pitcher Hank Borowy, who appeared in 1942 and 1943 with the Yankees, and with the Cubs in 1945, after he won 21 games playing in two leagues, 10 games for the Yankees and 11 for the Cubs. He appeared in four games against the Tigers, posting a 2-2 record.

Game 1 Oct. 3
Chicago	403 000 200 ·	9
Detroit	000 000 000 ·	0

Winner-Borowy Loser-Newhouser

Game 2 Oct. 4
Chicago	000 100 000 ·	1
Detroit	000 040 00* ·	4

Winner-Trucks Loser-Wyse

Game 3 Oct. 5
Chicago	000 200 100 ·	3
Detroit	000 000 000 ·	0

Winner-Passeau Loser-Overmire

Game 4 Oct. 6
Detroit	000 400 000 ·	4
Chicago	000 001 000 ·	1

Winner-Trout Loser-Prim

Game 5 Oct. 7
Detroit	001 004 102 ·	8
Chicago	001 000 201 ·	4

Winner-Newhouser Loser-Borowy

Game 6 Oct. 8
Detroit	010 000 240 000 ·	7
Chicago	000 041 200 001 ·	8

Winner-Borowy Loser-Trout

Game 7 Oct. 10
Detroit	510 000 120 ·	9
Chicago	100 100 010 ·	3

Winner-Newhouser Loser-Borowy

Total Attendance—333,457
Average Attendance—47,639
Winning Player's Share—$6,443
Losing Player's Share—$3,930

BATTING	Pos	G	AB	R	H	2B	3B	HR	RBI	BB	SO	SB	BA
Detroit													
Rudy York	1b	7	28	1	5	1	0	0	3	3	4	0	.179
Eddie Mayo	2b	7	28	4	7	1	0	0	2	2	2	0	.250
Skeeter Webb	ss	7	27	4	5	0	0	0	1	3	1	0	.185
Jimmy Outlaw	3b	7	28	1	5	0	0	0	3	2	1	1	.179
Roy Cullenbine	rf	7	22	5	5	2	0	0	4	8	2	1	.227
Doc Cramer	cf	7	29	7	11	0	0	0	4	1	0	1	.379
Hank Greenberg	lf	7	23	7	7	3	0	2	7	6	5	0	.304
Paul Richards	c	7	19	0	4	2	0	0	6	4	3	0	.211
Bob Swift	c	3	4	1	1	0	0	0	0	2	0	0	.250
Joe Hoover	ss	1	3	1	1	0	0	0	1	0	0	0	.333
Chuck Hostetler	ph	3	3	0	0	0	0	0	0	0	0	0	.000
John McHale	ph	3	3	0	0	0	0	0	0	0	1	0	.000
Hub Walker	ph	2	2	1	1	1	0	0	0	0	0	0	.500
Bob Maier	ph	1	1	0	1	0	0	0	0	0	0	0	1.000
Red Borom	ph	2	1	0	0	0	0	0	0	0	0	0	.000
Ed Mierkowicz	lf	1	0	0	0	0	0	0	0	0	0	0	.000
Zeb Eaton	ph	1	1	0	0	0	0	0	0	0	0	0	.000
Hal Newhouser	p	3	8	0	0	0	0	0	1	1	1	0	.000
Dizzy Trout	p	2	6	0	1	0	0	0	0	0	0	0	.167
Virgil Trucks	p	2	4	0	0	0	0	0	0	1	1	0	.000
Stubby Overmire	p	1	1	0	0	0	0	0	0	0	0	0	.000
Jim Tobin	p	1	1	0	0	0	0	0	0	0	0	0	.000
Al Benton	p	3	0	0	0	0	0	0	0	0	0	0	.000
Tommy Bridges	p	1	0	0	0	0	0	0	0	0	0	0	.000
George Caster	p	1	0	0	0	0	0	0	0	0	0	0	.000
Les Mueller	p	1	0	0	0	0	0	0	0	0	0	0	.000
Team Total		7	242	32	54	10	0	2	32	33	22	3	.223

Double Plays—4   Left on Bases—53

BATTING	Pos	G	AB	R	H	2B	3B	HR	RBI	BB	SO	SB	BA
Chicago													
Phil Cavarretta	1b	7	26	7	11	2	0	1	5	4	3	0	**.423**
Don Johnson	2b	7	29	4	5	2	1	0	0	0	8	1	.172
Roy Hughes	ss	6	17	1	5	1	0	0	3	4	5	0	.294
Stan Hack	3b	7	30	1	11	3	0	0	4	4	2	0	.367
Bill Nicholson	rf	7	28	1	6	1	1	0	8	2	5	0	.214
Andy Pafko	cf	7	28	5	6	2	1	0	2	2	5	1	.214
Peanuts Lowrey	lf	7	29	4	9	1	0	0	0	1	2	0	.310
Mickey Livingston	c	6	22	3	8	3	0	0	4	1	1	0	.364
Paul Gillespie	ph-c	3	6	0	0	0	0	0	0	0	0	0	.000
Frank Secory	ph	5	5	0	2	0	0	0	0	0	2	0	.400
Heinz Becker	ph	3	2	0	1	0	0	0	0	1	1	0	.500
Lenny Merullo	ss-pr	3	2	0	0	0	0	0	0	0	1	0	.000
Ed Sauer	ph	2	2	0	0	0	0	0	0	0	2	0	.000
Dewey Williams	ph-c	2	2	0	0	0	0	0	0	0	1	0	.000
Bill Schuster	ss-pr	2	1	1	0	0	0	0	0	0	0	0	.000
Clyde McCullough	ph	1	1	0	0	0	0	0	0	0	1	0	.000
Cy Block	pr	1	0	0	0	0	0	0	0	0	0	0	.000
Claude Passeau	p	3	7	1	1	0	0	0	1	0	4	0	.000
Hank Borowy	p	4	6	1	1	1	0	0	0	0	3	0	.167
Hank Wyse	p	3	3	0	0	0	0	0	0	0	2	0	.000
Hy Vandenberg	p	3	1	0	0	0	0	0	0	0	0	0	.000
Paul Erickson	p	4	0	0	0	0	0	0	0	0	0	0	.000
Paul Derringer	p	3	0	0	0	0	0	0	0	0	0	0	.000
Ray Prim	p	2	0	0	0	0	0	0	0	0	0	0	.000
Bob Chipman	p	1	0	0	0	0	0	0	0	0	0	0	.000
Team Total		7	247	29	65	16	3	1	27	19	48	2	.263

Double Plays—5   Left on Bases—50

PITCHING	G	GS	CG	IP	H	R	ER	BB	SO	W	L	SV	ERA
Detroit													
Hal Newhouser	3	3	2	20²/₃	25	14	14	4	22	2	1	0	6.10
Dizzy Trout	2	1	1	13²/₃	9	2	1	3	9	1	1	0	**0.66**
Virgil Trucks	2	2	1	13¹/₃	14	5	5	5	7	1	0	0	3.38
Stubby Overmire	1	1	0	6	4	2	2	2	2	0	1	0	3.00
Al Benton	3	0	0	4²/₃	6	1	1	0	5	0	0	0	1.93
Jim Tobin	1	0	0	3	4	2	2	1	0	0	0	0	6.00
Les Mueller	1	0	0	2	0	0	0	1	1	0	0	0	0.00
Tommy Bridges	1	0	0	1²/₃	3	3	3	3	1	0	0	0	16.20
George Caster	1	0	0	²/₃	0	0	0	0	1	0	0	0	0.00
Team Total	7	7	4	65²/₃	65	29	28	19	48	4	3	0	3.84
Chicago													
Hank Borowy	4	3	1	18	21	8	8	6	8	2	2	0	4.00
Claude Passeau	3	2	1	16²/₃	7	5	5	8	3	1	0	0	2.70
Hank Wyse	3	1	0	7²/₃	8	7	6	4	1	0	1	0	7.04
Paul Erickson	4	0	0	7	8	3	3	5	5	0	0	0	3.86
Hy Vandenberg	3	0	0	6	1	0	0	3	3	0	0	0	0.00
Paul Derringer	3	0	0	5¹/₃	5	4	4	7	1	0	0	0	6.75
Ray Prim	2	1	0	4	4	5	4	1	1	0	1	0	9.00
Bob Chipman	1	0	0	¹/₃	0	0	0	1	0	0	0	0	0.00
Team Total	7	7	2	65	54	32	30	33	22	3	4	0	4.15

1946

St. Louis N.L. 4
Boston A.L. 3

Highlights

THE FIRST PLAYOFF IN NATIONAL League history pitted the Brooklyn Dodgers against the St. Louis Cardinals, with the Cards sweeping two games to none, to gain the flag.

Cards edged Boston, four games to three, when Enos Slaughter made his famous dash to score all the way from first base on Harry Walker's two-out single to left center in the eighth inning of game seven.

Harry "The Cat" Brecheen was the pitching star for the Cards. After saving the final play-off victory against the Dodgers, he won three games in the Series, giving up 14 hits in 20 innings and posting a stingy 0.45 ERA.

Batting stars in the Series for the victorious Cards were Harry "The Hat" Walker, .420, and Enos Slaughter, .320. Joe Garagiola compiled a robust .383 batting average for the play-offs and the Series, including one game in which he collected four hits.

Stars who failed to shine included Stan Musial, who batted .222 in the Series after batting a league-leading .365 during the regular season, and American League MVP Ted Williams, who batted .200 after posting a .342 regular-season average that included 38 home runs and 156 RBI's.

Game 1 Oct. 6

Boston	010 000 001 1	-	3
St. Louis	000 001 0100	-	2

Winner-Johnson Loser-Pollet

Game 2 Oct. 7

Boston	000 000 000	-	0
St. Louis	001 020 00*	-	3

Winner-Brecheen Loser-Harris

Game 3 Oct. 9

St. Louis	000 000 000	-	0
Boston	300 000 01*	-	4

Winner-Ferriss Loser-Dickson

Game 4 Oct. 10

St. Louis	033 010 104	-	12
Boston	000 100 020	-	3

Winner-Munger Loser-Hughson

Game 5 Oct. 11

St. Louis	010 000 002	-	3
Boston	110 001 30*	-	6

Winner-Dobson Loser-Brazle

Game 6 Oct. 13

Boston	000 000 100	-	1
St. Louis	003 000 01*	-	4

Winner-Brecheen Loser-Harris

Game 7 Oct. 15

Boston	100 000 020	-	3
St. Louis	010 020 01*	-	4

Winner-Brecheen Loser-Klinger

Total Attendance—250,071
Average Attendance—35,724
Winning Player's Share—$3,742
Losing Player's Share—$2,141

BATTING	Pos	G	AB	R	H	2B	3B	HR	RBI	BB	SO	SB	BA
St. Louis													
Stan Musial	1b	7	27	3	6	4	1	0	4	4	2	1	.222
Red Schoendienst	2b	7	30	3	7	1	0	0	1	0	2	1	.233
Marty Marion	ss	7	24	1	6	2	0	0	4	1	1	0	.250
Whitey Kurowski	3b	7	27	5	8	3	0	0	2	0	3	0	.296
Enos Slaughter	rf	7	25	5	8	1	1	1	2	4	3	1	.320
Terry Moore	cf	7	27	1	4	0	0	0	2	2	6	0	.148
Harry Walker	lf-rf-ph	7	17	3	7	2	0	0	6	4	2	0	.412
Joe Garagiola	c	5	19	2	6	2	0	0	4	0	3	0	.316
Del Rice	c	3	6	2	3	1	0	0	0	2	0	0	.500
Erv Dusak	ph-lf	4	4	0	1	1	0	0	0	2	2	0	.250
Dick Sisler	ph	2	2	0	0	0	0	0	0	0	0	0	.000
Nippy Jones	ph	1	1	0	0	0	0	0	0	0	1	0	.000
Harry Brecheen	p	3	8	2	1	0	0	0	0	1	0	1	.125
Murry Dickson	p	2	5	1	2	2	0	0	1	0	1	0	.400
George Munger	p	1	4	0	1	0	0	0	0	0	2	0	.250
Howie Pollet	p	2	4	0	0	0	0	0	0	0	0	0	.000
Al Brazie	p	1	2	0	0	0	0	0	0	0	0	0	.000
Johnny Beazley	p	1	0	0	0	0	0	0	0	0	0	0	.000
Ted Wilks	p	1	0	0	0	0	0	0	0	0	0	0	.000
Team Total		7	232	28	60	19	2	1	27	19	30	3	.259

Double Plays—7   Left on Bases—50

BATTING	Pos	G	AB	R	H	2B	3B	HR	RBI	BB	SO	SB	BA
Boston													
Rudy York	1b	7	23	6	6	1	1	2	5	6	4	0	.261
Bobby Doerr	2b	6	22	1	9	1	0	1	3	2	2	0	.409
Johnny Pesky	ss	7	30	2	7	0	0	0	0	1	3	1	.233
Pinky Higgins	3b	7	24	1	5	1	0	0	2	2	0	0	.208
Wally Moses	rf	4	12	1	5	0	0	0	0	1	2	0	.417
Dom DiMaggio	cf	7	27	2	7	3	0	0	3	2	2	0	.259
Ted Williams	lf	7	25	2	5	0	0	0	1	5	5	0	.200
Hal Wagner	c	5	13	0	0	0	0	0	0	0	1	0	.000
Tom McBride	rf-ph	5	12	0	2	0	0	0	1	0	1	0	.167
Roy Partee	ph-c	5	10	1	1	0	0	0	1	1	2	0	.100
Leon Culberson	rf-cf	5	9	1	2	0	0	1	1	1	2	1	.222
Don Gutteridge	pr-2b	3	5	1	2	0	0	0	0	1	0	0	.400
Rip Russell	ph-3b	2	2	1	2	0	0	0	0	0	0	0	1.000
Catfish Metkovich	ph	2	2	1	1	1	0	0	0	0	0	0	.500
Paul Campbell	pr	1	0	0	0	0	0	0	0	0	0	0	.000
Boo Ferriss	p	2	6	0	0	0	0	0	0	0	1	0	.000
Mickey Harris	p	2	3	0	1	0	0	0	0	0	1	0	.333
Tex Hughson	p	3	3	0	1	0	0	0	0	1	0	0	.333
Joe Dobson	p	3	3	0	0	0	0	0	0	0	2	0	.000
Earl Johnson	p	3	1	0	0	0	0	0	0	0	0	0	.000
Jim Bagby	p	1	1	0	0	0	0	0	0	0	0	0	.000
Mace Brown	p	1	0	0	0	0	0	0	0	0	0	0	.000
Clem Dreisewerd	p	1	0	0	0	0	0	0	0	0	0	0	.000
Bob Klinger	p	1	0	0	0	0	0	0	0	0	0	0	.000
Mike Ryba	p	1	0	0	0	0	0	0	0	0	0	0	.000
Bill Zuber	p	1	0	0	0	0	0	0	0	0	0	0	.000
Team Total		7	233	20	56	7	1	4	18	22	28	2	.240

Double Plays—5   Left on Bases—53

PITCHING	G	GS	CG	IP	H	R	ER	BB	SO	W	L	SV	ERA
St. Louis													
Harry Brecheen	3	2	2	20	14	1	1	5	11	3	0	0	0.45
Murry Dickson	2	2	0	14	11	6	6	4	7	0	1	0	3.86
Howie Pollet	2	2	1	10⅓	12	4	4	4	3	0	1	0	3.48
George Munger	1	1	1	9	9	3	1	3	2	1	0	0	1.00
Al Brazle	1	0	0	6⅔	7	5	4	6	4	0	1	0	5.40
Johnny Beazley	1	0	0	1	1	0	0	0	1	0	0	0	0.00
Ted Wilks	1	0	0	1	2	1	0	0	0	0	0	0	0.00
Team Total	7	7	4	62	56	20	16	22	28	4	3	0	2.32
Boston													
Tex Hughson	3	2	0	14⅓	14	8	5	3	8	0	1	0	3.14
Boo Ferriss	2	2	1	13⅓	13	3	3	2	4	1	0	0	2.03
Joe Dobson	3	1	1	12⅔	4	3	0	3	10	1	0	0	0.00
Mickey Harris	2	2	0	9⅔	11	6	4	4	5	0	2	0	3.72
Earl Johnson	3	0	0	3⅓	1	1	1	2	1	1	0	0	2.70
Jim Bagby	1	0	0	3	6	1	1	1	1	0	0	0	3.00
Bill Zuber	1	0	0	2	3	1	1	1	1	0	0	0	4.50
Mace Brown	1	0	0	1	4	3	3	1	0	0	0	0	27.00
Mike Ryba	1	0	0	⅔	2	1	1	1	0	0	0	0	13.50
Bob Klinger	1	0	0	⅔	2	1	1	1	0	0	1	0	13.50
Clem Dreisewerd	1	0	0	⅓	0	0	0	0	0	0	0	0	0.00
Team Total	7	7	2	61	60	28	20	19	30	3	4	0	2.95

1947

New York A.L. 4
Brooklyn N.L. 3

Highlights

THE DODGERS MADE HISTORY during the regular season by inserting Jackie Robinson in their lineup at first base—the first black man to play in the major leagues. Robinson sparked the Dodgers to the pennant with his all-around play, which included a league-leading total of 29 stolen bases and a solid .297 batting average.

The Yankees won first two games but trailed, 9-7 in the seventh inning. of game three. Then rookie catcher Yogi Berra, batting for Sherman Lollar, blasted the first World Series pinch-hit home run. But it wasn't enough. The Dodgers hung on to win, 9-8.

Game four was high drama. Dodger Cookie Lavagetto, batting for regular Eddie Stanky in the bottom of the ninth, doubled to drive in two runs and break up Yankee right-hander Bill Bevens' bid for the fall classic's first no-hit game. Dodgers won 3-2.

Hero of game six, played in Yankee Stadium, was Al Gionfriddo who entered the game in left field in the bottom of the sixth. Dodgers led, 8-5. With two men on base, Joe DiMaggio drove a long fly to deep left center. It appeared to be at least a double, maybe a homer. But Gionfriddo backhanded the ball at the 415-foot mark to end the rally and preserve the Dodgers' victory.

Yanks eventually took game seven, 5-2, behind five shutout innings of relief pitching by Joe Page.

Game 1 Sept. 30
Brooklyn   100 001 100 · 3
New York   000 050 00* · 5
Winner-Shea   Loser-Branca

Game 2 Oct. 1
Brooklyn   001 100 001 · 3
New York   101 121 40* · 10
Winner-Reynolds   Loser-Lombardi

Game 3 Oct. 2
New York   002 221 100 · 8
Brooklyn   061 200 00* · 9
Winner-Casey   Loser-Newsom

Game 4 Oct. 3
New York   100 100 000 · 2
Brooklyn   000 010 002 · 3
Winner-Casey   Loser-Bevens

Game 5 Oct. 4
New York   000 110 000 · 2
Brooklyn   000 001 000 · 1
Winner-Shea   Loser-Barney

Game 6 Oct. 5
Brooklyn   202 004 000 · 8
New York   004 100 001 · 6
Winner-Branca   Loser-Page

Game 7 Oct. 6
Brooklyn   020 000 000 · 2
New York   010 201 10* · 5
Winner-Page   Loser-Gregg

Total Attendance—389,763
Average Attendance—55,680
Winning Player's Share—$5,830
Losing Player's Share—$4,081

BATTING	Pos	G	AB	R	H	2B	3B	HR	RBI	BB	SO	SB	BA
New York													
George McQuinn	1b	7	23	3	3	0	0	0	1	5	8	0	.130
Snuffy Stirnweiss	2b	7	27	3	7	0	1	0	3	8	8	0	.259
Phil Rizzuto	ss	7	26	3	8	1	0	0	2	4	0	2	.308
Billy Johnson	3b	7	26	8	7	0	3	0	2	3	4	0	.269
Tommy Henrich	rf-lf	7	31	2	10	2	0	1	5	2	3	0	.323
Joe DiMaggio	cf	7	26	4	6	0	0	2	5	6	2	0	.231
Johnny Lindell	lf	6	18	3	9	3	1	0	7	5	2	0	**.500**
Yogi Berra	c-ph-rf	6	19	2	3	0	0	1	2	1	2	0	.158
Aaron Robinson	c	3	10	2	2	0	0	0	1	2	1	0	.200
Sherm Lollar	c	2	4	3	3	2	0	0	1	0	0	0	.750
Bobby Brown	ph	4	3	2	3	2	0	0	3	1	0	0	1.000
Allie Clark	ph-rf	3	2	1	1	0	0	0	1	1	0	0	.500
Jack Phillips	ph-1b	2	2	0	0	0	0	0	0	0	0	0	.000
Lonnie Frey	ph	1	1	0	0	0	0	0	0	1	0	0	.000
Ralph Houk	ph	1	1	0	1	0	0	0	0	0	0	0	1.000
Spec Shea	p	3	5	0	2	1	0	0	1	0	2	0	.400
Allie Reynolds	p	2	4	2	2	0	0	0	0	1	0	0	.500
Joe Page	p	4	0	0	0	0	0	0	0	0	1	0	.000
Bill Bevens	p	2	4	0	0	0	0	0	0	0	2	0	.000
Karl Drews	p	2	2	0	0	0	0	0	0	0	2	0	.000
Bobo Newsom	p	2	0	0	0	0	0	0	0	0	0	0	.000
Vic Raschi	p	2	0	0	0	0	0	0	0	0	0	0	.000
Spud Chandler	p	1	0	0	0	0	0	0	0	0	0	0	.000
Butch Wensloff	p	1	0	0	0	0	0	0	0	0	0	0	.000
Team Total		7	238	38	67	11	5	4	36	38	37	2	.282

Double Plays—4   Left on Bases—63

BATTING	Pos	G	AB	R	H	2B	3B	HR	RBI	BB	SO	SB	BA
Brooklyn													
Jackie Robinson	1b	7	27	3	7	2	0	0	3	2	4	2	.259
Eddie Stanky	2b	7	25	4	6	1	0	0	2	3	2	0	.240
Pee Wee Reese	ss	7	23	5	7	1	0	0	4	6	3	3	.304
Spider Jorgensen	3b	7	20	1	4	2	0	0	3	2	4	0	.200
Dixie Walker	rf	7	27	1	6	1	0	1	4	3	1	1	.222
Carl Furillo	ph-cf	6	17	2	6	2	0	0	3	3	0	0	.353
Gene Hermanski	lf	7	19	4	3	0	1	0	1	3	3	0	.158
Bruce Edwards	c	7	27	3	6	1	0	0	2	2	7	0	.222
Pete Reiser	cf-lf-ph	5	8	1	2	0	0	0	0	3	1	0	.250
Cookie Lavagetto	ph-3b	5	7	0	1	1	0	0	3	0	2	0	.143
Eddie Miksis	ph-pr-2b-lf	5	4	1	1	0	0	0	0	0	1	0	.250
Al Gionfriddo	ph-lf	4	3	2	0	0	0	0	0	1	0	1	.000
Arky Vaughan	ph	3	2	0	1	1	0	0	0	1	0	0	.500
Bobby Bragan	ph	1	1	0	1	1	0	0	0	0	0	0	1.000
Gil Hodges	ph	1	1	0	0	0	0	0	0	0	1	0	.000
Ralph Branca	p	3	4	0	0	0	0	0	0	0	1	0	.000
Joe Hatten	p	4	3	1	1	0	0	0	0	0	0	0	.333
Hal Gregg	p	3	3	0	0	0	0	0	0	1	1	0	.000
Vic Lombardi	p-pr	3	3	0	0	0	0	0	0	0	0	0	.000
Hugh Casey	p	6	2	0	0	0	0	0	0	0	1	0	.000
Rex Barney	p	3	1	0	0	0	0	0	0	0	0	0	.000
Hank Behrman	p	5	0	0	0	0	0	0	0	0	0	0	.000
Harry Taylor	p	1	0	0	0	0	0	0	0	0	0	0	.000
Dan Bankhead	pr	1	0	1	0	0	0	0	0	0	0	0	.000
Team Total		7	226	29	52	13	1	1	26	30	32	7	.230

Double Plays—8   Left on Bases—46

PITCHING	G	GS	CG	IP	H	R	ER	BB	SO	W	L	SV	ERA
New York													
Spec Shea	3	3	1	15 1/3	10	4	4	8	10	2	0	0	2.35
Joe Page	4	0	0	13	12	6	6	2	7	1	1	1	4.15
Bill Bevens	2	1	1	11 1/3	3	3	3	11	7	0	1	0	2.38
Allie Reynolds	2	2	1	11 1/3	15	7	6	3	6	1	0	0	4.76
Karl Drews	2	0	0	3	2	1	1	1	0	0	0	0	3.00
Bobo Newsom	2	1	0	2 1/3	6	5	5	2	0	0	1	0	19.29
Butch Wensloff	1	0	0	2	0	0	0	0	0	0	0	0	0.00
Spud Chandler	1	0	0	2	2	2	2	3	1	0	0	0	9.00
Vic Raschi	2	0	0	1 1/3	2	1	1	0	1	0	0	0	6.75
Team Total	7	7	3	61 2/3	52	29	28	30	32	4	3	1	4.09
Brooklyn													
Hal Gregg	3	1	0	12 2/3	9	5	5	8	10	0	1	0	3.55
Hugh Casey	6	0	0	10 1/3	5	1	1	3	2	2	0	1	0.87
Joe Hatten	4	1	0	9	12	7	7	7	5	0	0	0	7.00
Ralph Branca	3	1	0	8 1/3	12	8	8	5	8	1	1	0	8.64
Rex Barney	3	1	0	6 2/3	4	2	2	10	3	0	1	0	2.70
Vic Lombardi	2	2	0	6 2/3	14	9	9	1	5	0	1	0	12.15
Hank Behrman	5	0	0	6 1/3	9	5	5	5	3	0	0	0	7.11
Harry Taylor	1	1	0	0	2	1	0	1	0	0	0	0	0.00
Team Total	7	7	0	60	67	38	37	38	37	3	4	1	5.55

Cookie Lavagetto

1948

Cleveland A.L. 4
Boston N.L. 2

Highlights

THE CLEVELAND INDIANS MADE it to the Series for the first time since 1920 by beating the Boston Red Sox, 8-3, in the A.L.'s first pennant playoff. Indians player-manager Lou Boudreau (.355, 106 RBI's) was the hero of the play-off game as he went four for four at the plate, including two home runs.

National League champion Boston Braves featured excellent pitchers Johnny Sain and Warren Spahn, who won 39 games between them during the regular season and generated the phrase "Spahn and Sain and two days of rain."

The Indians lost only two games to the Braves; fast-balling Bob Feller, who won 19 games during the regular season, lost them both—1-0 in the opener and 11-5 in game five. Loss in game one came after a controversial call at second base in the eighth inning when Feller attempted to pick off pinch runner Phil Masi. It appeared that Boudreau's tag was made before Masi slid back to second, but umpire Bill Stewart ruled him safe. Tommy Holmes promptly singled, driving home Masi to give the Braves their 1-0 triumph over Feller and the Indians.

Leroy "Satchel" Paige made his only World Series appearance, relieving in the seventh inning of game five. He retired the only two batters he faced: Spahn on a fly to center and Holmes on a grounder to short.

Game 1	Oct. 6		
Cleveland	000 000 000	·	0
Boston	000 000 01*	·	1

Winner-Sain   Loser-Feller

Game 2	Oct. 7		
Cleveland	000 210 001	·	4
Boston	100 000 000	·	1

Winner-Lemon   Loser-Spahn

Game 3	Oct. 8		
Boston	000 000 000	·	0
Cleveland	001 100 00*	·	2

Winner-Bearden   Loser-Bickford

Game 4	Oct. 9		
Boston	000 000 100	·	1
Cleveland	101 000 00*	·	2

Winner-Gromek   Loser-Sain

Game 5	Oct. 10		
Boston	301 001 600	·	11
Cleveland	100 400 000	·	5

Winner-Spahn   Loser-Feller

Game 6	Oct. 11		
Cleveland	001 002 010	·	4
Boston	000 100 020	·	3

Winner-Lemon   Loser-Voiselle

Total Attendance—358,362
Average Attendance—59,727
Winning Player's Share—$6,772.07
Losing Player's Share—$4,570.73

BATTING	Pos	G	AB	R	H	2B	3B	HR	RBI	BB	SO	SB	BA
Cleveland													
Eddie Robinson	1b	6	20	0	6	0	0	0	1	1	0	0	.300
Joe Gordon	2b	6	22	3	4	0	0	1	2	1	2	1	.182
Lou Boudreau	ss	6	22	1	6	4	0	0	3	1	1	0	.273
Ken Keltner	3b	6	21	3	2	0	0	0	0	2	3	0	.095
Walt Judnich	rf	4	13	1	1	0	0	0	1	1	4	0	.077
Larry Doby	cf-rf	6	22	1	7	1	0	1	2	2	4	0	.318
Dale Mitchell	lf	6	23	4	4	1	0	1	1	2	0	0	.174
Jim Hegan	c	6	19	2	4	0	0	1	5	1	4	1	.211
Thurman Tucker	cf	1	3	1	1	0	0	0	0	1	0	0	.333
Allie Clark	rf	1	3	0	0	0	0	0	0	0	1	0	.000
Bob Kennedy	rf-lf	3	2	0	1	0	0	0	0	1	0	1	.500
Hal Peck	rf	1	0	0	0	0	0	0	0	0	0	0	.000
Ray Boone	ph	1	1	0	0	0	0	0	0	0	1	0	.000
Al Rosen	ph	1	1	0	0	0	0	0	0	0	0	0	.000
Joe Tipton	ph	1	1	0	0	0	0	0	0	0	1	0	.000
Johnny Berardino	Did not play												
Hank Edwards	Did not play												
Bob Lemon	p	2	7	0	0	0	0	0	0	0	0	0	.000
Gene Bearden	p	2	4	1	2	1	0	0	0	0	1	0	.500
Bob Feller	p	2	4	0	0	0	0	0	0	0	2	0	.000
Steve Gromek	p	1	3	0	0	0	0	0	0	0	1	0	.000
Russ Christopher	p	1	0	0	0	0	0	0	0	0	0	0	.000
Eddie Klieman	p	1	0	0	0	0	0	0	0	0	0	0	.000
Bob Muncrief	p	1	0	0	0	0	0	0	0	0	0	0	.000
Satchel Paige	p	1	0	0	0	0	0	0	0	0	0	0	.000
Sam Zoldak	Did not play												
Don Black	Did not play—injured												
Team Total		6	191	17	38	7	0	4	16	12	26	2	.199

Double Plays—9   Left on Bases—34

	Pos	G	AB	R	H	2B	3B	HR	RBI	BB	SO	SB	BA
Boston													
Earl Torgeson	1b	5	18	2	7	3	0	0	1	2	1	1	**.389**
Eddie Stanky	2b	6	14	0	4	1	0	0	1	7	0	0	.286
Al Dark	ss	6	24	2	4	1	0	0	0	2	0	0	.167
Bob Elliott	3b	6	21	4	7	0	0	2	5	2	2	0	.333
Tommy Holmes	rf	6	26	3	5	0	0	0	1	0	0	0	.192
Mike McCormick	cf-lf	6	23	1	6	0	0	0	2	0	4	0	.261
Marv Rickert	lf	3	19	2	4	0	0	1	2	0	4	0	.211
Bill Salkeid	c-ph	5	9	2	2	0	0	1	1	5	1	0	.222
Phil Masi	pr-c-ph	5	8	1	1	1	0	0	1	0	0	0	.125
Frank McCormick	ph-1b	3	5	0	1	0	0	0	0	0	2	0	.200
Clint Conatser	cf	2	4	0	0	0	0	0	1	0	0	0	.000
Sibby Sisti	pr-2b-ph	2	1	0	0	0	0	0	0	0	1	0	.000
Connie Ryan	ph-pr	2	1	0	0	0	0	0	0	0	0	0	.000
Ray Sanders	ph	1	1	0	0	0	0	0	0	0	0	0	.000
Jeff Heath	Did not play—injured												
Jim Russell	Did not play—heart illness												
Bobby Sturgeon	Did not play												
Johnny Sain	p	2	5	0	1	0	0	0	0	0	1	0	.200
Warren Spahn	p	3	4	0	0	0	0	0	1	0	1	0	.000
Neis Potter	p	2	2	0	1	0	0	0	0	0	1	0	.500
Bill Voiselle	p	2	2	0	0	0	0	0	0	0	0	0	.000
Red Barrett	p	2	0	0	0	0	0	0	0	0	0	0	.000
Vern Bickford	p	1	0	0	0	0	0	0	0	0	0	0	.000
Bobby Hogue	Did not play												
Clyde Shoun	Did not play												
Al Lyons	Did not play												
Ernie White	Did not play												
Team Total		6	187	17	43	6	0	4	16	16	19	1	.230

Double Plays—3   Left on Bases—34

PITCHING	G	GS	CG	IP	H	R	ER	BB	SO	W	L	SV	ERA
Cleveland													
Bob Lemon	2	2	1	16⅓	16	4	3	7	6	2	0	0	1.65
Bob Feller	2	2	1	14⅓	10	8	8	5	7	0	2	0	5.02
Gene Bearden	2	1	1	10⅔	6	0	0	1	4	1	0	1	0.00
Steve Gromek	1	1	1	9	7	1	1	1	2	1	0	0	1.00
Bob Muncrief	1	0	0	2	1	0	0	0	0	0	0	0	0.00
Satchel Paige	1	0	0	⅔	0	0	0	0	0	0	0	0	0.00
Russ Christopher	1	0	0	1	0	2	1	1	0	0	0	0	0.00
Eddie Klieman	1	0	0	0	1	3	3	2	0	0	0	0	0.00
Sam Zoldak	Did not play												
Don Black	Did not play—injured												
Team Total	7	6	4	53	43	17	16	16	19	4	2	1	2.72
Boston													
Johnny Sain	2	2	2	17	9	2	2	0	9	1	1	0	1.06
Warren Spahn	3	1	0	12	10	4	4	3	12	1	1	0	3.00
Bill Voiselle	2	1	0	10⅔	8	3	3	2	2	0	1	0	2.53
Nels Potter	2	1	0	5⅓	6	6	5	2	1	0	0	0	8.44
Red Barret	2	0	0	3⅔	1	0	0	0	1	0	0	0	0.00
Vern Bickford	1	1	0	3⅓	4	2	1	5	1	0	1	0	2.70
Bobby Hogue	Did not play												
Clyde Shoun	Did not play												
Al Lyons	Did not play												
Ernie White	Did not play												
Team Total	7	6	2	52	38	17	15	12	26	2	4	0	2.60

1949

New York A.L. 4
Brooklyn N.L. 1

Highlights

THE DODGERS AND YANKEES were back again, both with slightly altered casts. The Yankees' most notable addition was manager Casey Stengel, who had compiled a successful record piloting the Oakland Oaks in the Pacific Coast League. With Stengel juggling his lineup to adjust for injuries to key players (including Joe DiMaggio in early season) and blending his young talent (Hank Bauer, Jerry Coleman and Bobby Brown) with his established stars, the Yankees beat the Boston Red Sox on the last day of the season to take the pennant by one game.

The Dodgers added two black players from the Negro leagues: catcher Roy Campanella, who batted .287 and smacked 22 home runs during the regular season, and pitcher Don Newcombe, who led the Dodgers' staff with 17 regular-season victories, including five shutouts.

Yankee pitchers Allie Reynolds and Joe Page, each with one victory and one save, led the Yanks to their Series triumph over the Dodgers, four games to one.

Game 1 Oct. 5
Brooklyn	000 000 000	-	0
New York	000 000 001	-	1

Winner-Reynolds Loser-Newcombe

Game 2 Oct. 6
Brooklyn	010 000 000	-	1
New York	000 000 000	-	0

Winner-Roe Loser-Raschi

Game 3 Oct. 7
New York	001 000 003	-	4
Brooklyn	000 100 002	-	3

Winner-Page Loser-Branca

Game 4 Oct. 8
New York	000 330 000	-	6
Brooklyn	000 004 000	-	4

Winner-Lopat Loser-Newcombe

Game 5 Oct. 9
New York	203 113 000	-	10
Brooklyn	001 001 400	-	6

Winner-Raschi Loser-Barney

Total Attendance—236,716
Average Attendance—47,343
Winning Player's Share—$5,627
Losing Player's Share—$4,273

BATTING	Pos	G	AB	R	H	2B	3B	HR	RBI	BB	SO	SB	BA
New York													
Tommy Henrich	1b	5	19	4	5	0	0	1	1	3	0	0	.263
Jerry Coleman	2b	5	20	0	5	3	0	0	4	0	4	0	.250
Phil Rizzuto	ss	5	18	2	3	0	0	0	1	3	1	1	.167
Bobby Brown	ph-3b	4	12	4	6	1	2	0	5	2	2	0	**.500**
Cliff Mapes	rf	4	10	3	1	1	0	0	2	2	4	0	.100
Joe DiMaggio	cf	5	18	2	2	0	0	1	2	3	5	0	.111
Gene Woodling	lf	3	10	4	4	3	0	0	0	3	0	0	.400
Yogi Berra	c	4	16	2	1	0	0	0	1	1	3	0	.063
Billy Johnson	3b	2	7	0	1	0	0	0	0	0	2	1	.143
Johnny Lindell	lf	2	7	0	1	0	0	0	0	0	2	0	.143
Hank Bauer	rf-pr-ph	3	6	0	1	0	0	0	0	0	0	0	.167
Charlie Silvera	c	1	2	0	0	0	0	0	0	0	0	0	.000
Gus Niarhos	c	1	0	0	0	0	0	0	0	0	0	0	.000
Johnny Mize	ph	2	2	0	2	0	0	0	2	0	0	0	1.000
Snuffy Stirnweiss	pr	1	0	0	0	0	0	0	0	0	0	0	.000
Charlie Keller	Did not play												
Vic Raschi	p	2	5	0	1	0	0	0	1	1	1	0	.200
Joe Page	p	3	4	0	0	0	0	0	0	0	2	0	.000
Allie Reynolds	p	2	4	0	2	1	0	0	0	0	1	0	.500
Ed Lopat	p	1	3	0	1	1	0	0	1	0	0	0	.333
Tommy Byrne	p	1	1	0	1	0	0	0	0	0	0	0	1.000
Fred Sanford	Did not play												
Cuddles Marshall	Did not play												
Duane Pillette	Did not play												
Ralph Buxton	Did not play												
Team Total		5	164	21	37	10	2	2	20	18	27	2	.226

Double Plays—5   Left on Bases—32

BATTING	Pos	G	AB	R	H	2B	3B	HR	RBI	BB	SO	SB	BA
Brooklyn													
Gil Hodges	1b	5	17	2	4	0	0	1	4	1	4	0	.235
Jackie Robinson	2b	5	16	2	3	1	0	0	2	4	2	0	.188
Pee Wee Reese	ss	5	19	2	6	1	0	1	2	1	0	1	.316
Spider Jorgensen	3b-ph	4	11	1	2	2	0	0	0	2	2	0	.182
Gene Hermanski	lf-rf	4	13	1	4	0	1	0	2	3	3	0	.308
Duke Snider	cf	5	21	3	3	1	0	0	0	0	8	0	.143
Luis Olmo	lf	4	11	2	3	0	0	1	2	0	2	0	.273
Roy Campanella	c	5	15	2	4	1	0	1	2	3	1	0	.267
Carl Furillo	rf-ph	3	8	0	1	0	0	0	0	1	0	0	.125
Eddie Miksis	3b-ph	3	7	0	2	1	0	0	0	0	1	0	.286
Marv Rackley	lf	2	5	0	0	0	0	0	0	0	2	0	.000
Billy Cox	ph-3b	2	3	0	1	0	0	0	0	0	1	0	.333
Mike McCormick	rf	1	0	0	0	0	0	0	0	0	0	0	.000
Bruce Edwards	ph	2	2	0	1	0	0	0	0	0	1	0	.500
Tommy Brown	ph	2	2	0	0	0	0	0	0	0	1	0	.000
Dick Whitman	ph	1	1	0	0	0	0	0	0	0	1	0	.000
Don Newcombe	p	2	4	0	0	0	0	0	0	0	3	0	.000
Ralph Branca	p	1	3	0	0	0	0	0	0	0	3	0	.000
Preacher Roe	p	1	3	0	0	0	0	0	0	0	3	0	.000
Jack Banta	p	3	1	0	0	0	0	0	0	0	0	0	.000
Carl Erskine	p	2	0	0	0	0	0	0	0	0	0	0	.000
Joe Hatten	p	2	0	0	0	0	0	0	0	0	0	0	.000
Rex Barney	p	1	0	0	0	0	0	0	0	0	0	0	.000
Erv Palica	p	1	0	0	0	0	0	0	0	0	0	0	.000
Paul Minner	p	1	0	0	0	0	0	0	0	0	0	0	.000
Team Total		5	162	14	34	7	1	4	14	15	38	1	.210

Double Plays—1   Left on Bases—31

PITCHING	G	GS	CG	IP	H	R	ER	BB	SO	W	L	SV	ERA
New York													
Vic Raschi	2	**2**	0	14²/₃	15	7	**7**	5	11	1	1	0	4.30
Allie Reynolds	2	1	1	12¹/₃	2	0	0	4	**14**	1	0	1	**0.00**
Joe Page	**3**	0	0	9	6	2	2	3	8	1	0	1	2.00
Ed Lopat	1	1	0	5²/₃	9	4	4	1	4	1	0	0	6.35
Tommy Byrne	1	1	0	3¹/₃	2	1	1	2	1	0	0	0	2.70
Fred Sanford	Did not play												
Cuddles Marshall	Did not play												
Duane Pillette	Did not play												
Ralph Buxton	Did not play												
Team Total	5	5	1	45	34	14	14	15	38	4	1	2	2.80
Brooklyn													
Don Newcombe	2	**2**	1	11²/₃	10	4	4	3	11	0	**2**	0	3.09
Preacher Roe	1	1	**1**	9	6	0	0	0	3	1	0	0	**0.00**
Ralph Branca	1	1	0	8²/₃	4	4	4	4	6	0	1	0	4.15
Jack Banta	**3**	0	0	5²/₃	5	2	2	1	4	0	0	0	3.18
Rex Barney	1	1	0	2²/₃	3	5	5	**6**	2	0	1	0	16.88
Erv Palica	1	0	0	2	1	0	0	1	1	0	0	0	0.00
Carl Erskine	2	0	0	1²/₃	3	3	3	1	0	0	0	0	16.20
Joe Hatten	2	0	0	1²/₃	4	3	3	2	0	0	0	0	16.20
Paul Minner	1	0	0	1	1	0	0	0	0	0	0	0	0.00
Team Total	5	5	2	44	37	21	21	18	27	1	4	0	4.29

1950

New York A.L. 4
Philadelphia N.L. 0

Highlights

THE EXCITING STORY OF THE regular season was the upstart Philadelphia Phillies' 'Whiz Kids' extra-inning triumph over the defending National League champion Dodgers on the final day of the season. Dubbed the "Whiz Kids" because of the youth of their key players—Del Ennis, Richie Ashburn, Willie Jones, Granny Hamner, Robin Roberts and Curt Simmons—the Phils lacked not only regular-season experience, but also World Series experience, since this was the first Phillies team to appear in the fall classic since 1915.

The Phillies' chances of winning were further hampered by the unexpected late-season induction of left-handed pitcher Curt Simmons into the armed forces.

Although the Phillies were swept by the Yankees, four games to none, they were not embarrassed. Game one was lost, 1-0, when N.L. MVP Jim Konstanty gave up a run on a double and two routine outs, the second a sacrifice fly that scored Bobby Brown from third. Game two was lost, 2-1, when Joe DiMaggio hit a tenth-inning home run off Robin Roberts, a regular-season 20-game winner for the Phils. Yankee Jerry Coleman won game three, 3-2, with a ninth-inning single off reliever Russ Meyer, and in game four, rookie left-hander Whitey Ford and Allie Reynolds, helped by Yogi Berra's sixth-inning homer, scattered seven Phillies hits to nail down the sweep, 5-2.

Game 1 Oct. 4
New York   000 100 000 · 1
Philadelphia   000 000 000 · 0
Winner-Raschi   Loser-Konstanty

Game 2 Oct. 5
New York   010 000 000 1 · 2
Philadelphia   010 000 000 0 · 1
Winner-Reynolds   Loser-Roberts

Game 3 Oct. 6
Philadelphia   000 001 100 · 2
New York   001 000 011 · 3
Winner-Ferrick   Loser-Meyer

Game 4 Oct. 7
Philadelphia   000 000 002 · 2
New York   200 003 00* · 5
Winner-Ford   Loser-Miller

Total Attendance—196,009
Average Attendance—49,002
Winning Player's Share—$5,738
Losing Player's Share—$4,081

BATTING	Pos	G	AB	R	H	2B	3B	HR	RBI	BB	SO	SB	BA
New York													
Johnny Mize	1b	4	15	0	2	0	0	0	0	0	1	0	.133
Jerry Coleman	2b	4	14	2	4	1	0	0	3	2	0	0	.286
Phil Rizzuto	ss	4	14	1	2	0	0	0	0	3	0	1	.143
Bobby Brown	3b-ph	4	12	2	4	1	1	0	1	0	0	0	.333
Hank Bauer	rf-lf	4	15	0	2	0	0	0	1	0	0	0	.133
Joe DiMaggio	cf	4	13	2	4	1	0	1	2	3	1	0	.308
Gene Woodling	lf-ph	4	14	2	6	0	0	0	1	2	0	0	.429
Yogi Berra	c	4	15	2	3	0	0	1	2	2	1	0	.200
Billy Johnson	3b	4	6	0	0	0	0	0	0	0	3	0	.000
Cliff Mapes	rf	1	4	0	0	0	0	0	0	0	1	0	.000
Johnny Hopp	1b-pr	3	2	0	0	0	0	0	0	0	0	0	.000
Joe Collins	1b	1	0	0	0	0	0	0	0	0	0	0	.000
Jackie Jensen	pr	1	0	0	0	0	0	0	0	0	0	0	.000
Billy Martin	Did not play												
Charlie Silvera	Did not play												
Charlie Houk	Did not play												
Vic Raschi	p	1	3	0	1	0	0	0	0	0	0	0	.333
Allie Reynolds	p	2	3	0	1	0	0	0	0	1	2	0	.333
Whitey Ford	p	1	3	0	0	0	0	0	0	0	2	0	.000
Ed Lopat	p	1	2	0	1	0	0	0	0	0	1	0	.500
Tom Ferrick	p	1	0	0	0	0	0	0	0	0	0	0	.000
Tommy Byrne	Did not play												
Fred Sanford	Did not play												
Joe Page	Did not play												
Joe Ostrowski	Did not play												
Team Total		4	135	11	30	3	1	2	10	13	12	1	.222
			Double Plays—4			Left on Bases—33								
Philadelphia													
Dick Waitkus	1b	4	15	0	4	1	0	0	0	2	0	0	.267
Mike Goliat	2b	4	14	1	3	0	0	0	1	1	2	0	.214
Granny Hamner	ss	4	14	1	6	2	1	0	0	1	2	1	.429
Willie Jones	3b	4	14	1	4	1	0	0	0	0	3	0	.286
Del Ennis	rf	4	14	1	2	1	0	0	0	0	1	0	.143
Richie Ashburn	cf	4	17	0	3	1	0	0	1	0	4	0	.176
Dick Sisler	lf	4	17	0	1	0	0	0	1	0	5	0	.059
Andy Seminick	c	4	11	0	2	0	0	0	0	1	3	0	.182
Stan Lopata	c-ph	2	1	0	0	0	0	0	0	0	1	0	.000
Ken Silvestri	c	1	0	0	0	0	0	0	0	0	0	0	.000
Jimmy Bloodworth	2b	1	0	0	0	0	0	0	0	0	0	0	.000
Dick Whitman	ph	3	2	0	0	0	0	0	0	1	0	0	.000
Putsy Caballero	pr-ph	3	1	0	0	0	0	0	0	0	1	0	.000
Jackie Mayo	ph-lf-pr	3	0	0	0	0	0	0	0	1	0	0	.000
Stan Hollmig	Did not play												
Jim Konstanty	p	3	4	0	1	0	0	0	0	0	1	0	.250
Robin Roberts	p	2	2	0	0	0	0	0	0	0	1	0	.000
Ken Heintzelman	p	1	2	0	0	0	0	0	0	0	0	0	.000
Russ Meyer	p	2	0	0	0	0	0	0	0	0	0	0	.000
Bob Miller	p	1	0	0	0	0	0	0	0	0	0	0	.000
Ken Johnson	pr	1	0	1	0	0	0	0	0	0	0	0	.000
Bubba Church	Did not play												
Blix Donnelly	Did not play												
Milo Candini	Did not play												
Jocko Thompson	Did not play												
Team Total		4	128	5	26	6	1	0	3	7	24	1	.203
			Double Plays— 1			Left on Bases—26								

PITCHING	G	GS	CG	IP	H	R	ER	BB	SO	W	L	SV	ERA
New York													
Allie Reynolds	2	1	1	10⅓	7	1	1	4	7	1	0	1	0.87
Vic Raschi	1	1	1	9	2	0	0	1	5	1	0	0	0.00
Whitey Ford	1	1	0	8⅔	7	2	0	1	7	1	0	0	0.00
Ed Lopat	1	1	0	8	9	2	2	0	5	0	0	0	2.25
Tom Ferrick	1	0	0	1	1	0	0	1	0	1	0	0	0.00
Tommy Byrne	Did not play												
Fred Sanford	Did not play												
Joe Page	Did not play												
Joe Ostrowski	Did not play												
Team Total	4	4	2	37	26	5	3	7	24	4	0	1	0.73
Philadelphia													
Jim Konstanty	3	1	0	15	9	4	4	4	3	0	1	0	2.40
Robin Roberts	2	1	1	11	11	2	2	3	5	0	1	0	1.64
Ken Heintzelman	1	1	0	7⅔	4	2	1	6	3	0	0	0	1.17
Russ Meyer	2	0	0	1⅔	4	1	1	0	1	0	1	0	5.40
Bob Miller	1	1	0	⅓	2	2	1	0	0	0	1	0	27.00
Ken Johnson	Did not pitch												
Bubba Church	Did not play												
Blix Donnelly	Did not play												
Milo Candini	Did not play												
Jocko Thompson	Did not play												
Team Total	4	4	1	35⅔	30	11	9	13	12	0	4	0	2.27

1951

New York A.L. 4
New York N.L. 2

Highlights

BEHIND 13½ GAMES IN MID-August, the Giants fashioned the greatest comeback in baseball history to catch the Dodgers on the final day of the season, and then defeated them, 5-4, when Bobby Thomson hit his "shot heard round the world," a three-run homer off Ralph Branca in the ninth inning.

The Yanks won the A.L. pennant by five games, blending the talent of two rookies, Gil McDougald and Mickey Mantle, with veterans Eddie Lopat, Vic Raschi, Allie Reynolds, Phil Rizzuto, Yogi Berra and Joe DiMaggio.

Game three featured controversial play when Eddie Stanky, nicknamed the "Brash Brat," slid hard into second base and kicked the ball out of Rizzuto's glove, igniting a fifth-inning five-run rally that gave the Giants a 6-2 victory, and a two-games-to-one lead in the Series.

In the next three games, however, the Yanks rolled over the Giants: 6-2, 13-1, and 4-3. In the Yanks' victory in game four, Joe DiMaggio hit a two-run homer, the last of his career: he retired following the Series, saying, "I'm not Joe DiMaggio any more."

Stars who failed to shine included rookies Mickey Mantle, who played in two games, collecting only a bunt single before wrenching his right knee in the fifth inning of game two, and Willie Mays, who played in all six games, batting only .182 with no extra-base hits.

Game 1 Oct. 4
Giants	200 003 000	5
Yankees	010 000 000	1

Winner-Koslo Loser-Reynolds

Game 2 Oct. 5
Giants	000 000 100	1
Yankees	110 000 01*	3

Winner-Lopat Loser-Jansen

Game 3 Oct. 6
Yankees	000 000 011	2
Giants	010 050 00*	6

Winner-Hearn Loser-Raschi

Game 4 Oct. 8
Yankees	010 120 200	6
Giants	100 000 001	2

Winner-Reynolds Loser-Maglie

Game 5 Oct. 9
Yankees	005 202 400	13
Giants	100 000 000	1

Winner-Lopat Loser-Jansen

Game 6 Oct. 10
Giants	000 010 002	3
Yankees	100 003 00*	4

Winner-Raschi Loser-Koslo

Total Attendance—341,977
Average Attendance—56,996
Winning Player's Share—$6,446
Losing Player's Share—$4,951

BATTING

	Pos	G	AB	R	H	2B	3B	HR	RBI	BB	SO	SB	BA
New York Yankees													
Joe Collins	1b-rf	6	18	2	4	0	0	1	3	2	1	0	.222
Gil McDougald	2b-3b	6	23	2	6	1	0	1	7	2	2	0	.261
Phil Rizzuto	ss	6	25	5	8	0	0	1	3	2	3	0	.320
Bobby Brown	ph-3b	5	14	1	5	1	0	0	0	2	1	0	.357
Hank Bauer	rf-lf	6	18	0	3	0	1	0	3	1	1	0	.167
Joe DiMaggio	cf	6	23	3	6	2	0	1	5	2	4	0	.261
Gene Woodling	ph-lf	6	18	6	3	1	1	1	1	5	3	0	.167
Yogi Berra	c	6	23	4	6	1	0	0	0	2	1	0	.261
Jerry Coleman	2b-pr	5	8	2	2	0	0	0	0	1	2	0	.250
Johnny Mize	ph-1b	4	7	2	2	1	0	0	1	2	0	0	.286
Mickey Mantle	rf	2	5	1	1	0	0	0	0	0	1	0	.200
Johnny Hopp	ph	1	0	0	0	0	0	0	0	1	0	0	.000
Billy Martin	pr	1	0	1	0	0	0	0	0	0	0	0	.000
Charlie Silvera	Did not play												
Ralph Houk	Did not play												
Ed Lopat	p	2	8	0	1	0	0	0	1	0	2	0	.125
Allie Reynolds	p	2	6	0	2	0	0	0	1	0	1	0	.333
Vic Raschi	p	2	2	0	0	0	0	0	0	2	1	0	.000
Johnny Sain	p	1	1	0	0	0	0	0	0	0	0	0	.000
Bobby Hogue	p	2	0	0	0	0	0	0	0	0	0	0	.000
Bob Kuzava	p	1	0	0	0	0	0	0	0	0	0	0	.000
Tom Morgan	p	1	0	0	0	0	0	0	0	0	0	0	.000
Joe Ostrowski	p	1	0	0	0	0	0	0	0	0	0	0	.000
Spec Shea	Did not play												
Art Schallock	Did not play												
Stubby Overmire	Did not play												
Team Total		6	199	29	49	7	2	5	25	26	23	0	.246

Double Plays—10 Left on Bases—41

	Pos	G	AB	R	H	2B	3B	HR	RBI	BB	SO	SB	BA
New York Giants													
Whitey Lockman	1b	6	25	1	6	2	0	1	4	1	2	0	.240
Eddie Stanky	2b	6	22	3	3	0	0	1	3	3	2	0	.136
Al Dark	ss	6	24	5	10	3	0	1	4	2	3	0	.417
Bobby Thomson	3b	6	21	1	5	1	0	2	5	5	0	0	.238
Hank Thompson	rf	5	14	3	2	0	0	0	0	5	2	0	.143
Willie Mays	cf	6	22	1	4	0	0	0	1	2	2	0	.182
Monte Irvin	lf	6	24	3	11	0	1	0	2	2	1	2	.458
Wes Westrum	c	6	17	1	4	1	0	0	0	5	3	0	.235
Clint Hartung	rf	2	4	0	0	0	0	0	0	0	0	0	.000
Ray Noble	ph-c	2	2	0	0	0	0	0	0	0	1	0	.000
Bill Rigney	ph	4	4	0	1	0	0	0	0	1	0	0	.250
Lucky Lohrke	ph	2	2	0	0	0	0	0	0	0	1	0	.000
Davey Williams	ph-pr	2	1	0	0	0	0	0	0	0	0	0	.000
Sal Yvars	ph	1	1	0	0	0	0	0	0	0	0	0	.000
Hank Schenz	pr	1	0	0	0	0	0	0	0	0	0	0	.000
Don Mueller	Did not play												
Dave Koslo	p	2	5	0	0	0	0	0	0	0	2	0	.000
Jim Hearn	p	2	3	0	0	0	0	0	0	0	1	0	.000
Larry Jansen	p	3	2	0	0	0	0	0	0	0	0	0	.000
Sal Maglie	p	1	1	0	0	0	0	0	0	0	1	0	.000
George Spencer	p	2	0	0	0	0	0	0	0	0	0	0	.000
Sheldon Jones	p	2	0	0	0	0	0	0	0	0	0	0	.000
Monte Kennedy	p	2	0	0	0	0	0	0	0	0	0	0	.000
Al Corwin	p	1	0	0	0	0	0	0	0	0	0	0	.000
Alex Konikowski	p	1	0	0	0	0	0	0	0	0	0	0	.000
Team Total		6	194	18	46	7	1	2	15	25	22	2	.237

Double Plays—4 Left on Bases—45

PITCHING

	G	GS	CG	IP	H	R	ER	BB	SO	W	L	SV	ERA
New York Yankees													
Eddie Lopat	2	2	2	18	10	2	1	3	4	2	0	0	0.50
Allie Reynolds	2	2	1	15	16	7	7	11	8	1	1	0	4.20
Vic Raschi	2	2	0	10⅓	12	7	1	8	4	1	1	0	0.87
Bobby Hogue	2	0	0	2⅔	1	0	0	0	0	0	0	0	0.00
Tom Morgan	1	0	0	2	2	0	0	1	3	0	0	0	0.00
Joe Ostrowski	1	0	0	2	1	0	0	0	1	0	0	0	0.00
Johnny Sain	1	0	0	2	4	2	2	2	2	0	0	0	9.00
Bob Kuzava	1	0	0	1	0	0	0	0	0	0	0	1	0.00
Spec Shea	Did not play												
Art Schallock	Did not play												
Stubby Overmire	Did not play												
Team Total	6	6	3	53	46	18	11	25	22	4	2	1	1.87
New York Giants													
Dave Koslo	2	2	1	15	12	5	5	7	6	1	1	0	3.00
Larry Jansen	3	2	0	10	8	7	7	4	6	0	2	0	6.30
Jim Hearn	2	1	0	8⅔	5	1	1	8	1	1	0	0	1.04
Sal Maglie	1	1	0	5	8	4	4	2	3	0	1	0	7.20
Sheldon Jones	2	0	0	4⅓	5	3	1	1	2	0	0	1	2.08
George Spencer	2	0	0	3⅓	6	7	7	3	0	0	0	0	18.90
Monte Kennedy	2	0	0	3	3	2	2	1	4	0	0	0	6.00
Al Corwin	1	0	0	1⅔	1	0	0	0	1	0	0	0	0.00
Alex Konikowski	1	0	0	1	1	0	0	0	0	0	0	0	0.00
Team Total	6	6	1	52	49	29	27	26	23	2	4	1	4.67

1952

New York A.L. 4
Brooklyn N.L. 3

Highlights

THE YANKEES NO LONGER HAD Joe DiMaggio, but his replacement, young and talented Mickey Mantle, showed great promise, despite his league-leading 111 strikeouts. Mantle played especially well in the Series. He led the Yanks with ten hits off Dodgers pitching, including two key hits in game seven—a solo homer in the sixth to break up a 2-2 tie and a run-producing single in the seventh—to provide the margin of victory.

Billy Martin's knee-level catch of Jackie Robinson's bases-loaded two-out pop on the infield grass between first and second in the bottom of the seventh in the final game made Mantle's hitting heroics stand up.

Joe Black, Brooklyn's ace relief pitcher (15-2 and 2.15 ERA), was used solely as a starter in the Series by manager Charlie Dressen. Black went nine full innings in the opener, beating Allie Reynolds, 4-2; seven innings in game four again against Reynolds, losing 2-0; and 5⅓ innings in game seven, losing again, 4-2, to Reynolds in relief of Eddie Lopat.

Game 1 Oct. 1
New York   001 000 010 · 2
Brooklyn   010 002 01* · 4
Winner-Black Loser-Reynolds

Game 2 Oct. 2
New York   000 115 000 · 7
Brooklyn   001 000 000 · 1
Winner-Raschi Loser-Erskine

Game 3 Oct. 3
Brooklyn   001 010 012 · 5
New York   010 000 011 · 3
Winner-Roe Loser-Lopat

Game 4 Oct. 4
Brooklyn   000 000 000 · 0
New York   000 100 01* · 2
Winner-Reynolds Loser-Black

Game 5 Oct. 5
Brooklyn   010 030 100 01 · 6
New York   000 050 000 00 · 5
Winner-Erskine Loser-Sain

Game 6 Oct. 6
New York   000 000 210 · 3
Brooklyn   000 001 010 · 2
Winner-Raschi Loser-Loes

Game 7 Oct. 7
New York   000 111 100 · 4
Brooklyn   000 110 000 · 2
Winner-Reynolds Loser-Black

Total Attendance—340,906
Average Attendance—48,701
Winning Player's Share—$5,983
Losing Player's Share—$4,201

BATTING	Pos	G	AB	R	H	2B	3B	HR	RBI	BB	SO	SB	BA
New York													
Johnny Mize	1b-ph	5	15	3	6	1	0	3	6	3	1	0	.400
Billy Martin	2b	7	23	2	5	0	0	1	4	2	2	0	.217
Phil Rizzuto	ss	7	27	2	4	1	0	0	0	5	2	0	.148
Gil McDougald	3b	7	25	5	5	0	0	1	3	5	2	1	.200
Hank Bauer	rf-ph	7	18	2	1	0	0	0	1	4	3	0	.056
Mickey Mantle	cf	7	29	5	10	1	1	2	3	3	4	0	.345
Gene Woodling	lf-ph	7	23	4	8	1	1	1	1	3	3	0	.348
Yogi Berra	c	7	28	2	6	1	0	2	3	2	4	0	.214
Joe Collins	1b-pr	6	12	1	0	0	0	0	0	1	3	0	.000
Irv Noren	lf-ph-rf	4	10	0	3	0	0	0	1	1	3	0	.300
Ralph Houk	ph	1	1	0	0	0	0	0	0	0	0	0	.000
Allie Reynolds	p	4	7	0	0	0	0	0	0	0	2	0	.000
Vic Raschi	p	3	6	0	1	0	0	0	1	1	2	0	.167
Ed Lopat	p	2	3	0	1	0	0	0	0	1	1	0	.333
Johnny Sain	ph-p	2	3	0	0	0	0	0	0	0	0	0	.000
Ewell Blackwell	p	1	1	0	0	0	0	0	0	0	0	0	.000
Bob Kuzava	p	1	1	0	0	0	0	0	0	0	0	0	.000
Ray Scarborough	p	1	0	0	0	0	0	0	0	0	0	0	.000
Tom Gorman	p	1	0	0	0	0	0	0	0	0	0	0	.000
Team Total		7	232	26	50	5	2	10	24	31	32	1	.216

Double Plays—7   Left on Bases—48

BATTING	Pos	G	AB	R	H	2B	3B	HR	RBI	BB	SO	SB	BA
Brooklyn													
Gil Hodges	1b	7	21	1	0	0	0	0	1	5	6	0	.000
Jackie Robinson	2b	7	23	4	4	0	0	1	2	7	5	2	.174
Pee Wee Reese	ss	7	29	4	10	0	0	1	4	2	2	1	.345
Billy Cox	3b	7	27	4	8	2	0	0	3	3	4	0	.296
Carl Furillo	rf	7	23	1	4	2	0	0	3	3	3	0	.174
Duke Snider	cf	7	29	5	10	2	0	4	8	1	5	1	.345
Andy Pafko	of-rf-ph	7	21	0	4	0	0	0	2	0	4	0	.190
Roy Campanella	c	7	28	0	6	0	0	0	1	1	6	0	.214
George Shuba	of-ph	4	10	0	3	1	0	0	0	0	4	0	.300
Rocky Nelson	ph	4	3	0	0	0	0	0	0	1	2	0	.000
Tommy Holmes	lf	3	1	0	0	0	0	0	0	0	0	0	.000
Bobby Morgan	3b-ph	2	1	0	0	0	0	0	0	0	0	0	.000
Sandy Amoros	pr	1	0	0	0	0	0	0	0	0	0	0	.000
Joe Black	p	3	6	0	0	0	0	0	0	1	6	0	.000
Carl Erskine	p	3	6	1	0	0	0	0	0	0	1	0	.000
Billy Loes	p	2	3	0	1	0	0	0	0	0	1	1	.333
Preacher Roe	p	3	2	0	0	0	0	0	0	0	0	0	.000
Ken Lehman	p	1	0	0	0	0	0	0	0	0	0	0	.000
Johnny Rutherford	p	1	0	0	0	0	0	0	0	0	0	0	.000
Team Total		7	233	20	50	7	0	6	18	24	49	5	.215

Double Plays—4   Left on Bases—52

PITCHING	G	GS	CG	IP	H	R	ER	BB	SO	W	L	SV	ERA
New York													
Allie Reynolds	4	2	1	20⅓	12	4	4	6	18	2	1	1	1.77
Vic Raschi	3	2	1	17	12	3	3	8	18	2	0	0	1.59
Ed Lopat	2	2	0	11⅓	14	6	6	4	3	0	1	0	4.76
Johnny Sain	1	0	0	6	6	2	2	3	3	0	1	0	3.00
Ewell Blackwell	1	1	0	5	4	4	4	3	4	0	0	0	7.20
Bob Kuzava	1	0	0	2⅔	0	0	0	0	2	0	0	1	0.00
Ray Scarborough	1	0	0	1	1	1	1	0	1	0	0	0	9.00
Tom Gorman	1	0	0	⅔	1	0	0	0	0	0	0	0	0.00
Team Total	7	7	2	64	50	20	20	24	49	4	3	2	2.81
Brooklyn													
Joe Black	3	3	1	21⅓	15	6	6	8	9	1	2	0	2.53
Carl Erskine	3	2	1	18	12	9	9	10	10	1	1	0	4.50
Preacher Roe	3	1	0	11⅓	9	4	4	6	8	1	0	0	3.18
Billy Loes	2	1	0	10⅓	11	6	5	5	5	0	1	0	4.35
Ken Lehman	1	0	0	2	2	0	0	1	0	0	0	0	0.00
Johnny Rutherford	1	0	0	1	1	1	1	1	1	0	0	0	9.00
Team Total	7	7	2	64	50	26	25	31	32	3	4	0	3.52

1953

New York A.L. 4
Brooklyn N.L. 2

Highlights

CLASSIC MATCH-UP OF THE BEST teams in baseball. The Yanks' title was their fifth straight, a record. The Dodgers notched their third championship in five years, and their potent lineup, which had five .300 hitters, achieved five individual regular-season offensive honors: Duke Snider, most runs scored, 132, and highest slugging percentage, .627; Jim "Junior" Gilliam, most triples, 17; Roy Campanella, most RBI's, 142; and Carl Furillo, the league's leading hitter, .344. But in the end, it was Yankee Billy Martin (.257) who stole the show by leading his team to victory with a record-setting 12 hits in six games.

Martin's three-run triple was the heart of a four-run outburst against Dodgers ace Carl Erskine in game one, and in game six Martin singled home the tie-breaking run in the bottom of ninth to give the Yankees a 4-3 victory and their fifth straight World Championship.

Carl Erskine fanned 14, a Series record, in game three to momentarily halt the Yanks.

Game 1 Sept. 30
Brooklyn   000 013 100 · 5
New York   400 010 13* · 9
Winner-Sain   Loser-Labine

Game 2 Oct. 1
Brooklyn   000 200 000 · 2
New York   100 000 12* · 4
Winner-Lopat   Loser-Roe

Game 3 Oct. 2
New York   000 010 010 · 2
Brooklyn   000 011 01* · 3
Winner-Erskine   Loser-Raschi

Game 4 Oct. 3
New York   000 020 001 · 3
Brooklyn   300 102 10* · 7
Winner-Loes   Loser-Ford

Game 5 Oct. 4
New York   105 000 311 · 11
Brooklyn   010 010 041 · 7
Winner-McDonald   Loser-Podres

Game 6 Oct. 5
Brooklyn   000 001 002 · 3
New York   210 000 001 · 4
Winner-Reynolds   Loser-Labine

Total Attendance—307,350
Average Attendance—51,225
Winning Player's Share—$8,281
Losing Player's Share—$6,178

BATTING

New York	Pos	G	AB	R	H	2B	3B	HR	RBI	BB	SO	SB	BA
Joe Collins	1b	6	24	4	4	1	0	1	2	3	8	0	.167
Billy Martin	2b	6	24	5	12	1	2	2	8	1	2	1	.500
Phil Rizzuto	ss	6	19	4	6	1	0	0	0	3	2	1	.316
Gil McDougald	3b	6	24	2	4	0	1	2	4	1	3	0	.167
Hank Bauer	rf	6	23	6	6	0	1	0	1	2	4	0	.261
Mickey Mantle	cf	6	24	3	5	0	0	2	7	3	8	0	.208
Gene Woodling	lf	6	20	5	6	0	0	1	3	6	2	0	.300
Yogi Berra	c	6	21	3	9	1	0	1	4	3	3	0	.429
Don Bollweg	ph-1b	3	2	0	0	0	0	0	0	0	2	0	.000
Johnny Mize	ph	3	3	0	0	0	0	0	0	0	1	0	.000
Irv Noren	ph	2	1	0	0	0	0	0	0	1	0	0	.000
Whitey Ford	p	2	3	0	1	0	0	0	0	0	0	0	.333
Ed Lopat	p	1	3	0	0	0	0	0	0	0	2	0	.000
Allie Reynolds	p	3	2	0	1	0	0	0	0	1	1	0	.000
Johnny Sain	p	2	2	1	1	1	0	0	2	0	1	0	.500
Jim McDonald	p	1	2	0	1	1	0	0	1	1	1	0	.500
Vic Raschi	p	1	2	0	0	0	0	0	0	0	1	0	.000
Tom Gorman	p	1	1	0	0	0	0	0	0	0	1	0	.000
Bob Kuzava	p	1	1	0	0	0	0	0	0	0	1	0	.000
Art Schallock	p	1	0	0	0	0	0	0	0	0	0	0	.000
Team Total		6	201	33	56	6	4	9	32	25	43	2	.279

Double Plays—5   Left on Bases—47

Brooklyn	Pos	G	AB	R	H	2B	3B	HR	RBI	BB	SO	SB	BA
Gil Hodges	1b	6	22	3	8	0	0	1	1	3	3	1	.364
Jim Gilliam	2b	6	27	4	8	3	0	2	4	0	2	0	.296
Pee Wee Reese	ss	6	24	0	5	0	1	0	0	4	1	0	.208
Billy Cox	3b	6	23	3	7	3	0	1	6	1	4	0	.304
Carl Furillo	rf	6	24	4	8	2	0	1	4	1	3	0	.333
Duke Snider	cf	6	25	3	8	3	0	1	5	2	6	0	.320
Jackie Robinson	lf	6	25	3	8	2	0	0	2	1	0	1	.320
Roy Campanella	c	6	22	6	6	0	0	1	2	2	3	0	.273
Don Thompson	lf	2	0	0	0	0	0	0	0	0	0	0	.000
Dick Williams	ph	3	2	0	1	0	0	0	0	1	1	0	.500
Wayne Belardi	ph	2	2	0	0	0	0	0	0	0	1	0	.000
George Shuba	ph	2	1	1	1	0	0	1	2	0	0	0	1.000
Bobby Morgan	ph	1	1	0	0	0	0	0	0	0	0	0	.000
Carl Erskine	p	3	4	0	1	0	0	0	0	0	1	0	.250
Billy Loes	p	1	3	0	2	0	0	0	0	0	0	0	.667
Preacher Roe	p	1	3	0	0	0	0	0	0	0	2	0	.000
Clem Labine	p	3	2	0	0	0	0	0	0	0	1	0	.000
Johnny Podres	p	1	1	0	1	0	0	0	0	0	0	0	1.000
Jim Hughes	p	1	1	0	0	0	0	0	0	0	1	0	.000
Russ Meyer	p	1	1	0	0	0	0	0	0	0	1	0	.000
Ben Wade	p	2	0	0	0	0	0	0	0	0	0	0	.000
Joe Black	p	1	0	0	0	0	0	0	0	0	0	0	.000
Bob Milliken	p	1	0	0	0	0	0	0	0	0	0	0	.000
Team Total		6	213	27	64	13	1	8	26	15	30	2	.300

Double Plays—3   Left on Bases—49

PITCHING

New York	G	GS	CG	IP	H	R	ER	BB	SO	W	L	SV	ERA
Ed Lopat	1	1	1	9	9	2	2	4	3	1	0	0	2.00
Vic Raschi	1	1	1	8	9	3	3	3	4	0	1	0	3.38
Whitey Ford	2	2	0	8	9	4	4	2	7	0	1	0	4.50
Allie Reynolds	3	1	0	8	9	6	6	4	9	1	0	1	6.75
Jim McDonald	1	1	0	7⅔	12	6	5	0	3	1	0	0	5.87
Johnny Sain	2	0	0	5⅔	8	3	3	1	1	1	0	0	4.76
Tom Gorman	1	0	0	3	4	1	1	0	1	0	0	0	3.00
Art Schallock	1	0	0	2	2	1	1	1	1	0	0	0	4.50
Bob Kuzava	1	0	0	⅔	2	1	1	0	1	0	0	0	13.50
Team Total	6	6	2	52	64	27	26	15	30	4	2	1	4.50

Brooklyn	G	GS	CG	IP	H	R	ER	BB	SO	W	L	SV	ERA
Carl Erskine	3	3	1	14	14	9	9	9	16	1	0	0	5.79
Billy Loes	1	1	0	8	8	3	3	2	8	1	0	0	3.38
Preacher Roe	1	1	1	8	5	4	4	4	4	0	1	0	4.50
Clem Labine	3	0	0	5	10	2	2	1	3	0	2	1	3.60
Russ Meyer	1	0	0	4⅓	8	4	3	4	5	0	0	0	6.23
Jim Hughes	1	0	0	4	3	1	1	1	3	0	0	0	2.25
Johnny Podres	1	1	0	2⅔	1	5	1	2	0	0	1	0	3.38
Ben Wade	2	0	0	2⅓	4	4	4	1	2	0	0	0	15.43
Bob Milliken	1	0	0	2	2	0	0	1	0	0	0	0	0.00
Joe Black	1	0	0	1	1	1	1	0	2	0	0	0	9.00
Team Total	6	6	2	51⅓	56	33	28	25	43	2	4	1	4.91

1954

New York N.L. 4
Cleveland A.L. 0

Highlights

THE CLEVELAND INDIANS WERE overwhelming favorites to win Series, having set an A.L. record for most victories during a regular season, 111. Cleveland lineup included batting champion Bobby Avila, .341; Larry Doby, who led the league in home runs, 32, and RBI's, 126; and steady, productive third baseman, Al Rosen, .300. Their pitchers were just as formidable: Bob Lemon, 23-7, 2.72 ERA; Early Wynn, 23-11, 2.72 ERA; and Mike "The Bear" Garcia, 19-8, who held the league-leading ERA of 2.64.

The Giants had two exciting stars, Willie Mays (.345 and 41 homers), and Johnny Antonelli (21 games, 2.29 ERA).

Mays and Antonelli were joined in the Series by Dusty Rhodes, a .341 part-time player and full-time pinch hitter for manager Leo Durocher. Rhodes won game one with a pinch-hit three-run homer in the bottom of the tenth. He blooped a RBI single and rapped a solo homer in game two to provide the Giants' 3-1 margin of victory, and broken open game three in the Giants' three-run third inning with a two-run pinch single that sent the Indians down to defeat, 6-2.

Mays made a miraculous over-the-head catch of Vic Wertz's 460-foot drive in game one, a play rated as one of the best ever in Series competition.

This was the last Series ever for Bob Feller, who failed to play despite a respectable 13-3 regular-season record, and it was the last Series ever played at New York's Polo Grounds.

Game 1 Sept. 29
Cleveland 200 000 000 0 · 2
New York 002 000 000 3 · 5
Winner-Grissom Loser-Lemon

Game 2 Sept. 30
Cleveland 100 000 000 · 1
New York 000 020 10* · 3
Winner-Antonelli Loser-Wynn

Game 3 Oct. 1
New York 103 011 000 · 6
Cleveland 000 000 110 · 2
Winner-Gomez Loser-Garcia

Game 4 Oct. 2
New York 021 040 000 · 7
Cleveland 000 030 100 · 4
Winner-Liddle Loser-Lemon

Total Attendance—251,507
Average Attendance—62,887
Winning Player's Share—$11,118
Losing Player's Share—$6,713

BATTING	Pos	G	AB	R	H	2B	3B	HR	RBI	BB	SO	SB	BA
New York													
Whitey Lockman	1b	4	18	2	2	0	0	0	0	1	2	0	.111
Davey Williams	2b	4	11	0	0	0	0	0	1	2	2	0	.000
Al Dark	ss	4	17	2	7	0	0	0	0	1	1	0	.412
Hank Thompson	3b	4	11	6	4	1	0	0	2	7	1	0	.364
Don Mueller	rf	4	18	4	7	0	0	0	1	0	1	0	.389
Willie Mays	cf	4	14	4	4	1	0	0	3	4	1	1	.286
Monte Irvin	lf	4	9	1	2	1	0	0	2	0	3	0	.222
Wes Westrum	c	4	11	0	3	0	0	0	3	1	3	0	.273
Dusty Rhodes	ph-lf	3	6	2	4	0	0	2	7	1	2	0	.667
Ruben Gomez	p	1	4	0	0	0	0	0	0	0	0	0	.000
Sal Maglie	p	1	3	0	0	0	0	0	0	0	2	0	.000
Johnny Antonelli	p	2	3	0	0	0	0	0	1	0	0	0	.000
Don Liddle	p	2	3	0	0	0	0	0	0	0	2	0	.000
Hoyt Wilhelm	p	2	1	0	0	0	0	0	0	0	1	0	.000
Marv Grissom	p	1	1	0	0	0	0	0	0	0	1	0	.000
Team Total		4	130	21	33	3	0	2	20	17	24	1	.254

Double Plays—2 Left on Bases—28

	Pos	G	AB	R	H	2B	3B	HR	RBI	BB	SO	SB	BA
Cleveland													
Vic Wertz	1b	4	16	2	8	2	1	1	3	2	2	0	**.500**
Bobby Avila	2b	4	15	1	2	0	0	0	0	2	1	0	.133
George Strickland	ss	3	9	0	0	0	0	0	0	0	2	0	.000
Al Rosen	3b	3	12	0	3	0	0	0	0	1	0	0	.250
Dave Philley	rf-ph	4	8	0	1	0	0	0	0	1	3	0	.125
Larry Doby	cf	4	16	0	2	0	0	0	0	2	4	0	.125
Al Smith	cf	4	14	2	3	0	0	1	2	2	2	0	.214
Jim Hegan	c	4	13	1	2	1	0	0	0	1	1	0	.154
Wally Westlake	rf	2	7	0	1	0	0	0	0	1	3	0	.143
Hank Majeski	ph-3b	4	6	1	1	0	0	1	3	0	1	0	.167
Rudy Regalado	pr-3b-ph	4	3	0	1	0	0	0	1	0	0	0	.333
Sam Dente	ss	3	3	1	0	0	0	0	0	1	0	0	.000
Dave Pope	ph-rf-lf	3	3	0	0	0	0	0	0	1	1	0	.000
Billy Glynn	ph-1b	2	2	1	1	1	0	0	0	0	1	0	.500
Dale Mitchell	ph	3	2	0	0	0	0	0	0	1	0	0	.000
Mickey Grasso	c	1	0	0	0	0	0	0	0	0	0	0	.000
Hal Naragon	c	1	0	0	0	0	0	0	0	0	0	0	.000
Bob Lemon	p-ph	3	6	0	0	0	0	0	0	1	1	0	.000
Early Wynn	p	1	2	0	1	1	0	0	0	0	1	0	.500
Don Mossi	p	3	0	0	0	0	0	0	0	0	0	0	.000
Mike Garcia	p	2	0	0	0	0	0	0	0	0	0	0	.000
Ray Narleski	p	2	0	0	0	0	0	0	0	0	0	0	.000
Art Houtteman	p	1	0	0	0	0	0	0	0	0	0	0	.000
Hal Newhouser	p	1	0	0	0	0	0	0	0	0	0	0	.000
Team Total		4	137	9	26	5	1	3	9	16	23	0	.190

Double Plays—2 Left on Bases—37

PITCHING	G	GS	CG	IP	H	R	ER	BB	SO	W	L	SV	ERA
New York													
Johnny Antonelli	2	1	1	10⅔	8	1	1	7	12	1	0	1	**0.84**
Ruben Gomez	1	1	0	7⅓	4	2	2	3	2	1	0	0	2.45
Don Liddle	2	1	0	7	5	4	1	1	2	1	0	0	1.29
Sal Maglie	1	1	0	7	7	2	2	2	2	0	0	0	2.57
Marv Grissom	1	0	0	2⅔	1	0	0	3	2	1	0	0	0.00
Hoyt Wilhelm	2	0	0	2⅓	1	0	0	0	3	0	0	1	0.00
Team Total	4	4	1	37	26	9	6	16	23	4	0	2	1.46
Cleveland													
Bob Lemon	2	2	1	13⅓	16	11	10	8	11	0	2	0	6.75
Early Wynn	1	1	0	7	4	3	3	2	5	0	1	0	3.86
Mike Garcia	2	1	0	5	6	4	3	4	4	0	1	0	5.40
Don Mossi	3	0	0	4	3	0	0	1	0	0	0	0	0.00
Ray Narleski	2	0	0	4	1	1	1	1	2	0	0	0	2.25
Art Houtteman	1	0	0	2	2	1	1	1	1	0	0	0	4.50
Hal Newhouser	1	0	0	0	1	1	1	1	0	0	0	0	0.00
Team Total	4	4	1	35⅓	33	21	19	17	24	0	4	0	4.84

Willie Mays

1955

Brooklyn N.L. 4
New York A.L. 3

Highlights

"NEXT YEAR" FINALLY ARRIVED for Brooklyn. Losers in all seven of their World Series appearances, including the last five against the Yankees, the Dodgers gained their first World Championship in seven games.

Don Newcombe, ace of the Dodgers' staff with a regular season record of 20-5, was still bedeviled by his "Yankee jinx," lasting only 5²/₃ innings in game one, taken by the Bronx Bombers, 6-5.

The Yankees were hampered by injuries: Mickey Mantle sat out games one and two with a leg injury, and Hank Bauer failed to play in game three because of a pulled leg muscle.

The most memorable play of the Series was left fielder Sandy Amoros' catch of Yogi Berra's slicing line drive in the sixth inning of final game. The play turned what looked like a certain extra-base hit into a double play and turned back the surging Yanks for good.

Dodgers were the first team to come back and win Series after losing first two games.

Game 1 Sept. 28
Brooklyn	021 000 020 -	5
New York	021 102 00* -	6

Winner-Ford   Loser-Newcombe

Game 2 Sept. 29
Brooklyn	000 110 000 -	2
New York	000 400 00* -	4

Winner-Byrne   Loser-Loes

Game 3 Sept. 30
New York	020 000 100 -	3
Brooklyn	220 200 20* -	8

Winner-—Podres   Loser-Turley

Game 4 Oct. 1
New York	110 102 000 -	5
Brooklyn	001 330 10* -	8

Winner-Labine   Loser-Larsen

Game 5 Oct. 2
New York	000 100 110 -	3
Brooklyn	021 010 01* -	5

Winner-Craig   Loser-Grim

Game 6 Oct. 3
Brooklyn	000 100 000 -	1
New York	500 000 00* -	5

Winner-Ford   Loser-Spooner

Game 7 Oct. 4
Brooklyn	000 101 000 -	2
New York	000 000 000 -	0

Winner-Podres   Loser-Byrne

Total Attendance—362,310
Average Attendance—51,759
Winning Player's Share—$9,768
Losing Player's Share—$5,599

BATTING

	Pos	G	AB	R	H	2B	3B	HR	RBI	BB	SO	SB	BA
Brooklyn													
Gil Hodges	1b	7	24	2	7	0	0	1	5	3	2	0	.292
Jim Gilliam	lf-2b	7	24	2	7	1	0	0	3	8	1	1	.292
Pee Wee Reese	ss	7	27	5	8	1	0	0	2	3	5	0	.296
Jackie Robinson	3b	6	22	5	4	1	1	0	1	2	1	1	.182
Carl Furillo	rf	7	27	4	8	1	0	1	3	3	5	0	.296
Duke Snider	cf	7	25	5	8	1	0	4	7	2	6	0	.320
Sandy Amoros	lf-cf	5	12	3	4	0	0	1	3	4	4	0	.333
Roy Campanella	c	7	27	4	7	3	0	2	4	3	3	0	.259
Don Zimmer	2b-ph	4	9	0	2	0	0	0	2	2	5	0	.222
Don Hoak	pr-ph-3b	3	3	0	1	0	0	0	0	2	0	0	.333
Frank Kellert	ph	3	3	0	1	0	0	0	0	0	0	0	.333
George Shuba	ph	1	1	0	0	0	0	0	0	0	0	0	.000
Johnny Podres	p	2	7	1	1	0	0	0	0	0	1	0	.143
Clem Labine	p	4	4	0	0	0	0	0	0	0	3	0	.000
Don Newcombe	p	1	3	0	0	0	0	0	0	0	0	0	.000
Russ Meyer	p	1	2	0	0	0	0	0	0	0	1	0	.000
Don Bessent	p	3	1	0	0	0	0	0	0	0	1	0	.000
Billy Loes	p	1	1	0	0	0	0	0	0	0	0	0	.000
Carl Erskine	p	1	1	0	0	0	0	0	0	0	0	0	.000
Karl Spooner	p	2	0	0	0	0	0	0	0	0	1	0	.000
Roger Craig	p	1	0	0	0	0	0	0	0	0	0	0	.000
Ed Roebuck	p	1	0	0	0	0	0	0	0	0	0	0	.000
Team Total		7	223	31	58	8	1	9	30	33	38	2	.260

Double Plays—12   Left on Bases—55

	Pos	G	AB	R	H	2B	3B	HR	RBI	BB	SO	SB	BA
New York													
Joe Collins	1b-rf-ph	5	12	6	2	0	0	2	3	6	4	1	.167
Billy Martin	2b	7	25	2	8	1	1	0	4	1	5	0	.320
Phil Rizzuto	ss	7	15	2	4	0	0	0	1	5	1	2	.267
Gil McDougald	3b	7	27	2	7	0	0	1	1	2	6	0	.259
Hank Bauer	rf-ph	6	14	1	6	0	0	0	1	0	1	0	.429
Irv Noren	cf-lf	5	16	0	1	0	0	0	1	1	1	0	.063
Elston Howard	lf-rf	7	26	3	5	0	0	1	3	1	8	0	.192
Yogi Berra	c	7	24	5	10	1	0	1	2	3	1	0	.417
Bob Cerv	cf-lf-ph	5	16	1	2	0	0	1	1	0	4	0	.125
Bill Skowron	1b-ph	5	12	2	4	2	0	1	3	0	1	0	.333
Mickey Mantle	cf-rf-ph	3	10	1	2	0	0	1	1	0	2	0	.200
Eddie Robinson	ph-1b	4	3	0	2	0	0	0	1	2	1	0	.667
Jerry Coleman	ss-pr	3	3	0	0	0	0	0	0	0	1	0	.000
Andy Carey	ph	2	2	0	1	0	1	0	1	0	0	0	.500
Tommy Carroll	pr	2	0	0	0	0	0	0	0	0	0	0	.000
Tommy Byrne	p-ph	3	6	0	1	0	0	0	2	0	2	0	.167
Whitey Ford	p	2	6	1	0	0	0	0	0	1	1	0	.000
Bob Grim	p	3	2	0	0	0	0	0	0	0	0	0	.000
Don Larsen	p	1	2	0	0	0	0	0	0	0	0	0	.000
Bob Turley	p	3	1	0	0	0	0	0	0	0	0	0	.000
Johnny Kucks	p	2	0	0	0	0	0	0	0	0	0	0	.000
Tom Morgan	p	2	0	0	0	0	0	0	0	0	0	0	.000
Tom Sturdivant	p	2	0	0	0	0	0	0	0	0	0	0	.000
Rip Coleman	p	1	0	0	0	0	0	0	0	0	0	0	.000
Team Total		7	222	26	55	4	2	8	25	22	39	3	.248

Double Plays—7   Left on Bases—41

PITCHING

	G	GS	CG	IP	H	R	ER	BB	SO	W	L	SV	ERA
Brooklyn													
Johnny Podres	2	2	2	18	15	3	2	4	10	2	0	0	1.00
Clem Labine	4	0	0	9⅓	6	3	3	2	2	1	0	1	2.89
Roger Craig	1	1	0	6	4	2	2	5	4	1	0	0	3.00
Russ Meyer	1	0	0	5⅔	4	0	0	2	4	0	0	0	0.00
Don Newcombe	1	1	0	5⅔	8	6	6	2	4	0	1	0	9.53
Billy Loes	1	1	0	3⅔	7	4	4	1	5	0	1	0	9.82
Don Bessent	3	0	0	3⅓	3	0	0	1	1	0	0	0	0.00
Karl Spooner	2	1	0	3⅓	4	5	5	3	6	0	1	0	13.50
Carl Erskine	1	1	0	3	3	3	3	2	3	0	0	0	9.00
Ed Roebuck	1	0	0	2	1	0	0	0	0	0	0	0	0.00
Team Total	7	7	2	60	55	26	25	22	39	4	3	1	3.75
New York													
Whitey Ford	2	2	1	17	13	6	4	8	10	2	0	0	2.12
Tommy Byrne	2	2	1	14⅓	8	4	3	8	8	1	1	0	1.88
Bob Grim	3	1	0	8⅔	8	4	4	5	8	0	1	1	4.15
Bob Turley	3	1	0	5⅓	7	5	5	4	7	0	1	0	8.44
Don Larsen	1	1	0	4	5	5	5	2	2	0	1	0	11.25
Tom Morgan	2	0	0	3⅔	3	2	2	3	1	0	0	0	4.91
Johnny Kucks	2	0	0	3	4	2	2	1	1	0	0	0	6.00
Tom Sturdivant	2	0	0	3	5	2	2	2	0	0	0	0	6.00
Rip Coleman	1	0	0	1	5	1	1	0	1	0	0	0	9.00
Team Total	7	7	2	60	58	31	28	33	38	3	4	1	4.20

1956

Highlights

YANKEE STARTER DON LARSEN (11-5 for the season) was drubbed for four runs in game two. But he stole the Series show in game five when he pitched a perfect no-hit, no-run game—the first ever in World Series history. Larsen made only 97 pitches and struck out seven. Gil Hodges near-ly broke up the perfect game in the fifth when he drove a ball to deep left center that Mickey Mantle ran down and backhanded, and in the eighth when he lined to Andy Carey at third. In the second inning, Robinson came close to spoiling Larsen's moment of glory when he lined a ball off Carey's glove that bounded to shortstop Gil McDougald, who rifled the ball to first to nip the fleet-footed Robinson by a half-step.

Don Newcombe, a fantastic 27-7 per-former during the regular season, failed again against the Yankees as he gave up six runs in 1 2/3 innings in game two, and five runs in three innings of game seven.

This was the last World Series ap-pearance for Robinson and the last time the Dodgers would represent Brooklyn.

Game 1 Oct. 3
New York	200 100 000 ·	3
Brooklyn	023 100 00* ·	6

Winner-Maglie Loser-Ford

Game 2 Oct. 5
New York	150 100 001 ·	8
Brooklyn	061 220 02* ·	13

Winner-Bessent Loser-Morgan

Game 3 Oct. 6
Brooklyn	010 001 100 ·	3
New York	010 003 01* ·	5

Winner-Ford Loser-Craig

Game 4 Oct. 7
Brooklyn	000 100 001 ·	2
New York	100 201 20* ·	6

Winner-Sturdivant Loser-Erskine

Game 5 Oct. 8
Brooklyn	000 000 000 ·	0
New York	000 101 00* ·	2

Winner-Larsen Loser-Maglie

Game 6 Oct. 9
New York	000 000 000 0 ·	0
Brooklyn	000 000 000 1 ·	1

Winner-Labine Loser-Turley

Game 7 Oct. 10
New York	202 100 400 ·	9
Brooklyn	000 000 000 ·	0

Winner-Kucks Loser-Newcombe

Total Attendance—345,903
Average Attendance—49,415
Winning Player's Share—$8,715
Losing Player's Share—$6,934

New York A.L. 4
Brooklyn N.L. 3

BATTING	Pos	G	AB	R	H	2B	3B	HR	RBI	BB	SO	SB	BA
New York													
Joe Collins	1b-ph	6	21	2	5	2	0	0	2	2	3	0	.238
Billy Martin	2b-3b	7	27	5	8	0	0	2	3	1	6	0	.296
Gil Mc Dougald	ss	7	21	0	3	0	0	0	1	3	6	0	.143
Andy Carey	3b	7	19	2	3	0	0	0	0	1	6	0	.158
Hank Bauer	rf	7	32	3	9	0	0	1	3	0	5	1	.281
Mickey Mantle	cf	7	24	6	6	1	0	3	4	6	5	1	.250
Enos Slaughter	lf	6	20	6	7	0	0	1	4	4	0	0	.350
Yogi Berra	c	7	25	5	9	2	0	3	10	4	1	0	**.360**
Bill Skowron	1b-ph	3	10	1	1	0	0	1	4	0	3	0	.100
Elston Howard	lf	5	5	1	2	1	0	1	1	0	0	0	.400
Jerry Coleman	2b	2	2	0	0	0	0	0	0	0	0	0	.000
Bob Cerv	ph	1	1	0	1	0	0	0	0	0	0	0	1.000
Norm Siebern	ph	1	1	0	0	0	0	0	0	0	0	0	.000
George Wilson	ph	1	1	0	0	0	0	0	0	0	1	0	.000
Billy Hunter	Did not play												
Tommy Carroll	Did not play												
Charlie Silvera	Did not play												
Whitey Ford	p	2	4	0	0	0	0	0	0	0	3	0	.000
Don Larsen	p	2	3	1	1	0	0	0	1	0	1	0	.333
Tom Sturdivant	p	2	3	0	1	0	0	0	0	0	1	0	.333
Johnny Kucks	p	3	3	0	0	0	0	0	0	0	1	0	.000
Bob Turley	p	3	4	0	0	0	0	0	0	0	1	0	.000
Tom Morgan	p	2	1	1	1	0	0	0	0	0	0	0	1.000
Mickey McDermott	p	1	1	0	1	0	0	0	0	0	0	0	1.000
Tommy Byrne	ph-p	2	1	0	0	0	0	0	0	0	0	0	.000
Bob Grim	Did not play												
Rip Coleman	Did not play												
Team Total		7	229	33	58	6	0	12	33	21	43	2	.253
	Double Plays—7 Left on Bases—40												
Brooklyn													
Gil Hodges	1b	7	23	5	7	2	0	1	8	4	4	0	.304
Jim Gilliam	2b-lf	7	24	2	2	0	0	0	2	7	3	1	.083
Pee Wee Reese	ss	7	27	3	6	0	1	0	2	2	6	0	.222
Jackie Robinson	3b	7	24	5	6	1	0	1	2	5	2	0	.250
Carl Furillo	rf	7	25	2	6	2	0	0	1	2	3	0	.240
Duke Snider	cf	7	23	5	7	1	0	1	4	6	8	0	.304
Sandy Amoros	lf	6	19	1	1	0	0	0	1	2	4	0	.053
Roy Campanella	c	7	22	2	4	1	0	0	3	3	7	0	.182
Charlie Neal	2b	1	4	0	0	0	0	0	0	0	1	0	.000
Gino Cimoli	of	1	0	0	0	0	0	0	0	0	0	0	.000
Dale Mitchell	ph	4	4	0	0	0	0	0	0	0	1	0	.000
Randy Jackson	ph	3	3	0	0	0	0	0	0	0	2	0	.000
Rube Walker	ph	2	2	0	0	0	0	0	0	0	0	0	.000
Chico Fernandez	Did not play												
Dixie Howell	Did not play												
Sal Maglie	p	2	5	0	0	0	0	0	0	0	2	0	.000
Clem Labine	p	2	4	0	1	1	0	0	0	0	2	0	.250
Don Bessent	p	2	2	0	1	0	0	0	1	1	1	0	.500
Roger Craig	p	2	2	0	1	0	0	0	0	0	0	0	.500
Don Newcombe	p	2	1	0	0	0	0	0	0	0	0	0	.000
Carl Erskine	p	2	1	0	0	0	0	0	0	0	1	0	.000
Ed Roebuck	p	3	0	0	0	0	0	0	0	0	0	0	.000
Don Drysdale	p	1	0	0	0	0	0	0	0	0	0	0	.000
Ken Lehman	Did not play												
Sandy Koufax	Did not play												
Team Total		7	215	25	42	8	1	3	24	32	47	1	.195
	Double Plays—8 Left on Bases—42												

PITCHING	G	GS	CG	IP	H	R	ER	BB	SO	W	L	SV	ERA
New York													
Whitey Ford	2	2	1	12	14	8	7	2	8	1	1	0	5.25
Bob Turley	3	1	1	11	4	1	1	8	14	0	1	0	0.82
Johnny Kucks	3	1	1	11	6	2	1	3	2	1	0	0	0.82
Don Larsen	2	2	1	10 2/3	1	4	0	4	7	1	0	0	**0.00**
Tom Sturdivant	2	1	1	9 2/3	8	3	3	8	9	1	0	0	2.79
Tom Morgan	2	0	0	4	6	4	4	3	0	0	1	0	9.00
Mickey McDermott	1	0	0	3	2	2	1	3	3	0	0	0	3.00
Tommy Byrne	1	0	0	1/3	1	1	0	0	1	0	0	0	0.00
Bob Grim	Did not play												
Rip Coleman	Did not play												
Team Total	7	7	5	61 2/3	42	25	17	32	47	4	3	0	2.48
Brooklyn													
Sal Maglie	2	2	2	17	14	5	5	6	15	1	1	0	2.65
Clem Labine	2	1	1	12	8	1	0	3	7	1	0	0	**0.00**
Don Bessent	2	0	0	10	8	2	2	3	5	1	0	0	1.80
Roger Craig	2	1	0	6	10	8	8	3	4	0	1	0	12.00
Carl Erskine	2	1	0	5	4	3	3	2	2	0	1	0	5.40
Don Newcombe	2	2	0	4 2/3	11	11	11	3	4	0	1	0	21.21
Ed Roebuck	3	0	0	4 1/3	1	1	1	0	5	0	0	0	2.08
Don Drysdale	1	0	0	2	2	2	2	1	1	0	0	0	9.00
Ken Lehman	Did not play												
Sandy Koufax	Did not play												
Team Total	7	7	3	61	58	33	32	21	43	3	4	0	4.72

1957

Highlights

THE MILWAUKEE BRAVES, TRANS-planted from Boston in 1953—in the first major-league franchise shift since 1903, won the N.L. championship with Warren Spahn (21) games, the only holdover from the 1948 Braves.

Turning point of Series came in game four, when the game appeared lost for the Braves after they blew a 4-1 lead with two out in the ninth. The Yankees put two men on with singles, and then Elston Howard smashed a three-run homer to tie the game, sending it into extra innings. The Yanks quickly added another run in the tenth, when Tony Kubek singled and was chased home by Hank Bauer's triple. The Braves, who had not managed a base hit since their four-run outburst in the fourth, were only three outs from defeat. Then pinch hitter Nippy Jones took first after being hit by a pitch. Felix Mantilla pinch-ran for Jones, and was promptly sacrificed to second by Red Schoendienst. Johnny Logan doubled home Mantilla to tie the game, and Eddie Matthews hit his first World Series home run over the right-field fence to win the game 7-5, thus tieing the series at two games apiece.

Lew Burdette, a 17-game winner during the regular season, used the World Series to round out his victory total at an even 20 games. Amidst Yankee complaints that he was throwing a spitter, he beat Stengel's nine three times: 4-2 in game, 1-0 in game five and 5-0 in the final game.

Game 1 Oct. 2
Milwaukee 000 000 100 - 1
New York 000 012 00* - 3
Winner-Ford Loser-Spahn

Game 2 Oct. 3
Milwaukee 011 200 000 - 4
New York 011 000 000 - 2
Winner-Burdette Loser-Shantz

Game 3 Oct. 5
New York 302 200 500 - 12
Milwaukee 010 020 000 - 3
Winner-Larsen Loser-Buhl

Game 4 Oct. 6
New York 100 000 003 1 - 5
Milwaukee 000 400 000 3 - 7
Winner-Spahn Loser-Grim

Game 5 Oct. 7
New York 000 000 000 - 0
Milwaukee 000 001 00* - 1
Winner-Burdette Loser-Ford

Game 6 Oct. 9
Milwaukee 000 010 100 - 2
New York 002 000 10* - 3
Winner-Turley Loser-E. Johnson

Game 7 Oct. 10
Milwaukee 004 000 010 - 5
New York 000 000 000 - 0
Winner-Burdette Loser-Larsen

Total Attendance—394,712
Average Attendance—56,387
Winning Player's Share—$8,924
Losing Player's Share—$5,606

Milwaukee N.L. 4
New York A.L. 3

BATTING	Pos	G	AB	R	H	2B	3B	HR	RBI	BB	SO	SB	BA
Milwaukee													
Joe Adcock	1b-ph	5	15	1	3	0	0	0	2	0	2	0	.200
Red Schoendienst	2b	5	18	0	5	1	0	0	2	0	1	0	.278
Johnny Logan	ss	7	27	5	5	1	0	1	2	3	6	0	.185
Eddie Mathews	3b	7	22	4	5	3	0	1	4	8	5	0	.227
Andy Pafko	rf-ph	6	14	1	3	0	0	0	0	0	1	0	.214
Hank Aaron	cf	7	28	5	11	0	1	3	7	1	6	0	**.393**
Wes Covington	lf	7	24	1	5	1	0	0	1	2	6	1	.208
Del Crandall	c	6	19	1	4	0	0	1	1	1	1	0	.211
Bob Hazle	rf	4	13	2	2	0	0	0	0	0	2	0	.154
Frank Torre	1b-ph	7	10	2	3	0	0	2	3	2	0	0	.300
Felix Mantilla	pr-2b	4	10	2	0	0	0	0	0	0	1	0	.000
Del Rice	c	2	6	0	1	0	0	0	0	1	2	0	.167
Nippy Jones	ph	3	2	0	0	0	0	0	0	0	0	0	.000
Carl Sawatski	ph	2	2	0	0	0	0	0	0	0	2	0	.000
John DeMerit	ph	1	0	0	0	0	0	0	0	0	0	0	.000
Mel Roach	Did not play												
Lew Burdette	p	3	8	0	0	0	0	0	0	0	1	2	0	.000
Warren Spahn	p	2	4	0	0	0	0	0	0	0	1	2	0	.000
Ernie Johnson	p	3	1	0	0	0	0	0	0	0	0	1	0	.000
Bob Buhl	p	2	1	0	0	0	0	0	0	0	0	1	0	.000
Juan Pizzaro	p	1	1	0	0	0	0	0	0	0	0	0	0	.000
Don McMahon	p	3	0	0	0	0	0	0	0	0	0	0	0	.000
Gene Conley	p	1	0	0	0	0	0	0	0	0	0	0	0	.000
Bob Trowbridge	p	1	0	0	0	0	0	0	0	0	0	0	0	.000
Taylor Phillips	Did not play												
Dave Jolley	Did not play												
Team Total		7	225	23	47	6	1	8	22	22	40	1	.209

Double Plays—10   Left on Bases—46

New York	Pos	G	AB	R	H	2B	3B	HR	RBI	BB	SO	SB	BA
New York													
Elston Howard	1b-ph	6	11	2	3	0	0	1	3	1	3	0	.273
Jerry Coleman	2b	7	22	2	8	2	0	0	2	3	1	0	.364
Gil McDougald	ss	7	24	3	6	0	0	0	2	3	3	1	.250
Jerry Lumpe	3b-ph	4	14	0	4	0	0	0	1	1	1	0	.286
Hank Bauer	rf	7	31	3	8	2	1	2	6	1	6	0	.258
Mickey Mantle	cf-pr	6	19	3	5	0	0	1	2	3	1	0	.263
Tony Kubek	1f-3b-cf	7	28	4	8	0	0	2	4	0	4	0	.286
Yogi Berra	c	7	25	5	8	1	0	1	2	4	0	0	.320
Enos Slaughter	lf	5	12	2	3	1	0	0	0	3	2	0	.250
Harry Simpson	1b-ph	5	12	0	1	0	0	0	1	0	4	0	.083
Andy Carey	3b	2	7	0	2	1	0	0	1	1	0	0	.286
Joe Collins	1b-ph	6	5	0	0	0	0	0	0	0	3	0	.000
Bill Skowron	1b-ph	2	4	0	0	0	0	0	0	0	0	0	.000
Bobby Richardson	pr-2b	2	0	0	0	0	0	0	0	0	0	0	.000
Darrell Johnson	Did not play												
Whitey Ford	p	2	5	0	0	0	0	0	0	0	1	0	.000
Bob Turley	p	3	4	0	0	0	0	0	0	0	2	0	.000
Tommy Byrne	2	2	0	1	0	0	0	0	0	1	0	0	.500
Don Larsen	p	2	1	0	0	0	0	0	0	2	1	0	.000
Tom Sturdivant	p	2	1	0	0	0	0	0	0	0	0	0	.000
Bobby Shantz	p	3	1	0	0	0	0	0	0	0	1	0	.000
Art Ditmar	p	2	1	0	0	0	0	0	0	0	0	0	.000
Bob Grim	p	2	0	0	0	0	0	0	0	0	0	0	.000
Johnny Kucks	p	1	0	0	0	0	0	0	0	0	0	0	.000
Al Cicotte	Did not play												
Team Total		7	230	25	57	7	1	7	25	22	34	1	.248

Double Plays—5   Left on Bases—45

PITCHING	G	GS	CG	IP	H	R	ER	BB	SO	W	L	SV	ERA
Milwaukee													
Lew Burdette	3	3	3	27	21	2	2	4	13	3	0	0	**0.67**
Warren Spahn	2	2	1	15⅓	18	8	8	2	2	1	1	0	4.70
Ernie Johnson	3	0	0	7	2	1	1	1	8	0	1	0	1.29
Don McMahon	3	0	0	5	3	0	0	3	5	0	0	0	0.00
Bob Buhl	2	2	0	3⅓	6	5	4	6	4	0	1	0	10.80
Juan Pizzaro	1	0	0	1⅔	3	2	2	2	1	0	0	0	10.80
Gene Conley	0	0	0	1⅔	2	2	2	1	0	0	0	0	10.80
Bob Trowbridge	1	0	0	1	2	5	5	3	1	0	0	0	45.00
Taylor Phillips	Did not play												
Dave Jolley	Did not play												
Team Total	7	7	4	62	57	25	24	22	34	4	3	0	3.48

New York	G	GS	CG	IP	H	R	ER	BB	SO	W	L	SV	ERA
New York													
Whitey Ford	2	2	1	16	11	2	2	5	7	1	1	0	1.13
Bob Turley	3	2	1	11⅔	7	3	3	6	12	1	0	0	2.31
Don Larsen	2	1	0	9⅔	8	5	4	5	6	1	1	0	3.72
Bobby Shantz	3	1	0	6⅔	8	5	3	2	7	0	1	0	4.05
Art Ditmar	2	0	0	6	2	0	0	2	0	0	0	0	0.00
Tom Sturdivant	2	1	0	6	4	4	4	1	2	0	0	0	6.00
Tommy Byrne	2	0	0	3⅓	1	2	2	2	1	0	0	0	5.40
Bob Grim	2	0	0	2⅓	3	2	2	0	2	0	1	0	7.71
Johnny Kucks	1	0	0	⅔	1	0	0	1	1	0	0	0	0.00
Al Cicotte	Did not play												
Team Total	7	7	2	62⅓	47	23	20	22	40	3	4	0	2.89

1958

New York A.L. 4
Milwaukee N.L. 3

Highlights

NEW YORK CITY RECLAIMED THE the World Championship when the Yankees triumphed, four games to three, over the Milwaukee Braves. With the Giants and Dodgers now playing in California, Casey Stengel's club was New York's only hope, and they came through after being down, three games to one. Their comeback from this deficit made them the first club to accomplish this feat since the 1925 Pittsburgh Pirates.

Hank Bauer led the Yanks with a .323 batting average and ten hits, including four home runs and eight RBI's. His finest performance was in game three, when the Yankees were down two games to none. He banged a two-run single in the fifth inning, and a two-run homer in the seventh to give them a 4-0 victory. These hits extended his World Series consecutive game hitting streak to 17, a Series record.

In game five, Elston Howard, playing left field, made a sparkling defensive play in the sixth inning to shut down a Braves rally. With no outs and Billy Bruton on first, he made a diving catch of Red Schoendienst's sinking line drive, and then relayed the ball to Gil McDougald to double Bruton off first, thus preserving a shaky 1-0 lead for pitcher Bob Turley. A game-saving play, it also seemed to inspire the Yanks at the plate, as they outscored the Braves for the remainder of the Series, 16-5, enough to sweep the final three games and the Championship.

Game 1 Oct. 1
New York	000 120 000 0	·	3
Milwaukee	000 200 010 1	·	4

Winner-Spahn Loser-Duren

Game 2 Oct. 2
New York	100 100 003	·	5
Milwaukee	710 000 23*	·	13

Winner-Burdette Loser-Turley

Game 3 Oct. 4
Milwaukee	000 000 000	·	0
New York	000 020 20*	·	4

Winner-Larsen Loser-Rush

Game 4 Oct. 5
Milwaukee	000 001 110	·	3
New York	000 000 000	·	0

Winner-Spahn Loser-Ford

Game 5 Oct.6
Milwaukee	000 000 000	·	0
New York	001 006 00*	·	7

Winner-Turley Loser-Burdette

Game 6 Oct. 8
New York	100 001 000 2	·	4
Milwaukee	110 000 000 1	·	3

Winner-Duren Loser-Spahn

Game 7 Oct. 9
New York	020 000 040	·	6
Milwaukee	100 001 000	·	2

Winner-Turley Loser-Burdette

Total Attendance—393,909
Average Attendance—56,273
Winning Player's Share—$8,759
Losing Player's Share—$5,896

BATTING

	Pos	G	AB	R	H	2B	3B	HR	RBI	BB	SO	SB	BA
New York													
Bill Skowron	1b	7	27	3	7	0	0	2	7	1	4	0	.259
Gil McDougald	2b	7	28	5	9	2	0	2	4	2	4	0	.321
Tony Kubek	ss	7	21	0	1	0	0	0	1	1	7	0	.048
Jerry Lumpe	3b-ss-ph	6	12	0	2	0	0	0	0	1	2	0	.167
Hank Bauer	rf	7	31	6	10	0	0	4	8	0	5	0	.323
Mickey Mantle	cf	7	24	4	6	0	1	2	3	7	4	0	.250
Elston Howard	lf-ph	6	18	4	4	0	0	0	2	1	4	1	.222
Yogi Berra	c	7	27	3	6	3	0	0	2	1	0	0	.222
Andy Carey	3b	5	12	1	1	0	0	0	0	0	3	0	.083
Norm Siebern	lf	3	8	1	1	0	0	0	0	3	2	0	.125
Bobby Richardson	3b	4	5	0	0	0	0	0	0	0	1	0	.000
Enos Slaughter	ph	4	3	1	0	0	0	0	0	1	1	0	.000
Marv Throneberry	ph	1	1	0	0	0	0	0	0	0	1	0	.000
Darrell Johnson	Did not play												
Bob Turley	p	4	5	0	1	0	0	0	0	2	0	1	.200
Whitey Ford	p	3	4	1	0	0	0	0	0	2	2	0	.000
Ryne Duren	p	3	3	0	0	0	0	0	0	0	1	2	.000
Don Larsen	p	2	2	0	0	0	0	0	0	1	0	0	.000
Johnny Kucks	p	2	1	0	1	0	0	0	0	0	0	0	1.000
Art Ditmar	p	1	1	0	0	0	0	0	0	0	0	0	.000
Murry Dickson	p	2	0	0	0	0	0	0	0	0	0	0	.000
Duke Maas	p	1	0	0	0	0	0	0	0	0	0	0	.000
Zack Monroe	p	1	0	0	0	0	0	0	0	0	0	0	.000
Bobby Shantz	Did not play												
Tom Sturdivant	Did not play—sore arm												
Team Total		7	233	29	49	5	1	10	29	21	42	1	.210

Double Plays—5 Left on Bases—40

	Pos	G	AB	R	H	2B	3B	HR	RBI	BB	SO	SB	BA
Milwaukee													
Frank Torre	1b-ph	7	17	0	3	0	0	0	1	2	0	0	.176
Red Schoendienst	2b	7	30	5	9	3	1	0	0	2	1	0	.300
Johnny Logan	ss	7	25	3	3	2	0	0	2	2	4	0	.120
Eddie Mathews	3b	7	25	3	4	2	0	0	3	6	11	1	.160
Hank Aaron	rf-cf	7	27	3	9	2	0	0	2	4	6	0	.333
Bill Bruton	ph-cf-pr	7	17	2	7	0	0	1	2	5	5	0	.412
Wes Covington	lf	7	26	2	7	0	0	0	4	2	4	0	.269
Del Crandall	c	7	25	4	6	0	0	1	3	3	10	0	.240
Joe Adcock	1b-ph	4	13	1	4	0	0	0	1	0	3	0	.308
Andy Pafko	cf-rf-lf	4	9	0	3	1	0	0	1	0	0	0	.333
Felix Mantilla	ss-ph	4	0	1	0	0	0	0	0	1	0	0	.000
Harry Hanebrink	ph	2	2	0	0	0	0	0	0	0	0	0	.000
Casey Wise	ph-pr	2	1	0	0	0	0	0	0	0	1	0	.000
Del Rice	Did not play												
Warren Spahn	p	3	12	0	4	0	0	0	3	0	6	0	.333
Lew Burdette	p	3	9	1	1	0	0	1	3	0	3	0	.111
Bob Rush	p	1	2	0	0	0	0	0	0	0	2	0	.000
Don McMahon	p	3	0	0	0	0	0	0	0	0	0	0	.000
Juan Pizarro	p	1	0	0	0	0	0	0	0	0	0	0	.000
Carl Willey	p	1	0	0	0	0	0	0	0	0	0	0	.000
Bob Buhl	Did not play—sore arm												
Ernie Johnson	Did not play												
Humberto Robinson	Did not play												
Bob Trowbridge	Did not play												
Gene Conley	Did not play—arm injury												
Team Total		7	240	25	60	10	1	3	24	27	56	1	.250

Double Plays—5 Left on Bases—58

PITCHING

	G	GS	CG	IP	H	R	ER	BB	SO	W	L	SV	ERA
New York													
Bob Turley	4	2	1	16⅓	10	5	5	7	13	2	1	1	2.76
Whitey Ford	3	3	0	15⅓	19	8	7	5	16	0	1	0	4.11
Don Larsen	2	2	0	9⅓	9	1	1	6	9	1	0	0	0.96
Ryne Duren	3	0	0	9⅓	7	2	2	6	14	1	1	1	1.93
Johnny Kucks	2	0	0	4⅓	4	1	1	1	0	0	0	0	2.08
Murry Dickson	2	0	0	4	4	2	2	0	1	0	0	0	4.56
Art Ditmar	1	0	0	3⅔	2	0	0	0	2	0	0	0	0.00
Zack Monroe	1	0	0	1	3	3	3	1	1	0	0	0	27.00
Duke Maas	1	0	0	⅓	2	3	3	1	0	0	0	0	81.00
Bobby Shantz	Did not play												
Tom Sturdivant	Did not play												
Team Total	7	7	1	63⅔	60	25	24	27	56	4	3	2	3.39

	G	GS	CG	IP	H	R	ER	BB	SO	W	L	SV	ERA
Milwaukee													
Warren Spahn	3	3	2	28⅔	19	7	7	8	18	2	1	0	2.20
Lew Burdette	3	3	1	22⅓	22	17	14	4	12	1	2	0	5.64
Bob Rush	1	1	0	6	3	2	2	5	2	0	1	0	3.00
Don McMahon	3	0	0	3⅓	3	2	2	3	5	0	0	0	5.40
Juan Pizarro	1	0	0	1⅔	2	1	1	1	3	0	0	0	5.40
Carl Willey	1	0	0	1	0	0	0	0	2	0	0	0	0.00
Bob Buhl	Did not play—sore arm												
Ernie Johnson	Did not play												
Humberto Robinson	Did not play												
Bob Trowbridge	Did not play												
Gene Conley	Did not play—arm injury												
Team Total	7	7	3	63	49	29	26	21	42	3	4	0	3.71

1959

Los Angeles N.L. 4
Chicago A.L. 2

Highlights

THE THIRD PLAYOFF IN NATIONAL League history decided the championship as the Los Angeles Dodgers, in their second year in their new home city, swept the Milwaukee Braves, two games to none: 3-2 and 6-5 in 12 innings.

Series matchup featured two teams that relied on speed, pitching and defense, and in the end, it was superior relief pitching by Dodger Larry Sherry that made the difference. After absorbing an 11-0 pasting by the White Sox in game one, Larry Sherry preserved a 4-3 Dodgers victory in game two after relieving starter Johnny Podres in the seventh. In game three, he saved Don Drysdale's 3-1 victory; he entered the game in the eighth inning with two men on base and no outs and pitched shutout ball the rest of the way. In game four, with the score tied at 4-4, Sherry pitched scoreless ball through the eighth and ninth innings; Gil Hodges' eighth-inning home run gave Sherry and the Dodgers a 5-4 victory. In game six, he again saved the Dodgers' 9-3 victory by pitching 5⅔ innings of shutout ball. He finished the Series with two victories and two saves, and a 0.71 ERA.

Chicago White Sox appearance in the Series was their first since 1919.

Game 1 Oct. 1
Los Angeles	000 000 000	- 0
Chicago	207 200 00*	- 11

Winner-Wynn Loser-Craig

Game 2 Oct. 2
Los Angeles	000 010 300	- 4
Chicago	200 000 010	- 3

Winner-Podres Loser-Shaw

Game 3 Oct. 4
Chicago	000 000 010	- 1
Los Angeles	000 000 21*	- 3

Winner-Drysdale Loser-Donovan

Game 4 Oct. 5
Chicago	000 000 400	- 4
Los Angeles	004 000 01*	- 5

Winner-Sherry Loser-Staley

Game 5 Oct. 6
Chicago	000 100 000	- 1
Los Angeles	000 000 000	- 0

Winner-Shaw Loser-Koufax

Game 6 Oct. 8
Los Angeles	002 600 001	- 9
Chicago	000 300 000	- 3

Winner-Sherry Loser-Wynn

Total Attendance—420,784
Average Attendance—70,131
Winning Player's Share—$11,231
Losing Player's Share—$7,275

BATTING	Pos	G	AB	R	H	2B	3B	HR	RBI	BB	SO	SB	BA
Los Angeles													
Gil Hodges	1b	6	23	2	9	0	1	1	2	1	2	0	.391
Charlie Neal	2b	6	27	4	10	2	0	2	6	0	1	1	.370
Maury Wills	ss	6	20	2	5	0	0	0	1	0	3	1	.250
Jim Gilliam	3b	6	25	2	6	0	0	0	0	2	2	2	.240
Norm Larker	rf-lf	6	16	2	3	0	0	0	0	2	3	0	.188
Don Demeter	cf-pr	6	12	2	3	0	0	0	0	1	3	0	.250
Wally Moon	lf-rf-cf	6	23	3	6	0	0	1	2	2	2	1	.261
Johnny Roseboro	c	6	21	0	2	0	0	0	1	0	2	0	.095
Duke Snider	cf-rf-ph	4	10	1	2	0	0	1	2	2	0	0	.200
Carl Furillo	ph-rf	4	4	0	1	0	0	0	2	0	1	0	.250
Ron Fairly	ph-rf-pr-cf	6	3	0	0	0	0	0	0	0	1	0	.000
Don Zimmer	pr-ss	1	1	0	0	0	0	0	0	0	0	0	.000
Joe Pignatano	c	1	0	0	0	0	0	0	0	0	0	0	.000
Chuck Essegian	ph	4	3	2	2	0	0	2	2	1	1	0	.667
Rip Repulski	ph-rf	1	0	0	0	0	0	0	0	1	0	0	.000
Larry Sherry	p-ph	5	4	0	2	0	0	0	0	0	1	0	.500
Johnny Podres	p-pr	3	4	1	2	1	0	0	1	0	0	0	.500
Roger Craig	p	2	3	0	0	0	0	0	0	0	2	0	.000
Sandy Koufax	p	2	2	0	0	0	0	0	0	0	1	0	.000
Don Drysdale	p	1	2	0	0	0	0	0	0	0	2	0	.000
Chuck Churn	p	1	0	0	0	0	0	0	0	0	0	0	.000
Johnny Klippstein	p	1	0	0	0	0	0	0	0	0	0	0	.000
Clem Labine	p	1	0	0	0	0	0	0	0	0	0	0	.000
Stan Williams	p	1	0	0	0	0	0	0	0	0	0	0	.000
Danny McDevitt	Did not play												
Team Total		6	203	21	53	3	1	7	19	12	27	5	.261

Double Plays—7   Left on Bases—42

	Pos	G	AB	R	H	2B	3B	HR	RBI	BB	SO	SB	BA
Chicago													
Ted Kluszewski	1b	6	23	5	9	1	0	3	10	2	0	0	.391
Nellie Fox	2b	6	24	4	9	3	0	0	0	4	1	0	.375
Luis Aparicio	ss	6	26	1	8	1	0	0	0	2	3	1	.308
Billy Goodman	3b-ph	5	13	0	3	0	0	0	1	0	5	0	.231
Jim Rivera	rf	5	11	1	0	0	0	0	0	3	1	0	.000
Jim Landis	cf	6	24	6	7	0	0	0	1	1	7	1	.292
Al Smith	lf-rf	6	20	1	5	3	0	0	1	4	4	0	.250
Sherm Lollar	c	6	22	3	5	0	0	1	5	1	3	0	.227
Bubba Phillips	3b-rf	3	10	0	3	1	0	0	0	0	0	0	.300
Jim McAnany	rf-lf	3	5	0	0	0	0	0	0	1	0	0	.000
Earl Torgeson	pr-1b-ph	3	1	1	0	0	0	0	0	1	0	0	.000
Sammy Esposito	3b-pr	2	2	0	0	0	0	0	0	0	1	0	.000
Norm Cash	ph	4	4	0	0	0	0	0	0	0	2	0	.000
Johnny Romano	ph	1	1	0	0	0	0	0	0	0	0	0	.000
Earl Battey	Did not play												
Early Wynn	p	3	5	0	1	1	0	0	1	0	2	0	.200
Bob Shaw	p	2	4	0	1	0	0	0	0	0	2	0	.250
Dick Donovan	p	3	3	0	1	0	0	0	0	0	1	0	.333
Gerry Staley	p	4	1	0	0	0	0	0	0	1	1	0	.000
Turk Lown	p	3	0	0	0	0	0	0	0	0	0	0	.000
Billy Pierce	p	3	0	0	0	0	0	0	0	0	0	0	.000
Ray Moore	p	1	0	0	0	0	0	0	0	0	0	0	.000
Barry Latman	Did not play												
Rudy Arias	Did not play												
Ken McBride	Did not play												
Team Total		6	199	23	52	10	0	4	19	20	33	2	.261

Double Plays—2   Left on Bases—43

PITCHING	G	GS	CG	IP	H	R	ER	BB	SO	W	L	SV	ERA
Los Angeles													
Larry Sherry	4	0	0	12⅔	8	1	1	2	5	2	0	2	0.71
Johnny Podres	2	2	0	9⅓	7	5	5	6	4	1	0	0	4.82
Roger Craig	2	2	0	9⅓	15	9	9	5	8	0	1	0	8.68
Sandy Koufax	2	1	0	9	5	1	1	1	7	0	1	0	1.00
Don Drysdale	1	1	0	7	11	1	1	4	5	1	0	0	1.29
Stan Williams	1	0	0	2	0	0	0	2	1	0	0	0	0.00
Johnny Klippstein	1	0	0	2	1	0	0	0	2	0	0	0	0.00
Clem Labine	1	0	0	1	0	0	0	0	1	0	0	0	0.00
Chuck Churn	1	0	0	⅔	5	6	2	0	0	0	0	0	27.00
Team Total	6	6	0	53	52	23	19	20	33	4	2	2	3.23
Chicago													
Bob Shaw	2	2	0	14	17	4	4	2	2	1	1	0	2.57
Early Wynn	3	3	0	13	19	9	8	4	10	1	1	0	5.54
Gerry Staley	4	0	0	8⅓	8	2	2	0	3	0	1	1	2.16
Dick Donovan	3	1	0	8⅓	4	5	5	3	5	0	1	1	5.40
Billy Pierce	3	0	0	4	2	0	0	2	3	0	0	0	0.00
Turk Lown	3	0	0	3⅓	2	0	0	1	3	0	0	0	0.00
Ray Moore	1	0	0	1	1	1	1	0	1	0	0	0	9.00
Team Total	6	6	0	52	53	21	20	12	27	2	4	2	3.46

Yogi Berra

1960

Pittsburgh N.L. 4
New York A.L. 3

Highlights

THIS SERIES MARKED YANKEES manager Casey Stengel's last year with the team, an era that gave New York Yankees fans ten pennants and seven World Championships.

Yanks set Series records with 55 runs scored, 91 hits, 27 extra-base hits and a .338 team batting average.

Game seven was one of the most dramatic in Series history. Trailing 4-0 after four innings, the Yanks rallied with Bill "Moose" Skowron's solo homer in the fifth, and Mickey Mantle's run-scoring single and Yogi Berra's three-run homer in the sixth. They added two more runs in the top of the eighth to make their lead, 7-4. The World Championship was only six outs away. But after Pirate Gino Cimoli led off the eighth with a pinch single, Bill Virdon's hard-hit grounder to shortstop Tony Kubek took a bad hop and struck Kubek in the throat, spoiling a certain double play. At first, the unfortunate play did not appear disastrous as the Yanks hung on to retire Bob Skinner and Rocky Nelson, but the Pirates rallied with Roberto Clemente's single and Hal Smith's three-run homer, sending the Bucs ahead, 9-7. The Yankees scored two runs in the top of the ninth on three singles and a fielder's choice play to tie the score, 9-9. Then, in the bottom of the ninth, Pittsburgh's Bill Mazeroski sent a towering drive over the left center-field fence off Ralph Terry's second pitch.

Game 1 Oct. 5
New York   100 100 002 · 4
Pittsburgh   300 201 00* · 6
Winner-Law   Loser-Ditmar

Game 2 Oct. 6
New York   002 127 301 · 16
Pittsburgh   000 100 002 · 3
Winner-Turley   Loser-Friend

Game 3 Oct. 8
Pittsburgh   000 000 000 · 0
New York   600 400 00* · 10
Winner-Ford   Loser-Mizell

Game 4 Oct. 9
Pittsburgh   000 030 000 · 3
New York   000 100 100 · 2
Winner-Law   Loser-Terry

Game 5 Oct. 10
Pittsburgh   031 000 001 · 5
New York   011 000 000 · 2
Winner-Haddix   Loser-Ditmar

Game 6 Oct. 12
New York   015 002 220 · 12
Pittsburgh   000 000 000 · 0
Winner-Ford   Loser-Friend

Game 7 Oct. 13
New York   000 014 022 · 9
Pittsburgh   220 000 051 · 10
Winner-Haddix   Loser-Terry

Total Attendance—349,813
Average Attendance—49,973
Winning Player's Share—$8,418
Losing Player's Share—$5,125

BATTING

BATTING	Pos	G	AB	R	H	2B	3B	HR	RBI	BB	SO	SB	BA
Pittsburgh													
Dick Stuart	1b	6	20	0	3	0	0	0	0	0	3	0	.150
Bill Mazeroski	2b	7	25	4	8	2	0	2	5	0	3	0	.320
Dick Groat	ss	7	28	3	6	2	0	0	2	0	1	0	.214
Don Hoak	3b	7	23	3	5	2	0	0	3	4	1	0	.217
Roberto Clemente	rf	7	29	1	9	0	0	0	3	0	4	0	.310
Bill Virdon	cf	7	29	2	7	3	0	0	5	1	3	1	.241
Gino Cimoli	lf-ph	7	20	4	5	0	0	0	1	2	4	0	.250
Smoky Burgess	c	5	18	2	6	1	0	0	0	2	1	0	.333
Rocky Nelson	1b-ph	4	9	2	3	0	0	1	2	1	1	0	.333
Bob Skinner	lf	2	5	2	1	0	0	0	1	1	0	1	.200
Hal Smith	c	3	8	1	3	0	0	1	3	0	0	0	.375
Dick Schofield	ph-ss	3	3	0	1	0	0	0	0	1	0	0	.333
Gene Baker	ph	3	3	0	0	0	0	0	0	0	1	0	.000
Joe Christopher	ph-pr	3	0	2	0	0	0	0	0	0	0	0	.000
Bob Oldis	c	2	0	0	0	0	0	0	0	0	0	0	.000
Vernon Law	p	3	6	1	2	1	0	0	1	0	1	0	.333
Roy Face	p	4	3	0	0	0	0	0	0	0	2	0	.000
Harvey Haddix	p	2	3	0	1	0	0	0	0	0	1	0	.333
Bob Friend	p	3	1	0	0	0	0	0	0	0	0	0	.000
Freddie Green	p	3	1	0	0	0	0	0	0	0	0	0	.000
Tom Cheney	p	3	0	0	0	0	0	0	0	0	0	0	.000
Clem Labine	p	3	0	0	0	0	0	0	0	0	0	0	.000
George Witt	p	2	0	0	0	0	0	0	0	0	0	0	.000
Vinegar Bend Mizell	p	2	0	0	0	0	0	0	0	0	0	0	.000
Joe Gibbon	p	2	0	0	0	0	0	0	0	0	0	0	.000
Team Total		7	234	27	60	11	0	4	26	12	26	2	.256

Double Plays—7   Left on Bases—42

	Pos	G	AB	R	H	2B	3B	HR	RBI	BB	SO	SB	BA
New York													
Bill Skowron	1b	7	32	7	12	2	0	2	6	1	6	0	.375
Bobby Richardson	2b	7	30	8	11	2	2	1	12	1	1	0	.367
Tony Kubek	ss-lf	7	30	6	10	1	0	0	3	2	2	0	.333
Gil McDougald	3b-pr	6	18	4	5	1	0	0	2	2	3	0	.278
Roger Maris	rf	7	30	6	8	1	0	2	2	2	4	0	.267
Mickey Mantle	cf	7	25	8	10	1	0	3	11	8	9	0	.400
Yogi Berra	lf-c-rf-ph	7	22	6	7	0	0	1	8	2	0	0	.318
Elston Howard	c-ph	5	13	4	6	1	1	1	4	1	4	0	.462
Bob Cerv	ph-lf	4	14	1	5	0	0	0	0	0	3	0	.357
Clete Boyer	3b-ss	4	12	1	3	2	1	0	1	0	1	0	.250
Johnny Blanchard	ph-c	5	11	2	5	2	0	0	2	0	0	0	.455
Hector Lopez	lf-ph	3	7	0	3	0	0	0	0	0	0	0	.429
Joe DeMaestri	ss-pr	4	2	1	1	0	0	0	0	0	1	0	.500
Dale Long	ph	3	3	0	1	0	0	0	0	0	0	0	.333
Eli Grba	pr	1	0	0	0	0	0	0	0	0	0	0	.000
Whitey Ford	p	2	8	1	2	0	0	0	0	2	2	0	.250
Bob Turley	p	2	4	0	1	0	0	0	0	1	1	0	.250
Bobby Shantz	p	3	3	0	1	0	0	0	0	0	0	0	.333
Ralph Terry	p	2	2	0	0	0	0	0	0	0	1	0	.000
Jim Coates	p	3	1	0	0	0	0	0	0	0	1	0	.000
Bill Stafford	p	2	1	0	0	0	0	0	0	0	1	0	.000
Luis Arroyo	p	1	1	0	0	0	0	0	0	0	0	0	.000
Art Ditmar	p	2	0	0	0	0	0	0	0	0	0	0	.000
Ryne Duren	p	2	0	0	0	0	0	0	0	0	0	0	.000
Duke Maas	p	1	0	0	0	0	0	0	0	0	0	0	.000
Team Total		7	269	55	91	13	4	10	54	18	40	0	.338

Double Plays—9   Left on Bases—51

PITCHING

PITCHING	G	GS	CG	IP	H	R	ER	BB	SO	W	L	SV	ERA
Pittsburgh													
Vernon Law	3	3	0	18⅓	22	7	7	3	8	2	0	0	3.44
Roy Face	4	0	0	10⅓	9	6	6	2	4	0	0	3	5.23
Harvey Haddix	2	1	0	7⅓	6	2	2	6	2	2	0	0	2.45
Bob Friend	3	2	0	6	13	10	9	3	7	0	2	0	13.50
Tom Cheney	3	0	0	4	4	2	2	1	6	0	0	0	4.50
Clem Labine	3	0	0	4	13	11	6	1	2	0	0	0	13.50
Freddie Green	3	0	0	4	11	10	10	1	3	0	0	0	22.50
Joe Gibbon	2	0	0	3	4	3	3	1	2	0	0	0	9.00
George Witt	3	0	0	2⅔	5	0	0	2	1	0	0	0	0.00
Vinegar Bend Mizell	2	1	0	2⅓	4	4	4	2	1	0	1	0	15.43
Team Total	7	7	0	62	91	55	49	18	40	4	3	3	7.11
New York													
Whitey Ford	2	2	2	18	11	0	0	2	8	2	0	0	0.00
Bob Turley	2	2	0	9⅓	15	6	5	4	0	1	0	0	4.82
Ralph Terry	2	1	0	6⅔	7	4	4	1	5	0	2	0	5.40
Bobby Shantz	3	0	0	6⅓	4	3	3	1	1	0	0	1	4.26
Jim Coates	3	0	0	6⅓	6	4	4	1	3	0	0	0	5.68
Bill Stafford	2	0	0	6	5	1	1	1	2	0	0	0	1.50
Ryne Duren	2	0	0	4	2	1	1	1	5	0	0	0	2.25
Duke Maas	1	0	0	2	2	1	1	0	1	0	0	0	4.50
Art Ditmar	2	2	0	1⅔	6	6	4	1	0	0	2	0	21.60
Luis Arroyo	1	0	0	⅔	2	1	1	0	1	0	0	0	13.50
Eli Grba				Did not pitch									
Team Total	7	7	2	61	60	27	24	12	26	3	4	1	3.54

1961

New York A.L. 4
Cincinnati N.L. 1

Highlights

YANKEES MANAGER RALPH HOUK became the third manager in history to win a World Championship in his freshman year, four games to one over manager Fred Hutchinson's scrappy Cincinnati Reds, who had not appeared in a Series since 1940, versus the new York Yankees.

MIckey Mantle and Roger Maris—the M&M Boys—paced the Yankees throughout the regular season. Mantle batted .317, knocked in 112 runs and ripped 54 home runs. Maris hit only .269, but led the league in RBI's with 142, and broke Babe Ruth's single-season home-run record by reaching the seats 61 times. Maris' final home run of the year was a Series game-winner—a solo blast off the Reds' right-hander Bob Purkey in the Yanks' 3-2 victory in game three.

Yankees bench proved valuable in series. Johnny Blanchard, pinch-hitting and playing part-time in right field, batted .400 and hit two home runs in ten at-bats, and Hector Lopez, substituting in both left and right field, batted .333 and drove in seven runs in the Series, including five in the deciding fifth game.

Left-hander Whitey Ford ran his consecutive scoreless innings streak to 32 innings, breaking Babe Ruth's old record of 29⅔ innings.

Yankees second baseman Bobby Richardson tied a Series record for most hits in a five-game Series by rapping out nine—eight singles and a double.

Game 1 Oct. 4
Cincinnati	000 000 000 ·	0
New York	000 101 00* ·	2

Winner-Ford Loser-O'Toole

Game 2 Oct. 5
Cincinnati	000 211 020 ·	6
New York	000 200 000 ·	2

Winner-Jay Loser-Terry

Game 3 Oct. 7
New York	000 000 111 ·	3
Cincinnati	001 000 100 ·	2

Winner-Arroyo Loser-Purkey

Game 4 Oct. 8
New York	000 112 300 ·	7
Cincinnati	000 000 000 ·	0

Winner-Ford Loser-O'Toole

Game 5 Oct. 9
New York	510 502 000 ·	13
Cincinnati	003 020 000 ·	5

Winner-Daley Loser-Jay

Total Attendance—223,247
Average Attendance—44,649
Winning Player's Share—$7,389
Losing Player's Share—$5,356

BATTING

	Pos	G	AB	R	H	2B	3B	HR	RBI	BB	SO	SB	BA
New York													
Bill Skowron	1b	5	17	3	6	0	0	1	5	3	4	0	.353
Bobby Richardson	2b	5	23	2	9	1	0	0	0	0	0	1	.391
Tony Kubek	ss	5	22	3	5	0	0	0	1	1	4	0	.227
Clete Boyer	3b	5	15	0	4	2	0	0	3	4	0	0	.267
Johnny Blanchard	ph-rf	4	10	4	4	1	0	2	3	2	0	0	**.400**
Roger Maris	cf-rf	5	19	4	2	1	0	1	2	4	6	0	.105
Yogi Berra	lf	4	11	2	3	0	0	1	3	5	1	0	.273
Elston Howard	c	5	20	5	5	3	0	1	1	2	3	0	.250
Hector Lopez	ph-rf-lf-pr	4	9	3	3	0	1	1	7	2	3	0	.333
Mickey Mantle	cf	2	6	0	1	0	0	0	0	0	2	0	.167
Jack Reed	cf	3	0	0	0	0	0	0	0	0	0	0	.000
Billy Gardner	ph	1	1	0	0	0	0	0	0	0	0	0	.000
Joe DeMaestri	Did not play												
Bob Hale	Did not play												
Whitey Ford	p	2	5	1	0	0	0	0	0	1	0	0	.000
Ralph Terry	p	2	3	0	0	0	0	0	0	0	1	0	.000
Bill Stafford	p	1	2	0	0	0	0	0	0	0	0	0	.000
Bud Daley	p	2	1	0	0	0	0	0	0	1	0	0	.000
Jim Coates	p	1	1	0	0	0	0	0	0	0	1	0	.000
Luis Arroyo	p	2	0	0	0	0	0	0	0	0	0	0	.000
Rollie Sheldon	Did not play												
Bob Turley	Did not play—sore arm												
Hal Reniff	Did not play												
Tex Clevenger	Did not play												
Al Downing	Did not play												
Team Total		5	165	27	42	8	1	7	26	24	25	1	.255

Double Plays—1   Left on Bases—34

	Pos	G	AB	R	H	2B	3B	HR	RBI	BB	SO	SB	BA
Cincinnati													
Gordy Coleman	1b	5	20	2	5	0	0	1	2	0	1	0	.250
Elio Chacon	2b-ph	4	12	2	3	0	0	0	0	1	2	0	.250
Eddie Kasko	ss	5	22	1	7	0	0	0	1	0	2	0	.318
Gene Freese	3b	5	16	0	1	1	0	0	0	3	4	0	.063
Frank Robinson	rf-lf	5	15	3	3	2	0	1	4	3	4	0	.200
Vada Pinson	cf	5	22	0	2	1	0	0	0	0	1	0	.091
Wally Post	lf-rf	5	8	3	6	1	0	1	2	0	1	0	.333
Johnny Edwards	c	3	11	1	4	2	0	0	2	0	0	0	.364
Don Blasingame	2b-pr	3	7	1	1	0	0	0	0	0	3	0	.143
Darrell Johnson	c	2	4	0	2	0	0	0	0	0	0	0	.500
Jerry Zimmerman	c	2	0	0	0	0	0	0	0	0	0	0	.000
Dick Gernert	ph	4	4	0	0	0	0	0	0	0	1	0	.000
Jerry Lynch	ph	4	3	0	0	0	0	0	0	1	1	0	.000
Gus Bell	ph	3	3	0	0	0	0	0	0	0	0	0	.000
Leo Cardenas	ph	3	3	0	1	1	0	0	0	0	1	0	.333
Joey Jay	p	2	4	0	0	0	0	0	0	0	2	0	.000
Jim O'Toole	p	2	3	0	0	0	0	0	0	0	1	0	.000
Bob Purkey	p	2	3	0	0	0	0	0	0	0	3	0	.000
Jim Broshan	p	3	0	0	0	0	0	0	0	0	0	0	.000
Bill Henry	p	2	0	0	0	0	0	0	0	0	0	0	.000
Ken Hunt	p	1	0	0	0	0	0	0	0	0	0	0	.000
Ken Johnson	p	1	0	0	0	0	0	0	0	0	0	0	.000
Sherman Jones	p	1	0	0	0	0	0	0	0	0	0	0	.000
Jim Maloney	p	1	0	0	0	0	0	0	0	0	0	0	.000
Howie Nunn	Did not play												
Jay Hook	Did not play												
Team Total		5	170	13	35	8	0	3	11	8	27	0	.206

Double Plays—7   Left on Bases—33

PITCHING

	G	GS	CG	IP	H	R	ER	BB	SO	W	L	SV	ERA
New York													
Whitey Ford	2	2	1	14	6	0	0	1	7	2	0	0	**0.00**
Ralph Terry	2	2	0	9⅓	12	7	5	2	7	0	1	0	4.82
Bud Daley	2	0	0	7	5	2	0	3	1	0	0	0	0.00
Bill Stafford	1	1	0	6⅔	7	2	2	2	5	0	0	0	2.70
Luis Arroyo	2	0	0	4	4	2	1	2	3	1	0	0	2.25
Jim Coates	1	0	0	4	1	0	0	1	2	0	0	1	0.00
Team Total	5	5	1	45	35	13	8	8	27	4	1	1	1.60
Cincinnati													
Jim O'Toole	2	2	0	12	11	4	4	7	4	0	2	0	3.00
Bob Purkey	2	1	1	11	6	5	2	3	5	0	1	0	1.64
Joey Jay	2	2	1	9⅔	8	6	6	6	6	1	1	0	5.59
Jim Brosnan	3	0	0	6	9	5	5	4	5	0	0	0	7.50
Bill Henry	2	0	0	2⅓	4	5	5	2	3	0	0	0	19.29
Ken Hunt	1	0	0	1	0	0	0	1	1	0	0	0	0.00
Ken Johnson	1	0	0	⅔	0	0	0	0	0	0	0	0	0.00
Sherman Jones	1	0	0	⅔	0	0	0	0	0	0	0	0	0.00
Jim Maloney	1	0	0	⅔	4	2	2	1	1	0	0	0	27.00
Team Total	5	5	2	44	42	27	24	24	25	1	4	0	4.91

1962

New York A.L. 4
San Francisco N.L. 3

Highlights

ANOTHER PLAYOFF BETWEEN the Dodgers and Giants decided the National League championship. The Giants, this time representing San Francisco, beat the Dodgers, two games to one. Just five years after leaving New York, the Giants were returning to face the Yankees, traditional rivals that they had met six times previously in Subway Series. Only center fielder Willie Mays and manager Alvin Dark remained from the Giants team that had opposed the Yankees in the 1951 Series.

The Giants ended Whitey Ford's World Series scoreless streak at 33²/₃ innings in the second inning of game one when Jose Pagan pushed across Mays from third on a bunt single.

Chuck Hiller hit the first World Series grand-slam home run by a National player in the seventh inning of game four to spark a 7-3 Giants victory.

The Yankees' game seven victory, 1-0, ended with Giants threatening in ninth with men on second and third when second baseman Bobby Richardson speared Willie McCovey's line drive.

Series was delayed by four days of rain, one in New York and three in San Francisco.

Mays, the National League home-run champion with 49, failed to connect in the Series.

Game 1 Oct. 4
New York   200 000 121 · 6
San Francisco   011 000 000 · 2
Winner-Ford   Loser-O'Dell

Game 2 Oct. 5
New York   000 000 000 · 0
San Francisco   100 000 10* · 2
Winner-Sanford   Loser-Terry

Game 3 Oct. 7
San Francisco   000 000 002 · 2
New York   000 000 30* · 3
Winner-Stafford   Loser-Pierce

Game 4 Oct. 8
San Francisco   020 000 401 · 7
New York   000 002 001 · 3
Winner-Larsen   Loser-Coates

Game 5 Oct. 10
San Francisco   001 010 001 · 3
New York   000 101 03* · 5
Winner-Terry   Loser-Sanford

Game 6 Oct. 15
New York   000 010 010 · 2
San Francisco   000 320 00* · 5
Winner-Pierce   Loser-Ford

Game 7 Oct. 16
New York   000 010 000 · 1
San Francisco   000 000 000 · 0
Winner-Terry   Loser-Sanford

Total Attendance—376,864
Average Attendance—53,838
Winning Player's Share—$9,883
Losing Player's Share—$7,291

BATTING	Pos	G	AB	R	H	2B	3B	HR	RBI	BB	SO	SB	BA
New York													
Bill Skowron	1b	6	18	1	4	0	1	0	1	1	5	0	.222
Bobby Richardson	2b	7	27	3	4	0	0	0	0	3	1	0	.148
Tony Kubek	ss	7	29	2	8	1	0	0	1	1	3	0	.276
Clete Boyer	3b	7	22	2	7	1	0	1	4	1	3	0	.318
Roger Maris	rf	7	23	4	4	1	0	1	5	5	2	0	.174
Mickey Mantle	cf	7	25	2	3	1	0	0	0	4	5	2	.120
Tom Tresh	lf	7	28	5	9	1	0	1	4	1	4	2	.321
Elston Howard	c	6	21	1	3	1	0	0	1	1	4	0	.143
Dale Long	1b	2	5	0	1	0	0	0	1	0	1	0	.200
Yogi Berra	c-ph	2	2	0	0	0	0	0	0	2	0	0	.000
Hector Lopez	ph	2	2	0	0	0	0	0	0	0	0	0	.000
Johnny Blanchard	ph	1	1	0	0	0	0	0	0	0	1	0	.000
Jack Reed	Did not play												
Phil Linz	Did not play												
Ralph Terry	p	3	8	0	1	0	0	0	0	1	6	0	.125
Whitey Ford	p	3	7	0	0	0	0	0	0	1	3	0	.000
Bill Stafford	p	1	3	0	0	0	0	0	0	0	1	0	.000
Marshall Bridges	p	2	0	0	0	0	0	0	0	0	0	0	.000
Jim Coates	p	2	0	0	0	0	0	0	0	0	0	0	.000
Bud Daley	p	1	0	0	0	0	0	0	0	0	0	0	.000
Jim Bouton	Did not play												
Rollie Sheldon	Did not play												
Bob Turley	Did not play												
Tex Clevenger	Did not play												
Luis Arroyo	Did not play—sore arm												
Team Total		7	221	20	44	6	1	3	17	21	39	4	.199

Double Plays—5   Left on Bases—43

BATTING	Pos	G	AB	R	H	2B	3B	HR	RBI	BB	SO	SB	BA
San Francisco													
Orlando Cepeda	1b	5	19	1	3	1	0	0	2	0	4	0	.158
Chuck Hiller	2b	7	26	4	7	3	0	1	5	3	4	0	.269
Jose Pagan	ss	7	19	2	7	0	0	1	2	0	1	0	**.368**
Jim Davenport	3b	7	22	1	3	1	0	0	1	4	7	0	.136
Felipe Alou	rf-lf	7	26	2	7	1	1	0	1	1	4	0	.269
Willie Mays	cf	7	28	3	7	2	0	0	1	1	5	1	.250
Harvey Kuenn	lf-rf	4	12	1	1	0	0	0	0	1	1	0	.083
Tom Haller	c	4	14	1	4	1	0	1	3	0	2	0	.286
Willie McCovey	1b-rf-lf	4	15	2	3	0	1	1	1	1	3	0	.200
Ed Bailey	c-ph	6	14	1	1	0	0	1	2	0	3	0	.071
Matty Alou	lf-rf-ph	6	12	2	4	1	0	0	1	0	1	0	.333
Ernie Bowman	ss-pr	2	1	1	0	0	0	0	0	0	0	0	.000
Bob Nieman	ph	1	0	0	0	0	0	0	0	1	0	0	.000
John Orsino	c	1	1	0	0	0	0	0	0	0	0	0	.000
Carl Boles	Did not play												
Jack Sanford	p	3	7	0	3	0	0	0	0	0	2	0	.429
Billy Pierce	p	2	5	0	0	0	0	0	0	0	1	0	.000
Billy O'Dell	p	3	3	0	1	0	0	0	0	0	0	0	.333
Juan Marichal	p	1	2	0	0	0	0	0	0	0	1	0	.000
Don Larsen	p	3	0	0	0	0	0	0	0	0	0	0	.000
Bobby Bolin	p	2	0	0	0	0	0	0	0	0	0	0	.000
Stu Miller	p	2	0	0	0	0	0	0	0	0	0	0	.000
Mike McCormick	Did not play—sore arm												
Jim Duffalo	Did not play												
Bob Garibaldi	Did not play												
Team Total		7	226	21	51	10	2	5	19	12	39	1	.226

Double Plays—9   Left on Bases—39

PITCHING	G	GS	CG	IP	H	R	ER	BB	SO	W	L	SV	ERA
New York													
Ralph Terry	3	3	2	25	17	5	5	2	16	2	1	0	**1.80**
Whitey Ford	3	3	1	19²/₃	24	9	9	4	12	1	1	0	4.12
Bill Stafford	1	1	1	9	4	2	2	2	5	1	0	0	2.00
Marshall Bridges	2	0	0	3²/₃	4	3	2	3	3	0	0	0	4.91
Jim Coates	2	0	0	2²/₃	1	2	2	1	3	0	1	0	6.75
Bud Daley	1	0	0	1	1	0	0	1	0	0	0	0	0.00
Team Total	7	7	4	61	51	21	20	12	39	4	3	0	2.95
San Francisco													
Jack Sanford	3	3	1	23¹/₃	16	6	5	8	19	1	2	0	1.93
Billy Pierce	2	2	1	15	8	5	4	2	5	1	1	0	2.40
Billy O'Dell	3	1	0	12¹/₃	12	6	6	3	9	0	1	1	4.38
Juan Marichal	1	1	0	4	2	0	0	2	4	0	0	0	0.00
Bobby Bolin	2	0	0	2²/₃	4	2	2	2	2	0	0	0	6.75
Don Larsen	3	0	0	2¹/₃	1	1	1	2	0	1	0	0	3.86
Stu Miller	2	0	0	1¹/₃	1	0	0	2	0	0	0	0	0.00
Team Total	7	7	2	61	44	20	18	21	39	3	4	1	2.76

Tom Tresh's game-winning home run.

1963

Los Angeles N.L. 4
New York A.L. 0

Highlights

THE LOS ANGELES DODGERS won the National League flag with superior pitching—five pitchers accumulated ten or more victories, paced by Sandy Koufax's league-leading 306 strikeouts and 25 victories. In the Series, these strong arms stifled the Yankees, limiting them to three runs in four games.

The four-game World Series sweep by the Dodgers was their first, and the second time the Yanks had appeared in a Series and failed to register a single victory (Giants swept them 4-0 in 1922, with an additional game ending in a 3-3 tie, called after ten innings because of darkness).

Koufax set a new Series single-game strikeout record with 15, breaking Carl Erskine's old mark set ten years ago to the day.

Former Yankee Bill "Moose" Skowron turned in a top performance against his old teammates, batting .385 with one home run and three RBI's.

Lone Yankee error in Series was costly. In the seventh inning of game seven with score tied at 1-1, first baseman Joe Pepitone lost Clete Boyer's throw from third in a background of white shirts, allowing Jim "Junior" Gilliam to reach third. Gilliam then scored the deciding run, tagging up after Willie Davis' deep fly to center.

Game 1 Oct. 2
Los Angeles	041 000 000 -	5
New York	000 000 020 -	2

Winner-Koufax Loser-Ford

Game 2 Oct. 3
Los Angeles	200 100 010 -	4
New York	000 000 001 -	1

Winner-Poders Loser-Downing

Game 3 Oct. 5
New York	000 000 000 -	0
Los Angeles	100 000 00* -	1

Winner-Drysdale Loser-Bouton

Game 4 Oct. 6
New York	000 000 100 -	1
Los Angeles	000 010 10* -	2

Winner-Koufax Loser-Ford

Total Attendance—247,279
Average Attendance—61,820
Winning Player's Share—$12,794
Losing Player's Share—$7,874

254/The World Series

BATTING	Pos	G	AB	R	H	2B	3B	HR	RBI	BB	SO	SB	BA
Los Angeles													
Bill Skowron	1b	4	13	2	5	0	0	1	3	1	3	0	.385
Dick Tracewski	2b	4	13	1	2	0	0	0	0	1	2	0	.154
Maury Wills	ss	4	15	1	2	0	0	0	0	1	3	1	.133
Jim Gilliam	3b	4	13	3	2	0	0	0	0	3	1	0	.154
Frank Howard	rf	3	10	2	3	1	0	1	1	0	2	0	.300
Willie Davis	cf	4	12	2	2	2	0	0	3	0	6	0	.167
Tommy Davis	lf	4	15	0	6	0	2	0	2	0	2	0	.400
Johnny Roseboro	c	4	14	1	2	0	0	1	3	0	4	0	.143
Ron Fairly	rf-ph	4	1	0	0	0	0	0	0	3	0	0	.000
Ken McMullen		Did not play											
Wally Moon		Did not play											
Lee Walls		Did not play											
Doug Camilli		Did not play											
Al Ferrara		Did not play											
Marv Breeding		Did not play											
Sandy Koufax	p	2	6	0	0	0	0	0	0	0	2	0	.000
Johnny Podres	p	1	4	0	1	0	0	0	0	0	0	0	.250
Don Drysdale	p	1	1	0	0	0	0	0	0	2	0	0	.000
Ron Perranoski	p	1	0	0	0	0	0	0	0	0	0	0	.000
Bob Miller		Did not play											
Pete Richert		Did not play											
Dick Calmus		Did not play											
Larry Sherry		Did not play											
Ken Rowe		Did not play											
Team Total		4	117	12	25	3	2	3	12	11	25	2	.214

Double Plays—1   Left on Bases—17

BATTING	Pos	G	AB	R	H	2B	3B	HR	RBI	BB	SO	SB	BA
New York													
Joe Pepitone	1b	4	13	0	2	0	0	0	0	1	3	0	.154
Bobby Richardson	2b	4	14	0	3	1	0	0	0	1	3	0	.214
Tony Kubek	ss	4	16	1	3	0	0	0	0	0	3	0	.188
Clete Boyer	3b	4	13	0	1	0	0	0	0	1	6	0	.077
Hector Lopez	ph-rf	3	8	1	2	2	0	0	0	0	1	0	.250
Mickey Mantle	cf	4	15	1	2	0	0	1	1	1	5	0	.133
Tom Tresh	lf	4	15	1	3	0	0	1	2	1	6	0	.200
Elston Howard	c	4	15	0	5	0	0	0	1	0	3	0	.333
Roger Maris	rf	2	5	0	0	0	0	0	0	0	1	0	.000
Johnny Blanchard	rf	1	3	0	0	0	0	0	0	0	0	0	.000
Phil Linz	ph	3	3	0	1	0	0	0	0	0	1	0	.333
Harry Bright	ph	2	2	0	0	0	0	0	0	0	2	0	.000
Yogi Berra	ph	1	1	0	0	0	0	0	0	0	0	0	.000
Jack Reed		Did not play											
Whitey Ford	p	2	3	0	0	0	0	0	0	0	0	0	.000
Jim Bouton	p	1	2	0	0	0	0	0	0	0	2	0	.000
Al Downing	p	1	1	0	0	0	0	0	0	0	1	0	.000
Hal Reniff	p	3	0	0	0	0	0	0	0	0	0	0	.000
Steve Hamilton	p	1	0	0	0	0	0	0	0	0	0	0	.000
Ralph Terry	p	1	0	0	0	0	0	0	0	0	0	0	.000
Stan Williams	p	1	0	0	0	0	0	0	0	0	0	0	.000
Bill Stafford		Did not play											
Bill Kunkel		Did not play											
Marshall Bridges		Did not play											
Tom Metcalf		Did not play											
Team Total		4	129	4	22	3	0	2	4	5	37	0	.171

Double Plays—7   Left on Bases—24

PITCHING	G	GS	CG	IP	H	R	ER	BB	SO	W	L	SV	ERA
Los Angeles													
Sandy Koufax	2	2	2	18	12	3	3	3	23	2	0	0	1.50
Don Drysdale	1	1	1	9	3	0	0	1	9	1	0	0	0.00
Johnny Podres	1	1	0	8⅓	6	1	1	1	4	1	0	0	1.08
Ron Perranoski	1	0	0	⅔	1	0	0	0	1	0	0	1	0.00
Bob Miller		Did not play											
Pete Richert		Did not play											
Dick Calmus		Did not play											
Larry Sherry		Did not play											
Ken Rowe		Did not play											
Team Total	4	4	3	36	22	4	4	5	37	4	0	1	1.00
New York													
Whitey Ford	2	2	0	12	10	7	6	3	8	0	2	0	4.50
Jim Bouton	1	1	0	7	4	1	1	5	4	0	1	0	1.29
Al Downing	1	1	0	5	7	3	3	1	6	0	1	0	5.40
Hal Reniff	3	0	0	3	0	0	0	1	1	0	0	0	0.00
Ralph Terry	1	0	0	3	3	1	1	1	0	0	0	0	3.00
Stan Williams	1	0	0	3	1	0	0	0	5	0	0	0	0.00
Steve Hamilton	1	0	0	1	0	0	0	0	1	0	0	0	0.00
Bill Stafford		Did not play											
Bill Kunkel		Did not play											
Marshall Bridges		Did not play											
Tom Metcalf		Did not play											
Team Total	4	4	0	34	25	12	11	11	25	0	4	0	2.91

1964

Highlights

ST. LOUIS WAS IN SERIES FOR THE first time since 1946. The Yankees were back in the classic for the fifth consecutive year, winning the league championship under freshman manager Yogi Berra.

In the ninth inning of game three, Mickey Mantle knocked knuckleballer Barney Schultz's first pitch into Yankee Stadium's right-field stands for a 2-1 Yankee victory. The four-bagger put Mantle in first place in the all-time Series home-run totals, surpassing Babe Ruth's 15. In game four, Ken Boyer's sixth-inning grand-slammer off lefty Al Downing gave the Cards a 4-3 triumph. In the tenth inning of game five, Cards catcher Tim McCarver rapped a three-run homer off Pete Mikkelsen to give the Cards a 5-2 victory. And in game six, Yankees Joe Pepitone hit a grand-slam home run to lift the Yanks to an 8-3 victory.

The day after the Cards won the seventh game of the Series, 7-5, the Yankees fired Berra, and Cardinals manager Johnny Keane quit the Cards. later, the Yanks hired Keane.

Game 1 Oct. 7
New York   030 010 010 · 5
St. Louis   110 004 03* · 9
Winner-Sadecki   Loser-Ford

Game 2 Oct. 8
New York   000 101 204 · 8
St. Louis   001 000 011 · 3
Winner-Stottlemyre   Loser-Gibson

Game 3 Oct. 10
St. Louis   000 010 000 · 1
New York   010 000 001 · 2
Winner-Bouton   Loser-Schultz

Game 4 Oct. 11
St. Louis   000 004 000 · 4
New York   300 000 000 · 3
Winner-Craig   Loser-Downing

Game 5 Oct. 12
St. Louis   000 020 000 3 · 5
New York   000 000 002 0 · 2
Winner-Gibson   Loser-Mikkelsen

Game 6 Oct. 14
New York   000 012 050 · 8
St. Louis   100 000 011 · 3
Winner-Bouton   Loser-Simmons

Game 7 Oct. 15
New York   000 003 002 · 5
St. Louis   000 330 10* · 7
Winner-Gibson   Loser-Stottlemyre

Total Attendance—321,807
Average Attendance—45,972
Winning Player's Share—$8,622
Losing Player's Share—$5,309

BATTING	Pos	G	AB	R	H	2B	3B	HR	RBI	BB	SO	SB	BA
St. Louis													
Bill White	1b	7	27	2	3	1	0	0	2	2	6	1	.111
Dal Maxvill	2b	7	20	0	4	1	0	0	1	1	4	0	.200
Dick Groat	ss	7	26	3	5	1	1	0	1	4	3	0	.192
Ken Boyer	3b	7	27	5	6	1	0	2	6	1	5	0	.222
Mike Shannon	rf	7	28	6	6	0	0	1	2	0	9	1	.214
Curt Flood	cf	7	30	5	6	0	1	0	3	3	1	0	.200
Lou Brock	lf	7	30	2	9	2	0	1	5	0	3	0	.300
Tim McCarver	c	7	23	4	11	1	1	1	5	5	1	1	**.478**
Jerry Buchek	pr-2b	4	1	1	1	0	0	0	0	0	0	0	1.000
Julian Javier	pr-2b	1	0	1	0	0	0	0	0	0	0	0	.000
Carl Warwick	ph	5	4	2	3	0	0	0	1	1	0	0	.750
Bob Skinner	ph	4	3	0	2	1	0	0	1	1	0	0	.667
Charlie James	ph	3	3	0	0	0	0	0	0	0	1	0	.000
Bob Uecker	Did not play												
Ed Spiezio	Did not play												
Bob Gibson	p	3	9	1	2	0	0	0	0	0	3	0	.222
Curt Simmons	p	2	4	0	2	0	0	0	1	0	1	0	.500
Ray Sadecki	p	2	2	0	1	0	0	0	1	0	1	0	.500
Barney Schultz	p	4	1	0	0	0	0	0	0	0	0	0	.000
Roger Craig	p	2	1	0	0	0	0	0	0	0	0	0	.000
Ron Taylor	p	2	1	0	0	0	0	0	0	0	1	0	.000
Gordie Richardson	p	2	0	0	0	0	0	0	0	0	0	0	.000
Bob Humphreys	p	1	0	0	0	0	0	0	0	0	0	0	.000
Mike Cuellar	Did not play												
Ray Washburn	Did not play												
Team Total		7	240	32	61	8	3	5	29	18	39	3	.254
		Double Plays—6			Left on Bases—47								
New York													
Joe Pepitone	1b	7	26	1	4	1	0	1	5	2	3	0	.154
Bobby Richardson	2b	7	**32**	3	13	2	0	0	3	0	2	1	.406
Phil Linz	ss	7	31	5	7	1	0	2	2	2	5	0	.226
Clete Boyer	3b	7	24	2	5	1	0	1	3	1	5	1	.208
Mickey Mantle	rf	7	24	8	8	2	0	3	8	6	8	0	.333
Roger Maris	cf	7	30	4	6	0	0	1	1	1	4	0	.200
Tommy Tresh	lf	7	22	4	6	2	0	2	7	6	7	0	.273
Elston Howard	c	7	24	5	7	1	0	0	2	4	6	0	.292
Hector Lopez	rf-ph	3	2	0	0	0	0	0	0	0	2	0	.000
Pedro Gonzalez	3b	1	1	0	0	0	0	0	0	0	0	0	.000
Johnny Blanchard	ph	4	4	0	1	1	0	0	0	0	1	0	.250
Mike Hegan	pr-ph	3	1	1	0	0	0	0	0	1	1	0	.000
Archie Moore	Did not play												
Chester Trail	Did not play												
Tony Kubek	Not in series—sprained wrist												
Mel Stottlemyre	p	3	8	0	1	0	0	0	0	0	6	0	.125
Jim Bouton	p	2	7	0	1	0	0	0	1	0	2	0	.143
Al Downing	p	2	2	0	0	0	0	0	0	0	2	0	.000
Whitey Ford	p	1	1	0	1	0	0	0	1	2	0	0	1.000
Pete Mikkelsen	p	4	0	0	0	0	0	0	0	0	0	0	.000
Steve Hamilton	p	2	0	0	0	0	0	0	0	0	0	0	.000
Rollie Sheldon	p	2	0	0	0	0	0	0	0	0	0	0	.000
Hal Reniff	p	1	0	0	0	0	0	0	0	0	0	0	.000
Ralph Terry	p	1	0	0	0	0	0	0	0	0	0	0	.000
Bill Stafford	Did not play												
Stan Williams	Did not play												
Team Total		7	239	33	60	11	0	10	33	25	54	2	.251
		Double Plays—6			Left on Bases—47								

PITCHING	G	GS	CG	IP	H	R	ER	BB	SO	W	L	SV	ERA
St. Louis													
Bob Gibson	3	3	2	27	23	11	9	8	31	2	1	0	3.00
Curt Simmons	2	2	0	14⅓	11	4	4	3	8	0	1	0	2.51
Ray Sadecki	2	2	0	6⅓	12	7	6	5	2	1	0	0	8.53
Roger Craig	2	0	0	5	2	0	0	3	9	1	0	0	0.00
Ron Taylor	2	0	0	4⅔	0	0	0	1	2	0	0	1	0.00
Barney Schultz	4	0	0	4	9	8	8	3	1	0	1	1	18.00
Bob Humphreys	1	0	0	1	0	0	0	1	0	0	0	0	0.00
Gordie Richardson	2	0	0	⅔	3	3	3	2	0	0	0	0	40.50
Team Total	7	7	2	63	60	33	30	25	54	4	3	2	4.29
New York													
Mel Stottlemyre	3	3	1	20	18	8	7	6	12	1	**1**	0	3.15
Jim Bouton	2	2	1	17⅓	15	4	3	5	7	**2**	0	0	**1.56**
Al Downing	3	1	0	7⅔	9	8	7	2	5	0	1	0	8.22
Whitey Ford	1	1	0	5⅓	8	5	5	1	4	0	1	0	8.44
Pete Mikkelsen	4	0	0	4⅔	4	4	3	2	4	0	1	0	5.79
Rollie Sheldon	2	0	0	2⅔	0	2	0	2	2	0	0	0	0.00
Steve Hamilton	2	0	0	2	3	1	1	0	2	0	0	1	4.50
Ralph Terry	1	0	0	2	2	0	0	0	3	0	0	0	0.00
Hal Reniff	1	0	0	⅓	2	0	0	0	0	0	0	0	0.00
Team Total	7	7	2	62	61	32	26	18	39	3	4	1	3.77

1965

Highlights

CONTRASTING TEAMS MET IN THE sixty-third annual fall classic. The Minnesota Twins, formerly the Washington Senators, who moved to the Twin Cities in 1961, won the American League championship by seven full games, powered by the long ball and a league-leading .254 team batting average. Tony Oliva led all American League batters with a .321 average, chipping in 16 home runs to the total amassed by the Twins' formidable lineup of power hitters: Don Mincher, 22 homers; Harmon Killebrew, 25 homers; Bob Allison, 23; Jimmie Hall, 20 homers; and Zoilo Versalles, 19 homers. The Dodgers relied on power pitching—primarily Sandy Koufax, 26-8, and a league-leading 382 strikeouts in 336 innings; and Don Drysdale, 23-12.

Koufax, manager Walt Alston's logical choice to open the Series, sat out game one in observance of a Jewish holiday. Instead, Drysdale pitched and lost, 8-2, with Versalles' three-run homer the big blow. The Twins beat Koufax 5-1 in game two.

In game six, the Twins' Jim "Mudcat" Grant beat the Dodgers single-handedly, 5-1, pitching nine strong innings and blasting a sixth-inning three-run homer.

Koufax pulled the Dodgers through in the final game, going the distance, striking out ten.

Game 1 Oct. 6
Los Angeles   010 000 001 · 2
Minnesota   016 001 00* · 8
Winner-Grant   Loser-Drysdale

Game 2 Oct. 7
Los Angeles   000 000 100 · 1
Minnesota   000 002 J2* · 5
Winner-Kaat   Loser-Koufax

Game 3 Oct. 9
Minnesota   000 000 000 · 0
Los Angeles   000 211 00* · 4
Winner-Osteen Loser-Pascual

Game 4 Oct. 10
Minnesota   000 101 000 · 2
Los Angeles   110 103 01* · 7
Winner-Drysdale Loser-Grant

Game 5 Oct. 11
Minnesota   000 000 000 · 0
Los Angeles   202 100 20* · 7
Winner-Koufax Loser-Kaat

Game 6 Oct. 13
Los Angeles   000 000 100 · 1
Minnesota   000 203 00* · 5
Winner-Grant   Loser-Osteen

Game 7 Oct. 14
Los Angeles   000 200 000 · 2
Minnesota   000 000 000 · 0
Winner-Koufax Loser-Kaat

Total Attendance—364,326
Average Attendance—52,047
Winning Player's Share—$10,297
Losing Player's Share—$6,634

Los Angeles N.L. 4
Minnesota A.L. 3

BATTING	Pos	G	AB	R	H	2B	3B	HR	RBI	BB	SO	SB	BA
Los Angeles													
Wes Parker	1b	7	23	3	7	0	1	1	2	3	3	2	.304
Dick Tracewski	ph-2b	6	17	0	2	0	0	0	0	1	5	0	.118
Maury Wills	ss	7	30	3	11	3	0	0	3	1	3	3	.367
Jim Gilliam	3b	7	28	2	6	1	0	0	2	1	0	0	.214
Ron Fairly	rf	7	29	7	11	3	0	2	6	0	1	0	.379
Willie Davis	cf	7	26	3	6	0	0	0	0	0	2	3	.231
Lou Johnson	lf	7	27	3	8	2	0	2	4	1	3	0	.296
Johnny Roseboro	c	7	21	1	6	1	0	0	3	5	3	1	.286
Jim Lefebvre	2b	3	10	2	4	0	0	0	0	0	0	0	.400
John Kennedy	3b-pr	4	1	0	0	0	0	0	0	0	0	0	.000
Willie Crawford	ph	2	2	0	1	0	0	0	0	0	1	0	.500
Wally Moon	ph	2	2	0	0	0	0	0	0	0	0	0	.000
Don Le John	ph	1	1	0	0	0	0	0	0	0	1	0	.000
Jeff Torborg	Did not play												
Sandy Koufax	p	3	9	0	1	0	0	0	1	1	5	0	.111
Don Drysdale	p-ph	3	5	0	0	0	0	0	0	0	4	0	.000
Claude Osteen	p	2	3	0	1	0	0	0	0	0	0	0	.333
Bob Miller	p	2	0	0	0	0	0	0	0	0	0	0	.000
Ron Perranoski	p	2	0	0	0	0	0	0	0	0	0	0	.000
Howie Reed	p	2	0	0	0	0	0	0	0	0	0	0	.000
Jim Brewer	p	1	0	0	0	0	0	0	0	0	0	0	.000
Johnny Podres	Did not play												
John Purdin	Did not play												
Nick Willhite	Did not play												
Mike Kekich	Did not play												
Team Total		7	234	24	64	10	1	5	21	13	31	9	.274

Double Plays—7   Left on Bases—52

Minnesota	Pos	G	AB	R	H	2B	3B	HR	RBI	BB	SO	SB	BA
Don Mincher	1b	7	23	3	3	0	0	1	1	2	7	0	.130
Frank Quilici	2b	7	20	2	4	2	0	0	1	4	3	0	.200
Zoilo Versalles	ss	7	28	3	8	1	1	1	4	2	7	1	.286
Harmon Killebrew	3b	7	21	2	6	0	0	1	2	6	4	0	.286
Tony Oliva	rf	7	26	2	5	1	0	1	2	1	6	0	.192
Joe Nossek	cf-rf	6	20	0	4	0	0	0	0	0	1	0	.200
Bob Allison	lf	5	16	3	2	1	0	1	2	2	9	1	.125
Earl Battey	c	7	25	1	3	0	1	0	2	0	5	0	.120
Sandy Valdespino	lf-ph	5	11	1	3	1	0	0	0	0	1	0	.273
Jimmie Hall	cf	2	7	0	1	0	0	0	0	1	5	0	.143
Jerry Zimmerman	c	2	1	0	0	0	0	0	0	0	0	0	.000
Rich Rollins	ph	3	2	0	0	0	0	0	0	1	0	0	.000
Jerry Kindall	Did not play												
John Sevcik	Did not play												
Mudcat Grant	p	3	8	3	2	1	0	1	3	0	1	0	.250
Jim Kaat	p	3	6	0	1	0	0	0	2	0	5	0	.167
Camilio Pascual	p	1	1	0	0	0	0	0	0	0	0	0	.000
Johnny Klippstein	p	2	0	0	0	0	0	0	0	0	0	0	.000
Jim Merritt	p	2	0	0	0	0	0	0	0	0	0	0	.000
Jim Perry	p	2	0	0	0	0	0	0	0	0	0	0	.000
Al Worthington	p	2	0	0	0	0	0	0	0	0	0	0	.000
Dave Boswell	p	1	0	0	0	0	0	0	0	0	0	0	.000
Bill Pleis	p	1	0	0	0	0	0	0	0	0	0	0	.000
Dick Stigman	Did not play												
Mel Nelson	Did not play												
Team Total		7	215	20	42	7	2	6	19	19	54	2	.195

Double Plays—3   Left on Bases—36

PITCHING	G	GS	CG	IP	H	R	ER	BB	SO	W	L	SV	ERA
Los Angeles													
Sandy Koufax	3	3	2	24	13	2	1	5	29	2	1	0	0.38
Claude Osteen	2	2	1	14	9	2	1	5	4	1	1	0	0.64
Don Drysdale	2	2	1	11²/₃	12	9	5	3	15	1	1	0	3.86
Ron Perranoski	2	0	0	3²/₃	3	3	3	4	1	0	0	0	7.36
Howie Reed	2	0	0	3¹/₃	2	3	3	2	4	0	0	0	8.10
Jim Brewer	1	0	0	2	3	1	1	0	1	0	0	0	4.50
Bob Miller	2	0	0	1¹/₃	0	0	0	0	0	0	0	0	0.00
Team Total	7	7	4	60	42	20	14	19	54	4	3	0	2.10
Minnesota													
Mudcat Grant	3	3	2	23	22	8	7	2	12	2	1	0	2.74
Jim Kaat	3	3	1	14¹/₃	18	7	6	2	6	1	2	0	3.77
Camilio Pascual	1	1	0	5	8	3	3	1	0	0	1	0	5.40
Jim Perry	2	0	0	4	5	2	2	2	4	0	0	0	4.50
Al Worthington	2	0	0	4	2	1	0	2	2	0	0	0	0.00
Jim Merritt	2	0	0	3¹/₃	2	1	1	0	1	0	0	0	2.70
Johnny Klippstein	2	0	0	2²/₃	2	0	0	2	3	0	0	0	0.00
Dave Boswell	1	0	0	2²/₃	3	1	1	2	3	0	0	0	3.38
Bill Pleis	1	0	1	1	2	1	1	0	0	0	0	0	9.00
Team Total	7	7	3	60	64	24	21	13	31	3	4	0	3.15

1966

Highlights

THE BALTIMORE ORIOLES, TRANS-planted from St. Louis (Browns) in 1954, had a youthful but strong pitching staff that included Dave McNally (13-6), Wally Bunker (10-6) and Jim Palmer (15-10), and they had the outstanding former Cincinnati Reds Frank Robinson, who won the Triple Crown with 49 homers, 122 RBI's and a .316 batting average.

The Dodgers had powerless but pesky hitting, good defense, speed and lots of solid pitching, including Sandy Koufax's outstanding 27-9 record that included 317 strikeouts and a 1.73 ERA.

Orioles pitching surprised the experts by shutting out the Dodgers for the last 33 innings of the Series, highlighting a four-games-to-none sweep.

The Orioles won game three, 1-0, on a homer by Paul Blair, and game four, 1-0, on a homer by Frank Robinson.

Last Series appearance for Koufax, who announced his retirement at season's conclusion because of an advanced arthritic condition in his left elbow.

Game 1 Oct. 5
Baltimore	310 100 000 -	5
Los Angeles	011 000 000 -	2
Winner-Drabowsky	Loser-Drysdale	

Game 2 Oct. 6
Baltimore	000 031 020 -	6
Los Angeles	000 000 000 -	0
Winner-Palmer	Loser-Koufax	

Game 3 Oct. 8
Los Angeles	000 000 000 -	0
Baltimore	000 010 00* -	1
Winner-Bunker	Loser-Osteen	

Game 4 Oct. 9
Los Angeles	000 000 000 -	0
Baltimore	000 100 00* -	1
Winner-McNally	Loser-Drysdale	

Baltimore A.L. 4
Los Angeles N.L. 0

BATTING

	Pos	G	AB	R	H	2B	3B	HR	RBI	BB	SO	SB	BA
Baltimore													
Boog Powell	1b	4	14	1	5	1	0	0	1	0	1	0	.357
Dave Johnson	2b	4	14	1	4	1	0	0	1	0	1	0	.286
Luis Aparicio	ss	4	16	0	4	1	0	0	2	0	0	0	.250
Brooks Robinson	3b	4	14	2	3	0	0	1	1	1	0	0	.214
Frank Robinson	rf	4	14	4	4	0	1	2	3	3	1	0	.286
Paul Blair	cf	4	6	2	1	0	0	1	1	1	3	0	.167
Curt Blefary	lf	4	13	0	1	0	0	0	0	2	3	0	.077
Andy Etchebarren	c	4	12	2	1	0	0	0	0	2	4	0	.083
Russ Snyder	cf-lf	3	6	1	1	0	0	0	1	2	0	0	.167
Sam Bowens	Did not play												
Bob Johnson	Did not play												
Woody Held	Did not play												
Vic Roznovsky	Did not play												
Larry Haney	Did not play												
Jim Palmer	p	1	4	0	0	0	0	0	0	0	2	0	.000
Dave McNally	p	2	3	0	0	0	0	0	0	0	1	0	.000
Wally Bunker	p	1	2	0	0	0	0	0	0	0	1	0	.000
Moe Drabowsky	p	1	2	0	0	0	0	0	0	0	1	0	.000
Steve Barber	Missed Series—arm injury												
Stu Miller	Did not play												
Eddie Watt	Did not play												
Dick Hall	Did not play												
Eddie Fisher	Did not play												
Gene Brabender	Did not play												
John Miller	Did not play												
Frank Bertaina	Did not play												
Team Total		4	120	13	24	3	1	4	10	11	17	0	.200

Double Plays—4   Left on Bases—18

	Pos	G	AB	R	H	2B	3B	HR	RBI	BB	SO	SB	BA
Los Angeles													
Wes Parker	1b	4	13	0	3	2	0	0	0	1	3	0	.231
Jim Lefebvre	2b	4	12	1	2	0	0	1	1	3	4	0	.167
Maury Wills	ss	4	13	0	1	0	0	0	0	3	3	1	.077
Jim Gilliam	3b	2	6	0	0	0	0	0	1	2	0	0	.000
Lou Johnson	rf-lf	4	15	1	4	1	0	0	0	1	1	0	.267
Willie Davis	cf	4	16	0	1	0	0	0	0	0	4	0	.063
Tommy Davis	lf-ph	4	8	0	2	0	0	0	0	1	1	0	.250
Johnny Roseboro	c	4	14	0	1	0	0	0	0	0	3	0	.071
Ron Fairly	ph-rf-1b	3	7	0	1	0	0	0	0	2	4	0	.143
John Kennedy	3b	2	5	0	1	0	0	0	0	0	0	0	.200
Dick Stuart	ph	2	2	0	0	0	0	0	0	0	1	0	.000
Jim Barbieri	ph	1	1	0	0	0	0	0	0	0	1	0	.000
Wes Covington	ph	1	1	0	0	0	0	0	0	0	1	0	.000
Al Ferrara	ph	1	1	0	1	0	0	0	0	0	0	0	1.000
Nate Oliver	pr	1	0	0	0	0	0	0	0	0	0	0	.000
Jeff Torborg	Did not play												
Don Drysdale	p	2	2	0	0	0	0	0	0	0	1	0	.000
Sandy Koufax	p	1	2	0	0	0	0	0	0	0	0	0	.000
Claude Osteen	p	1	2	0	0	0	0	0	0	0	1	0	.000
Ron Perranoski	p	2	0	0	0	0	0	0	0	0	0	0	.000
Phil Regan	p	2	0	0	0	0	0	0	0	0	0	0	.000
Jim Brewer	p	1	0	0	0	0	0	0	0	0	0	0	.000
Bob Miller	p	1	0	0	0	0	0	0	0	0	0	0	.000
Joe Moeller	p	1	0	0	0	0	0	0	0	0	0	0	.000
Don Sutton	Did not play												
Team Total		4	120	2	17	3	0	1	2	13	28	1	.142

Double Plays—4   Left on Bases—24

PITCHING

	G	GS	CG	IP	H	R	ER	BB	SO	W	L	SV	ERA
Baltimore													
Dave McNally	2	2	1	11⅓	6	2	2	7	5	0	0	0	1.59
Wally Bunker	1	1	1	9	6	0	0	1	6	1	0	0	0.00
Jim Palmer	1	1	1	9	4	0	0	3	6	1	0	0	0.00
Moe Drabowsky	1	0	0	6⅔	1	0	0	2	11	1	0	0	0.00
Team Total	4	4	3	36	17	2	2	13	28	4	0	0	0.50
Los Angeles													
Don Drysdale	2	2	1	10	8	5	5	3	6	0	2	0	4.50
Claude Osteen	1	1	0	7	3	1	1	1	3	0	1	0	1.29
Sandy Koufax	1	1	0	6	6	4	1	2	2	0	1	0	1.50
Ron Perranoski	2	0	0	3⅓	4	2	2	1	2	0	0	0	5.40
Bob Miller	1	0	0	3	2	0	0	2	1	0	0	0	0.00
Joe Moeller	1	0	0	2	1	1	1	1	0	0	0	0	4.50
Phil Regan	2	0	0	1⅔	0	0	0	1	2	0	0	0	0.00
Jim Brewer	1	0	0	1	0	0	0	0	1	0	0	0	0.00
Team Total	4	4	1	34	24	13	10	11	17	0	4	0	2.65

1967

St. Louis N.L. 4
Boston A.L. 3

Highlights

TRIPLE CROWN WINNER CARL Yastrzemski led the Boston Red Sox to a hard-won American League championship. Like Frank Robinson the year before, Yaz accumulated impressive statistics: .326 batting average, 44 home runs and 121 RBI's. Right-hander Jim Lonborg, 22-9, was the ace of the Sox Staff. First-year manager Dick Williams raised his team from a ninth-place finish the year before to the flag with a victory on the final day of the season; he became the first freshman manager to make the World Series since the Yankees Ralph Houk in 1961.

National League champion Cardinals were well balanced. Orlando Cepeda (25 homers and 111 RBI's), Curt Flood (.335), Tim McCarver (.295) and Lou Brock (21 homers, .299 batting average and a league-leading 52 stolen bases) gave St. Louis plenty of offensive punch.

Cardinals right-hander Bob Gibson, 13-7 during the regular season, dominated the Series in the Cards' four-games-to-three triumph. He pitched three complete games, winning 2-1 in game one with ten strikeouts; 6-0 in game four, striking out six; and 7-2 in game seven, again striking out ten.

Brock led everyone at the plate, batting .414, which included two doubles, one triple, one home run and seven stolen bases. Yastrzemski batted .400 with three home runs.

Game 1 Oct. 4
St. Louis   001 000 100 · 2
Boston   001 000 000 · 1
Winner-Ro. Gibson   Loser-Santiago

Game 2 Oct. 5
St. Louis   000 000 000 · 0
Boston   000 101 30* · 5
Winner-Lonborg   Loser-Hughes

Game 3 Oct. 7
Boston   000 001 100 · 2
St. Louis   120 001 01* · 5
Winner-Briles   Loser-Bell

Game 4 Oct. 8
Boston   000 000 000 · 0
St. Louis   402 000 00* · 6
Winner-Gibson   Loser-Santiago

Game 5 Oct. 9
Boston   001 000 002 · 3
St. Louis   000 000 001 · 1
Winner-Lonborg   Loser-Carlton

Game 6 Oct. 11
St. Louis   002 000 200 · 4
Boston   010 300 40* · 8
Winner-Wyatt   Loser-Lamabe

Game 7 Oct. 12
St. Louis   002 023 000 · 7
Boston   000 010 010 · 2
Winner-Ro. Gibson   Loser-Lonborg

Total Attendance—304,085
Average Attendance—43,441
Winning Player's Share—$8,315
Losing Player's Share—$5,115

BATTING	Pos	G	AB	R	H	2B	3B	HR	RBI	BB	SO	SB	BA
St. Louis													
Orlando Cepeda	1b	7	29	1	3	2	0	0	1	0	4	0	.103
Julian Javier	2b	7	25	2	9	3	0	1	4	0	6	0	.360
Dal Maxvill	ss	7	19	1	3	0	1	0	1	4	1	0	.158
Mike Shannon	3b	7	24	3	5	1	0	1	2	1	4	0	.208
Roger Maris	rf	7	26	3	10	1	0	1	7	3	1	0	.385
Curt Flood	cf	7	28	2	5	1	0	0	3	3	3	0	.179
Lou Brock	lf	7	29	8	21	2	1	1	3	2	3	7	**.414**
Tim McCarver	c	7	24	3	3	1	0	0	2	2	2	0	.125
Dave Ricketts	ph	3	3	0	0	0	0	0	0	0	0	0	.000
Bobby Tolan	ph	3	2	1	0	0	0	0	0	1	1	0	.000
Phil Gagliano	ph	1	1	0	0	0	0	0	0	0	0	0	.000
Ed Spiezio	ph	1	1	0	0	0	0	0	0	0	0	0	.000
Ed Bressoud	ss	2	0	0	0	0	0	0	0	0	0	0	.000
Alex Johnson	Did not play												
Bob Gibson	p	3	11	1	1	0	0	1	1	1	2	0	.091
Nelson Briles	p	2	3	0	0	0	0	0	0	0	0	0	.000
Dick Hughes	p	2	3	0	0	0	0	0	0	0	3	0	.000
Steve Carlton	p	1	1	0	0	0	0	0	0	0	0	0	.000
Jack Lamabe	p	3	0	0	0	0	0	0	0	0	0	0	.000
Ron Willis	p	3	0	0	0	0	0	0	0	0	0	0	.000
Joe Hoerner	p	2	0	0	0	0	0	0	0	0	0	0	.000
Ray Washburn	p	2	0	0	0	0	0	0	0	0	0	0	.000
Larry Jaster	p	1	0	0	0	0	0	0	0	0	0	0	.000
Hal Woodeshick	p	1	0	0	0	0	0	0	0	0	0	0	.000
Al Jackson	Did not play												
Team Total		7	229	25	51	11	2	5	24	17	30	7	.223

Double Plays—4   Left on Bases—40

Boston	Pos	G	AB	R	H	2B	3B	HR	RBI	BB	SO	SB	BA
George Scott	1b	7	26	3	6	1	1	0	0	3	6	0	.231
Jerry Adair	2b-ph	5	16	0	2	0	0	0	1	0	3	1	.125
Rico Petrocelli	ss	7	20	4	4	1	0	2	3	3	8	0	.200
Dalton Jones	3b-ph	6	18	2	7	0	0	0	1	1	3	0	.389
Jose Tartabull	pr-rf-ph	7	13	1	2	0	0	0	0	1	2	0	.154
Reggie Smith	cf	7	24	3	6	1	0	2	3	2	2	0	.250
Carl Yastrzemski	lf	7	25	4	10	2	0	3	5	4	1	0	.400
Elston Howard	c	7	18	0	2	0	0	0	1	1	2	0	.111
Joe Foy	ph-3b	6	15	2	2	1	0	0	1	1	5	0	.133
Mike Andrews	ph-2b	5	13	2	4	0	0	0	1	0	1	0	.308
Ken Harrelson	rf	4	13	0	1	0	0	0	0	1	3	0	.077
Norm Siebern	ph-rf	3	3	0	0	0	0	0	0	1	0	0	.000
George Thomas	ph-rf	2	2	0	0	0	0	0	0	0	1	0	.000
Russ Gibson	c	2	2	0	0	0	0	0	0	0	2	0	.000
Mike Ryan	c	1	2	0	0	0	0	0	0	0	1	0	.000
Jim Lonborg	p	3	9	0	0	0	0	0	0	0	7	0	.000
Jose Santiago	p	3	2	1	1	0	0	1	1	0	1	0	.500
Gary Waslewski	p	2	1	0	0	0	0	0	0	0	1	0	.000
Gary Bell	p	3	0	0	0	0	0	0	0	0	0	0	.000
Ken Brett	p	2	0	0	0	0	0	0	0	0	0	0	.000
Dave Moorehead	p	2	0	0	0	0	0	0	0	0	0	0	.000
Dan Osinski	p	2	0	0	0	0	0	0	0	0	0	0	.000
John Wyatt	p	2	0	0	0	0	0	0	0	0	0	0	.000
Lee Stange	p	1	0	0	0	0	0	0	0	0	0	0	.000
Jerry Stephenson	p	1	0	0	0	0	0	0	0	0	0	0	.000
Team Total		7	822	21	48	6	1	8	19	17	49	1	.216

Double Plays—3   Left on Bases—43

PITCHING	G	GS	CG	IP	H	R	ER	BB	SO	W	L	SV	ERA
St. Louis													
Bob Gibson	3	3	3	27	14	3	3	5	26	**3**	0	0	**1.00**
Nelson Briles	2	1	1	11	7	2	2	1	4	1	0	0	1.64
Dick Hughes	2	2	0	9	9	6	5	3	7	0	1	0	5.00
Steve Carlton	1	1	0	6	3	1	0	2	5	0	1	0	0.00
Jack Lamabe	3	0	0	2⅔	5	2	2	0	4	0	1	0	6.75
Ray Washburn	2	0	0	2⅓	1	0	0	1	2	0	0	0	0.00
Hal Woodeshick	1	0	0	1	1	0	0	0	0	0	0	0	0.00
Ron Willis	3	0	0	1	2	4	3	4	1	0	0	0	27.00
Joe Hoerner	2	0	0	⅔	4	3	3	1	0	0	0	0	40.50
Larry Jaster	1	0	0	⅓	2	0	0	0	0	0	0	0	0.00
Team Total	7	7	4	61	48	21	18	17	49	4	3	0	2.66
Boston													
Jim Lonborg	3	3	2	24	14	**8**	**7**	2	11	2	1	0	2.63
Jose Santiago	3	2	0	9⅔	**16**	6	6	3	6	0	**2**	0	5.59
Gary Waslewski	2	1	0	8⅓	4	2	2	2	7	0	0	0	2.16
Gary Bell	3	1	0	5⅓	8	3	3	1	1	0	1	1	5.06
John Wyatt	2	0	0	3⅔	1	2	2	3	1	1	0	0	4.91
Dave Morehead	2	0	0	3⅓	0	0	0	4	3	0	0	0	0.00
Lee Stange	1	0	0	2	3	1	0	0	0	0	0	0	0.00
Jerry Stephenson	1	0	0	2	3	2	2	1	0	0	0	0	9.00
Ken Brett	2	0	0	1⅓	0	0	0	1	1	0	0	0	0.00
Dan Osinski	2	0	0	1⅓	2	1	1	0	0	0	0	0	6.75
Team Total	7	7	2	61	51	25	23	17	30	3	4	1	3.39

1968

Highlights

THE DETROIT TIGERS WON THE American League pennant for the first time since 1945. Right-hander Denny McClain, who flew planes and sang and played piano in nightclubs between starts, won 31 games, the first 30-win season since Dizzy Dean's 1934 campaign. McClain won his league's Cy Young and MVP awards.

The National League's Cy Young and MVP winner, Bob Gibson, led the Cards into their second straight World Series. Gibson's record of 22 victories and 9 defeats, and league-leading 268 strikeouts, 13 shutouts and 1.12 ERA spearheaded the tough Cards staff.

In game one in St. Louis, Gibson set a new Series single-game strikeout record by fanning 17.

The Tigers, down three games to one, and 3-2 in game five, nipped a budding Cardinals rally in the fifth inning when left fielder Willie Horton threw out Lou Brock at home when he failed to slide. Tigers eventually pulled out the game in the seventh on Kaline's two-run single, then rallied for victories in game six behind McClain, 13-1, and Mickey Lolich in game seven, 4-1. In game seven, with Gibson and Lolich locked in a runless duel, Cards center fielder Curt Flood misjudged a line drive in the seventh inning, allowing the deciding runs to score. Lolich, who pitched in relative obscurity all season behind the media favorite McClain, became the Series hero, winning three games.

Game 1 Oct. 2
Detroit   000 000 000 · 0
St. Louis   000 300 10* · 4
Winner-Gibson   Loser-McLain

Game 2 Oct. 3
Detroit   011 003 102 · 8
St. Louis   000 001 000 · 1
Winner-Lolich   Loser-Briles

Game 3 Oct. 5
St. Louis   000 040 300 · 7
Detroit   002 010 000 · 3
Winner-Washburn   Loser-Wilson

Game 4 Oct. 6
St. Louis   202 200 040 · 10
Detroit   000 100 000 · 1
Winner-Gibson   Loser-McLain

Game 5 Oct. 7
St. Louis   300 000 000 · 3
Detroit   000 200 30* · 5
Winner-Lolich   Loser-Hoerner

Game 6 Oct. 9
Detroit   021 010 000 · 13
St. Louis   000 000 001 · 1
Winner-McLain   Loser-Washburn

Game 7 Oct. 10
Detroit   000 000 301 · 4
St. Louis   000 000 001 · 1
Winner-Lolich   Loser-Gibson

Total Attendance—379,670
Average Attendance—54,239
Winning Player's Share—$10,937
Losing Player's Share—$7,079

Detroit A.L. 4
St. Louis N.L. 3

BATTING	Pos	G	AB	R	H	2B	3B	HR	RBI	BB	SO	SB	BA
Detroit													
Norm Cash	1b	7	26	5	10	0	0	1	5	3	5	0	.385
Dick McAuliffe	2b	7	27	5	6	0	0	1	3	4	6	0	.222
Mickey Stanley	ss-cf	7	28	4	6	0	1	0	0	2	4	0	.214
Don Wert	3b	6	17	1	2	0	0	0	2	6	5	0	.118
Al Kaline	rf	7	29	6	11	2	0	2	8	0	7	0	.379
Jim Northrup	cf-lf	7	28	4	7	0	1	2	8	1	5	0	.250
Willie Horton	lf	7	23	6	7	1	1	1	3	5	6	0	.304
Bill Freehan	c	7	24	0	2	1	0	0	2	4	8	0	.083
Eddie Mathews	ph-3b	2	3	0	1	0	0	0	0	1	1	0	.333
Ray Oyler	ss	4	0	0	0	0	0	0	0	0	0	0	.000
Dick Tracewski	3b-pr	2	0	1	0	0	0	0	0	0	0	0	.000
Tom Matchick	ph	3	3	0	0	0	0	0	0	0	1	0	.000
Jim Price	ph	2	2	0	0	0	0	0	0	0	1	0	.000
Gates Brown	ph	1	1	0	0	0	0	0	0	0	0	0	.000
Wayne Comer	ph	1	1	0	1	0	0	0	0	0	0	1	1.000
Mickey Lolich	p	3	12	2	3	0	0	1	2	1	5	0	.250
Denny McLain	p	3	6	0	0	0	0	0	0	0	4	0	.000
Earl Wilson	p	1	1	0	0	0	0	0	0	0	1	0	.000
Pat Dobson	p	3	0	0	0	0	0	0	0	0	0	0	.000
John Hiller	p	2	0	0	0	0	0	0	0	0	0	0	.000
Don McMahon	p	2	0	0	0	0	0	0	0	0	0	0	.000
Daryl Patterson	p	2	0	0	0	0	0	0	0	0	0	0	.000
Fred Lasher	p	1	0	0	0	0	0	0	0	0	0	0	.000
Joe Sparmer	p	1	0	0	0	0	0	0	0	0	0	0	.000
John Warden	Did not play												
Team Total		7	231	34	56	4	3	8	33	27	59	0	.242

Double Plays—5   Left on Bases—44

	Pos	G	AB	R	H	2B	3B	HR	RBI	BB	SO	SB	BA
St. Louis													
Orlando Cepeda	1b	7	28	2	7	0	0	2	6	2	3	0	.250
Julian Javier	2b	7	27	1	9	1	0	0	3	3	4	1	.333
Dal Maxvill	ss	7	22	1	0	0	0	0	0	3	5	0	.000
Mike Shannon	3b	7	29	3	8	1	0	1	4	1	5	0	.276
Roger Maris	rf-ph	6	19	5	3	1	0	0	1	3	3	0	.158
Curt Flood	cf	7	28	4	8	1	0	0	2	2	2	3	.286
Lou Brock	lf	7	28	6	13	3	1	2	5	3	4	7	.464
Tim McCarver	c	7	27	3	9	0	2	1	4	3	2	0	.333
Ron Davis	rf	2	7	0	0	0	0	0	0	0	2	0	.000
Dick Schofield	pr-ss	2	0	0	0	0	0	0	0	0	0	0	.000
Phil Gagliano	ph	3	3	0	0	0	0	0	0	0	0	0	.000
Johnny Edwards	ph	1	1	0	0	0	0	0	0	0	1	0	.000
Dave Ricketts	ph	1	1	0	1	0	0	0	0	0	0	0	1.000
Ed Spiezio	ph	1	1	0	1	0	0	0	0	0	0	0	1.000
Bobby Tolan	ph	1	1	0	0	0	0	0	0	0	1	0	.000
Bob Gibson	p	3	8	2	1	0	0	1	2	1	2	0	.125
Nelson Briles	p	2	4	0	0	0	0	0	0	0	4	0	.000
Ray Washburn	p	2	3	0	0	0	0	0	0	0	1	0	.000
Joe Hoerner	p	3	2	0	1	0	0	0	0	0	1	0	.500
Ron Willis	p	3	0	0	0	0	0	0	0	0	0	0	.000
Steve Carlton	p	2	0	0	0	0	0	0	0	0	0	0	.000
Wayne Granger	p	1	0	0	0	0	0	0	0	0	0	0	.000
Dick Hughes	p	1	0	0	0	0	0	0	0	0	0	0	.000
Larry Jaster	p	1	0	0	0	0	0	0	0	0	0	0	.000
Mel Nelson	p	1	0	0	0	0	0	0	0	0	0	0	.000
Team Total		7	239	27	61	7	3	7	27	21	40	11	.255

Double Plays—7   Left on Bases—49

PITCHING	G	GS	CG	IP	H	R	ER	BB	SO	W	L	SV	ERA
Detroit													
Mickey Lolich	3	3	3	27	20	5	5	6	21	3	0	0	1.67
Denny McLain	3	3	1	16⅔	18	8	6	4	13	1	2	0	3.24
Pat Dobson	3	0	0	4⅔	5	2	2	1	0	0	0	0	3.86
Earl Wilson	1	1	0	4⅓	4	3	3	6	3	0	1	0	6.23
Daryl Patterson	2	0	0	3	1	0	0	1	0	0	0	0	0.00
Fred Lasher	1	0	0	2	1	0	0	0	1	0	0	0	0.00
John Hiller	2	0	0	2	6	4	3	1	0	0	0	0	13.50
Don McMahon	2	0	0	2	4	3	3	0	1	0	0	0	13.50
Joe Sparma	1	0	0	⅓	2	2	2	0	0	0	0	0	54.00
John Warden	Did not play												
Team Total	7	7	4	62	61	27	24	21	40	4	3	0	3.48
St. Louis													
Bob Gibson	3	3	3	27	18	5	5	4	35	2	1	0	1.67
Nelson Briles	2	2	0	11⅓	13	7	7	4	7	0	1	0	5.56
Ray Washburn	2	2	0	7⅓	7	8	8	7	6	1	1	0	9.82
Joe Hoerner	3	0	0	4⅔	4	2	2	5	3	0	1	1	3.86
Ron Willis	3	0	0	4⅓	2	4	4	4	3	0	0	0	8.31
Steve Carlton	2	0	0	4	7	3	3	1	3	0	0	0	6.75
Wayne Granger	1	0	0	2	0	0	0	1	1	0	0	0	0.00
Mel Nelson	1	0	0	1	0	0	0	0	0	0	0	0	0.00
Dick Hughes	1	0	0	⅓	2	0	0	0	0	0	0	0	0.00
Larry Jaster	1	0	0	0	2	3	3	1	0	0	0	0	0.00
Team Total	7	7	3	62	56	34	32	27	59	3	4	1	4.65

1969

New York N.L. 4
Baltimore A.L. 1

Highlights

THE NEW YORK METS USED SOLID pitching, good defense and opportunistic hitting to catch the Chicago Cubs in mid-season and defeat Atlanta in the National League playoffs.

Tom Seaver (25-7) and Jerry Koosman (17-9) led the pitching staff. Former White Sox Tommie Agee (26 homers and .271) and Cleon Jones (.340) were the most consistent Met batsmen.

The Baltimore Orioles, one of the best baseball teams ever assembled, defeated the Twins for the American League championship and went into the fall classic as heavy favorites.

The first game followed the expected form—the Orioles' Mike Cuellar beating Tom Seaver, 4-1. But then the Orioles managed only five runs over the next four games. The Mets posted successive 2-1, 5-0, 2-1 and 5-3 victories for their first World Championship.

Agee made two sparkling catches in game three to preserve Gary Gentry's 5-0 victory. He robbed Elrod Hendricks of an extra base hit in the fourth inning with a diving backhanded catch in left center, and Paul Blair in the seventh with another diving catch, this time in right center.

Al Weis, a .215 regular season hitter, batted .455 in the Series, including a key game-tying homer in the deciding game.

Game 1 Oct. 11
New York   000 000 100 · 1
Baltimore 100 300 00* · 4
Winner-Cuellar   Loser-Seaver

Game 2 Oct. 12
New York   000 100 001 · 2
Baltimore 000 000 100 · 1
Winner-Koosman   Save-Taylor
Loser-McNally

Game 3 Oct. 14
Baltimore 000 000 000 · 0
New York   120 001 01* · 5
Winner-Gentry   Loser-Palmer

Game 4 Oct. 15
Baltimore 000 000 000 0 · 1
New York   010 000 000 1 · 2
Winner-Seaver   Loser-Hall

Game 5 Oct. 16
Baltimore 003 000 000 · 3
New York   000 002 12* · 5
Winner-Koosman   Loser-Watt

Total Attendance—272,378
Average Attendance—54,472
Winning Player's Share—$13,260*
Losing Player's Share—$9,350

*Including Playoff Series:
  Winners—$18,338   Losers—$14,904

BATTING

	Pos	G	AB	R	H	2B	3B	HR	RBI	BB	SO	SB	BA
New York													
Donn Clendenon	1b	4	14	**4**	5	1	0	**3**	**4**	2	6	0	.357
Al Weis	2b	5	11	1	5	0	0	1	3	**4**	2	0	**.455**
Bud Harrelson	ss	5	17	1	3	0	0	0	0	3	4	0	.176
Ed Charles	3b	4	15	1	2	1	0	0	0	0	2	0	.133
Ron Swoboda	rf	4	15	1	**6**	1	0	0	1	1	3	0	.400
Tommie Agee	cf	5	18	1	3	0	0	1	1	2	5	1	.167
Cleon Jones	lf	5	19	2	3	1	0	0	0	0	1	0	.158
Jerry Grote	c	5	19	1	4	**2**	0	0	1	1	3	0	.211
Art Shamsky	ph-rf	3	6	0	0	0	0	0	0	0	0	0	.000
Ken Boswell	2b	1	3	1	1	0	0	0	0	0	0	0	.333
Rod Gaspar	ph-rf-pr	3	2	1	0	0	0	0	0	0	0	0	.000
Ed Kranepool	1b	1	4	1	1	0	0	1	1	0	0	0	.250
Wayne Garrett	3b	2	1	0	0	0	0	0	0	2	1	0	.000
Duffy Dyer	ph	1	1	0	0	0	0	0	0	0	0	0	.000
J.C. Martin	ph	1	0	0	0	0	0	0	0	0	0	0	.000
Jerry Koosman	p	2	7	0	1	1	0	0	0	0	4	0	.143
Tom Seaver	p	2	4	0	0	0	0	0	0	0	2	0	.000
Gary Gentry	p	1	3	0	1	1	0	0	2	0	2	0	.333
Ron Taylor	p	2	0	0	0	0	0	0	0	0	0	0	.000
Don Cardwell	p	1	0	0	0	0	0	0	0	0	0	0	.000
Nolan Ryan		Did not play											
Tug McGraw		Did not play											
Cal Koonce		Did not play											
Jim McAndrew		Did not play											
Jack DiLauro		Did not play											
Team Total		5	159	15	35	8	0	6	13	15	35	1	.220

Double Plays—0   Left on Bases—34

	Pos	G	AB	R	H	2B	3B	HR	RBI	BB	SO	SB	BA
Baltimore													
Boog Powell	1b	5	19	0	5	0	0	0	0	1	4	0	.263
Dave Johnson	2b	5	16	1	1	0	0	0	0	2	1	0	.063
Mark Belanger	ss	5	15	2	3	0	0	0	1	2	1	0	.200
Brooks Robinson	3b	5	19	0	1	0	0	0	2	0	3	0	.053
Frank Robinson	rf	5	16	2	3	0	0	1	1	**4**	3	0	.188
Paul Blair	cf	5	**20**	1	2	0	0	0	0	2	5	1	.100
Don Buford	lf	5	**20**	1	2	1	0	1	2	2	4	0	.100
Ellie Hendricks	c	3	10	1	1	0	0	0	0	1	0	0	.100
Andy Etchebarren	c	2	6	0	0	0	0	0	0	0	1	0	.000
Clay Dalrymple	ph	2	2	0	2	0	0	0	0	0	0	0	1.000
Dave May	ph	2	1	0	0	0	0	0	0	1	1	0	.000
Curt Motton	ph	1	1	0	0	0	0	0	0	0	0	0	.000
Chico Salmon	pr	2	0	0	0	0	0	0	0	0	0	0	.000
Merv Rettenmund	pr	1	0	0	0	0	0	0	0	0	0	0	.000
Bobby Floyd		Did not play											
Mike Cuellar	p	2	5	0	2	0	0	0	1	0	3	0	.400
Dave McNally	p	2	5	1	1	0	0	1	2	0	2	0	.200
Jim Palmer	p	1	2	0	0	0	0	0	0	0	0	0	.000
Eddie Watt	p	2	0	0	0	0	0	0	0	0	0	0	.000
Dick Hall	p	1	0	0	0	0	0	0	0	0	0	0	.000
Dave Leonhard	p	1	0	0	0	0	0	0	0	0	0	0	.000
Pete Richert	p	1	0	0	0	0	0	0	0	0	0	0	.000
Tom Phoebus		Did not play											
Jim Hardin		Did not play											
Marcelino Lopez		Did not play											
Team Total		5	157	9	23	1	0	3	9	15	28	1	.146

Double Plays—4   Left on Bases—29

PITCHING

	G	GS	CG	IP	H	R	ER	BB	SO	W	L	SV	ERA
New York													
Jerry Koosman	**2**	**2**	1	17⅔	7	4	4	4	9	**2**	0	0	2.04
Tom Seaver	**2**	**2**	1	15	12	5	5	3	9	1	1	0	3.00
Gary Gentry	1	1	0	6⅔	3	0	0	**5**	4	1	0	0	0.00
Ron Taylor	**2**	0	0	2⅓	0	0	0	1	3	0	0	1	0.00
Nolan Ryan	1	0	0	2⅓	1	0	0	2	3	0	0	1	0.00
Don Cardwell	1	0	0	1	0	0	0	0	0	0	0	0	0.00
Tug McGraw		Did not play											
Cal Koonce		Did not play											
Jim McAndrew		Did not play											
Jack DiLauro		Did not play											
Team Total	5	5	2	45	23	9	9	15	28	4	1	2	1.80
Baltimore													
Mike Cuellar	**2**	**2**	1	16	**13**	2	2	4	**13**	1	0	0	**1.13**
Dave McNally	**2**	**2**	1	16	11	5	5	5	**13**	0	1	0	2.81
Jim Palmer	1	1	0	6	5	4	4	4	5	0	1	0	6.00
Eddie Watt	**2**	0	0	3	4	2	1	0	3	0	1	0	3.00
Dave Leonhard	1	0	0	2	1	1	1	1	1	0	0	0	4.50
Dick Hall	1	0	0	1	1	0	1	0	0	0	1	0	0.00
Pete Richert	1	0	0	0	0	0	0	0	0	0	0	0	0.00
Tom Phoebus		Did not play											
Jim Hardin		Did not play											
Marcelino Lopez		Did not play											
Team Total	5	5	2	43	35	15	13	15	35	1	4	0	2.72

1970

Baltimore A.L. 4
Cincinnati N.L. 1

Highlights

THE BALTIMORE ORIOLES CAME back with a vengeance after their Series loss to the Mets the previous October, trouncing the Cincinnati Reds' "Big Red Machine" four games to one. The Series-seasoned Orioles cast of Frank Robinson, Brooks Robinson, Boog Powell, Mike Cuellar, Dave McNally and Jim Palmer were no match for the rising Reds stars: Johnny Bench, Pete Rose, Tony Perez, Lee May, Bobby Tolan, Bernie Carbo, Gary Nolan and Don Gullett.

Brooks Robinson put on **the** performance of his career. He compiled a .429 Series average that included nine hits, two doubles and two home runs. In the sixth inning of game one, he backhanded a certain double by Lee May and threw out the big man with a strong, accurate peg. In the next inning, Brooks shot a solo homer over the left-field fence to give Jim Palmer and the Orioles a 4-3 winner. In game two, he contributed a run-scoring single in Baltimore's decisive fifth-inning five-run rally. In game three, he made sparkling defensive plays in the first, second and fith innings, and doubled in the Orioles' game-breaking four-run sixth-inning rally. In game four, the only game that the Orioles lost (6-5), Brooks went four for four, including a home run.

Oriole pitchers Jim Palmer, Mike Cuellar and Dave McNally, who combined for 68 victories during the season, each won a Series game.

Game 1 Oct. 10
Baltimore   000 210 100 · 4
Cincinnati   102 000 000 · 3
Winner-Palmer   Loser-Nolan

Game 2 Oct. 11
Baltimore   000 150 000 · 6
Cincinnati   301 001 000 · 5
Winner-Phoebus   Loser-Wilcox

Game 3 Oct. 13
Cincinnati   010 000 200 · 3
Baltimore   201 014 10* · 9
Winner-McNally   Loser-Cloninger

Game 4 Oct. 14
Cincinnati   011 010 030 · 6
Baltimore   013 001 000 · 5
Winner-Carroll   Loser-Watt

Game 5 Oct. 15
Cincinnati   300 000 000 · 3
Baltimore   222 010 02* · 9
Winner-Cuellar   Loser-Merritt

Total Attendance—253,183
Average Attendance—50,637
*Winning Player's Share—$18,216
*Losing Player's Share—$13,688

*Includes Playoffs and World Series.

BATTING	Pos	G	AB	R	H	2B	3B	HR	RBI	BB	SO	SB	BA
Baltimore													
Boog Powell	1b	5	17	6	5	1	0	2	5	5	2	0	.294
Dave Johnson	2b	5	16	2	5	2	0	0	2	5	2	0	.313
Mark Belanger	ss	5	19	0	2	0	0	0	1	1	2	0	.105
Brooks Robinson	3b	5	21	5	9	2	0	2	6	0	2	0	.429
Frank Robinson	rf	5	22	5	6	0	0	2	4	0	5	0	.273
Paul Blair	cf	5	19	5	9	1	0	0	3	2	4	0	**.474**
Don Buford	lf	4	15	3	4	0	0	1	1	3	2	0	.267
Ellie Hendricks	c	3	11	1	4	1	0	1	4	1	2	0	.364
Andy Etchebarren	c	2	7	1	1	0	0	0	0	2	3	0	.143
Merv Rettenmund	ph-lf	2	5	2	2	0	0	1	2	1	0	0	.400
Terry Crowley	ph	1	1	0	0	0	0	0	0	0	0	0	.000
Chico Salmon	ph	1	1	1	1	0	0	0	0	0	0	0	1.000
Curt Motton	Did not play												
Bobby Grich	Did not play												
Jim Palmer	p	2	7	1	1	0	0	0	0	0	3	0	.143
Mike Cuellar	p	2	4	0	0	0	0	0	0	0	2	0	.000
Dave McNally	p	1	4	1	1	0	0	1	4	0	2	0	.250
Moe Drabowsky	p	2	1	0	0	0	0	0	0	0	1	0	.000
Dick Hall	p	1	1	0	0	0	0	0	0	0	1	0	.000
Marcelino Lopez	p	1	0	0	0	0	0	0	0	0	0	0	.000
Tom Phoebus	p	1	0	0	0	0	0	0	0	0	0	0	.000
Pete Richert	p	1	0	0	0	0	0	0	0	0	0	0	.000
Eddie Watt	p	1	0	0	0	0	0	0	0	0	0	0	.000
Jim Hardin	Did not play												
Dave Leonhard	Did not play												
Team Total		5	171	33	50	7	0	10	32	20	33	0	.292
			Double Plays—3			Left on Bases—31							
Cincinnati													
Lee May	1b	5	18	6	7	2	0	2	8	2	2	0	.389
Tommy Helms	2b	5	18	1	4	0	0	0	0	1	1	0	.222
Dave Concepcion	ss	3	9	0	3	0	1	0	3	0	0	0	.333
Tony Perez	3b	5	18	2	1	0	0	0	0	3	4	0	.056
Pete Rose	rf	5	20	2	5	1	0	1	2	2	0	0	.250
Bobby Tolan	cf	5	19	5	4	1	0	1	1	3	2	1	.211
Hal McRae	lf	3	11	1	5	2	0	0	3	0	1	0	.455
Johnny Bench	c	5	19	3	4	0	0	1	3	1	2	0	.211
Bernie Carbo	lf-ph	4	8	0	0	0	0	0	0	2	3	0	.000
Woody Woodward	ss-ph	4	5	0	1	0	0	0	0	0	0	0	.200
Darrel Chaney	ss	3	1	0	0	0	0	0	0	0	1	0	.000
Ty Cline	ph	3	3	0	1	0	0	0	0	0	0	0	.333
Angel Bravo	ph	4	2	0	0	0	0	0	0	1	1	0	.000
Jimmy Stewart	ph	2	2	0	0	0	0	0	0	0	1	0	.000
Pat Corrales	ph	1	1	0	0	0	0	0	0	0	0	0	.000
Gary Nolan	p	2	3	0	0	0	0	0	0	0	0	0	.000
Tony Cloninger	p	2	2	0	0	0	0	0	0	0	1	0	.000
Jim McGlothlin	p	1	2	0	0	0	0	0	0	0	1	0	.000
Clay Carroll	p	4	1	0	0	0	0	0	0	0	0	0	.000
Don Gullett	p	3	1	0	0	0	0	0	0	0	1	0	.000
Jim Merritt	p	1	1	0	0	0	0	0	0	0	0	0	.000
Wayne Granger	p	2	0	0	0	0	0	0	0	0	0	0	.000
Milt Wilcox	p	2	0	0	0	0	0	0	0	0	0	0	.000
Ray Washburn	p	1	0	0	0	0	0	0	0	0	0	0	.000
Mel Behney	Did not play												
Wayne Simpson	Not in Series—shoulder injury												
Team Total		5	164	20	35	6	1	5	20	15	23	1	.213
			Double Plays—4			Left on Bases—28							

PITCHING	G	GS	CG	IP	H	R	ER	BB	SO	W	L	SV	ERA
Baltimore													
Jim Palmer	2	2	0	15²/₃	11	8	8	9	9	1	0	0	4.60
Mike Cuellar	2	2	1	11¹/₃	10	7	4	2	5	1	0	0	3.18
Dave McNally	1	1	1	9	9	3	3	2	5	1	0	0	3.00
Moe Drabowsky	2	0	0	3¹/₃	2	1	1	1	0	0	0	0	2.70
Dick Hall	1	0	0	2¹/₃	0	0	0	0	0	0	0	1	0.00
Tom Phoebus	1	0	0	1²/₃	1	0	0	0	0	1	0	0	0.00
Eddie Watt	1	0	0	1	2	1	1	1	3	0	1	0	9.00
Marcelino Lopez	1	0	0	¹/₃	0	0	0	0	0	0	0	0	0.00
Pete Richert	1	0	0	¹/₃	0	0	0	0	0	0	0	1	0.00
Team Total	5	5	2	45	35	20	17	15	23	4	1	2	3.40
Cincinnati													
Gary Nolan	2	2	0	9¹/₃	9	8	8	3	9	0	1	0	7.71
Clay Carroll	4	0	0	9	5	0	0	2	11	1	0	0	**0.00**
Tony Cloninger	2	1	0	7¹/₃	10	6	6	5	4	0	1	0	7.36
Don Gullett	3	0	0	6²/₃	5	2	1	4	4	0	0	0	1.35
Jim McGlothlin	1	1	0	4¹/₃	6	4	4	2	2	0	0	0	8.31
Milt Wilcox	2	0	0	2	3	2	2	0	2	0	1	0	9.00
Jim Merritt	1	1	0	1²/₃	3	4	4	1	0	0	1	0	21.60
Wayne Granger	2	0	0	1¹/₃	7	5	5	1	1	0	0	0	33.75
Ray Washburn	1	0	0	1¹/₃	2	2	2	2	0	0	0	0	13.50
Team Total	5	5	0	43	50	33	32	20	33	1	4	0	6.70

1971

Pittsburgh N.L. 4
Baltimore A.L. 3

Highlights

ORIOLES WERE BACK FOR THIRD straight year. Their pitching staff boasted four 20-game winners: Jim Palmer (20-9), Mike Cuellar (20-9), Dave McNally (21-5) and Pat Dobson (20-8).

National League champion Pittsburgh Pirates features an explosive offense led by Willie Stargell (.295, 125 RBI's and league-leading 48 homers), Bob Robertson (.271 and 26 homers), Manny Sanguillen (.319) and Roberto Clemente (.341).

More than 60 million viewers watched game four, baseball's first game scheduled during television's prime time. The tremendous success of this experiment prompted Commissioner Bowie Kuhn to schedule all weekday games at night starting the following year. The Pirates won the game (4-3) on a pinch-hit single by reserve Milt May in the seventh.

Roberto Clemente, in his only World Series appearance, performed brilliantly. He batted .414, with 12 hits in 29 at-bats, including two doubles, a triple and two homers.

Pirate right-hander Steve Blass, 15-8 during the regular season, excelled in the Series with two complete game victories, including the 2-1 clincher over the Orioles' Mike Cuellar.

Game 1 Oct. 9
Pittsburgh	030 000 000 ·	3
Baltimore	013 010 00* ·	5

Winner-McNally Loser-Ellis

Game 2 Oct. 11
Pittsburgh	000 000 003 ·	3
Baltimore	010 361 00* ·	11

Winner-Palmer Loser-R. Johnson

Game 3 Oct. 12
Baltimore	000 000 100 ·	1
Pittsburgh	100 001 30* ·	5

Winner-Blass Loser-Cuellar

Game 4 Oct. 13
Baltimore	300 000 000 ·	3
Pittsburgh	201 000 10* ·	4

Winner-Kison Loser-Watt

Game 5 Oct. 14
Baltimore	000 000 000 ·	0
Pittsburgh	021 010 00* ·	4

Winner-Briles Loser-McNally

Game 6 Oct. 16
Pittsburgh	011 000 000 0 ·	2
Baltimore	000 001 100 1 ·	3

Winner-McNally Loser-Miller

Game 7 Oct. 17
Pittsburgh	000 100 010 ·	2
Baltimore	000 000 010 ·	1

Winner-Blass Loser-Cuellar

Total Attendance—351,091
Average Attendance—50,156
*Winning Player's Share—$18,165
*Losing Player's Share—$13,906

* Includes Playoffs and World Series.

BATTING

	Pos	G	AB	R	H	2B	3B	HR	RBI	BB	SO	SB	BA
Pittsburgh													
Bob Robertson	1b	7	25	4	6	0	0	2	5	4	8	0	.240
Dave Cash	2b	7	30	2	4	1	0	0	1	3	1	1	.133
Jackie Hernandez	ss	7	18	2	4	0	0	0	1	2	5	1	.222
Jose Pagan	3b	4	15	0	4	2	0	0	2	0	1	0	.267
Roberto Clemente	rf	7	29	3	12	2	1	2	4	2	2	0	.414
Al Oliver	ph-cf	5	19	1	4	2	0	0	2	2	5	0	.211
Willie Stargell	lf	7	24	3	5	1	0	0	1	7	9	0	.208
Manny Sanguillen	c	7	29	3	11	1	0	0	0	0	3	2	.379
Richie Hebner	3b	3	12	2	2	0	0	1	3	3	3	0	.167
Gene Clines	cf	3	11	2	1	0	1	0	0	1	1	1	.091
Vic Davalillo	ph-lf-cf	3	3	1	1	0	0	0	0	0	0	0	.333
Gene Alley	ss-pr	2	2	0	0	0	0	0	0	1	0	0	.000
Milt May	ph	2	2	0	1	0	0	0	0	1	0	0	.500
Bill Mazeroski	ph	1	1	0	0	0	0	0	0	0	0	0	.000
Charlie Sands	ph	1	1	0	0	0	0	0	0	0	1	0	.000
Steve Blass	p	2	7	0	0	0	0	0	0	0	1	0	.000
Bob Johnson	p	2	3	0	0	0	0	0	0	0	2	0	.000
Bob Moose	p	3	2	0	0	0	0	0	0	0	1	0	.000
Bruce Kison	p	2	2	0	0	0	0	0	0	1	2	0	.000
Nelson Briles	p	1	2	0	1	0	0	0	0	1	1	0	.500
Dock Ellis	p	1	1	0	0	0	0	0	0	0	1	0	.000
Dave Giusti	p	3	0	0	0	0	0	0	0	0	0	0	.000
Bob Miller	p	3	0	0	0	0	0	0	0	0	0	0	.000
Bob Veale	p	1	0	0	0	0	0	0	0	0	0	0	.000
Luke Walker	p	1	0	0	0	0	0	0	0	0	0	0	.000
Team Total		7	238	23	56	9	2	5	21	26	47	5	.235

Double Plays—7   Left on Bases—63

	Pos	G	AB	R	H	2B	3B	HR	RBI	BB	SO	SB	BA
Baltimore													
Boog Powell	1b	7	27	1	3	0	0	0	1	1	3	0	.111
Dave Johnson	2b	7	27	1	4	0	0	0	3	0	1	0	.148
Mark Belanger	ss	7	21	4	5	0	1	0	0	5	2	1	.238
Brooks Robinson	3b	7	22	2	7	0	0	0	5	3	1	0	.318
Frank Robinson	rf	7	25	5	7	0	0	2	2	2	8	0	.280
Merv Rettenmund	cf-rf-lf-ph	7	27	3	5	0	0	1	4	0	4	0	.185
Don Buford	lf	6	23	3	6	1	0	2	4	3	3	0	.261
Ellie Hendricks	c	6	19	3	5	1	0	0	1	3	3	0	.263
Paul Blair	cf-pr	4	9	2	3	1	0	0	0	0	1	0	.333
Andy Etchebarren	c	1	2	0	0	0	0	0	0	0	0	0	.000
Tom Shopay	ph	5	4	0	0	0	0	0	0	0	0	0	.000
Chico Salmon	Did not play												
Jerry DaVanon	Did not play												
Curt Motton	Did not play												
Clay Dalrymple	Did not play												
Dave McNally	p	4	4	0	0	0	0	0	0	0	3	0	.000
Jim Palmer	p	2	4	0	0	0	0	0	2	2	2	0	.000
Mike Cuellar	p	2	3	0	0	0	0	0	0	1	2	0	.000
Pat Dobson	p	3	2	0	0	0	0	0	0	0	0	0	.000
Tom Dukes	p	2	0	0	0	0	0	0	0	0	0	0	.000
Eddie Watt	p	2	0	0	0	0	0	0	0	0	0	0	.000
Dick Hall	p	1	0	0	0	0	0	0	0	0	0	0	.000
Grant Jackson	p	1	0	0	0	0	0	0	0	0	0	0	.000
Dave Leonhard	p	1	0	0	0	0	0	0	0	0	0	0	.000
Pete Richert	p	1	0	0	0	0	0	0	0	0	0	0	.000
Team Total		7	219	4	45	3	1	5	22	20	35	1	.205

Double Plays—2   Left on Bases—39

PITCHING

	G	GS	CG	IP	H	R	ER	BB	SO	W	L	SV	ERA
Pittsburgh													
Steve Blass	2	2	2	18	7	2	2	4	13	2	0	0	1.00
Bob Moose	3	1	0	9⅔	12	7	7	2	7	0	0	0	6.52
Nelson Briles	1	1	1	9	2	0	0	2	2	1	0	0	0.00
Bruce Kison	2	0	0	6⅓	1	0	0	2	3	1	0	0	0.00
Dave Giusti	3	0	0	5⅓	3	0	0	2	4	0	0	1	0.00
Bob Johnson	2	1	0	5	5	5	5	3	3	0	1	0	9.00
Bob Miller	3	0	0	4⅔	7	2	2	1	2	0	1	0	3.86
Dock Ellis	1	1	0	2⅓	4	4	4	1	1	0	1	0	15.43
Bob Veale	1	0	0	⅔	1	1	1	2	0	0	0	0	13.50
Luke Walker	1	1	0	⅔	3	3	3	1	0	0	0	0	40.50
Team Total	7	7	3	61⅔	45	24	24	20	35	4	3	1	3.50
Baltimore													
Jim Palmer	2	2	0	17	15	5	5	9	15	1	0	0	2.65
Mike Cuellar	2	2	0	14	11	7	6	6	10	0	2	0	3.86
Dave McNally	4	2	1	13⅔	10	7	3	5	12	2	1	0	1.98
Pat Dobson	3	1	0	6⅔	13	3	3	4	6	0	0	0	4.05
Tom Dukes	2	0	0	4	2	0	0	1	0	0	0	0	0.00
Eddie Watt	2	0	0	2⅓	4	1	1	0	2	0	1	0	3.86
Dick Hall	1	0	0	1	1	0	0	0	0	0	0	1	0.00
Dave Leonhard	1	0	0	1	0	0	0	1	0	0	0	0	0.00
Grant Jackson	1	0	0	⅔	0	0	0	1	0	0	0	0	0.00
Pete Richert	1	0	0	⅔	0	0	0	0	1	0	0	0	0.00
Team Total	7	7	1	61	56	23	18	26	47	3	4	1	2.66

1972

Highlights

THE CINCINNATI REDS WERE BACK after a year's absence with a strengthened lineup that included newcomers Joe Morgan (.292 and 58 stolen bases), Cesar Geronimo (.275), Pedro Borbon (8-3 and 11 saves). They complemented the already powerful array of Reds: Tony Perez (.283), Bobby Tolan (.283), Pete Rose (307) and Johnny Bench (.270 and league-leading 125 RBI's and 40 homers).

American League champion Oakland A's were a talented young club that included Reggie Jackson (.265, 25 homers), Mike Epstein (.270, 26 homers), Bert Campaneris (52 stolen bases), Joe Rudi (.305, led the A's in RBI's with 77), Jim "Catfish" Hunter (21-7), Ken Holtzman (19-11), Blue Moon Odom (15-6) and Rollie Fingers (11-9 and 21 saves).

First World Series appearance for A's since 1931, then under ownership of Connie Mack in Philadelphia.

Part-time catcher-first baseman Gene Tenace hit home runs in first two Series plate appearances, in second and fifth innings of game one—a Series record. His total of four for the seven-game Series tied a record held by Babe Ruth, Duke Snider and Hank Bauer.

Game 1 Oct. 14
Oakland	020 010 000	3
Cincinnati	010 100 000	2

Winner-Holtzman Save-Blue
Loser-Nolan

Game 2 Oct. 15
Oakland	011 000 000	2
Cincinnati	000 000 001	1

Winner-Hunter Save-Fingers
Loser-Grimsley

Game 3 Oct. 18
Cincinnati	000 000 100	1
Oakland	000 000 000	0

Winner-Billingham Save-Carroll
Loser-Odom

Game 4 Oct. 19
Cincinnati	000 000 020	2
Oakland	000 010 002	3

Winner-Fingers Loser-Carroll

Game 5 Oct. 20
Cincinnati	100 110 011	5
Oakland	030 100 000	4

Winner-Grimsley Save-Billingham
Loser-Fingers

Game 6 Oct. 21
Oakland	000 010 000	1
Cincinnati	000 111 50*	8

Winner-Grimsley Save-Hall
Loser-Blue

Game 7 Oct. 22
Oakland	100 002 000	3
Cincinnati	000 010 010	2

Winner-Hunter Save-Fingers
Loser-Borbon

Total Attendance—363,149
Average Attendance—51,878
*Winning Player's Share—$20,705
*Loser Player's Share—$15,080

*Includes Playoffs and World Series.

Oakland A.L. 4 / Cincinnati N.L. 3

BATTING	Pos	G	AB	R	H	2B	3B	HR	RBI	BB	SO	SB	BA
Oakland													
Mike Epstein	1b	6	16	1	0	0	0	0	0	5	3	0	.000
Dick Green	2b	7	18	0	6	2	0	0	1	0	4	0	.333
Bert Campaneris	ss	7	28	1	5	0	0	0	0	1	4	0	.179
Sal Bando	3b	7	26	2	7	1	0	0	1	2	5	0	.269
Matty Alou	rf	7	24	0	1	0	0	0	0	3	0	1	.042
George Hendrick	cf	5	15	3	2	0	0	0	0	0	1	0	.133
Joe Rudi	lf	7	25	1	6	0	0	1	1	2	5	0	.240
Gene Tenace	c-1b	7	23	5	8	1	0	4	9	2	4	0	.348
Angel Mangual	ph-cf	4	10	1	3	0	0	0	1	0	0	0	.300
Mike Hegan	1b-ph	6	5	0	1	0	0	0	0	0	2	0	.200
Dave Duncan	ph-c	3	5	0	1	0	0	0	0	1	3	0	.200
Ted Kubiak	2b	4	3	0	1	0	0	0	0	0	0	0	.333
Gonzalo Marquez	ph	5	5	0	3	0	0	0	1	0	0	0	.600
Don Mincher	ph	3	1	0	1	0	0	0	1	0	0	0	1.000
Allen Lewis	pr	6	0	2	0	0	0	0	0	0	0	0	.000
Tim Cullen	Did not play												
Dal Maxvill	Did not play												
Reggie Jackson	Not in Series—Hamstring pull												
Catfish Hunter	p	3	5	0	1	0	0	0	1	2	1	0	.200
Ken Holtzman	p	3	5	0	0	0	0	0	0	0	0	0	.000
Blue Moon Odom	p-pr	4	4	0	0	0	0	0	0	0	3	0	.000
Rollie Fingers	p	6	1	0	0	0	0	0	0	0	0	0	.000
Vida Blue	p	4	1	0	0	0	0	0	0	0	2	1	0	.000
Dave Hamilton	p	2	0	0	0	0	0	0	0	0	0	0	.000
Joe Horlen	p	1	0	0	0	0	0	0	0	0	0	0	.000
Bob Locker	p	1	0	0	0	0	0	0	0	0	0	0	.000
Darold Knowles	Not in Series—injured												
Team Total		7	220	16	46	4	0	5	16	21	37	1	.209

Double Plays—0 Left on Bases—45

	Pos	G	AB	R	H	2B	3B	HR	RBI	BB	SO	SB	BA
Cincinnati													
Tony Perez	1b	7	23	3	10	2	0	0	2	4	4	0	**.435**
Joe Morgan	2b	7	24	4	3	2	0	0	1	6	3	2	.125
Dave Concepcion	ss-pr-ph	6	13	2	4	0	1	0	2	2	2	1	.308
Denis Menke	3b	7	24	1	2	0	0	1	2	2	6	0	.083
Cesar Geronimo	rf-cf	7	19	1	3	0	0	0	3	1	4	1	.158
Bobby Tolan	cf	7	26	2	7	1	0	0	6	1	4	5	.269
Pete Rose	lf	7	28	3	6	0	0	1	2	4	4	1	.214
Johnny Bench	c	7	23	4	6	1	0	1	1	5	5	2	.261
Hal McRae	ph-rf	5	9	1	4	1	0	0	2	0	1	0	.444
Darrel Chaney	ss-ph	4	7	0	0	0	0	0	0	2	2	0	.000
Joe Hague	ph-rf	3	3	0	0	0	0	0	0	0	0	0	.000
George Foster	pr-rf	2	0	0	0	0	0	0	0	0	0	0	.000
Ted Uhlaender	ph	4	4	0	1	1	0	0	0	0	1	0	.250
Julian Javier	ph	4	2	0	0	0	0	0	0	0	0	0	.000
Bill Plummer	Did not play												
Jack Billingham	p	3	5	0	0	0	0	0	0	0	4	0	.000
Gary Nolan	p	2	3	0	0	0	0	0	0	0	3	0	.000
Ross Grimsley	p	4	2	0	0	0	0	0	0	0	2	0	.000
Tom Hall	p	4	2	0	0	0	0	0	0	0	1	0	.000
Don Gullett	p	1	2	0	0	0	0	0	0	0	0	0	.000
Jim McGlothlin	p	1	1	0	0	0	0	0	0	0	0	0	.000
Pedro Borbon	p	6	0	0	0	0	0	0	0	0	0	0	.000
Clay Carroll	p	5	0	0	0	0	0	0	0	0	0	0	.000
Wayne Simpson	Did not play												
Ed Sprague	Did not play												
Team Total		7	220	21	46	8	1	3	21	27	46	12	.209

Double Plays—5 Left on Bases—49

PITCHING	G	GS	CG	IP	H	R	ER	BB	SO	W	L	SV	ERA
Oakland													
Catfish Hunter	3	2	0	16	12	5	5	6	11	2	0	0	2.81
Ken Holtzman	3	2	0	12⅔	11	3	3	3	4	1	0	0	2.13
Blue Moon Odom	2	2	0	11⅓	5	2	2	6	13	0	1	0	1.59
Rollie Fingers	6	0	0	10⅓	4	2	2	4	11	1	1	2	1.74
Vida Blue	4	1	0	8⅔	8	4	4	5	5	0	1	1	4.15
Dave Hamilton	2	0	0	1⅓	2	1	1	0	1	0	0	0	27.00
Joe Horlen	1	0	0	1⅓	3	4	4	1	1	0	0	0	6.75
Bob Locker	1	0	0	⅓	1	0	0	0	0	0	0	0	0.00
Darold Knowles	Not in Series—injured												
Team Total	7	7	0	62	46	21	21	27	46	4	3	3	3.05
Cincinnati													
Jack Billingham	3	2	0	13⅔	6	1	0	4	11	1	0	1	**0.00**
Gary Nolan	2	2	0	10⅔	7	4	4	2	3	0	1	0	3.38
Tom Hall	4	0	0	8⅓	6	0	0	2	7	0	0	1	**0.00**
Pedro Borbon	6	0	0	7	7	3	3	2	4	0	1	0	3.86
Ross Grimsley	4	1	0	7	7	2	2	3	2	2	1	0	2.57
Don Gullett	1	1	0	7	5	1	1	2	4	0	0	0	1.29
Clay Carroll	5	0	0	5⅔	6	1	1	4	3	0	1	1	1.59
Jim McGlothlin	1	1	0	3	2	4	4	2	3	0	0	0	12.00
Wayne Simpson	Did not play												
Ed Sprague	Did not play												
Team Total	7	7	0	62⅓	46	16	15	21	37	3	4	3	2.17

1973

Oakland A.L. 4
New York N.L. 3

Highlights

OAKLAND A'S BECAME THE FIRST repeat World Champions since the 1961-62 New York Yankees, edging the New York Mets, four games to three.

A's had three 20-game winners going into series—Jim "Catfish" Hunter, Vida Blue and Ken Holtzman. Hunter and Holtzman produced three of the four A's victories, with only Blue getting shut out in the win column.

Mets won the National League pennant with lowest won-loss percentage (.512) in history.

After game two, A's owner Charlie Finley tried to replace second baseman Mike Andrews, claiming that Andrews was disabled by a shoulder injury. Andrews had drawn Finley's wrath when in the twelfth inning of second game he allowed three runs to score with two back-to-back errors that sent the A's down to defeat, 10-7. Commissioner Bowie Kuhn ordered Andrews reinstated and levied a fine against Finley, whose behavior had aroused the ire of fans and players alike.

Rusty Staub, in his first World Series, led all hitters, with a .423 batting average and six RBI's.

Game 1 Oct. 13
New York   000 100 000 · 1
Oakland   002 000 00* · 2
Winner-Holtzman Loser-Matlack
Save-Knowles

Game 2 Oct. 14
New York   011 004 000 004 · 10
Oakland   210 000 102 001 · 7
Winner-McGraw Loser-Fingers
Save-Stone

Game 3 Oct. 16
Oakland   000 001 010 01 · 3
New York   200 000 000 00 · 2
Winner-Lindblad Loser-Parker
Save-Fingers

Game 4 Oct. 17
Oakland   000 100 000 · 1
New York   300 300 00* · 6
Winner-Matlack Loser-Holtzman
Save-Sadecki

Game 5 Oct. 18
Oakland   000 000 000 · 0
New York   010 001 00* · 2
Winner-Koosman Loser-Blue
Save-McGraw

Game 6 Oct. 20
New York   000 000 010 · 1
Oakland   101 000 01* · 3
Winner-Hunter Loser-Seaver
Save-Fingers

Game 7 Oct. 21
New York   000 001 001 · 2
Oakland   004 010 00* · 5
Winner-Holtzman Loser-Matlack

Total Attendance—358,289
Average Attendance—51,184
*Winning Player's Share—$24,618
*Losing Player's Share—$14,950

*Includes Playoffs and World Series.

BATTING

	Pos	G	AB	R	H	2B	3B	HR	RBI	BB	SO	SB	BA
Oakland													
Gene Tenace	1b-c	1	19	0	3	1	0	0	3	11	7	0	.158
Dick Green	2b	7	16	0	1	0	0	0	0	1	6	0	.063
Bert Campaneris	ss	7	31	6	9	0	1	1	3	1	7	3	.290
Sal Bando	3b	7	26	5	6	1	1	0	1	4	7	0	.231
Jesus Alou	rf-ph	7	19	0	3	1	0	0	3	0	0	0	.158
Reggie Jackson	cf-rf	7	29	3	9	3	1	1	6	2	7	0	.310
Joe Rudi	lf	7	27	3	9	2	0	0	4	3	4	0	.333
Ray Fosse	c	7	19	0	3	1	0	0	0	1	4	0	.158
Vic Davalillo	cf-ph-1b	6	11	0	1	0	0	0	0	2	1	0	.091
Deron Johnson	ph-1b	6	10	0	3	1	0	0	0	1	4	0	.300
Angel Mangual	ph-cf	5	6	0	0	0	0	0	0	0	3	0	.000
Ted Kubiak	2b	4	3	1	0	0	0	0	0	1	1	0	.000
Mike Andrews	ph-2b	2	3	0	0	0	0	0	0	1	1	0	.000
Pat Bourque	ph-1b	2	2	0	1	0	0	0	0	0	0	0	.500
Billy Conigliaro	ph	3	3	0	0	0	0	0	0	0	1	0	.000
Allen Lewis	pr	3	0	1	0	0	0	0	0	0	0	0	.000
Bill North		Not in Series—injured											
Catfish Hunter	p	2	5	0	0	0	0	0	0	0	3	0	.000
Vida Blue	p	2	4	0	0	0	0	0	0	0	4	0	.000
Rollie Fingers	p	6	3	0	1	0	0	0	0	0	1	0	.333
Ken Holtzman	p	3	3	2	2	2	0	0	0	0	0	0	.667
Paul Lindblad	p	3	1	0	0	0	0	0	0	0	0	0	.000
Blue Moon Odom	p-pr	3	1	0	0	0	0	0	0	0	1	0	.000
Darold Knowles	p	7	0	0	0	0	0	0	0	0	0	0	.000
Horace Pina	p	2	0	0	0	0	0	0	0	0	0	0	.000
Team Total		7	241	21	51	12	3	2	20	28	62	3	.212

Double Plays—8   Left on Bases—58

	Pos	G	AB	R	H	2B	3B	HR	RBI	BB	SO	SB	BA
New York													
John Milner	1b	7	27	2	8	0	0	0	2	5	1	0	.296
Felix Millan	2b	7	32	3	6	1	1	0	1	1	1	0	.188
Bud Harrelson	ss	7	24	2	6	1	0	0	1	5	3	0	.250
Wayne Garrett	3b	7	30	4	5	0	0	2	2	5	11	0	.167
Rusty Staub	rf	7	26	1	11	2	0	1	6	2	2	0	.423
Don Hahn	rf-cf	7	29	2	7	1	1	0	2	1	6	0	.241
Cleon Jones	lf	7	28	5	8	2	0	1	1	4	2	0	.286
Jerry Grote	c	7	30	2	8	0	0	0	0	0	1	0	.267
Willie Mays	cf-pr-ph	3	7	1	2	0	0	0	1	0	1	0	.286
George Theodore	ph-lf	2	2	0	0	0	0	0	0	0	0	0	.000
Jim Beauchamp	ph	4	4	0	0	0	0	0	0	0	1	0	.000
Ed Kranepool	ph	4	3	0	0	0	0	0	0	0	0	0	.000
Ken Boswell	ph	3	3	1	3	0	0	0	0	0	0	0	1.000
Ted Martinez	pr	2	0	0	0	0	0	0	0	0	0	0	.000
Ron Hodges	ph	1	0	0	0	0	0	0	0	1	0	0	.000
Duffy Dyer		Did not play											
Tom Seaver	p	2	5	0	0	0	0	0	0	0	2	0	.000
Jon Matlack	p	3	4	0	1	0	0	0	0	0	2	0	.250
Jerry Koosman	p	2	4	0	0	0	0	0	0	0	3	0	.000
Tug McGraw	p	5	3	1	1	0	0	0	0	0	0	0	.333
Ray Sadecki	p	4	0	0	0	0	0	0	0	0	0	0	.000
Harry Parker	p	3	0	0	0	0	0	0	0	0	0	0	.000
George Stone	p	2	0	0	0	0	0	0	0	0	0	0	.000
Jim McAndrew		Did not play											
Buzz Capra		Did not play											
Team Total		7	261	24	66	7	2	4	16	26	36	0	.253

Double Plays—3   Left on Bases—72

PITCHING

	G	GS	CG	IP	H	R	ER	BB	SO	W	L	SV	ERA
Oakland													
Rollie Fingers	6	0	0	13⅔	13	5	1	4	8	0	1	2	0.66
Catfish Hunter	2	2	0	13⅓	11	3	3	4	6	1	0	0	2.03
Vida Blue	2	2	0	11	10	6	6	3	8	0	1	0	4.91
Ken Holtzman	3	3	0	10⅔	13	5	5	5	6	2	1	0	4.22
Darold Knowles	7	0	0	6⅓	4	1	0	5	5	0	0	2	0.00
Blue Moon Odom	2	0	0	4⅔	5	2	2	2	2	0	0	0	3.86
Paul Lindblad	3	0	0	3⅓	4	0	0	1	1	1	0	0	0.00
Horacio Pina	2	0	0	3	6	2	0	2	0	0	0	0	0.00
Team Total	7	7	0	66	66	24	17	26	36	4	3	4	2.32
New York													
Jon Matlack	3	3	0	16⅔	10	7	4	5	11	1	2	0	2.16
Tom Seaver	2	2	0	15	13	4	4	3	18	0	1	0	2.40
Tug McGraw	5	0	0	13⅔	8	5	4	9	14	1	0	1	2.63
Jerry Koosman	2	2	0	8⅔	9	3	3	7	8	1	0	0	3.12
Ray Sadecki	4	0	0	4⅔	5	1	1	1	6	0	0	1	1.93
Harry Parker	3	0	0	3⅓	2	1	0	2	2	0	1	0	0.00
George Stone	2	0	0	3	4	0	0	1	3	0	0	1	0.00
Jim McAndrew		Did not play											
Buzz Capra		Did not play											
Team Total	7	7	0	65	51	21	16	28	62	3	4	3	2.22

1974

Oakland A.L. 4
Los Angeles N.L. 1

Highlights

THIS FIRST ALL-CALIFORNIA World Series featured the A's, back in the fall classic for the third consecutive year, and the Los Angeles Dodgers, who for the first time since the 1966 Koufax-Drysdale World Series team did not rely solely on pitching, speed and defense. The 1974 Dodgers had power-hitting Jimmy Wynn (the "Toy Cannon"), who blasted 32 homers and knocked in 108 runs during the regular season, and Steve Garvey (.312, 21 homers and 111 RBI's) in their well-balanced lineup. Davey Lopes and Bill Buckner, with 59 and 31 stolen bases respectively, added speed to their offense.

The A's, who feuded as fiercely off the field as they played on the field, brought the same successful cast (plus or minus a few characters, including Mike Andrews, who had left the team and subsequently filed a $2 million libel suit against owner Charlie Finley for the 1973 Series incident) that won the 1972 and 1973 Championships.

Dodger reliever Mike Marshall, who led the National League with 21 saves, appeared in all five Series games, garnering a loss, a save and ten strikeouts in nine innings.

Game 1 Oct. 12
Oakland   010 010 010 - 3
Los Angeles   000 010 001 - 2
Winner-Fingers   Loser-Messersmith
Save-Hunter

Game 2 Oct. 13
Oakland   000 000 002 - 2
Los Angeles   010 002 00* - 3
Winner-Sutton   Loser-Blue
Save-Marshall

Game 3 Oct. 15
Los Angeles   000 000 011 - 2
Oakland   002 100 00* - 3
Winner-Holtzman Loser-Messersmith
Save-Fingers

Game 4 Oct. 16
Los Angeles   000 200 000 - 2
Oakland   001 004 00* - 5
Winner-Holtzman Loser-Messersmith
Save-Fingers

Game 5 Oct. 17
Los Angeles   000 002 000 - 2
Oakland   110 000 10* - 3
Winner-Odom   Loser-Marshall
Save-Fingers

Total Attendance—260,004
Average Attendance—52,000
*Winning Player's share—$22,219
*Losing Player's Share—$15,704

*Includes Playoffs and World Series.

BATTING	Pos	G	AB	R	H	2B	3B	HR	RBI	BB	SO	SB	BA
Oakland													
Gene Tenace	1b-c	5	9	0	2	0	0	0	0	3	4	0	.222
Dick Green	2b	5	13	1	0	0	0	0	1	1	4	0	.000
Bert Campaneris	ss	5	17	1	6	2	0	0	2	0	2	1	.353
Sal Bando	3b	5	16	3	1	0	0	0	2	2	5	0	.063
Reggie Jackson	rf	5	14	3	4	1	0	1	1	5	3	1	.286
Bill North	cf	5	17	3	1	0	0	0	0	2	5	1	.059
Joe Rudi	lf-1b	5	18	1	6	0	0	1	4	0	3	0	.333
Ray Fosse	c	5	14	1	2	0	0	1	1	1	5	0	.143
C. Washington	rf-ph-cf-lf	5	7	1	4	0	0	0	0	1	1	0	.571
Jim Holt	ph-1b	4	3	0	2	0	0	0	2	0	0	0	.667
Larry Haney	c	2	0	0	0	0	0	0	0	0	0	0	.000
Dal Maxvill	2b-pr	2	0	0	0	0	0	0	0	0	0	0	.000
Herb Washington	pr	3	0	0	0	0	0	0	0	0	0	0	.000
Jesus Alou	ph	1	1	0	0	0	0	0	0	0	1	0	.000
Angel Mangual	ph	1	1	0	0	0	0	0	0	0	1	0	.000
Ted Kubiak	Did not play												
Ken Holtzman	p	2	4	2	2	1	0	1	1	1	1	0	.500
Vida Blue	p	2	4	0	0	0	0	0	0	0	4	0	.000
Rollie Fingers	p	4	2	0	0	0	0	0	0	0	1	0	.000
Catfish Hunter	p	2	2	0	0	0	0	0	0	0	2	0	.000
Blue Moon Odom	p	2	0	0	0	0	0	0	0	0	0	0	.000
Glenn Abbott	Did not play												
Dave Hamilton	Did not play												
Darold Knowles	Did not play												
Paul Lindblad	Did not play												
Team Total		5	142	16	30	4	0	4	14	16	42	3	.211

Double Plays—6   Left on Bases—26

Los Angeles	Pos	G	AB	R	H	2B	3B	HR	RBI	BB	SO	SB	BA
Steve Garvey	1b	5	21	2	8	0	0	0	1	0	3	0	.381
Dave Lopes	2b	5	18	2	2	0	0	0	0	3	4	2	.111
Bill Russell	ss	5	18	0	4	0	1	0	2	0	2	0	.222
Ron Cey	3b	5	17	1	3	0	0	0	0	3	3	0	.176
Joe Ferguson	rf-c	5	16	2	2	0	0	1	2	4	6	1	.125
Jim Wynn	cf	5	16	1	3	1	0	1	2	4	4	0	.188
Bill Buckner	lf	5	20	1	5	1	0	1	1	0	1	0	.250
Steve Yeager	c	4	11	0	4	1	0	0	1	1	4	0	.364
Willie Crawford	ph-rf	3	6	1	2	0	0	1	1	0	0	0	.333
Von Joshua	ph	4	4	0	0	0	0	0	0	0	0	0	.000
Tom Paciorek	pr-ph	3	2	1	1	1	0	0	0	0	0	0	.500
Lee Lacy	ph	1	1	0	0	0	0	0	0	0	1	0	.000
Rick Auerbach	pr	1	0	0	0	0	0	0	0	0	0	0	.000
Gail Hopkins	Did not play												
Ken McMullen	Did not play												
Manny Mota	Did not play												
Andy Messersmith	p	2	4	0	2	0	0	0	0	0	2	0	.500
Don Sutton	p	2	3	0	0	0	0	0	0	0	2	0	.000
Al Downing	p	1	1	0	0	0	0	0	0	0	0	0	.000
Mike Marshall	p	5	0	0	0	0	0	0	0	1	0	0	.000
Jim Brewer	p	1	0	0	0	0	0	0	0	0	0	0	.000
Charlie Hough	p	1	0	0	0	0	0	0	0	0	0	0	.000
Doug Rau	Did not play												
Eddie Solomon	Did not play												
Geoff Zahn	Did not play												
Tommy John	Not in Series—injured												
Team Total		5	158	11	36	4	1	4	10	16	32	3	.228

Double Plays—5   Left on Bases—36

PITCHING	G	GS	CG	IP	H	R	ER	BB	SO	W	L	SV	ERA
Oakland													
Vida Blue	2	2	0	13 2/3	10	5	5	7	9	0	1	0	3.29
Ken Holtzman	2	2	0	12	13	3	2	4	10	1	0	0	1.50
Rollie Fingers	4	0	0	9 1/3	8	2	2	2	6	1	0	2	1.93
Catfish Hunter	2	1	0	7 2/3	5	1	1	2	5	1	0	1	1.17
Blue Moon Odom	2	0	0	1 1/3	0	0	0	1	2	1	0	0	0.00
Glenn Abbott	Did not play												
Dave Hamilton	Did not play												
Darold Knowles	Did not play												
Paul Lindblad	Did not play												
Team Total	5	5	0	44	36	11	10	16	32	4	1	3	2.05
Los Angeles													
Andy Messersmith	2	2	0	14	11	8	7	7	12	0	2	0	4.50
Don Sutton	2	2	0	13	9	4	4	3	12	1	0	0	2.77
Mike Marshall	5	0	0	9	6	1	1	1	10	0	1	1	1.00
Al Downing	1	1	0	3 2/3	4	3	1	4	3	0	1	0	2.45
Charlie Hough	1	0	0	2	0	0	0	1	4	0	0	0	0.00
Jim Brewer	1	0	0	1/3	0	0	0	1	0	0	0	0	0.00
Doug Rau	Did not play												
Eddie Solomon	Did not play												
Geoff Zahn	Did not play												
Tommy John	Not in Series—injured												
Team Total	5	5	0	42	30	16	13	16	42	1	4	1	2.79

1975

Cincinnati N.L. 4
Boston A.L. 3

Highlights

THE CINCINNATI REDS DEFEATED the Boston Red Sox, four games to three, in one of the most exciting World Series ever played. Five of seven games were decided by one run. Not only were games close, but only one run and one hit separated the two teams after 65 innings (Boston: 30 runs and 60 hits, Cincinnati: 29 runs and 59 hits).

The Red Sox lost the services in Series of outstanding rookie outfielder Jim Rice, who broke his wrist late in the season. Rice had compiled a .309 batting average with 22 homers and 102 RBI's before being sidelined by the injury.

Red Sox Bernie Carbo, former Red and their number one free agent draftee in 1965, hit two pinch-hit home runs in Series. The second home run came in game six, the most dramatic game of the Series. With the Red Sox trailing 6-3 in the eighth and just four outs from extinction, Carbo reached the center-field seats with a three-run blast off Rawly Eastwick, the Reds' ace relief pitcher. Boston eventually won the game, 7-6, in twelfth on solo homer by Carlton Fisk.

The two teams used twelve pitchers in game six, four by the Red Sox and eight by the Reds, tying a Series record.

Game 1 Oct. 11
Cincinnati	000 000 000 ·	0
Boston	000 000 60* ·	6

Winner-Tiant Loser-Gullett

Game 2 Oct. 12
Cincinnati	000 100 002 ·	3
Boston	100 001 000 ·	2

Winner-Eastwick Loser-Drago

Game 3 Oct. 14
Boston	010 001 102 0 ·	5
Cincinnati	000 230 000 1 ·	6

Winner-Eastwick Loser-Willoughby

Game 4 Oct. 15
Boston	000 500 000 ·	5
Cincinnati	200 200 000 ·	4

Winner-Tiant Loser-Norman

Game 5 Oct. 16
Boston	100 000 001 ·	2
Cincinnati	000 113 01* ·	6

Winner-Gullett Loser-Cleveland
Save-Eastwick

Game 6 Oct. 21
Cincinnati	000 030 210 000 ·	6
Boston	300 000 030 001 ·	7

Winner-Wise Loser-Darcy

Game 7 Oct. 22
Cincinnati	000 002 101 ·	4
Boston	003 000 000 ·	3

Winner-Carroll Loser-Burton
Save-McEnaney

Total Attendance—308,272
Average Attendance—44,039
*Winning Player's Share—$19,060
*Losing Player's Share—$13,326

*Includes Playoffs and World Series

BATTING	Pos	G	AB	R	H	2B	3B	HR	RBI	BB	SO	SB	BA
Cincinnati													
Tony Perez	1b	7	28	4	5	0	0	3	7	3	9	1	.179
Joe Morgan	2b	7	27	4	7	1	0	0	3	5	1	2	.259
Dave Concepcion	ss	7	28	3	5	1	0	1	4	0	1	3	.179
Pete Rose	3b	7	27	3	10	1	0	0	2	5	1	0	**.370**
Ken Griffey	rf	7	26	4	7	3	1	0	4	4	2	2	.269
Cesar Geronimo	cf	7	25	3	7	0	1	2	3	3	5	0	.280
George Foster	lf	7	29	1	8	1	0	0	2	1	1	1	.276
Johnny Bench	c	7	29	5	6	2	0	1	4	2	4	0	.207
Marv Rettenmund	ph	3	3	0	0	0	0	0	0	0	1	0	.000
Ed Armbrister	ph	4	1	1	0	0	0	0	0	2	0	0	.000
Darrell Chaney	ph	2	2	0	0	0	0	0	0	0	1	0	.000
Terry Crowley	ph	2	2	0	1	0	0	0	0	0	1	0	.500
Dan Driessen	ph	2	2	0	0	0	0	0	0	0	0	0	.000
Doug Flynn		Did not play											
Bill Plummer		Did not play											
Don Gullett	p	3	7	1	2	0	0	0	0	0	2	0	.286
Jack Billingham	p	3	2	0	0	0	0	0	0	0	0	0	.000
Rawlie Eastwick	p	5	1	0	0	0	0	0	0	0	0	0	.000
Bill McEnaney	p	5	1	0	1	0	0	0	0	0	0	0	1.000
Pedro Borbon	p	3	1	0	0	0	0	0	0	0	0	0	.000
Pat Darcy	p	2	1	0	0	0	0	0	0	0	1	0	.000
Gary Nolan	p	2	1	0	0	0	0	0	0	0	0	0	.000
Fred Norman	p	2	1	0	0	0	0	0	0	0	0	0	.000
Clay Carroll	p	5	0	0	0	0	0	0	0	0	0	0	.000
Clay Kirby		Did not play											
Team Total		7	244	29	59	9	3	7	29	25	30	9	.242

Double Plays—8   Left on Bases—50

	Pos	G	AB	R	H	2B	3B	HR	RBI	BB	SO	SB	BA
Boston													
Cecil Cooper	1b-ph	5	19	0	1	1	0	0	1	0	3	0	.053
Denny Doyle	2b	7	30	3	8	1	1	0	0	2	1	0	.267
Rick Burleson	ss	7	24	1	7	1	0	0	2	4	2	0	.292
Rico Petrocelli	3b	7	26	3	8	1	0	0	4	3	6	0	.308
Dwight Evans	rf	7	24	3	7	1	1	1	5	3	4	0	.292
Fred Lynn	cf	7	25	3	7	1	0	1	5	5	5	0	.280
Carl Yastrzemski	lf-1b	7	29	7	9	0	0	0	4	4	1	0	.310
Carlton Fisk	c	7	25	5	6	0	0	2	4	7	7	0	.240
Juan Beniquez	lf-ph	3	8	0	1	0	0	0	1	1	1	0	.125
Bernie Carbo	ph-lf	4	7	3	3	1	0	2	4	1	1	0	.429
Rick Miller	lf	3	2	0	0	0	0	0	0	0	0	0	.000
Doug Griffin	ph	1	1	0	0	0	0	0	0	0	0	0	.000
Bob Montgomery	ph	1	1	0	0	0	0	0	0	0	0	0	.000
Tim Blackwell		Did not play											
Bob Heise		Did not play											
Jim Rice		Not eligible for Series—injured											
Luis Tiant	p	3	8	2	2	0	0	0	0	2	4	0	.250
Bill Lee	p	2	6	0	1	0	0	0	0	0	3	0	.167
Reggie Cleveland	p	3	2	0	0	0	0	0	0	0	2	0	.000
Rick Wise	p	2	2	0	0	0	0	0	0	0	0	0	.000
Roger Moret	p	3	0	0	0	0	0	0	0	0	0	0	.000
Jim Willoughby	p	3	0	0	0	0	0	0	0	0	0	0	.000
Jim Burton	p	2	0	0	0	0	0	0	0	0	0	0	.000
Dick Drago	p	2	0	0	0	0	0	0	0	0	0	0	.000
Dick Pole	p	1	0	0	0	0	0	0	0	0	0	0	.000
Diego Segui	p	1	0	0	0	0	0	0	0	0	0	0	.000
Team Total		7	239	30	60	7	2	6	30	30	40	0	.251

Double Plays—6   Left on Bases—52

PITCHING	G	GS	CG	IP	H	R	ER	BB	SO	W	L	SV	ERA
Cincinnati													
Don Gullett	3	3	0	18 2/3	19	9	9	10	15	1	1	0	4.34
Jack Billingham	3	1	0	9	8	2	1	5	7	0	0	0	**1.00**
Rawly Eastwick	5	0	0	8	6	2	2	3	4	**2**	0	1	2.25
Bill McEnaney	5	0	0	6 2/3	3	2	2	2	5	0	0	1	2.70
Gary Nolan	2	2	0	6	6	4	4	1	2	0	0	0	6.00
Clay Carroll	5	0	0	5 2/3	4	2	2	3	1	1	0	0	3.18
Pat Darcy	2	0	0	4	3	2	2	1	0	0	1	0	4.50
Fred Norman	2	1	0	4	8	4	4	3	2	0	1	0	9.00
Pedro Borbon	3	0	0	3	3	3	2	2	1	0	0	0	6.00
Clay Kirby		Did not play											
Team Total	7	7	0	65	60	30	28	30	40	4	3	2	3.88
Boston													
Luis Tiant	3	3	2	25	25	10	10	8	12	**2**	0	0	3.60
Bill Lee	2	2	0	14 1/3	12	5	5	3	7	0	0	0	3.14
Reggie Cleveland	3	1	0	6 2/3	7	5	5	3	5	0	1	0	6.75
Jim Willoughby	3	0	0	6 1/3	3	1	0	0	2	0	1	0	0.00
Rick Wise	2	1	0	5 1/3	6	5	5	2	2	1	0	0	8.44
Dick Drago	2	0	0	4	1	1	1	1	1	0	1	0	2.25
Roger Moret	3	0	0	1 2/3	2	0	0	3	1	0	0	0	0.00
Jim Burton	2	0	0	1	1	1	1	3	0	0	1	0	9.00
Diego Segui	1	0	0	1	0	0	0	1	0	0	0	0	0.00
Dick Pole	1	0	0	0	0	1	1	2	0	0	0	0	0.00
Team Total	7	7	2	65 1/3	59	29	28	25	30	3	4	0	3.86

1976

Highlights

THE CINCINNATI REDS BECAME the first National League team to win two consecutive World Series since the New York Giants in 1921 and 1922 by sweeping the New York Yankees, four games to none. It was the Yanks' first Series appearance since 1964.

This was the first Series in which the designated hitter—used only in the American League during the regular season—was employed, as Commissioner Bowie Kuhn ordered that the DH be used in Series in alternating years. In game three, the Reds made good use of the American League innovation, as DH Dan Driessen walked, singled, doubled and homered in a perfect three-for-three day at the plate, pacing the Reds to an easy 6-2 victory.

Saturday afternoon's opening game was the only game played during daylight hours, as Sunday's game was switched to the evening to accommodate television scheduling.

Yankees manager Billy Martin was ejected from game four in the ninth inning for tossing a ball onto the field in anger. Following Martin's ejection, Reds catcher Johnny Bench shot a three-run homer into the left-field seats to put the game out of reach.

Bench batted .533 for the Series, had two homers, a triple, a double and six RBI's. Yankee catcher Thurman Munson also turned in an outstanding performance: .529 batting average, including six consecutive hits, tying a Series record.

Game 1 Oct. 16
New York   010 000 000 · 1
Cincinnati   101 001 20* · 5
Winner-Gullett   Loser-Alexander

Game 2 Oct. 17
New York   000 100 200 · 3
Cincinnati   030 000 001 · 4
Winner-Billingham   Loser-Hunter

Game 3 Oct. 19
Cincinnati   030 100 020 · 6
New York   000 100 100 · 2
Winner-Zachry   Loser-Ellis
Save-McEnaney

Game 4 Oct. 21
Cincinnati   000 300 004 · 7
New York   100 010 000 · 2
Winner-Nolan   Loser-Figueroa
Save-McEnaney

Total Attendance—223,009
Average Attendance—55,752
*Winning Player's Share—$26,758
*Losing Player's Share—$19,935

*Includes Playoffs and World Series.

Cincinnati N.L. 4
New York A.L. 0

BATTING

	Pos	G	AB	R	H	2B	3B	HR	RBI	BB	SO	SB	BA
Cincinnati													
Tony Perez	1b	4	16	1	5	1	0	0	2	1	2	0	.313
Joe Morgan	2b	4	15	3	5	1	1	1	2	2	2	2	.333
Dave Concepcion	ss	4	14	1	5	1	1	0	3	1	3	1	.357
Pete Rose	3b	4	16	1	3	1	0	0	1	2	2	0	.188
Ken Griffey	rf	4	17	2	1	0	0	0	1	0	1	1	.059
George Foster	lf	4	14	3	6	1	0	0	4	2	3	0	.429
Cesar Geronimo	cf	4	13	3	4	2	0	0	1	2	2	2	.308
Johnny Bench	c	4	15	4	8	1	1	2	6	0	1	0	.533
Dan Driessen	dh	4	14	4	5	2	0	1	1	2	0	1	.357
Ed Armbrister		Did not play											
Bob Bailey		Did not play											
Doug Flynn		Did not play											
Mike Lum		Did not play											
Manny Sarmiento		Did not play											
Bill Plummer		Did not play											
Team Total		4	134	22	42	0	3	4	21	12	16	7	.313

Double Plays—3   Left on Bases—22

	Pos	G	AB	R	H	2B	3B	HR	RBI	BB	SO	SB	BA
New York													
Chris Chambliss	1b	4	16	1	5	1	0	0	1	0	2	0	.313
Willie Randolph	2b	4	14	1	1	0	0	0	0	1	3	0	.071
Graig Nettles	3b	4	12	0	3	0	0	0	2	3	1	0	.250
Jim Mason	ss	3	1	1	1	0	0	0	1	0	0	0	1.000
Fred Stanley	ss	4	6	1	1	1	0	0	1	0	0	0	.167
Lou Piniella	rf-dh-ph	4	9	1	3	1	0	0	1	3	0	0	.333
Mickey Rivers	cf	4	18	1	3	0	0	0	0	1	2	1	.167
Roy White	lf	4	15	0	2	0	0	0	0	3	0	0	.133
Thurman Munson	c	4	17	2	9	0	0	0	2	0	1	0	.529
Elliot Maddox	dh-rf	2	5	0	1	0	1	0	0	1	2	0	.200
Carlos May	ph-dh	4	9	0	0	0	0	0	0	0	1	0	.000
Oscar Gamble	ph-rf	3	8	0	1	0	0	0	0	1	0	0	.125
Elrod Hendricks	ph	2	0	0	0	0	0	0	0	0	0	0	.000
Otto Velez	ph	3	0	0	0	0	0	0	0	0	3	0	.000
Sandy Alomar		Did not play											
Fran Healy		Did not play											
Dick Tidrow	p	2	0	0	0	0	0	0	0	0	0	0	.000
Sparky Lyle	p	2	0	0	0	0	0	0	0	0	0	0	.000
Doyle Alexander	p	1	0	0	0	0	0	0	0	0	0	0	.000
Doc Ellis	p	1	0	0	0	0	0	0	0	0	0	0	.000
Ed Figueroa	p	1	0	0	0	0	0	0	0	0	0	0	.000
Catfish Hunter	p	1	0	0	0	0	0	0	0	0	0	0	.000
Grant Jackson	p	1	0	0	0	0	0	0	0	0	0	0	.000
Team Total		4	135	8	30	3	1	1	8	12	16	1	.222

Double Plays—6   Left on Bases—33

PITCHING

	G	GS	CG	IP	H	R	ER	BB	SO	W	L	SV	ERA
Cincinnati													
Will McEnaney	2	0	0	4⅔	2	0	0	1	2	0	0	2	0.00
Jack Billingham	1	0	0	2⅔	0	0	0	0	1	1	0	0	0.00
Pedro Borbon	1	0	0	1⅔	0	0	0	0	0	0	0	0	0.00
Don Gullett	1	1	0	7⅓	5	1	1	3	4	1	0	0	1.23
Gary Nolan	1	1	0	6⅔	8	2	2	1	1	1	0	0	2.70
Pat Zachry	1	2	0	6⅔	6	2	2	5	6	1	0	0	2.70
Fred Norman	1	1	0	6⅓	9	3	3	2	2	0	0	0	4.26
Santo Alcala		Did not play											
Rawly Eastwick		Did not play											
Joel Youngblood		Did not play											
Team Total	4	4	0	36	30	8	8	12	16	4	0	2	2.00

	G	GS	CG	IP	H	R	ER	BB	SO	W	L	SV	ERA
New York													
Sparky Lyle	2	0	0	2⅔	1	0	0	0	3	0	0	0	0.00
Catfish Hunter	1	1	0	8⅔	10	4	3	4	5	0	1	0	3.12
Grant Jackson	1	0	0	3⅔	4	2	2	0	3	0	0	0	4.91
Ed Figueroa	1	1	0	8	6	5	5	5	2	0	1	0	5.63
Doyle Alexander	1	1	0	6	9	5	5	2	1	0	1	0	7.50
Dick Tidrow	2	0	0	2⅓	5	2	2	1	1	0	0	0	7.71
Doc Ellis	1	1	0	3⅓	7	4	4	0	1	0	1	0	10.80
Ron Guidry		Did not play											
Ken Holtzman		Did not play											
Team Total	4	4	0	34⅔	42	22	21	12	16	0	4	0	5.45

1977

Highlights

THE NEW YORK YANKEES, BACK in the Series for the second consecutive year, met the Los Angeles Dodgers. The Yanks beat the young, talented Kansas City Royals to take the American League pennant, while the Dodgers took the N.L. flag from a solid Philadelphia team. In the Series, behind great pitching and slugging, the Yanks rolled over the Dodgers, four games to two.

Yankees pitchers Ron Guidry (won game four, 4-2) and Mike Torrez (won game three, 5-3, and game six, 8-4) came through with complete-game victories when the Yankees' high-priced but sore-armed talent of Jim "Catfish" Hunter and Don Gullett failed to stop the Dodgers' attack. Gullett, however, pitched long enough in game one—8⅓ innings giving up three runs and five hits—before Sparky Lyle took over in relief, picking up the Yankees' initital Series victory, 4-3, with 3⅔ innings of scoreless ball.

Yankee slugger Reggie Jackson set a record for most home runs in a six-game Series. He belted five, including three in the final game at Yankee Stadium, which tied another Series record (held by Babe Ruth, who did it twice, in 1926 and 1928) of most home runs in one game. All his homers came on the first pitch. Jackson had homered in his last at-bat in the fifth game, and walked in his first at-bat in game six. Thus, he had hit four home runs in four successive official times at bat.

Game 1 Oct. 11
Los Angeles   200 000 001 000 · 3
New York   100 001 010 001 · 4
Winner-Lyle   Loser-Rhoden

Game 2 Oct. 12
Los Angeles   212 000 001 · 6
New York   000 100 000 · 1
Winner-Hooton   Loser-Hunter

Game 3 Oct. 14
New York   300 110 000 · 5
Los Angeles   003 000 000 · 3
Winner-Torrez   Loser-John

Game 4 Oct. 15
New York   030 001 000 · 4
Los Angeles   002 000 000 · 2
Winner-Guidry   Loser-Rau

Game 5 Oct. 16
New York   000 000 220 · 4
Los Angeles   100 432 00* · 10
Winner-Sutton   Loser-Gullett

Game 6 Oct. 18
Los Angeles   201 000 001 · 4
New York   020 320 01* · 8
Winner-Torrez   Loser-Hooton

Total Attendance—337,708
Average Attendance—56,283
*Winning Player's Share—$27,758
*Losing Player's Share—$20,899

*Includes Playoffs and World Series

BATTING	Pos	G	AB	R	H	2B	3B	HR	RBI	BB	SO	SB	BA
New York													
Chris Chambliss	1b	6	24	4	7	2	0	1	4	0	2	0	.292
Willie Randolph	2b	6	25	5	4	2	0	1	1	2	2	0	.160
Bucky Dent	ss	6	19	0	5	0	0	0	2	2	1	0	.263
Craig Nettles	3b	6	21	1	4	1	0	0	2	2	3	0	.190
Reggie Jackson	rf	6	20	10	9	1	0	5	8	3	4	0	**.450**
Mickey Rivers	cf	6	**27**	1	6	2	0	0	1	0	2	1	.222
Lou Piniella	lf	6	22	1	6	0	0	0	3	0	3	0	.273
Thurman Munson	c	6	25	4	8	2	0	1	3	2	8	0	.320
Mike Torrez	p	2	6	0	0	0	0	0	0	0	4	0	.000
Paul Blair	rf-ph	4	4	0	1	0	0	0	1	0	0	0	.250
Ron Guidry	p	1	2	0	0	0	0	0	0	0	1	0	.000
Don Gullett	p	2	2	0	0	0	0	0	0	0	2	0	.000
Sparky Lyle	p	2	2	0	0	0	0	0	0	0	2	0	.000
Roy White	ph	2	2	0	0	0	0	0	0	0	0	0	.000
George Zeber	ph	2	2	0	0	0	0	0	0	0	2	0	.000
Cliff Johnson	ph-c	2	1	0	0	0	0	0	0	0	0	0	.000
Ken Clay	p	2	Did not bat										
Jim Hunter	p	2	Did not bat										
Fred Stanley	ss	1	Did not bat										
Fran Healy		Did not play											
Gene Klutts		Did not play											
Ed Figueroa		Did not play											
Ken Holtzman		Did not play											
Team Total		6	205	26	50	10	0	8	25	11	37	1	.244
			Double Plays—2 Left on Bases—32										
Los Angeles													
Steve Garvey	1b	6	24	5	9	1	1	1	3	1	4	0	.375
Davey Lopes	2b	6	24	3	4	0	1	1	2	4	3	2	.167
Bill Russell	ss	6	26	3	4	0	1	0	2	1	3	0	.154
Ron Cey	3b	6	21	2	4	1	0	1	3	3	5	0	.190
Reggie Smith	rf-cf	6	22	7	6	1	0	3	5	4	3	0	.273
Lee Lacy	ph-rf	4	7	1	3	0	0	0	2	1	1	0	.429
Rick Monday	cf	4	12	0	2	0	0	0	0	0	3	0	.167
Johnnie Baker	lf	6	24	4	7	0	0	1	5	0	2	0	.399
Steve Yeager	c	6	19	2	7	1	0	2	5	1	1	0	.368
Vic Davalillo	ph	3	3	0	1	0	0	0	1	0	0	0	.333
Dick Rhoden	p	2	2	1	1	1	0	0	0	0	0	0	.500
Don Sutton	p	2	6	0	0	0	0	0	0	1	4	0	.000
Burt Hooton	p	2	5	0	0	0	0	0	0	0	2	0	.000
Glenn Burke		3	5	0	1	0	0	0	0	0	1	0	.200
Manny Mota	ph	3	3	0	0	0	0	0	0	0	1	0	.000
Tommy John	p	1	2	0	0	0	0	0	0	0	2	0	.000
Jim Goodson	ph	1	1	0	0	0	0	0	0	0	1	0	.000
Jerry Grote	c	1	1	0	0	0	0	0	0	0	0	0	.000
Johnny Oates	ph-c	1	1	0	0	0	0	0	0	0	0	0	.000
Mike Garman	p	2	Did not bat										
Charlie Hough	p	2	Did not bat										
Doug Rau	p	2	Did not bat										
Elias Sosa	p	2	Did not bat										
Rafael Landestoy	pr	1	Did not bat										
Lance Rautzhan	p	1	Did not bat										
Team Total		6	208	28	48	5	3	9	28	16	36	2	.231
			Double Plays—4 Left on Bases—31										

PITCHING	G	GS	CG	IP	H	R	ER	BB	SO	W	L	SV	ERA
New York													
Sparky Lyle	2	0	0	4⅔	2	1	1	0	2	1	0	0	1.93
Ron Guidry	1	1	1	9	4	2	2	3	7	1	0	0	**2.00**
Ken Clay	2	0	0	3⅔	2	1	1	1	0	0	0	0	2.45
Mike Torrez	2	2	2	18	16	7	5	5	15	2	0	0	2.50
Dick Tidrow	2	0	0	3⅔	5	2	2	0	1	0	0	0	4.91
Don Gullett	2	2	0	12⅔	13	10	9	7	10	0	1	0	6.39
Catfish Hunter	2	1	0	4⅓	6	5	5	0	1	0	1	0	10.38
Ed Figueroa	Did not play												
Ken Holtzman	Did not play												
Team Total	6	6	3	56	48	28	25	16	36	4	2	0	4.02
Los Angeles													
Mike Garman	2	0	0	4	2	0	0	1	3	0	0	0	0.00
Lance Rautzhan	1	0	0	⅓	0	0	0	2	0	0	0	0	0.00
Charlie Hough	2	0	0	5	3	1	1	0	5	0	0	0	1.80
Dick Rhoden	2	0	0	7	4	2	2	1	5	0	1	0	2.57
Burt Hooton	2	2	1	12	8	5	5	2	9	1	1	0	3.75
Don Sutton	2	2	1	16	17	7	7	1	6	1	0	0	3.94
Tommie John	1	1	0	6	9	5	4	3	7	0	1	0	6.00
Doug Rau	2	1	0	2⅓	4	3	3	0	1	0	1	0	11.59
Elias Sosa	2	0	0	2⅓	3	3	3	1	1	0	0	0	11.57
Team Total	6	6	2	55	50	26	25	11	37	2	4	0	4.09

Reggie Jackson

Leon Goslin

Individual Statistics

Individual Batting, Base-running Series Records

Most Series Played
14—Berra, Lawrence P., New York A.L., 1947, 1949, 1950, 1951, 1952, 1953, 1955, 1956, 1957, 1958, 1960, 1961, 1962, 1963 (75 games, 65 consecutive).

Most Games, Total Series
75—Berra, Lawrence P., New York A.L., 1947, 1949, 1950, 1951, 1952, 1953, 1955, 1956, 1957, 1958, 1960 1961, 1962, 1963 (14 Series, 65 consecutive games).

Most Consecutive Games Played
30—Richardson, Robert C., New York A.L., October 5, 1960 through October 15, 1964.

Most Series Batting .300 or Over
6—Ruth, George H., New York A.L., 1921, 1923, 1926, 1927, 1928, 1932.

Highest Batting Average, Total Series (20 or More Games)
.391—Brock, Louis C., St. Louis N.L., 1964, 1967, 1968 (3 Series, 21 games, 87 at-bats, 34 hits).
.363—Baker, J. Franklin, Philadelphia A.L., 1910, 1911, 1913, 1914; New York A.L., 1921, 1922 (6 Series, 25 games, 91 at-bats, 33 hits).
.361—Gehrig, H. Louis, New York A.L., 1926, 1927, 1928, 1932, 1936, 1937, 1938 (7 Series, 34 games, 119 at-bats, 43 hits).

Highest Batting Average, Series
4-game Series—.625—Ruth, George H., New York A.L., 1928.
5-game Series—.500—McLean, John B., New York N.L., 1913.
　　　　　　　　　　　Gordon, Joseph L., New York A.L., 1941.
6-game Series—.500—Robertson, Davis A., New York N.L., 1917.
　　　　　　　　　　　Martin, Alfred M., New York A.L., 1953.
7-game Series—.500—Martin, John L., St. Louis N.L., 1931.
　　　　　　　　　　　Lindell, John H., New York A.L., 1947 (played only six games due to broken rib).
8-game Series—.400—Herzog, Charles L., New York N.L., 1912.

Highest Slugging Average, Total Series (20 or More Games)
.744—Ruth, George H., Boston A.L., 1915, 1916, 1918; New York A.L., 1921, 1922, 1923, 1926, 1927, 1928, 1932; 10 Series, 41 games, 129 at-bats, 42 hits, 5 doubles, 2 triples, 15 home runs, 96 total bases.

Highest Slugging Average Series
4-game Series—1.727—Gehrig, H. Louis, New York A.L., 1928.
5-game Series— .929—Gordon, Joseph L., New York A.L., 1941.
　　　　　　　　　　　(Clendenon, Donn A., New York N.L., 1969, had slugging average of 1.071 but played only four games).
6-game Series—1.250—Jackson, Reginald M., New York A.L., 1977.
7-game Series— .913—Tenace, F. Gene, Oakland A.L., 1972.
8-game Series— .600—Herzog, Charles L., New York N.L., 1912.

Most At-Bats, Total Series
259—Berra, Lawrence P., New York A.L., 1947, 1949, 1950, 1951, 1952, 1953, 1955, 1956, 1957, 1958, 1960, 1961, 1962, 1963 (14 Series, 75 games).

Most Runs, Game
4—Ruth, George H., New York A.L., October 6, 1926.
   Combs, Earle B., New York A.L., October 2, 1932.
   Crosetti, Frank P., New York A.L., October 2, 1936.
   Slaughter, Enos B., St. Louis N.L., October 10, 1946.
   Jackson, Reginald M., New York A.L., October 18, 1977.

Most Runs Batted In, Game
6—Richardson, Robert C., New York A.L., October 8, 1960.

Most Total Bases, Game
12—Ruth, George H., New York A.L., October 6, 1926, three home runs.
    Ruth, George H., New York A.L., October 9, 1928, three home runs.
    Jackson, Reginald M., New York A.L., October 18, 1977, three home runs.

Most Bases on Balls, Game
4—Clarke, Fred C., Pittsburgh N.L., October 16, 1909.
   Hoblitzel, Richard C., Boston A.L., October 9, 1916 (14 innings).
   Youngs, Ross, New York N.L., October 10, 1924 (12 innings).
   Ruth, George H., New York A.L., October 10, 1926.
   Robinson, Jack R., Brooklyn N.L., October 5, 1952 (11 innings).

Most Consecutive Hits, One Series
6—Goslin, Leon A., Washington A.L., October 6 (1), October 7 (4), October 8 (1), 1924.
   Munson, Thurman L., New York, A.L., October 19 (2), October 21 (4), 1976.

Most Home Runs, Game (3 home runs, 3 times)
3—Ruth, George H., New York A.L., October 6, 1926, and October 9, 1928 (two consecutive in each game)
   Jackson, Reginald M., New York A.L., October 18, 1977 (consecutive, each on first pitch).

Most Stolen Bases, Game
3—Wagner, John P., Pittsburgh N.L., October 11, 1909.
   Davis, William H., Los Angeles N.L., October 11, 1965.
   Brock, Louis C., St. Louis N.L., October 12, 1967.
   Brock, Louis C., St. Louis N.L., October 5, 1968.

Most Hits, Total Series
71—Berra, Lawrence P., New York A.L., 1947, 1949, 1950, 1951, 1952, 1953, 1955, 1956, 1957, 1958, 1960, 1961, 1962, 1963 (14 Series, 75 games).

Most Runs, Total Series
42—Mantle, Mickey C., New York A.L., 1951, 1952, 1953, 1955, 1956, 1957, 1958, 1960, 1961, 1962, 1963, 1964 (12 Series, 65 games).

Most Consecutive Games, One or More Runs, Total Series
9—Ruth, George H., New York A.L., 1927, last 2 games; 1928, 4 games; 1932, first 3 games.

Most Runs Batted In, Total Series
40—Mantle, Mickey C., New York A.L., 1951, 1952, 1953, 1955, 1956, 1957, 1958, 1960, 1961, 1962, 1963, 1964 (12 Series, 65 games).

Most Consecutive Games, One or More runs Batted in, Total Series
8—Gehrig, H. Louis, New York A.L., 1928 (4), 1932 (4), 17 runs batted in.

Most Runs Batted In, Series
4-game Series— 9—Gehrig, H. Louis, New York A.L., 1928.
5-game Series— 8—Murphy, Daniel F., Philadelphia A.L., 1910.
                   May, Lee A., Cincinnati N.L., 1970.
6-game Series—10—Kluszewski, Theodore B., Chicago A.L., 1959.
7-game Series—12—Richardson, Robert C., New York A.L., 1960.
8-game Series— 8—Leach, Thomas W., Pittsburgh N.L., 1903.
                   Duncan, Louis B., Cincinnati N.L., 1919.

Most Runs Batted In, Series, Pinch-Hitter
6—Rhodes, James L., New York N.L., 3 games, 1954.

Most Hits, Series
4-game Series—10—Ruth, George H., New York A.L., 1928.
5-game Series— 9—Baker, J. Franklin, Philadelphia A.L., 1910.

Duke Snider

Mickey Mantle

Collins, Edward T., Philadelphia A.L., 1910.
Baker, J. Franklin, Philadelphia A.L., 1913.
Groh, Henry K., New York N.L., 1922.
Moore, Joseph G., New York N.L., 1937.
Richardson, Robert C., New York A.L., 1961.
Blair, Paul L., Baltimore A.L., 1970.
Robinson, Brooks C., Baltimore A.L., 1970.
6-game Series—12—Martin, Alfred M., New York A.L., 1953.
7-game Series—13—Richardson, Robert C., New York A.L., 1964.
Brock, Louis C., St. Louis N.L., 1968.
8-game Series—12—Herzog, Charles L., New York N.L., 1912.
Jackson, Joseph J., Chicago A.L., 1919.

Most Hits, Series, Pinch-Hitter
3—Brown, Robert W., New York A.L., 4 games, 1947 consecutive; one base on balls, one single, two doubles, 3 runs batted in).
Rhodes, James L., New York N.L., 3 games, 1954 (consecutive; one home run, two singles, 6 runs batted in).
Warwick, Carl W., St. Louis N.L., 5 games, 1964 (consecutive; two singles walk, single, 1 run batted in).
Marquez, Gonzalo, Oakland A.L., 5 games, 1972 (consecutive in second, third, fourth games, three singles, one run batted in).
Boswell, Kenneth G., New York N.L., 3 games, 1973 (consecutive; three singles).

Most Hits, Total Series, Pinch-Hitter
3—O'Dea, James K., Chicago N.L., 1935 (1), 1938 (0); St. Louis N.L., 1942 (1), 1943 (0), 1944 (1), 5 Series, 8 games.
Brown, Robert W., New York A.L., 1947 (3), 1949 (0), 1950 (0), 1951 (0), 4 Series, 7 games.
Mize, John R., New York A.L., 1949 (2), 1950 (0), 1951 (0), 1952 (1), 1953 (0), 5 Series, 8 games.
Rhodes, James L., New York N.L., 1954 (3), 3 games.
Furillo, Carl A., Brooklyn N.L., 1947 (2), 1949 (0); Los Angeles N.L., 1959 (1), 3 Series, 7 games.
Cerv, Robert H., New York A.L., 1955 (1), 1956 (1), 1960 (1), 3 Series 3 games.
Blanchard, John E., New York A.L., 1960 (1), 1961 (1), 1962 (0), 1964 (1), 4 Series, 10 games.
Warwick, Carl W., St. Louis N.L., 1964 (3), 1 Series, 5 games.
Marquez, Gonzalo, Oakland A.L., 1972 (3), 1 Series, 5 games.
Boswell, Kenneth G., New York N.L., 1973 (3), 1 Series, 3 games.

Most Consecutive Games, One or More Hits, Total Series
17—Bauer, Henry A., New York A.L., 1956, 7 games; 1957, 7 games; 1958, first 3 games.

Most Home Runs, Total Series
18—Mantle, Mickey C., New York A.L., 1951, 1952, 1953, 1955, 1956, 1957, 1958, 1960, 1961, 1962, 1963, 1964; 12 Series, 65 games.

Most Home Runs, Series, Pinch-Hitter
2—Essegian, Charles A., Los Angeles N.L., 4 games, 1959.
Carbo, Bernardo, Boston A.L., 3 games, 1975.

10 or More Home Runs, Total Series
Player	Series	HR.
Mantle, Mickey C.	12	18
Ruth, George H.	10	15
Berra, Lawrence P.	14	12
Snider, Edwin D.	6	11
Gehrig, H. Louis	7	10

Most Total Bases, Total Series
123—Mantle, Mickey C., New York A.L., 1951, 1952, 1953, 1955, 1956, 1957, 1958, 1960, 1961, 1962, 1963, 1964; 12 Series, 65 games.

Most Bases on Balls, Series
4-game Series— 7—Thompson, Henry, New York N.L., 1954.
5-game Series— 7—Sheckard, James T., Chicago N.L., 1910.
Cochrane, Gordon S., Philadelphia A.L., 1929.
Gordon, Joseph L., New York A.L., 1941.
6-game Series— 8—Ruth, George H., New York A.L., 1923.
7-game Series—11—Ruth, George H., New York A.L., 1926.

Sandy Koufax

Lou Brock

Tenace, F. Gene, Oakland A.L., 1973.
8-game Series— 7—Devore, Joshua, New York N.L., 1912.
Youngs, Ross M., New York N.L., 1921.

Most Bases on Balls, Total Series
43—Mantle, Mickey C., New York A.L., 1951, 1952, 1953, 1955, 1956,
1957, 1958, 1960, 1961, 1962, 1963, 1964; 12 Series, 65 games.

Most Strikeouts, Total Series
54—Mantle, Mickey C., New York A.L., 1951, 1952, 1953, 1955, 1956,
1957, 1958, 1960, 1961, 1962, 1963, 1964; 12 Series, 65 games.

Most Strikeouts, Series
4-game Series— 7—Meusel, Robert W., New York A.L., 1927.
5-game Series— 8—Hornsby, Rogers, Chicago N.L., 1929.
Snider, Edwin, Brooklyn N.L., 1949.
6-game Series— 9—Bottomley, James L., St. Louis N.L., 1930.
7-game Series—11—Mathews, Edwin L., Milwaukee N.L., 1958.
Garrett, R. Wayne, New York N.L., 1973.
8-game Series—10—Kelly, George L., New York N.L., 1921.

Most Home Runs, Series
4-game Series— 4—Gehrig, H. Louis, New York A.L., 1928.
5-game Series— 3—Clendenon, Donn A., New York N.L., 1969.
6-game Series— 5—Jackson, Reginald M., New York, 1977.
7-game Series— 4—Ruth, George H., New York N.L., 1926.
Snider, Edwin D., Brooklyn N.L., 1952.
Snider, Edwin D., Brooklyn N.L. 1955.
Bauer, Henry A. New York A.L., 1958.
Tenace, F. Gene, Oakland A.L., 1972.
8-game Series— 2—Daugherty, Patrick H., Boston A.L., 1903.

Most Stolen Bases, Total Series
14—Collins, Edward T., Philadelphia A.L. (10), 1910, 1911, 1913, 1914;
Chicago A.L. (4), 1917, 1919; 6 Series, 34 games.
Brock, Louis C., St. Louis N.L., 1964 (0), 1967 (7), 1968 (7); 3 Series, 21
games.

Most Stolen Bases, Series
4-game Series— 2—Deal, Charles A., Boston N.L., 1914.
Maranville, Walter J.V., Boston N.L., 1914.
Geronimo, Cesar F., Cincinnati N.L., 1976.
Morgan, Joe L., Cincinnati N.L., 1976.
5-game Series— 6—Slagle, James F., Chicago N.L., 1907.
6-game Series— 3—Collins, Edward T., Chicago A.L., 1917.
7-game Series— 7—Brock, Louis C., St. Louis N.L., 1967.
Brock, Louis C., St. Louis N.L., 1968.
8-game Series— 4—Devore, Joshua, New York N.L., 1912.

Individual Pitching Records

Most Games Pitched, Total Series
22—Ford, Edward C., New York A.L., 1950, 1953, 1955, 1956, 1957, 1958,
1960, 1961, 1962, 1963, 1964 (11 Series).

Most Complete Games Pitched, Total Series
10—Mathewson, Christopher, New York N.L., 1905, 1911, 1912, 1913.

Most Consecutive Complete Games Pitched, Total Series
8—Gibson, Robert, St. Louis N.L., 1964 (2), 1967 (3), 1968 (3), (won 7, lost 1).

Most Games Started, Total Series
22—Ford, Edward C., New York A.L., 1950, 1953, 1955, 1956, 1957, 1958,
1960, 1961, 1962, 1963, 1964 (11 Series).

Most Games Won, Total Series
10—Ford, Edward C., New York A.L., 1950, 1953, 1955, 1956, 1957, 1958,
1960, 1961, 1962, 1963, 1964 (won 10, lost 8), 11 Series, 22 games.

Pitchers Winning 5 or More Games, Total Series

Pitcher and Club	Years	W.	L.
Ford, Edward C., New York A.L.	1950-3-5-6-7-8-60-1-2-3-4	10	8
Ruffing, Charles H., New York A.L.	1932-36-37-38-39-41-42	7	2
Reynolds, Allie P., New York A.L.	1947-49-50-51-52-53	7	2

Babe Ruth

Rogers Hornsby

Gibson, Robert, St. Louis N.L. 1964-67-68 7   2

Most Saves Total Series, Since 1969
6—Fingers, Roland G., Oakland A.L., 1972 (2), 1973 (2), 1974 (2).

Fewest Hits Allowed, Game, Nine Innings
0—Larsen, Donald J., New york A.L., October 8, 1956 (perfect game).

One Hit Games, Nine Innings (Pitching Complete Game)
1—Reulbach, Edward M., Chicago N.L., October 10, 1906 (none out in seventh).
  Passeau, Claude W., Chicago N.L., October 5, 1945 (two out in second).
  Lonborg, James R., Boston A.L., October 5, 1967 (two out in eighth).
  Bevens, Floyd New York A.L., October 3, 1947 (two out in ninth).

Most Strikeouts, Game
17—Gibson, Robert, St. Louis N.L., October 2, 1968.
15—Koufax, Sanford, Los Angeles N.L., October 2, 1963.

Most Strikeouts, Game, Relief Pitcher
11—Drabowsky, Myron W., Baltimore A.L., October 5, 1966, last six and two-thirds innings.

Most Consecutive Scoreless Innings, Total Series
33⅔—Ford, Edward C., New York A.L., October 8, 1960, 9 innings; October 12, 1960, 9 innings; October 4, 1961, 9 innings; October 8, 1961, 5 innings; October 4, 1962, 1⅔ innings.

Most Consecutive Scoreless Innings, Series
27—Mathewson, Christopher, New York N.L., October 9, 12, 14, 1905.

General Records

Largest Attendance, Game
92,706—At Los Angeles, October 6, 1959, Chicago A.L., 1, Los Angeles N.L., 0, fifth game.

Largest Attendance, Series
4-game Series—251,507—New York N.L., vs. Cleveland A.L., 1954.
5-game Series—277,312—New York A.L., vs. St. Louis N.L., 1943.
6-game Series—420,784—Los Angeles N.L., vs. Chicago A.L., 1959.
7-game Series—394,712—Milwaukee N.L., vs. New York A.L., 1957.
8-game Series—269,976—New York N.L., vs. New York A.L., 1921.

Largest Players' Pool, Series
$2,778,300.31—New York A.L., vs. Los Angeles N.L., 1977 (including League Championship Series).

Largest Share, Winning Player, Series
$27,758.04—New York A.L., vs. Los Angeles, N.L., 1977 (including League Championship Series).

Largest Share, Losing Player, Series
$20,899.05—Los Angeles N.L., vs. New York A.L., 1977 (including League Championship Series).

Largest Receipts, Game
$694,809.00—At Los Angeles, Sunday, October 13, 1974, Los Angeles N.L., 3, Oakland A.L., 2, second game.

Largest Gate Receipts, Series
4-game Series—$2,498,416.69—Cincinnati N.L., vs. New York A.L., 1976
5-game Series—$3,007,194.00—Oakland A.L., vs. Los Angeles N.L., 1974.
6-game Series—$3,978,825.33—New York A.L., vs. Los Angeles N.L., 1977.
7-game Series—$3,954,542.99—Cincinnati N.L., vs. Oakland A.L., 1972.
8-game Series—$ 900,233.00—New York N.L., vs. New York A.L., 1921.

Winning Series After Losing First Two Games
New York N.L., vs. New York A.L., 1921 (best-out-of-nine Series).
Brooklyn N.L., vs. New York A.L., 1955 (best-out-of-seven Series).
New York A.L, vs. Brooklyn N.L., 1956 (best-out-of-seven Series).
New York A.L., vs. Milwaukee N.L., 1958 (best-out-of-seven Series).
Los Angeles N.L., vs. Minnesota A.L., 1965 (best-out-of-seven Series).
Pittsburgh N.L., vs. Baltimore A.L., 1971 (best-out-of-seven Series).

Bob Gibson

Lou Gehrig

Winning Series After Losing First Three Games
Never accomplished.

Most Series, Manager
10—Stengel, Charles D., New York A.L., 1949, 1950, 1951, 1952, 1953, 1955, 1956, 1957, 1958, 1960 (won 7, lost 3).

Most World Series Winners Managed
7—McCarthy, Joseph V., New York A.L., 1932, 1936, 1937, 1938, 1939, 1941, 1943.
    Stengel, Charles D., New York A.L., 1949, 1950, 1951, 1952, 1953, 1956, 1958.

Most Different World Series Winners Managed
2—McKechnie, William B., Pittsburgh N.L., 1925; Cincinnati N.L., 1940.
    Harris, Stanley R.; Washington A.L., 1924; New York A.L., 1947.

Most Different Clubs Managed in World Series
3—McKechnie, William B., Pittsburgh N.L., 1925; St. Louis N.L., 1928; Cincinnati N.L., 1939, 1940.

Most Series Played
31—New York A.L., 1921, 1922, 1923, 1926, 1927, 1928, 1932, 1936, 1937, 1938, 1939, 1941, 1942, 1943, 1947, 1949, 1950, 1951, 1952, 1953, 1955, 1956, 1957, 1958, 1960, 1961, 1962, 1963, 1964, 1976, 1977 (won 21, lost 10).

Most Series Played
31—New York A.L., 1921, 1922, 1923, 1926, 1927, 1928, 1932, 1936, 1937, 1938, 1939, 1941, 1942, 1943, 1947, 1949, 1950, 1951, 1952, 1953, 1955, 1956, 1957, 1958, 1960, 1961, 1962, 1963, 1964, 1976, 1977 (won 21, lost 10).

Most Series Won
21—New York A.L., 1923, 1927, 1928, 1932, 1936, 1937, 1938, 1939, 1941, 1943, 1947, 1949, 1950, 1951, 1952, 1953, 1956, 1958, 1961, 1962, 1977 (lost 10).

Most Series Umpired
18—Klem, William J., 1908, 1909, 1911, 1912, 1913, 1914, 1915, 1917, 1918, 1920, 1922, 1924, 1926, 1929, 1931, 1932, 1934, 1940.

Most Games Umpired
104—Klem, William J. (18 Series).

Most Consecutive Series Won
8—New York A.L., 1927, 1928, 1932, 1936, 1937, 1938, 1939, 1941.

Most Times Winning Series in Four Consecutive Games
6—New York A.L., 1927, 1928, 1932, 1938, 1939, 1950.

Most Series Lost
10—New York A.L., 1921, 1922, 1926, 1942, 1955, 1957, 1960, 1963, 1964, 1976.

Most Games Played, Total Series, Most Games Lost, One Club
175—New York A.L., 31 Series (Won 103, lost 71, tied 1).

Most Games Decided by One Run, Series, Both Clubs
4-game Series—3—New York A.L., (Won 3), vs. Philadelphia N.L., 1950.
5-game Series—4—Boston A.L., (Won 4), vs. Philadelphia N.L., 1915.
                Oakland A.L., (Won 3), vs. Los Angeles N.L., (Won 1) 1974.
6-game Series—4—Boston A.L., (Won 4), vs. Chicago N.L., 1918.
7-game Series—6—Oakland A.L., (Won 4), vs. Cincinnati N.L., (Won 2), 1972.
8-game Series—4—Boston A.L., (Won 3), vs. New York N.L., (Won 1), 1912.

Ty Cobb

Reggie Jackson

Individual .400 Hitters, or Better
(Playing in all games, each Series)

	Year	G	AB	R	H	2B	3B	HR	TB	Pct.
Babe Ruth, New York A.L.	1928	4	16	9	10	3	0	3	22	.625
Hank Gowdy, Boston N.L.	1914	4	11	3	6	3	1	1	14	.545
Lou Gehrig, New York A.L.	1928	4	11	5	6	1	0	4	19	.545
Johnny Bench, Cincinnati N.L.	1976	4	15	4	8	1	1	2	17	.533
Lou Gehrig, New York A.L.	1932	4	17	9	9	1	0	3	19	.529
Thurman Munson, New York A.L.	1976	4	17	2	9	0	0	0	9	.529
John McLean, New York N.L.	1913	5	12	1	6	0	0	0	6	.500
Dave Robertson, New York N.L.	1917	6	22	3	11	1	1	0	14	.500
Mark Koenig, New York A.L.	1927	4	18	5	9	2	0	0	11	.500
Pepper Martin, St. Louis N.L.	1931	7	24	5	12	4	0	1	19	.500
Joe Gordon, New York A.L.	1941	5	14	2	7	1	1	1	13	.500
Billy Martin, New York A.L.	1953	6	24	5	12	1	2	2	23	.500
Vic Wertz, Cleveland A.L.	1954	4	16	2	8	2	1	1	15	.500
Tim McCarver, St. Louis N.L.	1964	7	23	4	11	1	1	1	17	.478
Heinie Groh, New York N.L.	1922	5	19	4	9	0	1	0	11	.474
Paul Blair, Baltimore A.L.	1970	5	19	5	9	1	0	0	10	.474
Harry Steinfeldt, Chicago N.L.	1907	5	17	2	8	1	1	0	11	.471
Frank Frisch, New York N.L.	1922	5	17	3	8	1	0	0	9	.471
Hack Wilson, Chicago N.L.	1929	5	17	2	8	0	1	0	10	.471
Stan Hack, Chicago N.L.	1938	4	17	3	8	1	0	0	9	.471
Lou Brock, St. Louis N.L.	1968	7	28	6	13	3	1	2	24	.464
Phil Cavarretta, Chicago N.L.	1938	4	13	1	6	1	0	0	7	.462
Max Carey, Pittsburgh N.L.	1925	7	24	6	11	4	0	0	15	.458
Monte Irvin, New York N.L.	1951	6	24	3	11	0	1	0	13	.458
Jake Powell, New York A.L.	1936	4	22	8	10	1	0	1	14	.455
Al Weis, New York N.L.	1969	5	11	1	5	0	0	1	8	.455
Frank Baker, Philadelphia A.L.	1913	5	20	2	9	0	0	1	12	.450
Reggie Jackson, New York A.L.	1977	6	20	10	9	1	0	5	25	.450
Duffy Lewis, Boston A.L.	1915	5	18	1	8	1	0	1	12	.444
Riggs Stephenson, Chicago N.L.	1932	4	18	2	8	1	0	0	9	.444
Joe Harris, Washington A.L.	1925	7	25	5	11	2	0	3	22	.440
Charlie Keller, New York A.L.	1939	4	16	8	7	1	1	3	19	.438
Johnny Evers, Boston N.L.	1914	4	16	2	7	0	0	0	7	.438
Fred Luderus, Philadelphia N.L.	1915	5	16	1	7	2	0	1	12	.438
Bill Dickey, New York A.L.	1932	4	16	2	7	0	0	0	7	.438
George McQuinn, St. Louis A.L.	1944	6	16	2	17	2	0	1	12	.438
Tony Perez, Cincinnati N.L.	1972	7	23	3	10	2	0	0	12	.435
Eddie Collins, Philadelphia A.L.	1910	5	21	5	9	4	0	0	13	.429
Yogi Berra, New York A.L.	1953	6	21	3	9	1	0	1	13	.429
Granny Hamner, Philadelphia N.L.	1950	4	14	1	6	2	1	0	10	.429
Gene Woodling, New York A.L.	1950	4	14	2	6	0	0	0	6	.429
Brooke Robinson, Baltimore A.L.	1970	5	21	5	9	2	0	2	17	.429
Phil Cavarretta, Chicago N.L.	1945	7	26	7	11	2	0	1	16	.423
Dan Staub, New York N.L.	1973	7	26	1	11	2	0	1	16	.423
Frank Chance, Chicago N.L.	1908	5	19	4	8	0	0	0	8	.421
Eddie Collins, Philadelphia A.L.	1913	5	19	5	8	0	2	0	12	.421
Jimmy Dykes, Philadelphia A.L.	1929	5	19	2	8	1	0	0	9	.421
Aaron Ward, New York A.L.	1923	6	24	4	10	0	0	1	13	.417
Casey Stengel, New York N.L.	1923	6	12	3	5	0	0	2	11	.417
Tommy Thevenow, St. Louis N.L.	1926	7	24	5	10	1	0	1	14	.417
Alvin Dark, New York N.L.	1951	6	24	5	10	3	0	1	16	.417
Yogi Berra, New York A.L.	1955	7	24	5	10	1	0	1	14	.417
Lou Brock, St. Louis N.L.	1967	7	29	8	12	2	1	1	19	.414
Roberto Clemente, Pittsburgh N.L.	1971	7	29	3	12	2	1	2	22	.414
Emil Verban, St. Louis N.L.	1944	6	17	1	7	0	0	0	7	.412
Harry Walker, St. Louis N.L.	1946	7	17	7	7	2	0	0	9	.412
Alvin Dark, New York N.L.	1954	4	17	2	7	0	0	0	7	.412
Bill Bruton, Milwaukee N.L.	1958	7	17	2	7	0	0	1	10	.412
Frank Baker, Philadelphia A.L.	1910	5	22	6	9	3	0	0	12	.409
Bobby P. Doerr, Boston A.L.	1946	6	22	1	9	1	0	1	3	.409
Eddie Collins, Chicago A.L.	1917	6	22	4	0	1	0	0	10	.409
Bobby Richardson, New York A.L.	1964	7	32	3	13	2	0	0	15	.406
Claude Rossman, Detroit A.L.	1907	5	20	1	8	0	1	0	10	.400
Buck Herzog, New York N.L.	1912	8	30	6	12	4	1	0	18	.400
Frank Frisch, New York N.L.	1923	6	25	2	10	0	1	0	12	.400
Babe Ruth, New York A.L.	1927	4	15	4	6	0	0	2	12	.400

Frank Frisch

Billy Martin

Lloyd Waner, Pittsburgh N.L.	1927	4	15	5	6	1	1	0	9	.400
Mickey Cochrane, Phila. A.L.	1929	5	15	5	6	1	0	0	7	.400
Red Rolfe, New York A.L.	1936	6	25	5	10	0	0	0	10	.400
Tony Lazzeri, New York A.L.	1937	5	15	3	6	0	1	1	11	.400
Joe Gordon, New York A.L.	1938	4	15	3	6	2	0	1	11	.400
Bill Dickey, New York A.L.	1938	4	15	2	6	0	0	1	9	.400
Frank McCormick, Cincinnati N.L.	1939	4	15	1	6	1	0	0	7	.400
Mickey Mantle, New York A.L.	1960	7	25	8	10	1	0	3	20	.400
Tommy Davis, Los Angeles N.L.	1963	4	15	0	6	0	2	0	10	.400
Carl Yastrzemski, Boston N.L.	1967	7	25	4	10	2	0	3	21	.400

Players Making Four Hits in a World Series Game

Date	Player and Club	AB	H	2B	3B	HR
Oct. 1, 1903	Tommy Leach, Pittsburgh (NL)	5	4	0	2	0
Oct. 8, 1903	Clarence Beaumont, Pittsburgh (NL)	5	4	0	0	0
Oct. 13, 1906	Frank Isbell, Chicago (AL)	5	4	4	0	0
Oct. 14, 1906	Edgar Hahn, Chicago (AL)	5	4	0	0	0
Oct. 12, 1908	Ty Cobb, Detroit (AL)	5	4	1	0	0
Oct. 25, 1911	Larry Doyle, New York (NL)	5	4	2	0	0
Oct. 26, 1911	Danny Murphy, Philadelphia (AL)	5	4	1	0	0
Oct. 5, 1921	Frankie Frisch, New York (NL)	4	4	0	1	0
Oct. 7, 1921	George Burns, New York (NL)	6	4	1	1	0
Oct. 7, 1921	Frank Snyder, New York (NL)	5	4	0	0	0
Oct. 13, 1923	Ross Youngs, New York (NL)	5	4	0	0	1
Oct. 14, 1923	Joe Dugan, New York (AL)	5	4	0	0	1
Oct. 7, 1924	Goose Goslin, Washington (AL)	4	4	0	0	1
Oct. 8, 1924	Fred Lindstrom, New York (NL)	5	4	0	0	0
Oct. 15, 1925	Max Carey, Pittsburgh (NL)	5	4	3	0	0
Oct. 3, 1933	Mel Ott, New York (NL)	5	4	0	0	1
Oct. 3, 1934	Joe Medwick, St. Louis (NL)	5	4	0	0	1
Oct. 6, 1934	Hank Greenberg, Detroit (AL)	5	4	2	0	0
Oct. 9, 1934	Jim Collins, St. Louis (NL)	5	4	0	0	0
Oct. 5, 1938	Bill Dickey, New York (AL)	4	4	0	0	0
Oct. 5, 1941	Charlie Keller, New York (AL)	5	4	2	0	0
Oct. 8, 1945	Stan Hack, Chicago (NL)	5	4	1	0	0
Oct. 10, 1946	Enos Slaughter, St. Louis (NL)	6	4	1	0	1
Oct. 10, 1946	Whitey Kurowski, St. Louis (NL)	5	4	2	0	0
Oct. 10, 1946	Joe Garagiola, St. Louis (NL)	5	4	1	0	0
Oct. 10, 1946	Wally Moses, Boston (AL)	5	4	0	0	0
Oct. 4, 1951	Monte Irvin, New York (NL)	5	4	0	1	0
Sept. 29, 1954	Vic Wertz, Cleveland (AL)	5	4	1	1	0
Oct. 5, 1959	Jim Gilliam, Los Angeles (NL)	5	4	0	0	0
Oct. 8, 1960	Mickey Mantle, New York (AL)	5	4	1	0	1
Oct. 11, 1965	Maury Wills, Los Angeles (NL)	5	4	2	0	0
Oct. 4, 1967	Lou Brock, St. Louis (AL)	4	4	0	0	0
Oct. 14, 1970	Brooks Robinson, Baltimore (AL)	4	4	0	0	1
Oct. 14, 1973	Reggie Jackson, Oakland (AL)	6	4	1	1	0
Oct. 17, 1973	Dan Staub (NL)	4	4	0	0	1
Oct. 21, 1976	Thurman Munson (AL)	4	4	0	0	0

Carl Furillo and Yogi Berra

Trivia Quiz

1 Who was the youngest player ever to pitch in a World Series?

2 Who was the oldest World Series pitcher?

3 On October 9, 1926, the oldest player ever to pitch a complete World Series game did just that. Who was he?

4 Who was the youngest pitcher ever to win a complete World Series game? Hint: He played for Philadelphia.

5 Who was the oldest pitcher to start in a World Series game?

6 Who won the first World Series night game, and when was it played?

7 Who was the youngest manager of a World Series-winning team?

8 What is the most number of times a player has come to bat in a Series game, and who holds that record?

9 What 1909 player came to bat five times in a single World Series game but was not charged with even one official at bat?

10 What Philadelphia Athletics player, with the same name as a famous comedian, came up twice in an inning when his team scored runs and made an out each time?

11 What St. Louis player is the only person to come to bat twice in an inning on two occasions in the same Series, and what were the results?

12 Only two players have ever been responsible for driving in all of their team's runs in a Series game. Who were they?

13 What one player was responsible for all three of his team's hits against the Yankees on October 14, 1923?

14 Who is the only player to hit four doubles in a single World Series game?

15 Fourteen players have hit home runs in their first at bats in a Series. But what one player has hit two homers in his first two times at bat?

16 What player slammed five consecutive extra base hits in a World Series?

17 What 1921 Giants player hit a double and a triple in the same inning?

18 What Baltimore pitcher walked twice with the bases loaded in the same World Series game?

19 What member of "Murderers' Row" drew five consecutive bases on balls in one?

20 What 1910 Chicago player drew three walks in two consecutive games?

21 What other Chicago player was picked off base twice in the same game?

22 What New York player grounded into three double plays in one game?

23 What 1903 Pittsburgh player reached base on errors three times in one Series game?

24 Who was eligible to play in a total of seven World Series games but actually played in only one?

25 Who is the only player to bat .300 or better in six World Series?

26 Of all the players who played twenty or more Series games, who has the highest batting average?

27 What player scored at least once in nine consecutive games to set the record for that feat?

28 Who drove in the most runs in a Series as a pinch hitter?

29 What player made seven consecutive hits in two consecutive Series?

30 Who hit in seventeen consecutive games in three consecutive Series?

31 What Detroit player went to bat thirty-one times in a row and never got a hit?

32 Who are the only two pitchers to hit two homers in a Series?

33 What Giants and Cardinals player went to bat 197 times in 50 Series games and never hit a home run?

34 Who hit two or more homers in a game on four separate occasions?

35 In 1924, a player came to bat as a pinch hitter three times but walked each time. Who was he?

36 What three players came to bat three times as pinch hitters and struck out each time? Hint: The years were 1929, 1932 and 1976.

37 What Milwaukee player holds the record for being struck out the most times in a Series, and what is that record?

38 What Chicago player was caught stealing nine times in four World Series?

39 What is the record for grounding into double plays in total Series played, and who holds it?

40 Who played in his first World Series in 1951 and in his last in 1973?

41 Who was the youngest player ever to play in a World Series?

42 Who is the only shortstop to make two unassisted double plays in a Series?

43 Who is the only outfielder to make an unassisted double play?

44 What Cincinnati outfielder started two double plays in the same game?

45 What pitcher pitched in all seven games in the 1973 Series?

46 What pitcher gave up eight doubles against Pittsburgh, and what Pittsburgh pitcher was tagged for three triples in a game against Boston?

47 What St. Louis pitcher gave up three home runs in a single inning?

48 What three men managed World Series clubs in both leagues?

49 What is the record for the most hits made in a single Series game?

50 Can you name the three years in which there was a tied game in the World Series?

51 What Cincinnati player holds the record for pitching six consecutive strikeouts at the start of a Series game?

52 What pitcher has allowed the greatest number of home runs in total World Series, and what is that record?

53 How many pinch hitters were used in the 1929 World Series, and what were the results each produced?

54 In the first game, a team collected five hits against their opponents, and all five were for extra bases. Then in the sixth and final game, the same team got seven hits, and all of those were also for extra bases. What was the name of the team and when was the Series played?

For answers, turn page.

Ed Walsh.

Answers

1 Kenneth A. Brett, Boston, A.L., was nineteen years and twenty days old when he pitched one inning in relief on October 8, 1967.

2 John P. Quinn, Philadelphia A.L., was forty-four years and three months old when he pitched two innings, finishing the game, October 4, 1930.

3 Grover Cleveland Alexander, St. Louis, N.L., was thirty-nine years, seven months and thirteen days old when he pitched for the Cards against New York that day (October 9, 1926). The score: St. Louis 10 and New York 2.

4 Leslie A. Bush, twenty years, ten months and twelve days old on October 9, 1913, when he pitched for Philadelphia, A.L., against New York, N.L., winning 8-2.

5 John P. Quinn, forty-three years, three months and seven days old when he started for Philadelphia, A.L., on October 12, 1929. He pitched five innings.

6 It was played on October 13, 1971, between Pittsburgh, N.L., and Baltimore, A.L. Pittsburgh won, 4-3.

7 Stanley R. Harris—twenty-seven years, eleven months and two days—Washington, A.L., vs. New York, N.L. Known as "The Boy Wonder," Bucky Harris was born November 8, 1896.

8 Seven. Don Hahn of the New York Mets, October 14, 1973.

9 Fred Clarke of Pittsburgh came up five times on October 16, 1909.

He received four bases on balls and sacrificed once.

10 George Burns. He flied out and struck out on October 12, 1929.

11 The player was Stan Musial, and it happened in 1942. In the ninth inning of game one, he made two outs. Then in the fourth inning of game four, he singled and doubled. Game one was played on September 30, and game four on October 4.

12 Hank Bauer of the New York Yankees, on October 4, 1958 (Yankees won 4-0). Ken Boyer of the St. Louis Cardinals, on October 11, 1964 (Cardinals won 4-3).

13 Irish Meusel of the New York Giants hit a single, a double and a triple on October 14, 1923.

14 Frank Isbell of the Chicago White Sox, October 13, 1906.

15 Gene Tenace of the Oakland A's did it, October 14, 1972.

16 Lou Brock of the St. Louis Cardinals, in the 1968 Series: three doubles, a triple and a home run.

17 Ross Youngs of the New York Giants, in the seventh inning, October 7, 1921.

18 Jim Palmer of the Baltimore Orioles, in the fourth and fifth innings, October 11, 1971.

19 Lou Gehrig of the New York Yankees, October 7-9, 1928.

20 Jimmy Scheckard of the Chicago Cubs, October 18-20, 1910.

21 Max Flack of the Chicago Cubs, September 9, 1918.

22 Willie Mays of the New York Giants, October 8, 1951.

23 Fred Clarke of Pittsburgh, October 10, 1903.

24 Charlie Silver of the New York Yankees was eligible for seven Series, but he played in only one game in 1949.

25 Babe Ruth.

26 Lou Brock's .391 is the highest batting average in total Series for players in twenty games or more.

27 Babe Ruth.

28 Dusty Rhodes of the New York Giants drove in six runs in the 1954 Series, setting the record for a pinch hitter.

29 Thurman Munson of the New York Yankees did it in 1976 and 1977.

30 Hank Bauer of the Yankees—in 1956, 1957 and 1958.

31 Marvin Owen in 1934 and 1935.

32 Bob Gibson of the St. Louis Cardinals and Dave McNally of the Baltimore Orioles.

33 Frankie Frisch.

34 Babe Ruth.

35 Benny Tate of Washington.

36 Gabby Hartnett of the Cubs, in 1929; Rollie Hemsley of the Cubs, in 1932; and Otto Velez of the Yankees, in 1976.

37 Eddie Mathews struck out eleven times in a Series (1958).

38 Frank Schute of the Chicago Cubs was caught stealing nine times in four World Series, five times in five attempts in 1910.

39 The record is seven, and it is held by Joe DiMaggio of the New York Yankees.

40 Willie Mays.

41 Freddie Lindstrom. He was eighteen years, ten months and thirteen days when he played his first game on October 4, 1924.

42 Joe Tinker of the Chicago Cubs. He did it on October 10 and October 11 in 1907.

43 Tris Speaker of the Boston Red Sox, October 15, 1912.

44 Eddie Roush, October 7, 1919.

45 Darold Knowles of Oakland pitched in all seven games in the 1973 Series against the Mets.

46 Walter Johnson of the Washington Senators gave up eight doubles in a game against Pittsburgh in 1925. Deacon Phillippe of the Pittsburgh Pirates was tagged for three triples in a game against Boston in 1903.

47 Dick Hughes, on October 11, 1967.

48 Joe McCarthy, Yogi Berra and Alvin Dark.

49 Four. No player has ever made five hits in a Series game.

50 1907, 1912 and 1922.

51 Hod Eller did it in the 1919 Series against the White Sox.

52 Burleigh Grimes. Eight.

53 Seven. All seven struck out.

54 The Philadelphia Athletics established this peculiar record in the 1930 Series against the Cardinals.

Credits

MEL ALLEN

Known to millions of radio listeners and TV viewers as "the Voice of the New York Yankees," Mel Allen has witnessed the setting of innumerable baseball records. Yet few realize that Mr. Allen has set a record of his own. From the time he covered his first World Series in 1938 until the time he broadcast his last in 1963, Mel Allen covered a total of twenty-one fall classics—more than any other broadcaster. His deep knowledge of both baseball and the electronic media gives him a unique perspective on the World Series as it appears from the broadcast booth.

ROY CAMPANELLA

Roy Campanella joined the Brooklyn Dodgers in the middle of the 1948 season after two years in the minors and eight years in the old Negro leagues. Campy was voted the National League's Most Valuable Player by the Baseball Writers Association in 1951, and many fans and sportswriters considered him the best catcher in the National League during his career. Lauded by Walter O'Malley as "one of the best clutch hitters in baseball," Mr. Campanella played in a total of five World Series. He is the author of **It's Good to Be Alive.**

LILLIAN CARTER

Loved and admired by the entire nation as the mother of President Jimmy Carter, "Miz Lillian" is a remarkable personality in her own right. A lifelong baseball fan and an outspoken individualist whose comments and opinions have added a refreshing note of candor to the national scene, Lillian Carter surprised everyone by joining the Peace Corps and going to India at an age when most people are thinking about retiring. Her experiences in India are vividly recounted in the recently published **Away from Home,** by Lillian Carter and her daughter Gloria Carter Spann.

LEO DUROCHER

Durocher began playing baseball on the sandlots of West Springfield, Mass. His first major league game was with the 1925 Yankees. His teammates included Babe Ruth, Lou Gehrig, and Earle Combs. After a stint in the minors, he returned to the Yankees for the 1928 and '29 seasons. From 1930 to '33 he played for the Cincinnati Reds and from 1933 to '37 he was part of the St. Louis Cardinals "Gashouse Gang." In 1938, Durocher went to the Brooklyn Dodgers as player-manager, a role he filled for five years. After retiring as a player, he continued to manage the Dodgers until 1948, (he sat out the 1947 season), leading them to the National League pennant in 1941. In his seven years with the Giants (1948-1955) he led them to the pennant and the 1954 World Championship. Durocher ranks fifth, all-time, in total games managed and games won. Now, 72, and an author and former radio-television broadcaster, he lives in Palm Springs, California.

JOSEPH DURSO

Joseph Durso is a veteran baseball writer for **The New York Times.** His books on baseball include **The Days of Mr. McGraw, Amazing: The Miracle** of the Mets, **Casey,** and **Yankee Stadium: Fifty Years of Drama.**

JAMES T. FARRELL

An editor, author and reporter, James T. Farrell has written scores of books on dozens of subjects. His most famous work, the Studs Lonigan trilogy, was made into a movie in 1960 and is currently being considered by NBC as a possible new mini-series. His fiction, nonfiction and criticism have been translated into more than twenty different languages. Recently he published his fifty-first book, a collection of stories called **Olive and Mary Anne.**

JOE GARAGIOLA

A radio and television personality **par excellence,** Joe Garagiola is familiar to sports fans everywhere. After playing baseball for St. Louis, as well as Pittsburgh, Chicago and New York, he made a successful switch to broadcasting. A former member of the NBC **Today** show cast, Joe Garagiola is the star of his own radio program, the play-by-play announcer on the **Saturday Game of the Week** telecasts and the author of **Baseball Is a Funny Game.**

JOSEPH L. REICHLER

Joe Reichler covered baseball and other sports for the Associated Press for nearly a quarter of a century. He is the author of many books about baseball, including, **The History of Baseball, Baseball's Great Moments** and **The Game and the Glory.** Mr. Reichler is special assistant to the Commissioner of Baseball, Bowie K. Kuhn.

All photographs courtesy of the
National Baseball Hall of Fame.

Index

The 1928 New York Yankees in Spring Training.

A's, see Oakland A's
Aaron, Henry, 51, 68, 79, 104, 107, 138
Abstein, Bill, 168, 169
Adams, Charles "Babe," 34, 90, 103, 156-57
Adams, Franklin P., 6
Agee, Tommy, 40, 97
Agnew, Sam, 48
Alexander, Grover Cleveland "Pete," 27-29, 49, 125, 140
Allen, Mel, 8, 79
Allison, Bob, 44
Alston, Walter, 43, 77
Altrock, Nick, 19, 90
Amoros, Sandy, 43, 94, 140, 177, 178
Antonelli, Johnny, 94

Aparicio, Luis, 136
Appling, Luke, 22, 134
Armbruster, Ed, 162-63
Athletic, see Philadelphia Athletics
Atlanta Braves, 79, 97
Attell, Abe, 144-47
Auker, Eldon, 172
Avila, Bobby, 94, 105

Babgy, Jim, 36, 54, 163
Baker, Del, 172
Baker, Frank "Home Run," 35, 51, 52, 54, 70, 82-83, 89, 90, 124, 134, 136-37, 169

Baltimore Americans, 14
Baltimore Orioles, 20, 40, 44, 59, 67, 86-88, 95-97, 105, 112-13, 120, 130, 136, 165, 173
Bancroft, Dave, 127, 136
Bando, Sal, 87, 105, 130, 137
Banks, Ernie, 22, 134
Barber, Red, 8, 175, 177, 182
Barber, Sam, 48
Barnes, Jesse, 127, 154
Barnett, Larry, 162
Barrow, Ed, 179
Barry, Jack, 89, 124, 136
Bartell, Dick, 36, 135
Bauer, Hank, 37, 44, 54, 59, 95, 122, 138
Beaumont, Ginger, 12
Beazley, Johnny, 93, 113, 126
Bedient, Hugh, 41, 159
Belanger, Mark, 136
Bell, Herman, 28, 49, 54
Bell, Lester, 67
Bench, Johnny, 70, 71, 86, 87, 101, 107
Bender, Chief, 17, 24, 35, 89, 124, 140
Bengough, Benny, 120
Bentley, Jack, 26, 75, 160
Benton, Rube, 65
Berra, Yogi, 32-33, 43, 57, 59, 60, 70, 73, 75-76, 84, 115, 122, 134, 138, 140, 162, 174-77
Bevens, Floyd "Bill," 32, 111-12, 162, 177
Bigby, Carson, 164
Billingham, Jack, 87
Bishop, Max, 56, 124, 165
Black, Joe, 77
Blair, Paul, 40, 97, 165
Blanchard, Johnny, 40, 77, 123
Blass, Steve, 86, 97
Blue, Vida, 130
Boley, Joe, 56, 124, 165
Bollweg, Don, 37, 84-85
Bonham, Ernie, 93
Boston Braves, 54, 67, 70-71, 89-90, 107, 125, 126, 135, 138, 160, 182
Boston Pilgrims, 10, 12-15, 24, 34, 54, 102-3
Boston Red Sox, 4, 5, 35, 36, 39-41, 47-48, 54, 59, 63, 75, 77, 81, 82, 84, 86, 87, 89, 101, 104, 105, 107-8, 110, 127, 130, 137, 138, 141, 155-56, 159, 162-63, 169

Boswell, Ken, 77

Bottomley, Jim, 62, 67, 125

Boudreau, Lou, 136

Boyer, Clete, 123

Branca, Ralph, 76

Braves, see Atlanta Braves; Boston Braves; Milwaukee Braves

Brecheen, Harry "The Cat," 36, 127

Bresnahan, Roger, 17, 127, 156

Bridges, Tommy, 43-44, 92, 141, 172

Bridwell, Al, 129

Bright, Harry, 38

Briles, Nellie, 97

Britt, Jim, 8

Brock, Lou, 60, 70, 127, 134, 137, 151

Brooklyn Dodgers, 8, 31-32, 36, 37, 43-45, 47-48, 51, 54, 57, 59, 60, 73, 75-77, 79, 82-85, 94, 99, 104, 105, 111-13, 117, 122, 127, 135, 136, 140, 149-51, 157, 162, 163, 173, 174, 176-84

Brown, Bobby, 75, 76

Brown, Jimmy, 126

Brown, Joe L., 152

Brown, Mordecai, 35, 36, 75, 90, 103, 107, 129

Browns, see St. Louis Browns

Brush, John T., 14-17

Bruton, Billy, 41

Buhl, Bob, 36

Bunker, Wally, 96

Bunning, Jim, 134

Burdette, Lew, 36-37, 39, 41, 140

Burgess, Smokey, 86

Burns, George, 127, 165

Burns, Sleepy Bill, 144-47

Bush, Joe, 48, 65, 73

Byrne, Bobby, 168-69

Byrne, Tommy, 43, 76

C

Camilli, Dolph, 104

Camnitz, Howard, 34, 60, 90, 156

Campanella, Roy, 32, 43, 76, 85, 105, 132

Campaneris, Bert, 87, 130, 136

Carbo, Bernie, 59, 75, 77, 87

Cardinals, see St. Louis Cardinals

Carey, Andy, 32, 77

Carey, Max, 138, 164

Carroll, Clay, 77

Carter, Billy, 78

Carter, Jimmy, 78, 79

Casey, Hugh, 83, 162, 184

Cash, Norm, 39

Cavaretta, Phil, 70, 172

Cepeda, Orlando, 104, 105

Cerv, Bob, 40, 76

Cey, Ron, 105

Chance, Frank, 19, 35, 70, 90, 103, 128, 135, 169

Chandler, A.B. "Happy," 173, 179

Chandler, Spud, 140

Chesbro, Jack, 15

Chicago Cubs, 4, 18-19, 29-31, 35-36, 48-50, 52, 54, 56, 57, 70, 73, 75, 88, 90, 103, 104, 107, 120, 122, 124, 125, 128-30, 134, 136-38, 150, 154-56, 165, 167-69, 172

Chicago White Sox, 4, 18-20, 30, 35, 38, 39, 44, 54, 70, 72, 77, 88, 90, 107, 127, 129, 135, 142-47, 157, 169-70, 173

Cicotte, Eddie, 19, 143, 145-47

Cimoli, Gino, 86

Cincinnati Reds, 8, 20, 36, 38, 40, 48, 59, 65, 71, 73, 77, 79, 81, 86, 87, 101, 105, 108, 109, 113, 122, 123, 130, 135-37, 141-47, 162-63, 170, 179, 182

Clarke, Fred, 10, 12, 34-35, 90, 156, 168

Clemente, Roberto, 70, 86, 97, 107, 138

Clendenon, Don, 40, 47

Cleveland, Reggie, 77

Cleveland Indians, 36, 43, 45, 54, 59, 73-76, 82, 88, 93-94, 105, 137, 150, 163

Cleveland Naps, 20

Coakley, Andy, 17

Cobb, Ty, 20, 34, 60-61, 67, 68, 90, 103, 132, 168

Cochrane, Mickey, 31, 43, 56, 70-72, 91, 92, 124-26, 138, 153, 155, 161, 165

Cole, Leonard "King," 35

Coleman, Jerry, 76, 112, 113, 178

Collins, Eddie, 20, 52, 63-65, 70, 89, 124, 135, 143, 169, 170

Collins, Jimmy, 10, 12, 137

Collins, Joe, 37, 45, 84

Collins, Pat, 120

Collins, Rip, 126

Combs, Earle, 28, 49, 120, 121

Conlan, Jocko, 173

Connolly, Tommy, 169, 170

Coombs, Jack, 23, 35-36, 89, 124, 140

Cooper, Cecil, 105

Cooper, Mort, 68, 126, 138

Cooper, Walker, 126

Corum, Bill, 175

Coveleski, Stan, 36, 140

Cox, Billy, 45, 84

Coyle, Harry, 8

Craig, Roger 76

Crawford, Sam, 34, 90, 168

Critz, Hughie, 171

Cronin, Joe, 56, 132

Crosetti, Frank, 57, 65, 136, 172-73

Cubs, see Chicago Cubs

Cuccinello, Tony, 150

Cuellar, Mike, 67, 97

Culberson, Leon, 63, 84

Cunningham, Bill, 41-42

Cutshaw, George, 48

Cuyler, Kiki, 31, 125, 164

D

Dahlen, Bill, 127

Darcy, Pat, 81

Dark, Alvin, 70, 94, 127, 135

Dascoli, Frank, 173

David, Harry, 169

Davis, George, 90, 107

Davis, Harry, 156

Davis, Virgil, 44

Davis, Willie, 113, 165

Dean, Dizzy, 38, 57, 92, 126, 150, 153, 172

Dean, Paul, 92, 153

Deegan, Bill, 173

DeLancey, Bill, 126, 172

Dente, Sam, 150

Derringer, Paul, 36

Detroit Tigers, 20, 34-36, 38-39, 43-44, 54, 60-61, 75, 86, 90, 92-93, 103, 109, 120, 126, 127, 129, 135, 137, 140, 150, 152-53, 155, 156, 165, 167-68, 172

Devlin, Artie, 127

Devore, Josh, 41, 81

Dickey, Bill, 70, 122, 138, 162

Dickson, Murry, 36

DiMaggio, Joe, 8, 43, 44, 57, 59, 65, 68, 76, 99, 107, 111, 112, 117, 122, 132, 137, 162, 173-75, 184

Dinneen, Bill, 10, 12, 13, 34, 140

Doby, Larry, 43, 94, 105

Dodgers, see Brooklyn Dodgers; Los Angeles Dodgers

Doheny, Ed, 12

Donlin, Mike, 17, 127

Donohue, Jiggs, 90, 107

Donovan, Wild Bill, 169

Dougherty, Pat, 12, 13, 54

Douglas, Phil, 48, 54, 61, 127

Doyle, Denny, 87

Doyle, Larry, 41, 54, 157

Drabowsky, Moe, 97, 112-13

Dressen, Charlie, 151, 173

Dreyfuss, Barney, 10-13

Drysdale, Don, 44

Dugan, Joe, 41-42, 120, 121, 137

Duren, Ryne, 77

Durocher, Leo, 43, 44, 74-75, 94, 121, 127, 136, 153, 162

Dyer, Eddie, 63, 102, 110

Dykes, Jimmy, 124, 165

Earnshaw, George, 29, 56, 71, 124, 125, 140

Eastwick, Rawly, 77

Edge, Bob, 8

Edwards, Bruce, 76

Ehmke, Howard, 30-31, 37, 84

Eller, Hod, 38, 144

Engle, Claude, 82, 160

English, Woody, 167, 172

Erskine, Carl, 37, 84-85

Essegian, Chuck, 59, 75-77

Etchebarren, Andy, 165

Evans, Dwight, 40, 87

Evans, Nat, 145

Evers, Johnny, 23, 89, 90, 129

Faber, Urban "Red," 35, 140

Face, Roy, 40, 77

Fairly, Ron, 44, 113

Feller, Bob, 94, 132

Felsch, Happy, 19, 54, 65, 143, 145, 170

Ferguson, Alex, 42

Fingers, Rollie, 87, 130

Finley, Charlie, 130

Fisk, Carlton, 40, 59, 77, 81, 87, 162-63

Fitzgerald, "Honey Fitz," 4, 156

Fletcher, Art, 169, 170

Flood, Curt, 39, 165

Ford, Whitey, 8, 36, 37, 49, 60, 94, 123, 134, 141, 178

Foster, George, 87

Foxx, Jimmy, 31, 56, 91, 124, 125, 135, 165

Freehan, Bill, 39

Freeman, Buck, 12

Friend, Bob, 116

Frisch, Frankie, 26, 50, 62, 70, 83, 125-28, 134, 135, 150,172

Froemming, Bruce, 173

Fullerton, Hugh, 4

Furillo, Carl, 32, 45, 60, 84, 178

Gandil, Chick, 145, 147

Garcia, Mike, 75, 94

Gardner, Larry, 48, 54, 82, 160

Gainor, Del, 48

Gedeon, Joe, 146

Gehrig, Lou, 28, 52, 54, 62, 70, 72, 79, 99, 101, 104, 107, 109, 120-22, 134, 135

Gehringer, Charley, 92, 135

Gelbert, Charlie, 135

Gentry, Garry, 40, 97

Geronimo, Cesar, 162

Giants, see New York Giants

Gibson, Bob, 38-39, 60, 86, 95, 127, 134, 140-41, 165

Gibson, George, 60-61, 168

Gilliam, Junior, 43, 112

Gionfriddo, Al, 8, 43, 111-12, 162, 174

Gomez, Lefty, 122, 141, 150, 154

Gonzalez, Mike, 63, 84, 172

Goodman, Ival, 65

Gordon, Joe, 70-73, 104, 135, 162

Gorman, Tom, 76

Goslin, Goose, 44, 56, 92, 137

Gowdy, Hank "Old Goldenrod," 26, 54, 67, 68, 70-71, 89, 107, 138, 157, 160-61

Grabowski, John, 120

Grant, Cary, 79

Gray, Dolly, 34, 156-57

Greb, Harry, 6

Green, Dick, 130

Greenberg, Hank, 92, 101, 135, 172

Greenwade, Tom, 177

Griffey, Ken, 87

Griffith, Clark, 90

Grim, Bob, 43

Grimes, Burleigh, 56, 92, 125, 163-64

Grimm, Charlie, 31, 70, 125, 135, 172

Groat, Dick, 86, 99-100

Groh, Heinie, 73, 127, 128, 136, 170

Grove, Lefty, 29, 31, 71, 91, 124, 125

H

Haas, Mule, 56, 124, 165, 171

Hack, Stan, 136-37, 168

Hafey, Chick, 67, 125

Hagne, Joe, 87

Hahn, Eddie, 107

Haines, Jesse, 28, 49, 62, 125

Hallahan, Bill, 92, 125-26

Hamner, Granny, 174

Haney, Fred, 36

Hartnett, Gabby, 125, 132

Harrelson, Bud, 97

Harris, Bucky, 26, 76

Harris, Joe, 108

Hartsel, Topsy, 17

Heilmann, Harry, 22, 134

Helms, Tommy, 86

Hendricks, Elrod, 40

Hendrix, Claude, 48

Henrich, Tommy, 59, 83-84, 122, 162, 184

Henriksen, Olaf, 159

Herman, Billy, 172

Hermanski, Gene, 84

Herrmann, Garry, 15, 156

Heydler, John, 34, 156

High, Andy, 62

Highlanders, see New York Highlanders

Hildebrand, George, 108

Hiller, Chuck, 59
Hoblitzell, Dick, 48
Hodges, Gil, 32, 43, 60, 99, 104
    116
Hodges, Russ, 8
Hoffman, Solly, 90
Hofman, Artie, 129
Holke, Walter, 65
Hollocher, Charlie, 49
Holmes, Tommy, 20
Holtzman, Ken, 87, 130, 141
Hooper, Harry, 41, 48, 54, 82,
    156, 160
Hopp, Johnny, 126
Hornsby, Rogers, 28, 29, 31, 67,
    68, 99, 104, 125, 132
Horton, Willie, 39
Hotteman, Art, 94
Hough, Charlie, 82
Houk, Ralph, 79
Howard, Elston, 38, 41, 43, 60,
    77
Hoyt, Waite, 28, 50, 73, 82, 90,
    108, 120, 121, 140
Hubbell, Carl, 140, 171
Huggins, Miller, 120
Hughes, Jim, 76
Hunter, Jim "Catfish," 87, 119,
    130, 140
Hurley, Ed, 173

Indians, see Cleveland Indians
Irvin, Monte, 60, 62, 74, 75, 84,
    94
Isbell, Frank, 90, 107

Jackson, Reggie, 51, 54, 59, 70,
    79, 82, 100-1, 107, 130, 138
Jackson, Shoeless Joe, 54, 65,
    143, 145, 147
Jackson, Travis, 91
James, Bill, 89
Javier, Julian, 38
Jennings, Hugh, 75, 103, 154,
    168
Johnson, Ban, 10-11, 14-16, 156
Johnson, Walter, 20, 25-26, 91,
    132, 140, 164

Jones, Fielder, 19, 90, 107
Jones, Harry, 152
Jones, Sam, 56
Jones, Tommy, 168
Joss, Addie, 134
Judge, Joe, 165
Jurges, Billy, 167

K

Kaline, Al, 38, 39
Kansas City Royals, 130
Kauff, Benny, 54
Keller, Charlie, 65, 70, 122, 137,
    138, 162, 184
Kellert, Frank, 60
Kelly, George, 26, 83, 127
Kerry, Paul, 42
Kilduff, Pete, 45
Killifer, Bill, 48
Killilea, Henry, 10, 12
Kiner, Ralph, 22, 134
Klem, Bill, 54, 157, 168, 172
Kling, Johnny, 107, 129
Klinger, Bob, 63, 110
Knowles, Darold, 130
Koenig, Mark, 28, 49, 62, 68, 71,
    72, 109, 120, 171
Koosman, Jerry, 97, 105
Koslo, Lefty Dave, 62
Koufax, Sandy, 37-39, 44, 86, 95,
    96, 141, 165, 178
Kralick, John, 178
Kubek, Tony, 86, 123, 177
Kuhn, Bowie, 79
Kurowski, Whitey, 93, 126
Kuzava, Bob, 45, 84

L

Lajoie, Napoleon, 20, 134
Landis, Kenesaw Mountain, 42,
    62, 93, 108, 142, 147, 155,
    157, 170-73
Lanier, Max, 126
Lapp, Jack, 157
Larsen, Don, 31-33, 37, 112, 149-
    50, 177
Lasorda, Tommy, 79
Lavagetto, Cookie, 57, 111-12,
    162, 177

Law, Vernon, 40
Lazzeri, Tony, 27-29, 57, 59, 62,
    72, 120-22, 125
Leach, Tommy, 12
Leever, Sam, 12
Lefebvre, Jim, 44
Leiber, Hank, 44
Leifield, Al, 34
Lemon, Bob, 43, 59, 74-75, 94
Lewis, Duffy, 48, 54, 82, 137,
    160
Liddle, Don, 43, 76
Lieb, Fred, 43, 62
Lindblad, Paul, 130
Lindstrom, Freddie, 26, 91, 137,
    160
Linz, Phil, 38
Livingston, Mickey, 173
Lockman, Whitey, 62
Loes, Billy, 151
Lolich, Mickey, 33-34, 39, 86,
    141, 165
Lollar, Sherman, 76, 162
Lombardi, Ernie, 65, 109
Lopat, Ed, 122, 140
Lopez, Hector, 123
Lord, Bristol, 156
Los Angeles Dodgers, 18, 20, 37-
    38, 51, 54, 75-79, 82, 95-97,
    101, 105, 112-13, 130, 141,
    165, 178
Luderus, Fred, 54
Lynn, Bird, 170
Lyons, Ted, 22, 134

Mack, Connie, 2, 16-17, 29-31,
    35-36, 51, 67, 72, 89, 107,
    119, 124, 125, 135, 137,
    155, 156, 165, 169, 171
MacPhail, Leland Stanford
    "Larry," 179-84
Maddox, Nick, 34
Magerkurth, George, 184
Maglie, Sal, 32, 43, 94
Maharg, Billy, 144-47
Majeski, Hank, 76
Malone, Pat, 52, 56
Mangual, Angel, 87
Mann, Les, 48, 156
Mantle, Mickey, 8, 32, 37, 38,
    40, 54, 70, 73, 84, 94, 101,
    104, 105, 107, 122, 123,
    137, 138, 177, 178

Manush, Heinie, 171-72

Mapes, Cliff, 76

Maranville, Rabbit, 89-90

Marberry, Fred, 42

Marion, Marty, 126

Maris, Roger, 40, 101, 123

Marquard, Rube, 51-52, 54

Marquez, Gonzalo, 77

Martin, Billy, 43-45, 59, 67, 68, 71, 73, 84, 122, 135, 173, 178

Martin, Pepper, 44, 56, 71-72, 91-92, 125, 134, 138, 153, 161, 172

Mathews, Eddie, 37, 38, 41, 105, 132-34

Mathewson, Christy, 2, 14, 17, 24-25, 34, 41, 48, 51-52, 82, 107, 127, 137, 140-41, 156, 159-60

Maxvill, Dal, 60

May, Lee, 86, 137

Mays, Carl, 42, 61, 90

Mays, Willie, 43, 68, 73, 74, 94, 104, 117, 132, 150

Mazeroski, Bill, 40, 52, 86, 94, 135

McCabe, Bill, 48

McCarthy, Joe, 31, 56, 73, 93, 122, 134, 155, 171

McCarver, Tim, 60

McCormick, Frank, 36, 65

McDonald, Arch, 175

McDonald, John, 180-84

McDougald, Gil, 32, 40, 41, 43, 59, 60, 122

McDowell, Sam, 178

McGinnity, Joe, 17, 24, 127

McGraw, John, 1, 2, 4, 8, 14, 15, 17, 24, 26, 41, 51-52, 62, 65, 70, 72, 73, 90, 91, 103, 109, 120, 127, 135, 157, 160, 171

McInnis, Stuffy, 49, 89, 124, 135

McIntire, Harry, 35, 169

McKechnie, Bill, 42, 49, 70

McLain, Denny, 38, 39

McLean, Larry, 67, 71, 72

McMillin, Fred, 144, 147

McNally, Dave, 59, 67, 96, 97, 112, 141

McNally, Mike, 49, 60, 61

McNamee, Graham, 6

McNeely, Earl, 26, 42, 160

McQuillan, Hugh, 41-42, 154

McQuinn, George, 68

McRae, Hal, 87

Medwick, Joe, 92-93, 126, 137, 172

Melton, Cliff, 153

Menke, Denis, 87

Merkle, Fred, 48, 54, 82, 129, 157, 159, 160

Merriwell, Frank, 86

Mets, see New York Mets

Meusel, Bob, 28, 29, 60-62, 65, 72, 90, 120, 128, 154, 170

Meusel, Irish, 26, 127

Meyers, Chief, 72, 82, 159, 160

Miller, Bing, 31, 56, 124, 165

Miller, Elmer, 61

Miller, John, 168

Miller, Otto, 45

Miller, Ralph, 160

Milwaukee Braves, 36-37, 41, 59, 104, 105, 138, 177, 178

Minnesota Twins, 44, 97

Mitchell, Clarence, 45, 163-64

Mize, Johnny, 37, 76, 84, 85, 123

Mollwitz, Fred, 23

Moore, Eddie, 164

Moore, Ray, 77

Moore, Terry, 44, 172-73

Moore, Wilcy, 120

Moran, Charlie, 171-72

Moran, Pat, 144

Moret, Rogelio, 77

Morgan, Joe, 40, 87, 105, 163

Moriarty, George, 60, 167-70, 172

Mowrey, Mike, 48

Munson, Thurman, 70, 71, 101

Murphy, Charles W., 169

Murphy, Danny, 124, 157, 169

Murphy, Johnny, 162

Murray, Red, 159

Murtaugh, Danny, 40, 94

Musial, Stan, 67, 68, 101, 126, 132

Myer, Buddy, 171

Myers, Hy, 47, 54

Narleski, Ray, 76

Neal, Charley, 44

Needham, Tom, 169

Nehf, Art, 26, 42, 56, 62, 82, 90, 127, 128, 141, 157, 165

Nelson, Rocky, 45

New York Giants, 2, 4, 5, 8, 14-17, 19, 20, 24, 26, 34, 35, 41-44, 48, 51-52, 54, 56-57, 59, 61-65, 70, 72-75, 81-84, 87-92, 94, 101, 103-5, 108, 119, 120, 122, 124-29, 135-38, 150, 153-54, 156, 157, 159, 169-71

New York Highlanders, 14-15, 19, 90

New York Mets, 23, 40, 44, 67, 77, 97, 105, 113, 130

New York Yankees, 5, 8, 15, 18, 20, 26-29, 31-32, 36-38, 40-41, 43, 45, 47-52, 54, 56, 57, 59-62, 65, 67, 70-73, 75-79, 82-86, 90-91, 93-95, 99-101, 103-5, 108-12, 115-17, 119-25, 127-28, 130, 134, 136-38, 140, 141, 149-51, 153-54, 157, 162, 170-73, 175-80, 184

Newcombe, Don, 59, 84, 115-16, 140

Newsom, Buck, 140

Newsom, Louis "Bobo," 36, 152-53

North, Bill, 130

Northrup, Jim, 39, 165

Oakland A's, 23, 54, 59, 77, 87, 97, 105, 113, 119, 130, 137

O'Day, Hank, 107, 168

O'Farrell, Bob, 29

O'Leary, Charley, 75

O'Malley, Walter, 179

O'Neill, Jack, 107

Odom, Blue Moon, 87

Ogden, Curly, 26

Oldring, Rube, 124

Olmo, Luis, 76

Orioles, see Baltimore Orioles

Ormsby, Red, 172

Orsatti, Ernie, 126

Ott, Mel, 56, 127

Overall, Orvie, 35, 103, 129

Owen, Frank, 90

Owen, Marvin, 172

Owen, Mickey, 84, 161-62, 184

Owens, Brick, 172

P

Pafko, Andy, 84

Pagan, Jose, 86-87
Page, Joe, 76, 84
Palmer, Jim, 67, 96, 97, 140, 165
Parker, Wes, 112
Partee, Rog, 63
Paskert, Dode, 107
Patterson, Roy, 90
Pearson, Monte, 122, 140
Peckinpaugh, Roger, 82, 164-65
Pennock, Herb, 73, 120, 121, 141
Perez, Tony, 86, 87
Pesky, Johnny, 63, 84
Pfeister, Jack, 35, 103, 107, 129
Pfirman, Charley, 49, 54, 70, 172
Philadelphia Athletics, 2, 16-17, 20, 24, 30-31, 34-36, 51,52, 54, 56, 88-92, 104, 107, 119, 120, 124-25, 127, 129, 135-38, 154-57, 160, 165, 168
Philadelphia Phillies, 31, 54, 59, 95, 104, 112, 122
Phillippe, Deacon Charles, 12-13, 24, 34
Pilgrims, see Boston Pilgrims
Pinelli, Babe, 33
Pinson, Vada, 105
Pipgras, George, 120, 121
Pipp, Wally, 82
Pittsburgh Pirates, 1, 2, 9-15, 20, 24, 34-35, 40, 42, 47, 52, 54, 56, 60-61, 72, 73, 77, 86-87, 90, 94, 97, 99, 102, 103, 108, 109, 120, 129, 135, 138, 141, 156, 164, 168, 184
Plank, Eddie, 24, 35, 89, 124
Podres, Johnny, 43, 77, 94, 112, 141
Pollet, Howie, 126
Pope, Dave, 75
Powell, Boog, 40, 67, 97, 137
Powell, Jack, 154
Powell, Jake, 68
Prince, Bob, 175
Pulliam, Harry, 16, 156
Puritans, see Boston Pilgrims
Purkey, Bob, 77

Rangers, see Texas Rangers
Rariden, Bill, 65
Raschi, Vic, 37, 45, 84, 85, 122, 140

Rath, Morrie, 143
Rawlings, Johnny, 82-83, 91, 127, 154
Red Sox, see Boston Red Sox
Reds, see Cincinnati Reds
Reese, Pee Wee, 43, 45, 76, 134, 136, 162
Reiser, Pete, 104
Reulbach, Ed, 35, 129
Reynolds, Allie, 45, 59, 62, 76, 84, 115, 122, 140, 178
Rhem, Flint, 49
Rhodes, James "Dusty," 43, 59, 74-76, 94
Rice, Grantland, 25
Rice, Sam, 42
Richardson, Bobby, 60, 94, 123
Rickey, Branch, 179, 182-83
Rigler, Charlie, 42, 169, 170
Ripple, Jimmy, 36, 109
Rivera, Jim, 44
Rizzuto, Phil, 37, 76, 122, 135, 162, 174, 178
Roberts, Robin, 59
Robertson, Dave, 65, 71, 72
Robertson, Gene, 121
Robinson, Aaron, 162
Robinson, Brooks, 40, 44, 67, 86, 97, 105, 136, 137
Robinson, Frank, 40, 67, 97
Robinson, Jackie, 8, 20, 32, 44-45, 60, 79, 84, 104, 132, 162
Robinson, Wilbert, 45
Roe, Preacher, 76
Rogell, Billy, 150
Rohe, George, 90, 107, 113, 137
Rolfe, Red, 122, 136, 162
Root, Charlie, 31, 50, 52, 56, 165
Rose, Pete, 40, 87, 137
Roseboro, John, 37, 38, 112
Rosen, Al, 43, 94, 105
Rothstein, Arnold, 144-46
Roush, Edd, 132, 142-45, 170
Rowe, Schoolboy, 92, 109, 153, 172
Rowland, Clarence "Pants," 169
Rudi, Joe, 130, 137
Rudolph, Dickie, 89
Ruel, Muddy, 26, 160
Ruelbach, Ed, 103
Ruether, Dutch, 120
Ruffing, Red, 93, 122, 140
Runyon, Damon, 6
Ruppert, Jake, 157

Ruth, Babe, 5, 6, 20, 28, 29, 41-42, 47-52, 54, 56, 61, 62, 70, 72, 79, 82, 90, 99, 101, 103-4, 107-9, 117, 120-22, 128, 134-38, 141, 154, 157, 171, 179
Ryan, Nolan, 40
Ryan, Rosy, 157

Saier, Vic, 23
St. Louis Browns, 12, 36, 68, 110
St. Louis Cardinals, 28, 34, 36, 38-39, 43-44, 49-50, 54, 56, 57, 60, 62, 63, 67-68, 70-73, 77, 84, 86, 91-93, 95, 101-2, 104, 108-10, 119-22, 134, 135, 137, 138, 141, 150, 153, 161, 165, 172-73, 175, 179, 182
Sallee, Slim, 19
San Francisco Giants, 47, 97, 127, 141
Schaefer, Germany, 155, 168
Schalk, Ray, 147, 170
Schang, Wally, 48, 54, 61, 138
Schmidt, Charley, 168, 169
Schoendienst, Red, 41, 177
Schulte, Wildfire Frank, 19, 90, 129
Schultz, Barney, 54
Scott, Everett "Deacon," 48
Scott, Jack, 108
Scully, Vin, 8, 79, 177, 178
Seaver, Tom, 97, 105
Sebring, Jimmy, 13, 54
Selkirk, George, 57, 122
Senators, see Washington Senators
Sewell, Joey, 136
Seybold, Socks, 124
Shannon, Mike, 38, 60
Shaw, Bob, 77
Shawkey, Bob, 73, 90
Shean, Dave, 49
Sheckard, Jimmy, 90, 107, 129
Sherdel, Bill, 49, 54, 70, 125
Sherry, Larry, 112
Shibe, Ben, 17, 156
Shocker, Urban, 120
Shotton, Burt, 43, 111
Shuba, George, 76
Siebern, Norm, 41
Simmons, Al, 29-30, 56, 91, 124, 125, 137, 165

Sisler, Dick, 104
Sisler, George, 20, 134
Skowron, Bill, 37, 40, 59, 123, 175
Slater, Bill, 8
Slaughter, Enos, 62-63, 84, 110, 126, 127, 173, 177
Smith, Earl, 42, 62, 154, 164, 170
Smith, Elmer, 36, 54, 59, 163
Smith, Frank, 90
Smith, Hal, 52, 86
Smith, Red, 152
Smith, Sherry, 48
Snider, Duke, 8, 32, 45, 54, 84, 104, 137
Snodgrass, Fred, 82, 160
Snyder, Frank, 61, 73
Southworth, Bill, 126
Spahn, Warren, 37, 141
Speaker, Tris, 82, 137, 160
Stahl, Chick, 12, 13
Stahl, Jack, 159
Stainback, Tuck, 172
Stallings, George, 126
Stanky, Eddie, 174
Stanley, Mickey, 39
Stanton, Bob, 8
Stargell, Willie, 86-87, 104
Steinfeldt, Harry, 68, 129, 136
Stengel, Charles Dillon "Casey," 6, 8, 23, 42, 45, 56, 65, 73, 77, 84, 93, 108, 122, 135, 138, 150, 151, 157
Stephenson, Riggs, 31, 70, 125, 137
Stirnweiss, George, 43
Stoneham, Horace, 179
Stottlemyre, Mel, 39, 60, 94
Strang, Sammy, 156
Strunk, Amos, 124
Sturm, Johnny, 162
Summers, Bill, 60, 172
Sutton, Don, 140
Swoboda, Ron, 44, 97

Tannehill, Lee, 19, 90, 107
Taylor, John I., 15
Taylor, Zack, 165
Tenace, Gene, 54, 59, 87, 105, 113, 130
Tennes, Monty, 145
Terry, Bill, 26, 91, 126-28, 135

Terry, Ralph, 52, 86, 171
Tesreau, Jeff, 4
Texas Rangers, 130
Thayer, Ernest Lawrence, 23
Thevenow, Tommy, 67-68, 108, 135
Thomas, Ira, 75
Thompson, Hank, 62, 74
Tigers, see Detroit Tigers
Tinker, Joe, 35, 54, 90, 129, 155
Tolan, Bobby, 87
Tolson, Chick, 31
Toney, Fred, 90, 127
Torgeson, Earl, 173
Torrez, Mike, 140
Traynor, Pie, 137
Tresh, Tommy, 38
Turley, Bob, 41
Twins, see Minnesota Twins
Tyler, George, 48, 89

Vance, Dazzy, 132
Vaughan, Jim "Hippo," 48, 169
Veeck, Bill, 157
Verban, Emil, 67, 68, 109-10
Vernon, Mickey, 134
Virdon, Bill, 40, 86, 99-100

Waddell, Rube, 17, 124, 134
Wagner, Heinie, 169
Wagner, Honus, 10, 12, 13, 20, 67, 68, 102-3, 132, 168
Walberg, Swede, 124
Walker, Harry, 63, 84, 110, 127
Walker, Tilly, 47
Walsh, Ed, 31, 90, 107
Walters, Bucky, 36, 140
Wambsganns, Bill, 45, 163
Waner, Lloyd, 120
Waner, Paul, 120, 132
Ward, Aaron, 62, 82, 83, 128, 171
Warneke, Lon, 150
Warwick, Carl, 77
Wasdell, Jimmy, 162
Washington, Claudell, 130

Washington Senators, 26, 34, 42, 56, 91, 108, 137, 160, 164, 171, 173
Watkins, George, 56
Weaver, Buck, 143, 145, 169
Weaver, Earl, 97, 173
Weis, Al, 40, 67, 97, 113
Werber, Billy, 136
Wert, Don, 38
Wertz, Vic, 43, 71, 73, 150
White, Doc, 90
White, Ernie, 93, 126
White, Jo-Jo, 43-44
White Sox, see Chicago White Sox
Whitehead, Burgess, 44
Whiteman, George, 49, 107-8
Williams, Billy, 134
Williams, Claude, 143, 145
Williams, Davey, 43
Williams, Dick, 87, 130
Williams, Ted, 67, 68, 101-2, 134
Willis, Vic, 34, 60
Wilson, Chief, 168
Wilson Hack "Sunny Boy," 31, 56, 70, 91, 125, 132, 165, 171
Wilson, Jimmy, 62, 109, 125
Witt, Whitey, 41-42
Wood, Smokey Joe, 35, 140, 159-60
Woodling, Gene, 76, 77
Wortman, Bill, 48
Wynn, Early, 75, 94

Yankees, see New York Yankees
Yastrzemski, Carl, 70, 101, 104, 137
Yerkes, Steve, 82, 160
Young, Cy, 1, 2, 9, 10, 12, 13, 24, 54
Youngs, Ross, 26, 127, 171
Yvars, Sal, 44, 84

Zeider, Rollie, 48
Zimmer, Don, 43, 60
Zimmerman, Heinie, 23, 65